The Sensational Rise of
William Randolph Hearst

The Uncrowned
KING

KENNETH WHYTE

Random House Canada

www.randomhouse.ca

LIBRARY AND ARCHIVES CANADA CATALOGUING IN PUBLICATION

Whyte, Kenneth
The uncrowned king / Kenneth Whyte.

ISBN 978-0-679-31343-4

1. Hearst, William Randolph, 1863–1951. 2. Newspaper publishing—
United States—History—19th century. 3. Newspaper publishing—United
States—History—20th century. 4. American newspapers—New York
(State)—New York—History—19th century. 5. American newspapers—
New York (State)—New York—History—20th century. 6. Newspapers—
Ownership—Biography. 7. Publishers and publishing—United States—
Biography. 8. New York (N.Y.)—History—1898–1951. I. Title.

Z473.H4W49 2008   070.5'722092   C2008-901667-X

Printed and bound in the United States of America

10 9 8 7 6 5 4 3 2 1

To my mother and father

TABLE OF CONTENTS

The people who live in a golden age usually
go around complaining how yellow everything looks.
RANDALL JARRELL

I n 1895, William Randolph Hearst, the son of a wealthy U.S. senator and a celebrated Washington socialite, stepped out of his parents' shadow with his purchase of a New York newspaper, the *Morning Journal*. It was a feeble money-losing daily, clinging to life in a city brimming with great newspapers and great newspapermen. Yet within a few short months, Hearst had turned it around and engaged Joseph Pulitzer, the undisputed king of the American press, in the most spectacular newspaper war of all time. They battled for three years, at enormous expense of energy, emotion, and money, through the thrilling presidential election campaign of 1896 and the Spanish-American War of 1898—a conflict that Hearst was accused of fomenting and that he covered in person. When they finally called a truce, Hearst had supplanted Pulitzer as the dominant force in American publishing. He was well on his way to becoming one of the most powerful and fascinating private citizens of the twentieth century, and the journalist with the worst reputation in the history of the trade.

I became interested in Hearst a full century after these events. I was leaving the magazine business to launch a new national newspaper in a relatively crowded Canadian market. In preparation, I read widely in the history of the North American press, paying particular attention to editors proficient in the almost forgotten arts of attracting readers and building circulation against established competition. That led me inevitably to the two masters, Hearst and Pulitzer; to their fabled clash in New York; and to the birth of what is known and regretted as "yellow journalism." I glanced at a few microfilmed copies of the *Journal* and was impressed by some of what I saw, but not sufficiently so as to question the conventional view of Hearst: that his paper was commercially successful but otherwise a hollow spectacle; that he was a free-spending sensationalist and a tireless self-promoter who lowered the standards and tone of American newspapers; that he twisted facts and invented stories in the course of ruining reputations and promoting unnecessary wars.

Five years later, with a new appreciation of the dynamics and difficulties of newspaper competition, I returned to Hearst versus Pulitzer. I decided to weigh the opinions of Hearst's many critics against the actual contents of his newspaper and those of his competitors, and to pay more attention to the records of the several impartial observers who followed his progress in New York. Instead of perusing the *Journal* for headlines proving that yellow journals were the nearest approach to hell in any Christian state, as E.L. Godkin famously declared, I tried to determine how Hearst was able to build, almost overnight, a publishing franchise with more than a million readers in a savvy newspaper city served by seventeen major dailies, some of them owned by the most talented and wealthiest editors the United States has ever seen. What emerged from my efforts was an entirely different Hearst from the cartoon figure of lore.

Nothing By Halves

I t was not at all unusual at the end of the nineteenth century for an American newspaper proprietor to own a steam yacht. James Gordon Bennett Jr., sybarite publisher of the *New York Herald* and a two-time commodore of the New York Yacht Club, dropped the astonishing sum of $625,000 on his 285-foot *Lysistrata,* which he staffed with a crew of a hundred officers and sailors. Joseph Pulitzer, owner and editor of the New York *World,* bought the *Romola* and took his delicate constitution aboard for a single sleepless night before selling it for a quarter of what he had paid. A few years later he would order the *Liberty,* a 300-foot vessel equipped with state-of-the-art soundproofing that allowed him many restful nights on his frequent journeys across the Atlantic.[1]

William Randolph Hearst's first yacht was relatively modest, a fifty-foot cruiser called the *Aquila.* He used it to shuttle back and forth over San Francisco Bay between his Sausalito home and the offices of his *San Francisco Examiner.* Though small, the *Aquila* was the fastest speedboat on the Pacific Coast, and a delight for its young owner, who liked to run circles around the Sausalito ferry. But the *Aquila*'s days were numbered after Hearst's mother boarded it to visit family in Santa Clara County: the seas were choppy and she arrived soaked to the skin. Phoebe Apperson Hearst decided her son would have, instead, the largest steam yacht that could be shipped by rail from New York to San Francisco. An order was placed with the famed Herreshoff Manufacturing Company of Bristol, Rhode Island.[2]

Most yacht builders in America and Europe toward the end of the nineteenth century were straddling the ages of sail and steam. More precisely, they were steeped in the physics and aesthetics of sail but slowly learning to incorporate into their craft the obvious advantages of steam

technology. Their yards produced what were best understood as traditional sailing yachts with steam as an auxiliary source of power used to
steady the boat or give it a push when conditions warranted. Their floating anachronisms were fine with their clients, the vast majority of whom
shared their romance with sail. If a Gilded Age tycoon was going to blow
a few hundred thousand dollars at sea, he wanted all the reassuring signatures of sailing-yacht elegance: a magnificent clipper bow, painted trail-
boards, varnished deckhouse, and towering fully rigged masts.[3]

The same tycoon wanted all that grace and opulence translated below
decks as well, which is why so many Gilded Age yachts were tricked out like
English country homes. The grandest of them were lined with floor-to-
ceiling mahogany, oak, and walnut. The furnishings might be Chippendale
or Louis XIV. There were fireplaces, pianos, gilded staircases, chandeliers,
rich carpets and curtains, and horrid masses of Victorian objets d'art and
bric-a-brac, not to mention modern conveniences such as ice and telegraph
machines. On top of all this were the personal touches. Joseph Pulitzer
ordered the *Liberty* fitted with an extensive library and high sink pedestals
so that the publisher, who was well over six feet tall, need not stoop to wash
his hands. Bennett Jr.'s *Lysistrata* featured a Turkish bath and padded stalls
for the pair of Alderney cows that provided fresh ingredients for his
brandy milk punch. On the *Lysistrata*'s bow perched an immense carved
wooden owl fitted so that its eyes blazed with electric searchlights.

The Herreshoff shipyard, where the Hearsts placed their order, had
built its share of floating mansions. But Captain Nat Herreshoff was an
engineer at heart, more interested in performance than in creature comforts or ostentatious display. What is more, while he and his blind brother
John had produced a number of the finest boat designs in the history of
wind power, they had embraced new technology without reserve. No
yard anywhere built better seagoing steam engines. The Herreshoffs, in
fact, may have been the only builder in the world confident enough to
accept the order, coming as it did with Will Hearst's single deal-breaking
stipulation: if the new yacht wasn't capable of twenty-six knots, making
it the fastest steam craft in the world, delivery would be refused.

The Herreshoffs worked on the Hearst commission over the winter
of 1890, loading it up with technology and design cues from the navy
torpedo boat USS *Cushing*, which they had built a few years earlier. They
installed their leading-edge five-cylinder quadruple expansion engines

and threw in innovative lightweight hollow-steel crankshafts, similar in design to what Henry Ford would use in his revolutionary V-8s thirty years later. The new yacht's power plant produced a thumping 875 brake horsepower and enough on-deck vibration to loosen a passenger's teeth.

At 109.4 feet, the Hearst vessel was not large by the standards of the day; nor, at $65,000, was it particularly expensive. But it stood apart. Low in profile, narrow at the beam, with a single smokestack and a deck uncluttered but for a flimsy sun canopy, it had none of the traditional features of yachting elegance. Without so much as a faux mast, it could not be sailed under any circumstances. It was all steam and only steam. Its sleek and menacing appearance anticipated the next century far more than it echoed the age of sail. It was a bullet-shaped rebuke to prevailing tastes, radically designed to its own aggressive purposes. Below deck, it was so spartan that Hearst was advised he would need to renovate from stem to stern if he ever wanted to sell; no yachtsman with a wife or girlfriend would ever be permitted to purchase it.

The new yacht's name was as singular as its design. The Victorian fashion in nomenclature ran to literary references, English or European history, and, as always, names of sweethearts. Pulitzer had christened his first yacht *Romola,* after the George Eliot novel. Bennett Jr. succumbed to both the literary and the classical for his *Lysistrata.* Hearst fell back on spirited American vernacular: *Vamoose.*

The *Vamoose* was to be shipped to Hearst in California via the Isthmus of Panama on a specially designed crib extending over three cars of the Panama Railway Company. It was an extraordinary operation, requiring, among other measures, the partial dismantling of three bridges along the track. All logistical obstacles were overcome and the payload appeared to be on its way when word came that a Colonel Rives, president of the railway company, was refusing Hearst's freight. It seems that the literary critics at Hearst's *San Francisco Examiner* had been unkind to an otherwise popular new novel, *The Quick or the Dead,* written by Amélie Rives, whose father ran the railroad in Panama.

The *Vamoose* was pointed back east and berthed in New York, where Hearst, on his increasingly frequent visits, raced it against all comers and loaned it to local yacht clubs for use as a viewing boat during regattas. It was indeed the fastest thing on water, clocking in at twenty-seven knots. Other yacht owners pretended to higher speeds, but in

September 1891 the American Yacht Club hosted a much-publicized race with a five-hundred-dollar prize, the course a straightaway of ninety miles. When the *Vamoose* arrived at the starting line, all competition stood down.

At the time that he took delivery of *Vamoose*, Hearst was known to be shopping for a newspaper in New York. His impending arrival on the scene caused little comment. His type—the man of wealth and regional influence—routinely arrived in the big city and just as routinely flamed out. But for all the magnificent and flamboyant talents then washing around the higher reaches of New York publishing, none owned a yacht like the *Vamoose*. None kept for a pleasure craft what was essentially a torpedo boat, minus the ordnance. At least one local columnist had an inkling of its significance. After watching a regatta from the deck of the *Vamoose*, he wrote, "The Hearsts are odd people in many ways, and they are admirable in many ways. They have not been accustomed to do things by halves."[4]

CHAPTER ONE

When He Wants Cake, He Wants Cake

There was only one place where one might live in a different way, more
keenly and vigorously than anywhere else in America, and that was
New York. It was the great city—the only cosmopolitan city—a
wonder-world in itself. . . .
All really ambitious people, people who were destined to do or be anything in any line, eventually drifted there—editors, newspaper men,
actors, playwrights, songwriters, musicians, money-makers—the town
was full of them, and the best of it was the best ones succeeded there.
You couldn't keep the able down in New York.
—THEODORE DREISER, *Newspaper Days*[1]

I t is difficult to say precisely when William Randolph Hearst first
hit on the idea of breaking into New York publishing, but it is clear
that by 1889 he would not be satisfied until he did. He was twenty-
six years old and already a minor newspaper phenomenon. Three years
earlier he had been handed the *San Francisco Examiner* by his father, who
had owned it for six years, accomplishing little beyond a string of annual
losses. With no more than a few months of professional journalistic
experience, the younger Hearst announced himself as proprietor and
editor and promptly established the *Examiner* as the most attractive,
intelligent, and exuberant daily on the Pacific coast. Its circulation more
than doubled. Its losses evaporated. It rivaled the mighty *San Francisco
Chronicle* as the leading newspaper in the West. The trade journals credited Hearst with a "masterstroke of enterprise."[2] It seems everyone who
knew the *Examiner* was impressed by it, save Hearst, who was keenly
aware that whatever he had accomplished in San Francisco, he had not
done anything in New York.

7

His expansion plans were in fact larger than one city. Hearst envisioned a chain of newspapers, the individual titles of which would share content, management, and other resources, reducing costs and magnifying the proprietor's voice and influence. But a chain was unthinkable without New York. It was the liveliest and most competitive newspaper city in the world, and the center of media and commercial influence in the United States. New York was a goal in itself.

Out of the blue, on Thanksgiving Day 1889, Charles M. Palmer, an experienced midwestern newspaper executive specializing in circulation, received a telegram from Hearst inviting him to join the *Examiner* and asking what salary he would expect. Palmer signed on, excited at the comprehensiveness of Hearst's expansion plans and the prospect of an imminent break into the New York market. He was also impressed by Hearst's manner, a curious mixture of deference and self-assurance. George Pancoast, Hearst's private secretary and frequent companion, also learned of the New York initiative around this time.[3] As they were crossing San Francisco Bay on a ferry, Hearst took from his pocket a railway timetable and drew circles around the names of several large cities, saying, "George, some day a paper there, and there, and there." New York he circled twice.

Hearst's plans were made public that autumn when the *New York Press* revealed that he had been "trying to induce his father to set him up in business here, either by buying some old paper or establishing a new one." A staggeringly wealthy senator from California, the Honorable George Hearst had cheerfully spent his best years in frontier mining camps and scrappy western towns, exercising an uncanny ability to charm metal out of rock. Before taking up politics, he had been instrumental in the development of four of the richest mines yet discovered in America: Nevada's Comstock Lode, Utah's Ontario Mine, Montana's Anaconda, and South Dakota's Homestake. The *Press* guessed George Hearst was worth $20 million. It reported that the senator had been in upstate New York over the summer to watch his thoroughbreds run, and that he had this to say about his son's New York newspaper ambitions: "There's plenty of money if the boy really has his heart set on it. But I am in hopes he will conclude after a while that one big paper is enough for one man to run."[4]

It's unlikely that Will Hearst viewed his father's caution as a serious obstacle. The old man was a soft touch. Will also had himself to blame for his father's "one big paper is enough" reservation. He had been complaining incessantly to the senator about his competitive difficulties in San Francisco. He had started a newspaper war with the *Chronicle* and, to his surprise and consternation, its owner, Michael de Young, was fighting back. De Young had announced a series of new investments in his paper, including the construction of an impressive new headquarters and Will had pleaded for more paternal support to keep pace. "I am working awfully hard and getting a little bit tired and a little bit discouraged," he wrote his father. "That damned *Chronicle* building is a tremendous advertisement and helps them immensely. Everybody talks about it and everybody thinks it is pretty fine and there is great difficulty getting subscribers away from a paper that is doing a big thing like that. The effect upon the advertiser is even worse. Mr. De Young told a friend the other day that since he had started his building his income [from the paper] had almost doubled. . . . How long do you suppose it will be before we can put up a building—a stunner that will knock his endways and make him as sick as he is now making me[?]"[5]

George Hearst's hesitancy about his son's New York plans may also have been lip service to Phoebe Apperson Hearst. The senator was constantly reminded by his wife that he had lost hundreds of thousands on the *Examiner* before it had begun to pay, and that was on top of the hundreds of thousands he was throwing away on his ponies.[6] Though one of the richest families in America, and a small one at that, the three Hearsts were diversely ambitious and variously extravagant; there was not enough money to go around. At the start of 1890, they were spending at a pace of almost $1 million annualized.[7] Phoebe was generally the voice of restraint, seeking to rein in her men not out of prudence so much as out of concern for her own spending and philanthropic priorities. Sometimes the men listened to her; more often, as in this instance, not.

The senator's misgivings appear to have lasted no longer than it took the *Press* to get them in print. He was soon reported to have made unsuccessful bids for the *New York Times* and the New York *Sun,* as well as a $5-million play for the mighty *New York Herald.*[8] The accuracy of these reports is uncertain, but any discussions toward the purchase of a New York title would have made Will's dream seem tantalizingly close. And just then everything changed.

Late in 1890, Senator Hearst was diagnosed with "a complication of diseases" rooted in "a serious derangement of the bowel"—in a word, cancer. He received first-rate medical attention and fought bravely against the illness, but it advanced quickly. Around seven o'clock on the evening of February 28, 1891, he slipped into a coma. Phoebe was called from dinner and was joined at his bedside in their Washington mansion by Will, a family friend, and the household staff. All were present when George died at 9:10 p.m, with Phoebe holding his hand. "So quickly and easily did he pass away," said one report, "that Mrs. Hearst did not know he was dead until so informed by Dr. Ward."[9]

GEORGE HEARST WAS REMEMBERED fondly as a tall, rumpled man with a great beard, a constant smile, and kindly, genial ways. Eulogies played up the incongruity of his humble origins and lack of formal education, and his spectacular rise to riches and high political office. There was much amusement at his love of horses, card games, and drink. It was said that "only such an amount of culture had attached to him as would necessarily be forced upon a man whose household was presided over by a model wife, who was a society leader having practically limitless wealth at her command."[10] That characterization of George Hearst has persisted over the years, with much of the warmth wrung from it. He is portrayed in his son's most recent biography as an "uncouth, loud, and semi-literate" hick who drank too much, neglected his family, and bought his way into the Senate. The recent HBO drama *Deadwood* presents him as a sociopathic tycoon who murders his way to riches.[11]

Senator Hearst was indeed a child of the Missouri frontier, but he hardly grew up wild. The family was patrician by local standards. George Hearst's father was a man of means, the largest slave owner in Meramec Township, and a force in local politics. His mother had some education and was known for her cashmere shawls and leghorn bonnets. George did not spend a lot of his childhood in the classroom, mostly because there was no schoolhouse nearby, but he had a good head and he eventually completed enough of grade school to graduate from the Franklin County Mining School in 1838. He was expected to study for the bar, but then his father passed away, leaving debts that George took upon himself to clear. Sufficiently literate to teach himself geology and mineralogy from bor-rowed texts, George earned his first financial stake by applying the effi-cient lead-mining practices he learned from books to mining properties considered worthless by experienced Missouri operators.

George Hearst took his knowledge west, made and lost several fortunes, and gained an international reputation as a mining analyst. He also became expert in the bewilderingly complex legal dimensions of his trade (the protection of a single claim could require litigation of twenty or thirty separate suits). His colleagues marveled at his shrewdness and cool judgment, which seemed only to improve in times of uncertainty or crisis. They also valued his personal qualities: he was cheerful, open, unaffected, honest, sensible, independent of mind, and innately dignified. He was a beloved figure in the mining belt. Colleagues sought his advice on personal as well as commercial matters. He dispensed his counsel in "wise, original and homely thoughts and phrases," flavored with the musical drawl of his native Missouri.[12] His personal magnetism kept him in some of the best company available in the western states. His business partners included California attorney general and U.S. senator William Morris Stewart, U.S. senator James Graham Fair, and Nevada City mayor Hamlet Davis. Among his friends were U.S. Supreme Court justice Stephen J. Field, Chief Justice of the Supreme Court of California Niles Searls, and Ninth Circuit judge Lorenzo Sawyer. Mark Twain was a drinking buddy, a business associate, and an admirer of George's self-reliance and political judgment.

Senator Hearst's "model wife" might not have registered the precise moment of his passing, but she knew exactly what to do once he was gone. Phoebe was a formidable woman in her own right. Tiny, dark-haired, and handsome in a severe manner, she was given to lavender gowns, antique lace, tight corsets, and show-stopping rubies and diamonds. She was Washington's most celebrated hostess, the "philanthropic grande dame" of the capital and its "arbiter of unsullied elegance," by one newspaper report. Just two years prior to her husband's death, she had opened their Dupont Circle mansion with a costume ball to commemorate Washington's birthday. The *Washington Post* deemed it "by far the most brilliant event of its kind" ever held in the city. The flowers alone were rumored to have cost $25,000 (the reporter who wrote the story would have been lucky to earn $25 a week). The party favors included "reticules of flowered silk, amber and tortoise shell combs and clusters of three ostrich tips for the hair. Those of the gentlemen were silver medals cut with colonial cocked hats and shields, pen wipers of white kid embroidered in flowers and tiny buckets of California redwood in the form of pin cushions."[13] So never mind that the humble senator might have been perfectly content with a quick drop in a pine box. Phoebe's reputation demanded she give him a glorious send-off.

The ceremonies began with George Hearst's body lying in state for the better part of a week. A memorial service was held in Washington at Saint John's Episcopal Church, the president and Mrs. Benjamin Harrison in attendance. Afterward, the casket, Phoebe, Will, and a large party of senators, congressmen, friends, and retainers boarded a special train, dyed Titian red, for the week-long ride back west. George's body was displayed for four more days at Grace Episcopal Cathedral in San Francisco, attracting thousands of mourners, even in hard rains.

The funeral service was Phoebe's main event. The governor of the state and the city's mayor were among the honorary pallbearers; the widow's society friends sat in assigned pews. She transformed the church into a garden, with palms and evergreens crowding every niche, and a pair of seven-foot white flower crosses bracketing the altar. Great streams of blossoms hung from every arch and rafter. It was an exhibition of "gems and treasures of the florist's art such as have rarely been brought together to do honor to the dead," gushed the *Examiner*. Will's daily had made its own contribution to the display.[14] Sitting like a billboard in front of the casket was a blue and white floral representation of the paper's front page, featuring a portrait of the senator.

After the service, Phoebe left the church on Will's arm to lead a slow ten-block procession to Laurel Hill Cemetery. The hearse was drawn by four jet-black horses. "The strains of the dirges and the long roll of the muffled drums were the only sounds above the patter of the rain," reported the *Examiner*. Fifteen thousand people gathered in the steady drizzle to watch the cortege pass. The crowd at the cemetery gates had to be cleared to permit the family to enter. Sixteen days after his last breath, the senator was finally laid to rest. Pheobe and Will were last to leave the casket.[15]

If Grace Episcopal had been to Phoebe's taste, the funeral train's return east sans casket was nearer to George's style. An Indiana temperance crusader whose own train happened to be trailing the Hearst party complained that its passengers engaged in a coast-to-coast debauch, fueled by wines donated by California vineyards. The front page of the starchy *New York Times* reported that privately marked cases of wine and hundreds of empties were loaded on and off the train near El Paso, Texas. Witnesses declared that tier upon tier of wine cases were stacked in the dining car and that the Hearst party "did not have a drip of water on their train but drank wine altogether, using orange wine to quench their thirst."[16] Congress was indignant at the allegations, especially as it was obliged to pick up the tab. The cost of the trip was a record $21,322.55, which led to legislation limiting government spending on congressional funerals to the costs of embalming and transporting the body home (the bill was never enacted).[17]

In the weeks before the senator's death, newspapers had speculated as to the settlement of the Hearst estate. Valued at between eighteen and twenty million, it included several outstanding mining properties and perhaps a million acres in land. The betting was that Will, as the only child, would be the sole heir. In fact, he was shut out. Everything regarding the ownership, management, and disposition of the assets fell to Phoebe. The senator had written, "I commend my son, William R. Hearst, to my said wife, having full confidence that she will make suitable provisions for him, but in the event of the marriage of my said wife after my death, I hereby give and bequeath to my said son all of my said property that may remain in the possession of my said wife at that date."[18]

Will Hearst now had a lot to absorb. Notwithstanding that his father had been away in mining camps for much of his life, there had been a bond between them. Will was his father's boy in many respects. There was a physical resemblance: the fair hair, the long face, the tall stature and sloped shoulders. Each possessed cool judgment and a powerful mind with a practical bent. Will also had some of George's gentleness and amiability (although little of his freewheeling charm). They had drawn close as Will had matured, primarily through their shared interests in publishing and politics. Many people, starting with Phoebe, had held the senator's simple ways against him, but Will had not. He favored competence and accomplishment over manners and appearances, an attitude he had adopted from George. He loved and admired his father, and his bereavement had to have been profound. It would have especially pained him that George had doubted his maturity and financial abilities, and had not seen fit to leave him an independent legacy. He must have cringed to recall his panicked pleas for another "million or a million and a half or two million" with which to fight the *Chronicle*.[19]

Will appears to have blamed himself for his father's decision (a verdict echoed by his biographers), yet odds on a full inheritance had always been slim. The senator's relations with his son were far less important to the disposition of his estate than were his relationship with his wife and the unorthodox terms of their marriage.

DURING THE CIVIL WAR, George Hearst had returned from the far west to visit his ailing mother in the Meramec Valley. He was an overripe but nonetheless eligible bachelor, forty years old and flush with one of his early mining successes. One newspaper described him as a tall, smiling man "with long swinging arms, big feet and hands, a somewhat awkward gait."[20] Phoebe Apperson was almost half his size and age, a petite, pretty twenty-year-old schoolteacher who could also sew, cook, plant, hoe, and milk. Their age gap was alarming, not least of all because George, as a young man, appears to have been sweet on Phoebe's mother. Naturally, her parents opposed the match, but Phoebe had read enough of *Harper's Weekly* to know there were grander and more interesting places to live than rural Missouri. The ceremony was performed by a Presbyterian minister in a private home on June 15, 1862, absent relations from either side.

More remarkably, the day prior to the ceremony, the couple had signed a prenuptial agreement guaranteeing Phoebe a share of George's estate for her own separate property, free from his interference and control during her natural life. Judith Robinson, the Hearst family chronicler, has turned up evidence that Phoebe may have been pregnant prior to the wedding, which could explain the unusual proceedings, but Phoebe would have been capable of striking a hard bargain even if she weren't expecting. William Randolph Hearst's date of birth is given as April 29, 1863. His birth record was lost in the 1906 San Francisco earthquake.[21]

Through the early years of their marriage, Hearst's parents lived largely separate lives—George in his mining milieu, his bride in San Francisco, where she engaged in an ambitious program of self-improvement and social advance. Phoebe had a vigorous mind and great curiosity about the world. She studied painting and art, read books, and attended the opera. She hosted luncheons, established a literary salon, and traveled incessantly—west to Hawaii, south to Acapulco, east to Washington, New York, and, ultimately, Europe. She made education the focus of her philanthropic activities and eventually became a leading benefactor and regent of the University of California.

Although the overall tone of the couple's correspondence is generally one of mutual regard and affection, they never got around to establishing a permanent family home. Neither would make the sacrifice to follow the other. Phoebe had barely left the farm before she was confessing an aversion to "common people."[22] She disliked mining towns and politics, and she hated horse racing. She became increasingly embarrassed by her tobacco-chewing husband's dirty shirtfronts and his contempt for polite society. She complained of his neglect of his family and suspected him of keeping company with other women, which was probably the case. By the second decade of their marriage, during which Phoebe traveled extensively, they were sometimes keeping track of one another's activities through the newspapers.[23]

It is not unfair to say that aside from a shared interest in the welfare and progress of their son, the strongest bond between Phoebe and George Hearst was the family fortune. Money and business are preoccupations in their letters, and from their first days together Phoebe was a champion spender of her husband's cash. She packed her wardrobes with the finest clothing and jewelry. She once returned from Europe with paintings, statuary, and antiques filling two railway cars. She was constantly moving house or renovating, and her entertainments at home were lavish even by the standards of the Gilded Age. Of course, all of the Hearsts were great spenders, but Phoebe distinguished herself by caring more for being rich: "I'm not a bit proud but I do love the prestige that filthy lucre gives one."[24] Hypocrisy about money was one of her charms. After having begged George to give her a large diamond as a Christmas gift, she wrote him that her conscience was troubling her "for saying a word about wanting Mrs. Barreda's beautiful diamonds. I only meant that I should like them very much if we had money and no debts." [25]

Just how mismatched a couple the Hearsts had become was apparent to all of Washington when George's election to the Senate threw the two together in the capital. Phoebe bought and renovated her "palace at Dupont Circle," a thirty-room grand mansion with towers, turrets, and a red-tiled roof. High Victorian in style, it had occasional Oriental touches to break with the ordinary. Walls in the library tower were hung with blue India velvet; a dining room was lined with Venetian leather. The house was packed with Phoebe's treasures, including an impressive collection of Napoleona and paintings by Sir Joshua Reynolds, Millet, and Van Dyke. Staffing was generous, from the two Chinese chefs to the stable master, who cared for six high-stepping, hackney-bred bay horses lodged in steam-heated stables.[26] The palace was appropriate to the personage Phoebe had become, but her husband was not at home in it. "It is hardly fair to say that Senator Hearst has occupied the house," snickered one newspaper. He paid the bills but was otherwise "not much of a factor in the domestic organization." The night his wife opened the home with a dress ball on Washington's birthday, George led a small party of favored guests to the cellar, where they smoked and drank in peace beside the coal hole. "I can't see the fun in my wife's rackets," he muttered.[27]

Notwithstanding their conflicts and differences, the Hearst marriage endured. George had high regard for Phoebe's abilities and allowed her to take a keen interest in his businesses, an unusual step for a Victorian husband. He kept her informed of all his commercial operations and invited her to play executive roles, even to interview prospective managers. At his death, Phoebe was due her husband's estate. She had married it as well as him and, through her participation in George's affairs, she had contributed to their prosperity. Given her nature, it is inconceivable that she would have let him die without his affairs being arranged to her own satisfaction, and she would never have been happy without full control of the estate. Any doubts as to her managerial capacity were squelched six weeks after the senator's funeral when she unsentimentally organized an auction of his beloved thoroughbreds. With that out of the way, she directed her firm gaze to her son.

Phoebe had always been capable of generosity toward Will—his yacht, *Vamoose*, for instance, had been her idea. She actually encouraged extravagance in him so long as it was in line with her own standards and social aspirations. But when he developed a cavalier habit of drawing on the family accounts to support the *Examiner* and began living openly with his girlfriend, Phoebe dug in her heels. She had questioned George's courage when he'd failed to curb what she considered to be Will's excesses.[28] Now that she controlled the purse strings, she wasn't about to compound her husband's errors. She reined in Will's allowance and ended his unscheduled cash draws from family accounts. She also made him take all his financial requests to her bookkeeper, deepening his humiliation at having being denied an inheritance. For the time being, the acquisition of a New York daily and the launch of a newspaper empire were out of the question.

Discomfitting as this new arrangement may have been for Will, he was not entirely without means. His father had deeded him the *Examiner,* which now produced a solid return. If he needed cash or wanted to finance another venture, he had the options of improving the paper's income or, presumably, selling it. His father had also previously made over to him the enormous Babicora ranch in Mexico, a property for which the Mormons were said to have offered a million dollars.[29] That, too, offered Will some flexibility. But there was no getting around the fact that the geysers of ready cash had been plugged. He was for the first time in his adult life operating under serious constraints.

PHOEBE'S INTENTION WAS NOT SIMPLY to control Will's spending but to direct his life. She had always been by far the more assertive parent. Throughout Will's youth, she had been at pains to show him an ideal of manhood apart from the tobacco-spitting, hog-and-hominy-eating southern oaf, which was how she rated the senator's example in her more exasperated moments. (Phoebe is in large part responsible for George's reputation for vulgarity. She never forgave him for failing to keep pace with her social pretensions and left in her letters a long record of complaint that has been uncritically mined by historians and biographers.) She had known from the first exactly what kind of man her Will should become: "A good man," she told a confidante. "They are scarce."[30] Good men, in Phoebe's books, were clean, carefully dressed, roundly educated, well traveled, reliable, and attentive to women, especially their mothers. She had been deeply impressed by the devastatingly well-bred gallants in the higher reaches of London society, men who resided in "perfect palaces," kept a dozen or more servants, and held close to distinctions of class and formality of manner. Phoebe believed that this sort of behavior was "putting your right foot foremost," something she adopted as a personal maxim.[31]

To make of her son a proper English gentleman, Phoebe had surrounded him with tutors from an early age and had fussed over his dress and manners. When circumstances allowed, she had enrolled him in private schools and tried to protect him from rougher boys—this against the advice of George, who figured the sooner Will learned to handle himself, the better. Will took lessons in dance and fencing and drawing. He studied French and German, and he traveled a great deal. He saw Ireland, where scenes of poverty moved him to want to give away his clothes, and the Louvre, which he wanted his mother to buy. He attended the Vienna International Exhibition and a papal audience in Rome. He visited no end of galleries and auction houses, and with his mother's encouragement spent vast sums at age eleven on Venetian glass. Eventually, Phoebe shipped him off to the prestigious St. Paul's Episcopal School near Concord, New Hampshire, and afterward to Harvard, where she decorated his suite of rooms at Matthews Hall in crimson and equipped him with a library, a maid, and a valet.

Phoebe got some of what she wanted out of her boy. She took great pride and comfort in his precociousness and handsome looks, his curiosity and good nature. As he grew, he developed a quick intelligence and a strong memory. His sense of humor was lively (unlike his mother's) and he displayed uncommon personal honesty. He did his lessons without too much complaint. He read Shakespeare and travel literature with Phoebe and he wrote his father at age fifteen of the thrill of reading Roman history at the exact locations where great events had occurred. Most importantly, so far as Phoebe was concerned, Will was openly affectionate toward his mother. "I want to see you so bad," he wrote her while in his teens. "If I could only talk how much more I could say than I can write in a letter. . . . I was very sorry to hear you had been sick. I suppose it was the effect of the waters and Dr. Sarrand's big bill."[32]

But other aspects of Will's behavior were disconcerting. Phoebe's early letters describe him, with a certain pride, as "very mischievous" and "full of pranks."[33] Most of this activity was harmless enough— plying his pet rabbit with champagne, fishing for goldfish in the fountains of the Tuileries gardens. There was, however, a pyrotechnic bent to Will's naughtiness. Visiting family friends over April Fool's Day one year, he drew the fire department to their home by setting off Bengal rockets indoors. In Paris during a European tour in 1879, Will and a friend, Eugene Lent, were discovered shooting pigeons from the window of their lodgings with a toy brass cannon. On the same trip, an attempt to create a small-scale model of a fire at sea using a large bowl, a supply of alcohol, and a ship lifted from the mantle in their room resulted in a midscale blaze that brought the Parisian *pompiers*. An unceremonious eviction followed. At a more elegant hotel on the Champs Élysées, Will and Eugene got hold of an ancient hunting rifle with a black cartridge and ramrod. They managed to fire a shot into the plaster cherubs on the ceiling of their suite. In an effort to dislodge the ramrod, the concierge pulled the whole ceiling down, adding considerably to the Hearsts' travel costs. Expensive as those stunts may have been, there was no malice in them. The malice was saved for Monsieur Gallivotti, proprietor of an *académie de danse*. Unhappy with his course of instruction, Will threw a stone through the establishment's window.[34]

Young Hearst attended St. Paul's at his mother's insistence, but its highly structured routine, with regular fasts and three high Episcopal services a day, was too solemn for his tastes: "There is never anything new to write about in this place. Every day is like another except now and then there is only substitution of Church for playtime and Sacred History for Latin, Greek, etc." He wrote Phoebe with his complaints of the sermons:

> I believe that every old minister in the country comes here to practice on us, and shove off old sermons that no one else will listen to, and I would not either if I did not have to. The Dr. preaches pretty well but hollers too much.[35]

He returned home after a year at St. Paul's and resumed studies with private tutors.

Harvard, where the demands were few and the freedom generous, was a better experience. Will was one of a minority of students from outside New England, yet he managed to accomplish all he desired socially. He was elected to the Porcellian Club and to Med Fac. The latter was "the most secret, most esteemed, and apparently, most criminal of the secret societies," its chief occupation being to monkey with campus plaques and statuary.[36] He kept to a demanding schedule of beer parties and dinners, on and off campus. As often as possible, he would haunt the demimondes of Boston and New York, nurturing a taste for café life and musical comedy. Unlike many of the wealthier students at Harvard, who lived off campus to avoid mandatory chapel attendance, Will lived on campus and skipped the compulsories anyway. He grew a wispy mustache and dressed like a dude. He acquired a girlfriend named Tessie and a pet alligator named Champagne

Charley after its favorite drink. His classmate, the philosopher and aes-
thete George Santayana, saw Hearst as a parvenu and later wrote that he
was "little esteemed in the college."[37] A reporter who interviewed other
students about Hearst heard him described as quiet and reserved but "one
of the best fellows in college," "good-hearted," a "whole-souled, generous" individual, and "the coolest and longest-headed man" on campus.[38]
Although the academic requirements at Harvard were not rigorous,
Hearst's performance was poor enough to win him probation in his sophomore year, followed not long after by a rustication from which he would
not return.

Heart wrote the occasional "Dear Mummer" letter from college,
boasting of his dinners and parties, complaining of eastern winters,
wondering why his parents so seldom wrote, and alternately reassuring
Phoebe about his studies and apologizing for the results. The odd letter
was forlorn, as this one on his twenty-first birthday: "I have the dumps
today and I feel rather homesick and I wish I could enjoy my birthday at
home and with you and father instead of with a lot of fellows who don't
care whether I am twenty one or thirty so long as the dinner is good
and the wine plenty."[39] More commonly, he adopted a breezy, playful
tone, as in this description of how he had killed a long train trip: "I
found some consolation in thinking about the dear one I had left behind,
of the sweet sweet pain of parting, of the tender eyes suffused with tears
and the winsome smile that played around the back of the neck of my
own my darling Charley."[40]

He would sometimes take breaks from campus to visit his mother in
New York. He always had a great time. She was invariably distraught,
writing George on one occasion:

> Late hours and dissipation affect him. Of course, I don't know how much
> he drank, but I do know he was not intoxicated at all, nor even *funny,* as
> they call it but even the amount he must have drunk did him *no good.*
> Theaters, horse shows, late suppers and *women* consumed the two hundred
> dollars quickly. . . .
>   The day after the college fellows left, I was suffering dreadfully.
> [A friend] said she did not think I could possibly live through the year if
> that state of things went on, but I don't believe heartaches kill and I am
> plucky if not strong.[41]

When Will ran afoul of the university, Phoebe, the educational philan-thropist, took it hard and personally. "It would almost kill me," she wrote her son, "if you should not go through college in a creditable manner."[42] The senator, never keen on Harvard, seems to have taken Will's struggles in stride, although his name was invoked in a sensible letter of advice to Will from a family friend:

> Your father realizes, if you do not, the contemptuous estimate of a man (even in a money-making community like this) which is sure to stick to one who has failed in a contest that is distinctively a test of brains. . . . A Harvard degree, if it means nothing else, does mean that a man has made the beginning of a liberally intelligent life. . . . Whatever occupation you may choose as a business, I venture to say, unless I am greatly mistaken in you, you will never lose an interest in intellectual things, but will feel from year to year that they hold a place of growing importance in your life.[43]

Neither parent (nor the family friend) was successful in urging Will to resume his education. Harvard had set what he considered to be intolera-ble conditions for his return: no suppers or parties in his rooms, no leaving campus during the semester. "I assured the gentlemen of the Faculty of Harvard College that I didn't regret so much having lost my degree as having given them an opportunity to refuse it to me," he wrote Phoebe.[44] She counted his refusal to accept the stated terms a disgrace and one of the great disappointments of her life.

Although his failure brought no credit to him, Harvard was hardly a waste of time for Will Hearst. While neglecting his studies, he had dis-covered two of the great passions of his life. He began to follow national politics. Lockstep with his father, then emerging as a power among California Democrats, he took up the party's cause on campus. He rallied "all the Democratic dudes in college"—a mere twenty-eight in a class of over two hundred—on behalf of Cleveland in 1884. He organized a rau-cous bonfire and flag-raising in the center of Harvard Yard, with plenty of fireworks, already something of a Hearst signature. "There were three cheers for Grover," he wrote his mother, "and as the crowd howled in response, the band played, rockets shot up into the night and the glorious flag unfurled and waved acknowledgment." At the end of the evening there were three cheers for the Hearsts, father and son, working at both ends of the continent in the same cause. Will was "quite overcome and ran away and hid" so that he wouldn't have to speak.[45]

However reticent at that moment, Hearst was already nurturing political ambitions. He worked hard at the organization of his Democratic club, and prepared as part of his studies an analysis of the 1884 election that displayed what biographer David Nasaw has called "a grasp of national politics remarkable for a college student."[46] Will wrote his father an amusing letter on the accommodations they would require when united as senior senator and junior congressman in one Washington household. He suggested something "imposing, that it may seem to appreciate the importance of its position in sheltering two such immortals," yet "unassuming, as if it were at the same time sensible of the views of the occupants towards the people."[47]

The senator does not appear to have answered the letter, not being in the practice of answering personal mail. "I was pleasantly surprised by a letter from you," his son wrote him on another occasion, "and I suppose it was for me although you signed yourself, 'Your loving husband.'"[48] George Hearst's absentmindedness—like his absence—was fundamental to his parenting style. His son frequently reminded him to write and to send gifts on special occasions, not always to good effect. "Well, goodbye," Will signed off in another letter. "I have given up all hope of having you write to me, so I suppose I must just scratch along and trust to hearing of you through the newspapers."[49] Nevertheless, the senator supplanted his wife as the dominant parent while Will was at Harvard. He represented a masculine ideal far more attractive to any red-blooded American youth than the English model proffered by Phoebe. Strong, shrewd, self-reliant, and undomesticated, George was the epitome of the self-made frontiersman, a type worshipped by college-educated easterners as diverse as Stephen Crane, Frederic Remington, and Theodore Roosevelt. He influenced not only Will's interest in politics, but his embrace of a second passion: publishing.

George had purchased the *San Francisco Examiner* in 1880 in part to further his political ambitions but also with his son's future in mind. "I hope the Boy will be able . . . to take charge of the paper soon after he leaves college," he wrote Phoebe, "as it will give him more power than anything else."[50] Will rose to the bait. When his friend Eugene Lent ran into trouble running the *Harvard Lampoon,* Will pitched in to keep the chronically indebted humor magazine afloat. He rented a room for the magazine in Brattle Street and supplied its contributors with subscriptions to the French comic papers, which he rated the best in the world. He competed successfully against rival university publications for the advertising business of Cambridge merchants. "I am a man of business now," he wrote his mother. "Eugene and I are business managers, or managing editors; we drum up subscriptions and advertisements, keep the books, send the exchanges, and attend to all the business of the paper." Phoebe soon found herself enlisted to sell *Lampoon* subscriptions to the San Francisco Harvard Club. The results of Hearst's efforts were impressive: circulation doubled to 450 and the magazine cleared a $650 profit after all debts were paid. "Show this to Papa," Will proudly instructed his mother, "and tell him just to wait till Gene and I get hold of the old *Examiner* and we'll boom her in the same way she needs it."[51]

It is telling that Hearst's successes at Harvard occurred outside the classroom. He was not an intellectual, one for whom ideas are living things, of interest for their own sake. He had a strong mind engaged on many intellectual matters and was a great learner, able to process huge amounts of information, but he had little time for anything he did not consider to have at least the potential for practical application. What's more, a university's requirement of steady application to a disciplined course of inquiry ran against his nature. He was powerfully self-directed. He needed to learn and live by his own interests and enthusiasms. He had a visceral attraction to action and conflict, to new sensations and experiences. He hated routine, as his St. Paul's experience had demonstrated, and he tended to ignore externally imposed standards and timetables. It is not that Hearst was incapable of discipline; he quit drinking and smoking during college, and he worked with ferocious concentration on projects that interested him. The discipline simply had to be in service of his own autonomous aims and ambitions.

Self-direction and independence go to the essence of Hearst. His great contemporary Lincoln Steffens studied and interviewed him not long after the events described in this book and decided that the most notable thing about Hearst wasn't his money, his talent, his intelligence, his choice of lieutenants, or his command of public attention. Rather, it was his "dogged determination to get done the things he wants to do." The man, concluded Steffens, "has a will. His very ability seems to be that of

will, rather than of mind." And his will was harnessed to his own purposes. Steffens mentioned repeatedly Hearst's "independence," his
"absolute self-sufficiency," his "self-reliance," his indifference to what
others might think.[52]

George Hearst might have been an absent parent but he, too, had given
his son's character some thought, reaching the same conclusions as Steffens
would. "There's one thing sure about my boy Bill," he wrote. "I've been
watching him, and I notice that when he wants cake, he wants cake; and he
wants it now. And I notice that after a while he gets his cake."[53]

IN THE AFTERMATH OF HARVARD, cake was the *Examiner*. While still at
school, Will had arranged to receive regular shipments of the paper. He
spent countless hours in its pages, applying to it the same hard artisan's
intelligence that his father had once applied to the study of mining. He
would read the paper, tear it apart, study its architecture and its individual parts, and compare it in great detail to the New York dailies—the
Evening Post, for instance, and Pulitzer's *World*, which he read obsessively. He would send the senator packages of clippings to illustrate arguments about page layouts or the proper use of typography. He developed
his own sense of the *Examiner*'s worth. He began complaining in letters
to his father of "our miserable little sheet" and the "imbecility" of its
managers. He offered advice on improvements. "I will give you the benefit of my large head and great experience on this subject," he teased, "and
not charge you a cent."[54]

When George asked him to take time from his studies to assist in the
search for new management at the *Examiner*, Will made the rounds of
editors in New York and pumped them dry of knowledge. He shocked
his mother with his anxiety over the task; she had seldom known him to
take anything seriously. "He says it seems dreadful to stay another year in
college," she wrote George ruefully, "when he might be at work doing
something to help you along with all the business you have."[55]

Journalism, long a refuge for intelligent individuals who by nature are
wasted on the academy, was a natural home for Hearst. Journalism was
an open field where his broad-ranging mind could indulge his political
interests or whatever else happened to catch his eye. Journalism was an
opportunity to make a difference, which mattered to Hearst; despite his

carefree poses, he had absorbed some of Phoebe's noblesse oblige and passion for a cause. Journalism supplied fireworks too—action, conflict, unpredictability, novelty, spectacle. A newspaper was a great thundering enterprise in itself, involving hundreds of people in the hurly burly of newsgathering and the massive manufacturing operation required to print and deliver hundreds of thousands of copies daily. Although somewhat shy and aloof, Hearst had shown at Harvard, with his Democratic club and the *Lampoon,* that he was drawn to enterprises larger than himself.

Hearst knew the *Examiner* was a perfect fit for him. His father knew it as well and was quite pleased to think that his son might be a newspaper editor.[56] His mother considered it beneath him. She fought his involvement in the paper and seems to have brought the senator around to her way of thinking with the practical argument that Will should be directed to a profitable branch of the family business: ranching, say, or mining. As a consequence, he was shipped for three months to the 900,000-acre Babicora ranch where he enjoyed the weather and managed to work up some romantic notions of what it meant to be a pioneer in Mexico, but his only real achievement was maintaining regular delivery of the *Examiner* 240 miles south of the border. When his parents suggested he take over operations at the ranch, he turned them down.

At George's urging, Will made stagecoach tours of some of the Hearst mining properties, accompanied on occasion by friends from school. As he wrote his mother, they made an impression on the locals:

All the inhabitants of this town who look upon life as serious and upon labor as an undesirable necessity are tonight collected in groups discussing the mysterious conduct of the Eastern dudes. They are in doubt how to explain the actions of four eccentrics who will deliberately and with malice aforethought push a heavy freight car up a steep grade some two miles in length for the mere pleasure of sliding down on the said car at the risk of their necks and who moreover not satisfied with having once imperiled their lives and insulted the dignity of labor repeated this performance for the second time. We are, for this imprudence, for of course it was we, objects of great interest not wholly unmingled with pity or contempt.[57]

Will enjoyed these adventures with his friends, but mining was another matter. He could work up an enthusiasm for the investment side of the business, an enthusiasm he would maintain well into middle age, but he was never cut out for prospecting, digging in the ground, and frontier life. Will's attachment to civilization was a clear victory for Phoebe. He found the mining towns grubby and dull, and the travel arduous. Worried about germs, he stockpiled Listerine, a new product as yet marketed only to the medical community. "Listerine," he wrote his mother, requesting a large bottle be shipped to him, "is a kind of disinfectious tooth wash, cholera cure and sore throat preventative."[58] His halfhearted efforts to learn the business that had made his father rich came to an end at the Anaconda:

> After having been thoroughly soaked with dust, choken up by the Narrow Gauge, and prostrated by the heat, I am now, at last, safely arrived at the Anaconda Mine. . . . Pa this is the damnedest hole I have ever struck. As far as one can see—which isn't very far because of the dust and smoke— there is nothing but reddish yellow leprous looking hills with an occasional splotch of dead-grey sage brush that rather serves to heighten the dreariness of the scene.
>
> In the town below . . . stands the bank, the church, the hotel, a few dwelling houses, saloons innumerable and the jail—and next to the saloons I have no doubt that the jail is the most frequented and best patronized place of the entire neighborhood.
>
> . . . I would just as soon live in a jail as anywhere else in this country and I am sure the four walls of a prison could not present any greater or more melancholy monotony than one obtains from the summit of the Anaconda mine. . . .
>
> You see, the trouble with me is that I don't know anything about this mining business. I don't know a drift from a vein or a dump from a tunnel and as a consequence, it is difficult for me to display any extraordinary interest in the proceedings.[59]

Through all these travels, wherever his parents sent him, Hearst's attentions returned time and again to the *Examiner*. He continued to send George critiques of its performance and suggestions for new editors. Eventually he tired of railing at the paper's myriad flaws and wrote his father proposing himself as the solution. This letter pleading for a chance to run the newspaper is in stark contrast to the one Will wrote from the Anaconda:

Now, if you should make over to me the *Examiner*—with enough money to carry out my schemes—I'll tell you what I would do. In the first place, I would change the general appearance of the paper and make seven wide columns where we now have nine narrow ones. Then I would have the type spaced more, and these two changes would give the pages a much cleaner and neater appearance. Secondly, it would be well to make the paper as far as possible original, to clip only some such leading journal as the New York *World* which is undoubtedly the best paper of that class to which the *Examiner* belongs—that class which appeals to the people and which depends for its success upon enterprise, energy and a certain startling originality and not upon the wisdom of its political opinions or the lofty style of its editorials. And to accomplish this we must have—as the *World* has—active intelligent and energetic young men; we must have men who come out west in the hopeful buoyancy of youth for the purpose of making their fortunes and not a worthless scum that has been carried there by the eddies of repeated failures. Thirdly, we must advertise the paper from Oregon to New Mexico and must also increase our number of advertisements if we have to lower our rates to do it. Thus we can put on the first page that our circulation is such and our advertisements so and so and constantly increasing. And now having spoken of the three great essential points, let us turn to details.

The illustrations are a detail, though a very important one. Illustrations embellish a page; illustrations attract the eye and stimulate the imagination of the lower classes and materially aid the comprehension of an unaccustomed reader and thus are of particular importance to that class of people which the *Examiner* claims to address. Such illustrations, however, as have heretofore appeared in the paper, nauseate rather than stimulate the imagination and certainly do anything but embellish a page.

Another detail of questionable importance is that we actually or apparently establish some connection between ourselves and the New York *World*, and obtain a certain prestige in bearing some relation to that paper. We might contract to have important private telegrams forwarded or something of that sort, but understand that the principal advantage we

are to derive is from the attention such a connection would excite and
from the advertisement we could make of it.

Whether the *World* would consent to such an arrangement for any
reasonable sum is very doubtful for its net profit is over one thousand
dollars a day and no doubt it would consider the *Examiner* as beneath its
notice. Just think, over one thousand dollars a day and four years ago it
belonged to Jay Gould and was losing money rapidly.

And now to close with a suggestion of great consequence, namely,
that all these changes be made not by degrees but at once so that the
improvement will be very marked and noticeable and will attract universal
attention and comment. . . .[60]

The letter is astonishing, first of all, for what is missing. There are
none of the typical failings of journalistic novices: the misplaced literary
airs, the single-issue political obsessions, the thirst for fame and self-
aggrandizement. There is none of the contempt for the commercial
aspects of newspapering common among journalists, nor the mistrust of
editorial aspirations often found in businessmen. The letter is written in a
purposeful voice, sometimes self-deprecating, sometimes bombastic, and
preternaturally self-assured. The extent of Hearst's ambition verges on
the absurd—he intends to make the miserable *Examiner* outperform every
newspaper on the Pacific coast—yet he has a sensible plan for success.

What's still more impressive about Hearst's letter is that it considers
the newspaper as a whole. He takes into account editorial style and tone,
political positioning, design, illustration, advertising, circulation,
staffing, promotion, capital investment, strategic alliances, and profitability. He perceives an opening in the San Francisco market for a newspaper with a mass audience, drawing particularly on the thousands of
migrants pouring into California annually. Everything in his plan, from
design to staffing, works toward producing the right paper for these readers. His mini-dissertation on the uses of illustration is particularly astute,
and a forecast of a lifelong preoccupation. He also understands that
enterprising journalism—or what he elsewhere called "startlingly original" journalism with an "alarming" spirit of enterprise—was essential to
cutting through in an otherwise crowded newspaper environment.[61] His
political ideas, while strongly held, are here subordinated to the overall
goal of building a viable and competitive franchise.

None of what he planned to do was revolutionary in itself. Many of his ideas had been gleaned from the great exemplar Pulitzer's *World* and from conversations with Pulitzer's editors in New York. Hearst appears to have worked at the paper for several months. (This has been disputed by his biographers, but the trades reported that he had been on staff at a New York daily and Hearst himself wrote years later that he had apprenticed under Ballard Smith at the *World*.)[62] He had also ingratiated himself in Boston with the operators of the *Globe,* one of the nation's livelier dailies. All that those papers had to teach, Hearst had taken to heart. His letter is a feat of apprehension and preparation: a lot of good newspapermen have retired without so clear and balanced an understanding of how to make a successful newspaper as Hearst possessed at the outset. On one of his previous sojourns in New York, Hearst had tried to persuade Ballard Smith, a topflight news executive in Pulitzer's employ, to run the *Examiner.* Smith told the twenty-three-year-old to forget about hiring an editor and manage the paper himself. In light of this memo, it was reasonable advice.

In a subsequent letter written days before he started at the *Examiner,* Hearst told his father his precise goals: "I have all my pipes laid, and it only remains to turn on the gas. One year from the day I take hold of the thing our circulation will have increased ten thousand. . . . In two years we will be paying. And in five years we will be the biggest paper on the Pacific slope. We won't be paying for two years because up to that time I propose turning back into the improvement of the paper every cent that comes in."[63] He warned his father that the *Examiner* would henceforth be "honest and fearless" and likely to offend his friends in high places. His name went on the masthead as proprietor March 4, 1887. On March 12 it was changed to proprietor and editor, and on March 14 it stuck as editor and proprietor.

HEARST'S *Examiner* WAS QUICK to establish its reputation for enterprise. When Monterey's famed Hotel Del Monte caught fire, Hearst hired a special train and freighted dozens of reporters and photojournalists there. They filled an ambitious fourteen-page special edition with eyewitness accounts, oversized headlines, and massive (for the time) three- and four-column pictures. As Hearst intended, the *Examiner*'s coverage caused almost as much commotion as the fire itself. The special edition sold out, as did the first extra press run, and another.

Enterprise of an alarming nature followed on the heels of that success. An *Examiner* man was sent on a successful mission to trap a California grizzly when the species was reported to be extinct. An *Examiner* man was launched in a hot-air balloon to give San Franciscans their first aerial view of their city. An *Examiner* man ventured out on Hearst's yacht to rescue a half-naked, half-dead fisherman stranded on a storm-swept rock near Point Bonita. An *Examiner* man threw himself over the side of the Oakland ferry to prove local authorities incapable of a timely rescue. An *Examiner* man beat a handful of posses to the mountain hideout of the infamous train robbers Sontag and Evans and brought back an exclusive interview. Hearst himself scooped the entire nation on the McKinley tariff bill, perhaps the most important piece of domestic business to come out of Washington in these years. He ran a leaked draft of the full text of the legislation in tiny type over three pages.

The *Examiner* plied its audience with generous doses of human interest: crime and calamity, medical marvels, society gossip, titillating illustrations of scantily attired actresses and ballerinas, and sheet music. But Hearst also reached out to readers with crusades for free schoolbooks, safe school buildings, and an income tax on high earners. The paper successfully campaigned for an eight-hour day for ironworkers and for public ownership of the water supply.

Most spectacularly, Hearst fulfilled his promise to offend his father's friends by hammering daily and gleefully on the good repute of Collis Potter Huntington, proprietor of the Southern Pacific Railroad. At the time, all of California was known as "Huntington's plantation." The *Examiner*'s editorialists accused the railway czar and his confederates, including George Hearst's U.S. Senate colleague Leland Stanford, of operating by bribery and intimidation, and of exploiting their monopoly for obscene personal gain. The paper also argued, not incorrectly, that the railway was hobbling the regional economy with unreliable freight service and exorbitant rates. In full rhetorical swing, the *Examiner* could imagine Huntington singlehandedly frustrating California's natural progress from backwater frontier to garden paradise and could charge him with a murderous laxity in his concern for passenger safety.

Spearheading the attacks on the Southern Pacific were two of Hearst's best hires: Arthur McEwan, a leading radical editorialist, lured to the *Examiner* from a competing paper; and Ambrose Bierce, an explosive polemicist and crabbed literary genius personally rescued by the editor from the semi-obscurity of San Francisco weeklies.

Born in Ohio in 1842, Bierce was one of thirteen children (all of whose names began with A) of Marcus Aurelius Bierce. He had seen action at Shiloh before serving on a military inspection of western outposts that landed him in San Francisco, where he married, raised three children of his own, and produced verse, journalism, and some of his generation's better short fiction. He took a sardonic view of everything and carried a pistol to protect himself from victims of his invective. By his own account, he answered his door one day to find on his stoop "the youngest man, it seemed to me, that I had ever confronted."

"Well?" asked Bierce.

> "I am from the *San Francisco Examiner*," [Hearst] explained in a voice like the fragrance of violets made audible, and backed a little away.
>
> "Oh," I said. "You come from Mr. Hearst?"
>
> Then that unearthly child lifted his blue eyes and cooed, "I *am* Mr. Hearst."[64]

In his first months at the Examiner, Hearst completely overhauled its staff. He kept the best of the old guard. He shipped in a small brigade of Harvard buddies, not least of them E.L. Thayer, who would give the paper his famous verse "Casey at the Bat." He recruited some sharp and experienced New York talent, including his managing editor, the debonair and alcoholic Sam Chamberlain. Others he hired on impulse. A pressman, George Pancoast, was promoted to Hearst's personal secretary after making him laugh one day in the pressroom. They became lifelong friends.

Having filled his stable at considerable expense with strong personalities and high-spirited talent, Hearst saw no reason not to let it all out for a romp. The atmosphere in the newsroom was loose and exuberant. The staff worked hard and took risks. It was "a happy and extravagant world," by one account, "a madhouse inhabited by talented and erratic young men, drunk with life in a city that never existed before or since."[65]

Not everyone was impressed by Hearst's methods. Even members of his own staff considered it contemptible to pollute the front page with sports stories, theater reviews, and a long rollicking account of Kaiser Wilhelm's ninetieth-birthday celebrations. Respected newspaper veterans complained of irresponsible reporting and "unwarranted insinuations" in news copy. There were occasional resignations and requests for reassignment. The paper was embarrassed when a series on the tribulations of an orphan newsboy struggling to support two younger brothers turned out to be a complete fraud, and there were even whispers that the celebrated interview with Evans and Sontag was a fake (it wasn't).

Hearst's promotional strategies were also controversial. Publishing a newspaper without promotion, he would say, was well intentioned but futile, "like winking at a girl in the dark." If the *Examiner* were to bask in an aura of vitality and success, it needed to be boomed to the rafters. The paper hired marching bands and hosted champagne celebrations to introduce itself to readers. It treated the public to free boat rides and oyster suppers and, inevitably, massive fireworks displays. It gave itself the tag line "Monarch of the Dailies," and boasted continually of its rising circulation. It patted itself on the back for every success. An immodest portion of the Monterey hotel fire coverage was devoted to the *Examiner*'s own methods and exploits. All of this struck higher-brows as hucksterism and a mindless affront to the serious craft of journalism. Hearst was derided by his competitors as a dilettante and an exhibitionist. One ran a mock interview in which Hearst explained his craft to a British newspaper editor:

> I soon told [the editor] who I was, and what a paper I had made of the *Examiner*, and how I usually make things hum. . . . I told him how I had startled the whole country by running special trains to Petaluma and Milpitas, and spending a lot of money on balloon ascensions, tight-rope walkers and oyster suppers, and whooped things up generally. . . . [T]he old chap didn't catch on at all.
>
> "What do you run special trains for?" he asked.
>
> "That's for enterprise," said I.
>
> "What are the balloons for?" asked he.
>
> "They prove that you've got the liveliest newspaper," said I.
>
> "What are the tight-rope walkers, the oysters and the other things for?" asked he.
>
> "They show that you've got the largest circulation," said I.

"But wouldn't it be better," he suggested, "to buy news with your money . . . ?"

"Why," I said, "I don't buy news because we can fake it."[66]

But Hearst was not easily dismissed; nor was his newspaper. The *Examiner* had the best talent in the West. It was a smart and well-written paper. Its crusades were often courageous and marked by an unmistakable sense of public service. One of his staffers noted, to his own mild astonishment, that Hearst had "a real sympathy for the submerged man and woman, a real feeling of his own mission to plead their cause."[67]

Even those who worked closely with him on the *Examiner* staff had trouble taking the measure of the man in the middle of this three-ring newspaper. "Boyish and slightly diffident in manner, and still a bit under the influence of the impish high spirits of youth," tried the journalist Florence Kelly.[68] At one moment Hearst might dissolve into a girlish giggle; at another he might break into a sober-faced jig or run out to fly a kite. He was soft-spoken and unfailingly courteous in manner. He operated by suggestion rather than command. With his short hair parted in the middle and his dandyish dress, he was the picture of youthful insouciance.

Those who looked closely at Hearst, however, noticed the fingers drumming, the feet tapping, the clenched lips. The truth is that he was running flat out at the *Examiner*. He was learning a business on the fly. He was leading the relaunch of a major daily newspaper against determined competition in an already crowded market. He was always prosecuting a handful of political crusades, each one of which required his detailed care and attention as it attracted return fire (and occasionally lawsuits) from politicians, public servants, and competitors. The load he carried, intellectually, emotionally, and physically, was immense. "I don't suppose I will live more than two or three weeks if this strain keeps up," he wrote his mother, one of the very few to ever see him lower his guard. "I don't get to bed until about two o'clock and I wake up at about seven in the morning and can't get to sleep again, for I must see the paper and compare it with the *Chronicle*. If we are the best, I can turn over and go to sleep with quiet satisfaction but if the *Chronicle* happens to scoop us, that lets me out of all sleep for the day."[69]

Hearst was obsessively competitive. He treated every strategic choice at the *Examiner* as a matter of life or death. Half measures were out of the question: "We have either got to go in and win," he once wrote his father, "or we have got to go out of the business."[70] He pushed himself and his operation for every possible advantage in his fight with the *Chronicle*. He mastered printing technology in search of crisper pages and faster press times. He was a nuisance about headlines, treating each one as though it alone would tease another hundred readers from the competition to his own sheet. He leaned on his father to call in political favors to bring in advertising and promote the paper's distribution, and was furious when the senator's friends patronized the *Examiner*'s rivals: "As these sons of bitches are principally indebted to you for whatever they have, I think this is the goddamdest low down business I ever heard of. I don't apologize for the swear words for I think the circumstances excuse them."[71]

Every advance by the *Chronicle* threw a chill into him. After the competitor hired a phalanx of new reporters and arranged for the rights to content from Pulitzer's *World*, Will wrote home, "The newspaper business is no fun. The *Chronicle* is fighting tremendously hard, and it does not hesitate to adopt any idea we bring out. . . . It has altered its makeup until it is almost exactly like ours. . . . [I]ts matter is so similar that we are not allowed to reap much advantage from our moves. . . . You bet your life those *Chronicle* people are smart and they are not retarded by any false pride."[72] Certain that Mike de Young was throwing every cent he had into the *Chronicle*, Will drew heavily on the family accounts, investing as much as $200,000 a year in his paper's growth.

But however difficult the fight, Hearst soon met most of his goals. Circulation did increase by ten thousand within his first year on the job. The paper did turn a profit, though in three rather than two years. And by the time of George's death, the *Examiner* was indeed the biggest paper on the West Coast. Will Hearst was a bona fide newspaper success. No one was prouder than the senator, who put his thoughts on record before he died:

> I tried all sorts of people to make [the *Examiner*] a success. . . . I had not time to attend to it, and could not pretend to run it. After I had lost about a quarter of a million by the paper, my boy Will came out of school, and said he wanted to try his hand at the paper. I thought it was the very worst thing he could do; and told him so, adding that I could not make it pay. He said, however, that the reason that the paper did not pay was because it

was not the best paper in the country. He said that if he had it, he would make it the best paper in the country . . . and then it would pay. I then put him in it, and made him a deed of the whole property from top to bottom and agreed to stand by him for two years. Now I don't think there is a better paper in the country.[73]

The senator estimated the paper had cost him as much as $700,000 before it broke even with his son at the helm. He placed its value by 1890 at upward of a million dollars. He wrote, "My son Will is one of the hardest workers I ever saw, and he thought at the time that he would tire of it as there was so much drudgery in it, but he did not."[74]

FIVE MONTHS AFTER HIS FATHER'S DEATH, in the sweltering summer of 1891, Hearst was still toying with his New York project, notwithstanding his mother's financial disciplines. He made the rounds of Manhattan newspapermen to see if any papers were on the market, and wrote Phoebe that he had visited John Cockerill, the former Pulitzer editor, now a principal at the one-cent *Morning Advertiser.* Cockerill offered him a share in his sheet, but Hearst politely declined, hoping instead to acquire a quality two- or three-cent daily—the *Herald,* for instance, or the biggest prize, Pulitzer's *World.*

Hearst's tour of New York occasioned a great deal of gossip on newspaper row and speculation as to his intentions. The *World* fired a shot across his bow by attempting to hire his best men from San Francisco. "I think the *World* people made their offers to Palmer and Chamberlain largely to hustle me off home and prevent me from going in with Cockerill whom they hate and fear," he told Phoebe. "Chamberlain acted splendidly and Palmer didn't."[75] It apparently cost the *Examiner* a tidy sum to keep its team intact.

Hearst continued to spend more of his time in New York. His *Examiner* now boasted the largest East Coast bureau of any western paper. Its offices, paneled in California redwood, were in Pulitzer's magnificent building on Park Row. Hearst used them as his base. He joined several clubs to improve his business contacts. He played on his yacht, frequented the musical theater, and continued to shop for newspapers, to no avail. The right property didn't come up, at least not at the right price. Though his mother couldn't be counted an ally to his expansion plans, Hearst kept her apprised of his activities. It is unclear whether that represented the usual candor he brought to their relationship or some understanding between them that he could expand at his own expense or with some form of limited financial assistance from her.

Phoebe was never keen on journalism as a vocation, but she was impressed by her son's hard work and his achievements. His professional life, however, was of less concern to her than his social activities. She still held out hopes for her son's career as a gentleman, and she was particularly interested in his marital prospects. She understood his options to be limitless: he was intelligent, handsome, good natured, and polite; he had made a tour of Harvard Yard; he had acquitted himself well in the field of journalism; and he would also be the eventual sole heir to one of America's largest private fortunes. In the fashion of the day, a young man with Will's prospects would be expected to effect a merger with European nobility or, at worst, a prominent American family. Phoebe thus directed any number of attractive and well-born women his way. The society pages reported that Will's choice of a wife "will make [Mrs. Hearst] a happy woman, or his marriage may prove the greatest sorrow, so much is her heart wrapped up in his future."[76]

In the meantime, Phoebe continued to encourage Will to travel and to mix with men of culture and leisure, particularly Englishmen. In 1891 she embarked on one of her extended European tours and invited Will to meet her early in 1892 in Germany, where family friend Orrin Peck would paint his portrait. Hearst agreed and, as he often did when at his leisure, sent her long and chatty letters. "[S]omething has happened to the weather in these parts," he wrote from Capri. "Somebody has been monkeying with the machinery and the whole thing is off the center. In the north it rained every day. It didn't just rain some days or even nearly every day. It rained every day. Of course, that wasn't all it did. It snowed quite frequently by way of variety, and also quite frequently it hailed large hails about the size of marbles. The fruit crops and vine crops are supposed to be ruined and undoubtedly the tourist crop was very seriously interfered with."[77]

Hearst also met with snow in Paris and with rain and hail in Nice, Geneva, and Florence. "I don't know what is the matter with the weather but I know I can't fix it. I see there were ninety thousand emigrants to

America last month. I don't wonder. I wish there had been ninety thousand and one, and that one had been, Your affectionate son, Will."[78]

To a mother whose sense of well-being could be made or broken by her son's disposition toward her, these words must have been musical. But other letters Will sent Phoebe could only have caused distress. One in particular, written from the *Luciana*, underlined the ludicrousness of her ambitions for her son:

> Lady Cunard is on board. She is at my table. She spoke about you and asked how you were. She is a nice little thing but kind of lightheaded and chatters loudly with a sort of turkey gobbler by the name of Guiness [sic] who makes the stout and a gibbering idiot by the name of Van Allen who doesn't make anything except a holy show of himself. Lady Cunard asked me why I didn't go into society and I could have told her that if I had no other reason the present company would furnish enough. She isn't bad, though, she certainly shines intellectually when compared with the men.
>
> In deference to your wishes I took Thomas the Jap along as valet. He has been very valuable so far as keeping my mind occupied looking after him. He comes in every morning about seven o'clock and wakes me up when I want to sleep and I don't see him anymore for the rest of the day. Fortunately, I am a natural born American citizen able to look after myself and a valet too. All I object to is the money he is costing me. He will foot up a thousand dollars before the trip is over and that would enable me to bring home an Egyptian mummy—something intrinsically valuable and which would make fully as good a valet as Thomas in a pinch. Anyhow it wouldn't wake me up in the morning and would stay put.[79]

Short and light as it is, the letter reveals much of Hearst as he entered his thirties. Lady Cunard asked the obvious question: Why not take a position in society? There were no barriers to his entry. Indeed, given his fortune, a social berth was more or less reserved for him. But Hearst had made up his mind about the swells long before. As early as college, he had written his father expressing disdain for "wealthy boors" and "aristocratic imbeciles." He and Orrin Peck had exchanged correspondence mocking a mutual friend who had suddenly developed a long line of "dookal" ancestors in Europe: "Think of those bare feet that used to patter around Virginia City, now nearing Queen quality . . . and carrying around a pudgy descendent of a line of imaginary Kings."[80]

In social matters, Will was very much George Hearst's son, and a child of the bumptious, egalitarian American West. The same society writer who noted Phoebe's desire to see her son well married noted that Will was "hopelessly American," by which he meant "hopelessly democratic in theory and practice, and uncompromisingly down on aristocratic tendencies."[81] Will was well aware of the cultural superiority of Europe: on this trip, as throughout his life, he would buy up great chunks of continental culture (including a collection of paintings and statuary, and a five-ton stone wellhead from a courtyard in Verona). He simply had an abiding preference for American ways and a sharp sense of America's ever-growing economic and political influence in the world.

The manner in which Will was traveling in Europe that season offered only further discouragement to Phoebe. She herself had ramped up her touring style after George's death. A newspaper reported that she "never allows expense to interfere with her disposition to travel by land or sea in the most luxuriously comfortable manner. She has a saloon railway carriage and state cabin on the channel steamer when she goes from London to Paris, or vice versa, and on the Continent, when obtainable, special and exclusive traveling facilities usually associated with royalty."[82] Will, meanwhile, was scampering around Europe demonstrating his relative independence and lack of pretense. In addition to the valet, his odd little retinue included George Pancoast, a cheerful man of remarkable talents—printer, photographer, mechanical genius, song-and-dance performer—none of which would have impressed Mrs. Hearst. The fourth member was Tessie Powers, Will's girlfriend from Cambridge, where she reportedly worked as a waitress.

Tessie Powers is an obscure figure, but she did have one thing in common with all the other young women in Hearst's life to this point: she was not what Phoebe wanted for her son. As a general rule, Will's tastes ran to the stage. His first experience of romance was an adolescent crush on the teenaged actress Lillian Russell. He attended her performances in San Francisco so frequently that the ushers came to know him by name. At nineteen, before his freshman year at Harvard, Hearst summered in Monterey and fell head over heels for Sybil Sanderson, a glamorous and talented San Francisco opera singer. It is said that he proposed to her and was talked out of following her to Paris, where she was to study.

As his Harvard days were ending, Hearst had begun courting the aspiring dramatic actress Eleanor Calhoun, one of Phoebe's protégés. The newspapers described her as a beauty of the highest order, with a promising career to that point "unmarred by vanity, by affectation, by any other taint." Phoebe admired her as a talent but not as a prospective daughter-in-law. The actress, she declared, was "erratic, visionary, indolent, and utterly wanting in order and neatness with extravagant tastes and no appreciation of values. All she cares for is to spend money, enjoy luxury and receive admiration." When Miss Calhoun told the press the young couple was engaged to be married, Phoebe rallied George to announce the family's opposition to the match. She told friends she would die if Miss Calhoun got her hooks into her son. She was shocked when Will, rejecting her guidance, became "ugly and cruel" toward her: she decided he must be in the "toils of the Devil fish," as she now called Miss Calhoun. She worried that her son was becoming as "selfish, indifferent, and undemonstrative as his father." The senator was heard to mutter that his wife was going crazy.[83]

Will Hearst eventually gave up on the Calhoun engagement, no doubt influenced by his mother's pressure. Phoebe was greatly relieved at the outcome but she had only created a larger problem for herself. Shortly after Eleanor Calhoun left town, and just as Will was settling in at the *Examiner*, he transported Tessie Powers from Massachusetts to California.

Almost all that is known of Tessie comes from hostile sources, in particular Anne Apperson Flint, Phoebe's niece and occasional confidante. Mrs. Flint, as a young woman, had traveled as a member of the Hearst household. She was in her early eighties when W.A. Swanberg interviewed her for his 1961 biography of Hearst, discussing events that had occurred when she was fifteen. By the time of the interview, she was nursing a financial grudge against her cousin Will, and it is obvious from her comments that her memory was shaky and that she was a reasonably good match for Phoebe in her ideas about social propriety and the stiff requirements of filial devotion. Anne Flint's story as relayed to Swanberg was that Tessie was a Cambridge waitress and the kept woman of Jack Follansbee, Will's closest friend at Harvard. When Follansbee's family suffered a financial reversal, forcing him to leave the university, he recommended the girl to his friend. Flint seems to have gathered all this straight from Phoebe, who was prone to exaggeration on her son's affairs. It does appear that Will took Tessie everywhere, including to the Harvard-Yale game and on trips to New York and Europe.[84]

For most of the time that Will edited the *Examiner*, Tessie shared his house across the bay in Sausalito, much to the displeasure of their straight-laced neighbors. He commuted daily to San Francisco aboard the *Aquila*. The two parted for a time at the height of the war with the *Chronicle*. "I have sent my girl away," Will wrote his father, "and I am working at the paper all the time."[85] He suggested to his mother that he was reforming his lifestyle, promising her that he would be "a highly respectable citizen and a credit to my family."[86] Nevertheless, Tessie was soon back on the scene.

Phoebe, outraged at the resumption of their relationship, challenged Will on his finances and accused him of wasting money on the girl. "I do hope you can induce Will to change his manner of living," she wrote George late in 1889. "I suppose you hear from him occasionally. I never do. How is it possible for him to devote his time and attention to a prostitute and utterly ignore his mother. He will surely have his punishment."[87]

That Phoebe and Anne Apperson Flint considered Tessie a prostitute is indisputable, but then so is their hysteria on the subject. Will himself treated Tessie as his girlfriend. He lived with her and gave every impression of being in love with her. Given that he was consistently attracted to beautiful, talented, spirited women, it is unlikely that she broke that mold. Elsewhere in her interview, Flint admits that all who knew Tessie considered her "very lady-like," "a very nice girl, well behaved, quiet," and as devoted to Will as he was to her. One of Will's friends suggests that she drank and that he was determined to straighten her out.[88] In any event, Will expected everyone in his life to treat Tessie with the same respect and consideration he received. Flint considered it preposterous of him to believe "that the world would accept [Tessie] because he said so. And because he could place her in that position." He was a bad man, Flint insisted, for refusing to listen to his mother and for not caring what the world thought.[89]

Because his mother now wished to avoid the embarrassment of running into her son's "prostitute" in some European restaurant or hotel, Hearst steered clear of Phoebe during his 1892 travels and promised that he would be alone when he caught up with his mother in Munich for his portrait painting. He did eventually sit for Orrin Peck. The resulting portrait now hangs in the Gothic Study at San Simeon; it shows the young proprietor seated in a vested suit and bow tie, the ends of his mustaches curled gently upward. He looks quite pleased with himself. Judith Robinson describes the painting as an "inspired work," a remarkable likeness capturing Hearst's self-confidence and "his way of fixing his cold blue eyes on whomever he was looking at, seemingly without emotion." Like the man, she writes, "the portrait was unsettling but riveting. He did not avert or waver, he did not lie, even to his mother and even when he knew that she was unhappy with him."[90]

While the Peck portrait was one reason for Hearst's tour of Europe, his primary motive was to indulge a new hobby. George Pancoast, an accomplished amateur photographer, had recently made a study of San Francisco Bay with ships' masts and the peak of Angel Island rising above a fog bank. It had fascinated Hearst. Within twenty-four hours of seeing the picture, he had located the best photographic equipment in San Francisco and placed orders in the East for what else he required. Hearst and Pancoast toured the Continent, their trunks filled with photographic plates and duplicate parts for all their cameras. They photographed wildlife, celebrities, battlefields in France and Italy, and the mountains of Switzerland. To cap their adventure, they departed Paris for an expedition up the Nile. They photographed the temples of Karnak and Luxor, and the Island of Philae. For the first time in history, they flash-lit the tombs of the kings of Egypt, demonstrating the awesome depth of the carved rock. When the British government learned of their activities, cameras were banned from the tombs, but not before Hearst and Pancoast had produced 3,200 negatives.

Also tucked into Hearst's luggage on the voyage home was a collection of mummies, two of them as perfectly preserved as any in existence. On the whole, however, Egypt seems to have made little impression on him. "The Nile is pretty fair," he wrote his mother, "but a little too much like the Sacramento. I don't think I'd enjoy it much if it were not for the queer types of people and the opportunity it gives me for photography."[91]

NOTWITHSTANDING THAT IT WAS the most significant transaction of Hearst's life—the single move that allowed him to emerge as a national

figure and make a fortune on his own—the story of his acquisition of a
New York paper has never been properly told. His most recent biography has Phoebe storming back from Europe and taking up rooms in
San Francisco's Palace Hotel, determined to run her son's mistress out
of town without his knowledge. She or an intermediary offers Tessie
money to leave San Francisco, and threatens her with criminal action if
she does not accept it. Tessie takes the bribe and skips town. A despondent Hearst abandons Sausalito and moves into the Palace with his
mother and Orrin Peck, who has arrived from Europe to console him.
"Instead of fighting to get Tessie back," writes David Nasaw, "Will
took [Tessie's] departure as a *fait accompli*. . . . [H]e accepted the implicit
bargain that Phoebe offered him. He gave up his girl and expected something in return."[92] The "return" was his mother's financial support for
his New York venture.

That Phoebe was upset at her son's behavior is clear from her letters.
That she traveled to San Francisco determined to send Tessie packing is
the uncorroborated witness of the unreliable Anne Apperson Flint. The
rest of the story was simply made up by W.A. Swanberg. In his 1961
biography, Swanberg speculates that Phoebe might have threatened
Tessie with criminal action for "illegal cohabitation." He admits in his text
that he has no evidence to support his conjecture. He credits a "private
source" for the rumor of the $150,000 payoff and then dismisses it himself
as an obvious exaggeration.[93] Nasaw's more recent biography presents
Swanberg's imaginings of threats and payoffs without reservations (and
without new evidence.)

Phoebe was eminently capable of meddling in the affairs of her own
child's heart, but there is no reason to believe that Will traded Tessie for a
paper. The couple returned from Europe to San Francisco in 1892 and
parted the following year when Hearst's New York ambitions were off
the boil: the vicious economic depression of 1893 had hurt the *Examiner*'s
returns and limited his financial options. Worse, the newspaper competition in San Francisco had reached a new and still more expensive pitch.
De Young's new building for the *Chronicle* was, as Hearst had feared, the
wonder of San Francisco. Even Phoebe's doddering father, with whom
Will was close, could not stop talking about it, much to his grandson's
distress. Fully electrified, the new building boasted the world's largest
clock face, visible as far away as Oakland. It terrified Will. Year after

year, brick by brick, prestige and momentum had been piling up on his competitor's building site. He had never persuaded George to advance him the million or two to build his own "great big magnificent building."[94] But he did move the *Examiner* to a new site in 1893 at considerable expense, with an additional thirty thousand in cost overruns. Meanwhile, he had learned that both the *San Francisco Call* and the *Chronicle* had ordered new presses double the size of his own new press, forcing him to contemplate further investment on printing equipment. "The times are dull," he wrote his mother, "and the *Examiner* is doing badly, so that with this thirty thousand to be paid . . . and some other minor indebtedness there is a most disheartening prospect confronting me."[95]

Phoebe was sticking to her guns and refusing to bail her son out of his financial difficulties, and in this regard, her efforts to shape his behavior had creditable effect. So desperate was he to dig out of his hole that he devised a plan to save money. He would "lay aside, not to spend but to invest[,] one half of all income from the paper, the ranch and all property that I may have or acquire."[96]

By 1894, the economic prospects for newspapers were somewhat improved. Hearst's spirits lifted and he began to talk again, urgently and optimistically, of expansion: "I have made up my mind to work very hard on the paper from now on. I must positively build myself papers in Chicago and New York and, if I have the ability, in London, too. I am beginning to get old and if this great plan is to be carried out I have no time to lose, and I am going to devote myself to business, first putting the *Examiner* on so satisfactory a basis that it will get along without much attention from me and will produce enough to enable me to buy my first paper elsewhere."[97]

Hearst wouldn't have been thinking of self-financing a New York acquisition in 1894 if, a year earlier, Phoebe had implicitly or explicitly promised to finance a paper in return for his dumping Tessie. What's more, Flint and other evidence suggests Will hooked up again with Tessie in New York in 1895.[98] It is unlikely that he would have dared to resume the relationship if funding for his next newspaper was contingent on his ending it. Finally, Flint, in another part of her interview with Swanberg, says that Will was unaware that Phoebe had intervened with Tessie until long afterward. How could there have been an "understanding" with his mother if he wasn't aware of what she'd done?

It is more likely that events in Phoebe's own life paved Will's way to New York. Early in 1895, at age fifty-three, she suffered a heart attack and was treated by William Pepper, a famous surgeon at the University of Pennsylvania.[99] Will wired her from New York: "Doctor Pepper says you're all right. Be up in a few days. Says you need better son and better business manager, that's all."[100] By spring, Phoebe had recovered enough to tour Europe, but as often happens in the wake of traumatic events, she reorganized her affairs. She asked her business managers to consider the sale of her stake in the rich Anaconda copper mine. She had some minor debts she wanted to clear and she did not trust the men who had been George's partners in the Anaconda. She also believed she could get a good price for her shares. Perhaps seeking to lessen her burdens, perhaps admitting defeat in her struggle to drag him down the social path she had marked for him, she also took seriously a request from Will that he be made less of a dependent and more of a partner in the family businesses. Both matters—the Anaconda and Will's status—would be decided in an odd sequence of events through the summer of 1895.

Specifically, Will had requested that half of the net income from his mother's investments flow to him; Phoebe went a step further, asking her personal accountant (and cousin) Edward Clark to look into dividing her property, making her son an equal partner. By August 1, Clark was able to inform Phoebe that legal counsel had declared it "unwise and dangerous" for her to sign any agreement making Will a partner in the estate or formalizing an arrangement allowing him half or any part of the income from it. She would be exposed to any claims that might arise against Will and his newspapers. She would also put in jeopardy her right to use the family money as she saw fit during her life time and to will it to whomever she chose. As things stood, Will had not "the slightest legal claim in any way" and Phoebe's professional advisors urged her to keep it that way.[101] She needed no further coaxing. Will may have been dear to her heart, but Phoebe still had a hard head. She would find another way to do right by her son.

Irwin Stump, her mining adviser, had been in New York all summer anxiously trying to sell the Anaconda shares while Phoebe and Will traveled separately in Europe. With Will's status up in the air, Stump wasn't entirely sure which Hearst he answered to and both of them took their time about replying to his letters and wires, never mind that he was executing a multi-million dollar transaction on their behalf. The truth was that mother and son were not communicating with one another either, at least not beyond a couple of sharp exchanges in which Will begged for news of his financial future and Phoebe told him to cool his heels. Sometime in August, she finally cabled Stump a clarification on Will's position: "Cannot arrange for partnership now. Attorney informs me would conflict with those existing. I wish William to be credited with ten thousand per month beginning July last. Will pay it soon as some sales of stock. Meantime he can draw part if needed. Also, will turn over one million for paper New York soon as possible."[102]

Will headed back to New York in late August, arriving on Sunday, September 1, and checking into the Hoffman House. On Labor Day, he visited Stump at his offices, otherwise vacated for the holiday. They reviewed Stump's ongoing efforts to unload Phoebe's Anaconda stake in a volatile copper market, and it appears to have been Stump's unhappy lot to inform Will that he would not be taken into partnership by his mother. Will balked at the suggestion of an income of $10,000 a month, not because of the amount but because he believed he ought to be consulted in the management of the estate. Stump cleverly played on Will's impatience, advising him that a reconsideration of his mother's decision would be complicated and time-consuming. He asked Will to be satisfied that his longing for a New York paper could now be realized. Phoebe, he said, would also contribute to the acquisition and improvement of a building that could be made the "nucleus" of a newspaper empire. Still more tantalizingly, Stump mentioned that success in one enterprise might lead Phoebe to assist in the launching of further newspaper endeavors. Overcome by this invocation of his ultimate dream—"a paper there, and there, and there"—Will immediately dropped the partnership request. The two men finished their meeting, walked uptown to view a piece of property that Will thought might serve as a nucleus, and parted in good humor.[103]

On September 18, 1895, Stump was able to write Phoebe that a syndicate involving the Rothschilds had purchased 300,000 shares in the Anaconda mine, pending an inspection of the property. Her take from the transaction would be $7,290,000. Phoebe was relieved to clear her debts—"I shall not know how to behave," she exulted to a friend. Her investment adviser, Hosmer B. Parsons, deposited the sum on her behalf, setting aside a million for her son.[104]

Will was not a partner in the family business, and he was only receiving a small portion of the proceeds of the Anaconda sale, but he had the go-ahead for his New York project and he was already absorbed in discussions with potential newspaper vendors. Stump met almost daily with Will through September and kept Phoebe apprised of his activities. In a couple of weeks he wrote her again: "I went down to the Hoffman this morning & met William—who is in splendid health. In fact I never saw him look better or more cheerful."[105]

CHAPTER TWO

Is God In?

T he *New York Morning Journal* was founded in 1882 by the portly Albert Pulitzer, younger and less celebrated brother of the legendary Joseph Pulitzer. Albert made no pretence of being an intellectual leader or a political force. Inordinately fond of ice cream and the actress Lillie Langtry, he produced a bright, gossipy paper that sold for a penny to people who worked in factories and department stores. It was to Albert's *Morning Journal* that New Yorkers turned for a heartrending spread on the funeral of a popular "daughter of joy," Fourteenth Street Kitty. It was the *Morning Journal* that serialized the pilfered diaries of a European soprano who, disguised as a man, had embarked on a racy career in New York society. Reports of the paper's circulation are inconsistent, but it appears to have sold between 175,000 and 225,000 copies at its peak, which would have made it one of New York's best-read papers.[1]

By the early 1890s, the *Morning Journal* was earning Albert a fat income of $100,000 a year. Another man might have been delighted at that, but Albert could not help but notice that his one-cent daily was neither as rich nor as authoritative as the two-cent marvel his more talented sibling, Joseph, had meanwhile built down the street. Joseph Pulitzer had entered the New York market in 1883 and, within months, his *World* was the sensation of Park Row. Albert held his peace for a decade, rarely speaking to his brother—they had been rivals since youth. Then, in the winter of 1894–95, Albert unaccountably snapped. He increased his price per copy to two cents, competing head to head with Joseph's mighty *World*, and at least half of the *Journal*'s audience evaporated overnight. Having derailed his own gravy train, Albert Pulitzer thought he was finished until the noted publisher John R. McLean rode in from Washington and offered a handsome sum of $400,000 for his struggling title. A deal was quickly signed and Albert fled to Europe where he suffered through an unhappy retirement of insomnia and mental instability before shooting himself to death in front of his mirror in 1909.[2]

When it was announced in May 1895 that McLean had purchased the *Morning Journal*, the *Washington Post* declared there was "not the least room for doubt" of his success in the undertaking. He was one of the capital's foremost businessmen: president of the Washington Gas Light Company, a major stockholder in banks, railroads, and hotels, and an experienced newspaper operator from a leading newspaper family. The *Post*'s faith in McLean was broadly shared by the New York publishing community.[3]

McLean, in fact, had much in common with the lesser-known William Randolph Hearst, who would pick up his pieces inside of six months. Like Hearst, McLean was born to immense wealth and was not the least ashamed of it. His family owned the Cincinnati *Enquirer* in addition to what was then the largest printing business in the world. Like Hearst, McLean had traveled extensively in Europe and had left Harvard under a cloud. Like Hearst, he had taken over the family paper in his early twenties. With the help of an outstanding editor, John Cockerill (who would also serve Joseph Pulitzer), McLean had more than quadrupled the *Enquirer*'s circulation. Again like Hearst, his paper was noted for its enterprise and its allegiance to the Democratic Party. On paper, McLean was a formidable newspaperman, yet he was a bust in New York.

John McLean tried to elevate the tone of the *Morning Journal*, dumping some of its gossip and entertainment news and loading up on Democratic politics. When circulation plummeted, he tried to restore it by delivering the same content but cutting his price to a penny.[4] This "much for little" strategy was hailed in the trades as a brilliant move. In its September 5 edition, *The Fourth Estate*, a weekly which billed itself as "A Newspaper for the Makers of Newspapers," applauded McLean for his willingness to spend money and the fact that he employed "some of the best men in the metropolitan field." It predicted that he would "work a revolution in the journalism of Manhattan."[5] But the *Morning Journal*'s circulation didn't budge in response to McLean's price cut. He was suddenly selling the same number of papers for half the revenue and his big investment was bleeding cash. By the time the September 5 edition of

The Fourth Estate actually hit the streets McLean had privately decided to throw in the towel.

During McLean's summer of misery, Hearst, in anticipation of Phoebe's largesse, had assigned Charles Palmer to scout for newspaper properties in New York. Palmer was spoiled for choice. According to *Printer's Ink,* a trade journal for newspaper advertisers, there were then forty-eight daily newspapers in New York, a city of 1.5 million with a total circulation area almost double that size. Ten morning and seven afternoon English-language newspapers claimed circulations of at least 12,500.[6] Thanks to the depression of 1893, at least a half dozen of these larger papers appear to have been available. The hot gossip in town was that the young Californian was trying to buy Pulitzer's *World,* a rumor Hearst went out of his way to deny. Palmer turned up four interesting possibilities, one of which was the *Recorder,* founded as a morning paper by tobacco tycoon James Duke in 1891 and "a great favorite with the women." Selling in excess of 75,000 copies a day, its asking price was reportedly $400,000.[7] The *Times,* not as virile as it had been under founder Henry J. Raymond but still a respectable conservative paper, was selling roughly 50,000 a day. It was priced at $300,000. The same amount would buy the *Advertiser,* a penny sheet for "busy men" that sold just 20,000 copies a day. Hearst asked Palmer to look into both the *Recorder* and McLean's *Morning Journal,* but the latter was his clear favorite.

Palmer met McLean at his residence, the August Belmont house on Fifth Avenue. McLean's opening gambit was to offer Hearst a partnership, asking $300,000 for a half-share in his paper. Palmer took that back to Hearst, who considered it a good start. He was not keen on a partnership, however, even with "as good a man as McLean."[8] Will and Palmer kept up the negotiation and undertook a thorough investigation of the *Morning Journal*'s plant and books. They called in Sam Chamberlain from San Francisco for his opinion on the proposed purchase. By the end of September, McLean had been beaten down to about $200,000 and Will was visiting Stump almost daily for updates on the Anaconda deal. Will and Palmer estimated that it would cost an additional $25,000 a month for twelve to eighteen months to bring the *Journal* up to their standards.

McLean folded rather quickly. The prospect of selling his paper at a six-figure loss only months after taking its helm hit him hard, but he was in no position to bargain. Readers and advertisers were continuing to bolt and he was writing weekly checks to cover his operating losses. He had as yet paid Albert Pulitzer only an eighth of the purchase price. On top of everything else, he was suffering from gout, his swollen foot wrapped in flannel compresses. On the morning of October 3, 1895, Will and Palmer strolled into Stump's offices to report that McLean had accepted their final offer of $150,000 for full ownership of the *Morning Journal*. Hearst had also taken as part of the bargain the *Morning Journal*'s German-language sister, the *New York Morgen Journal,* which enjoyed one of the larger circulations among the many foreign-language dailies then publishing in New York.[9]

The question of whether or not Hearst struck a good deal with McLean has never much troubled his chroniclers. Hearst is typically cast as a reckless young playboy determined to satisfy his rampaging impulses without regard to cost or consequence. The stereotype is not entirely baseless. Hearst dressed the part, dropped out of school, and lived openly with his mistress. Most people would say he spent extravagantly, including his mother, whose complaints about his bills and irresponsible behavior have greatly influenced his biographers. All that, combined with the pervasive assumption that inherited wealth corrodes character, has tended to preempt discussion of Hearst's care and good sense in his business dealings.

Hearst's deal with McLean is also difficult to rate for the lack of a good yardstick. Reliable data on the assets, profitability, and market value of long-dead dailies is hard to come by, but there are some rough benchmarks for newspaper sales in the last decades of the century (a period of slight economic deflation). A large, profitable New York paper—the *Herald* or the *World*—was thought to be worth three to five million but, as these earned as much as a million a year, they were not for sale. The smaller but prestigious *New York Tribune* was valued at $1 million in the early 1870s.[10] The similarly revered New York *Evening Post*, selling only 25,000 copies a day and making a mere $50,000 annually, brought $900,000 after William Cullen Bryant died in 1868.[11] The *Times* hit a peak valuation of $1.5 million in 1876, when its circulation was between 40,000 and 75,000.[12] At the other end of the scale, and more relevant to Hearst's deal, were the declining or damaged franchises. The pre-Pulitzer New York *World,* losing $40,000 a year and selling only

11,000 copies, went for $346,000 in 1883.[13] The *New York Mercury*, with less than 20,000 in circulation, sold for $300,000 in 1894. Against these transactions, Hearst's $150,000 purchase of the money-losing *Morning Journal*, with its 70,000 in daily circulation, shows reasonably well.

But perhaps the best comparison for Hearst's deal is Adolph Ochs's contemporaneous purchase of the *New York Times*. In 1896, the *Times* was in receivership, with substantial monthly losses and daily sales of about 10,000 copies. Ochs, a penny-pincher and one of the shrewdest operators in the history of American publishing, invested $75,000 of borrowed money on condition that he would gain 51 percent of the newspaper's stock if and when the paper had been profitable for three years. So Ochs bought half the stock and conditional control of the *Times* for $75,000 a year just months after Hearst bought 100 percent of the troubled *Journal* for $150,000. Ochs obtained a shaky but prestigious franchise; Hearst gained a humbler title with a larger audience. Ochs had to endure three years of sweat and uncertainty before taking firm command of his franchise; Hearst, with the advantage of more capital, took as a bonus to his purchase the *Morgen Journal*, a going concern with a circulation in excess of 40,000. Hearst got at least as good a deal as Ochs and each man bought the right paper for his purposes.[14]

The *Morning Journal* was a good fit for Hearst not only for its price—which left him with funds to invest in its improvement—but also because of its heritage, which was both mass market and Democratic. There was nothing in its past to prevent its new owner from making it a popular progressive daily. "The reason I bought the *Journal*," Hearst later told *Printer's Ink*, "was because of its large circulation. It had very much more circulation than the other papers that were offered me. I thought it would be easier to change the reputation, and make that good, than to take a paper with a good reputation and little or no circulation, and build it up."[15]

Hearst rated the day he and McLean agreed to terms among the happiest of his life. He had been studying, plotting, aching for an opportunity in New York for at least six years. He had persisted through the competitive pressures of San Francisco, through loss and upheaval in his own family, and through the economic panic of 1893. Now his dream was finally in hand. Never one for big emotional displays, he reportedly danced a little jig and rushed down to Park Row to survey the field of play.

Park Row, at least the newspaper portion of it, was a brief street in lower Manhattan reaching northeast from Broadway and Ann to Nassau Street and Printing House Square with its statue of Benjamin Franklin, patron saint of American publishing. City Hall and its grassy park occupied the west side. Most of the important dailies in New York fought for air in a jumble of buildings on the east. The *Sun*, the *Mail and Express*, the *Commercial Advertiser*, the *Daily News*, the *World*, the *Morning Journal*, the *Times*, and the *Tribune* were all there, with the *Star* and the *Evening Post* just around the corner. There was a rationale behind this geographic squeeze. Park Row was convenient to City Hall and the U.S. courthouse, prime sources of metro news. It was also near the Post Office, where papers picked up "exchanges" of copy from around the country. Over the years, the street had sprouted taverns, oyster broils, billiard halls, and other amenities, making Park Row not only the journalistic nerve center of greater New York but its own bustling ink-soaked village, swarming at all hours with newspapermen, newsboys, petitioners, hawkers, delivery trucks, and horse-cab operators poised for rush assignments.

Of particular interest to Hearst on his visit that day would have been two mismatched buildings directly across from City Hall. The squat structure with a clear view of the park was home to the New York *Sun*, edited by Charles Anderson Dana. The *Sun* had been the most popular newspaper in America when Hearst had entered Harvard in 1882. Next door, casting its long shadow over the *Sun*, was the Pulitzer Building, headquarters of the New York *World*, the most popular newspaper in America by the time Hearst left college in 1886.

Park Row had seen its share of conflict in the nineteenth century, but nothing more venomous and momentous than what had transpired between Pulitzer and Dana in those few years. They were two proud, brilliant journalists who unfortunately shared the identical goal of publishing the most interesting and influential Democratic newspaper in New York. There could only be one winner and neither man was inclined to yield. Their great clash, ruinous to each in different ways, riveted Hearst while he was at school. It was a crucial part of his newspaper education, shaping his ideas, tastes, and ambitions. The letters he wrote to his father advocating changes to the *San Francisco Examiner* were strongly influenced by the so-called "new journalism" that Pulitzer was unleashing on

Dana in New York. Hearst's move eastward from San Francisco emulated Pulitzer's 1883 journey from St. Louis to Manhattan. The strategic plan Hearst carried in his head as he stalked Park Row that day, the proud new owner of the *New York Journal,* was drawn directly from Pulitzer's attack on Dana: he would employ similar approaches to content, political alliances, circulation, pricing, and promotions in his own campaign for newspaper supremacy. The most significant difference between his plan and Pulitzer's was that Hearst's target was not Dana. Hearst was aiming to supplant Pulitzer himself as the predominant publisher in America, and he intended to do so by beating the master at his own game.

IT IS DIFFICULT TO APPRECIATE the magnitude of what Hearst was attempting in New York—or the magnitude of what Pulitzer had earlier accomplished—without first taking the measure of Charles Anderson Dana, the original master, the most successful and admired editor on Park Row for two decades after the Civil War.

Dana, still working long hours despite his seventy-five years, may well have been at his desk the day Hearst closed the deal. His offices were at the top of a spiral staircase on the third floor of the weathered Sun Building. He was almost completely bald now, with a bushy white beard on his somber block of a face, but age seemed only to underscore his eminence. Whatever luster his paper had lost since the war with Pulitzer, his record of accomplishment was unassailable. In addition to three decades at the helm of the *Sun* and fifteen years as managing editor of Horace Greeley's celebrated *New York Tribune,* Dana had published a life of Ulysses S. Grant and a spirited defense of the French anarchist Pierre-Joseph Proudhon. He had co-edited a sixteen-volume *American Cyclopaedia* that had sold three million copies. There probably wasn't a sharper intellect in any newsroom in New York, nor anyone else with his depth and range of knowledge. He picked up languages as effortlessly as most people pick up viruses: Latin, Greek, German, French, Russian, Spanish, Portuguese, Danish, Italian, Icelandic, and a smattering of Old Norse. Some of the younger denizens of Park Row now thought him old-fashioned—he disdained advertising and viewed photography as a passing fancy—yet for many he remained an authority on journalistic taste and craftsmanship, the newspaperman's newspaperman.

For someone who was ending his career as one of the most conservative and cynical voices in the American press, Dana's beginnings had been remarkably idealistic. In 1841, after leaving Harvard early for reasons of ill health and tight finances, he had joined the renowned Brook Farm Institute of Agriculture and Education, a model community of New England transcendentalists testing new ideas about cooperative living and intellectual growth. Dana worked in the fields, lectured in Greek and German, and sang in the choir. He also wrote for the farm's publication, the *Dial,* which brought him into the literary circles of Hawthorne and Emerson. Dana might have enjoyed a long career in the community had a fire not ripped through the main lodge in 1846, smothering in smoke and ash the high ideals of the founders. Dana directed his talents toward New York and the newspaper business.

He joined Horace Greeley's *Tribune* and rapidly rose through the ranks at a time when any association with that paper was said to confer "a patent of literary nobility."[16] His dispatches from Europe during the revolutions of 1848 brought him distinction, and on his return home Greeley made him managing editor. He was the first journalist to hold that title in the United States. For the next thirteen years, with his politically ambitious master frequently out of the office, Dana was responsible for the daily contents of the *Tribune.* He published the Brontë sisters, Dickens, Hawthorne, and a long-running weekly column by an economist he had met in Europe named Karl Marx. Over time, Greeley and Dana developed a personal rivalry and eventually fell out over differences on the prosecution of the Civil War. After serving as assistant secretary of war in the Lincoln administration, Dana returned to newspapers and in 1868 found backing to purchase the New York *Sun.*

Established by Benjamin Day in 1833, the *Sun* had an impressive pedigree of its own. It was America's first successful penny newspaper and, as such, was a forerunner of the popular and inexpensive dailies later established by Pulitzer and Hearst. Day's *Sun* broke into a newspaper universe dominated by small-circulation sheets published for political, commercial, and cultural elites. These were directly subsidized by partisan interests and available mostly by subscription (single copies sold for as much as six cents). Day, by contrast, courted middle-class artisans, entrepreneurs, and professionals with a more affordable paper suited to their tastes and relatively free of partisan influence. Stories about crime, scandal, sports, and entertainment received consideration in his pages alongside news of public policy, literature, and commerce. Day and his most successful imitator in the penny field—James Gordon Bennett of the *New York Herald*—sold their papers directly to readers in the street rather than through the mails by subscription. Their sales would rise and fall each day depending on the interest and immediacy of their news. This led to increased competition to be first off the press with a hot story: the penny sheets did not wait for news to come in through the mail; they sent reporters out in pursuit of it. Critics accused Day and Bennett of pandering to the rabble and coarsening public taste, the default response of elites to every stage in the popularization of print culture. But the many admirers of the penny publishers credited them with an honest attempt to inform, entertain, and lead vast reading audiences ignored by the established press—they wrought a democratic revolution in newspapering.

By the time Dana took control of the *Sun,* it was a marginally profitable two-penny paper selling a respectable 50,000 copies among the "mechanics and small merchants" of the city.[17] His first fifteen years were an unmitigated success. He published four crisp pages a day. He combined the quality and literary values of more expensive newspapers with the broad interests of less expensive dailies to produce an admirably distinctive publication. Beautifully written, with sparkling humor and sharp opinions, the *Sun* lit up an otherwise gloomy postbellum newspaper marketplace. In its pages, as one historian has noted, "life was not a mere procession of elections, legislatures, theatrical performances, murders and lectures. Life was everything—a new kind of apple, a crying child on the curb, a policeman's epigram, the exact weight of a candidate for president, the latest style in whiskers, the origin of a new slang expression . . . everything was fish to the great net of Dana's mind."[18]

Dana hired literary men and had an unusual number of college graduates on staff. He discovered more great talent than any editor of his time, including four of the century's most celebrated reporters: Richard Harding Davis, Jacob Riis, David Graham Phillips, and Julian Ralph. Always be interesting, he lectured them, never be in a hurry. Dana wanted leisurely prose, long on description and anecdote, with the author's personal viewpoint well above the surface. He told his stories chronologically, which meant the real news was often buried in the final paragraph. Despite the

Sun's high tone, Dana did not shy away from crime or vice. A good murder would be treated with a long narrative and diagrams of the action.[19] He famously considered "news" to mean everything that might interest a reader: "I have always felt that whatever the Divine Providence permitted to occur I was not too proud to report."[20] The *Sun*'s editorials were terse, sometimes cynical, and devastatingly witty. Unenthusiastic about General Winfield Hancock, the Democratic nominee in 1880, Dana praised him as "a good man, weighing 250 pounds."[21]

By the early 1880s, Dana was enjoying a circulation of 140,000, the highest in New York and annual returns approaching 40 percent.[22] His financial success allowed him to maintain a fierce political independence, to hire and keep the best talent, and to offer comprehensive national and international reporting as well as topflight sports, arts, crime, and human-interest journalism. His success infuriated rival journalists who accused him of running a "washerwoman's paper" full of "ribaldry, falsehood, indecency, levity, and dishonesty" and other tricks designed to produce sensations. He was said to be damaging the public sphere by pandering to the very masses their own dull sheets sought to edify. The lofty E.L. Godkin, editor of the *Nation,* called the *Sun* "nearly all that was evil in New York journalism."[23]

Their harangues were in vain. The *Sun* was the best newspaper in America and its more traditional peers quietly adopted its successful features and practices even as they printed their denunciations. The younger generation of journalists embraced the *Sun* wholeheartedly. In fact, the paper had no greater admirer than Joseph Pulitzer, then a twenty-four-year-old reporter for the German-language press in St. Louis, Pulitzer wrote Dana a fan letter: "I read the *Sun* regularly. In my opinion it is the most piquant, entertaining, and, without exception, the best newspaper in the world."[24]

YOUNG AS HE WAS, Pulitzer had already embarked on a spectacular career of his own. In the previous four years he had become a naturalized U.S. citizen, gained admittance to the Missouri bar, established himself as a promising political journalist, taken a seat in the Missouri state legislature, and been charged in a shooting.

The St. Louis press corps had never seen anything like Joseph Pulitzer.

He was well over six feet tall and exceedingly thin. He had a crown of wavy dark hair, prominent ears, piercing eyes, a colossal nose, a jutting chin, and a bulging Adam's apple. It was as though every feature of his face were struggling for distinction. He held himself erect and dressed with a shabby old-world elegance but underneath was a body that seemed to throw off more energy than its circuits could handle. His head jerked, his long bony fingers twitched, his chest wheezed and coughed, and he spoke in loud spasms with the guttural accent of his native Hungary. Even sitting still he seemed a buzzing, rattling hive of activity. Uncertain what to make of him, Pulitzer's colleagues decided to mock him. His nose became a primary target—"Pull-it-sir," they called him. Or Joey the German. Or Joey the Jew. Yet the young phenom was not without admirers. Henry Brokmeyer, nephew of Bismarck, translator of Hegel, and a towering figure in the St. Louis German community, was particularly impressed: "They think because he trundles about with himself a big cobnose . . . that he has no sense; but I tell you he possesses greater dialectical ability than all of them put together."[25]

Whereas Dana had left Harvard to join the Brook Farm idealists, Pulitzer had left his native Hungary looking for a fight. He was born April 10, 1847, the son of a prosperous Magyar Jewish grain dealer and an Austro-German mother who was also Jewish but a practicing Catholic. He was raised in comfortable homes in Makó and Budapest, and was educated in private schools with additional tutoring in French and German as well as Hungarian. He appears to have enjoyed a happy childhood until heart disease claimed his father. His mother remarried. Joseph, headstrong and excitable, took a dislike to his stepfather and could not wait to leave home. Drawn to the romance of battle, he applied to the British army in India and to the French Foreign Legion, as well as to the Austrian army, where he had family connections. Underage and underweight, with poor eyesight, he was rejected by all three. He finally found a Union army recruiter who received a bounty for every chump that could negotiate his gangway. Pulitzer arrived in Boston harbor in the summer of 1864. He jumped ship and made his way to New York, where he enlisted on his own rather than through his agent, thus pocketing his recruitment bonus.

Pulitzer spent less than a year with the First New York (Lincoln) Cavalry. He hated every minute of his service. The regimentation and physical discomfort of army life wore on him, as did his comrades. They immediately spotted in the brainy, petulant young man an enormous capacity for indignation, and they amused themselves trying to fill it. Pulitzer obliged them with displays of rage, almost ruining his career at one point by striking a tormentor of higher rank. His fellow soldiers had discovered an important thing about Joseph Pulitzer: he could seldom keep his cool under attack.

On his discharge from the army, Pulitzer returned to New York. Unable to find work, he headed west to St. Louis, which promised a vibrant German community and plenty of work, and delivered generously on both. After a series of dead-end jobs—mule hostler, waiter, construction laborer—Pulitzer began running errands for several lawyers, one of whom allowed him access to legal texts so that he might read law. Pulitzer also fell in with a circle of German intellectuals who discussed radical democratic politics and played chess at the Mercantile Library. His unusually aggressive game brought him to the attention of Carl Schurz, a Bonn-educated veteran of the German revolution and future U.S. senator. Schurz owned a piece of the *Westliche Post,* the most influential German newspaper west of New York. He offered Pulitzer a job as a reporter. "I, the unknown, the luckless, almost a boy of the streets, selected for such a responsibility—it all seemed like a dream," Pulitzer would later write.[26]

The dream only got better. Pulitzer poured himself into his new assignment, working sixteen-hour days and swiftly mastering the craft of reportage. He showed up everywhere, including an 1869 meeting of Missouri Republicans who were looking to fill a vacancy in the state legislature. Pulitzer emerged as their representative, never mind that he was three years under the age limit of twenty-five. To a man with more than a passing acquaintance with European autocracy, it was another proud moment. As one biographer has written, Pulitzer viewed American democracy not merely as another form of government: "It was something unique and precious, a huge stride in civilization, a hope for the oppressed not only in America but all over the world."[27] *Liberty* would one day be the name of Pulitzer's grand yacht. The figure of Liberty would grace the nameplate of his most famous paper.

The tireless Pulitzer had no trouble juggling his responsibilities in state government with reporting for the *Post.* He drew on both offices to campaign against fraud and malfeasance in the frontier world of Missouri politics. He was a brilliant crusader, with formidable analytic skills and a querulous disposition. His efforts weren't appreciated in all corners of St. Louis, however. He walked one evening into Schmidt's Hotel, where political types gathered, and came face to face with a local brute named Captain Augustine. The recent recipient of a public contract to build an asylum, Augustine believed that the *Westliche Post*'s reporting on his deal had impugned his honor. Before a roomful of startled legislators, he called Pulitzer a "damned liar."[28]

Wilting under Augustine's assault, Pulitzer skulked out of the hotel and returned a short time later with a concealed pistol. He found Augustine in a parlor and made a feeble attempt at saving face. He pulled the gun but managed only to graze his target. Augustine disarmed his shaky young assailant and after a vigorous show of displeasure left him on the floor in a bleeding, humiliated heap. Charged with breach of the peace, Pulitzer was subsequently required to pay a small fine.

That setback notwithstanding, Pulitzer advanced from lowly reporter to newspaper owner and editor in one dramatic leap thanks to the outcome of the 1872 election. The *Westliche Post* had enthusiastically backed the Liberal Republicans, led by *Tribune* editor Horace Greeley. And when the party crashed, *Post* shareholders ran for cover, offering Pulitzer a controlling interest in the paper on very reasonable terms, likely involving no cash. A few months later, when the dust settled and the paper was still standing, Pulitzer sold them back their shares at a tidy profit.

Suddenly a man of means, he packed up, went back to Europe, and toured the continent, visiting family in Budapest and pampering himself on the Riviera. On his return to St. Louis, he rented a comfortable apartment and established himself as a gentleman of leisure. He read Plato and Aristotle in the original and attended the theater, where he befriended the Shakespearean actor John McCullough. He purchased a saddle horse and trotted daily about the suburbs. He also kept up his political interests, giving up on the Republicans and campaigning for the Democrat Samuel Tilden in 1876.

Already looking toward New York, Pulitzer tried without success to purchase the *Belletristische Journal*, a Manhattan-based German weekly. Late in 1876 he visited Charles Dana and tried to interest him in a German-language edition of the *Sun*, which Pulitzer would run. The *Sun*'s financial backers weren't interested, but Dana seems to have taken a shine to the young man—certainly there was no inkling of the bloody-minded hatred they would soon share. Dana assigned his new friend to watch Congress wrestle with the disputed outcome of the 1876 election. Pulitzer believed, with justification, that the Republicans were stealing the presidency from Tilden. His outraged dispatches were featured prominently in the *Sun*. He also raised eyebrows with a speech at a pro-Tilden rally in the Capitol in which he called for 100,000 Democratic faithful to march in protest on Washington, "fully armed and ready for business."[29]

That bit of lunacy seems only to have brought Pulitzer luck. On the same Washington trip he met the woman he would marry. Kate Davis was the beautiful and well-connected daughter of a Washington judge, and a distant relative of Jefferson Davis, last president of the Confederacy. The wedding was held June 19, 1878, at Washington's Episcopal Church of the Epiphany. After the ceremony, the groom told the bride that his friend McCullough, the actor, would be tagging along on their honeymoon, a foreshadowing of odd living arrangements to come. He also informed Kate's family of his previously unmentioned Jewish heritage. The union survived both revelations.

Before the year was out, the *Saint Louis Dispatch*, a bankrupt evening paper, came up for auction and Pulitzer snagged it for $2,500. The publisher of his principal evening competitor, the *St. Louis Post*, knowing Pulitzer by reputation, wasted no time in proposing a merger. A deal was struck and the *St. Louis Post-Dispatch* was born. Pulitzer's days of leisure were over. He began to remake his paper in a manner then popular with editors in Cincinatti, Chicago, and Kansas City, among other western cities: he was infused with a near-desperate commitment to engage readers through lively human-interest stories, aggressive newsgathering, public-spirited crusades, and progressive politics. He dominated every aspect of the paper's operations, buying out his partner at the end of their first year. He began acquiring first-rate journalistic talent, notably John A. "Colonel" Cockerill, a former drummer boy and bugler in the Civil War and the man who had helped John McLean make a success of the Cincinnati *Enquirer*. The *Post-Dispatch*'s numbers began to skyrocket, rising to 9,000 in under two years and earning $45,000 annually. As with the *Westliche Post*, however, Pulitzer's hard-hitting style got him into trouble.

William Hyde, editor of the *Missouri Republican*, the self-appointed voice of the state's Democrats (notwithstanding his paper's name), took exception to the *Post-Dispatch*'s presuming to speak for the interests of his party. One day, without warning, he walked up to Pulitzer and knocked him down in the street. More seriously, Cockerill received a visit in his office from the intimidating figure of Colonel Alonzo W. Slayback. A politically connected lawyer, Slayback was calling to defend a partner who had received handsome fees from both sides in a municipal gas-franchise dispute. The *Post-Dispatch* had attacked the partner in print, repeatedly and mercilessly, and when Slayback denounced the paper at a public meeting, he came in for his own share of abuse in its pages. He now barged into Cockerill's office intending to slap him silly. Cockerill, apparently anticipating the confrontation, had his loaded gun lying near at hand. On seeing the weapon, Slayback pulled his own, but before he could get a round off, the editor shot him dead. Cockerill pleaded self-defense and was never prosecuted, but his deed offended respectable opinion in town and competing papers could not write enough about the killer in the *Post-Dispatch*'s editorial suite. Pulitzer stood by his man but, brittle as ever under attack, he became a nervous wreck. A chronic cough interrupted his sleep. His weight plummeted and he endured excruciating headaches. His doctor warned of a possible collapse and advised an extended vacation. At Kate's insistence, the Pulitzers booked passage to Europe for the spring of 1883.

They never got on the ship. Nor did they get much rest. While passing through New York, Pulitzer discovered that the *World*, a morning paper, was for the taking. He was convinced that this was his moment and Kate Pulitzer was sure of it, too. She noticed that her husband's physical complaints had all but vanished the moment he had caught scent of the *World*. (It does not diminish his suffering to note that there was often a psychological dimension to Pulitzer's ailments. Throughout his career, he would display an amazing ability to will himself up from physical or nervous prostration to perform impressive feats of industry.)

The *World* was owned by the infamous Jay Gould, whom readers of Pulitzer's *Post-Dispatch* knew as "one of the most sinister figures that ever flitted bat-like across the vision of the American people." Another man might have let such invective get in the way of a business deal, but Gould was accustomed to far worse. A fellow financier rated him the "worst man on earth since the beginning of the Christian era."[30] A slender, neat, black-bearded tycoon with polite manners and a soft voice, Gould was not the corporate monster he is often made out to be, but it is fair to say his first-class commercial mind was light on scruple.[31] Gould claimed to have acquired the *World* inadvertently, as an incidental to a larger deal, when in fact, he had made a serious attempt to salvage the paper, granting it a new building and buying it Hoe presses. He was patient with its losses but he liked to use it to promote his own stocks, and the paper had no credibility. Its circulation slumped. By the time Pulitzer came along, it was selling 11,000 copies a day and losing $40,000 a year.

Gould brazenly asked $500,000 for his crippled sheet. Pulitzer gulped hard and begged for time. He visited his brother, Albert, who had successfully launched the *Journal* a year earlier, and asked his advice. Albert responded that New York was not big enough for two Pulitzers. Undeterred, Joseph bought the money-bleeding *World* the next day, for $346,000, payable in installments. It was a steep price but justified in part by the paper's potential and the new plant Gould had installed. In another three days, Pulitzer announced himself in the *World*'s pages as its new editor and proprietor with the following prospectus:

> There is room in this great and growing city for a journal that is not only cheap but bright, not only bright but large, not only large but truly democratic—dedicated to the cause of the people rather than that of purse potentates—devoted more to the news of the new than the old world, that will expose all fraud and sham, fight all public evils and abuses—that will serve and battle for the people with earnest sincerity.[32]

The whole of the New York media world yawned. In fact, the only paper to greet the *World*'s new owner was the *Sun*. "Mr. Pulitzer," wrote Dana, "possesses a quick and fluent mind with a good share of originality and brightness; but he has always seemed to us rather deficient in judgment and in staying power. . . . Anyway, we tender all sorts of friendly wishes." Given Dana's disdain for competitors and the fact that Pulitzer was stepping onto his populist Democratic turf, those were warm regards indeed. Pulitzer, thirty-six years old to Dana's sixty-four, printed an unctuous reply: "If the editor of the *World* has shown deficiency of judgment heretofore, it has been because he has tried not only to imitate, but even to excel the *Sun* in its truthfulness, fearlessness, independence and vigor."[33]

The war was on.

PULITZER'S AMBITION WAS NOT merely to break into New York but to push the boundaries of mass appeal for newspapers in a great commercial market. New York was riding the crest of America's phenomenal post-bellum economic expansion and drawing to its streets many of the hundreds of thousands of immigrants arriving on the nation's shores each year. Mushrooming ethnic communities were chipping away at the political and cultural domination of the city's Anglo-Protestant elite. They peppered New York politics with German socialism and Irish nationalism, and shook the established parties with a new pitch of working-class assertiveness. They worked hard and earned good incomes and supported booming markets in packaged goods, ready-made clothing, domestic appliances, and newspapers. They patronized a fresh abundance of popular cultural attractions: Coney Island and West Brighton; the Bowery's variety shows; Harrigan and Hart on Broadway. They were remaking and democratizing New York, and Pulitzer would give them a daily that caught the manifold spirit of their burgeoning city.

Everything, for Pulitzer, started with popular appeal: "If a newspaper is to be of real service to the public, it must have a big circulation, first because its news and its comments must reach the largest possible number of people, second because circulation means advertising, and advertising means money, and money means independence."[34] Like all successful publishers, Pulitzer sometimes placed money ahead of all other considerations, but he was genuinely committed to his notion of public service. He rightly believed that financial success allowed a newspaper to stand with its readers against powerful political and business interests.

Pulitzer's version of the much-for-little strategy was to keep the *World*'s price at two cents while doubling its size to eight pages, twice that of the now identically priced *Sun* and one or two cents cheaper than the larger *Times, Tribune,* and *Herald* (all of which were now selling for three or four cents). Pulitzer would soon increase his paper from eight to ten pages and sometimes twelve. These measures were aggressive, but not recklessly so. Sharp declines in the cost of newsprint and a range of technological efficiencies had made larger newspapers more affordable to produce. Pulitzer was further blessed by a booming advertising market as retailers and promoters turned more and more to the dailies to chase mass audiences for their wares and services. Advertising spending in newspapers increased from $39 million in 1880 to $150 million in 1900. Circulation revenue was still the engine of newspaper growth and the key to attracting advertising, but the day was fast approaching when advertising would become "the very soul of the concern," as Lincoln Steffens phrased it.[35]

Pulitzer's high page count permitted him to diversify the contents of his paper and broaden its appeal. All of the major papers in New York covered politics and public affairs along with business, crime, scandal, disaster, and sport. Pulitzer offered more of everything and gave conspicuous prominence to his human-interest fare—the murders, shipwrecks, big games and society weddings. Pulitzer saw New York as a bustling, boisterous city, with drama and wonder on every street corner, and he wanted all of that captured for his pages. A *World* reporter would no longer gather news at the bar of his club. He would venture out and discover it among ordinary working-class people. Pulitzer's instructions to his new staff were blunt: "Gentlemen, you realize that a change has taken place. . . . Heretofore you have all been living in the parlour and taking baths every day. Now I wish you to understand that, in future, you are all walking down the Bowery."[36]

They would walk briskly, too. Whereas Dana counseled his men never to hurry, Pulitzer, flapping about his newsroom, eyes gleaming through pince-nez, made clear by example that his men could never move fast enough. News would be sold fresh and the writing would be snappy. Cockerill, shipped in from St. Louis, demanded sharp verbs, clear descriptions, strong emotions, and a tight delivery—"Condense! Condense!" became the *World*'s battle cry. "It seemed as if a cyclone had entered the building," recalled one reporter of Pulitzer's first days.[37] A number of old hands immediately quit. They were promptly replaced.

Pulitzer was acutely aware that New York readers had a choice of newspapers and that commuters and pedestrians made quick decisions each day about which to purchase. It followed that everything about his *World* must work a little harder than its competitors to call attention to itself. The paper would make generous use of cartoons and illustration. Headlining became bold and, at times, operatic. On the last day of Gould's proprietorship, the *World* presented front-page stories with strictly informational headlines: "Affairs at Albany," "Mr. Vanderbilt's Trip," and "Bench Show of Dogs." On Pulitzer's first day, the headlines started telling stories: "The Deadly Lightning," "A Fortune Squandered in Drink," "Married and Taken to Jail," and "Cornetti's Last Night."

Cornetti, a condemned man, received even more dramatic treatment with the next day's report of his hanging:

SCREAMING FOR MERCY.
HOW THE CRAVEN CORNETTI
MOUNTED THE SCAFFOLD.

Gagged and Pinioned by the Guards and
Dragged Resisting to a Prayer-less Doom[38]

The *World*'s politics were attention-getting as well, and neatly tailored to middle- and working-class audiences. Pulitzer called for taxes on luxuries, taxes on inheritances, taxes on large incomes, taxes on monopolies. He made his paper an enemy of vote-buying, police brutality, unfair labor practices, and monopolistic greed. He clamored for safer food and housing. He was merciless in his lampoons of the so-called purse potentates with their vulgar Manhattan chateaux and their valets outside their opera boxes. He hammered the same themes relentlessly. The "red thread of continuous policy," he liked to say, would win allies, create enemies, and make the New York *World* important.[39]

To counterbalance the paper's constant finger-wagging, Pulitzer gave it an exuberant public spirit and engaged in unabashed celebrations of New York. The Brooklyn Bridge opened two weeks after he acquired the paper. A massive undertaking, thirteen years in the works and the longest suspension bridge on earth, it was a remarkable engineering feat in America and the pride of New York's Italian and German communities, which had done much of the work. Pulitzer published a special edition and devoted his entire front page to the bridge. He ran a front-page four-column woodcut of its span, reportedly the first time the *World* had illustrated a news story, and enjoyed a phenomenal sale.

Critics dismissed the *World* as crude and sensationalistic. They could not stomach its gaudy tones and raw emotion, its politics or its salesmanship. They worried for the future of the elite dailies to which they themselves subscribed. But readers were galvanized by Pulitzer's paper. Whatever it lacked in subtlety and intellectual heft (far less than is often imagined), the *World* was flat-out exciting. It left Dana's *Sun*, for one, looking tired and gray. Pulitzer's circulation popped from 28,000 in May to around 40,000 by autumn. "[The *World*] had no infancy," he would later boast. "At once it sprang into full vigor."[40] While he was doing little that had not been done before, he was doing it so well and energetically that it was accepted in New York as a "new journalism."

Having ignored Pulitzer's entry to the market, the competition now panicked. The *Times* and the *Herald*, selling at four and three cents respectively, cut their cover prices to two cents. The *Tribune* dropped from four cents to three. Pulitzer crowed that they had handed him the city. He was guessing, correctly, that the price cuts would only underscore his success in the eyes of readers and advertisers while doing nothing to help his competitors' circulations.

Dana did not join the rush to cut prices. With little advertising in his pages, he could not afford the loss of circulation revenue. But, beyond that, he felt no pressure to make a cut. He was still the market leader, selling 147,000 copies a day. Pulitzer's readers, he surmised, were either new to the daily habit or drawn from other papers. The *World*'s fast start had not yet put a dent in the *Sun*, so Dana would stand pat. But not for long.

MOST NEWSPAPERS toward the end of the nineteenth century claimed to be politically independent. That meant they were no longer operated or subsidized by partisan political interests. But an editor's endorsement could still make or break a paper in a presidential year. Immediately on taking the *World*'s reins, Pulitzer had begun advancing New York governor Grover Cleveland for the 1884 Democratic nomination. Given that the *Tribune*, the *Times*, and most other papers in town tilted Republican, Dana's *Sun* was the only important paper expected to follow suit. The *Sun* was closely identified with the Democrats and had championed Cleveland for governor two years earlier, but Dana was unpredictable.

For all his talents, Dana sometimes allowed personal grievances to play havoc with his paper's politics, and he could make a nuisance of himself trying to convert the *Sun*'s electoral support into offices for himself, friends and family. After the 1882 election, for instance, he had written Cleveland, then the newly elected governor of New York, suggesting an appointment or two in his administration. Cleveland failed even to respond to the letter and Dana sulkily backed a nonstarter, Greenback Labor candidate Benjamin F. Butler, in 1884. Blinded by spite and completely underestimating the

World as a competitive threat, he made his paper irrelevant in a presidential year. The *Sun*'s circulation, proudly recorded atop its editorial page, sunk from 137,000 at the start of 1884 to 85,000 by November. Dana would soon quit publishing his circulation number altogether.

Cleveland won the 1884 election and the *World* sold a whopping 264,378 copies the morning after the vote. Many of those were bought by former *Sun* readers who would never return to Dana's fold. Pulitzer also had a personal victory to celebrate: he had let his name stand for Congress in the Ninth District of New York, and the voters had chosen him as their representative.[41]

Dana's problems ran deeper than his nonsensical endorsement of Butler. The advent of the *World* had exposed a fundamental weakness in his style. The *Sun* still sided with what it called the "producing classes" against the financial and political elites, but from first to last, Dana's paper reflected the sophisticated interests, tastes, and humor of its supremely intelligent editor. Its relationship with its audience was arm's-length and paternalistic; its tone was seldom warmer than wry detachment. Dana may have been *for* the people—as in his famous slogan, "The *Sun* Shines for All"—but he was not *of* the people. Pulitzer's *World* had locked arms with working men and women, taking their enthusiasms, aspirations, and emotions as its own. It pleaded their cases and fought their battles and it became their paper.

Within months of the 1884 election, Pulitzer's average daily circulation broke the 100,000 mark. Now the leading Democratic publisher on the eastern seaboard, he threw a party in City Hall Park and fired a cannon once for every thousand in circulation. The mayor made a speech and *World* staffers all received tall silk hats.

With everything going his way, Pulitzer turned up the heat—upgrading his presses, throwing increasing amounts of content at readers, and poaching staff from his rivals, especially the *Sun*. One of Dana's best, Solomon S. Carvalho, became the *World*'s business manager. Ballard Smith left the *Herald* to become Pulitzer's assistant managing editor, second only to Cockerill. Compensation at the *World* began to soar. Cockerill's $10,000 a year was twice the salary of a U.S. senator and on par with that of the governor of New York and of leading insurance and bank executives. Many *World* hacks were earning $50 to $80 a week. This was double the going rate at the *Herald,* where Bennett boasted that he could hire "all the brains

I want . . . at twenty-five dollars per week" (wages for skilled labor hovered around $5 to $10 a week).[42] Pulitzer paid the artist Walt McDougall $50 a week simply to draw cartoons, a salary that raised eyebrows even in the *World*'s offices. But Pulitzer's reasoning was sound: McDougall also drew readers.

The mid-eighties were the best years of Pulitzer's career. He now employed a staff of 1,200, about twice that of any other paper. He so routinely exposed graft and malfeasance in public office as to set a new standard for social responsibility and investigative journalism. A reporter named Elizabeth Cochrane, who joined the *World* in 1887 at the age of twenty-three, faked insanity to gain entry to the asylum on Blackwell's Island. Her shocking account of the execrable conditions there, published under the nom de plume Nellie Bly, resulted in a grand jury investigation and an overhaul of the asylum.

At its grandest, the *World* produced awe-inspiring crusades. When Congress refused to vote the $100,000 necessary for a pedestal on which to stand Frédéric-Auguste Bartholdi's Statue of Liberty, commissioned by the people of France, the *World* leapt to action, organizing a public subscription. One and two dollars at a time, the statue was erected, and Pulitzer was able to dominate coverage of yet another impressive addition to the metropolitan skyline.[43]

Although paying the highest salaries on Park Row, Pulitzer continued to lead every aspect of the *World*'s operations. "He was forever unsatisfied," wrote his friend and colleague Don Seitz, "not so much with the results as with the thought that if a further effort had been made, a sterner command, or greater encouragement given, as the case might be, more could have been accomplished."[44] The publisher's wife, Kate, worried that the constant striving and the competitive pressures were too much for him: "He is pushing his body in a manner no human being can stand," she wrote friends, and she was right to worry.[45] Her husband's bad nerves and insomnia returned within a few years of his arrival in New York. Rather than buy another paper, Pulitzer this time addressed his ill health by taking the cure at Aix-les-Bains. He also salved himself with money: the *World* was making him rich. His income rivaled that of J.P. Morgan, who lived a block from Pulitzer's new brownstone mansion on East 36th Street.[46] Pulitzer built a library of first editions and collected Gobelin tapestries, diamonds, gems, and old masters. He snapped up two shares in a private resort for millionaires at Jekyll Island, Georgia, where his neighbors were Morgans, Rockefeller and Astors. Pulitzer, scourge of the purse potentates, was now solidly of their number.

NO ONE WATCHED Pulitzer's bounding good fortune and increasing prominence in national affairs with more distaste than Charles A. Dana. Whatever goodwill the two had shared in earlier days was gone. The *Sun* had begun to snipe at Pulitzer's unimpressive military record and his absenteeism from Congress (he resigned his seat early in his term, pleading the demands of running newspapers). Dana spread a rumor that his rival had hired the socially prominent Ballard Smith to ease his way into New York's better drawing rooms. The *Sun* even chided Pulitzer, nominally Episcopalian and slippery about his Jewishness, for failing to attend synagogue. It called him the "Jew who does not want to be a Jew," or "Judas Pulitzer."[47]

Bile and jealousy led Dana's pen. Fear, too. His folly during the 1884 campaign had prompted speculation on Park Row that the *Sun*'s stockholders might show him the door. Dana was the paper's largest investor but owned only a third of its shares. He now borrowed to purchase majority control and in 1886 also mortgaged his building to raise capital for better presses and printing equipment. He abandoned his four-page format and began printing eight or more pages a day. More daringly, he launched a four-page evening edition in March 1887. It sold for a penny and quickly produced a respectable sale of 40,000. When Pulitzer established an identically sized and priced *Evening World*, the animosity between the two men exploded.

A fall election for New York district attorney became a proxy war for the newspaper titans. The incumbent, De Lancey Nicoll, a Democrat whose dedication to reform had cost him the allegiance of corrupt old Tammany Hall, was now running as the nominee of Republicans and Independents. Pulitzer and Dana both backed Nicoll until a week after the launch of the *Evening World*. Dana then bolted to John Fellows, the Democrat, regardless of the fact that Fellows enjoyed the support of Grover Cleveland. Dana next tried to smear both Pulitzer and Nicoll by dragging out the decade-old Cockerill shooting story. Pulitzer saluted Dana as "a mendacious blackguard"and Dana fired back that Pulitzer exuded "the venom of a snake" and wielded "the bludgeon of a bully." The Jews of New York, he wrote, "have no reason to be ashamed of Judas Pulitzer if he has denied his race and religion. . . . [T]he shame rests exclusively upon himself. The insuperable obstacle in the way of his social progress is not the fact that he is a Jew, but in certain offensive personal qualities. . . . His face is repulsive, not because the physiognomy is Hebraic, but because it is Pulitzeresque. . . . Cunning, malice, falsehood, treachery, dishonesty, greed and venal self-abasement have stamped their unmistakable traits. . . . No art can eradicate them."[48]

With the pride of each newspaper now riding on the quality of its editor's vitriol, Pulitzer gamely pursued Dana into the rhetorical wasteland of ethnic slur: "To what race of human beings does Charles Anderson Dana belong? . . . The Danas, although a New England family of considerable Puritan and literary pretensions, have unquestionably a Greek derivation. The modern Greek is a treacherous, drunken creature. . . . Mr. Charles Ananias Dana may be descended from a Greek corsair. If so, his career of treachery, hypocrisy, deceit and lying could easily be accounted for."[49] The *World* also alleged, without corroboration, that Dana had once fought a young woman for a life preserver on a sinking ship.

When Fellows won the election, the *Sun*'s headline gloated that his man had beaten "Pulitzer's Dude" by a 20,000 plurality. The people had rebuked "the liars" and Dana had yet another occasion to lambaste his rival as a "treacherous venomous greedy junk dealer," with all the usual racist and hysterical flourishes. However disappointed at the election result, Pulitzer was able to boast a post-election press run of 317,940, which he claimed was the largest ever printed by any newspaper in the world. He then rallied himself for what he hoped would be the last word in his dogfight with Dana, driving home that the people of New York preferred his paper to his rival's because, "The *World* has never advocated a bad cause nor proved recreant to a good one. It will continue to war against corruptionists with renewed vigor. It rests upon a solid foundation of Honesty and Public Service and against it the disappointed, malice-cankered envious sons of darkness cannot prevail."[50]

In an odd turn of fate, darkness did prevail, for both men. Pulitzer matched, insult for insult, an acknowledged master of verbal abuse, yet he suffered a great deal in the exchange. Each blow from Dana bruised his fragile psyche. He had never learned to laugh away personal attacks, however many he endured. Two weeks after his last rejoinder, Pulitzer picked up the day's editorial page and was astonished to discover he could "hardly see the writing, let alone read it." He visited a doctor, who detected damage in both eyes. The physician also found Pulitzer to be suffering from asthma, a bad stomach, insomnia, exhaustion, and depression. He counseled six weeks in a dark room. Pulitzer obeyed, leaving the *World* in the hands of a committee of executives as he took his rest, followed by an extended holiday in California and trips to Paris and Wiesbaden, where he visited specialists and took cures. His general health would improve somewhat but his eyesight would continue to deteriorate. In October 1890, he announced his retirement from an active role in his paper.

Dana's darkness was less tragic than Pulitzer's but nonetheless profound. The introduction of more pages and an evening edition would bring the *Sun* back over 100,000 in circulation, but the *World* continued its own climb, soon exceeding 200,000. Dana would never lead again. His paper was permanently eclipsed, and its character would change markedly over the next decade—the last of his editorship and of his life. The *Sun* would lose much of its charm and sparkling wit. It would abandon working people to the *World* and shine instead for New York's merchant classes, who appreciated its conservative economic policy and its hard line on labor issues. Dana opposed the eight-hour day as folly and had curt advice for the jury in the trial of the eight anarchists accused of the 1886 Haymarket Square bombing: "Let them hang."[51]

To compound Dana's hurt, Pulitzer's reputation, in the eyes of many observers, now exceeded his own. A Buffalo weekly wrote that Pulitzer's "tireless energy and love of justice have made the New York *World* the foremost paper of the world. There is not a working journalist in the United States who does not regret the cause of his retirement."[52] Even his adversaries in New York had touching things to say. Throughout the 1880s, the *Herald* had been turning up its nose at the *World* while furiously adopting its practices: more pictures, larger headlines, and more human-interest journalism. Now its proprietor, James Gordon Bennett Jr., acknowledged his debt:

A great vacuum is made in the present actuality of American journalism. What the Greeleys and the Raymonds and the Bennetts did for journalism thirty years ago, Pulitzer has done today. As for us of the *Herald*, we droop our colors to him. He . . . has roused the spirit of enterprise and personality which, up to this time, had not been known. We have not always agreed with the spirit which has made his ideas a journalistic success, and we cannot refrain from regretting that he did not encourage us in the new departure which he has made, instead of merely astonishing us, frightening us, and we may add . . . perhaps a little bit disgusting us. But le Roi est mort, vive le Roi![53]

It would especially have galled Dana to see Pulitzer raking in accolades when his retirement was more or less a charade. Pulitzer had merely surrendered the title of editor. He remained proprietor and de facto publisher of the *World,* with a firm grip on all of its business operations. It also became clear to his staff within days of his "retirement" that he remained sovereign in editorial matters as well. He kept in constant contact with the paper through flurries of telegraph cables, letters, and emissaries as he traveled from New York to Bar Harbor to Jekyll Island to Europe. He made all significant decisions with regard to coverage, politics, staffing, and style. His personal commitment to the *World* would wane not one bit over the next two decades. Pulitzer had not retired: he had merely taken leave of Park Row. And though he was no longer physically present, he would mark his place in stunning fashion.

ON DECEMBER 10, 1890, the *World* celebrated yet another monumental addition to the New York skyline, this one its own. The Pulitzer Building was tall: 16 stories and 309 feet. On the day it opened, it was the tallest building in New York—6 stories taller than any other commercial building in the city. It was the tallest building in the United States, and the tallest commercial structure anywhere. Most importantly, it was so tall that it blocked the *Sun*'s exposure to its namesake. Darkness indeed.

The opening ceremonies of the Pulitzer Building were attended by thousands of eminent New Yorkers, including twelve governors, ex-governors, and governors elect, the mayor, and virtually every municipal politician of note. A special train brought a carload of cabinet members, senators, and congressmen from Washington for the day. Tour guides spirited these eminences from the *World*'s printing works in the basement up six elevators to its newsroom and commercial offices above. The visitors learned that the building's 142,000 square feet of floor space were constructed from 5 million pounds of steel and wrought iron and over 6 million bricks, that its corridors were lined with marble and its walls with 3 million feet of hardwood. They were allowed a glimpse under the burnished-copper dome on the 16th floor where Pulitzer kept opulent semicircular offices with frescoes on the ceiling, embossed leather wainscoting, and windows overlooking Governor's Island, Brooklyn, and Long Island. The decor was impressive, but it was the sheer height of the building that staggered visitors. One gentleman rode the elevator as high as it would go and emerged to ask, "Is God in?"[54]

Perhaps the most remarkable thing about the Pulitzer Building is that the man who built it felt no obligation to show up for its opening. The day before the ceremonies, Pulitzer sailed for Europe aboard the White Star steamship *Teutonic*. His lame explanation was that the excitement of the opening might overwhelm him. That his guests might feel slighted appears to have been of no concern. Such were the privileges of being the foremost newspaperman in the world's leading media market at a time when dailies were king.

Ironically, no one had so clearly articulated the majesty of Pulitzer's position as the man who most resented his success. Dana liked to give lectures on the newspaper as an almighty force in American life. The power of the press, he believed was "the power of speaking out the sentiment of the people, the voice of justice, the inspiration of wisdom, the determinations of patriotism, and the heart of the whole people." Newspapers, he said, would always be the most reliable expression of the public will because they had to earn their mandates from their readers, one sale at a time, every morning.[55] (The degree to which editors sought to speak "the sentiment of the people," rather than study or direct it, is a crucial difference between nineteenth- and twentieth-century journalism.)

Dana further argued that the press was uniquely suited to its high purpose by virtue of its collective genius, "not exceeded in any branch of human effort." Every day, an army of supremely intelligent and specially trained reporters reached around the globe to gather in "the treasures of intellectual wealth that are stored up there, and a photograph of the occurrences of life that are there taking place." Their findings were printed and distributed by some of the richest and most complex business organizations known to man, employing heroic amounts of labor and material, not to mention the best managerial talent and the latest technology: "What a wonder, what a marvel it is that here for one or two cents you buy a history of the entire globe of the day before! It is something that is miraculous, really, when you consider it. . . . All brought here by electricity, by means of the telegraph! So that the man who has knowledge enough to read, can tell what was done in France yesterday, or in Turkey. . . . That is a wonderful thing."[56]

Atop these grand journalistic enterprises, with their high purpose, enormous intelligence, and boundless resources, sat the great editors themselves. Only presidential candidates and Shakespearean actors rivaled them in fame. They were towering, intimidating figures. Young Theodore Dreiser, not lacking in confidence or ambition, was so impressed by the auras of Dana and Pulitzer, so cowed by their "air of assurance and righteousness and authority and superiority as well as general condescension toward all," that the mere mention of their names frightened him. "Something about [these dailies] as yet overawed me," he wrote, "especially the *World,* the owner and editor of which had begun his meteoric career in St. Louis years before, and which since had become the foremost paper in New York. . . . It had become the 'biggest' and most daring in point of news and action, and this tempted me."[57]

Dreiser had once walked up and down Park Row, gazing up at the newspaper buildings as Hearst had done on purchasing the *Journal.* He longed for the opportunities these offices represented, but he could not bring himself to even step inside the *World*'s door. When finally he did, his courage failed him and he turned around and walked out. Dreiser uses the word "overawed" four times in his memoir as he discusses Pulitzer and his newspaper.[58]

THERE WAS A TIME WHEN HEARST, TOO, was in awe of Pulitzer. Hearst had held the *World* in high esteem from its first appearance, telling his friends on the *Harvard Lampoon* that it was the best paper in America. His letters to his father abound with explications of Pulitzer's methods and success. He liked the *World*'s energy and enterprise, its emotional charge and its intellectual bite. He liked its social conscience, its sympathy for the underdog, and its promotional style. He broadly shared its politics, prosecuting on campus a small-scale version of the lonely 1884 Cleveland campaign that Pulitzer fought in New York. Hearst befriended a number of Pulitzer's key staffers, including Ballard Smith, John Cockerill, and business manager George W. Turner, extracting whatever he could of their ideas, attitudes, opinions, and knowledge.

It was probably regard for Pulitzer that led Hearst to locate the *Examiner's* East Coast bureau under the *World's* dome. It made practical sense—the Pulitzer Building was new, well-equipped space in the thumping heart of the New York publishing community. But Hearst also understood all that Pulitzer's skyscraper signified: in terms of readership, influence, and profits, the *World* was the most successful daily on the planet. Its building was a gold-topped monument to that triumph, to its supplanting of the *Sun,* to the immigrant Pulitzer's enormous personal prestige, to the rise of a popular new form of crusading journalism, and to the commercial and cultural vitality of the newspaper industry in the Gilded Age. In simplest terms, the Pulitzer Building symbolized everything Hearst wanted for himself. And as the delighted owner of the *New York Journal,* he now had means to pursue it.

CHAPTER THREE

A Great Deal More Than Money

The Hoffman House was the grandest of Manhattan's grand hotels and a favorite haunt of the city's social and Democratic elite. Under the coffered ceilings of its cavernous lobby was a great mahogany bar staffed by seventeen bartenders. The cocktail of choice was the razzle dazzle. A buffet of sixty dishes was free to patrons. The tragedian Maurice Barrymore stopped by on occasion to recite Shakespeare from table tops and to brawl with his critics, but he took second billing at the Hoffman House to another work of art. Lit by a crystal chandelier and reflected in a large mirror over the bar was Bouguereau's *Nymphs and Satyr,* featuring in its central grouping four of the most ravishing demigoddesses ever to frolic on canvas. They were so beautiful, so voluptuous, and so gloriously naked that a steady flow of tourists wandered through the lobby for a glimpse. The painting cut the grandeur of the Hoffman House with a thrill of decadence, as did the fact that the hotel's owner, Edward Stokes, had served time in Sing Sing for shooting the financier Jim Fisk, his rival for the attentions of the actress Josie Mansfield. On arriving in New York to negotiate the purchase of the *Morning Journal,* Hearst checked in at the Hoffman House, and he remained there for the balance of the year.

The consensus of the two best Hearst biographies—W.A. Swanberg's *Citizen Hearst* (1961) and David Nasaw's *The Chief* (2000)—is that the young Californian floundered on assuming control of the *Morning Journal* on November 7, 1895. Swanberg has Hearst closely imitating Pulitzer's *World,* exceeding the master only in "schoolboy simplicity" and the "loving attention" he gave to crime and scandal.[1] Nasaw, too, sees scandal and fearmongering reports of "terrifying crime against ordinary folk" as Hearst's formula for success.[2] Neither biography credits Hearst with a single meritorious piece of journalism in his first several months on the job, although Nasaw does mention that the *Journal*'s violent and gossipy melodramas were well written, "if a bit long-winded." The biographers agree that it was only after stealing Pulitzer's talent, and engaging in several months of relentless promotion, unbridled spending, and lurid journalistic excess, that Hearst's new paper began to enjoy significant circulation gains.

It is one of the curiosities of the Hearst literature that characterizations of his work as shallow and lurid themselves tend toward the shallow and lurid. Part of the problem is the source material. Accounts of Hearst's beginnings at the *Morning Journal* lean heavily on the memoirs of ancient journalists. High in color, hazy in detail, twisted by time and personal agendas, these works are as unreliable as they are indispensable, given the dearth of alternatives. Fortunately, they can be tested, to some extent, against the actual contents of Hearst's paper, the pages of his rivals, and the records of the several trade publications that reported and commented on New York's bustling newspaper scene in the late nineteenth century, functioning as something of a Greek chorus to the action on Park Row. These sources permit an entirely different and more reliable account of Hearst's methods and results as he assembled his staff, reorganized his newspaper, and shot to immediate prominence on journalism's biggest stage.

The stage was far more crowded than is generally supposed. Hearst's primary target may have been Pulitzer's *World*, but the reality of the marketplace was that he was competing against all 48 dailies in New York, not to mention a vibrant suburban press—Brooklyn alone had at least three significant sheets.[3] Each of these newspapers was vying for the attention of some portion of greater New York's three million souls, a vast metropolitan population, as diverse as any in the world, ranging from the hundreds of thousands of Irish refugees, German artisans, Shtetl Jews, Russian peasants, Italian laborers and Southern blacks who were crowded into the Bowery's grimy tenements to Mrs. Astor's Four Hundred, opulently ensconced on upper Fifth Avenue in grand French chateaux and Italianate villas with electric lights, steam heat, and new-fangled telephones. Every morning, the population of Manhattan Island swelled by a million as great hordes of shopkeepers, lawyers, accountants, salesman, laborers, mechanics, and secretaries flowed in by ferry, train, cable car, and the Brooklyn Bridge. At the end of the day they poured home again to

White Plains, Queens, Staten Island, and Jersey City. Somehow this nightly ebb barely registered in the street. New York was already the city that never sleeps. Visitors cursed the impossibility of slumber "in the midst of all the thunder and the rush and the roar of her million-crowded streets, along which surges as a restless tide the turbid and foaming flood of city life. The bells of tramcars continually sounding, the wearyless trampling of the ironshod hoofs over granite roadway, the whirling rumble of the wheels, the roar of the trains which on the elevated railways radiate uproar from a kind of infernal firmament on high, all suffused and submerged in the murmurous hum that rises unceasing from the hurrying footsteps in the crowded street, that inarticulate voice of New York."[4]

It was a noisy, restless population, highly literate—perhaps more so than today, given the complexity of the language in the popular dailies—and hungry for news. All of the major papers routinely produced three or four editions a day, and as many as a dozen if a story warranted, giving birth to a 24/7 news environment more than a century before the phrase became current.[5] It was also a discriminating population. Readers knew and appreciated the political and class orientation of the papers, and gave their pennies to the editors who best spoke their sentiments. A hot new sheet could double its circulation inside a year; a failing one could shed readers at the same rate. The distinctiveness and excellence of a daily's content mattered in a way long since lost to journalism. On Hearst's arrival, the market leaders were the two-cent papers: the *World* (between 200,000 and 250,000), the *Herald* (between 150,000 and 200,000), and the *Sun* (about 120,000). The three-cent *Tribune* is believed to have had a circulation of less than 75,000, and the elite *Evening Post* perhaps a third of that.

Hearst's first priority on closing his deal with McLean was to gather his management team. He did not steal its members from rival papers. He imported his best executives from San Francisco, where the *Examiner* was now strong enough to operate with less supervision. On the commercial side, business manager Charles Palmer, advertising executive Andy Katz, and printing specialist George Pancoast all pulled up stakes for Park Row. The debonair Sam Chamberlain, now approaching fifty years of age and still a stranger to sobriety, left his post as managing editor of the *Examiner* to perform the same function at the *Morning Journal*.

It was something of a homecoming for Chamberlain. The son of Park Row veteran Ivory Chamberlain, he had apprenticed as a reporter in New

York and had worked on about half the major papers in town, including the pre-Pulitzer *World,* the *Herald,* and Albert Pulitzer's *Morning Journal.* He had also been a friend and adviser to James Gordon Bennett Jr. in Paris, serving as his official secretary and matching his resolute dissipation until they eventually tired of one another. A tall, slim, blue-eyed bachelor, Chamberlain had long been considered the best-dressed man in journalism. He favored English tweeds, frock coats, flowered cravats, and gardenias in his lapel. He wore a monocle and an expensive cat's-eye ring, the latter a gift from Bennett Jr. after Chamberlain had saved him from publishing a nasty editorial he had written while drunk. Hearst admired his editor's considerable talent. Chamberlain possessed news instincts as sharp as any in the business and a keen sense of what people would pay to read. Hearst also had no illusions about his editor's habits: it is said that when they had first sat down together at the Hoffman House, all seventeen bartenders stopped by to pay Sam their respects.[6]

Hearst also ordered a handful of his most talented *Examiner* writers and artists to board a train to New York without mentioning the purpose of the trip. They were already two days out of San Francisco before they figured out that their boss had bought a new paper and that they would not be returning home for a while. Winifred Black was a former chorus girl who wrote under the name Annie Laurie. A Chamberlain discovery, she had begun her career in imitation of Pulitzer's star Nellie Bly but had soon developed into a first-rate reporter in her own right. She had once gained an interview with President Harrison by sneaking into his private railcar and popping up from under a table to introduce herself. Charles Dryden was perhaps America's first great baseball writer and a man whose gifts awed even the unimpressable Ring Lardner. It was Dryden who described Washington as "first in war, first in peace, and last in the American League."[7] Homer Davenport, a former circus hand on his way to becoming the most important American caricaturist since Thomas Nast, was the staff hick. He had been raised in tiny Silverton, Oregon, and Dryden claimed he had to be blindfolded and backed into elevators. Also aboard the eastbound train were Sunday editor Frank Noble and the volatile Scots editorialist Arthur McEwan.

Arriving on track from Chicago was Willis J. Abbot, who, although slightly younger than Hearst, had already seen as much journalistic action. Starting as a reporter in New Orleans, he had worked his way through New York to Kansas City, where, at the age of twenty-three, he was a partner in the launch of a new daily. After its failure, he turned up as managing editor of the *Chicago Times*. When that paper's owner, the mayor of Chicago, was assassinated in 1893, Abbot gained control of the paper and quickly effected a merger with the *Chicago Herald*. That merger led to another, and another, culminating in the preposterously named Chicago *Times-Herald, Record and Inter-Ocean*. Merged out of a job, Abbot signed on as editor-in-chief of Hearst's *Morning Journal*, a grandiose title giving him responsibility for the editorial page. Although he would finish up as editor of the *Christian Science Monitor* and write a dignified memoir of his career, he was at the time a flaming radical.[8] Together with McEwan, Abbot gave Hearst the most progressive and provocative editorial team in newspapers.

As New York media circles were staunchly parochial even in the nineteenth century, Chamberlain's was the only name on the above roster to raise a murmur on Park Row. Hearst's biggest catch, as far as the trades were concerned, was Julian Ralph, lured over from the *Sun*. Dana used him as his paper's lead writer on such momentous occasions as the funeral of Ulysses S. Grant, for which Ralph wrote ten thousand words of evocative prose in seven hours flat. Because Dana did not allow bylines, Ralph owed his popular following to his freelance work for *Harper's*. He arrived at the *Morning Journal* a bona fide star.

The notable acquisitions from Pulitzer's stable were the ailing humorist Bill Nye, who would die in a matter of weeks, and the arts writer Alan Dale of the *Evening World*. Dale was the best drama critic in the country. Droll and fearless, he is believed to have been the first of countless journalists barred from New York theaters over unfavorable reviews. Hearst did make an early run at Ballard Smith, tracking the dynamic, young Pulitzer editor to England and telegraphing a job offer, but it was refused.[9]

It is likely that Hearst paid above-market rates for the talent he hired away from other papers. He was following the example of Pulitzer, who had been skimming the cream from Dana's staff for the better part of two decades. The governing assumption was that hiring the best people would produce the most compelling paper and that sales would jump accordingly. In addition to paying premiums, Hearst ran against the industry practice of "hire and fire" by offering his better recruits multi-year contracts. Job security was then virtually unknown at metropolitan dailies, and long-term deals brought a look of solidity to Hearst's fledgling organization and made him a safer bet for journalists reluctant to leave "secure positions for shaky ones," as *The Fourth Estate* said.[10]

Expensive as these outside recruits may have been, they numbered no more than a dozen or two in these early months. Hearst held on to many of McLean's people and opened the vault only for individuals whose unusual talents or popular appeal could be expected to make an impact on the paper. "Wars are won by generals," he liked to say, "not merely by armies."[11] Hearst, moreover, was paying above-market salaries for his top talent at a time when the going rates were low. Journalists had seen little improvement in their pay over the previous decade; even Pulitzer's largesse was by now a thing of the past. Publishers were benefiting from falling costs for paper and typesetting, yet they weren't sharing the wealth, choosing instead to form publishers' associations aimed at fixing salaries and other costs. Their intransigence was Hearst's opportunity. He denounced publishers' associations shortly after he arrived in New York: "A newspaper is not only in competition with other newspapers, but with all other business. It wants the best brains there are. It's got to offer them inducements, so they won't go into other lines of business."[12] Such comments raised expectations on Park Row of an orgy of competitive spending but, as *The Fourth Estate* noted, while Hearst was known to have money to burn, "He went about his business in a way that proved there was to be no bonfire."[13]

The most surprising thing Hearst did with his money at this point was to decline to spend it on real estate. In the course of negotiating with McLean to purchase the paper, and a matter of days after dragging Stump out to see a building he thought could be purchased and refurbished for a million or two, he dropped the idea of the "nucleus." Stump explained this change of heart in a letter to Phoebe. The *San Francisco Examiner* was then piling on circulation, despite the *Chronicle*'s flashy new headquarters: "Will says it does not appear that fine buildings are necessary to build up a paper, from which I would infer that he is not very anxious to spend a large amount of money on the 'Nucleus.' He is acting with deliberation and caution on the newspaper proposition in New York, & does not feel disposed to jump until he sees where he is going to land."[14] Given his earlier panic at the *Chronicle*'s new offices and his high regard for Pulitzer's

methods, Hearst's abandonment of the nucleus idea was no small decision—he was developing his own ideas about what was necessary for a
publishing success.

Instead of a fancy new building, Hearst and his new recruits reported
for work in the *Morning Journal*'s rented space on the second and third
floors of the Tribune Building at Park Row and Spruce, a block from
Pulitzer's tower. The main newsroom, among the shabbiest on the street,
was a large, open space with innumerable flat and rolltop desks crowded
back to back and side by side as though the goal of the exercise were to
create as cramped, noisy, and sweaty a milieu as possible. Gas lighting
had recently given way in the offices to electric, which blazed at all hours
to supplement the dull glow from the dingy windows. The floor was littered with scrap paper and brass spittoons. The air was dense with cigar
and pipe smoke and the stale odors of working men. During business
hours, editors, reporters, copy boys, clerks, librarians, and artists could be
found bent over their tasks or milling about, most of them in shirtsleeves
and suspenders and, as a general rule, the older the journalist, the more
hair on his face. Most of the younger set preferred only a mustache, and a
few were entirely clean-shaven. Hearst arrived in New York sporting a
wispy blonde mustache but sheared it off in a matter of weeks.

One of the best descriptions we have of Hearst's newsroom comes
from fiction. Stephen Crane, an occasional contributor, used the *Journal* as
a model for his daily in the novel *Active Service*:

> For the most part they bore the unmistakeable stamp of the American col-
> lege. They had that confident poise which is easily brought from the ath-
> letic field. Moreover, their clothes were quite in the way of being of the
> newest fashion. There was an air of precision about their cravats and
> linen. . . . The men coming one and one, or two and two, flung badinage
> to all corners of the room. Afterward, as the wheeled from time to time in
> their chairs, they bitterly-insulted each other with the utmost good-nature,
> taking unerring aim at faults and riddling personalities with the quaint and
> cynical humor of a newspaper office. Throughout this banter, it was
> strange to note how infrequently the men smiled . . ."[15]

With his staff coming together, Hearst turned his attention to the
newspaper itself. McLean's *Morning Journal* had been an uninspired

product. It ran eight pages on most days, with a dull, formulaic front page. The first, leftmost, of its seven columns, considered the lead position, was reserved for Democratic Party news, even if the editors had to stoop to coverage of inconsequential state or county affairs to fill it (other parties rarely rated coverage). Often a second column in the middle of the front page was devoted to the Democrats as well. A political cartoon, crudely drawn and reliably unfunny, ran almost daily at the top of the page over three or four of the middle columns. Shortly before Hearst took over, one of these cartoons portrayed a pair of Republicans on a beach about to be swamped by a Democratic tidal wave, unsubtly labeled "Dem. Tidal Wave." In case anyone missed the point, a caption read, "What the Wild Waves are Saying."[16]

The old *Morning Journal* did have its moments, usually in its human-interest coverage. In the last week of McLean's reign, the paper carried a fascinating report of a rivalry between two butchers, each claiming to be the best in New York, who had determined to settle the matter with a public contest. A large, noisy crowd gathered in Harlem River Park as each butcher in turn picked up his cleaver and raced against the clock to kill and slaughter a young bull. The winner finished in three minutes, twenty-one seconds.

That piece notwithstanding, most of what passed for human interest in McLean's paper simply was not interesting. Too much of it was trivial (police chase mad dog, none injured) or simply tragic (two men die in freight-yard accident) or told without sensitivity or insight. The point of human interest is to stimulate, challenge, delight, outrage, or otherwise engage the hearts and minds of readers. A litany of misfortunes befalling otherwise anonymous people triggers little but sadness. It is no surprise that the *Morning Journal*'s audience was dwindling, even at a penny a copy.

HEARST'S BIOGRAPHERS ARE CORRECT that his name first appeared on the *Journal* on November 7, 1895. He also dropped *Morning* from the paper's title that day.[17] But Hearst's relaunch of the *Journal* was by then already a month old. He had come to terms with McLean on October 3. Four days later Stump gave McLean $30,000 in cash (with the balance due in thirty days), and Hearst assumed control of the paper.[18] He wasted no time in making changes. The lame front-page cartoon disappeared from the October 8 edition, never to return. On October 9, the lead story on Democratic politics migrated from the extreme left of the page to the extreme right. Running in the former lead slot was the story of a young woman who had trained a circus horse to pull her small carriage around town in response to voice command, without benefit of reins or bridle. She had run down an undertaker in the street. The paper's staid front-page template had been broken, the first step toward a more energetic presentation of news.

The *Journal* continued to evolve through the month of October. While still selling for a penny, it was some days expanded to twelve pages. New strategies were evident in the realm of human-interest coverage. The *Journal* began to dwell less on the miseries and hard luck of ordinary people and more on the antics and misfortunes of extraordinary individuals. The death of telegraph tycoon John W. Mackay Jr. hit the front page October 20. He had been thrown headlong into the trunk of a tree while riding at his French estate. He shared page one that week with Colonel Samuel Colt, of the gun-manufacturing Colts, who was suing his wife for divorce after she had disappeared for a three-hour buggy ride with the dashing James J. Van Alen. And the duke of Marlborough, in town for his much-anticipated nuptials with Consuelo Vanderbilt, graced the *Journal*'s pages almost every day for the last two weeks of the month, never more prominently than after his arrest by New York police for reckless bicycle riding in Central Park. All of these stories were milked over several editions, creating narratives intended to draw readers back day after day.

Political stories now sometimes dominated the front page and sometimes went missing entirely, depending on their perceived importance and on whatever else was happening in the world. While still giving reams of space to internal Democratic maneuverings, the *Journal* began to show interest in the affairs of other parties and it began to press its own priorities and issues, including campaigns against collusion and price-fixing in railroads and liquor industries. On October 27, a remarkably detailed cartoon of the Republican elephant, drawn by the former circus hand Homer Davenport, ran at a striking five columns. The beast's trunk tickles the bearded chin of prospective Republican presidential nominee Benjamin Harrison. Davenport was one of several artists whose work now ran on page one, in place of the old unfunny *Journal* cartoon.

The clear and simple elegance of his work immediately established a new tone of visual sophistication for the paper.

Realistic sketches of politicians, society leaders, and courtroom figures also began to appear regularly on page one. Hearst's critics have accused him of using art to pander to dullards and foreigners, as though attracting new readers to newspapers were a reprehensible activity. Illustrated material probably did expand his audience, but it also drew attention to stories, aided in their telling, heightened their dramatic presentation, and appealed to the eye. Like halftone photographs, which were just beginning to appear in periodicals, illustrations were a fabulous journalistic tool, attractive to the broadest range of readers, and they were increasingly common even in the three-cent *Herald*.

Hearst probably withheld his name from the masthead until November 7 in order to get his staff in place and an initial round of improvements underway, and to have a big story at his disposal before he announced to his competitors that his charge was on. November 7 certainly provided the big story: a beautiful eighteen-year-old railroad heiress had just been married against her will to the reckless bicyclist, the cash-strapped duke of Marlborough.

The *Journal*'s coverage of the Vanderbilt-Marlborough nuptials is not mentioned in either of the major Hearst biographies—Nasaw sees nothing but "rather pedestrian" news in Hearst's first week. Yet the wedding was a popular sensation, one of the social occasions of the decade, and a significant news event besides. The *Journal*'s coverage was appropriately massive. Almost the entire front page was given over to a richly detailed illustration of the couple leaving the altar of flower-strewn Saint Thomas Church as attendants, family, and distinguished well-wishers looked on. Julian Ralph, hired because he could write more copy faster and better than anyone else in town, authored the main article. His report started on front and continued over three pages inside, and was accompanied by a play-by-play from "a lady of the Four Hundred," reproductions of the menu and musical program, and illustrations of the bride's triumphant mother, of prominent guests, and of police holding back the great throngs outside.

There were several factors that lifted the Vanderbilt-Marlborough wedding out of the ordinary, including the stature of the families, the commercial dimension of the marriage, the bride's known opposition to the match, and her mother's insane social ambition. Writers as diverse as Henry James and Mark Twain had treated the spectacle of rich American parents dealing their sons and daughters for European titles, and Mrs. Vanderbilt, in engineering this match, had brought the practice to its apogee. It was a story that reached near the heart of American cultural identity, and everyone in New York had an opinion on it. Newspaper readers, whether enraptured by the story or outraged by it, wanted every available detail. The upmarket *Herald*, celebrated then and now for its news judgment, also gave the event enormous coverage, running it over three pages, with seven illustrations.

Immediately on the heels of the Marlborough-Vanderbilt extravaganza came two stories even more seriously misrepresented in the Hearst biographies. On November 10, the *Journal* led with the arrest of two men in connection with a deadly saloon robbery. Nasaw cites this as the "first front page of Hearstian proportions," a prime example of the new proprietor's dedication to cheap and irresponsible fearmongering. Gussied up with a near full-page drawing of "two lugubrious criminals" under a "large type bold headline," the story, writes Nasaw, "was not covered by the other dailies and vanished from the *Journal* as miraculously as it appeared."[19]

In fairness, the saloon attack wasn't the Great Train Robbery, but neither was it plucked from thin air. The *Journal* had given it great play the day before, in large part because police were fascinated by the crime. Investigators had developed a theory that the culprits, who had burst into the saloon and fired shots into the ceiling, were performers in Buffalo Bill's visiting Wild West Show. Police had also linked the crime to similar armed robberies in Baltimore, Chicago, and Hoboken. The violent, multi-city crime spree was a far fresher narrative at the end of the nineteenth century than it is in our time, and New York's finest devoted extraordinary resources to their investigation.[20] The drawings of the alleged criminals ran at less than a fifth of the page, and the headline was actually the standard one-column minimum the *Journal* used for top copy on both the front and inside pages. Nor did the story quickly disappear. When new information emerged two weeks later, one of the lugubrious duo was back on front.[21] Upmarket papers like the *Tribune* and the *Sun* didn't give much space to the saloon attack: they were more interested in the intoxicated warden of the Ludlow Street jail and whether or not

Warren Palmer would be held responsible for the debts of his runaway wife. The *Herald*, however, gave it good play and also found space for "Yale Students Steal a Mail Box ."[22]

The second *Journal* story to be looked at askance in the biographies was a yachting dispute. The earl of Dunraven's *Valkyrie III* had recently lost an America's Cup series to the American *Defender*. Returning to England, Dunraven wrote a long letter to the London *Field* accusing the *Defender* of cheating. The New York yachting community, which had hosted the race, was outraged at the charge but unable to defend itself, as only bits and pieces of the letter had been cabled across the Atlantic. Hearst paid to have the entire letter cabled to the *Journal*. He splashed it over seven columns without illustration, under the first full-page banner headline he would run in New York: "Full Text of Lord Dunraven's Charges. . . ."[23] Hearst's enthusiasm for this controversy has been criticized as evidence of his losing his bearings and of suddenly pitching his penny paper at the yachting set. In fact, the Dunraven story was a coup for the *Journal*.

Yachting may have been a rich man's sport, but it had an immense popular following in the late nineteenth century, taking up more space in the sports pages than baseball. The America's Cup was particularly appealing, attracting tens of thousands of spectators including strong representation from New York's vast Irish community, which could be counted on to jeer the British entries. International contests of any kind were infrequent before the start of the modern Olympics in 1896. Patriotic passions typically ran high, and they might be said to have hit a peak in 1895, with the United States and Great Britain rattling sabers over the border between Venezuela and British Guiana. London refused to submit the matter to arbitration on terms satisfactory to the Venezuelans and their Washington allies. President Cleveland was a short five weeks from advising Congress that Britain represented a threat to his country's "peace and safety," a speech that left many (including Hearst) convinced of the inevitability of war. In this atmosphere, questions of fair dealing between the United States and Britain took on unusual significance.

All of the New York newspapers devoted space to Dunraven's charges—the *Herald* had three reporters on the story—and all were waiting to receive Dunraven's text by mail. There was no doubt on Park Row as to the value of the *Journal*'s enterprise. The November 20 edition of the trade journal *Printer's Ink* reported that it was being discussed as "the journalistic triumph of the year."[24]

All in all, Hearst had set a hot pace in his first official week. More impressively, he maintained it. New publications generally tend to stockpile scoops and features in advance of their relaunch and then run dry after several issues. The *Journal* continued to knock out feats of journalistic enterprise once or twice a week for the rest of the year. A few days after Dunraven, for instance, Hearst tackled another major sporting event. Princeton versus Yale was the greatest rivalry in American football (the professional game was not yet off the ground). All the papers sent correspondents. Hearst sent something more.

Before there were matinee idols, there was Richard Harding Davis, the most dashing figure in Victorian New York. American journalism has not seen the likes of him since: strong-jawed and smoulderingly handsome, with a wardrobe that gave Sam Chamberlain a run for his money, Davis was rumored to be the model for the Gibson Boy, that debonair counterpart to the new American girls in Charles Dana Gibson's magazine illustrations. At thirty-one years of age, he had published fiction in *Scribner's*, developed a popular newspaper column, served as managing editor of *Harper's Weekly*, and published six successful books. Hearst hired him to cover Princeton-Yale at the princely fee of $500 for the single piece.

At first blush, it might seem an odd match of writer and subject, but Davis was an ardent sports fan. He had covered prizefights as well as football, and he had once quit a reporting job in Philadelphia to follow an American cricket team on a tour of the British Isles. Even at $500, securing Davis was a clever move. His name was a guaranteed draw, a sure way to distinguish the *Journal*'s report of what would be a well-covered event. To get his money's worth, Hearst paraded the story over two pages, including the whole of a Sunday front and ran the author's byline almost an inch high. The text was accompanied by depictions of the action, the crowd, and the coaches, and a bird's-eye view of Manhattan Field. Two intricate charts followed the ball through each half of the game. A former Yale coach offered a technical assessment of the action, and the famous boxer James Corbett weighed in with his thoughts on the outcome. The most interesting part of Davis's story from today's perspective is his reaction to the crowd of 40,000 packed into Manhattan Field. Mass audiences were clearly as new to sport as they were to newspapers:

> It was like a great crater of living people, and those who were on a level with the players saw the blue sky above them as a man sees it from the bottom of a well. A circle a half of a mile in circumference, and composed of people rising one above the other as high as a three-story house, is a very remarkable sight, and when half of these people leap suddenly to their feet and wave blue flags and yell, and then sink back as the man they have been cheering is tackled and thrown, and the other half jump up in their turn and wave orange and black flags, the effect is something which cannot be duplicated in this country or in any other.[25]

No story would loom larger in Hearst's paper over the next five years than Cuba's struggle for independence from Spain, and it too was front and center in these early weeks. On December 8, Hearst led his front page with a report from the Spanish front by Lieutenant Winston Churchill of the British army's Fourth Hussars. On leave from his cavalry regiment, Churchill had crossed the Atlantic with a friend to collect "a great many Havana cigars" and observe the Spanish government's spirited but increasingly futile efforts to stamp out an insurrection among the islanders. Churchill sent five reports back to the *Daily Graphic* in London. His article in the *Journal* was largely a summary of those pieces. Though he was only twenty years of age, Churchill was hardly an anonymous correspondent. The *Journal* introduced him as the eldest son of the noted Tory statesman Lord Randolph Churchill and, more intriguingly, as cousin and possible heir to the recently wed duke of Marlborough. Churchill traveled two weeks through the swamps and rugged hills of the Cuban countryside in the company of General Valdez—"the greatest man Spain had produced in latter days." His report is a lively account of some minor skirmishes and Churchill's own experiences under fire, once while bathing in a river.[26]

A final story of note from these initial weeks involves the arrest of Miss Amelia Elizabeth Schauer, who occupied the *Journal*'s front page the same morning as Churchill's report. This article, too, has been cited as an example of Hearst's duping a credulous public with front-page "melodrama" manufactured out of "back-page filler," but it was much more than that.

A few months prior to Miss Schauer's arrest, New York police commissioner Theodore Roosevelt had ordered a crackdown on habitual
criminals, making a particular target of prostitutes. In twelve months,
403 women were convicted of soliciting compared to 172 during the
previous twelve.[27] Evidence of actual crime was often slight. Policemen
and city magistrates considered the mere presence of an unescorted
woman on the street late at night sufficient to warrant a conviction.
Miss Schauer had been picked up for soliciting and was thrown in
among the hardened criminals at the Blackwell's Island workhouse.
She claimed her only offense was to have asked a man for directions. A
well-spoken woman, fetching in prison garb (or so the *Journal*'s artists
presented her), Miss Schauer attracted an abundance of maudlin sympathy. Social activists took up her cause and brought her to the attention of the *Journal*, where she became the object of Hearst's first New
York advocacy campaign. The *Journal* gathered character witnesses,
paid her legal bills, and published front-page illustrations of her menacing, thick-browed prison mates. The State Supreme Court reviewed
the case and found Miss Schauer innocent of all charges. The *Journal*
celebrated her release and its own role in the proceedings with almost
equal enthusiasm.[28]

Purple patches notwithstanding, the Schauer story was rooted in a
vexing legal conflict between individual rights and public safety, and it
deserved its spot on the front page. Despite the court's ruling, the incarceration of young women on slight evidence continued apace. Within a
year, another young literary phenomenon, Stephen Crane, would
embroil himself and the *Journal* in a similar storyline, albeit with a less
joyful outcome.

All the stories cited as evidence of Hearst's underwhelming performance in New York were far more interesting and substantive than
might be gathered by glancing at their headlines. A stronger argument
that Hearst produced a shoddy spectacle of gossip and fearmongering
in these weeks might have pointed to an article guessing at who would
fill the dancing pumps of Ward McAllister, the late king of society's
Four Hundred, or another enumerating (with graphs) the positions off
Coney Island from which the Queen's Navy might shell Madison
Square Garden if the Venezuela situation got out of hand. But it is a
simple business to find schlock in any paper.

One would never guess from the Hearst literature—which includes innumerable journalism histories as well as a half-dozen biographies— that the *Journal*'s first weeks included expansive coverage of Speaker Thomas Brackett Reed's ongoing domination of the House of Representatives or the full text of President Cleveland's annual address to Congress. Or a string of lengthy reports from a national labor convention at Madison Square Garden, with commentary from noted British trade unionist James Mawdsley. Or a campaign against Cornell University's practice of dissecting live cats to teach physiology, complete with angry anti-vivisectionist editorials and a range of pro and con opinions from leading medical professionals. Or a front-page story about a New York rabbi coming to the defense of an agnostic clergyman who had outraged his fellow Christians by challenging the infallibility of the Bible. Or a holiday edition featuring a tour of Bowery slums and other places untouched by Christmas spirit, written by Jacob Riis, celebrated author of *How the Other Half Lives*, and published alongside his own documentary-style photo-illustrations of indigent Manhattanites.[29]

It is true that news of society and calamities were a part of the paper's formula for success. They were a part of every major Park Row daily's formula for success. They were part of the stiff-necked, three-cent, thoroughly Republican *New York Tribune*'s formula for success. In addition to generous coverage of the Vanderbilt-Marlborough wedding and the Dunraven scandal, the *Tribune* during Hearst's first weeks on Park Row sported front-page stories of train crashes, maritime wrecks, forest fires, scamming bookkeepers, rampaging armed lunatics, bar fights, and lonely men expiring in elevators. The difference between the Hearst and Reid papers was primarily one of emphasis. The *Tribune* tended to carry more political, international, and financial news than the *Journal*, and fewer crime and disaster stories. Each paper was professionally and intelligently edited for its own particular audience, the *Journal*'s mass and democratic, the *Tribune*'s elite and commercial.

Hearst, in fact, improved the quality of crime and disaster coverage at the *Journal*. He engaged readers less with frights than by illuminating character and creating narrative, by playing up the arts of police detection and courtroom argument, by delineating justice issues and moral controversies and vigorously taking sides in them. He made similar improvements to the paper's gossip and society news, eliminating a clutch of cheesy columns with names like "Gossip of the Swells" and the "Jolly Joker," in favor of Alan Dale's popular reviews and "Caught in the Metropolitan Whirl," a smart new column containing short, breezy observations about city life. The whole paper was being reworked. The quality of its prose, while still uneven, was improving steadily. The design, on the whole, was more polished. Coverage was more comprehensive throughout: foreign and financial news were expanded, along with sports and the arts.

As for publicity, there was no unusual amount of showmanship in Hearst's initial assault on New York. He hired brass bands and hung posters for his Sunday edition and dreamt up the circulation slogans that ran atop his front page: "*You can't get more than all the News. You can't pay less than one cent.*" He got some applause in the trades for using color-coded fireworks to announce the results of the November state elections, but they specifically noted that he had relaunched the *Journal* without any "blare of trumpets or big-typed praise."[30] For now, Hearst was pouring his money into his product, not its promotion. At the end of 1895, Joseph Pulitzer was still the unrivaled king of ballyhoo. A pioneer in the art of newspaper self-promotion, Pulitzer proudly recorded every journalistic accomplishment and each upward tick in his circulation on page one. He not only organized parades and posters but kept the dome of the Pulitzer Building illuminated every night to remind New Yorkers of his presence. One evening, when the cloud cover was just so, Pulitzer used a 200,000-candlepower light to project his paper's slogan into the Manhattan sky: "The World, 2 cents, circulation nearly one-half million per day."[31]

In all essentials, then, the conventional view of Hearst's first months in New York is seriously off the mark. Hearst managed to turn the *Journal* around and double his circulation inside of three months without relent-less self-promotion, without pillaging Pulitzer's staff, without cheapening his editorial contents, and without breaking his own bank. He had identi-fied an opportunity in the New York market for a one-cent paper of com-parable quality to the two- and three-cent papers he himself admired—the *World* and the *Herald*. He hit the 100,000 mark in December and 150,000 by the end of January. Rather than racing to the bottom, he drove the *Journal* and the penny press, as a class, upmarket. The *Journal* was a demanding, sophisticated paper by contemporary standards. Writers like

Julian Ralph and Richard Harding Davis, quite at home in the three-cent
sheets, did not dumb down for its pages. Not everything in the new paper
clicked; it would continue to evolve, sometimes for the better, sometimes
not. But by New Year's, the trades were unanimous that the *Journal*'s contents rivaled those of New York's more expensive dailies and that the
paper was making rapid gains in circulation and stature. "Nothing has
been more remarkable in the history of metropolitan newspaperdom than
the tremendous increase in the circulation of the *Journal*. . ."[32]

Of everything written about Hearst in this initial period, the most
interesting piece was by Addison Archer for *Printer's Ink*. The leading
commentator on publishing affairs in New York, Archer tracked the
young proprietor down at the Tribune Building.

> Everybody in Park Row is talking about Mr. William R. Hearst, the young
> San Francisco millionaire, who has bought the New York *Morning Journal*,
> and has put his brain, energy and experience into making it a dangerous
> competitor for any number in this field. . . . I went to see him in the middle of
> a busy afternoon. I found him in the main editorial room of the *Journal*—a
> young man with a smooth face, an easy, college-bred manner, and a quiet,
> business-like air. I told him who I was, and he made an appointment to see
> me at his office or at mine, whichever was more convenient to me, on the
> following day, at a stated hour. He did this in a pleasant, easy, unassuming
> way that one would hardly be led to expect in a famous young journalist.[33]

As the two men sat on either side of an immense flat-topped desk in
the center of a large office, Archer quizzed Hearst on his experiences in
San Francisco and his plans for New York, his hiring practices, his sense
of the competitive environment. Hearst revealed that he had already
ordered a set of color presses in order to add color illustrations to the
Journal. He confessed that he had entered journalism because he was
not up to the long, dull preparation required, say, for a legal career: "The
newspaper business seemed to offer more attractions than any other—
more immediate attractions, and as many ultimate rewards." Archer also
interviewed Hearst's colleagues and rivals, some of whom were predicting that he would empty the family purse in no time. Nonetheless, the
interviewer came away convinced that he had been speaking to a "journalistic genius" and a man with strong business acumen:

I find it the universal verdict of those who know, that Mr. Hearst deserves all that I have said of him. That it is his brain and good judgment that have given him success in the past and present, and on which he may rely for success in the future. I lay great stress upon this point, because journalistic success is always dependent upon personal qualifications. The wealth of the Vanderbilts and Astors combined would not make success for a journalist if he were not personally capable of making the most of his journalistic opportunities.

That last line is as important as anything that has ever been written about Hearst's adventures in journalism. Nasaw, Swanberg, and every other important historian or biographer who has dealt with Hearst's career has overestimated the importance of his family fortune to his progress as a publisher.[34] A.J. Liebling famously held that Hearst's greatest accomplishment was to demonstrate that money could be used "like a heavy club" to found a newspaper empire.[35] Archer knew better. John McLean's millions had not saved him from a humiliating failure with the *Morning Journal*. Multi-millionaire tobacco tycoon James Duke was, in 1895, driving the *Recorder* into receivership. Jay Gould hadn't been able to make a success of the *World*. Money was not nearly enough.

There's no question that his family fortune was useful to Hearst. It was his father's money that had bought him the *Examiner,* that had allowed him to purchase the *Journal,* that provided him capital to invest in its improvement, and that covered his losses and gave him a measure of security as he strove to expand at breakneck speed. But money was useless without those elusive "personal qualifications." As Archer well knew, everyone in the upper echelons of New York publishing was fabulously rich.

The *Sun*'s Charles Dana was perhaps the least materialistic of the Park Row editor-owners, yet he lived in a manner beyond the dreams of his well-heeled readers. A millionaire many times over, he owned, in addition to his comfortable Manhattan residence, a mansion at Glen Cove on the Gold Coast of Long Island Sound, from which he commuted daily by steam yacht in the summer months. His neighbors included F.W. Woolworth, J.P. Morgan, and Charles Pratt, one of the founders of Standard Oil. Dana, however, kept mostly to himself and his collections of fine wines and Chinese porcelain.

Pulitzer had spent the spring of 1895 in Bar Harbor, where he had just purchased a fifteen-acre seaside estate with breathtaking views and a stable for twenty-five horses. He had retained Stanford White of McKim, Mead, & White, the most fashionable and expensive architecture firm in America, to renovate the property. White's special assignment was to build a luxurious four-story, granite-walled "tower of silence" with Pulitzer's private quarters above and a steam-heated swimming pool in the basement. Extensive soundproofing would be installed to shield the hypersensitive publisher from outside irritants, including his family in the main house. Pulitzer summered at Moray Lodge in England until the cries of the peacocks in nearby Kensington Gardens drove him to a second, quieter manor nearby.[36] He returned in autumn to his bucolic retreat in Lakewood, New Jersey, and made occasional trips to his mansion on East 55th, where he kept his Millet paintings and one of the city's two or three finest libraries. Each of Pulitzer's residences, including his resort at Jekyll Island, Georgia, was fully furnished and staffed at all times. He traveled with a massive entourage and sent out advance parties to book the finest accommodations and to ensure that everything would be perfect on his arrival.

Whitelaw Reid, proprietor and editor of the *Tribune*, owned fewer properties than Pulitzer but easily matched him for opulent living. A bona fide American aristocrat, boasting social connections as impeccable as his grooming, he had served three years as minister to France before joining the ill-fated 1892 Republican ticket as Benjamin Harrison's vice-presidential nominee. Since then he had been sulking, traveling, and throwing hundreds of thousands of dollars into the development of Ophir Farm, a gray stone castle set on seven hundred acres of prime Westchester soil. To assist in the project he hired not only Stanford White but the similarly pricey Frederick Law Olmsted, America's foremost landscape architect. Money was no object. Apart from having substantial income from the *Tribune*, Reid had married Elisabeth Mills, daughter of Darius Ogden Mills, the most successful banker on the West Coast and a leading shareholder in the Southern Pacific Railroad.[37]

All of these men—Dana, Pulitzer, Reid—were pikers compared to the "mad commodore," James Gordon Bennett Jr., champion yachtsman and owner of the money-spewing *New York Herald*. Bennett raised profligate living to a wild art. When he rode his bicycle around the block from his Fifth Avenue townhouse, his butler stood curbside with a silver tray and a glass of brandy to celebrate each lap. When he became bored with the townhouse, Bennett moved to his "country" manor in Washington Heights. He owned a spectacular Newport mansion and across the street from it a private club, the Casino, built after his boorish behavior forced his expulsion from the Newport Reading Room. He frequently entertained King Charles of Portugal at his Versailles estate, and English aristocracy at his shooting box in Scotland. *Herald* managers were sometimes summoned to his villa at Beaulieu-sur-Mer, between Nice and Monte Carlo, for staff meetings at the foot of his bed. From time to time, he was also spotted in the vicinity of his apartment on the Champs Élysées, driving his coach at reckless speeds, occasionally in the buff. Bennett, too, had hired Stanford White, not once but several times. The great architect outfitted the interior of the publisher's yacht, *Namouna,* and designed his Casino at Newport. White was also commissioned to build a new headquarters for the *Herald*. Bennett had wanted it modeled after the Doge's Palace in Venice, but White insisted on something a little less ostentatious, in the manner of Verona's Palazzo del Consiglio. Bennett reluctantly agreed and immediately lost interest in the project. He traveled from residence to residence in the company of a large staff and some three dozen Pomeranians, Chihuahuas, cocker spaniels, and other small dogs.[38]

Bennett and Pulitzer, Hearst's most direct competitors for mass circulation, both derived incomes approaching $1 million a year from their papers. Bennett was said to enjoy the largest assured income in America next to Commodore Vanderbilt and William B. Astor. Pulitzer netted approximately $20 million in his first twenty years at the *World*, and his proceeds from his outside investments in some years exceeded those from publishing. Hearst may have paid $150,000 for his newspaper, but Pulitzer dropped the same sum on one pearl necklace for his wife, and Mrs. Pulitzer owned a lot of jewelry. Bennett was blithely losing $100,000 a year on the Paris edition of his *Herald,* and he was spending at least three times that on the annual upkeep of his yacht. The clock at his new Herald Building had cost more than Hearst paid for the *Journal*.[39] Clearly, there were deep pockets up and down Park Row.

Unfortunately, more direct comparisons of financial resources are impossible. Despite all the fuss about Hearst's money and its impact on the newspaper industry, we have only the murkiest picture of his accounts. We know what he paid for the *Journal*. We know that he drove harder bargains and made his money go further than has been credited. We know that his mother had committed a million for his new paper, but that he didn't receive the sum until the summer of 1896, and he probably didn't spend more than a few hundred thousand in the interim, during which the *Journal* was substantially relaunched. We know that Stump expected the *Journal*'s monthly operating losses to be $20,000[40] and that, at the heights of the coming war, the paper would for several consecutive months lose approximately $150,000, much to Phoebe's chagrin. It is likely that Will spent several million on the *Journal*—possibly as much as $5 million—before it began to pay.

Five million is not as much as Bennett Jr. and Pulitzer sank into their yachts, but it is a large sum. Much of Hearst's cash went to capital assets, including what was probably the newspaper world's most advanced printing plant, and all of it has to be considered an investment in establishing himself against entrenched competition in the richest publishing market in the world, an inherently expensive undertaking. His chief rivals could afford to match him dollar for dollar, and their competitive costs were lower than his (it requires far less to defend an established business than to grow a new one). There was always a chance he might get wiped out, but if Hearst succeeded, he would have a franchise capable of spinning out a million a year in profits and the nucleus of a national chain of newspapers. High risk, high reward.

What really distinguished Hearst from his fellow proprietors at the end of 1895—and what must have frightened them most—was not the wealth at his disposal but that he was young, talented, driven, and willing to put everything he had on the line in pursuit of his journalistic ambitions. He was far more interested in making a great paper than in turning a profit. He believed that if he conquered Park Row, his finances would sort themselves out. "I didn't care about making money," he said some years later, "at least not just to make money."[41] One of his financial advisers expanded on this point: "Money as such bores him. His idea of money is that it is something to do something with. He is a builder. He wants to build buildings. . . . His idea is to build, build, build all the time."[42]

No one was more astounded by Will's attitude toward money than his mother's banker, who was charged with delivering the funds she had earmarked for him. "I asked Will how he wanted the million paid to him," Hosmer Parsons wrote Pheobe, "and he said 'I don't want any

million, I would not know what to do with it.'" Will told Parsons he
would prefer to simply draw what he needed from his mother as he went
along. "There are not many in America," wrote Parsons, "who would
neglect a chance to claim a million of dollars." The banker eventually
convinced Hearst to deposit the sum in a trust company, and when the
matter was finally settled, Parsons observed to Phoebe: "Will is a very
peculiar man and cannot be judged by usual standards."[43]

Hearst was also peculiar among the New York newspaper barons in
that he was willing to invest his full attention in his daily. Bennett had
established and perfected the role of absentee proprietor, cabling his editors comments and instructions from across the Atlantic as though they
were just across the hall. He rarely visited the *Herald*'s headquarters, or
New York, for that matter. Pulitzer emulated Bennett in this regard. He
traveled incessantly, never working a day under the golden dome of the
World Building, yet he managed to exercise unquestioned control of his
paper's operations. Reid broke with Pulitzer and Bennett only in his willingness to delegate management responsibilities to trusted colleagues; he
thought nothing of holding his editorship and various diplomatic postings
simultaneously. Even Dana, in his dotage, was increasingly aloof from the
Sun, publishing four books in a three-year span. Bennett, Pulitzer, Reid,
and Dana—among the most admired editors in the history of American
journalism—were the unmistakable leaders of their newspaper operations. But none of them was really at home at the moment the *Journal*
rushed out of the gate.

A Kind of Rumba Accompanied
by Snapping Fingers

Joseph Pulitzer had many excellent qualities as an employer of newspaper executives. He was brilliant for starters. His various managers and handlers often left his presence feeling like they had encountered another order of human intelligence—who else could play several games of chess at once without looking at a board? They admired his courage and originality, his reforming zeal, his popular touch, his commercial instincts, and they reveled in his showmanship. Many of his executives would have agreed with his long-serving editor "Colonel" Cockerill that their boss was "the greatest journalist the world has ever known."[1] He could be volatile, overbearing, and abusive at times, but otherwise he was good company.

Also, a certain prestige came with employment under Pulitzer's golden dome. The *World* was the most popular and influential newspaper in the country, and status often trumps money when journalists make career choices. It is uncommon to see a talented executive voluntarily leave the management ranks of a great daily for a lesser one, at any salary. Pulitzer offered his men both eminence and the top pay on Park Row. Cockerill was pulling in a princely $15,000 a year by the end of his career, while the *World*'s business managers and managing editors routinely earned $10,000 or more. These not only were the top salaries in journalism but some of the highest in any line of work. Raises, bonuses, and prizes were awarded for outstanding work, which might be anything from writing a brilliant headline to producing a surge in advertising. Pulitzer feted his favorites with dinners, distributed silk hats and silver medals to celebrate circulation milestones, and gave fur coats as Christmas gifts.

But there was a definite downside. The boss expected his talent to match his own phenomenal energy and commitment. Cockerill once described what was wanted of a *World* managing editor: "He should live at his desk and sleep under it. He has no right to have family, relatives, friends nor social obligations, and if ever he attempted to go north of Park Row, men should be stationed there with clubs to drive him back to his den."[2] Pulitzer instructed one of his editors to spend six hours a day reading all available newspapers and dreaming up ideas; a few hours talking with his senior staff, handing out assignments and instructions; and several hours more "book reading to cultivate and equip your mind."[3] Somewhere in between, the poor soul was to squeeze in his ample administrative duties, meals, and home life.

While the executives were expected to share in the burdens of piloting a great paper, public recognition was reserved for the proprietor. One of the most revealing letters ever written by Joseph Pulitzer was addressed to the loyal and talented Cockerill in 1886, at the height of their triumph in New York. It was a reaction to isolated comments from Park Row sources crediting the *World*'s success to Cockerill's journalistic and commercial skill, and representing Pulitzer as the financier of the enterprise:

I presume you have seen the remarkable notices given you by your friends in the press. These efforts to belittle me . . . I mean to stop. You might have stopped them in time yourself. I have waited for some time, hoping that your own sense of right would have induced you to tell your friends what you, of all men, must know to be false.

You know that my primary object and ambition in journalism was always intellectual and honorable—not for mere money-making. . . . I always was, and always shall be, editor first and proprietor only secondly. But, if what your friends say is true, you ought to own the paper and I ought to be in your employ.

You know how fond I am of you. You know how much I appreciate your tact, talent and brightness—even if you do not seem to appreciate me. . . . But I will not tolerate even by my silence for you what I know to be a gross injustice. I want you to know exactly how I feel in this matter.

If I am not a self-made man you never knew one. If I was not the real, actual head in building up my two newspapers nobody ever could be.

You, better than anybody, must know that every cardinal constructive idea that created the *World* and the *Post-Dispatch* was mine and mine only.

This letter, published in the trade papers several years after Cockerill's death (and unnoticed since), was received on Park Row as evidence of Pulitzer's consuming vanity and imperious, demeaning management style.[4]

He did have a perverse streak: it was one thing to ask employees to work hard, but Pulitzer adopted extreme methods to ensure his men were constantly on their toes and earning their pay. Senior managers were assigned overlapping responsibilities and required to report to him on one another's work habits, morale, and overall performance. Inevitably, these reports, reaching him in Bar Harbor or Monte Carlo or wherever he might be, were tainted by self-interest and malice, but Pulitzer would take them to heart. His managers grew accustomed to receiving in person or by wire scorching criticisms of their efforts, including indictments of their work ethic and personal habits that their employer could not possibly have observed first-hand. Pulitzer expected executives to take this medicine with a cheerfulness entirely absent from his own manner. "Don't be sensitive," he wrote one of his managing editors, "if I should in future seem brusque, harsh, or even unjust in my criticism. I sincerely hope I never shall be; but if I should, remember that fault-finding is perhaps both my privilege and my weakness, that correction is the only road to improvement, and that my quick temper and illness are entitled to some consideration."[5] Both the volume and the sharpness of his fault-finding increased in the early 1890s as his deteriorating eyesight and long forays abroad left him more dependent on his managers.

In addition to promoting internal rivalries, Pulitzer fought what he imagined to be the complacency of his staff with a constant shuffling of responsibilities. The columns of the trade journals routinely burst with news of promotions, demotions, sidelinings, and resignations among *World* executives. Just four years before Hearst's arrival in New York, Cockerill refused to accept a demotion and quit as editor of the *World*. His Pulitzer-imposed rival, the haughty and talented Ballard Smith, took up his responsibilities. The following year, 1892, Ballard Smith was found wanting and was shipped off to London as a correspondent, replaced by George Harvey. S.S. Carvalho was put in charge of business operations with complete control of spending. John Dillon, only recently hired as business manager, was redirected to the editorial page, while John Norris was picked up from the *Philadelphia Record* to serve as Carvalho's rival in the counting room. It took only a year for Carvalho and Norris to stop speaking to one another. They communicated by notes. When George Harvey failed to meet expectations as editor, possibly as a result of a bout of pneumonia, Pulitzer reached for a grand solution. He had invited Colonel Charles H. Jones of the *Missouri Republican* to spend a week with him in Bar Harbor, and on that brief acquaintance Jones arrived at the dome in July 1893 with a letter of instruction giving him full run of the paper.[6] Carvalho, Harvey, and their various rivals were dumbfounded but quickly rallied and cooperated long enough to undermine the newcomer. They sank Jones in a matter of weeks, capitalizing on the fact that he had flouted a cardinal rule by editorializing against Pulitzer's political preferences. The dysfunctional team of Carvalho and Norris was back in harness by the time Hearst purchased the *Journal*.[7]

That any of this made for a sharper paper is doubtful, but it did combine with Pulitzer's encouragement of staff informants to institutionalize at the *World* his own suspicious, querulous nature and his admittedly "brusque, harsh, or even unjust" treatment of staff. "What are called 'office politics,'" remembered the journalist Charles Edward Russell, "were in a state of highly irrational ferment."[8] Another described the city room as a "witch's brew of suspicion, jealousy, and hatred—a maelstrom of office politics that drove at least two editors to drink, one to suicide, a fourth to insanity, and another to banking."[9]

And yet Pulitzer still had his pick of the best editorial and commercial talent in the business. It wasn't until Hearst arrived and offered a dignified alternative to life under the Dome that Pulitzer's style began to have consequences. He lost his three best managers—three of the most talented and dedicated executives in the annals of American newspapering—within two years of the start of the war with Hearst. In all three cases, Pulitzer initiated the damage by losing confidence in his men, demoting or quarreling with them, and making them miserable enough to quit. He effectively drove his best people into Hearst's warm and lucrative embrace, crippling the *World*, sinking its morale, and handing its primary competitor the management capacity to expand and improve.

MORRILL GODDARD WAS THIRTY YEARS OLD at the beginning of 1896, a small, pale, sickly-looking man, but already a legend on Park Row. Born in Maine and educated at Dartmouth, he had arrived in New York fresh from school and determined to work at a great newspaper. The best any city editor would offer him was the occasional freelance assignment. For a long winter, Goddard eked out a living on piecework. His luck began to turn, however, when he befriended "Peg Leg" Fogarty, chief attendant of the city morgue. Fogarty tipped the young hack to news of prominent and untimely visitors to his shop and Goddard began churning out scoop after scoop, leading to full-time employment at the *World*. There was a similarly ghoulish touch to the most notorious coup of Goddard's reporting career. On the occasion of President Ulysses S. Grant's funeral procession through New York, Goddard donned a black suit, a black tie, and his most somber expression and quietly climbed into the first carriage to take a seat beside the widow and her police escort, both of whom assumed he was the undertaker's assistant. Goddard covered the entire procession practically from Mrs. Grant's lap.[10]

In 1894, serving as the *World*'s city editor, Goddard led the paper's successful campaign to elect William L. Strong as mayor of New York. Pulitzer was impressed. He offered Goddard a managing editor's role. Goddard replied that he was content to remain in the city room. "If you have no more confidence in yourself than that," spat Pulitzer, "I will not give you the post." But Goddard's stubbornness seems only to have raised him in the eyes of his employer. After a short interval, Pulitzer made him another offer: managing editor of the Sunday *World*. This time he bit.[11]

The attraction of the Sunday *World* was plain: it was the bestselling edition of any paper in America. Pulitzer had practically invented Sunday journalism. When he started in New York, the vast majority of dailies ran six days a week, but as New Yorkers adopted a more casual approach to the Sabbath and department stores took to advertising on Sundays on the assumption that people had more time to read, a seventh day of publication began to make sense. Pulitzer made the most of the opening, adding a four-page Sunday supplement to his regular run of news, priced it at three cents, and he was soon selling 90,000 copies a week. By the time Goddard took the helm, circulation was up to 250,000 at five cents apiece.[12] High circulation together with an abundance of advertising made the Sunday *World* the single most lucrative issue of any paper anywhere. Most weeks it weighed in at forty-eight pages. Even with an advertising-to-editorial ratio approaching 50 percent, there was a lot of space for editors to fill. In keeping with the more leisurely pace of the day, Pulitzer loaded up on human-interest features, illustrated journalism, travelogues, science and technology stories, sermons, reviews, and society news. This was Goddard's element: he had a gift for feature journalism. It took him only a few months to prove that Pulitzer had yet to scratch the surface of the potential market for a Sunday paper.

Goddard's Sunday editions gave great value for five cents. "American journalism," wrote an English observer, "has reached its highest development in the Sunday newspaper. There is no parallel to it in England or in any other country. It is at once a newspaper and a literary miscellany, a society journal and household magazine."[13] New York churchmen and newspaper traditionalists considered Goddard's work an abomination: among other complaints, he is accused of relying on stories of dime museum freaks, "the three-horned steer, five-legged calf, cross-eyed cow, two-headed girl."[14] Their views were upheld by American journalism historians through most of the last century, but lately some of the original enthusiasm for his journalism has been rekindled. "Even at a distance of one hundred years," writes Hearst biographer David Nasaw, "there is something extraordinarily exhilarating about reading through a turn-of-the-century Sunday newspaper. Like continuous vaudeville in the 1890s, amusement parks in the 1900s, and the movie palaces of the 1920s, the Sundays were intentionally oversized, overstocked, and overwhelming."[15]

Pulitzer knew he had a rocket in Goddard, and he liked him well enough to double his salary for individual weeks in which the Sunday edition posted strong sales. Circulation was hovering around 500,000 per issue at the end of 1895, by which time the Sunday edition was accounting for almost half of Pulitzer's weekly profits.[16] Inevitably, not everyone in the dysfunctional *World* office was pleased with Goddard's success, and the boss was soon in possession of memos accusing the Sunday editor of damaging the newspaper's reputation with his outlandish features and journalistic stunts. Goddard was summoned to Paris to explain himself. He found Pulitzer sitting in an armchair in his darkened hotel room, wearing a robe and slippers. Goddard glanced at the familiar gray-black whiskers and fully expected the full force of the great man's wrath to blast from beneath them. Instead, Pulitzer climbed out of his chair and grabbed Goddard's hands in warm welcome. "I'm so glad you found it possible to accept my invitation," he cooed. "I have just received reports by cable of our Sunday circulation. It's going up, up, up! Most encouraging!" They spent a week together and Goddard returned home with a pair of Grecian urns and a bonus check. His days at the *World* were nonetheless numbered.[17]

LEGEND HAS IT that Hearst's interest in Morrill Goddard was whetted by the Sally Johnson story. Goddard was in the practice of presenting fashionable cartwheel hats to actresses and models in return for society news tips. One day an artist's model dropped by the *World* and in exchange for such a hat gave Goddard the address of another model, named Sally Johnson, who had a story to tell from her previous evening's work. Goddard hustled out and knocked on Miss Johnson's door just as the sixteen-year-old beauty was rising from bed. In return for a hat of her own, the girl recounted her performance at a stag dinner in the 16th Street studio apartment of the bachelor and noted artist James L. Breese. At the height of the evening, waiters carried in an enormous papier-mâché pie and set it in the center of the long dining table. Miss Johnson burst from the crust and began dancing up and down the table. She was covered, the *World* noted, "only by the ceiling."

According to another of his biographers, John K. Winkler, Hearst read the Sally Johnson tale late on the Saturday night of its publication and immediately sent his card to request a meeting with Goddard. They sat down the following Monday at noon in Hearst's suite at the Hoffman House. Goddard told Winkler that the butler produced "a bottle of vintage wine and a silver dish of kidneys sauté and eggs" while Hearst discussed his thoughts on newspapering and his ambition to produce a new Sunday magazine insert. He offered Goddard its editorship at double his *World* salary.

"Your proposition is tremendously interesting, Mr. Hearst, if you can carry out your plans," replied Goddard. "But some of the shrewdest men on the *World* claim that you can't possibly last longer than three months more in this town."

Hearst smiled a soft, inscrutable smile and pulled from his vest pocket a crumpled Wells, Fargo & Co. draft in the amount of $35,000. He instructed Goddard to take whatever he required as an advance on salary. "That ought to convince you that I intend to remain in New York quite some time," he said. A deal was struck, with Goddard insisting on bringing his complete staff from the Sunday *World*.[18]

The accuracy of Winkler's story is difficult to gauge. His account of the Hoffman House conversation appears to have come from Goddard himself. The Sally Johnson article, however, ran in the October 13, 1895 *World*, months after the Breese party, and months before Goddard informed the *World* of his intentions near the end of January 1896. It is far more likely that Hearst was impressed by the overall performance of the Sunday *World*, and not by a single story. What is certain is that Goddard did leave, taking with him every writer, editor, and artist on staff—eleven men in total, abandoning only Emma Jane Hogg, the office secretary. Pulitzer was traveling when he was notified of the defections. He dispatched the loyal Carvalho to reel Goddard back into the fold. According to his *World* colleague Don Seitz, Carvalho offered the right inducements and the Sunday staff returned for a day to the Dome but Hearst sweetened his offer and closed the deal for good. Meanwhile, as W.A. Swanberg has quipped, the *World* was left to wonder "who would help Miss Hogg get out next Sunday's paper."[19]

All of the Hearst and Pulitzer biographies have Goddard moving for cash, but Seitz testifies that Pulitzer was prepared to compete on compensation. Goddard would have been the best-paid man on Park Row whichever way he turned (and given the enormous profits associated with a winning Sunday edition, he was probably worth it). So why did he leave? Why desert the mother of all Sunday editions for an upstart with as yet modest circulation and questionable staying power? The best explanation comes from the other party to the Hoffman House conversation. In an unpublished interview with a journalist many years afterward, Hearst offered his version of events:"My earliest recollection—my earliest contact with [Goddard] was when he was on the *World*. . . . Mr. Pulitzer liked him very much and valued him, not as highly as he deserved, but nevertheless he appreciated him, and Mr. Goddard left the *World* and came into our service. The average person would say that we took Mr. Goddard from the *World*; as a matter of fact we didn't. He had a quarrel with Mr. Pulitzer who left him. Of course, we were very glad to get him."[20]

Hearst did not comment on the nature or the timing of the quarrel between Pulitzer and Goddard. He may have been referring to the incident several months earlier when Goddard had gone trembling to Paris only to be saved by a sudden uptick in sales. In any case, it had to be clear to

Goddard that Pulitzer's favor was a fickle thing, that he was only as good as last week's numbers, and that his jealous colleagues would work diligently to undermine him. Life under the Dome was precarious, Grecian urns or no. Hearst's long-term prospects may have been in doubt, but he was already believed to be at 150,000 in weekday circulation, just slightly behind the *World*'s 185,000. He was growing at a faster rate than Pulitzer had managed on his own arrival in New York. Park Row had never seen anything like it, and if he was serious about enhancing his Sunday edition, Goddard's job at the Sunday *World* was only going to get more difficult. Add to this the opportunity Hearst was giving Goddard to build a Sunday franchise almost from scratch—whatever Goddard achieved at the *World* was always going to be credited to Pulitzer—and the young editor had several good reasons apart from money to cross the street.

The importance of Goddard's move can not be overstated. Hearst had hired away the foundations of a Sunday franchise that produced roughly half a million in annual profits. In one bold move he had radically expanded his paper's circulation and revenue potential, and he had done it entirely at the expense of his primary competitor. In the bargain he picked up one of the best art departments in newspapers—this in the midst of a revolution in illustrated journalism sparked by new printing technologies and an insatiable public demand, which Pulitzer had been among the first to recognize.

Pulitzer now panicked. He rushed to the city from his home in Lakewood, New Jersey, for an all-night meeting with Carvalho and business manager John Norris. Worrying that Hearst's circulation was weeks from surpassing their own, they discussed options for answering his challenge and quickly focused on the question of price reductions. Norris wanted a 50 percent cut: make the *World* available for a penny, he argued, and it would begin selling a million copies almost overnight. Advertisers would flock to the paper and Hearst would be left in their dust. Pulitzer was reluctant. At least at two cents, he covered the costs of producing a single copy of his newspaper. It wasn't unreasonable to think that the *World* could sell a lot more papers if priced at a penny, and it wasn't wrong to assume that higher circulation would invite more advertising, but he would need a huge boost in advertising to cover the high costs of producing many more papers for sale at one cent. And if circulation did not jump in response to the price cut, he would get no increase in advertising and he would be left to fight new and determined competition on 50 percent less circulation revenue.

Unable to come to a resolution, the *World* brain trust regrouped the next day on Pulitzer's private rail car as it left New York for Jekyll Island. According to Don Seitz, Norris's assistant at the time, the executives continued to urge a price cut and Pulitzer relented just short of Philadelphia. Carvalho and Norris hopped off the train and returned to New York to prepare the one-cent *World* for its February 10 debut.[21] Pulitzer announced the new price with bravado:

> We prefer power to profits. The *World*'s habit of growth was never more vigorous than now. But the price of paper and other items in the cost of production have decreased considerably within the past few years, and though a sixteen-page paper like the *World* could not by itself be sold at one cent, the enormous sales of the evening and the Sunday editions and the advertising patronage so far surpassing all other journals, permit a sacrifice of revenue from one source to achieve the sooner the one million circulation.[22]

The reviews were mixed. *The Fourth Estate* congratulated Pulitzer on meeting Hearst's challenge head-on. It was "a stroke of aggressive strategy, both brilliant and bold,"[23] and it spelled an end to Hearst's honeymoon. The mighty *World*, with all its advertisers and with its sights set on a million circulation, would now fight the newcomer on a more equal footing. *Newspaper Maker* and *Printer's Ink* saw only distress behind Pulitzer's move. Hearst, wrote the latter, had in four months of lavish investment and journalistic enterprise "brought the *World* down from its lofty position." All the talk of aiming for a million sales a day "does not throw sufficient dust in the eyes of those who know the situation."[24]

The *World*'s circulation did not zoom to a million. On the first day it climbed 88,000 from a base of about 185,000 but sales quickly flattened out, leaving Pulitzer with the revenue shortfall he feared. He also had an advertising problem. He had raised his rates in anticipation of the massive increase in readership. Now the advertisers who had supported him when he was a two-cent paper were wondering why it should cost more to buy space in a one-cent paper with only a slightly higher circulation. With his fabulous profits imperiled, Pulitzer began slashing expenses, even to the point of running less editorial content.[25]

Worse for Pulitzer, his price cut did nothing to slow the *Journal*'s advance. Emboldened by the *World*'s distress, Hearst turned up the gas, buying billboards all over town to promote his paper. As soon as Goddard hopped aboard, the *Journal* began a targeted circulation campaign, mailing a circular to 30,000 ladies out of the better directories in New York and Brooklyn calling attention to the paper's Woman's Page, to Julian Ralph's popular London Letters, and to the drama critic Alan Dale.[26] As *Newspaper Maker* reported,

> Upward goes the circulation of the *New York Journal* until one wonders when and where it will stop. Monday last it was over 186,000, which was a gain of 4,897 over the previous Saturday. . . . Probably never before has a newspaper made such rapid strides in circulation and popularity. Were it not for temporarily limited press capacity the increase would be even greater. . . . Verily it is a wonderful paper. Not the least astonishing thing about it is the fact that it is fast cutting into the circulation of the paper published under the gilded dome, notwithstanding that that paper was forced to reduce its price.[27]

It is doubtful that Hearst was cutting into the *World*'s circulation as much as *Newspaper Maker* suggests. He was probably frustrating its growth but doing his greatest damage to New York's lesser penny papers—the *Press*, the *Recorder*, the *Mercury*, the *Advertiser*—none of which could hope to compete with what Hearst and Pulitzer were offering at the same price point. Their distress signals began to flash in the trades. Meanwhile, morale under the Dome plunged from bad to worse. Pulitzer reorganized his executive ranks to fill the hole left by Goddard. Among his moves was the elevation of seventeen-year *World* veteran Richard A. Farrelly to the helm of the morning edition. In a bid to rally the troops, Pulitzer organized a dinner to celebrate the promotion. The day before the festivities, however, invitees received cancellation notices by telegraph. Farrelly, too, had jumped to the *Journal*.

MUCH OF THE BURDEN of managing the *World*'s increasingly frantic proprietor and his turbulent newspaper fell on the shoulders of Solomon Solis Carvalho, a Portuguese Jew with an encyclopedic knowledge of publishing. Like many of Pulitzer's best people, he had been recruited from the *Sun,* where he'd distinguished himself as a reporter, city editor, and managing editor. Pulitzer had assigned him responsibility for launching his evening edition and had given him only ten days to do it. Carvalho had not only got the paper out on time but established it as the city's evening leader.[28] Quiet, cautious, and a glutton for work, Carvalho saw his responsibilities expand until he was serving as the *World*'s utility executive, running the business department and editorial operations, overseeing presses, amusing the boss—whatever the moment required. He also did his share of dirty work. When, in a bout of cost consciousness, Pulitzer decided twenty-five reporters had to go, it was Carvalho who picked up the ax.[29] He was a short, square figure with a heavy limp, a neat goatee, and a passion for Russian wolfhounds, but advertisers liked him. So did journalists, never mind the firings. Pulitzer knew his worth and paid him handsomely. By 1896, Carvalho's position at the paper seemed to outsiders "as secure and certainly permanent as that of any of the able men engaged in New York."[30]

But Goddard's departure had left Carvalho with a superhuman workload. Aside from dealing with Pulitzer's panic and second guessing, he had to return order to a shaken newsroom, squeeze every nickel to offset revenue losses, and placate his angry advertisers. He also had to keep a step ahead of his internal rival, John Norris, and clean up another mess entirely at the Pulitzer-owned *St. Louis Post-Dispatch.*

The St. Louis problems were of Pulitzer's making. He had maneuvered the disastrous Colonel Jones out of the Dome by offering him complete control of and an equity share in the *Post-Dispatch.* Jones moved west and began running the paper as though he were sole proprietor, and Pulitzer almost immediately began to regret the deal. In mid-March, he sent Carvalho to St. Louis to renegotiate the colonel's agreement. Norris took advantage of his rival's absence, launching a bid to unseat him.

Carvalho had been in talks with a group of dry goods advertisers who had formed a combine to fight the *World*'s ad rate increases. A deal was nearly complete when Norris wired Pulitzer at Jekyll Island with misgivings about the terms on which Carvalho was prepared to settle, and asked that talks be suspended until the details could be reviewed. Pulitzer obliged, instructing Carvalho to stand down until further notice.

Carvalho returned from St. Louis brimming with resentment toward both Norris and Pulitzer, and, on the last day of March, informed Pulitzer by telegraph that if his authority was not restored by 5 p.m., he would consider his service at the *World* complete.

This would have been a fine moment for Pulitzer to pause and reflect on the events of the past couple of months and the havoc inflicted on his newspaper by the advent of Hearst and the defection of Goddard. In this new competitive environment, he could no longer spy on his employees, pit them against one another, berate them, and humiliate them yet still command unstinting loyalty. A compromise or some gesture of conciliation toward Carvalho might have been warranted. Instead, 5 p.m. came and went, Carvalho said his farewells at 5:30, and left the Dome for good.[31]

Biographies of both Hearst and Pulitzer hold that Carvalho resigned to join the *Journal*, but in fact he simply quit, saying nothing of his plans. Initially, the trades expected his immediate return to the *World*— surely Pulitzer had challenges enough without losing his best executive. After several weeks had passed and no reconciliation had transpired, word circulated that Carvalho was retiring; he was known to have "accumulated a considerable fortune" in the *World*'s employ.[32] Finally, in June, it was reported that he had joined the *Journal* in an advisory capacity.[33]

Carvalho's first chore at the *Journal* was to superintend an expansion of the mechanical plant. Much of the money Hearst had initially earmarked for his "nucleus" was instead invested in printing capacity. His pressworks were now spilling over to the Rhinelander Building across the street from the Tribune Building; an adjoining warehouse had been rented for paper storage.[34] Hearst had made an early decision to push his circulation to unprecedented levels: "The rapidly increasing circulation of the *New York Journal* has necessitated securing greater press facilities at once. A Goss press has been secured at Chicago and brought to New York, and by combining two old presses discarded by New York papers, the present capacity has been increased a few thousand copies. The *Journal* entered an order some time ago with R. Hoe & Company for six new presses, and this order has been increased by an order for two more sextuple presses. When the presses ordered have been delivered the *Journal* will have a capacity of nearly a million copies daily."[35]

Several weeks after joining the *Journal*, Carvalho was spotted in the newsroom filling in for a vacationing city editor. The sight of this journalistic legend in his shirtsleeves organizing the day's news campaign was an inspiration to Hearst's still freshly assembled staff. Hearst subsequently shifted Carvalho's attention to planning an evening edition that would compete with the *Evening World*, the *Evening Sun*, and the *Evening Telegram* (sister paper to Bennett Jr.'s morning *Herald*). Within a matter of months, Carvalho became one of the *Journal*'s two or three most important executives. Like Goddard, he would grow old in Hearst's employ.

IT IS ANOTHER MEASURE of the magnificence of the New York *World* and of Pulitzer's strength in the New York market that the publisher was able to respond to the losses of Goddard and Carvalho and Farrelly by plucking still other brilliant young executives from his ranks. One whose moment now arrived was Arthur Brisbane, the son of a wealthy American philosopher, raised in Europe and trained as a journalist by Dana. He leapt to the challenge of reconstituting the Sunday *World* after Goddard's departure. He put up a brilliant fight, much to the delight of Pulitzer, who treated him like a son, their first serious confrontation being still a year in the future.

However frenzied life was under the Dome, Pulitzer had not cornered the market on newsroom chaos. Hearst too had his share. He once confessed, in a letter home, to a woeful lack of "system" in the *Examiner*'s operations, and his New York newspaper was no improvement. The seasoned Carvalho did his tour of the city room in part to help bring order to its operations: its growing corps of reporters was not always effectively deployed; copy editing was erratic; headlining was weak on inside pages. Evidence of Hearst's loose and idiosyncratic management style was evident in every corner of the newsroom. When Willis Abbot reported for his first day of duty as editorials editor, no one at the *Journal* had been told to expect him. A series of clerks took him for a crank and tried to shoo him off the premises. It was only when Abbot ran across his old friend Charles Palmer and explained that Hearst had hired him away from his job in Chicago that his right to a desk was recognized. Not long after this, Abbot met in the art department a brawny fellow who could not draw a line but who was rumored to have crewed on a sailboat that had rescued Hearst from a dangerous position off the Barbary Coast. Abbot wrote a friend that he had "secured very remunerative employment in a lunatic asylum."[36]

But while Abbot's "asylum" line is a constant in the Hearst literature, his broader assessment of the *Journal*'s operations has been overlooked. There was never any doubt, he wrote, as to who was in charge, and, how-ever unorthodox his methods, Hearst possessed "extraordinary enterprise and [an] absolutely clear vision of what he purposed to do." He had assembled an "extraordinarily brilliant group of men" and right from the start inspired in them a "certain audacity of effort, and brilliancy of achievement."[37] In spite of the frantic life at the *Journal*, the atmosphere was by all accounts upbeat and constructive.

Hearst kept a sanctum for himself in the Tribune Building, an office with a view of City Hall and Printing House Square. He filled it with his purchases of furniture, statuary, and suits of armor and placed a guard of aides outside the door to ward off the supplicants, job seekers, public relations flaks, and salesmen who gathered daily in hopes of an audience. He spent little time there, however. He preferred to work in shirtsleeves in the city room, blending in with the young men on his staff as he reviewed sales figures or sorted through the next edition's news. He operated throughout the day by polite handwritten memos and informal conversations in which he listened intently and spoke succinctly—he had a "facility in epigrammatic expression," said one employee.[38] He pre-ferred almost any type of human interaction to meetings. The larger and more structured a meeting, the less likely he was to engage. He would sit and fidget as others talked, leaving colleagues to wonder if they even had his attention. "W.R. doesn't talk much," said one employee. "You can sit by the hour with [him] and he'll 'yes' you along and sit and smile. And if you go back and tell him next week 'That is what I said,' he will say, 'That is not the story you told me last week.'"[39]

Hearst would still be at the office well after midnight, taking a final run through the page proofs or grabbing the bulldog edition (the first off the press) for review. He would spread the sheets on the floor, sometimes crawling among them, other times standing and shuffling the pages about with his feet. He studied the placement of stories, gauged the impact of headlines and illustrations, and perused opening paragraphs. Eventually he would pull a blue pencil from behind his ear and order a rewrite, or throw out an illustration, or pull a piece from deep inside the paper to the front page. If he spotted a weak headline, he would scrawl an alternative in the margin. If he didn't like a story, he marked it "punk" or "dull." When the edition was finally put to bed and the wagons had clattered off into the darkness, Hearst would often join the reporters and mechanics at the plant restaurant on the Frankfort Street side of the building for an early morning hotdog with plenty of mustard.

Stephen Crane used Hearst as the model for the editor of the *New York Eclipse* in his newspaper novel, describing him as "a kind of poet using his millions romantically," generous to his employees, full of ideas and plans, some of them beautiful, others preposterous. At one moment he would be sitting on the edge of a table, dangling a leg and dreamily surveying the wall, and at another he would be pacing excitedly around the room, "hands deep in his trousers' pockets, his chin sunk in his collar, his light blue eyes afire with interest" as he explained his latest scheme.[40]

Other accounts of Hearst at work note his odd habits, including his simian-like tendency to use his feet as another pair of hands. In the comfort of his suite in the Hoffman House, he was known to spread a paper on the floor, kick off his shoes and socks, and turn the pages with his toes. At work he would sometimes appear at the door to an editor's office, grab both sides of the door frame, and with solemn face perform a soft-shoe shuffle until he had sorted out what he wanted to say. Many years after he had left Hearst's employ, James Coleman, a young secretary at the *Journal*, still had vivid recollection of his boss's rituals:

> My eyes strained wide and I tried vainly to keep from swallowing my bubble gum when Hearst suddenly spread the proofs . . . on the floor, and began a sort of tap dance around and between them. It was a mild, un-costumed combination of Carmen Miranda, a rumba, a Russian dagger dance, and Notre Dame shift, with lively castanet accompaniment produced by snapping fingers. After I had observed W.R.'s strange dance, I learned it was his customary method of absorbing pictures and captions on pictures pages. The cadence of it speeded up with his reactions of disturbance and slowed down to a strolling rhythm when he approved. Between dances, he scribbled illegible corrections on the margins and finally gave the proofs back to me.[41]

Hearst's insistence on working to his own rhythms was not always appreciated by his employees. Like all dailies, the *Journal* ran on precise schedules to ensure that each edition made it onto the press and off the loading dock on time for delivery deadlines. These schedules were always in jeopardy with Hearst in the building. He had no compunctions about holding pages for another round of changes or dashing down to the composing room to rework a typeset page before it was mounted on the press. His editors and floor managers would warn against delays— "We'll never make the mail train!"—or tell him he was too late to intervene because the edition was already on the press. "Well, stop it," he would answer. "You'll never send that paper out with my name." There was always time to make the paper better, he insisted.[42]

The absence of regularity in Hearst's workday did reflect a lack of discipline, but at the same time it made a certain sense for him to structure his role as he did. He hired competent managers in every sector of the paper's operations to handle day-to-day operations, to respect production processes, pay the bills, and clean up messes; he left himself free to address the *Journal*'s most urgent needs at a given time. What he considered most urgent were things likely to engage and grow his reading audience. He was heavily involved in staff recruitment, the upgrading and expansion of his presses, promotional campaigns, and, of course, editorial matters. His editors did the bulk of the assigning and editing of stories and got the paper out each day while Hearst rode above them, setting the priorities and the tone. He determined the *Journal*'s interests, aversions, and enthusiasms; the scale of its enterprise; its political outlook, including whom it defended and whom it fought; the pitch of its humor; the depth of its outrage; the style of its art—among other elements that contributed to the paper's character or voice. Once Pulitzer and other publishers had cut their prices to better compete with the *Journal*, a singular and attractive voice became ever more crucial to the paper's success. Everything Hearst did during his workday, from his informal newsroom conversations to his early morning rewrites, was intended to enhance the *Journal*'s voice, lifting it out of the ordinary and distinguishing it in ways attractive to readers. He spent little effort on advertising, on the assumption that it would come on its own once he had assembled a mass audience. He attended all of his business with what one colleague called "unswerving enthusiasm and ruthless low-key drive."[43]

Hearst's manner in his newsroom was steady and polite. He was "impeccably calm," wrote Charles Edward Russell.[44] He never barked orders or threw fits, preferring instead to lead by questions and gentle encouragement. "He was a gentleman," writes James L. Ford. "I do not think I ever heard him use an expression unfit for a polite drawing-room."[45] He was generous with praise and thanks, and he treated the pressmen with the same consideration as he did his seniormost editors, chatting with them, remembering their names, addressing them as "Mister." They called him W.R. or Chief. He was said to be a good listener, prone to fixing his large pale blue eyes on his interlocutor with an unsettling intensity.[46] New employees "who feared that the rich Senator's son might be a painful popinjay were charmed by his quaint courtesy and the absence of anything top-lofty or condescending," writes biographer Swanberg.[47]

Hearst seems genuinely to have enjoyed his hours in the newsroom; it was one of few social environments where he felt at ease. He liked the company of his journalists, and when he was in the mood, he could hold his own in the newsroom banter. Irvin S. Cobb recalled him as a gracious companion, "abounding in witty, pungent comments on what's transpiring around him and what's happening to him, personally." He had a keen sense of humor, "not the spurious brand which sees what is ridiculous in other people—but genuine drollery. He can laugh at himself. The joke which is aimed at him or the one which he actually aimed on that target is the one over which he laughs the heartiest and remembers the longest and repeats the oftenest. A million things have been said for or against Hearst. . . . Yet not the most rabid of his enemies or the nastiest of his critics has accused this man . . . of having a false dignity or an exaggerated idea of his own sanctity."[48]

Cobb's assessment notwithstanding, only a handful of journalists ever got to know Hearst well. He had inherited none of his father's gregariousness and open-hearted charm. He was pleasant but not expansive. He lacked the agreeable, flexible nature that encourages familiarity. Even years of newsroom camaraderie failed to loosen him up much. In the company of strangers, he remained quiet, preferring to let others do the talking. His family knew him to be capable of speaking at length and with great particularity on a wide range of topics, but he seldom felt inclined to do so in work settings. Abbot recalled that it was "a real ordeal to introduce [Hearst] to a public man, even when he himself sought the introduction, for he would invariably sit silent, with downcast eyes, leaving me to carry on the conversation."[49]

Stories of Hearst's leniency with his staff in San Francisco and New York are legion. He was unafraid of prima donnas, eccentrics, bohemians, drunks, or reprobates so long as they had useful talents. A reporter who disappeared for a few days on a bender could count on being welcomed back without censure. Ambrose Bierce was surprised to learn that Hearst had kept on staff a man who was stealing money from the *Examiner*. "I have a new understanding with him," he told Bierce. "He is to steal only small sums hereafter; the largest are to come to me."[50] An assistant editor at the *Examiner* once fired a reporter in the middle of the newsroom, only to have the man refuse to leave the premises. They wound up in the boss's office, where Hearst asked the reporter why the assistant editor shouldn't be allowed to dispense with an employee when he saw fit to do so. "The reason," exclaimed the reporter, "is that I refused to be fired." Hearst looked at the editor and held up his hands in resignation. They all had a laugh and the reporter kept his job.[51] "I never knew him to hold rancor against anybody," said the artist Jimmy Swinnerton. "He is a very queer fellow."[52]

The more Hearst wanted a journalist, the more he was prepared to forgive. No one in his employ was more indulged than the obstreperous Scots editorialist Arthur McEwen. A towering figure, gaunt and sandy-haired, McEwen professed with wit and religious fervor a brand of radically progressive politics that Hearst admired and wanted for his editorial pages. Even in a West Coast city famous for its saloon culture, in a profession noted for insobriety, Arthur McEwen stood out. He drank heavily and fell hard and often. When he failed to show for work, Hearst would dispatch squads of reporters with instructions to search under every table in every dive in town until they could drag their colleague back to the office. Hearst himself once went looking for McEwen to discuss a point of policy and found him out cold under the rolltop of his desk.[53]

One of McEwen's many oddities was that he was even more difficult to manage when he was sober. Feeling unappreciated, he quit the *Examiner* in 1894 and started his own weekly, dedicated to slaying "the dragons of greed and dishonesty which master this town." He ran out of

money inside of three months and was quietly welcomed back to the
Examiner. All was fine for a few more months until Hearst had the temer-
ity to send him a note offering the following advice:

> I would prefer somewhat fewer editorials. Be careful not to be drawn into
> too many fights. We are now after the Democrats and the Republicans,
> the lawyers and the businessmen, with occasional sideswipes at the people.
> This sort of limits our sympathizers and will also make the editorial page
> too truculent to be interesting. I think a more calm and judicial tone on
> politics and a greater variety of subjects would improve the page. Think
> it over.

McEwen did not need to think about it much. "The public judgment,"
he fired back, "is that the editorial columns of the *Examiner* now have
what they very much needed—brains, courage and character. I have
given all my energies and sixteen hours a day to your paper and placed it
on a higher level than it has ever held before. You don't deserve such
work, for you are unable to appreciate it. Your telegram is equally
ungrateful and stupid. Accept my resignation."[54] McEwen punctuated this
note by restarting his weekly and dismissing Hearst as "a humbug in
journalism . . . a clever amateur." Hearst not only ignored the abuse but
talked McEwen back into the fold and soon after transported him to
New York to write editorials for the *Journal.*

Sam Chamberlain, the *Journal*'s managing editor, was as convivial as
McEwen was cranky yet he struggled almost equally with the bottle.
His habits wore on his colleagues, who carried his workload when he
was indisposed. On one of his European trips, Hearst received a cable
from an executive: "Chamberlain drunk again. May I dismiss him?"
Hearst responded immediately: "If he is sober one day in thirty that is
all I require."[55]

There was no weakness or self-abasement in Hearst's leniency. So
long as the job was getting done, he had no need of conformity or sup-
plications from his staff. "His is the unconscious egotism of an absolute
self-sufficiency," wrote Lincoln Steffens.[56] Having watched his son
work at the *Examiner,* George Hearst was able to elaborate on this
point, albeit with fatherly affection: "If he lacked confidence in himself
he might require more ceremony from others; but doubtless, the very

reason why he is so indulgent to those who serve him in various capacities is that it never occurred to him that he was insecure in his own position. He selects his men wisely for the work he wants them to do and so long as they attend that work he does not bother himself by trying to discipline them. Thus, without much wear and tear, he does a vast deal of work by other heads and hands: he multiplies himself in them."[57]

Like Pulitzer, Heart often showed generosity and concern for employees who fell ill or found themselves in need, and he was quick with thanks and praise for good work, but there are important qualifications to his standing as a liberal employer. Irvin Cobb noted that Hearst was an appreciative boss "provided you deliver the particular brand of goods he hankers for."[58] His rank-and-file journalists were as overworked and modestly compensated as those at any other leading daily, and their job security was nonexistent. Even talented editors could be ingloriously sidelined after Hearst landed one of his star recruits. And while Hearst himself treated employees with consideration, others operating in his name could behave ruthlessly. One history of Park Row reports that staffers who ran afoul of their superiors at the *Journal* would be made men's-room attendants in order to humiliate them into quitting.[59]

Still, Hearst quickly established himself as the most attractive employer on the street, and a clear favorite over the suspicious and volatile Pulitzer, his chief rival for newspapering talent. Journalists responded with dedication and enterprise. They followed their proprietor's lead in subordinating all other concerns—office politics, administrative niceties, sobriety—to the overarching goal of creating a great and popular newspaper. And the *Journal,* effectively a new publication without a preexisting style or personality, quickly found its voice.

Late in April 1896, *Printer's Ink* reported a conversation between two advertising executives on business prospects and the difficulties of the times: "I cannot help feeling," said one, "that that man Hearst has struck it. He has done what he alone could have done. The success is as conspicuous, as mysterious, as actually present as the electric light. It is here, we see it, we know it, and it is Hearst that has done it. He has created a great property and it will grow and grow. He alone has done it. It was not his money, though that was useful. It was not the men he has gathered around him, though they too were needed implements, but the success is attributable solely to him, to Hearst, to his personality, to the man. Nothing succeeds like success, and it is upon a recognized, a phenomenal success that the young man from the other side of the continent is already rearing a colossal structure—upon a foundation already plainly seen to be wide and broad and strong enough to sustain any weight and height its projector may aspire to construct. He will do what . . . has not been done [before]. It is as certain as fate."[60]

CHAPTER FIVE

Like a Blast Furnace,
a Hundred Times Multiplied

W ill Hearst's politics owed much to his father's politics, which were far more substantive than the senator's reputation allows. Knocked for buying his way into the U.S. Senate and drinking his way around Washington—facts that are not really in dispute—George Hearst nonetheless gave a lifetime of meaningful support to the Democratic Party and its causes, setting an example his son would follow well into middle age.

George began attending political meetings in boyhood and was a delegate to a Missouri Democratic convention at age twenty-six. Almost two decades later, in 1865, he was elected to the California state legislature. As a southerner and a Democrat, he sided with the Confederacy in the Civil War and voted in the legislature against the Thirteenth Amendment, abolishing slavery, as well as the Fourteenth Amendment, requiring states to provide all citizens equal protection under the law. He was a strong advocate of states' rights throughout his career, identifying with the South and West against the Northeast and promoting individual liberties against government paternalism. He was also a relentless critic of Republican coziness with Wall Street and of Washington's systems of preferment and protections for industry. To his wife's annoyance, he poured as much as $500,000 a year into the Democratic machine.[1]

George Hearst's political career took off after he failed to win the Democratic nomination for governor of California in 1882. He was subsequently appointed by the man who beat him, General George Stoneman, to finish the term of a deceased U.S. senator, and later elected to the Senate for his own six-year term. He sat on several committees and was the Democratic point man on the Southern Pacific Railroad file, one of the thorniest tangles of commercial, political, legal, and constitutional issues then extant. But Senator Hearst was no silk-hat statesman. The issues he tackled were mostly related to his regional or commercial interests. The few speeches he made in the chamber were remembered as "blissfully short."[2] He exerted influence through personal relationships and his seat at the regular Senate poker game. It is worth noting that almost all Gilded Age senators either paid for their seats or had someone else pay for them—and however thirsty George Hearst may have been, he was never short of drinking companions in Washington.

Will was proud of his father's contributions to public life and freely admitted that George was the major influence on his own politics. He absorbed noblesse oblige from both parents but chose the senator's example of service through partisan wrangling and journalism over the philanthropic route advocated by Phoebe, who still considered politics demeaning. Will not only followed his father into the Democratic Party, but beat many of the same policy drums, although with the benefit of a few semesters at Harvard, he talked a better game. Will defined himself as a Jeffersonian Democrat, by which he meant a defender of individuals, small businessmen, and farmers against overreaching central governments and concentrated capital in the form of monopolies and trusts.[3] (Trusts were a relatively new corporate structure designed to give a small ownership group the ability to fix prices or otherwise restrain trade in an entire industry.) He viewed Republican-style capitalism as "industrial feudalism on the lines of the old military feudalism and for the same purposes—the exploitation and control of the many by the few."[4] All of this was straight from the Democratic hymnal, and his father would have happily sung along.

Another important similarity between the Hearsts is their regional chauvinism. It might be said that George didn't know better: he was well into middle age before he spent much time east of Missouri. Will, by contrast, was educated in New England and had seen more of Europe than all but a few other Americans, yet he agreed with his father on the merits of western life. His earliest letters home from college tout the social and geographic superiority of California over the Northeast: "I long to get out West somewhere where I can stretch myself without coming in contact with the narrow walls with which the prejudice of the bean eaters has surrounded us. . . . I hate their weak, pretty New England scenery with its gently rolling hills, its pea green foliage, its vistas, tame enough to begin with but totally disfigured by houses and barns which could not be told apart save for the respective inhabitants. . . . I long to see our own woods, the jagged rocks and towering mountains, the majestic pines, the grand impressive scenery of the 'far West.' I shall never live anywhere but in California."[5] Hearst would consistently champion the West against the Northeast throughout his life.

However strong his father's influence, Will was nonetheless a different breed of Democrat. The senator was a pragmatist, taking politics as it came; he kept on good terms with the old-line party bosses and accepted their ways. Will represented the progressive or reform wing of the party, rallying behind a range of policies recently brought to market by the Populists. He saw a limited but legitimate role for the state in protecting the interests of common folk from predatory capitalism; he supported labor's demands for an eight-hour day and collective bargaining; he embraced redistributive measures, including the graduated income tax; he recommended all manner of health and public safety and education improvements, as well as anti-corruption policies and the popular election of U.S. senators, among other democratic reforms. He was progressive enough to be considered dangerous by Republicans and conservative Democrats alike. His papers "breathed the spirit of radical democracy," wrote his editor Willis Abbot, adding that Hearst was "entirely sincere in his sympathy for the masses."[6]

Hearst's political skills were put to a grueling test almost immediately upon his purchase of the *Journal*: he had landed in New York at the opening of the 1896 election season. Presidential campaigns were main events for daily newspapers in the pre-broadcast era, when newspapers more or less monopolized election news. As Pulitzer had demonstrated with his support of Grover Cleveland, an editor riding the right candidate for a nomination or the presidency could attract large numbers of fierce partisans and perhaps even influence the course of a great event. Alternatively, a single misplaced endorsement could drive readers away and ruin a newspaper franchise. Hearst knew that his own political reputation and the success of his paper would be on the line in 1896. He had watched and applauded Pulitzer's triumph over Dana from Harvard Yard in '84, and he now hoped to imitate Pulitzer's success and establish himself as the foremost Democratic editor in New York. But Pulitzer, of course, was still around, still on top, and very much in Hearst's way.

THE FIRST SIX MONTHS OF 1896 could not have been duller from a political point of view. All eyes were on the Republican nomination race— not that it was much of a race. Former congressman and Ohio governor William McKinley had built a commanding lead long in advance of the party's June convention in St. Louis. McKinley was the favorite son of the politically fecund state of Ohio, home to four of the five previous presidents. He was the clear favorite of the Midwest, the region in which the election was likely to be won or lost. He had gained ground in the South, making him the only candidate for the nomination with substantial support outside of his own region. He was so well organized so early in the contest that none of his competitors ever got off the ground.[7]

Another damper on the election season was the fact that the Republicans appeared to have no opposition. It was widely assumed that whoever won the nomination would be president by default. The Democrats were prostrate and bleeding from the nastiest collapse in American electoral history. In 1892 they had won an enormous victory, putting Grover Cleveland back in the White House in a landslide and sweeping both houses of Congress for the first time since the Civil War. But Cleveland was undone almost at the moment of his inauguration. A run on the gold supply precipitated the Panic of '93, the worst economic depression the U.S. had yet experienced. Markets tumbled. Banks called in loans. The Reading Railroad fell into receivership, followed quickly by the Erie, the Northern Pacific, the Union Pacific, and the Santa Fe. Before long, a quarter of the U.S. railway industry was in the hands of bankruptcy courts. Some 15,000 businesses failed, including, by the end of the year, 642 banks, most of them in the South and the West. Farms foreclosed at a dizzying rate. Countless factories were shut down, sending armies of unemployed in search of work and stoking labor militancy. Soup kitchens were said to be the only industry benefiting from a Cleveland White House.[8]

It was not entirely fair to point the finger at Cleveland, since many of the factors contributing to the panic predated his administration. But the public was in no mood to quibble: Cleveland was in office; Cleveland was to blame. The Democrats were thumped in the elections of 1894, dropping 125 seats in the House while the Republicans picked up 130 and gained control of both chambers—an unprecedented swing in partisan fortunes. To make matters worse, the Populists emerged in 1894 as a serious force, crowding the Democrats from the left. Disgraced, demoralized, divided, and leaderless, Democracy looked doomed for '96.

Hearst's *Journal*, however, was in no hurry to concede the election. On April 7, it published an editorial objecting to the assumption of a McKinley coronation and reminding readers and rival newspapers that there was more than one political party in the country. As many as six million Americans counted themselves Democrats, the *Journal* insisted, and their loyalty would ensure a close contest by autumn. Given the facts on the ground, the forecast was preposterous, yet it would be borne out. McKinley won the Republican nomination handily in June only to see the Democrats spring to life in July at their Chicago convention—one of the most dramatic moments in American politics. Nebraskan congressman William Jennings Bryan, the Great Commoner, the Boy Orator of the Platte, emerged as the party's nominee and stormed the hustings with unexpected energy. Fresh-faced and charismatic, he was the perfect foil to the stolid McKinley, and he would make the race exhilaratingly close.

LIKE ANY CANDIDATE, William McKinley wanted to campaign on his own terms, and anyone who knew him understood that to mean that he would run on a platform trumpeting protective tariffs as the key to renewing American prosperity. Protective tariffs were what McKinley knew best. He had never mastered or taken a hard stand on another issue. He had capped his fourteen-year congressional career by lending his name to a massive tariff hike. He was called "The Napoleon of Protection," and there was indeed a slight physical resemblance.[9]

By some combination of shrewdness and luck, McKinley's one great issue was the key to Republican fortunes in the late nineteenth century. The party promoted protective tariffs for three reasons. First, they shielded American industry from cheap imports, which was appreciated by the party's base in the industrialized sectors of the Northeast and Midwest. Second, they were thought to create jobs and to preserve the highest possible wages for American workers, which played well among the burgeoning urban labor vote in those same regions. Finally, they also supplied the free-spending Republicans in Congress with the funds to introduce popular social programs, such as veterans' pensions. For three decades the Republicans had enjoyed the firm support of vast contingents of Union army vets. The Northeast, the Midwest, and the vets were key components for a GOP victory.

As far as the *Journal* and most Democrats were concerned, Republican tariffs merely shielded the party's Wall Street cronies from normal competitive pressures, aiding in the proliferation of trusts and monopolies and saddling the American public with higher prices for protected goods. As the party of small government and decentralization, the Democrats also complained that high tariffs led to a larger, more corrupt, and more meddlesome federal state. They told their faithful that the Republicans would use tariff proceeds to put their friends on the Washington payroll and to introduce expensive and paternalistic social legislation that would undermine individual enterprise and befoul the national character. The Democrats were strong among farmers, laborers, and merchants in the South, the West, and pockets of the Midwest; they also attracted working-class votes in such commercial centers as New York, San Francisco, and Chicago.[10]

The brutal depression together with the mere fact that the dead hand of the Cleveland Democrats had lowered tariffs were sufficient to win broad support for raising tariffs again. McKinley did seem the man for the moment. If he was able to fight the election on tariffs, he was unbeatable. The *Journal* analyzed the results of recent Republican state conventions and on April 2 declared McKinley the nominee, two months in advance of the convention. The next day it printed a full page of telegrams from Republican worthies, all of whom said that McKinley would build his campaign around the tariff. Then, on April 15, the *Journal*'s chief political correspondent, Julius Chambers, reported that another issue entirely was rumbling over the horizon and threatening to dominate the election.[11]

The so-called silver craze surprised a lot of observers in 1896, but monetary issues were never far from the top of the political agenda in the

Gilded Age. The U.S. currency had been on a gold standard since 1873, with some limited provisions for the coinage of silver. Through much of that time, gold stocks were low and the money supply was tight. Some currency experts (and a great many amateurs) had been agitating for the full and free monetization of silver to offset the dearth of gold and bring more liquidity to the financial system. Leaders of the silver movement wanted a return to a pre-1873 regime in which silver was freely coined at a ratio of sixteen units to each one of the more valuable gold.

By 1896, the battle lines were drawn. Most economists and financiers, along with most New York newspapers, opposed the free coinage of silver. They believed the gold standard guaranteed an "honest dollar" and a secure and stable economic order. They claimed that the government would never be able to support the price of silver at sixteen to one, given its abundant supply. The full reintroduction of bimetallism (the coinage of silver and gold) would lead to a devalued currency, runaway inflation, and economic mayhem. Gold's adherents also suspected the motives of the silver movement: they saw it as a conspiracy of indebted farmers, who hoped cheap money would ease the burden of their improvident debts, and greedy western silver producers hell-bent on higher prices for their metal regardless of the consequence for the national economy.

Silverites, predominant in the South and West, bridled at the suggestion that the gold standard provided a stable economy. The previous three decades, they pointed out, had been marked by prolonged bouts of deflation. The economy and the population had grown faster than the supply of gold. Dollars had become increasingly scarce and expensive, making debts increasingly difficult to service—what was "honest" about that? The gold standard and the scarcity of the dollar were also believed to have scuppered prices for agricultural products and other commodities, some of which had dropped by more than half between the early 1880s and the early 1890s (eastern manufacturers were less sensitive to pricing matters because they were protected by Republican tariffs). Farmers and small producers were thus getting it both ways: their debts were becoming more expensive because of deflation, while their incomes were shrinking because of low prices. They believed the remonetization of silver would increase the money supply, restore price stability and the integrity of the dollar, and alleviate the economic distress brought by the depression of 1893. While most economists opposed the free silver movement, there was hardly unanimity. Indeed, the newly formed American Economic Association was divided not only on bimetallism but also on such basic questions as the relationship between tight money supply and low farm prices.[12]

Nineteenth-century voters were remarkably conversant with the arcana of monetary policy, but they recognized that much more than policy was at stake in the currency debate. The struggle between gold and silver exposed class and regional tensions in American life. The metals were proxies in a larger contest for control of the government and the national economy between the urban, industrialized East and the agrarian and resource-dependent states of the South and West. Thus voters would come to care as much about monetization of silver as they had any other issue since the Civil War. Adding still more significance to the debate were partisan considerations: the Republicans, strongest in the lending states of the East, largely supported the gold standard, while the Democrats, strongest in the borrowing regions of the West and South, were keener on silver, but neither side was united—some of the fiercest fighting would occur within parties.

Three days after its April 15 report, describing how pro-silver sentiment was taking the Democrats by storm, the *Journal* published a canvass of delegates to the party's July convention correctly forecasting that a majority would be pledged to free (that is, unlimited) coinage of silver at a ratio of sixteen to one against gold.[13] A pair of editorials published April 16 and 18 foresaw the Democrats fracturing on regional lines, with the relatively small but influential northeastern wing of the party holding firm for gold. The paper spanked the Cleveland administration for allowing the schism to develop. The president's sympathies were with gold, but instead of seeking compromise with the growing legion of silverites in his own party, Cleveland dismissed them as cranks. He also reneged on promises to seek agreement with other industrialized nations to jointly pursue the remonetization of silver (it was thought that international cooperation would take some of the risk out of such a move). The *Journal* argued that the silverites deserved better: bimetallism was "the proper Democratic creed," and the silver movement was "real, vital, [and] urged largely by men of convictions." The only bright side the *Journal* could find in the silver craze was that it promised to elbow out tariffs as the main issue of the election, forcing McKinley and the Republicans onto unfamiliar ground.[14]

Pulitzer's *World*, seeing itself as the guardian of all things Democratic, was also monitoring the rise of silver sentiment, but Hearst and Pulitzer were pulling in different directions on the issue. Pulitzer had no patience for farm-belt currency cranks and he detested the silverites as a "menace."[15] He may have broken into New York as an establishment-baiting friend of the people, but the *World*'s publisher had grown comfortable over the years. He now enjoyed a station in New York society, and he had toned down his earlier democratic radicalism. He firmly believed that the gold standard was smart policy.

In an increasingly shrill series of commentaries leading up to the convention, Pulitzer argued that his party's blind and fatuous silver obsession would lead to certain ruin. Any movement away from gold would bring panic and distress to the economy. Americans would have to get used to fewer jobs, meager wages, and a lower standard of living—"There is no measuring the calamity that will overtake the people." His editorials accused silver advocates of anarchistic tendencies and of threatening violence against pro-gold forces: "this is not politics—it is lunacy. It is not campaigning—it is suicide."[16]

Hearst, too, had his connections among the New York Democratic elite. His paper was promoting for the party's nomination his acquaintance William Collins Whitney, a Harvard-trained lawyer and Democratic reformer who had fought the Tweed ring and served as Cleveland's secretary of the navy. Whitney leaned toward gold, but Hearst presented him as more flexible than Cleveland and a man capable of finding a compromise on the money question that would unite their party.[17] Notwithstanding its preference for a middle way, the *Journal* was clearly sympathetic to the free silver advocates. It chided the *World* and the *Sun* for attributing ignorance and base motives to silver advocates: "Except for their one financial fad, the Western and Southern silver Democrats are the salt of the political earth. Their leaders have given their lives to the public service in honorable poverty. [They] are men of fastidious honor in all their personal and official relations. . . . They have always formed the backbone of every force that has resisted schemes of public plunder. They have stood inflexibly for economical government, just taxation and equality of opportunities." No good Democrat could part with such comrades over one plank, "however serious." The *Journal*'s recommendation of a fair-minded Democratic dialogue applied to the silverites as well. They were advised to disown their rumored plans to use force of numbers to muzzle gold supporters in Chicago and push through their own platform and candidate without debate.[18]

While their differences were becoming clear, Hearst and Pulitzer were not yet in direct opposition to one another on the issue. In fact, their advice was remarkably similar in the weeks leading up to Chicago. Neither wanted the Democrats to split over currency. Neither wanted to have to chose between the gold-minded Democrats in their home base of New York and what would likely be a pro-silver ticket. So each advocated compromise, coaxing the party to explore the middle ground of limited rather than free coinage of silver. Each saw merit in adopting bimetallism in the company of other major Western financial powers such as England and Germany. Pulitzer beseeched Cleveland to use his remaining months in office in pursuit of an international treaty to that effect. But Cleveland wasn't interested, and besides, it was too late—the silverites were fed up with Washington's lack of action and disinclined to settle for anything short of free coinage of silver at a rate of sixteen to one. There would be no compromise. Hearst and Pulitzer would be driven to take sides.

Hearst sent a huge delegation to Chicago, led by Julius Chambers, regular correspondents Alfred Henry Lewis and Henry George, and artists Homer Davenport and M. de Lipman. He also signed up a long string of Democratic luminaries to provide on-the-spot commentary, including California senator Stephen Mallory White, former New York governor Roswell Pettibone Flower, and the wild-eyed John Altgeld, governor of Illinois, and John R. McLean, the man who had sold Hearst the *Journal*. Most of these gentlemen not only would comment on the convention but would play roles in the proceedings—four *Journal* contributors (David B. Hill, John McLean, Stephen M. White, John W. Daniel) were considered candidates for either the presidential or vice-presidential nomination.[19]

Hearst's corps would fill a newspaper now running at sixteen pages a day in two eight-page sections, with most of the first section given over to political news. The correspondents worked out of the *Journal*'s headquarters and reception room, a rented storefront under the magnificent facade of the Palmer House block. Decorated with bunting and posters and a dazzling combination of mirrors and electric lights, it became an unofficial Democratic headquarters during the convention, filled at all hours with hacks and delegates of every description. Hearst also erected in Chicago, New York, and Brooklyn giant billboards on which his lightning sketch artists presented for the public continuously updated scenes from the action unfolding on the floor of "the most important convention ever held by the Democracy of the United States."[20]

The convention itself was held in the Chicago Coliseum, a building that would burn to the ground the following year, but in the meantime it was the most impressive structure of its kind anywhere and another powerful symbol of America's emerging mass culture. Reporters marveled at its capacity—"so great that, although less than three-quarters of its floor space is utilized for this convention, there has been found place for 14,000 people, seated in comfortable chairs."[21]

The fight between the rival currency factions for control of the convention was over early. On the first night, July 7, one *Journal* contributor, silver senator John W. Daniel of Virginia, easily out-polled another *Journal* contributor, gold senator David B. Hill of New York, for the position of temporary chair of the Democratic National Committee, and the rout was on. The Democratic old guard, led by the pro-gold New York delegation, sat silent and grim as Daniel's triumph was greeted by flying hats, waving handkerchiefs, and a long, noisy demonstration. It was the first of several wild displays. The silver forces, having grabbed the convention's reins, struggled to marshal their numbers and advance their business—the *Journal*'s Chambers reported a spirit of "political anarchy" in the hall. After a procedural vote on the second evening that admitted more silver delegates at the expense of the gold forces, fourteen thousand voices exploded at once and the scene again dissolved into chaos. "[No] efforts of the presiding officer were sufficient to quell the tumult until the great gathering had yelled itself to hoarseness and finally voicelessness," wrote Chambers. The roar "was like that of a blast furnace a hundred times multiplied." It was only when the band was cued and had played through "Yankee Doodle" two or three times that the proceedings resumed. Gold-friendly newspapers complained that delegates resembled a revolutionary mob.[22]

The excitability of delegates notwithstanding, a platform was hammered out and read from the podium on the morning of July 9. It called for smaller government, restrictions on federal authority, fixed terms of public office, merit-based appointments, an income tax, and an end to railway loan extensions, among other measures. It was short on foreign policy, but it did object to the Spanish presence in the Western Hemisphere, extending "sympathy to the people of Cuba in their heroic struggle for liberty and independence."[23]

The heroism of Cuban rebels was not seriously disputed in American public life; the Populists would also offer hearty support in their platform, and the Republicans were the most aggressive of all, calling for more military and naval spending, an expansionist foreign policy, and a full application of the Monroe Doctrine to bring peace and independence to the Cuban people. The unanimity on Cuba kept it from becoming an issue in the campaign, but with help from Hearst and other editors it would rise with a vengeance the moment the currency debate was decided.[24]

The centerpiece of the Democratic platform was its monetary plank, a full-out endorsement of free silver:

> We are unalterably opposed to the single gold standard, which has locked fast the prosperity of an industrial people in the paralysis of hard times. . . . It is not only un-American, but anti-American, and it can be fastened on the United States only by the stifling of what indomitable spirit and love of liberty which proclaimed our political independence in 1776 and won it in the War of the Revolution.
>
>   . . . We demand the free and unlimited coinage of both gold and silver at the present legal ratio of 16 to 1 without waiting for the aid or consent of any other nation.[25]

Hearst's friend William C. Whitney called the platform "the worst I ever heard."[26] New York's Senator Hill, asked if he would join the gold delegates who had walked out of the Coliseum, replied that he was "a Democrat still; very still."[27] But Nebraska congressman William Jennings Bryan judged it "the strongest platform upon which any party has gone to the country in recent years."[28] Hearst's editorial page sought to bridge the unbridgeable. Financial matters were but one plank of the platform, it argued. On everything else, the party was united in its fierce protest against a "corrupt and selfish plutocracy," against "the injustice of class privileges, which make stepping stones of the many for the profit of the few."[29]

That night, in the stifling, smoke-filled Coliseum, a series of prominent Democrats spoke for and against the platform. Senator Hill made one last attempt to pierce the silver line. *Journal* commentator Amos

Cummings called it "a gallant effort carefully prepared and manfully executed against overwhelming numbers." Hill calmly explained to the delegates that all Democrats supported bimetallism: they differed only on how to implement it. "Those whom I represent, and for whom I speak," declared Hill, "insist that we should not attempt the experiment of the free and unlimited coinage of silver without the cooperation of other great nations." The only safe and prudent path to monetary reform was a multilateral one: "In this great day, when we are connected with all portions of the earth by our ships, by our telegraph cables and by all the methods of intercourse, we think it unwise to attempt this alone."[30]

Hill's compromise was consistent with the *Journal*'s proposals. The paper admired his performance, noting that a dozen sparrows flew into the great hall while he was speaking to chirp a musical accompaniment: "It was conciliatory in tone and brotherly in feeling. It sparkled with patriotism and glowed with the spirit of true Democracy. Indeed, some of [Hill's] friends began to whisper that even yet he might become the nominee of his party for the Presidency." But, as Amos Cummings admitted, Hill's pitch "utterly failed" to move the convention. He was driven back at every point by the wild cheers of the silver corps.[31]

The last orator, taking the stage just before midnight, was William Jennings Bryan. He had been assigned to speak for the silver plank as a consolation prize, having lost his bid for the chair of the convention earlier in the week. "He tripped lightly up the steps of the platform," reported the *Journal*:

As he stood before the convention, pale, modest and unassuming, he looked the perfect picture of [the late Philadelphia congressman] Samuel J. Randall, a real tribune of the people. His voice filled the hall, apparently without effort. His gestures were the acme of grace as he paced backward and forward in easy familiarity with his hearers. There was no self-consciousness in either action or utterance. The words poured forth in rhythmical volume, burnishing his ideas and facts until they shone like diamonds. His topics, similes and metaphors were marvelous. The whole speech was iridescent. The delegates sat as if enchanted, breaking into applause at odd moments as though touched by electric wires. It was a display of eloquence pure and undefiled.[32]

Bryan, like Hill, regretted the fracture in the Democratic Party over the silver issue and disavowed any hostility to his opponents. He paid tribute to the abilities and reputations of the gold advocates who had spoken earlier. He doubted that he could match their stature as individuals but hoped to carry the day by his ideas: "The humblest citizen in all the land, when clad in the armor of a righteous cause, is stronger than all the hosts of error. I come to speak to you in defense of a cause as holy as the cause of liberty, the cause of humanity."

The humanity that concerned Bryan most particularly were the common folk—small merchants and farmers who lived close to the land and who had been hardest hit by the recent depression. These people, as deserving as any in America, had seen their homes, families, and livelihoods threatened by economic injustice. Their interests, Bryan argued, could no longer be subordinated to those of the eastern monied classes. Turning to address the gold delegates directly, he challenged their claim that unilateral abandonment of the gold standard would be ruinous to U.S. business:

When you come before us and tell us that we are about to disturb your business, we say to you that you have made the definition of a business man too limited in its application. The man who is employed for wages is as much a business man as his employer; the attorney in a country town is as much a business man as the corporation counsel in a great metropolis; the merchant at the crossroads store is as much a business man as the merchant of New York; the farmer who goes forth in the morning and toils all day . . . is as much a business man as the man who goes upon the board of trade and bets upon the price of grain. . . . We come to speak for this broader class of business men. We do not come as aggressors. Our war is not a war of conquest; we are fighting in the defense of our homes, our families, and posterity. We have petitioned, and our petitions have been scorned; we have entreated, and our entreaties have been disregarded; we have begged, and they have mocked when our calamity came. We beg no longer; we entreat no more; we petition no more. We defy them.[33]

Invoking Cicero and the twin Democratic icons Andrew Jackson and Thomas Jefferson, Bryan rolled on to defend the income tax and other aspects of the party's platform before taking issue with the gold corps' plea for international bimetallism. Leading Democrats, he argued, had been talking of international agreements for twenty years, but all efforts had been fruitless. He noted that not even the Republicans defended the gold standard any longer—they had pledged themselves to bimetallism by international agreement. If the gold standard was so discredited that not even Republicans would speak for it, why did America need the permission of the great powers to abandon it? Why were Americans surrendering their sovereignty and ceding legislative control of their affairs to foreign powers? With that, Bryan arrived at his startling conclusion:

> If they dare to come out in the open field and defend the gold standard as a good thing, we will fight them to the uttermost. Having behind us the producing masses of this nation and the world, supported by the commercial interests, the laboring interests, and the toilers everywhere, we will answer their demand for a gold standard by saying to them: You shall not press down upon the brow of labor this crown of thorns; you shall not crucify mankind upon a cross of gold.

Bryan raked his fingers down the sides of his face at "crown of thorns" and stood with arms outstretched for "cross of gold." He held the pose for a moment. There was a stunned silence in the stadium and Bryan began walking off stage as the delegates absorbed his words. He was almost lost in the crowd before a great furor erupted. "Pale and exhausted," reported the *Journal*, "but with flashing eyes and a smiling face, he was raised to the shoulders of the Nebraska delegation, while the guidons of three-fourths of the states were dancing around him. There was an ocean of applause while it lasted, those bearing the guidons marched in procession around the delegates, shouting choruses of satisfaction. It was a tribute never before paid to a living orator." The demonstration lasted the better part of an hour. The next day's *Journal* ran Bryan's speech in full (along with Hill's).[34]

The *Journal* was the only New York paper to remain in Bryan's presence throughout the nomination voting. The candidate and his wife were lodged at the modest Clifton House hotel. According to the paper's anonymous correspondent, Bryan was confident and buoyant from the first ballot: "He read the bulletins as they were brought to him from the little telegraph office downstairs. His comments at first were few and short. As his vote gradually kept increasing there was no change in his countenance. Rather, he became more solemn, and once or twice his brow was knit for a moment, as though he already felt the responsibilities of a candidate."[35]

Bryan gained momentum through the third ballot and was beginning to look like the eventual winner. His rooms began to fill with supporters and onlookers eager to witness the birth of a presidential nominee. When the results of the fourth ballot were brought, they showed Bryan ahead of the other contender, Richard "Silver" Bland of Missouri, for the first time. His win was now inevitable:

> For a second Bryan's face was pale and had a sad, anxious look. It was a moment for him to reflect on the sudden honors which came to him in the days of his youth. He looked out on the street. There were the usual crowds of people going and coming. They looked up at the window and saw a black-haired, smooth-faced man, but no one on the street, perhaps, knew that this man was then nearing the greatest moment, the most eventful period of his thirty-six years of life.
>
> The candidate began to look furtively and anxiously at the door. He was awaiting the messengers with white bulletins. Friendly chaffing ceased. There was growing feeling of awe. So satisfying was the fourth ballot that the suspense became intense when the bulletin came announcing the order for the fifth.[36]

Reports now streamed into the Clifton announcing the declarations of the delegates state by state—California, Kentucky, North Carolina, all for Bryan. The candidate asked the *Journal* correspondent for a sheet of paper. He told his guests that he'd be back in a minute and stepped into his private room. The correspondent followed him.

> "You are nominated, Mr. Bryan," said the *Journal* man.
>
> The nominee looked up. He was writing a statement to be given to the press. He knew that he was already nominated, but he wouldn't admit it by word of mouth. But he was putting on paper his first official utterance as the nominated candidate of the Democratic party. Before he had finished it another bulletin came in. It was brief.

"Bryan is nominated."

That was all. It was enough. A crowd gathered, each man in it being anxious to be the first to touch his hand.

That hand was still writing.

"Wait a moment, I've important business just now," he said, laughing, and looked up when he finished and stood erect. He looked the typical leader of men—the leader of a great political party. He had leaned over to write his idea of one term for the Presidency. When he began no one knew that he was already a nominee for that high office. When he looked up, his face was full of conscious pride.[37]

The *Journal*, in its coverage of the Democratic convention, was by far the most animated and comprehensive of the New York dailies. Several papers, including the Republican *Tribune*, credited the Nebraskan with a stirring address, and reviewed or quoted his salient points. The *Times*, on the other hand, reported that the speaker, a "wild theorist" in baggy trousers, had managed to excite the "diseased" minds of the "silver yawpers."[38] Only the *Journal* left readers with the impression that Bryan's performance was of a caliber American politics had not heard since Lincoln.

The *World* also ran transcripts of the Hill and Bryan speeches but covered the latter with evident distaste, quoting from it only a single forgettable sentence, and mentioning in a few short paragraphs that his audience was impressed—"the floor of the convention seemed to heave up." The paper's editorial, entitled "Hysteria in Politics," accused the delegates of "fanaticism" and "madness." Bryan had been carried from obscurity to the nomination on the "frenzy" generated by his eloquence at the convention, an effect identical to that produced when "religious exhorters work upon the sensibilities of their hearers until hysterical women fall into a state resembling catalepsy. . . . Men, too, under the influence of these magnetic appeals, fall to shouting 'hallelujah!' 'Glory to God!' and walk up and down the . . . aisles under the control of a frenzy that renders them utterly unconscious of their actions."[39]

The *World* decided to leave speculation on the psychological origins of this condition to specialists in the "abnormal conditions of the mind and the contagion of emotion." It concerned itself instead with mocking the already famous closing of Bryan's speech: "Is the best money a 'crown of thorns' for labor? Is mankind 'crucified' in gold-standard England,

France, Germany, and Austria, and exalted in free-silver Mexico, Central American and Japan? If it comes to a question of torture and death, is it any worse to suffer upon a 'cross of gold' than to be twisted and torn on a rack of silver?" The whole of Bryan's speech, declared the *World*, was "sublimated nonsense."[40]

Yet however outraged he may have been by the convention, Pulitzer was reluctant to abandon Bryan and his followers. Perhaps realizing that insisting on the lunacy of Democrats was a risky strategy for a Democratic paper, not to mention inconsistent with the *World*'s "trust the people" editorial line, he went out of his way to boast of his access to the new leader. He ran on his front page transcripts of letters from Bryan explaining his policies and asking for the newspaper's support.[41]

The *World* began to sort itself out as the election heated up. It opposed Bryan and his platform as "hostile to the traditions and foreign to the principles" of the Democratic Party. On July 21, it noted that only five of the seventeen policy planks agreed upon in Chicago had ever before been part of a national Democratic platform. The people were still trustworthy—rank-and-file Democrats were fundamentally decent folk who, shattered by corporate greed and Cleveland's misrule, had stubbornly ignored the sound advice of the *World*'s editorials and succumbed to the dubious charms of a boyish prairie demagogue, but they would eventually come to their senses. Pulitzer promised to keep the party's true flame alive on their behalf until Bryan's inevitable crash.[42]

Pulitzer was acting from conviction on these matters, but he was also playing the odds. He considered the Democrats doomed, and he was not about to go down with them. "There is no doubt as to the result of the election," he told his executives, "except as to the size of McKinley's popular and electoral majorities."[43]

Bryan sent an emissary to Pulitzer, asking again for his support and suggesting that the *World* would lose prestige and influence if it failed to back a winning ticket. Pulitzer was unyielding. "As we sat there on his little private porch at Bar Harbor," remembered his employee, George C. Eggleston, "Mr. Pulitzer named every state that would give its electoral vote to each candidate, and the returns of the election." Pulitzer ordered an editorial predicting the results of the election on the basis of his projections. "Let that be our answer," he said, "to Mr. Bryan's audacious message."[44] Confident as he was of his position, Pulitzer was nonetheless abandoning the Bryan Democrats as Charles Dana and the *Sun* had shunned Cleveland a dozen years earlier.

HEARST, MEANWHILE, had problems of his own. According to one biographer, John K. Winkler, he had attended the Chicago convention and was a dozen feet from the stage, watching impassively, as Bryan made his rousing address. Hearst could see where the party was headed and that Bryan was likely to take the nomination. The *Journal*'s hopes of a compromise in Chicago were dashed, and the paper needed a new editorial line.[45]

The two biographers who had the most cooperation from Hearst, Winkler and Cora Older, tell essentially the same tale of his deliberations. Winkler's version is more detailed. He has Hearst hustling back to New York and called a meeting of his top executives. "Gentlemen," Hearst said, "I have asked you in to discuss our attitude in the coming campaign. Shall we support McKinley and the gold standard or Bryan and free silver?" Managing editor Sam Chamberlain reportedly counseled him to either sit on the fence or switch allegiance to the McKinley Republicans. Editorialist Arthur McEwen argued that Bryan and the Democratic platform deserved support but acknowledged that such a position was untenable in New York or anywhere else in the Northeast given the overwhelming sentiment in favor of the gold standard. Charles Palmer, the *Journal*'s business manager, warned that anything other than an endorsement of McKinley would be devastating to the paper's circulation and advertising prospects. Hearst is said to have let this conversation run for about half an hour, listening intently and occasionally whistling softly. Finally he said his piece: "I am sorry to disagree with you but I have made up my mind. Mr. McEwen, write a good strong editorial for Bryan and silver. Get it into tomorrow's paper. Have it played up right, Sam. Good day, gentlemen." With that, he picked up his straw hat with its bright ribbon and left the room, still whistling softly.[46]

Hearst's own account of his decision, like the Winkler and Older biographies, emerged long after events. He claimed to have spent a sleepless night pondering his move before choosing to support Bryan, despite silver, as a sincere Democrat and champion of the people.

"When . . . the morning of the next day broke, I walked down to my editorial room and said to the boys, 'Unlimber the guns; we are going to fight for Bryan.'"[47] Hostile biographers—including Carlson and Bates and Ferdinand Lundberg—maintain that Hearst was privately in favor of gold but cynically took up the silver cause seeking competitive and financial advantage. He hoped either to sell more papers by distinguishing himself from Pulitzer or, worse, to increase the value of his family's silver mines by getting Bryan elected.

If Hearst did hold a meeting about the *Journal*'s position on Bryan and silver, it probably did not happen in the manner Winkler describes. Winkler leaves the impression that the *Journal*'s deliberations over the endorsement began and ended at that one particular executive meeting and that a full range of options were on the table at that time, including support for McKinley and gold. He portrays Hearst as approaching the decision cavalierly and without much forethought. But, as we have seen, the paper had been publishing editorials on currency and partisan matters for many months in advance of Chicago. "It will take something worse than the free coinage of silver at 16 to 1 to ruin this country," the paper had stated only a week earlier.[48] The *Journal*'s positions were so deeply entrenched by the time of the convention that a move toward McKinley in the wake of Chicago would have meant recanting several months' work and effectively relaunching the paper. If Hearst did discuss an endorsement with his executives, the options under consideration would have been narrow. Would the *Journal* support the ticket and silver, or would it support the ticket despite silver?

What's more, the meeting could not have happened when Hearst and his biographers say it did. There was no time for Hearst to return from Chicago for a conference with his executives, as in Winkler's account; nor was there occasion for him to endure a sleepless night, as in his own account. The *Journal*'s new position was on the street within hours of Bryan's speech, even before he'd won the nomination: "The platform adopted yesterday at Chicago, admirable in everything else, outlines a financial policy that is not satisfactory to Eastern Democrats, nor to the more thoughtful ones of the West and South. It involves confusion, distress, and, as regards existing contracts, partial repudiation." Recognizing these unpleasant facts, the *Journal* asked, what was a Democratic newspaper to do?

If the alternative were between the free, unlimited and independent coinage of silver at 16 to 1 and McKinleyism . . . our situation would indeed be embarrassing. But it is not quite as bad as that. The election of a free silver President would not necessarily mean the free coinage of silver. All such a President could do would be to sign a bill passed by both houses of Congress. It is absolutely impossible for the silver men to capture the House of Representatives without gross dereliction on the part of the friends of sound money. The question for us, therefore, is whether we ought to try to elect a President who is independent, upright and progressive . . . and enlightened in his views on all subjects but one, but whose ideas on one topic that is never likely to come before him for official action are unsound, or whether we should prefer a man mortgaged to a corrupt oligarchy that would make his Administration a national scandal. . . .

The choice is between the regular Democratic nominee and McKinley, and in such circumstances the duty of Democrats admits of no doubt. It is to vote for sound money Congressmen and the national ticket.[49]

It was not an especially elegant position, wishing the Democrats frustration on their key plank, but it was consistent with the *Journal*'s standing policy. The next morning, the paper repeated the essentials of its new argument in an editorial welcoming Bryan as the nominee.[50]

It is unlikely that Hearst's hunger for higher circulation decided the matter. Hearst could be as self-interested as any publisher in New York, but the commercial prospects of his choice were unpromising. Even if Pulitzer were to repeat Dana's error and abandon the Democrats in a presidential year (which was not certain when the *Journal* made its call), and even if that were to leave Hearst the only significant New York editor behind Bryan, he remained at risk. The Democrats were prohibitive underdogs coming out of Chicago. The party was split and the ticket was unpopular in New York, especially among the commercial elites, although it did find a measure of support among the working-classes and recent immigrants. These facts threatened Hearst's circulation and advertising. He stuck with Bryan primarily on principle. However much he disliked the silver plank, Hearst did consider the Republicans and their support for the gold standard a greater evil.

Biographers have always found it difficult to accept Hearst as a serious political actor. One reason is that he does not fit the profile. He had

none of the familiar attributes of leading political journalists. The *Sun*'s
Dana and the *Evening Post*'s E.L. Godkin owned more impressive intellects; Pulitzer was more didactic and Whitelaw Reid more high-minded;
and all of these editors were also accomplished political writers. Hearst
got an incomplete at Harvard and he did relatively little writing for publication. He was young and high-spirited and burdened with the percep-
tion that he was making what one historian has called a "spectacle of his
life."[51] He was also running a newspaper notably short of the earnestness
we associate with a strong sense of political purpose. But all of this only
makes Hearst unusual: none of it disqualifies him as a political voice.

Another knock against Hearst has been the apparent incongruity
between his progressive views and his privileged circumstances. It is
incredible to some that a publisher with millions at his disposal would
advocate policies inimical to the interests of the monied classes—he must
be hypocritical, or cynical, or both. But wealth is not a reliable indicator
of ideology even in our time. Hearst was not a traitor to his class or his
birthright; he was true to his father's political legacy and to his own
ideals. His attraction to Bryan was predictable given that Bryan, too,
claimed the mantle of Jeffersonian Democrat, trusting the people as the
depository of power and authority in American life, defending equal
rights before the law, declaiming privilege "whether it stemmed from an
accident of birth or the favoritism of public and private authorities."[52]

From his early days at the *Examiner* until long after he had removed
himself from the day-to-day management of the *Journal*, Hearst held
sincere and reasonably coherent political views. He could wobble on
issues and individuals in response to particular election scenarios and
personal feuds, as did Pulitzer, Dana, and everyone else. But the candidates and programs he endorsed in San Francisco and New York were
steadily progressive (his preferences would later shift in light of experience and changes in the political environment). The writers, editorialists,
and columnists with whom Hearst surrounded himself at this time were
among the most radical political voices in America—Willis J. Abbot,
Ambrose Bierce, Arthur McEwen, Henry George, Alfred Henry Lewis.
The opinions expressed by Hearst's newspapers matched the views he
professed in interviews, and none of them were seriously contradicted in
private correspondence. Hearst had reservations about silver, but he was
a Bryan Democrat.

And a worried one. The youthful insouciance apparent in Winkler's account of Hearst's whistling through a critical meeting is deceptive. Hearst did cultivate a carefree image—the bright hatbands and impromptu jigs—and that image has always been taken at face value by his biographers, as it was by some of his colleagues. But Hearst was on edge through the convention season. His closest associates worried at the physical and intellectual loads he was carrying. In a previously unpublished letter, the *Journal*'s business manager, Charles Palmer, wrote to Phoebe with his concerns:

> I did not feel at liberty to say anything regarding the matter of Mr. Hearst's health that would alarm you, but have considered it as too serious to be disregarded for some little time and have urged him as strongly as possible to take the best possible care of himself. You may remember that I have spoken to you about it also each time I have seen you when you have been in the city. I do not think that there is anything serious to be apprehended, but he certainly should take care of himself, or should have some one with him to see that he does so; and more important than all, he should stop worrying about the paper, its condition and its future. Everything is most satisfactory as far as the present condition and future prospects of THE JOURNAL are concerned. Of course there are minor imperfections developing from time to time to cause temporary annoyance, but none of them have as yet been such as to interfere with the continuous and steady progress of the paper, which is gaining in circulation as rapidly as we are in condition to print the papers required, and in advertising at an even faster rate.[53]

Notwithstanding Palmer's reassurances, Hearst did have a lot to worry about. His early progress was encouraging, but his larger strategy called for him to continue his blazing pace until he had blown by Pulitzer and established himself as America's bestselling daily, a status that would attract a lion's share of advertising, leading to the reduction, and, in time, the elimination of his losses. Only then, from a position of strength, would he begin to trim his expenses and raise either his advertising rates or his circulation price to improve his margins and consolidate his standing in the market. It was an uncomplicated plan, but there were obstacles in his way.

It is clear from another paragraph in Palmer's letter that Phoebe was already complaining about the paper's losses and that Will was reluctant to cut spending for fear that it might hurt his circulation and undermine his grand plan. "As to reduction of general expense, this is possible at any time," writes Palmer. "I have kept it before Mr. Hearst's attention, but have not strongly urged it until he should be ready to undertake it in a systematic way, fearing that in his anxious condition the least sign of checking the growth of circulation, from whatever cause, might be attributed by him to the reduction of expenses, which would certainly cause a reaction even more costly than at present."[54]

In addition to these familial pressures, there was strong evidence that Pulitzer was rising to the *Journal*'s competitive challenge. *The Fourth Estate* noted a steady improvement in the *World*'s editorials, which it took as proof that the master's hand was firmly on the tiller. The *World* had also begun printing its first edition at midnight, in order to expand its field of circulation as far as Boston and Baltimore. Its circulation was up to 312,000 by early June, a 50,000 increase over April.[55] Every 50,000 the *World* increased was another 50,000 the *Journal* had to climb in order to claim first place, and given Palmer's comment about the limits of their printing presses, Hearst did not need higher targets, especially now that he was supporting the underdog in a national election and pitting himself against the leading New York Democrats and the city's commercial elites.

CHAPTER SIX

A Large Brute of Some
Utterly New Species

T he late nineteenth century was an age of mechanization and industrialization, and a wondrous time for the many Americans fascinated with technology, Will Hearst among them. In addition to building the world's fastest steam yacht, he imported one of the first motor cars to the United States, a French number, painted red. He took his new portable camera up in a hot air balloon to photograph San Francisco, and not long after arriving in New York he caught a bird's-eye view of Manhattan from an experimental flying machine. He challenged speed records with express trains carrying his newspapers to distant cities. His daily business made use of the transatlantic telegraph, the telephone, the typewriter, and a dazzlingly sophisticated printing plant. He was making plans during the election campaign to send a motion picture camera to Washington to capture the inauguration on film for the first time. Hearst was living at the dawn of the machine age and embracing all the marvels and conveniences it offered, an attitude that undoubtedly contributed to his avid coverage of the bicycle craze of 1896.

Bicycles had evolved dramatically over the previous decade. Gone were the ungainly huge-wheeled contraptions that had required skill and daring of the young men who rode them; the so-called safety bicycle arrived in contours recognizable to us today—a seat perched between two equal-sized spoke wheels with pneumatic rubber tires, a diamond-shaped frame, and pedals attached to a sprocket-and-chain system. Produced on assembly lines and sold at affordable prices, the new bicycle allowed urbanites unprecedented freedom and mobility, not to mention fun. As a mass-market newspaper committed not only to studying but to sharing the enthusiasms of its readers, the *Journal* monstered the wheeling mania.

Throughout the spring and summer of '96, the paper bulked up on articles on bicycle engineering, manufacturing, and sales, including a large anatomy of a bicycle with each of its hundred parts labeled and explained, and a report on how the bicycle fad was killing the market for pianos while boosting the sales of soft drinks. It offered advice on how to ride a "wheel," how to "scorch" (ride fast), and how to brake, which was still something of a problem. It visited bicycle academies and bicycle clubs, and discussed the problems of bicycle traffic, poor roads, bicycles cluttering trains and cable cars, and bicycle accidents, injuries, and deaths. It covered local, college, and international bicycle races, profiled champion cyclists, and produced close-up illustrations of their overdeveloped leg muscles. And then there were the bicycle novelties: bicycles built for two or four, bicycles with sails, amphibious bicycles, bicycles mounted for indoor use (the "boudoir scorcher"), a bicyclist with a monkey on his back, a bicyclist with no legs, and a woman who bicycled around town in red bloomers.

Fashion was a big part of bicycling. The diva Lillian Russell cruised Central Park in a tan bicycle suit "that fitted as if she had been melted and run into it." (Her tumble from her gold-plated bicycle made the *Journal*'s front page.)[1] Other women favored high leather riding boots, and one was seen sporting a diamond-studded bicycle sweater. An essay by a *Journal* fashion writer suggested that the bicycle would liberate women from uncomfortable and insensible attire, leading to more independence for her sex generally. That was one reason that bicycles were also a moral issue. Early feminists called the bicycle the freedom machine and Charlotte Smith, the self-appointed guardian of public virtue and a virulent anti-bicycler, worried that young girls were escaping the parental gaze and scorching down "paths that lead directly to sin." After playing up Smith's concerns and asking her, uncharitably, if she weren't too stout to pedal, the *Journal*, always supportive of what was called the "new woman," gave right of rebuttal to Commander Frederick Booth-Tucker of the Salvation Army. A young girl might be led astray by the devil, he argued, but "not [by] an inanimate thing of steel and rubber."[2]

The bicycle craze hardly went unnoticed in other newspapers. All of them carried bicycle stories, and in 1895 the *Evening Telegraph* sponsored a bicycle parade that attracted thousands of riders on decorated wheels, but no one attacked the fad with more élan than Hearst. He dreamed up a transcontinental bicycle relay that would carry a letter from San Francisco to New York over the old Wells-Fargo pony express route and, where necessary, railroad grades and trestles. Some four hundred bicyclists passed through the Sierra Nevada and Rocky Mountains, hitting Ogden, Omaha, Chicago, and Buffalo before reaching Manhattan in just under two weeks. As the paper boasted, "They have crossed yawning gorges on spidery, unguarded trestles, bumping over the ties where a slip would have sent them on the rocks three hundred feet below; they have coasted down wild mountain roads, strewn thick with threatening boulders; they have flattened themselves against the sides of snowsheds to give the right of way to insistent freight trains; they have encountered every vicissitude, from inhaling alkali dust into parched throats on fiery deserts to wading knee-deep in mud under drenching rains, and with it all they have averaged over 280 miles a day for the whole distance from ocean to ocean."[3]

The *Journal* capped its relay with a nighttime bicycle parade up Broadway. The boulevard was packed with spectators and costumed cyclists carrying Chinese lanterns on sticks and "illuminated decorations of every description." The Harlem Wheelmen, 150 strong, rode in formation with torches and fairy lamps to take the prize for best bicycle club. The following morning, the *Journal* gave the parade an illustrated double-page spread, including photo-illustrations of the prettiest girls on the gaudiest bikes. There were also cartoons: Uncle Sam on a bike, and another of plump Charlotte Smith pedaling along with a tear in her eye. And, low in the bottom right corner, yet another cartoon, this one of a beastly-looking rider in a plaid suit covered with dollar signs. Instead of a Chinese lantern, he carried a skull marked "LABOR" on the end of a stick. *Journal* readers would have recognized him instantly and laughed out loud. He was Mark Hanna, a leading Republican political figure and one of few subjects getting more attention than bicycles in the *Journal* that summer.[4]

IT WAS NOT ENOUGH for a late-nineteenth-century newspaper proprietor to support one party or another in a national election; he was expected to attack the leadership and policies of its rivals as well. This was a challenge for Hearst and his Democratic paper in '96. The Republican nominee, William McKinley, was an elusive target.

Solid, uncharismatic, and fifty-three years old, McKinley was a veteran
of the Civil War and a lawyer by trade. He boasted executive experience
as governor of Ohio on top of fourteen years as a legislator in
Washington, and he had been one of the country's best-known congressmen, thanks to the protective tariff bearing his name. Apart from the tariff, he had avoided hard stands on controversial issues and maintained
good relations with business and financial elites as well as with the labor
movement. He was decent, agreeable, intelligent, and reasonably eloquent. He possessed an innate sense of personal dignity appropriate to the
highest office in the land. If that were not enough, he had been ennobled
by personal tragedy. After losing both daughters to illness, McKinley's
wife, Ida, had suffered a series of debilitating emotional and physical
breakdowns. He was known to be active in her care. Even his one brush
with scandal—he had teetered at the edge of bankruptcy after guaranteeing the notes of a friend whose business collapsed—was conceded by the
Journal to have been a fault of his heart rather than of his head.[5]

McKinley, in short, looked unassailable in the early months of the
campaign. That his party was determined to ride into office on the general detestation of the Cleveland Democrats while making as few policy
commitments as possible made it still harder for critics to get a bead on
him. But Hearst had two unusual weapons at his disposal. The first was
a reporter, Alfred Henry Lewis, whom he dispatched to Canton, Ohio, as
soon as McKinley appeared to have the nomination sewn up.

If any journalist in America was capable of finding a chink in
McKinley's armor, it was Alfred Henry Lewis. He had reached Hearst's
employ by an unusual route. In his twenties he had been a square-jawed,
binge-drinking prosecuting attorney in the Cleveland police courts and
then a city solicitor in Kansas City. In the latter post, he had managed to
stay sober long enough to win a particularly important case, after which,
by his own account, he went out to celebrate with "just one" glass. That
one glass led to a bunch more, and to a rash decision to buy a ticket on a
westbound train. Before he knew it, Lewis was punching cows on a ranch
in New Mexico, not that he minded terribly. He spent some time in the
saddle, drying out and living the life of a cowboy hobo and itinerant
journalist. He saw much of the Oklahoma Territory, Texas, and Arizona.

Not yet thirty, he returned to Kansas City, taking up the law again as well as his pen, but not the bottle.

Lewis began to write fiction, spinning his adventures on the frontier into short stories for newspapers. His earliest effort was a crusty old cattleman's recollection of the first funeral in the tiny town of Wolfville (modeled on Tombstone, Arizona). The corpse was the result of a disputed poker pot. Local worthies decided to bury the dead gambler at least a mile from town on the theory that "you can't make no funeral imposin' unless you're plumb liberal on distances." Lewis's story was published in the Kansas City *Times* in 1890 under the signature Dan Quin, his nom de plume. He got no money for the piece, but it was syndicated to such acclaim that his next Wolfville tale brought $360.[6]

In 1891, Lewis gave up the law again and ventured to Washington as a correspondent for the Chicago *Times* and the Kansas City *Times*. He brought a unique set of skills to the job. He could sketch scenes and characters with a light touch, and his legal training was evident in his close attention to fact, but what really set him apart was his rhetoric. Among the angriest and most radical of progressive journalists, he wrote in scorching gales of rage interspersed with bitter humor. *Journal* editor Willis Abbot esteemed him as a "past master of the art of invective, and a singularly vigorous hater." He was distinguished among early muckraking journalists for rebuking the victims of robber barons and corrupt politicians as spineless and thus deserving of their abuse.[7]

Lewis flourished in Washington. In 1894, he was offered the editorship of the recently merged Chicago *Times-Herald*. He turned it down but a year later accepted Hearst's invitation to write on national affairs for the *Journal*. The two men developed a respectful and lasting professional relationship. Lewis did brilliant work at the *Journal*, wrote Abbot, because "Hearst at once recognized his peculiar qualities and employed him on those jobs which he could best do and his writing fairly scintillated in the paper."[8]

Lewis's specific assignment in Canton was to write a "pen picture," or profile, of the Republican nominee. He spent a few days knocking around town, looking up McKinley's friends, associates, and rivals, drinking endless cups of black coffee (one addiction having replaced the other). He talked as much as he listened. Apart from everything else, Lewis was a capital conversationalist. He could talk with anyone about anything, all day long.[9] "He would talk to you of civilization and savagery, truth and lies, human nature, foes and friends, or anything else that can engage the mind," said his colleague Julian Hawthorne. On all subjects, Lewis would speak with vehement conviction, although some doubted whether he believed what he was saying or simply felt a need to talk.[10]

Having sucked what information he could from the locals, Lewis finally dropped in on McKinley. He was surprised to find the prospective nominee living in almost rural simplicity in a rented home in Canton. He described McKinley as a short, handsome individual with wide shoulders and a deep chest: "He has keen eyes, as bright as mirrors, which look steadily at men." His conversation was genial and trite, and devoid of humor: "his tongue has been checked too often in a life of office-hunting to make any resentful slips." His mind was mediocre, which was all Lewis believed the presidency required—too much originality and intellectual agility being a hindrance to steady leadership. The candidate's tender solicitude toward his invalid wife impressed Lewis, as it did all visitors. But for the fact that he smoked "like Vesuvius," Lewis thought McKinley could pass for a "well-paid pulpiteer."[11]

Lewis's pen picture, published April 13, 1896, did not lay a glove on McKinley. By the writer's usual standards, it was almost fawning. But Lewis did not leave Ohio empty-handed. To gain his interview, Lewis had endured a pre-interview with the candidate's gatekeeper, Mark Hanna. This man seemed to have "charge and complete control" of the candidate. Hanna had taken the unusual step of requiring Lewis to avoid all questions of politics in his meeting with McKinley. He had then followed up with the candidate to make sure his orders had been followed. Lewis described Hanna as a "square corpulent figure of a man, with light eyes, light hair, a heavy jaw and whiskers of mutton-chop cut." He was larger, stronger, and more vigorous, both mentally and constitutionally, than McKinley. He was also "vain, and a bit peacocky." Lewis hated him instantly.[12]

Hanna was a Cleveland shipping and steel magnate who, on failing to win the Republican nomination for Ohio senator John Sherman in 1884 and 1888, had decided that William McKinley possessed whatever winning qualities Sherman lacked. Hanna's personal fortune and prodigious organizational skills had been dedicated to McKinley ever since. When Democratic gerrymandering cost his man his congressional seat in 1890, Hanna quickly organized and bankrolled McKinley's successful 1891 run for governor of Ohio. At the 1892 Republican national convention,

McKinley officially supported the frontrunner, Benjamin Harrison, while Hanna worked on McKinley's behalf behind the scenes; together they engineered a respectable second-place finish for the governor without ever declaring his candidacy, positioning him as a leading contender for 1896. When McKinley's career hit another bump in 1893, Hanna was again there to pull him from the ditch: the failure of his friend's tin-plate business had left McKinley on the hook for $130,000. He was contemplating a return to the law to clear his debts until Hanna organized a syndicate of wealthy Republicans whose generous contributions relieved his distress and saved his political career.[13]

More than a year before the 1896 Republican convention, with McKinley in Canton maintaining a disinterested pose, Hanna assembled at his own expense a full-fledged campaign machine and retired from business to better oversee its operations. He opened offices in Chicago, Cleveland, Boston, and Washington and organized campaign workers into a tight and unprecedentedly businesslike structure, complete with tendered contracts and organizational charts. Whereas most Republican bosses had been content to work within their own states or regions and to broker support with other bosses, Hanna bought an impressive home in Thomasville, Georgia, and brought McKinley out for a "vacation" during which they assiduously wooed southern delegates. These tactics and superb organization, and McKinley's broad appeal, allowed Hanna to effectively secure his man's nomination before the regional bosses got their own candidates into the field.[14]

But however brilliant Hanna may have been as a campaign manager, he lacked political tact, as Lewis sensed from their first meeting. His manner was overbearing, by some measures arrogant. His speech was gruff and uncompromisingly frank. He was of the firm opinion that all questions in politics in a democracy came down to money. He had a habit of dismissing old-time Republican political bosses as feckless amateurs. He was capable of hurling ungentlemanly language at the most venerable party stalwarts if they were foolish enough to stand in his way. It struck Lewis as curious that so obviously upright a man as McKinley would hitch himself to this swaggering tycoon. Nor could Lewis understand why McKinley would allow Hanna and his friends to clear his debts. "No man of high sensitive regard for himself would have allowed it," he wrote. "One is left to wonder if the whole moral effect of it all was not to leave McKinley the subject of a syndicate; practically the property of those who took him out of hock."[15]

The notion that McKinley was beholden to his wealthy manager captivated Lewis. He nursed an obsession with Hanna and wasted no time in getting a second interview with him in Cleveland. He found the manager in prime form, "rotund, ruddy, rough." Hanna obliged his visitor with one of his periodic outbursts, describing the eastern Republican bosses Matt Quay and Thomas Platt, both of whom opposed McKinley's nomination, as "the merest political babies." He had expected them to be "astute, far-sighted politicians" and instead he found himself "contending with pigmies."[16] The interview was published in the *Journal* the day after Lewis's McKinley piece.

Lewis continued to poke around Ohio, curious about Hanna's diverse business concerns, the formation of his fortune, his past political adventures, and the nature of his relationship with McKinley. The more he saw, the more outraged he grew, and as his outrage grew, so did his excitement. Lewis had at last found a subject commensurate with his capacity to vituperate.

A few weeks later, Lewis published another article on Hanna, this one entitled "McKinley's Political Manager and His War on Organized Labor." The article opened with a comprehensive assault on Hanna's person and character. Hanna is described this time as "broad, tall, carelessly clothed, and of a red, violent visage." His nature has "all the force and lack of scruple of a torrent." He has a "bushel of brains; coarse they are, but strong as a horse. One could make two McKinleys out of Hanna and have plenty of Hanna left." He is "lacking utterly in human sympathy, a king for selfish egotism, void of an imagination and the ability to put oneself in another's place." He is in love with money, not as a miser but "because he may make men creep and crawl and spring to do his word. This feeds his vanity, and he is vain with all the vulgarity and ostentatious strut of a turkey cock—a fowl, by the way, he much resembles."[17]

All of that is warm-up for Lewis's account of how this "relentless," "rapacious," "ruthless," "ignorant" man has swallowed whole the probable Republican candidate:

> It is as if Hanna had established the picket posts of his commands all about his candidate. No one reaches the McKinley eye or speaks one word to the

McKinley ear without the password of Hanna. He has McKinley in his clutch as ever did hawk have chicken, and he will carry him whither he chooses. That is the pact between them; the understanding upon which Hanna and his syndicate is breaking and buying and begging and bullying a road for McKinley to the White House. And when he's there, Hanna and the others will shuffle him and deal him like a deck of cards.[18]

To what ends would Hanna shuffle and deal McKinley? As the headline suggests, the news value of the piece was Lewis's substantial recounting of a four-year conflict between Hanna and the Seamen's Union, by the end of which Hanna had broken the guild and slashed the wages of his Great Lakes ship workers. Lewis portrayed the tycoon in the worst possible light but Hanna's performance in this incident did provoke the Cleveland Trades Assembly to boycott all of his businesses in 1884. The seamen's dispute became for Lewis a symbol of the ruthlessness and self-interest of Hanna and the capitalists with whom he associated. It was a foretaste, he believed, of what Americans could expect from a White House in which Hanna and his friends exerted influence.[19]

For the next five months, Lewis would repeat and elaborate on this line of attack. His articles were relatively few in number, published irregularly and usually on inside pages, yet they made a deep impression. *Journal* readers were galvanized by Lewis's furious prose and disturbing allegations. Democratic papers across the country reprinted his articles and took up his arguments, forcing responses from Republican papers. Lewis almost single-handedly flushed Hanna from the back rooms of the Republican Party to the front lines of the rhetorical war between the national parties. But it was left to another of Hearst's journalistic weapons to brand Hanna forever in the public mind.

HOMER DAVENPORT MAY BE THE ONLY MAN in the history of journalism literally born to be a cartoonist. His mother, Florinda Davenport, an Oregon farm wife, was a devotee of the famed illustrator Thomas Nast, whose work appeared regularly in *Harper's Weekly*. Around the time she became pregnant with Homer, she read an article by a popular physician on how to give birth to a genius, complete with dietary instructions and mental exercises. She followed it diligently in the hopes of bearing another Thomas Nast. To her delight, Homer, born March 8, 1867, could draw almost before he could walk. She encouraged his nascent talent, making for him a padded bib so that he could lie on his stomach all day and draw with his carpenter's pencil.[20]

Florinda contracted smallpox and died before her son's fourth birthday. Her last wish was that her husband, Thomas, encourage Homer's gifts. Thomas Davenport had read just enough of the classics to have academic ambitions for his son, but as soon as it became clear that Homer was indifferent about his studies, Florinda got her way. When Homer turned seven, father and son left the farm for the metropolis of Silverton, Oregon, population 300. The idea, Homer later explained, was that the budding artist "might live in the Latin Quarter of that village, and inhale any artistic atmosphere that was going to waste."[21]

Homer grew to be a skinny kid with ridiculously long legs and a love of animals, particularly fast horses and fighting cocks. He continued to grind down his carpenter's pencils, sometimes for ten hours a day, on paper, fences, barn doors, outbuildings, and rocks. He was well liked in Silverton, but the townsfolk considered him idle and vague; they doubted he would amount to much—drawing, after all, was not real work. Nor was jawing through long afternoons with the crowd at the shoemaker's shop, "men of great learning and wide experience," Davenport quipped, "who spent all their time playing marbles."[22]

But ambition did finally stir in Davenport. One day, a one-ring circus arrived in Silverton, and when it pulled up stakes, Homer, now in his late teens, left with it. He worked as a clown and animal trainer and spent much of his spare time drawing the circus's small menagerie of horses, a tiger, and an elephant. He liked it well enough until assigned the onerous task of brushing the elephant with linseed oil. The circus quickly lost its charm, although no one would ever draw a better Republican elephant.[23]

Davenport also tried jockeying, despite his long legs, and shoemaking, and he worked for spells as a store clerk and a railway fireman, but he did not last at any of these pursuits. His first attempt at professional illustrating also ended in failure. At his father's urging, he took a position in the art department of the Portland *Oregonian*. Silvertonians were so impressed at this development that they decorated the streets with flowers and bunting and declared a half-day holiday. Davenport bade everyone farewell with a little speech and boarded a train for the big city.

He was back in Silverton before the flowers had wilted, the *Oregonian* having found his talents dispensable.[24]

Pushed by his father to give illustration another chance, Davenport eventually made his way to San Francisco and signed on with Hearst's *Examiner* at $10 a week. At the outset, he was not a cartoonist but a newspaper artist, expected to provide illustrative accompaniment to news and commentary: diagrams and maps, "artist's conceptions" of scenes described by reporters, and sketches from portraits and news photography (direct newspaper reproduction of photography was as yet a few years and a series of technological advances away). Newspaper artists were valued for how quickly and accurately they completed an assignment. Wit and originality were frowned upon. None of this played to Davenport's strengths. Buildings, furniture, and other inanimate objects were beyond him. He was adept at living flesh, but even there his instincts ran against realistic portrayals and toward caricature. He also could not spell, which made him useless with maps and charts. (Davenport once asked the editor Arthur Brisbane if there were two *t*'s in water. Brisbane answered without looking up, "Only the wettest, Homer.")[25]

Whatever his shortcomings, Hearst appears to have been impressed with Davenport from the start. When a famous horse died and the *Examiner* was desperate for an image, Davenport, the former jockey, was able to draw it from memory—he had happened to have seen it run a year earlier. Hearst was so pleased he purchased the original. The formally trained artists on the *Examiner* staff were less impressed. They sneered at Davenport's limits and his self-taught style. Feeling underappreciated, he skipped from the *Examiner* to the *Chronicle* to the *Chicago Daily Herald* and then back to the *Chronicle*, where his renderings of Democratic and Republican leaders became the talk of the 1894 state conventions. Hearst lured him back to the *Examiner* as a full-time cartoonist at a salary of $75 a week, double what the *Chronicle* was paying him.[26]

Still in his twenties, Davenport took his new responsibilities seriously. He began to pay more attention to public affairs, traveling to Sacramento to watch the legislature, studying the process and its participants. He made his biggest splash at the paper with a portrait of San Francisco Democratic boss Sam Rainey, the man at the center of a web of municipal corruption routinely decried by the *Examiner*.

Rainey had always refused to have his face in the papers. Like most

everyone in America, he was aware of Thomas Nast's devastating caricatures of Tammany's Boss Tweed, and he wasn't about to let West Coast
cartoonists get a bead on him. Davenport sauntered down to Rainey's
office next to a stable on California Street and found the pudgy boss
standing outside in his favorite pose—back to a wall, belly thrust forward, head thrown back, fat legs crossed at the ankle, stubby fingers
working a thick cigar. Rainey's henchmen spotted Davenport and chased
him off, but not before his camera-like eye had captured what it needed.
The finished sketch was remarkable for its simplicity. Davenport simply
let Rainey lean against the wall in all his corpulent glory, radiating arrogance and vice from every pore. Hearst gave it an entire front page. San
Franciscans were disgusted. Their first glimpse of Rainey's self-satisfied
mug is said to have hurried the end of the city's old Democratic cabal, a
legend that probably gives Davenport too much credit, but indeed Rainey
and company were soon shipping out to Canada to avoid prosecution.[27]

Whatever his limits as a newspaper artist, Davenport the cartoonist
seemed to get a new job offer with each piece he published. Not long
after he had rejoined the *Examiner,* an eastern paper tried to hire him
away at $100 a week. "My God, Davvy," said Hearst. "That's as much
as the managing editor gets."[28] But Hearst matched the offer and, on
purchasing the *Journal,* took Davenport to New York, where subsequent bids for his services would catapult his salary to $500 a week, far
beyond what any other newspaper writer or artist was making. Hearst
was happy to pay it. Nothing attracted readers and distinguished a
newspaper from its competitors like a brilliant cartoonist, and while
Hearst would assemble at the *Journal* the best team of illustrators any
newspaper had ever seen—Davenport, Richard Outcault, M. de Lipman,
T.E. Powers, Jimmy Swinnerton, Frederick Opper, among others—
there was never any question as to his favorite.

Hearst not only paid Davenport generously, he took an active interest
in making him a star, runnning interference with editors who wanted to
bury his work in the back pages or waste his time sketching corpses at the
morgue. Hearst understood the unique nature of Davenport's talent.
Inspiration wasn't the illustrator's strongest suit—in fact, he was "sadly
destitute of ideas," by Abbot's reckoning. And while his pen was liveliest
when indignant, Davenport wasn't a naturally excitable personality. He fed
off the ideas and outrage of others. Hearst instructed his top editorial

people to meet regularly with the artist, and Hearst himself sometimes joined in as they talked through stories and the paper's various crusades. All this coddling might have spoiled other talents, but it brought out the best in Davenport. His biographers say he did his finest work in Hearst's employ.[29]

Whether Hearst teamed Davenport with Alfred Henry Lewis or they found each other independently is impossible to say, but only a few months into the life of the new *Journal* the two men were close and happy collaborators. Lewis loved to talk and he loved an audience, and he was only too happy to share his abundant outrage with the laconic cartoonist. Davenport first drew McKinley and Hanna shortly after Lewis had conducted his initial interviews in Ohio. He worked from Lewis's verbal and written descriptions and whatever photo-illustrations of the men that were then in circulation. The results were unpromising. Davenport published one cartoon depicting Hanna as an ogre protecting a tiny Napoleonic McKinley from a trio of Republican pygmies (the regional bosses). Another represented manager and candidate in the roles of Paul and Virginia, after the popular Victorian melodrama, with McKinley taking the feminine part. Davenport's McKinley was reasonably convincing, but the face of his Hanna was dead on the page and the body beneath it wasn't much better—an all-purpose body for overfed men of affairs, indistinguishable from the cartoonist's treatment of Speaker Tom Reed.[30] Davenport's efforts did not improve until he got his own hard look at Hanna during the Republican convention in St. Louis.

Davenport began looking for Hanna from the moment he arrived in St. Louis, and once he found him he never let him out of his sights. He followed him around the convention floor and made surreptitious sketches from the corners of crowded hotel lobbies. He was thrilled by what he saw. Not only was Hanna the most imposing presence at the assembly, outclassing in political and personal strength the likes of regional bosses Platt and Quay, but his physiognomy was more interesting than that of any man Davenport had ever beheld. Whether talking, laughing, or just standing still, Hanna exuded great vitality and enormous force. He had the strong and vivid character lines that make a cartoon pop. Davenport knew exactly what to do with him.

Hanna was a tall man. Davenport made him taller, and he further exaggerated his stature by shrinking everyone around him. He doubled Hanna's girth, giving him a thick bull's neck and immense power in his arms, legs, and bulging torso. Hanna's low forehead was drawn lower still. His thin hair was reduced to clumps. His short sideburns were extended and roughed up—"like an unplaned cedar board," Davenport explained. The tip of Hanna's stubby nose was raised a little more and his ears were made to stick out like a monkey's. His grin grew apelike. His eyes were borrowed from all over the bestiary. "Hanna's eye shifts like the eye of a parrot," Davenport noted, "and you can't make a move he does not follow." He also compared Hanna's eyes to those of a circus elephant in a parade scanning the street for peanuts.[31]

Davenport's caricature yielded a large brute of some utterly new species. His Hanna was cheerful, vigorous, overpowering, and ruthless. He was keenly intelligent and aware of everything but himself. He came with a few props: his big clown's feet liked to rest on bulging bags of money or the white skulls of laborers. And he had a sidekick, McKinley, who stood as tall as his own Napoleonic hat (a mere five foot six, McKinley was sensitive about his height).[32] Davenport gave McKinley all the grace and good looks that Hanna lacked, and however ridiculous his situation—chained to the wall in Hanna's office, begging for the core of an apple Hanna was about to eat whole—McKinley always carried himself with dignity.

Powerful as this new work was, Davenport still felt he hadn't nailed Hanna. He brooded about him in the wake of the convention before adding a final touch. Davenport had been dressing Hanna as per Lewis's reports in a plaid businessman's suit and striped shirt. The only flourish had been a set of dollar-sign cufflinks. Now Davenport took the dollar signs from the cufflinks and placed one in each of the large checks on Hanna's suit. This single device conveyed at a glance everything Lewis and Davenport wanted to say about the Republican manager's social and political philosophies. Brazen greed and moneyed arrogance were now woven into the fabric of Hanna's clothes. It was a brilliant stroke, but a night editor thought it overkill and pulled the cartoon; Hearst saw it and ordered it published. Davenport would later say the idea for the dollar signs came to him during his conversations with Lewis, but more likely it was suggested by his colleague, M. de Lipman, who in May had drawn McKinley as a mute Buddha in a loincloth with Hanna as his attendant wearing a polka-dot robe with dollar signs in each dot. Whatever its origins, Davenport's "plutocratic plaid," as it became known, was an instant hit.[33]

Davenport depicted Hanna as a tailor attempting to draw a reluctant

Uncle Sam into his shop for his own suit of plutocratic plaid. He portrayed Hanna as a woman in a bonnet and dress of plutocratic plaid; a childlike McKinley tugs at her skirts, pointing to a store window where the "labor vote" is for sale. These gags were moderately successful, but Davenport was not a natural comedian. A moralist at heart, his best pieces deal in darker emotions. They are simple in conception and somber in mood. In one, Hanna fills almost the whole frame, wearing his straw hat at a jaunty angle and the broadest of grins as he bounces down Wall Street with bags of money in each hand; far in the background, the personification of labor hangs from a street lamp. In another cartoon, you see only Hanna's tree trunk of a wrist and his meaty fist with its rough skin and stubbly hair. A cufflink bearing his name peeks out from under a coat sleeve of plutocratic plaid. The fist clenches a fob chain, dangling from which is the tiny, dejected figure of McKinley, yoked at the neck, legs and arms shackled, still somehow dignified. Hanna appears to have just pulled the candidate from his pocket to show his friends.[34]

Davenport's cartoons ran a few times a week, usually on inside pages, but nothing in any paper came close to matching their impact. Like Lewis's pieces, they were widely reprinted and circulated as Democratic campaign materials, and Hanna couldn't appear anywhere without fielding unwanted questions about the cartoons. There were rumors of a late-night meeting between artist and subject in which Hanna attempted to induce Davenport to drop the plaid. Hanna apparently considered suing the *Journal* and wrote a letter of protest to Hearst, to no avail. Perhaps the best testament to the power of Davenport's caricature and the speed with which it took hold was an article in Pulitzer's *World* less than two months after the St. Louis convention. Its headline was "How Mark Hanna Really Looks":

> When men, especially politicians, become famous they are subjects for cari-
> caturists; but usually men become famous by slow degrees and the public
> has a chance to become familiar with their exact features through authentic
> likenesses of them published from time to time during their ascent of the
> ladder of fame. Mark Hanna, however, bounded into national prominence
> so quickly that the caricaturists got in their work ahead of the portrait
> artists. The consequence is that the masses of the people have come to know
> him as the caricaturists represent him, not as he is. This would not be so bad

if caricaturists of the present day had not become so enslaved to grotesque Aubrey Beardsleyism as to try to outdo each other in exaggeration. Each one appears to have tried to go his rival one better in making Mr. Hanna hideous, and the result is that the general public has a most false idea of him in the mind's eye. The public thinks of him as being a weird nightmare—a being with a tapering pate, bulging eyes, huge chops and a gruesome grin.[35]

The article explained that Hanna was, in reality, fairly good-looking and as typically American as either Bryan or McKinley. The *World* neglected to acknowledge that the Hanna phenomenon had been generated largely by Davenport and the *Journal*, nor did it mention that a few weeks earlier it had attempted its own weak and short-lived imitations of the caricature, complete with a diminutive McKinley in a Napoleonic hat.[36]

Davenport guessed early that his caricatures of Hanna would define his career. On August 8, less than two months after he had followed Hanna around the Republican convention, he published a cartoon of "Dollar Mark" seen full-figure from behind, standing at ease, his weight on one hip, his hands clasped loosely behind his back. His gaze is directed high on the wall in front of him at Thomas Nast's famous caricature of Boss Tweed—the one with a money bag for a head and a dollar sign, slightly contorted, to represent the features of his face. Hanna stands in homage to Tweed; Davenport draws in tribute to Nast. Seeing the caricatures together in one cartoon, it seems Davenport had his idol in mind all along: the distinctive dollar sign from Tweed's face is the same as the dollar signs in Hanna's plaid suits. If Davenport is suggesting a comparison between his caricature and Nast's, he comes up short. Nast is the master of American caricature. But given that Nast was the Davenport family deity, it was probably enough for Homer to have found a character of his own at least comparable to Tweed. Florinda would have been proud.

Daily newspapers had been running cartoons for decades prior to 1896, but the finest cartoonists and their best work had always appeared in magazines—*Harper's Weekly, Vanity Fair, Judge, Puck.* Davenport's Hanna set a new standard for draftsmanship, substance, and sustained impact in newspaper art. So far as histories of American caricature are concerned, the daily medium begins to matter with Dollar Mark. But while Davenport won plaudits within his own profession, he and Alfred Henry Lewis and their proprietor were excoriated everywhere else.

The *Journal*'s coverage of McKinley and Hanna has been described by historians and Hearst biographers as a one-sided, distorted, unethical, vitriolic, and "maliciously injurious" effort to bludgeon the Republican ticket. They charge that Hearst and company deliberately distorted and misrepresented the McKinley-Hanna association and that the candidate was in fact a smart political operator with an agreeable personality, a winning platform, and sufficient clout to have gained the Republican nomination without Hanna's help. A surprising number of scholars cite Davenport's work as their primary beef with the *Journal*'s coverage. They complain of "cruelty" and "distortions," and of a "brutal" and "perverted" ingenuity in the cartoons.[37]

The *Journal*'s critics are not entirely wrong. Davenport's work was indeed distorted and cruel, but cartoonists, like satirists, do not deal in polite and literal representations of the world. Alfred Henry Lewis was gratuitously nasty and guilty of all manner of overstatement: McKinley was not really just a stalking horse for plutocrats, and Hanna's mistreatment and neglect of his employees did not lead to a thousand deaths, but, again, partisan invective and riotous hyperbole were the tools of his trade. Ohio governor Joseph B. Foraker, himself a world-class mudslinger, said it was expected of newspapers to "call the man with whom they do not happen to agree, a liar, a thief, a villain, a scoundrel, a Yahoo, a marplot, a traitor, a beast, anything and everything they may be able to command in the way of an epithet."[38] Bryan, as we shall see, was treated in the same manner by the Republican press. Howling partisanship and bitter rhetorical excess were givens in this era, and understood by readers as more stylistic than substantive.

The further charge that Hearst served up relentlessly biased coverage of the Republican campaign is based on an exceedingly narrow reading of the *Journal*'s election coverage. Most historians confine themselves to the work of Lewis and Davenport, as though they represent the whole of the paper. Hearst, in fact, gave regular space to dispassionate coverage of Republican affairs, as well as to pro-Republican opinion. None of his critics has noted that the *Journal* published a full-page rebuttal of Alfred Henry Lewis by the famous Republican correspondent Murat Halstead, a regular contributor to the paper. "It is nonsense," wrote Halstead, "to attribute the immense and overwhelming McKinley movement, which is gaining every hour, to the management of one man, Mr. Hanna. Of course, Mr. Hanna deserves great credit for his organizing capacity but he has been responding to an unmistakable and irresistible public sentiment that he did not create, and that is the recognition by the people of McKinley's sincerity and force of character—his comprehensive and particular intelligence and faithful and unflinching following of the great principle [protectionism] of which he is the leading expounder and most conspicuous representative."[39]

The *Journal*'s editorial page occasionally echoed Lewis's basic read of the McKinley-Hanna relationship, describing the former as a "puppet" and the latter as an "overbearing, conscienceless, dominant man of money bags."[40] Generally speaking, however, the editorial page avoided extremes. It often presented McKinley as a wholly respectable politician and, early in May, it actually leapt to McKinley's defense when he was characterized in other quarters as "a disreputable old shuffler" and an "unscrupulous bird of prey."[41] At a personal level, it rated him "wholly admirable—even lovable." Hearst ran a touching front-page feature on the candidate's courtship and marriage, and his tender care for his invalid wife of twenty-five years.[42]

While it is difficult to find Hanna declared "lovable" in the *Journal* (or anywhere else, for that matter), there are numerous instances of respectful treatment. The paper ran a lengthy summary of Hanna's essay in defense of the gold standard, and played on the front page his self-interested analyses of the nomination race.[43] It ran a cheerful little interview with Mrs. Hanna (her first), and placed a magisterial portrait of the man on its front at the opening of the St. Louis convention.[44] When Hanna made a mid-campaign visit to New York, a *Journal* photographer and reporter tracked him through every minute of a long business day. Their richly detailed coverage, headlined "24 Hours with the Great Republican Boss," started with Hanna rising without benefit of alarm at 7 a.m. in suite 712 of the Waldorf. He sat on the edge of the tub as it filled with water: "It is at this moment that some of his most subtle political combinations are mapped out." He took the elevator down to the second floor, where his favorite barber, Dan, gave him a two-cent shave and accepted a twenty-five-cent tip. Hanna then took a fistful of mail and telegrams to the dining room and did his correspondence while enjoying a "frugal" breakfast of cantaloupe, boiled eggs, chops, and coffee. On it went until his head hit the pillow at 11 p.m. The piece could not have been done without Hanna's cooperation.[45] The *Journal* was fair to its opponents by conventional standards.

Perhaps the greatest injustice concerning Hearst's performance in 1896 is that outrage at Lewis and Davenport has overshadowed the paper's coverage of the Republican convention. The *Journal* on that occasion produced by far the most interesting, innovative, and wide-ranging file of any New York paper. Its June 11 front page introduced four marquee correspondents sent to the convention along with a large corps of *Journal* reporters, editors, and illustrators. Representing the paper's politics were Alfred Henry Lewis and Henry George, a one-time candidate for mayor of New York and perhaps American's leading champion of the income tax. Providing insight from a Republican perspective were Murat Halstead and J.J. Ingalls, an eighteen-year Republican senator from Kansas. As a group, they gave Hearst geographical, ideological, and stylistic diversity and, in George and Halstead, experience of U.S. political conventions dating back to the Civil War.[46]

All of the New York papers fielded teams of journalists to St. Louis, but none sent anywhere near so diverse and celebrated a group of pundits as the *Journal*, and no other gave its talent significant promotion. Typical of the competition was the *World*, which dispatched James Creelman to write the bulk of its color and analysis and gave him only his usual byline at the end of his pieces. Creelman's opinions were consistent with the *World*'s editorial line. Editors like Pulitzer, Dana, and Whitelaw Reid believed their papers should speak with one voice on political matters: the editor's voice. They were notoriously stingy in crediting their contributors. Hearst broke sharply with this tradition, giving his pundits not only bylines but page-one bylines with pictures, and he would run as many as three of their commentaries on the front page on the same day. In so doing, he hastened the end of the so-called Age of the Editor and helped to usher in the multi-perspective approach we identify with the modern op-ed page. No other significant American paper was operating this way at the time.

But critics of the *Journal*'s coverage may still have a point. Even if one acknowledges that Hearst's journalism was far more nuanced and balanced than has been credited, and even if one accepts that viciousness and rhetorical extremism were standard fare in nineteenth-century journalism, there remains the charge that Hearst and company were fundamentally wrong about the nature of the McKinley-Hanna partnership and that they smeared both men.

There is no doubt that the *Journal* exaggerated the whole "puppet" issue: it was exploiting Hanna's vulnerabilities to undermine his candidate. McKinley was a capable man with a mind of his own, a strong following, and valuable political instincts. Still, the *Journal*'s basic complaint is not easily dismissed.

McKinley was unusually indebted to Hanna, who repeatedly bailed him out, financially and politically. No one credits McKinley with any organizational or fundraising acumen. In fact, he is said to have had a "curious lack of talent for party organizational work."[47] If, as an alternative to Hanna's support, he had offered himself up to the regional bosses, he would have emerged a seriously compromised candidate, running with their issues, their speeches, and their vice-presidential choice, and he would have had to hold his nose at their boodling ways. Hanna's money bought McKinley freedom from everything but Hanna.

In attacking the *Journal*'s contention that Hanna was the larger or stronger personality, McKinley's defenders make much of testimony and correspondence suggesting that Hanna addressed McKinley in deferential tones and followed his lead on matters of policy. Almost all of this evidence comes from McKinley's intimates, men protective of his reputation, and none of it was available to reporters in the summer of 1896. Indeed, all but a few scraps date from after the election, by which time McKinley and Hanna had suffered an unholy beating from the Hearst press, leaving McKinley sensitive to any appearance of subordination to Hanna.

At the time Hearst and his journalists were sizing up McKinley, he had yet to gain the sheen of high office. He was a decent man and a plausible candidate, but Alfred Henry Lewis was not alone in considering him a mediocrity. Even McKinley's friendly biographers admit that he had "few intellectual resources"[48] and little in the way of taste or erudition. The Republican-friendly journalist William Allen White regarded McKinley as "a kindly dull gentleman . . . on the whole dumb, and rarely reaching above the least common denominator of the popular intelligence. . . . He walked among men like a bronze statue . . . determinedly looking for his pedestal."[49]

Hanna, on the other hand, *did* cut an extraordinary figure at the time. No one had ever come closer to establishing the role of political boss and kingmaker on the national level. He had dominated the Republican convention, shaped the party's platform, selected the running mate

(Garrett Hobart of New Jersey), and grasped every lever of the campaign machinery. St. Louis became known as "Hanna's convention."[50] Especially during the nomination period, he exercised unusual control over public access to his candidate while himself commenting in the press on every aspect of the Republican campaign.[51] It was not unreasonable to see Hanna as the stronger personality from the vantage point of mid-campaign. The question of strength, however, is somewhat beside the point. The *Journal* portrayed McKinley as the subordinate figure in their relationship more because he was beholden to Hanna than because of perceived weakness in character.

McKinley's defenders dismiss the $130,000 bailout as inconsequential because the recipient was honorable, but someone had to ask the questions posed by the *Journal:* Was the money put up as "a gift or a loan? If as a gift, does Mr. McKinley feel any sense of obligation for their kindness. . . . If as a loan, what was the security, and when and how does Mr. McKinley expect to pay it back?"[52] It was arrogant of Hanna to brush off the bailout as a private matter between friends. Even in the Republican press, it was widely assumed that Hanna would gain from his many services to McKinley, influencing appointments, patronage, and policy in a new government, and perhaps taking a senior cabinet seat for himself. New York Republicans touted Hanna as the next secretary of the treasury.[53]

The prospect of Hanna and friends throwing their weight around Washington was naturally and legitimately ominous to the *Journal* and its Democratic audience. Some of Hanna's pro-business views were radical for the time, such as his belief that government existed primarily to protect and promote commercial enterprise. He loathed the income tax, supported protective tariffs, and saw nothing inherently wrong in the proliferation of trusts and monopolies. It is true that Hanna held some relatively enlightened views on labor, but, as Lewis reported, he did have some bad history with his ship workers and he had resorted to lethal force to settle the Massillon, Ohio, coal miners' strike of 1876. Governor McKinley, for his part, had repeatedly used the National Guard to negotiate with strikers in Ohio. And Hanna's election coffers were being filled by some of the most controversial employers in the United States, including Andrew Carnegie and Henry Clay Frick, hosts of the 1892 Homestead debacle, one of the bloodiest strikes in U.S. labor history.[54]

A good many Republicans shared the misgivings that Lewis, Davenport, and Hearst raised about Hanna. The seeds of Lewis's arguments were gathered in conversation with McKinley's Republican foes in Ohio who knew the details of Hanna's $130,000 gift—it had been a controversy in the last gubernatorial campaign.[55] The vanquished regional bosses Tom Platt and Matt Quay initiated denunciations of Hanna's methods and money; they also lambasted McKinley as weak and evasive on policy. The only serious opponent McKinley faced on his path to the nomination—Tom Reed, Speaker of the House of Representatives—made "liberal accusations about his alleged weakness" and about Hanna's use of funds to purchase delegates.[56] Theodore Roosevelt, who made speeches for McKinley in '96, complained to friends that the nominee had the "backbone of a chocolate éclair," and that Hanna was selling him "as if he were a patent medicine."[57]

Finally, critics of the *Journal*'s coverage need also take into account the degree to which Hanna and McKinley had made targets of themselves. Hanna, who had never held an office or troubled himself with serious policy deliberations, who mocked and bullied reigning Republican grandees, who proclaimed that government existed as the handmaiden to business, and who declared that money was all that mattered in politics, shouldn't really have been surprised to find himself caricatured as an oversized brute bicycling through the *Journal* in a "Dollar Mark" suit. Likewise, McKinley, sitting mute and debt-free in his humble Canton home as Hanna strode about moving heaven and earth to get him elected, might have expected his own portrayal.

The *Journal* did err in its coverage of Hanna and McKinley, and some of its positions were at best arguable. There was merit, nonetheless, to its core arguments about the Republican duo. The paper was asking important questions and playing its oppositional role superbly throughout the summer of 1896. Lewis and Davenport produced the most powerful journalistic statements in what was emerging as an epochal presidential campaign and it is much to their credit that one cannot discuss McKinley and '96 today without mention of the *Journal*'s role. That role would only grow as voting day approached.

CHAPTER SEVEN

Skin the East and
Skin the Rich

About two o'clock of the hottest night of the famous hot summer of 1896, when all New York sweltered and the breathless air dripped with a rank humidity, a young man ran at fierce speed down the middle of Park Row. The panting wayfarers about the [Brooklyn] Bridge entrance and the tired newspaper men homeward bound looked at the running figure with manifest discomposure; his hot haste and hard work seemed to raise the temperature. He was a good-looking young man, well dressed, [and] except for his exertions in such an atmosphere, apparently sane. He carried a straw hat in one hand and an open newspaper in the other, and wholly oblivious of disparaging comment, he held his way to the Tribune Building, up the steps of which he bounded three at a time, and disappeared.

I had never seen him before, but I knew from certain descriptions that this was W. R. Hearst, the new proprietor of the *New York Journal*. The next day Park Row buzzed with the cause of his feat of unseasonable athletics. It was so simple that it made men laugh and stare; yet nothing could have been more characteristic. Reading his paper on his way home from the office he had found something he did not like. With him there had been no time to waste in waiting for street-cars or cabs. From almost Chatham Square he had run to his office to have the error corrected in the next edition.

—CHARLES EDWARD RUSSELL, *Harper's Weekly*[1]

T he weather was a big story in the summer of 1896. By season's end, close to a thousand deaths had been attributed to extreme temperatures and humidity—the worst toll in memory. Dogs, mad from the heat, were being shot in the street by policemen. So many horses had perished that the trams were idle. If indeed Hearst's hot haste and hard work had contributed to the swelter, he at least had something to show for it when the temperatures dropped to a bearable range in September. His newspaper was still in the red, but its losses were manageable and accepted as the price of its phenomenal growth in circulation, advertising revenue, editorial talent, influence, and prestige. His new press capacity was coming on stream. His staff had intercepted a circular from Pulitzer to news agents around the country asking how many copies of the *Journal* they received and sold, and what special tactics the paper employed to boost sales. Hearst flaunted the memo on his front page as evidence of Pulitzer's desperation, and also used the occasion to boast of a daily circulation of 378,694—"the largest morning circulation of any newspaper printed in the English language."[2]

That boast was made possible in part because Hearst found himself playing an ever more significant role in what was shaping up as one of the most exciting elections in American history. The currency issue had polarized the major parties and the electorate and had driven every other significant newspaper in the Northeast either into the gold camp or onto the sidelines.[3] This left the *Journal* as the leading print champion of Bryan, the leading critic of McKinley, and the leading opponent of the gold standard. To be so sharply distinguished from its competitors in the heat of a closely watched campaign was a marvelous break for an emerging paper in a crowded market. And having loaded up on journalists with powerful voices and progressive views, Hearst had the fighting spirit and intellectual muscle to hold his ground.

The most unexpected development of the summer was that the presidential race was close. Coming out of the conventions, the supposedly unbeatable Republicans suddenly appeared vulnerable. They might have had a solid candidate, a state-of-the-art organization, buckets of money, and vast newspaper support, but they had no answer for William Jennings Bryan.

On paper, the Democratic nominee was a weak link in his party's campaign. He was a relatively unknown ex-congressman from the lightly populated and politically inconsequential state of Nebraska. He was only a year over the minimum age requirement for the presidency (thirty-five), he had no executive experience, and he had never played an important role in a national campaign. Yet it was Bryan's unique talents and determination that were propelling the Democrats within reach of a massive upset.

A true populist with an unaffected love of his fellow man and an abiding faith in the processes of democracy, Bryan knew intuitively that his party's best chance lay in his own direct connection with voters. While it was not unusual by the 1890s for a presidential candidate to venture out and shake a few hands in advance of polling day, the preferred approach was still to sit statesmanlike on one's own front porch as the party's professionals raised the obligatory commotion. It had been good enough for George Washington, and it had worked for Grover Cleveland, who reportedly made a grand total of eight speeches and journeyed all of 312 miles in three national election campaigns. Bryan boarded a train immediately after his nomination and quickly smashed all records for travel and speechmaking in pursuit of the White House. After his first forty-five days of campaigning, the *World* ran a map of the United States showing all of the 172 towns and cities in which he had delivered his 205 speeches. The paper estimated that he had spoken more words on the stump and traveled farther than all presidential contenders put together in the previous 100 years.[4] By the time the ballots were counted Bryan would travel 18,000 miles and talk to as many as five million Americans.[5]

The Republicans harrumphed at Bryan's lack of dignity, but Americans could not get enough of this handsome young man and his eloquent message of compassion and hope. "It was the first time in my life and in the life of a generation," remembered William Allen White, "in which any man large enough to lead a national party had boldly and unashamedly made his cause that of the poor and oppressed."[6] Spontaneous gatherings of supporters and curiosity seekers turned out at all hours at every stop along Bryan's routes. They listened keenly to his arguments on the currency, on the travails of labor, and on the merits of an income tax. They thrilled at his powerful delivery. They swooned at his wavy chestnut hair and his gallantry—one warm day, he interrupted himself in mid-speech to share his drinking water with women in the front rows of his pressing crowd. As he piled up the miles, his audiences multiplied, and he proved incapable of disappointing them. He would speak as many as thirty times a day. He caught catnaps of twenty minutes to an hour between stops and ate food by the tableload to keep up his strength. After a long talk on a hot afternoon, he would cool off by wiping down with a gin-soaked rag and then venture out to press the flesh. He would drag himself from his bed in the middle of the night and appear on the rear platform of his railcar in his nightshirt to offer an appreciative wave to supporters. Rolling into a station during his morning shave, he would stick his lathered face out the window for a cheerful salute. It might have been undignified by conventional measures, but it moved the people.

The Democratic press, led by Pulitzer and Hearst, did an effective job of capturing the popular mania for Bryan. The Republican papers didn't so much describe the phenomenon as deplore it, but all reporters who spent any time with Bryan that summer understood they were witnessing something extraordinary. The *Journal*'s Julian Hawthorne watched in awe as crowds in the Midwest mobbed Bryan's moving train at risk of life and limb and old men climbed on the joists of railway sheds to get a glimpse of the candidate:

> The mass of them were poor people—men in dirty shirts and bad hats . . . rough-handed famers, small storekeepers, day laborers, clerks and their wives, sisters and children. . . . The numbers grew as we passed on, and the stifling night was succeeded by the sweltering day. . . . You could not look in their multitudinous homely faces, pinched, and hardened by laborious days and narrow circumstances, without feeling that they were in earnest, in desperate earnest. They did not know how to express their feelings gracefully and becomingly. . . . All they could do was to grin and laugh excitedly and to utter ever and anon, singly or in concert, that shrill "Hi, hi, hi!" which passes in country districts for a cheer.
>
> But you saw the motive power of these abortive demonstrations in their eyes, in the strained, tense look concentrated with painful unanimity on that single figure in the black alpaca sack coat and the grey felt hat who stood on the step of the car bowing and giving both his hands to all who could fight their way through the wedged mass to grasp them. It was a look such as drowning men bend on approaching succor, a pathetic, you might say a terrible look.[7]

JULIAN HAWTHORNE was the son of the novelist Nathaniel Hawthorne, and another of Hearst's prized literary recruits. Educated at Harvard and

trained as an engineer, he had been abused by reviewers early in his writing career for possessing none of his father's genius. In later years, he
would serve twenty-four months in an Atlanta penitentiary for orchestrating a Canadian mining swindle. In between, life was good. He was
fifty-one years old in 1896, the author of twenty-six novels, and one of
New York's leading men of letters. While not a profound or original
thinker, he knew how to hold a reader's attention. Months before joining
the *Journal*, he had beaten more than a thousand contestants to win the
New York Herald's novel-writing competition with an entry dashed off in
three weeks and submitted under a pseudonym. Before Hearst called,
Hawthorne had never reported for dailies, but after getting a taste of life
in the *Journal* stable, he would never seriously return to fiction.
Newspaper work was exciting and remunerative, and whatever fame he
brought to the paper as a novelist was compounded by his exposure
through the *Journal*. His dispatches frequently ran on the front page,
accompanied by a picture byline that revealed fine features and a fabulously bushy mustache.[8]

The *Journal* deployed Hawthorne less as a political analyst than as a
sketch writer or scene setter. Every day Bryan would make another series
of stops along the tracks, and every day Hawthorne would painstakingly
record the differences in the towns, their inhabitants, their reception of
the candidate, and the content and manner of Bryan's addresses.
Hawthorne did his best to make each encounter sound fresh and to put
faces on the crowds. An unabashed admirer of Bryan, he had an annoy-
ing tendency to gush at his performances, but he nonetheless studied him
as intently as any other reporter, and Hearst would keep him on Bryan's
trail for the duration of the campaign.

Pulitzer relied for his coverage of the Democratic candidate on James
Creelman, a young man who may have lacked a Harvard education and
a literary pedigree but who stood second to none as a newspaper
correspondent.

Creelman was born in Montreal, but his parents split when he was a
toddler and his mother moved to New York City. Miserable with his
father, Creelman scraped together a handful of coins and at age twelve
walked most of the four hundred miles to New York, arriving at the
doorstep of his mother's rooming house "with worn-out shoes and a
nickel in his pocket."[9] He needn't have troubled himself; he wasn't much

happier with his mother, who demanded he attend school. He refused, preferring to apprentice as a printer for an Episcopalian church newspaper. By age eighteen, he had parlayed that experience into a job as a cub reporter for the *New York Herald*.

Creelman quickly won a reputation for fearlessness in pursuit of stories. He broke his arm after boarding an experimental airship that crashed in a farmer's field and dragged him for several miles. He was rescued from the East River after testing a newly invented but unperfected diving suit. These sacrifices led to more substantial assignments: he paddled down the Missouri to interview Sitting Bull, and he was shot at by one of the Hatfields while covering their feud with the McCoys in Kentucky.

The *Herald* eventually sent Creelman to London as its special correspondent. He conducted interviews with Pope Leo XIII and Tolstoy, and served for two years (1891–92) as editor of the Paris *Herald*, accomplishments that won him high esteem in journalistic circles. He was still unknown to the great public, however, since the *Herald*'s proprietor, James Gordon Bennett, permitted no bylines. In 1894, Creelman jumped to Pulitzer's *World*, where he was allowed to sign his name to the end of his stories.

The *World* gained a reporter thirty-four years old and at the top of his game: bold, intelligent, with an almost religious devotion to his craft. Unlike other newspapermen of "special correspondent" status, Creelman had no literary aspirations. He was an American reporter, and so far as he was concerned there was no more exalted calling. His job was to bear witness to the greatest events and personages on the planet. The work, he admitted, was profane, invasive, and frequently dangerous, but it was also of real social purpose. Journalism could foster communication and understanding, and to Creelman's mind, communication and understanding were salves to all the world's ills. Assigned to cover the Sino-Japanese War, he visited the hot center of the battle at Pyongyang. He beheld the Chinese fighting in the rain under colorful oilpaper umbrellas and suffering enormous casualties in misguided cavalry offensives. After the Japanese victory, he journeyed to Seoul for an unprecedented interview with the king of Korea:

> The American public must be allowed to see the inmost throne of the royal palace; American journalism must invade the presence of the hermit monarch—to touch whose person was an offense punishable by death—

see his face, question him, and weave his sorrows into some up-to-date political moral. The artificial majesty of kings, after all, counts for little before the leveling processes of the modern newspaper power. It may be intrusive, it may be irreverent, it may be destructive of sentiment; but it gradually breaks down the walls of tradition and prejudice that divide the human race.[10]

Pulitzer was lucky to still have Creelman. They had quarrelled in February over the reporter's desire for more independence in his assignments and in the expression of his opinions. Notwithstanding that he had just lost Goddard and his whole Sunday crew to Hearst, Pulitzer decided that Creelman had "outgrown a subordinate position" and rendered himself destructive to the *World*'s harmony. He accepted Creelman's resignation but kept him on retainer, a "special assignment" that would save the *World*'s campaign.[11]

Creelman spent the spring of 1896 in Cuba, reporting on the Spanish government's increasingly brutal efforts to suppress rebellion on the island, before covering the party conventions and the presidential campaign. During his six weeks on the Bryan tour, Creelman sketched the scenes along Bryan's trail more evocatively than the novelist Hawthorne: "The next stopping place was Charleston, the scene of one of Lincoln's never-to-be-forgotten debates with Douglas. Here was another crowd of 10,000. Mr. Bryan's wife stepped from the car to a great roofed platform on wheels, which was pushed through the immense multitude, rocking and dipping among its surging faces like a ship in a storm. It rained, and as the gray drizzle descended hundreds of umbrellas moved above the multitude like gleaming black turtles."[12]

Creelman also gave considerable thought to what made Bryan tick, hoping to lift the lid on Bryan's "simplicity and apparent innocence." As he sat with him at breakfast one morning, he studied his face and discerned two contrary natures. In the candidate's high forehead and clear hazel eyes, Creelman saw the strong moral qualities of the born commander. Something in his jaw and the set of his mouth, however, suggested the desperado:

What would such a man be in the White House? What latent power for good or evil lies hidden in that restless, tireless brain to be called forth by some sudden crisis? . . . His youth and his radicalism invite investigation, and it is not hard to understand why every man who comes into the special car searches his face. That is one of the most impressive things about this wonderful journey. Men watch him as they might watch a developing child, marveling at his courage and endurance and wondering what new mental or moral trait he will display next. Already every man in his party knows that behind this seeming innocence and careless frankness of the young leader there is not only an ambition that never sleeps, but a rapidly expanding political shrewdness that takes not of the smallest trifles.[13]

BY THE END OF AUGUST, Bryan was widely considered to have caught McKinley, but the Republicans were hardly giving up the fight. Hanna canceled his vacation and stepped up his fundraising and promotional efforts. He urged McKinley to board a train and meet the people in the manner of Bryan, but McKinley, certain that he could never compete with the Democrat in electoral athletics, wisely insisted upon a front-porch campaign that emphasized his stolid and reliable qualities. Hanna had to settle for bringing the people to his candidate, and he succeeded in spectacular fashion. Some 750,000 pilgrims from thirty states fell on Canton that summer.[14] They arrived by foot, on horseback, and in buggies, but mostly by train (encouraged by the cheap fares Hanna wrangled from supportive railway executives). Some of the delegations were large enough to include choirs and marching bands, and all of them bore gifts, including flowers, walking canes, fresh-baked pies, the polished stump of a Tennessee tree, and the largest plate of galvanized iron yet produced in the United States.[15] The visitors trampled the grass on McKinley's lawn and cheered his pitch for a new era of Republican prosperity. While not a riveting speaker, McKinley carefully choreographed his front-porch entrances and exits, and tweaked his scripted remarks to better suit the particular geographic or occupational concerns of each set of callers, and tried to leave them all with something memorable.

With his candidate thus occupied, Hanna spent his days delivering the most audacious fundraising pitches Wall Street had ever heard. Instead of begging for donations, Hanna "levied" banks and insurers a percentage of their assets; wealthy individuals were "assessed" at 2 percent of their estimated annual income, the level of a proposed Democratic income tax on high earners.[16] One of his associates recalled Hanna returning from lunch with $50,000 in cash from a railroad magnate and forwarding a check in the same amount from another tycoon later in the day.[17] The likes of Carnegie, Rockefeller, Morgan, Huntington, and Armour all ponied up to preserve the high-tariff business environment they sincerely believed was best for America, and also to preserve their personal fortunes from harebrained Democratic monetary theorists. By early August, reports from Republican sources estimated the party's war chest at $10 million or more. The exact amount Hanna raised and spent was probably less than that but has never been determined. All that is certain is that previous spending records were shattered: at a minimum the party more than doubled its 1892 expenditure.

Hanna employed the money to great effect. In addition to the usual brass bands, parades and rallies, posters, buttons, and balloons, the McKinley campaign printed and mailed a mind-boggling 250 million documents. Its staff of writers and artists generated 275 different pamphlets—many of them reproduced in English, Italian, Polish, Greek, and Yiddish, among other languages—along with mounds of pro-Republican copy and cartoons for sympathetic newspapers. It paid for and carefully monitored the deployment of a regular roster of 1,400 speakers whose job it was to spread the McKinley gospel from town to town.[18] Hanna organized separate bureaus catering to special-interest and minority groups: "colored" bureaus, women's bureaus, bureaus for bicycling enthusiasts and traveling salesmen. The campaign even paid for spies at Democratic headquarters.[19]

The *Journal* continued to chronicle Hanna's operations and to denounce his efforts to marry "representatives of consolidated capital" to the Republican machine. The paper presented itself and the Democrats as the champions of the rights of the many against the privileges of the few. Less than three weeks into the campaign, the chair of the Democratic National Committee had written Hearst that his support was making Bryan's election a possibility.[20] All of which may have made the *Journal* and its readers feel good, but Hearst knew as well as anyone that his lone voice was no match for Hanna's magnificent promotional racket, backed by a near unanimous chorus of eastern newspapers. Moreover, it appeared to the same reporters who credited Bryan with massive gains in popular support that his organization was by late summer running out of steam.

Bryan, in fact, did not have an organization.[21] He had a mass following and a loose, scattered network of allies and operatives. Outside of the South, the local and state Democratic machines gave him spotty support, if any. Prominent New York Democrats refused to take the stage with him when he first appeared at Madison Square Garden; Tammany had endorsed the ticket but kept a pointed silence on the platform and largely sat out the campaign; the business community closed ranks against the candidate. Bryan's Democratic Party, rued the *Journal*, had become "too Democratic to suit them."[22] As a result, Bryan was critically short of money, logistical support, strategic advice, and field intelligence. He was often guessing as to where he should spend his time. He would arrive in new towns to find no party officials among the people gathered to greet him; his skeletal traveling staff was not competent to direct his glad-handing or tune his remarks to local sensibilities. If his trains were late or connections were missed, Bryan often handled his own rescheduling. He also managed most of his own correspondence, and more than once reporters saw him carry his own bags off the train and walk unaccompanied to his hotel.[23] Having raised roughly $150,000 by September, he had no money to hire stump speakers or to match the literature spewing from the Republican camp. Standard Oil alone contributed $250,000 to Hanna's campaign.[24] The House of Morgan matched that amount.[25] Bryan's $150,000 didn't do a lot more than keep him on the road.

Incensed at the financial disparity between the Democratic and Republican campaigns, Hearst stepped into the breach. Throughout the summer, the *Journal* had been promoting Bryan but making a show of even-handedness on the currency issue. Much of its editorial page had been given over to a feature entitled "Battle of the Standards," where interested parties were encouraged to present arguments for and against the free coinage of silver. Hearst now junked "Battle of the Standards" in favour of a direct campaign to raise funds for Bryan:

Never in the history of American politics has there been such a discrepancy in the means at the disposal of two contending parties as now. The Republican party has enlisted the services of almost all the holders of accumulated wealth in the country. . . . The result is that the country is flooded with sound money documents designed to convince the voter that bimetallism would reduce the independent American citizen to the level of the Chinese coolie and the Mexican peon. . . .

The *Journal* feels that the meager fund within reach of the Democratic managers ought to be increased, and that every citizen who desires an enlightened national verdict in November ought to have an opportunity to contribute to it. . . . And in order to start the current of popular contributions the *Journal,* until further notice, will give a dollar of its own for every dollar entrusted to it by the people.[26]

From the beginning of September forward the *Journal* published a record of contributions it received in care of the Democratic campaign. The sums were paltry, most in the range of 25 cents to a few dollars. Some people, no doubt, simply wanted to see their names in the paper. Others donated anonymously for fear of reprisals in the workplace. After five weeks, the paper had raised $15,000 in contributions, which it matched and sent along to the Democratic National Committee. Almost apologetically, the paper explained that it was closing the fund: its purpose had been to educate voters, and the window with which to print and distribute documents was fast closing. Roughly $5,000 more came in over the next few days, bringing the fund's total (with Hearst's matching contributions) to $40,000. Hanna could have raised the same amount at a single meal, but it was by far the largest contribution to a Democratic campaign that spent about $350,000.[27]

In the absence of a functioning Democratic machine, Hearst, ironically, was assuming for the Democrats some of the chores Hanna handled for the Republicans. In addition to raising money, he addressed Bryan's lack of effective campaign literature. Hearst began publishing a weekly "campaign extra" compiled from the *Journal*'s files. Hundreds of thousands of copies were printed and distributed at his expense. The newspaper's offices, in the meantime, were transformed into an unofficial campaign headquarters: Democratic candidates and spokesmen rushed in and out at all hours, bearing news tips and statements for release, requesting advice or attention, and suggesting initiatives helpful to their cause.[28]

However welcome this practical support to the Democrats, by far the *Journal*'s most important contribution to the campaign was its journalism. Over the course of the race, the paper had occasion to explain and defend practically every plank in the Democratic platform and to answer every argument posed by the Republicans in favor of gold and protective tariffs (without ever endorsing unlimited coinage of silver). The *Journal* not only called attention to the unprecedented role of money in the GOP campaign but helped to expose sharp tactics employed in McKinley's name. Republican-friendly employers, for instance, were warning workers of widespread layoffs in the event of a Democratic victory, submitting them to mandatory "education" seminars led by GOP speakers, and demanding their attendance at Republican parades and rallies.[29] Again, Hearst's was the only major paper in the Northeast with enthusiasm for this work.

One of the most interesting fights the *Journal* picked with Republicans in 1896 was over sectionalism and the Civil War. It was a Republican habit in national campaigns to seek opportunities to stoke remembrance of the Civil War among the party's supporters in the North. Waving the bloody shirt, as the tactic was known, emphasized the Republicans' standing as the party of national unity and patriotism and painted the Democrats as the party of division and rebellion. It was particularly effective in this campaign. With the Democrats wedded to a currency policy popular in the South and West yet anathema to the Northeast, the Republicans had their opening. No sooner had Bryan been nominated than McKinley began associating silver with regional discord and flaying his opponent with Civil War imagery: "Then section was arrayed against section. Now men of all sections can and will unite to rebuke the repudiation of our obligations and debasement of our currency."[30] Republican sheets were quick to take up the theme. "The country is in greater danger than it has been since 1861," worried the *Tribune*. "This is not merely our opinion, and is not merely a party opinion. It is the profound belief of patriotic men without distinction of party and in every section of the country."[31]

To dramatize the supposed menace of the Democratic platform, Hanna funded a Patriotic Heroes' Battalion comprising Union army generals.[32] The veterans traveled 8,000 miles and held 276 meetings in the last months of the campaign. At each stop, they would ride out in full uniform to a bugle call. There was no subtlety to their message. As one of their number argued, "The rebellion grew out of sectionalism and the veterans who are here and their comrades all over the land know too well what it cost us to put that rebellion down. Five hundred thousand lives and uncounted millions of treasure. A million homes left desolate. . . . We cannot tolerate, will not tolerate, any man representing any party who attempts again to disregard the solemn admonitions of Washington to frown down every attempt to set one portion of the country against another." These remarkable words brought hosannas from the Republican papers in New York.

It was left to the *Journal* alone among leading U.S. newspapers, to refute this characterization of the Democratic platform and to answer the charge of sectional incitement. Hearst's paper did not dispute that the country was divided. It attributed the "curse" of sectionalism, however, not to any desire for rebellion in the outlying regions but to the eagerness of eastern Republicans to indict as rebels those who disagreed with their monetary policy. Instead of honestly debating silver and other campaign issues, Republicans were dismissing Bryan as "a demagogue, a Socialist, an Anarchist," and his followers as "a horde of brainless, characterless zealots" bent on evading their honest debts. The paper asked what these harsh characterizations contributed to the spirit of national unity, and suggested that the Republican effort to win a partisan monopoly on patriotism was a greater act of rebellion than anything the Democrats had in mind.[33]

The *Journal* appealed to the Republicans to quit their saber-rattling, drop their "campaign of opprobrium" against Bryan and his followers, and engage in a more civil debate.[34] There was hypocrisy in this plea, given what the *Journal* was inflicting on Hanna and McKinley, and it was Bryan, after all, who had claimed that he and his followers were being crucified. But the belligerence of the Republican campaign did need to be answered. Not only were a bunch of Civil War heroes riding around advising old soldiers to vote as they shot, but senior New York Republican Edward Lauterbach made the ominous proclamation that if the Chicago platform received a mandate from voters, "we will not abide the decision."[35]

New York's anti-Bryan papers were every bit as shrill as Lauterbach:

- The New York *Sun* heard among the Democrats the "murmur of the assailants of existing institutions, the shriek of the wild-eyed, the tramp of the Coxeyite army marching again upon Washington." It also saw the coming of an era of "[r]epudiation, robbery, inequitable taxation, a free hand for the forces of socialism, a clear field for the advance of the skirmish line of Communism and Anarchy."[36]
- The *New York Times* called Bryan "an irresponsible, unregulated, ignorant, prejudiced, pathetically honest and enthusiastic crank" presiding over a "freaky," howling "aggregation of aliens."[37]

- The *New York Herald* warned that the Jacobins of the West and South had raised the flags of "silverism, Populism, and Communism. These are crimes against the nation, as secession was. They menace national repudiation and dishonor, disaster to business and suffering to the people. They [are] an assault upon constitutional government and republican institutions. . . ."[38]
- The *New York Tribune* congratulated the Democrats on becoming the "avowed champion of the right of pillage, riot and train-wrecking." The party's members were driven by "all the unclean passions that deform the human soul," their "burn-down-your-cities"platform was an assault upon the Constitution and the Ten Commandments, and their leader a "wretched rattle-pated boy, posing in vapid vanity and mouthing resounding rottenness."[39]

Perhaps the *Journal*'s best answer to all of these eruptions was the pen of editorialist Arthur McEwan. McEwan invented an arch-Republican character called "A Gentleman," who was "a sort of combination of all the snobs of history." The Gentleman saw it as his social duty to speak for the "enlightened few against the imbruted many." He scolded the *Journal* in its own pages for foolishly encouraging common laborers to consider themselves competent to pass judgment on important issues of public finance. He thought it absurd that anyone might consider a man born in Nebraska and educated at a freshwater college suitable for the presidency. When a group of boisterous Yale students hooted down Bryan as he addressed a mass gathering of Democrats at New Haven, the Gentleman regretted the disturbance—"discourtesy even to a scoundrel is never to be defended." All the same, he could not help but be impressed that a few hundred well-born students from his alma mater, shouting their "inspiring class yells," had cowed 15,000 unwashed proletarians. "Blood will tell," he shrugged. The *Journal* received bales of mail in response to McEwan's work. Some writers satirized the satirist; some threatened to lynch him.[40]

The *Journal* met the *Sun* head-on over its assessment of the Democratic platform as a summons to anarchy. Dana was sincere in this charge. The Democrats, to his mind, were bent on manipulating the currency to effect a massive repudiation of debt. They also sought to defy a recent Supreme Court decision on the constitutionality of taxes on certain forms of income (the Democratic platform sided with a minority of the court in favor of income taxes). The *Sun* argued that the anarchist who had recently fired at President Faure of France would, if allowed into America and "armed" with citizenship papers, vote for Bryan and the Chicago platform. Hyperbolic as it was, the *Sun* never lost its wit. It aimed the following piece of doggerel at Bryanites:

> Pile the load on plutocrats' backs;
> sock it to 'em with the income tax.
> Of goldbug law we make a sport;
> when the time comes we'll pack the court.
> On with the program without a hitch;
> skin the East and skin the rich.
> Lift the heart and lift the fist;
> swear to be an Anarchist.
> Our greed is ruin; our flag is red.
> On brother Anarchists, and raise Ned.[41]

The *Journal* responded by pulling from the shelf a copy of Charles A. Dana's 1849 defense of "the Great French Anarchist" Proudhon. The paper found it interesting that the one time Dana had written about an avowed anarchist, he had warmly applauded his ideas. He had been keeping a sharp lookout for anarchists ever since, applying the label to Grover Cleveland, Illinois governor John Altgeld, the writers William Dean Howells and Henry George, and the Reverend Lyman Abbott, among others. When writing about these men, none of whom claimed to be anarchists and none of whom had ever otherwise been associated with anarchism, Dana denounced them as anarchists with grim ferocity. The *Journal* attributed this difference in treatment to the fact that the book on Proudhon had been written when Dana was in the prime of his intellectual life: "His years were sufficient to have given him education and discretion, and still few enough to leave him unspoiled by the sordid associations of long business life."[42]

One of the more bizarre attacks on Bryan during the campaign came from the *New York Times,* which asked, "Is Mr. Bryan Crazy?" The *Times* believed that no one could review Bryan's speeches and public pronouncements without "feeling that these are not adaptations of intelligent reason to intelligent ends." The candidate would not stop talking, and he would not listen to anyone who disproved his theories. He was convinced that the world was falling to pieces and that he alone was competent to rectify its problems. Of course, the same could be said of just about every candidate for high office, but the *Times* took its suspicions to an "eminent alienist," who concluded Bryan was unhinged and that a Democratic victory would put "a madman in the White House." Just what kind of madman, however, vexed the *Times*. Every psychological expert the paper queried had a different diagnosis. Was Bryan suffering from delirium, megalomania, paranoia, paranoia reformatoria, paranoia querulenta, querulent logorrhea, oratorical monomania, graphomania? For *Times* readers, the precise nature of Bryan's psychosis emerged as one of the most hotly contested issues of the campaign.[43]

The *Journal* supposed that the *Times* had adopted this novel line of inquiry in preference to the hard work of controverting Bryan's arguments, and went on to note that similar diagnoses might be reached in examination of McKinley's self-consecration to the cause of protective tariffs, or William Lloyd Garrison's opposition to slavery: "And Lincoln, the uncouth Western statesman who received at the hands of the New York press much such a greeting as has been thrust upon Bryan, had the single purpose of preserving the Union. Was he insane?"[44]

Every time Hearst answered a critic of the Democratic leader or his campaign, the paper itself came under attack. The *Journal*, as Hearst would later romanticize it, was like a "solitary ship surrounded and hemmed in by a host of others, and from all sides shot and shell poured into our devoted hulk. Editorial guns raked us, business guns shattered us, popular guns battered us, and above the din and flame of battle rose the curses of the Wall Street crowd that hated us."[45]

Not all of the complaints came from Republicans and Park Row competitors. Phoebe Hearst asked Ed Clark, her financial manager, to approach Will about moderating his support for Bryan. She was worrying about the purchasing power of her U.S. millions in the event of a Democratic victory. She was also taking flak from her many social and financial connections on Wall Street, where her son's rag was regarded as the voice of Armageddon. Hosmer B. Parsons, Phoebe's attorney and the future president of Wells Fargo Bank, wrote her with his personal

The young San Francisco publisher
W.R. Hearst, dressed like a dude.

W.R. considered
himself a hit on
stage at Harvard.

Phoebe Apperson Hearst blazed with diamonds.

Senator George Hearst lived as he pleased.

Hearst's *Vamoose*: like a torpedo boat, without the ordnance.

The newspaper buildings of Park Row, the most exciting street in New York.

A confident W.R. on
the eve of his
New York adventure,
painted by
Orrin Peck.

W.R. sent up by his own
cartoonist, Homer Davenport.

Davenport: literally born to draw.

Joseph Pulitzer called Dana a "mendacious blackguard."

Charles Anderson Dana called Pulitzer a "venomous, greedy junk dealer."

The aristocratic Republican,
Whitelaw Reid.

The precociously dissolute James
Gordon Bennett.

The brilliant misanthrope,
Edwin Godkin.

The shrewd whelp, Adolph Ochs.

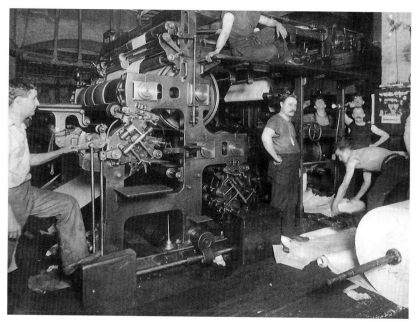

The *Journal*'s magnificent pressworks: as many as forty editions a day.

Richard Harding Davis, posing as a war correspondant.

Arthur Brisbane, who cherished his superficiality.

Alfred Henry Lewis: a singularly vicious hater.

James Creelman: profane, invasive, fearless.

Millicent Willson (left) with sister, Anita, and mother, Hannah: at first it wasn't clear which girl interested Hearst.

estimation of the *Journal*'s inanity: "There must be much improvement
in the morale and dignity of the *Journal* before it can hope to rank with
some of the other NY papers and become a commercial success. I am
sure it is now conducted upon a mistakenly low estimate of public intelligence and taste."[46] To her credit, Phoebe did not press her concerns with
Will and in public gave him nothing but support.

THE MOST DIRECT AND DETERMINED of the *Journal*'s assailants in the
last weeks of the campaign was Joseph Pulitzer. Whatever the state of
his health, few things engaged the *World* publisher like a presidential
contest. His one-time colleague and biographer Donald Seitz reports
that he spent the whole election season "in unceasing labor, never for a
waking moment out of touch with the telegraph. . . . The fever of the
fight revived his bodily strength and he labored as few in the fullness of
their powers could do, sustained by his devotion to the right." Pulitzer
bombarded his editors with orders, ideas, information, and criticisms. He
personally supervised his star reporter, Creelman. Yet despite his efforts,
the *World* wasn't enjoying the campaign.[47]

There was, for starters, Pulitzer's throbbing indignation at the
Democrats' rejection of his counsel on the currency question. That Bryan
and his outrageous platform were finding an audience didn't sit well with
him either. Pulitzer had made his fortune as an evangelist for democratic
ideals, but the '96 campaign was shaking his faith in the intelligence and
morality of the people and in the viability of the Republic. Worse, he had
nowhere to turn. Despite his preference for the gold standard, Pulitzer
couldn't bring himself to support the Republicans. His editorial page was
still scorching McKinley for his reluctance to support anti-trust legislation
and to speak against combinations of capital and private monopolies. In
the end, the best the *World* could say of McKinley was that he wasn't
Bryan. Pulitzer was thus without a horse in a big derby. For an old cam-
paigner, it was a kind of death.

And then there was Hearst, making a reputation for himself in a role
traditionally reserved for Pulitzer. Hearst was the champion of the
Democratic ticket and of the Democratic platform, rushing to press each
day with a righteous sense of purpose. Pulitzer was certain the Democrats
were headed for defeat and that Hearst's bubble would burst along with

Bryan's, but he did not like for a moment being eclipsed by an upstart. Especially an impudent upstart. In addition to splashing on his front-page Pulitzer's memo to news agents, Hearst had confirmed in late August that he was planning to launch an evening edition to take on the *Evening World*.

The *Evening Journal* made its debut on September 28, 1896, with five weeks remaining in the campaign. That same say, the morning *Journal* published on its front page the news that its circulation had passed the 400,000 mark, and a letter to Hearst from the president of the printing-press giant R. Hoe & Co. (which also built Pulitzer's plant), acknowledging receipt of yet another order to upgrade the *Journal*'s printing capacity:

> You may not be aware of the fact, but the orders received from you during the past year embrace a larger number of machines, with a greater producing capacity, than we have furnished to any one customer during a similar period of time. Your circulation having, since we received your first order, on October 1st, 1895, increased from fifty thousand (50,000) to four hundred thousand (400,000) daily, we think we have reason to congratulate ourselves upon being able, with the machines already furnished, to so nearly keep up with your requirements.[48]

Pulitzer was not one to take all this lying down. The advent of the *Evening Journal* infuriated him. While less prestigious journalistically than their morning cousins, evening papers raked in advertising on the assumption that consumers were more likely to make their purchases at the end of a workday than at the beginning. The *Evening World*, sharing costs with the morning *World*, was probably the most profitable daily in town. Now both *Worlds* were under attack—actually, all three, counting Sunday. In his rage, Pulitzer grasped at a story he believed would all at once expose the folly of the Democrats, return the *World* to its rightful place at center stage in the election campaign, and destroy the interloper, Hearst.

Various newspapers had reported that western silver miners were enthusiastic promoters of the free-silver movement. A week before the debut of the *Evening Journal*, Pulitzer's *World* began tracing connections between western mine owners and pro-silver members of the Senate and House. It learned that a memo had circulated among silver miners urging them to donate generously to the Democratic campaign. It discovered that senators from Nevada and other western states had investments in silver mines. It seemed obvious to the *World* that these rich silver-mine-owning Senators from Nevada were engaged in a plot to foist bimetallism on the American people—a "sharp, unscrupulous business scheme of amazing impudence and audacity."[49] The silver kings aimed to get rich by convincing the national government to buy their metal at the above-market ratio of sixteen to one against gold. To that end, they had recruited neighboring silver-producing states to take up the cry of free silver. They then broadened their pitch to areas of "debt, poverty and ignorance"—the western and southern agricultural states.[50] The Nevada conspirators next captured the Chicago convention by illegal manipulation of the rules governing the proper recognition of delegates and, voilà, free silver had "assumed the aspect of a national movement."

The *World* promised to shine the light of publicity on the devious operations of what it called The Great Silver Trust Conspiracy—"the richest, the most powerful and the most rapacious trust in the United States."[51] It began running lists of silver mines and their owners and estimates of what they would gain if Bryan won and fulfilled his promises. It presented a series of cartoons featuring a blimp-like personification of the Silver Trust.[52] Throughout September and October, articles and illustrations of this nature appeared almost daily in the *World*.

There was some legitimate reporting in Pulitzer's crusade, particularly with regard to the silver lobby's political connections, but the notion of a conspiracy was a stretch. The only evidence presented by the *World* was the memo to silver miners asking them to donate to the Democrats—more of a canvass than an intrigue. There was also the difficulty of reconciling the *World*'s reports on the wealth and ferocity of the silver trust with its many articles on the manifest poverty of the Democratic campaign. The nadir of Pulitzer's crusade was a wacky piece alleging the existence of a league of "secret silver societies" with branches in every state in the Union. The "Silver Knights of America" and "Patriots of America" and "The Supreme Temple of the Silver Knights of America" were said to have three million voters pledged by oath to support silver with their ballots. The league was controlled, of course, by silver senators from Nevada.[53]

One constant in the *World*'s coverage of the silver conspiracy was its implication of William Randolph Hearst.[54] The *San Francisco Call* had earlier speculated that the Hearst family, with its substantial investments in silver mines, would be a big winner if silver were to prevail on election day. The *World* ran these reports verbatim and continued to make prominent mention of Hearst's supposedly compromising holdings in its extensive coverage of the silver trust. It also included Hearst's picture in its rogues' gallery of silver conspirators.

Hearst's response was to publish a brief news report on the allegations, along with a curt editorial entitled "Hearst Estate and Politics."[55] The latter denied that Hearst was supporting Bryan and advocating bimetallism because he owned silver mines. It pointed out that less than a tenth of the Hearst estate consisted of silver mines, and that most of the rest was invested in gold mines (which was the case). Homer Davenport also weighed in, with a series of cartoons in which a ninety-seven-pound Pulitzer, in boxing tights, thrashed a straw man representing the Silver Trust.[56]

Pulitzer's silver conspiracy had the intended effect of energizing the *World*'s campaign coverage, but it was not taken seriously on Park Row. No other paper touched it. Even allowing for the overheated environment of the campaign, Pulitzer had overreached. It was not the sort of mistake he would make under normal circumstances; it was the sort of mistake he made when sorely provoked. Hearst had got under his skin, and he burrowed deeper as the campaign approached its climax.

THE ARTIST RICHARD OUTCAULT was the single-most popular talent in Pulitzer's *World*. Two years prior to the 1896 election, he had been a technical draftsman for a publication called *Electric World* when his occasional cartoons of street urchins in the humor magazine *Truth* caught the eye of Walt McDougall, the *World*'s political cartoonist. McDougall recommended Outcault to Morrill Goddard (then still in Pulitzer's employ). Goddard was looking for talent to fill a new illustrated supplement in the Sunday *World*, an eight-page affair, four of them in color. Outcault climbed on board and on May 5, 1895, began publishing what would be the first successful recurring comic in an American newspaper, *Hogan's Alley*.

On its first appearance, *Hogan's Alley* was a half-page, single-panel tableau of ragged Irish-American children imitating acrobats and jugglers in the lot behind their tenement—the circus was in town that week. While most newspaper portrayals of the immigrant poor emphasized misery and shame, Outcault's kids had a joyful vitality that transcended their meager circumstances: they were clever, confident, and irreverent. In the weeks following, the *Hogan's Alley* gang would cheerfully send up the America's Cup race, the Vanderbilt-Marlborough wedding, the Princeton-Yale football game, and whatever else was in the news.

In the lower right corner of the very first *Hogan's Alley* was a bald, jug-eared boy in bare feet and a long nightshirt. His infectious bucktooth grin would reappear in almost every panel Outcault produced. His original name was Mickey Dugan, but after January 5, 1896, when Outcault began coloring his nightshirt a brilliant yellow and placing him in the foreground, he became known as the Yellow Kid. Sometimes his costume bore captions in *Hogan's Alley* vernacular. When Chinese viceroy Li Hung-chang visited New York, the shirt read "ME & LI HAS MADE A BIG HIT WIT EACH OTER. SAY! HE TINKS I'M A CHINAMAN— DON'T SAY A WOID . . ." There were other recurring characters in Outcault's strip, including the Naughty Riccadonna Sisters, who ran a ballet school offering plain and fancy dancing and the coochee-coochee, but the Yellow Kid was the star attraction of the Sunday *World*.[57]

It was only a matter of time before Hearst developed his own humor supplement for the *Journal*. He was a devotee of the genre: he had been collecting German comic books since boyhood, reading French and English humor magazines since Harvard, and he kept a close eye on their American counterparts, *Puck, Judge,* and *Life*. By the summer of 1896 he had installed a press capable of producing an all-color section he would call The American Humorist—"eight pages of iridescent polychromous effulgence that makes the rainbow look like a lead pipe," according to a *Journal* promotion.[58] He hired Outcault away from the *World* as the Humorist's centerpiece. With Pulitzer laying claim to the title *Hogan's Alley*, Outcault debuted the Yellow Kid and the rest of his characters in the *Journal* under the name *McFadden's Row of Flats*. The first panel, on October 18, showed the entire motley gang moving to its new premises with suitcases, pets, and toys in hand. One of the kids carried a placard: "SAY! HOGAN'S ALLEY HAS BEN CONDEMED BY DE BOARD OF HELT. AN WE WAS GITTEN TIRED OF IT ANY WAY." The major difference in Hearst's presentation of the Yellow Kid was the addition of a weekly narrative by E.W. Townsend, a *Journal* writer who had years earlier produced a popular column for the *Sun* featuring a boisterous Bowery tough named Chimmie Fadden. Townsend now produced a weekly short story based on Outcault's characters to run alongside *McFadden's Row of Flats*.

Pulitzer assigned the artist George Luks to continue *Hogan's Alley* for the *World*, and Luks produced a credible facsimile of Outcault's original with the result that New York readers were now treated to the weekly spectacle of rival Yellow Kids. Hearst and Pulitzer both promoted their comics on posters and billboards. Merchandisers created Yellow Kid buttons, toys, and cigarette boxes. The comedy team of Weber and Fields put the Yellow Kid on stage. The social critic Max Nordau took one look at the Yellow Kid's bald head, bad teeth, and misshapen feet and, shuddering to think what other abnormalities were hidden beneath his yellow shirt, declared him the ultimate symbol of Western degeneracy. The Kid was a bona fide hit.

Although Pulitzer fought to protect the *Hogan's Alley* franchise, his response to Hearst's humor supplement was halfhearted. He let Outcault go, apparently without a fight, and he did not immediately match Hearst's eight-page full-color American Humorist. The expense may have been a factor, but Pulitzer was not entirely convinced of the charms of uppity ethnic urchins. The *Journal* would soon add to its comic arsenal Rudolph Dirks's *Katzenjammer Kids*, a chronicle of mischievous German-American youths, and Frederick Opper's *Happy Hooligan*, based on a lovable hobo and his sidekick, Gloomy Gus. Hearst was the more committed populist, in comics as well as in the national election race.

AS THE CAMPAIGN CAME TO A CLOSE, New Yorkers were almost dizzy with suspense. A Davenport cartoon showed burglars walking free, people dying in the street, and actresses in tears as cops, ambulance drivers, and theater audiences got caught up in the new rage for talking politics.[59] The popular excitement was stoked by continuous street parades as the parties worked to mobilize voters. A fireworks specialist named John Delaney had been hired by the Republicans to give one of their processions a dazzling finale. According to a *Journal* report, he waited on a rooftop at the appointed hour and at the first sight of balloons and a marching band let loose his rockets. The marchers, unfortunately for Delaney, turned out to be Democrats. He realized his mistake and fainted on the spot.[60]

The *Journal* managed to keep its poise in the closing days, despite reasonably certain knowledge that Bryan would lose the election. Oddsmakers at the stock exchange were giving at least 3 to 1 for McKinley. The vast majority of voter canvasses, as opinion surveys were then called, foretold a Republican victory. Hanna, who had better intelligence than anyone in America, claimed a lock on 311 electoral-college votes with an additional 26 strong possibilities and 32 long shots.[61] The *Journal* gave precedence to optimistic assessments of Democratic strength from Democratic sources, including Bryan, who predicted his own election, but nonetheless reported the facts. Outcault poked fun at all prognostications in a pre-election Yellow Kid cartoon, drawing a mock newspaper billboard that read "LATEST RETURNS GIVE EACH CANDIDATE AN OVERWHELMING MAJORITY . . . DESE FIGURES AINT BEN CONFIRMED BUT ARE MERELY GUESSES BY EXPERT GUESSERS WICH WE ALL ARE—AFTERWARDS."[62]

The *Journal*'s Julian Hawthorne finished the campaign on a high. He stuck with Bryan through his final sweep of the Midwest en route to his Nebraska home, where he would cast his ballot on voting day. The Bryan train crossed the level prairie into Lincoln on a clear and peaceful Sunday morning. The town glittered under the first hoarfrost of the season. Hawthorne checked into his hotel and strolled through the streets and among the small cottages before arriving at the one belonging to the candidate. Hawthorne's article, like the *Journal*'s convention report from Bryan's hotel room, demonstrates the astonishing access afforded newspapermen at the time:

> I had called only to leave a message, not to go in, but as I stood there a large man, with black hair and eagle eyes, came to the door and gave me a cordial handclap and an invitation to enter. There were two little girls, one of eleven with a face of quaint intelligence and clear gray eyes, the other a little yellow haired creature, just old enough to be hugged and played with. There was the mother, too, a slender, motherly woman. The house contained four or five pleasant little rooms, with nothing conspicuous in the way of furniture or decoration, but in the study, which used to be the dining room, were two cases of books, a cabinet of souvenirs and a big study table, with two blotting pads, one on each side.
>   "Why two?" asked I.

"Mrs. Bryan sits at that side and I sit on this," the master of the house replied. "We do our work together."

It was a very quiet, domestic, homelike little place; it was as good as being in the country. The world, with its noise and trouble, its society, commerce and politics, seemed far off. There was nothing in the dwelling or in the demeanor of its simple-hearted occupants to suggest the strife of opposing parties, the conflict of good and evil. It was the home of an honest and useful American citizen of small means. There are millions of such in this country; such citizens form the bulk of our population; we could not get on without them, but we never hear of them; they live and die unknown beyond their own little circle. Upon the owner of this particular house, of late the eyes of the world have literally been fixed, with hate and fear, with hope and love. He is our greatest public man today.[63]

Not to be outdone, the *World*'s indefatigable James Creelman also followed Bryan to the wire but slipped away long enough for a last interview with McKinley in Canton. His mission was to finally break the candidate's silence on the issue of corporate trusts, a source of great frustration to the *World*. Creelman's article matched Hawthorne's both for its effusive praise of the candidate (McKinley is described as "a god of speech") and for the intimacy of access he was granted:

[McKinley's] voice rang out over the heads of the surging thousands with the tone of a bugle in it. His eyes flashed and his face was radiant with the pride of conscious power. But when I saw him Sunday he was dumb, and in the morning he sat in church with bowed head while the minister drawled, "Not all who say Lord, Lord, shall enter into the kingdom of heaven."

In the afternoon I watched him as he stood in his little study with his back to the hearth, pleasant blaze in the grate. The snow whirled down from the dull heavens and swept against the window panes.

All around the house, the ground trampled smooth by hundreds of thousands of feet, was matted with yellow and crimson leaves fallen from the half bare branches. There was a hush to the place.

The ruddy glow of the fire was on Mr. McKinley's back, and the cold hard light of the winter day was on his face. It was a handsome face, strong, masculine, and refined. The large hazel eyes seemed to be in wait under the great bushy eyebrows. There was a suggestion of ambush in them, as when one looks in the shadowed surfaces of deep pools.

Mr. McKinley thrust his hands in his pockets in a boyish way and snuggled backward towards the comfortable fire. He looked fresher than he did before the nomination. He is stouter and stronger. Presently he lit a cigar and spread his hands out before the dancing flames, rubbing them briskly and glancing out at the soft white mist that drizzled through the tree-tops.

Not a word did he have to say about trusts—not one. [64]

On the morning of November 3, 1896, Hearst presented to *Journal* readers his plans for announcing election results in New York that evening. A system of colored electric lights attached to a "monster balloon" tethered high above the city would flash news of the outcome to greater New York and New Jersey. The lights would flash red for a Bryan victory, green for McKinley. He also offered state-by-state results projected on huge bulletin boards on Park Row, as well as stereopticon and kinetoscope exhibitions, musical bands, and other entertainment. [65]

Pulitzer likewise announced plans to transform his own building and several others around New York into huge screens on which to project results. His elaborate system of multicolored signals and searchlights— the "greatest electrical display ever produced"—would announce by a series of codes, published in the *World*, the presidential result and the Senate, House, and swing-state outcomes as well. [66]

Almost 14 million Americans voted that day, or 79 percent of those eligible, a record that still stands. Hundreds of thousands of New Yorkers began pouring into Park Row and Madison Square Garden even before dusk. They brought tin horns and noisemakers and raised a rumpus as each state reported. When the *Journal* declared McKinley elected, the Seventh Regiment Band broke into "The Star Spangled Banner." Amid the throng was Richard Harding Davis, who described the scene in a letter to his brother:

On the election night every newspaper had from four to seven places for showing bulletins instead of one as formerly. . . . [T]hey all had cinematographs showing life-sized figures in motion and McKinley walking in his garden. . . . [B]rass bands played in front of all the newspaper uptown

offices and clubs—the *Journal* had a map of the United States with the silver and gold states picked out in white or tallow electric lights & the number of the electoral vote of each. It stretched from Broadway to 5th
Avenue. It was the most remarkable sight ever witnessed in New York. All
of the "plain people" apparently went down town to learn the returns. . . .
[E]veryone was laughing and shrieking and waving flags and yellow rib-
bons. It was exactly like the football crowd on Thanksgiving Day and it
packed the streets so that the cable cars could not move.[67]

The margin of victory was comfortable: 7,111,607 to 6,509,052 for
McKinley in the popular vote (or 51 percent to 47 percent), and a decisive
271 to 176 in the electoral college. McKinley and Hanna had run a mistake-
free campaign, persuading a majority of voters that they were the safe bet
for stability, commercial progress, and high wages. McKinley took not
only the urban and industrialized Northeast but the prosperous farm
country of the Midwest and several western states as well. Bryan could
not break out of the stricken agricultural regions of the West and South.

As New Yorkers celebrated in the streets, Hearst and his editors put
together a front page with a statesmanlike illustration of the Republican
president-elect under the headline "McKinley Carries the Country."[68]
Pulitzer's *World* adjudged its own performance more significant than
McKinley's. It designed a front page with a huge cartoon of Liberty
leaning from her pedestal to shine the light of publicity on a vanquished,
serpentine Silver Trust. On the pedestal were scrolls quoting Pulitzer's
warnings to the Democrats that adoption of the free-silver heresy would
be suicide.[69] The *Tribune,* a sore winner, remixed its previous editorials
for one last broadside at Bryan and the Democrats: "There are some
movements so base, some causes so depraved, that neither victory can
justify them nor defeat entitle them to commiseration. . . ."[70]

Hearst's morning-after editorial acknowledged "the high privilege of
the citizens of this Republic to decide for themselves what is good for
them." It added that while the *Journal* "regrets the decision," believing
that bimetallism would be better for the country than monometallism
and that trusts and syndicates require checking rather than encouraging,
"the duty of all good citizens now is to acquiesce loyally and quickly in
Major McKinley's election, forget the rancors and excitements of politics
as soon as possible—parting with no convictions, but remembering that

there is a time for all things—and settle down to business. The country needs a rest."[71]

Hearst, too, needed a rest. Hot haste and hard work had been his daily routine for more than a year now. He was just a few days from his official first anniversary as the acknowledged proprietor of the *Journal*. He had given the paper every ounce of his care and concentration and prodigious energy from the start. Weary but proud, he telegraphed his mother from the newsroom before leaving on election night:

> Am going home to sleep a little for a change. Will be up in the morning. Too bad about Bryan but don't worry about Journal. The orders for tomorrow are nearly nine hundred thousand. I don't know how we can print them. Hope you are well. I'm tired out but all right otherwise.[72]

By the time Hearst awoke, he was well on his way to a record sale. His presses had started running within minutes of the declaration for McKinley, and they ran virtually nonstop for twenty-four hours. The *Journal* printed and distributed, exclusive of giveaways, 956,921 copies of its morning paper, 437,491 copies of the *Evening Journal,* and 112,312 copies of its German edition. Election extras were rushed by chartered express trains to Washington, Buffalo, and Boston. With more than 1.5 million copies sold in a single day, Hearst boasted of an achievement "not only unparalleled in the history of the world, but hitherto undreamed of in the realm of modern journalism."[73]

Pulitzer, meanwhile, had booked passage for Europe on the liner *Columbia*. His careful advance parties had somehow failed to note the presence of a brass band on the ship. It played nonstop, and no pleading or inducement would make it quit. When Pulitzer finally arrived, irritated and exhausted, in Monte Carlo, the constant chiming of the ships' bells in the harbor drove him to distraction. He took out his frustration on his secretaries, who scrambled to find him a quieter refuge. They finally located an isolated country villa in Cap Martin, near the Italian border, where he would rest and regroup in the company of the empress of Austria.

A few days after the election, Assistant Secretary Perkins of the Republican National Committee walked into his boss's office and said, "Mr. Hanna, allow me to introduce you to Mr. Homer Davenport." Mutual acquaintances had insisted upon a meeting of the caricaturist and his prized subject. By the *Journal*'s account, Hanna put on a semi-serious face and extended his hand. "So you are the scamp, are you, that's been doing it? Well, ain't you ashamed of yourself?" The men had a good laugh and admired one another's genius while messenger boys and party operatives crowded into the office to watch and listen. Even Murat Halstead and Vice President Hobart dropped by to witness the occasion. Davenport described his efforts to observe Hanna and the techniques he'd employed in his portrayals. Hanna answered that some of the cartoons were "pretty tough" but allowed that he had "many a good laugh" over them. "Just don't let Mrs. Hanna get her hands on you," he added.[74]

Mark Hanna emerged from the election a hero to Republicans, and he is credited today with ushering in a new era of well-funded, tightly scripted political campaigning. The diplomat and author John Hay, a former secretary to Abraham Lincoln, saluted Hanna's "glorious" performance and called him a "born general in politics."[75] McKinley did offer Hanna a seat in cabinet and also sought his advice on senior appointments to the administration. Hanna landed his associates in plum jobs but refused a cabinet role, citing the press as a factor in his decision: "All the newspapers would have cartoons of me selling the White House kitchen stove."[76] Hanna had something better in mind for himself: a seat in the U.S. Senate would bring him prestige and influence and allow him to establish an independent power base that could outlast the McKinley regime. In particular, Hanna asked the president-elect for the seat filled by Ohio senator John Sherman. McKinley obliged him, creating the vacancy by taking the infirm and fast-deteriorating Sherman, aged seventy-four, as his secretary of state. After his inauguration, McKinley kept Hanna at arm's length, and he was in every way the master of his administration.

As for the great currency debate, monetary historians, led by Milton Friedman, now tend to believe that stubborn insistence on the gold standard through the deflationary years of 1879 to 1896 was "a mistake that had highly adverse consequences" for the economy and the American people.[77] In any event, the currency soon sorted itself out. After the election, vast production of South African and Klondike gold accomplished much the same increase in the money supply that Bryanites had sought through free coinage of silver. Prices picked up after McKinley's victory and rose an average of 2 percent a year until the start of the Great War, taking heat off farmers and small producers.[78] The reality is that both Democrats and Republicans overestimated the potential consequences of the other's monetary policies. Moreover, as the historian Stanley L. Jones writes, the Democrats were no wiser to believe that free coinage of silver would answer all their problems than the Republicans were to consider protective tariffs a panacea. On the deeper struggle for control of the government and the economy between the industrialized lending states of the East and the more agrarian debtor states of the West and South, the outcome is mixed. Over the next several decades, almost every plank in the Democratic platform would be accepted as policy by the national government, but the Republicans would dominate the White House for most of that time.[79]

CHAPTER EIGHT

Four Sensations and the Morals Police

Will Hearst might have backed a loser in '96, but the trade press had no doubts as to which New York newspaper emerged from the campaign a winner. The *Journal* had covered the race "in splendid style," earning a reputation for courage, cleverness, and accuracy, said *The Fourth Estate*, which cited the enormous circulation of Hearst's election edition as evidence that people relied on the paper even in its hour of political defeat.[1] The young man from San Francisco, it continued, was the talk of the newspaper community: "[The *Journal*'s] accomplishments have been truly remarkable. . . . which even rivals must acknowledge, though they have a habit of paying tribute in the form of sneers."[2]

The sneers were many and heartfelt. The *Journal*'s success was causing havoc up and down Park Row as Hearst's competitors struggled to keep up. Pulitzer wasn't the only one reeling: expenses were leaping and profits shrinking all along the street. After the panic of '93, publishers had been looking forward to another era of fat and easy returns but instead they were being forced, as *The Fourth Estate* joked, to put their "rheumatic limbs to unaccustomed exercise."[3]

Early in 1897, the *Evening Telegram*, sister paper to Bennett's *Herald*, followed Pulitzer's lead and dropped its price from two cents to a penny. Bennett called publicly for collusion among proprietors to reduce the size of their papers, increase their prices, and bring salaries under control.[4] The *Tribune* held its three-cent price but offered its readers special promotions such as free tokens for the Brooklyn Bridge (valued at two and a half cents).[5] The *Evening Post*, easily the most conservative of the New York dailies in style and politics, and thus seemingly insulated from the new competitive threat, shocked the street by announcing it would buy new presses and increase its size.[6] And those titles were the lucky ones. After months of missing its payroll, the *Mercury* closed.[7] The *Times* was forced into receivership, from which it would emerge under new ownership.[7] The *Recorder* joined the *Times* in receivership and died there.[8]

Not all of this ruin could be laid at Hearst's feet—there were other economic factors at play, including the lingering effects of the depression— but after twelve months of watching with distaste and alarm the progress of the *Journal*, his rivals no longer had any doubts as to the threats he presented, politically, journalistically, and commercially. He had caused them serious problems. He had made them look bad. They were now bent on returning the favor. Some, like Pulitzer and Bennett, fought back with price cuts and new spending, while doing their best to compete with Hearst's journalism. Several others, unable to keep up commercially, fashioned an entirely different response: they declared a moral war.

Moral wars were nothing new in the nineteenth-century newspaper world. In fact, they were a routine reaction to every stage in the development of popular journalism. Since the advent of the penny press, papers in pursuit of mass audiences had been leavening their political and business reports with ever-increasing amounts of crime, scandal, calamity, and other human-interest content. Dana articulated the strategy best: an editor should attempt to offer "a daily photograph of the whole world's doing in the most lively and luminous manner."[9] He should consider as news everything "of sufficient importance to arrest and absorb the attention" of the general public. If his wares did not "correspond to the wants of the people," he would never succeed. And if that took his paper into the mud, so be it. "I have always felt," said Dana, "that whatever the Divine Providence permitted to occur I was not too proud to report."[10] James Gordon Bennett had followed this basic recipe when he launched the *Herald* in the 1830s. Shocked at the contents of his paper, to say nothing of its success, Bennett's opponents had accused him of wallowing in filth and sensation, of coarsening public taste, of corrupting women and children, of belittling the good and great, of endangering democracy by emboldening the mob, and of spoiling the market for more intelligent and uplifting newspaper fare. Bennett was hailed as an "obscene vagabond," a "venal wretch," a "vile nuisance," a "leprous slanderer," and an "infamous

Scotchman."[11] Dana and Pulitzer had been similarly received in their primes. Now it was Hearst's turn.

Moral wars never really worked—Bennett, Dana, and Pulitzer had all thrived despite the criticism—but Hearst's attackers could be excused for thinking him an easier target. He tried harder than any of his predecessors to arrest and absorb readers. He chased even the most sordid human-interest stories exactly as he covered politics: with naked enthusiasm and an unparalleled application of journalistic resources. And there was now so much to chase. New York was expanding at a phenomenal pace, and as it grew, the volume of lurid news grew with it. Much to the disgust, the well-orchestrated and very public disgust, of his competitors, Hearst was all over these stories, and sometimes directly involved in them. Take, for instance, the Stephen Crane episode.

EVEN BEFORE HE BECAME the *Journal*'s most notorious correspondent in the autumn of 1896, Stephen Crane was famous. *The Red Badge of Courage*, his slim but powerful novel of the Civil War, had been published twelve months earlier. It arrived, said H.L. Mencken, "like a flash of lightning out of a clear winter sky; it was at once unprecedented and irresistible."[12] Drawing comparisons to the work of Hugo, Tolstoy, and Zola, it climbed bestseller lists in the United States and London. Many who read the book assumed Crane to be a wizened veteran of the Civil War— an understandable error given his vivid rendering of the horrors of battle—but he was twenty-four years old and a veteran of nothing more dangerous than the Syracuse University baseball diamond. His novel was a triumph of the imagination, the product of his ridiculously large literary talent. Crane, wrote Joseph Conrad, "was a seer with a gift for rendering the significant on the surface of things with an incomparable insight into primitive emotions."[13] He was also a newspaperman.

Crane had begun to freelance news squibs to New York dailies at the age of sixteen, while living in Asbury Park. He eventually graduated to feature articles and short stories in the Sunday editions. He considered his newspaper work preparation for a literary career: "I decided that the nearer a writer gets to life the greater he becomes as an artist, and most of my prose writings have been toward the goal partially described by that misunderstood and abused word, realism."[14] In his twenties, Crane would begin trampling the distinction between journalism and literature. His fiction was "nearer to life" in a newspaper sense: he was drawn to scenes of action and danger, crisis and war. He employed an episodic narrative style and the sparse and concrete language of reportage. His tone—world-weary, ironic, skeptical to the point of insolence—was also more journalistic than conventionally literary. Before Dreiser, Hemingway, Mailer, and a host of others, Crane owned the swaggering persona of the big-time adventure-seeking writer-reporter. As Mencken said, he single-handedly "lifted newspaper reporting to the level of a romantic craft, alongside counterfeiting and mining in the Klondike."[15]

For most of the summer of '96, Crane had been on assignment to Hearst's *Journal,* one of a handful of name-brand pens providing sketches of life at popular resorts in upstate New York and on the New Jersey seaboard. It was not terribly romantic work, but then Crane's entire writer-reporter persona was riddled with holes. His creed of "getting closer to life" to become a great artist was fine in theory, but he was going about it backward: he had produced a great war novel long before he had covered a war. And his journalistic skills were limited. The sketches he submitted to dailies were sometimes rejected as too literary, too daring. He was unreliable on deadline and he was known to miss central events of important stories. But he at least made an effort to master the craft of journalism. It offered him things the literary life could never match, starting with money. The fees he received were modest but far better than those he got for his early fiction, news editors being quicker to see value in the strength and originality of Crane's voice. Most important, journalism fed Crane's restless and daring nature. He had a need, as the critic Mark Van Doren has noted, to live "in the midst of all but unbearable excitement."[16] The *Journal* was about to give him an assignment that would bring him all he could handle.

There was a vogue in the 1890s for stories from America's burgeoning inner cities. To people fortunate enough to live elsewhere, urban slums were an exciting spectacle, full of exotic characters, strange customs, and squalid scenes. Like foreign fields of battle and the unsettled reaches of America's West, the slums were unprotected by the hard veneers of civilization; life remained raw and elemental, and the primitive emotions still ran riot. The market for slum novels, slum journalism, and slum photography was bottomless. Wealthy New Yorkers took up a new form of urban tourism known as the "slumming party." Under the pretext of social concern, bluestocking men and women would rush through the Bowery, giddy at their proximity to wretchedness and vice.[17]

On a September afternoon in 1896, Henry Haxton, a *Journal* editor, ran into Hearst on a stairway at the Tribune Building and delivered a pitch on Crane's behalf for a series of "novelettes based upon real incidents of New York life." Crane was a recognized authority on the lower orders. The success of *The Red Badge of Courage* had recently emboldened publishers in New York and London to issue his first full novel, *Maggie: A Girl of the Streets*—a book they had all rejected in 1893 as risqué and entirely bereft of social uplift. Hearst gave his assent and Haxton promptly wrote to Crane: "I am sure that if you read the police news in next Sunday and Monday mornings' papers and go to Jefferson Market Police Court on Monday morning, you will get the material for a good Tenderloin story to start with. I suppose that if you are going there on Monday you would be glad to have a reporter, who knows the ropes, meet you there."[18]

The Tenderloin was a square mile of saloons, nickleodeons, dance halls, peep shows, opium dens, gambling joints, and whorehouses, running through the West 30s on either side of Broadway, and in the 1890s, according to the chief chronicler of New York lowlife, Luc Sante, it set "what was probably the city's all-time standard for vice in one district."[19] The Jefferson Market Police Court was where denizens of the Tenderloin had their morning reckonings. Crane met a *Journal* court reporter at Shanley's Restaurant around 9 a.m. on Monday, September 14. They hustled to court and spent a few hours watching the day's lot of transgressors grind through the machinery of justice. On the following evening, Crane furthered his research by observing the same population in its natural habitat. He crawled the Broadway dives.

For this part of his assignment Crane needed no guide. A wiry little man with a thin mustache under his prominent nose, he met up with a couple of chorus girls in a Turkish smoking parlor on West 29th Street. Some time before midnight they wandered over to Broadway Garden, which had a reputation as a "resort for notorious women."[20] There they ran into Dora Clark, an acquaintance of the chorus girls. Miss Clark was a ravishing young woman, barely twenty years old, with masses of curly dark red hair. The foursome later left Broadway Garden together. Crane put one of the chorus girls on an uptown streetcar and turned around to find a policeman arresting Dora Clark and the remaining chorus girl for soliciting. Amid the "wildest and theatrical sobbing," the chorus girl told the policeman that Crane was her husband. Crane backed her up. "If it was necessary," he would later explain, "to avow a marriage to save a girl who is not a prostitute from being arrested as a prostitute, it must be done, though the man suffer eternally." The policeman lost interest in the "married" girl but pressed his case against Miss Clark. He warned Crane that she was a known prostitute. "If you people don't want to get pinched, too, you had better not be seen with her."[21]

The patrolman, Charles Becker, led Crane and the two women to the 30th Street station house, where he locked up Dora Clark. Crane calmed the hysterical chorus girl long enough to say goodnight and went home. By his own account he tried to sleep but instead spent the night wrestling with his conscience. He knew Miss Clark was probably a courtesan: "The sergeant at the station house seemed to know her as well as he knew the Madison Square tower." But Crane firmly believed the arrest to be wrong. He guessed that he could hardly be the first man of character to witness a wrongful arrest, but he supposed that "reputable citizens" wouldn't dream of interfering with the law. A man might lose his job if it became known that he was out until 2:30 a.m. with chorus girls. But didn't he have a civic responsibility to speak up? Wasn't it the right thing to do?[22]

On the morning of September 16, 1896, Crane sat quietly in the Jefferson Market Police Court as the red-headed Dora Clark was led sobbing from the prisoner's box to the bar. Face flushed, eyes downcast, she stood accused of what the next day's *Journal* would call "the most degrading of all offences." Patrolman Becker explained the circumstances of her arrest to the court. Magistrate Cornell asked the young woman if she had anything to say. Miss Clark admitted that she had been in Broadway Garden and acknowledged that the hour was late for a woman to be on the town but said she had been lonesome and in need of company: "I was out where there were people and lights and music." She denied the charge of solicitation and responded bitterly to the statement of prior offenses. Her earlier arrest, she said, had happened after a policeman had spoken insultingly to her and she had rebuffed him. Since that incident, she declared, the police had made a target of her. The presiding magistrate asked Becker if there was any doubt in the case. None at all, he said: "She's an old hand and always lies about it."[23]

"Young woman," said the magistrate, "I have listened patiently because it is a terrible thing to judge a girl on such a charge unheard. But the officer's testimony and your past record. . . ." Before Cornell could render judgment, Crane rose from his seat. He wore a dark blue suit and a blue-striped shirt. His tawny hair was carefully combed and parted in the middle. "Your honor, I know the girl to be innocent. I am the man who was with her and there is no truth in what the officer has charged." The magistrate asked his name. He looked pale and nervous but his voice was firm: "I am Stephen Crane, the novelist."[24]

Crane told the court that he had been studying human nature in the Tenderloin for descriptive use in his journalism and gave his account of the evening's events. When he finished, the magistrate discharged Dora Clark. She thanked the court but added, "They'll only arrest me again."[25]

A *Journal* reporter caught up with Crane at his home later in the day. The novelist allowed that he knew nothing of the girl's character: "I only know that while with me she acted respectably, and that the policeman's charge was false." Crane also acknowledged that he was risking both his personal and literary reputations by standing up for Miss Clark, but he felt it his duty: "[If] a man should stand tamely by in such a case, our wives and sisters would be at the mercy of any ruffian who disgraces the uniform. The policeman flatly lied, and if the girl will have him prosecuted for perjury I will gladly support her."[26]

The reporter asked Crane if he had thought his feelings on rising in court at risk of public censure were at all like those experienced by the hero of *The Red Badge of Courage* before his first battle. Crane played along. "Yes I did. I was badly frightened, I admit, and would gladly have run away, could I have done so with honor." With admirable thoroughness, the *Journal*'s reporter returned to the station house to get police comment. One officer lent credence to Miss Clark's fear of rearrest. "I only hope she'll be out tonight, and be run in here." The policemen were as yet only mildly curious as to the identity of her defender, Stephen Crane. "An actor?" they wondered. "Never heard of him."[27]

The *Journal*'s next-day story was headlined "Badge of Courage in a New York Police Court." Crane had "boldly avowed he had been the escort of a Tenderloin Woman" who had been arrested. He had risked censure "by manfully championing a woman of whose antecedents he knew nothing." An editorial called for an official investigation into the arrest, and concluded that if Crane was telling the truth, Policeman Becker was guilty either of perjury, which should be prosecuted, or of "a blunder so gross and unpardonable as to call for his removal from the force." Consistent with this position, the *Journal*'s photo-illustrators produced a portrait of Crane sitting at a well-appointed writer's desk—a respectable literary gentleman.[28]

That picture of Crane hardly fit the reality of his life. Since dropping out of Syracuse five years earlier, his home turf had been midtown Manhattan. Typical of his living arrangements was an apartment at the Art Students League on East 23rd, which he shared with a group of young men he affectionately referred to as "the Indians." They slept three to a bed, pooling their shoes and overcoats. Crane was almost always broke. He got by on two meals a day and a heavy diet of coffee and cigars. He slept in his clothes, and wrote notes on his cuffs. His friends described him as frail and undernourished, narrow in the chest and shoulders, like "someone who's been skimped on."[29] His hair was usually a tangled mess. When not writing or playing cards or drinking beer with the Indians, Crane wandered the Bowery and the Tenderloin.

These adventures were research inasmuch as everything Crane saw and experienced was useful to his work, but the line between partaking and observing was blurry, and he never pretended to be operating under cover of a social agenda. Crane loved the streets as they were. He got a charge from their illicit pleasures. In sexual matters, he was ready and indiscriminate. "He took up with many a drab," recalled a friend, "and was not overly particular as to her age, race or color. Many a time I have heard him say he would have to go out and get a nigger wench 'to change his luck.'"[30] A few months before the Dora Clark incident, Crane had given *McClure's* a detailed story entitled "Opium's Varied Dreams." "The influence of dope is evidently a fine languor. . . . The problems of life no longer appear. Existence is peace . . . until the next morning." Crane left his readers to guess if he had actually tried the drug.[31]

Still, Crane's pose of literary probity might have held if Dora Clark had not insisted on charging the police with harassment. The strongest part of her case was the witness of Stephen Crane, and she had not forgotten his promise of support. On learning that she intended to press ahead, the police suddenly became very interested in Crane's identity. Reporters began to hear rumors from police sources of the author's high times with Tenderloin women, and of an opium pipe in his rooms.

Crane was now worried enough to send a telegram explaining his involvement in the Clark affair to one of New York's three police commissioners, Theodore Roosevelt, whose acquaintance he had recently made when Roosevelt had asked Crane to autograph his copy of *The Red Badge of Courage*. Thirty-seven years of age, beaming energy and confidence through his wall of white teeth, Theodore Roosevelt was on a mission to clean up a New York police force notorious for its manifold corruption and to improve its enforcement of the law. Prostitution was a particular target for him: convictions for solicitation had more than doubled in the previous twelve months. He upheld the view that a woman's presence on the streets late at night was sufficient cause for arrest. Long before he'd ever met Dora Clark, Crane had protested in print this overzealous policing of prostitution and other aspects of Roosevelt's crusade. Roosevelt, not surprisingly, offered no assistance in response to Crane's letter, only advice: drop the Dora Clark matter and keep it out of the newspapers.[32]

Another of New York's three police commissioners, Frederick Grant, heard the charges brought by Dora Clark against Patrolman Becker on October 15. Miss Clark appeared in a black dress, a large black hat with black feathers, and a veil. Her only jewelry was a diamond star at her throat. The newspapermen rated her a cut above the other streetwalkers in the hearing room. Under cross-examination, it came out that she had been arrested six times for soliciting and fined once. Her real name was Ruby Young and she confessed to being a kept woman. She gave credible accounts of how the police had harassed her.

Becker's lawyer, also named Grant, summoned policemen and a series of what the *Journal* called "women with yellow hair and big diamonds" to corroborate his client's version of the arrest. The *Journal* reporter found Becker forthright and intelligent, in no manner the bully. He claimed to have seen Dora Clark speak to three men before he arrested her. Asked what he meant by "soliciting," he replied, "Any woman who appears on the street alone late at night and talks to a man is a prostitute."[33]

Crane was the next to last witness called. His contention, under cross-examination, that he was in the Tenderloin collecting material for stories drew a hearty laugh from the policemen in attendance. The lawyer suggested that Crane had been living on money given him by women of the Tenderloin, and was particularly interested in one of his former residences on West 27th, which was "redolent of opium." Crane denied having smoked opium. He looked frail during these exchanges, the *Journal* reported, frequently putting his hands to his face. Captain George S. Chapman, Patrolman Becker's supervisor, dredged up the last witness—a janitor who testified that Crane had lived off a prostitute at the aforementioned 27th Street address. Commissioner Grant excluded his testimony, but the newspapers reported it regardless.[34]

The coverage focused on Crane and ignored the accused policeman and Dora Clark (the commissioner had reserved his decision). The *World*'s headlines were harshest:

"CRANE HAD A GAY NIGHT—RACY STORY BROUGHT OUT IN THE TRIAL OF BECKER . . .—A JANITOR TESTIFIED THAT THE NOVELIST LIVED WITH A TENDERLOIN GIRL—AN OPIUM SMOKING EPISODE."

The *New York Press* wasn't far behind:

"RED BADGE MAN ON A POLICE RACK—STEPHEN CRANE'S CHARACTER ASSAILED AT BECKER TRIAL— VILE CHARGES ARE MADE—NOVELIST STICKS TO HIS DEFENSE OF THE TENDERLOIN WOMAN HE SAYS WAS ARRESTED UNLAWFULLY."

The *Journal* was more sympathetic but nonetheless hurtful to Crane's reputation:

"CRANE RISKED ALL TO SAVE A WOMAN—HIS BOHEMIAN LIFE IN NEW YORK LAID BARE FOR THE SAKE OF DORA CLARK."[35]

A final *Journal* editorial was outraged that Clark's charges had not been taken seriously because she was from "the lower half world." The courtroom assault on Mr. Crane's private life was a "deliberate and despicable scheme of police intimidation, of which any voluntary witness in a trial for police outrage may become a victim."[36]

Apart from the *Journal,* which immediately assigned Crane to cover a football game, most editorial opinion considered Crane to have disgraced himself. A few days later, he slipped out of New York, rarely to return. Within a week of the hearing, Dora Clark was arrested again and returned to Jefferson Market Police Court. Becker survived the whole incident and rose to the position of police lieutenant. He developed a specialization in extorting money from Manhattan brothels and casinos. He was eventually convicted of ordering the murder of a bookie and was executed in the electric chair at Sing Sing on July 30, 1915.[37]

THE SAME CAPTAIN GEORGE S. CHAPMAN who had called the last damaging witness against Stephen Crane featured in another headline-winning drama at the other end of the social spectrum shortly after Dora Clark's hearing. On the evening of December 19, 1896, Herbert Barnum Seeley, a young nephew of the late P.T. Barnum, hosted an all-night stag party for his brother, Clinton. The guests, twenty in all, were drawn primarily from the membership register of the Larchmont Yacht Club. They were affluent young men, about half of them married. The venue was a private dining room at Sherry's, a fashionable restaurant. The carte du jour consisted of thirteen courses interspersed with displays of "art"—singing, dancing, and comedy provided by a variety of performers, most of them known to local theater audiences. The dinner guests wore evening dress. What the performers did or didn't wear became a matter of some dispute.

The trouble started around 11 p.m. when a man named Moore walked into the Nineteenth Precinct station in the Tenderloin and advised Captain Chapman that an "indecent" performance by a dancer called Little Egypt was about to take place in a private room at Sherry's on 37th Street. Moore said that a theatrical agent named Phipps had offered Moore's daughter, Anabelle, a sweet and comely girl of eighteen, $15 to dance without her tights at the very same event. It would later emerge that Anabelle had wanted at least $20 to dance without her tights and that her father, who lived off the avails of the girl's dancing, was upset at losing lucrative business to Phipps, who had also booked Little Egypt for the evening.[38]

Not long after midnight, Chapman and a couple of patrolmen burst into Sherry's through a side door and climbed upstairs in search of lewd behavior. They stumbled first into a dressing room, where a handful of women rested in various states of undress. One of them was the singer-dancer Cora Routt, who ordered Chapman out of the room. He answered that she was a disgrace to her sex and instructed her to leave the premises immediately. A handful of gentlemen heard the commotion and rushed to Chapman's side, easing him out the door and attempting to assuage his concerns about indecent activities. Unconvinced, Chapman stormed the private dining room occupied by the Seeley party and lectured the guests on prohibited forms of entertainment. They invited him to sit down, have a drink, and enjoy the show. Chapman made his exit without finding either filth or Little Egypt.

The story, such as it was, troubled the three-cent papers more than it did the penny press. That Chapman would barge, without a warrant, into a dinner party in a private room in a respectable restaurant on a seemingly spurious allegation of indecency was viewed as a gross assault on the privileges and freedoms of club life. The *Herald* predicted that the diners would all be making out complaints against the police. Louis Sherry protested that he catered to only "the very best people in New York" and threatened to lodge a complaint against Chapman and to sue the city.[39] Phipps, who had supplied much of the night's entertainment, accused Chapman of trying to harm his agency. He, too, was threatening legal action. The *Journal* played the story on an inside page and could muster only a yawn of indignation in its editorials.

The Seeley story did not make the *Journal*'s front page until December 24, when it became apparent that none of the young men who attended the bachelor party was prepared to swear a complaint against Chapman. The paper attributed their reluctance to the fact that Little Egypt had indeed appeared at the dinner and "given it to them hot." It was reported that she had actually been on the premises during Chapman's raid, hiding in a private dressing room on the fourth floor. She waited there until 3:30 a.m. before finally emerging to dance the coochee-coochee.[40]

The *Journal* was now clearly amused. It noted that Clinton Seeley, a member of the Consolidated Exchange, had returned to the floor the previous day for the first time since the dinner in his honor. "No sooner did the other brokers spy him than a dozen of them surrounded him and began an imitation of the 'Couchee-Couchee.' Mr. Seeley tried to escape but could not break his way through the line of grinning and cavorting brokers." A large illustration with the story showed "Little Egypt" dancing in a bejeweled bustier, arms raised and midriff bared.[41]

Tired of waiting for the dinner guests to file complaints, Police Chief
Conlin called his own hearing into the raid and fired off subpoenas to all
involved in the affair. The proceedings opened January 7, 1897, at police
headquarters. The hearing room was packed beyond capacity with some
four hundred lawyers, witnesses, policemen, soubrettes, and thrill-
seeking spectators. From the outset, the *Journal* declared it an opera
bouffe of a trial. There were serious issues of law enforcement at stake
but none that would be satisfactorily addressed in this venue, especially
when Police Commissioner Grant, presiding over the affair, was obviously delighted at the salacious testimony. The paper held its mirthful
tone, reporting that onlookers in the hearing room fought over seats, sent
messengers for sandwiches so as not to lose their places, and listened to
the witnesses with open-mouthed grins. Cora Routt, who had ordered
Chapman out of her dressing room, was described as "a self-possessed
young woman . . . with a self-conscious smirk and a purple velvet hat of
alarming proportions and fearsome design." In addition to the smirk and
the hat, Miss Routt wore "a checked waist, a dark skirt, a fur cape, and
carried a muff. She kissed the [Bible] when told to do so with a resounding smack and settled into the witness chair with much complacency and
an audible rustle of silk skirts." She excited onlookers with accounts of
her dances and costumes, all the while denying that she'd done anything
dirty. Her testimony was related in the *Journal* amid a spectacular page-
dominating illustration of flying champagne bottles, dancing girls, tuxe-
doed gentlemen, and police officers.[42]

The next day Anabelle Moore testified as to the nature of her stage
act and what, in particular, she had been asked to do at the Seeley dinner. She described her repertoire, including one piece she called her
"sun dance." She allowed that her figure, in tights, was munificently
displayed throughout the number, though she denied that exposing her
figure was the point of the dance. She went on to explain another gyra-
tion, known as her "butterfly dance." When Miss Moore was asked
under cross-examination how she dressed for the butterfly dance, her
lawyer shouted, "I object."

"Well, how do you undress then?" her interrogator asked.[43]

New Yorkers were agog at the scenes described, even if the dancers
were wearing gauze and body stockings. It wasn't every day that the public got a glimpse inside the private dining rooms of the city's smart set.

The Seeley dinner became a universal topic of conversation. Hardly a preacher in town failed to denounce it from the pulpit. And all this even before the key witness had taken the stand.

When Little Egypt finally entered the hearing room, every gleaming eye in the place fell upon her. She was so lustily surveyed that the *Journal* wondered if Captain Chapman shouldn't raid his own trial. "She carried her chin high," the paper reported, smiling and boldly meeting the stares of the assembled as she approached the stand. "Her lips were painted a fiery red that set off by contrast the ivory whiteness of her fine teeth. Her eyes were bright, restless." She wore a sealskin sack coat, which the heat of the room compelled her to remove. Her tight-fitting dress was made of "some crinkly blue stuff," with white horizontal stripes across the waist and skirt. "Her hat was a wonderful creation of velvet, embroidery and feathers, worn tilting over her left eye."[44]

Little Egypt, a native of Algeria, was born Asheya Waba. She claimed to be fluent in French and to possess only a smattering of English. "She speaks a patois that may be intelligible on the docks of Marseilles," observed the *Journal*, "but that certainly would not be understood in Paris." Asked under oath what she was hired to do by Phipps, the entertainment booker, she answered slowly, affecting a lisp that made her even more difficult to understand. Phipps, she said, had told her, "You do a leetle Egyptian pose on a leetle pedestal—in ze altogether." A moment later, she answered the question again with a slight twist: Phipps had asked her to "pose for art's sake on a leetle pedestal in ze altogether." Asked what she meant by "ze altogether," Little Egypt cast down her eyes for a second, and then raised them and showed her fine teeth in a smile so comprehensive that every man in the room felt it was intended for him. She addressed the question: "Me say, 'Me do what ees proper for art sake.' And he say, 'ver' well.'"

Little Egypt further testified that Captain Chapman had rushed into Sherry's shortly after she arrived to perform. Her hosts had hidden her on the fourth floor: "Quick zay take me to ze room of ze color of lemons. Zere I was an hour: much wine was given me."[45]

These statements were followed by accusations that men had touched and pinched her during her performance and that several of the guests were, as the *Herald* put it, "careless about their attire."[46] These latter details Hearst's paper omitted from its coverage. It simply alluded to

"testimony that would not interest the *Journal*'s readers" and ran hiero-
glyphics in place of the offending words. Among other illustrated merri-
ment, the paper produced cartoons of ancient Egyptian characters
enacting scenes from the trial: one showed two pharaoh-like figures with
cigars in their mouths spiriting a dancer upstairs; one showed lawyers in
Egyptian garb demonstrating dance steps; another had Captain Chapman
nodding off during the hearing. A further series of five large illustrations
showed Little Egypt in various poses, entering the courtroom and flaunting the voluptuous body inside the tight striped dress.

Captain Chapman himself testified the same day as Little Egypt. The
Journal was unimpressed. The ruler of the Tenderloin, it commented, was
entirely at ease on the stand, "stroking his fine whiskers and twisting his
mustache while he answered questions. Some of his phrases were grandil-
oquent and might have been impressive had they been grammatical."[47]

At the end of the day, Chapman was vindicated, although no one was
ever convicted of procuring or performing indecent acts. In the absence
of hard findings, the *Journal* organized a "jury" of twelve society women
to pass judgment on what had transpired in the private dining room. Mrs.
Jennie June Croly spoke for the majority: "I wouldn't touch one of them
with a rake," she said of the Seeley men. "They have disgraced their own
sex, and ours, too." The only lasting consequence of the hearing was that
Little Egypt doubled her rates.[48]

Amid the Seeley saga, the *Journal* also chased the story of a Christmas
morning fire at an East 33rd Street tenement that left dozens of families
on the street. The *Journal* bought them all Christmas dinner, found them
lodging, and launched a drive to collect food, rent money, and household
effects for the victims. As part of the relief effort, the paper announced
that it would team with impresario Oscar Hammerstein to host a matinee
fundraising benefit at his Olympia Theatre on Saturday, January 2.
Hammerstein promised to contribute the box office receipts from the performance. The *Journal* bought two hundred seats for the displaced. The
chanteuse Louise Beaudet announced she would sing a new song and
wear the prettiest of her new dresses at the benefit. Among the other
singers, acrobats, and comedians hired to draw the largest possible crowd
and lift the spirits of the fire sufferers was the sensational exotic dancer
Little Egypt.

AT THE HEIGHT OF THE SEELEY AFFAIR, Reverend Louis A. Banks, a Brooklyn pastor, preached on the subject of "Christ's controversy with the brutality and sensuality of Greater New York." If the Savior were to visit Gotham, the Reverend maintained, there would be hell to pay for the city's obsessions with violence and sexuality. The Seeley dinner had catered to the basest passions of man, furnishing "a shocking illustration of the decadence and degradation" of the respectable classes. But it was not just lust and lasciviousness that troubled the Reverend. He did not like boxing, either. The *Journal* quoted him at length: "That in the latter days of what we are often pleased to call an enlightened century, on the most famous street in the leading city on the American continent, it should be lawful to slug a man to death for the amusement of [those] who pay . . . is horrible and revolting in the extreme."[49]

Hearst himself was not fond of boxing. The *Journal* wanted the sport outlawed, a position it shared with legions of reformers, church groups, and politicians, and prizefighting was indeed illegal in most of the country. The paper did not dispute that fighting encouraged skill and pluck and reliance on one's fists instead of weapons, but it nonetheless felt that legal recognition for pugilism invited "gamblers, drunkards, roughs and all the social debris to move out of darkness into the light and take a footing which removes the salutary dread of the policeman's club."[50]

The occasion for the latter comment was a heavyweight bout between Bob Fitzsimmons and Tom Sharkey in San Francisco at the end of 1896. Fitzsimmons sent Sharkey to the mat with a body blow in the eighth round, but Wyatt Earp, the infamous lawman and part-time fight referee, declared a low blow and awarded the match and the $10,000 purse to Sharkey. Earp was accused of fraud. Fitzsimmons took the matter to court. The whole country was talking about the fight over the fight— even Brooklyn pastors were paying attention—and that put the *Journal* in a quandary. It disliked boxing, but it had to admit just "how widespread and deep seated is the savage human interest in fighting." And now Fitzsimmons was to fight again in an even bigger match.[51]

Promoters had been trying since 1894 to pit Fitzsimmons against reigning champion Gentleman Jim Corbett, a college-educated fighter who claimed an artistic and scientific approach to the sport. They first scheduled the match in Florida but ran into heavy opposition from local worthies, especially after one of Fitzsimmons's sparring partners died as a result of injuries suffered in a public exhibition. The promoters turned to Texas and began to build a 50,000-seat arena to host the bout, but the state governor denounced prizefighting as a brutal and degrading sport and ordered a special session of the legislature specifically to make it a felony. The promoters moved on to Hot Springs, Arkansas, with no better luck. Corbett and Fitzsimmons were arrested on entering the state. Finally, the fighters announced that they would meet on March 17, 1897, in Carson City, a mining camp in what was already recognized as the "morally liminal" state of Nevada.[52]

Notwithstanding its opposition to prizefighting, the *Journal* revealed a month before the event that it had bought exclusive access to both boxers for an undisclosed price. The paper was aware of at least one level of hypocrisy: "Although this paper is unfriendly to trusts in a general way, it makes an exception in favor of itself. It has practically secured a monopoly of information concerning the great championship fight. All who desire accurate and official news from the principals, the training quarters, and the ringside will have to read the *Journal* to get it."[53]

It wasn't uncommon for a paper to deplore and cover an event simultaneously—give the people what they want, as Dana commanded. But Dana had said nothing about monopolizing the conversation around an event that was illegal in most states and that the U.S. Congress was working furiously to suppress. A congressional effort to ban the Corbett-Fitzsimmons fight had failed in 1896. Now lawmakers were attempting to forbid the transmission by mail or interstate commerce all pictures and descriptions of prize fights. A coalition of religious and reform groups, including the 300,000-member Women's Christian Temperance Union, rallied in Washington in support of the bill. Prizefighting was decried as a "degrading, brutal, and disgusting business" that had "no place in a Christian civilized community."[54] The reformers lost the vote in the House, saving the *Journal*'s exclusive, and leaving the paper free to editorialize against the sport while making itself the center of attention for the title match.

Every day for weeks in advance of the event, the *Journal* ran profiles of the fighters, life-sized pictures of their fists and forearms, and illustrations of their stances, dodges, and punches, including three new blows invented by Corbett, which he claimed had never been used by any other pugilist. Fitzsimmons was followed to church, where he sang in the choir, and to the grave of Brigham Young, where he spoke of his curiosity about Mormonism. The paper consulted experts on everything from training methods to betting lines.

Almost daily, the *Journal* reported on the efforts of its competitors to undermine its exclusives. Corbett claimed that the *World* approached him with a rumor that he struck his wife, in hopes of eliciting a printable comment. Fitzsimmons lectured reporters from rival dailies that the *Journal*'s arrangement was good for their craft: "The *Journal* and the *Examiner* get all the news and the pictures and the best stuff, and you guys have to hop out and do something for a living to make any kind of showing, whatever. I tell you it is a good thing for the proprietors, and for the first time in years the reporters have got to battle for everything they get. It keeps you digging."[55] Fitzsimmons was right about that. Notwithstanding Hearst's deal, the *World* and the *Herald* managed to fill pages with observations, interviews with secondary figures, and brief quotes from the fighters themselves, which were dressed up as exclusives (whether they were overheard or based on actual interviews is hard to say).

On the day of the match, the *Journal* erected bulletin boards at Madison Square and in Union Square, Harlem, and Park Row, where fifty thousand people assembled in anticipation of telegraphed news from Carson City. "Bankers touched elbows with Park Row waiters still wearing their aprons," the paper reported. Two rapid writers manned each of the *Journal*'s boards, sketching scenes and narrating the fight round by round.[56] The *World* and the *Herald* had bulletins of their own.

Occasional correspondent and former Kansas senator John J. Ingalls was ringside for the *Journal*. He clearly favored Corbett, with his dark and drawn countenance "lined deeply with the furrows of care and concern." Fitzsimmons had "a silly, open-mouthed grin and an uncouth, awkward, shambling gait, like a clown." The appearance of the men stripped for the ring struck Ingalls as grotesque: "With the exception of a small breech cloth, they were naked to their ankles, where their stockings were rolled loosely down over the tops of their thin, flat-soled shoes."[57]

In the fourteenth round, Fitzsimmons landed a savage blow to Corbett's midsection and knew in an instant that the fight was over. "Fitzsimmons," wrote Ingalls, "turned with buffoon gesture and bloody grin to the audience. When Corbett, who was still erect, suddenly tottered, a swift spasm shuddered through his limbs, he sank slowly upon his left knee, his head fell forward upon his knotted chest . . . he leaned for an instant upon his right hand in a precise attitude of the dying gladiator in the familiar state described by Byron when his manly brow 'consents to death, but conquers agony.'" This narrative accompanied a round-by-round summary of the bout, analysis by Nevada governor Reinhold Sadler, and scads of illustrations, including maps of the bodies of both fighters that marked every blow that landed and the round in which it was received.[58] Coverage in competing papers was similarly exhaustive.

A *Journal* editorial in the wake of its orgy of coverage of the Nevada bout was resigned to the sport's popularity. "[The] enormous crowds about the *Journal*'s bulletins—crowds exceeding in numbers those on the night of the Presidential election—afforded sufficient evidence that the interest in a great pugilistic battle is not confined to any class of society, but spreads among all. Perhaps prize fighting is brutal, but, after all, man is the most brutal of brutes. . . . It is necessary to take cognizance of the nature of man when we try to judge his interest in the exploits of the prize ring."[59]

ON JUNE 26, 1897, several boys were swimming in the East River at the foot of 11th Street when one of them, on his way back to the pier, noticed a bundle bobbing ahead of him. He pushed it to the pier and lifted it out. The package was wrapped in oilcloth and bound with twine. The boys ripped it open and found inside the mutilated upper torso of a human male, headless but with arms still attached. Throwing on their clothes, the youngsters ran up 11th Street to find a policeman.

The lead headline on the next day's *Journal* read "Beheaded, cast into the river." Beneath it was a reproduction of the pattern of the oilcloth: gilt lilies and diamonds on a red background. According to doctors interviewed by the paper, the deceased was about thirty-five years of age, five foot ten and two hundred pounds, healthy, with light blond hair and a light complexion. A portion of skin had been cut away from his chest, perhaps a birthmark or a tattoo that might have aided in his identification.[60]

On the afternoon of June 27, at the other end of Manhattan, a man named Meyer and his two sons, Herbert, age thirteen, and Edgar, age eight, were picking wild cherries under the Washington Bridge. Herbert spied a bright bundle at the bottom of a retaining wall, clear of the underbrush. The boys raced toward it and fought for possession. "It's mine," screamed Herbert. "I saw it first." They summoned their father, who opened the package and found the bottom section of a male torso, from the lower ribs to the upper thighs. Meyer alerted the police, who transported the grisly find to Bellevue Hospital, where it caused great excitement among physicians, administrators, and, according to the *Journal*, loitering patients.[61]

The upper and lower torsos were perfectly matched, as were the portions of oilcloth in which they were wrapped. Attending surgeons determined that whoever had butchered the body had neatly removed the head with a fine saw. He appeared to have begun to detach the legs in the same careful manner before impatiently snapping them off with brute strength. The *Journal* now had at least thirty reporters chasing down clues that might put a name to the corpse. They located the manufacturer of the red gilt oilcloth as well as its sales agents; they visited all the Manhattan dry goods dealers who carried the pattern. They came up empty.

The *Journal*'s third day of coverage was thin. No new body parts were found. In recognition of "the outrageousness of the crime" and the "vast public interest" in its solution, the paper offered a reward of $1,000 for help in identifying the victim. It performed experiments with buoyant materials to determine where in the East River the upper torso might have been dumped in order to arrive at 11th Street on an ebb tide. It dredged the river in hopes of discovering the missing head. It investigated all of New York's active missing persons cases in hopes of finding someone who fit the victim's profile. It drafted Professor P.S. McAllister, an expert in surgery at New York University, along with physicians from the coroner's office and Bellevue's anatomical experts, to make more precise estimates of the height and weight and physical characteristics of the deceased. In addition to medical men, the *Journal* consulted experts in tattoos and palmistry and crime detection, including Robert Pinkerton of the legendary detective agency, who, resorting to a crude form of racial profiling, offered the following: "It is seldom the Italian will do such a thing. . . . The German seems to regard [dismemberment] as the best means of disposing of a body."[62] Pinkerton, as things transpired, had hit the bull's eye.

New Yorkers were riveted to the case of the headless corpse. Large crowds gathered daily on the banks of the river to watch the boats dredging for the victim's lost parts. Coverage was exhaustive all along Park Row—"a veritable newspaper holocaust," complained one trade publication.[63] Even dailies with low tolerance for slayings chased the story: the *Times* judged it "the most brutal and cold-blooded murder of the decade."[64] New York's finest were also hard at work on the case. The *Journal* gave investigators high marks for effort, but the police force was small and inexpert. Its members were largely political appointees with minimal training and the barest commitment to professionalism. It is not altogether surprising that a newspaper, the *Journal*, produced all of the significant breaks in the case.

George Waugh Arnold, a stocky former athlete employed as a Hearst reporter, frequently capped his workday with some exercise and a body rub at the Murray Hill Turkish Baths. Two days after the torso had been discovered, he stopped by the baths and called for his favorite rubber, only to learn that the man was not available. Disappointed, Arnold asked the other attendants what had become of his masseur and was told that the man had not been at work in several days. A light went on in Arnold's mind. It is not clear whether he had already examined the corpse or whether he now ran to do so. In any event, he noted that the hands of the victim were calloused like those of a rubber.

The *Journal* marched a party of employees from the Murray Hill Turkish Baths to the morgue and positively identified the corpse as belonging to Willie Guldensuppe, a German masseur with a tattoo of a woman on his chest, a souvenir of his years at sea. Guldensuppe's co-workers volunteered his address, along with stories about his complicated love affair with his German landlady, a midwife named Augusta Nack. She was said to have a possessive ex-husband and another man in her life, possibly named Fred. She lived over a drugstore at 34th and Ninth. Arnold received a $1,000 bonus from Hearst.

At 1 a.m. on Tuesday, June 29, several hours after the identification of the body, a *Journal* reporter rang Augusta Nack's bell and kept ringing it until she answered and invited him inside. Posing as a friend of Guldensuppe, he asked whether she knew his whereabouts. Mrs. Nack replied that she had not seen him since they had quarreled several days earlier. She said little else in response to the reporter's questions, although she did admit to the failure of her marriage and to living with Guldensuppe. The *Journal*'s reporter described Mrs. Nack as strong, ruddy, broad-shouldered, and erect. She had smooth, clear skin and dark, burning eyes, deep set and close together. Her black hair was shiny and well brushed.[65]

All of this information was splashed in the *Journal*'s fourth day of coverage, along with a sketch of the interiors of Mrs. Nack's rooms and a floor plan of her apartment. The paper's suspicions were clearly focused on the ex-husband, Herman Nack, the former owner of a Tenth Avenue bologna shop. He had lost his business and his wife, but his jealous temper was still very much with him. A further break in the case that same day resulted from the *Journal*'s diligent canvass of dry goods retailers. A reporter had interviewed Mrs. Max Riger, who worked the counter of her husband's establishment in Astoria. A day or two before Guldensuppe's torso had floated down the East River, she had sold a quantity of red gilt oilcloth to a woman who appeared to be in a hurry and who looked remarkably like Mrs. Nack.[66]

Hearst himself was up to his ears in the Guldensuppe case. He was seen charging down Park Row at the fore of his journalistic "murder squad," an investigative team formed for just such a story. On learning Mrs. Nack's address, he rented every available apartment in her building and guarded the entrance to keep competing reporters out. His murder squad not only led police to Mrs. Nack but remained in the room while detectives conducted their initial interrogation of her.

The *Journal* continued to lead the coverage as suspicions shifted from Mr. Nack to his wife's second male friend, another German, whose name was not "Fred" but Martin Thorn. A black-eyed barber with curly hair, Thorn had lately joined the ranks of Mrs. Nack's boarders and had replaced Guldensuppe in her affections. The two men had quarreled, violently, on at least one occasion, and Thorn had since boasted to his fellow barbers that he had killed his rival. Police arrested Thorn and Mrs. Nack, charging both with murder.

The trial began in November. The defense, led by William F. Howe, the most celebrated criminal defender in the United States, seemed to present the stronger arguments in the early going, but the case would never reach the jury. The *Journal* interrupted the proceedings with yet another spectacular scoop. At the behest of the paper, a Presbyterian clergyman made a mid-trial visit to Mrs. Nack in prison. He took along his four-year-old son, an angelic-looking boy who apparently climbed into the accused's lap and told her that if she was guilty of a crime, God would want her to confess. The next morning, as reported by the *New York Times*, William Howe walked up to his other client, Martin Thorn, and handed him a copy of the *New York Journal*, its headlines announcing Mrs. Nack's confession:

> A deep, dull red blush rose quickly over Thorn's face, but there was not a flicker of his eyelids, not an extra beat in the blood vessels of his jaw or neck. . . . Thorn looked at [the newspaper] and evidently comprehended it. His next act looked like that of a partly frozen and insensible man, in whom courtesy was instinctive. . . . He handed the newspaper back to his counsel, inclining his head as he did so, but moving slowly and stiffly, as a man asleep and barely comprehending might do. With that act the color left his face. The wholesome pink that had shone through his skin vanished and was replaced by a dull, cheesy pallor, which remained. During all the day his face looked as if it might be cut without a drop of blood flowing from the blade. It was a ghastly face—the eyes and likes of a living man, the hue and skin of a dead man above a living, moving, nervous body.[67]

Mrs. Nack and Martin Thorn had murdered Willie Guldensuppe in order to pursue their love undisturbed. She had lured the victim to a cottage in the Queen's neighborhood of Woodside, where Thorn, taking no chances, awaited him with a pistol, a poison dagger, a hammer, a noose, carbolic acid, and a carving knife. After shooting Guldensuppe and stabbing him in the heart with the poison dagger, Thorn had dissected him in the bathtub and dumped his parts around town. The victim's head was never found. Mrs. Nack got fifteen years. In August 1898, Thorn took a seat in the electric chair at Sing Sing. Fifty-nine seconds later he was dead.[68]

CRANE, SEELEY, Corbett-Fitzsimmons, and Guldensuppe are among the most sensational of the sex, violence, and squalor stories covered by Hearst in New York. There were many others, some one-day wonders, some week-long page-dominating dramas, some raising serious public issues, some occasioning brilliant journalism, and others best described as meretricious junk. While Hearst managed to dominate more than his share of these narratives, almost all of them would have excited the public even without his attentions. It was an age of sensation. The public space was awash in febrile emotions and they spilled not only into murders and scandals but such great and consequential events as the Panic of '93 and the clash of '96, with all of it leading to a great bloody eruption over Cuba in '98. Hearst did not set the mood, but he reveled in it and amply exposed its less savory dimensions to his readers, and that was enough to make him a plausible target for a morals campaign.

Ervin Wardman led the charge. A tall, severe native of Salt Lake City, Wardman followed Hearst by a few years at Harvard before taking up journalism and climbing swiftly to the editorship of the *New York Press*. A staunch Republican sheet, the *Press* fought McKinley's corner in '96, mocking Hearst as "our silverite, or silver-wrong" competitor, which was about as close to humor as the grim Wardman ever managed. He took pleasure in taunting the socially prominent Phoebe Hearst for having raised a rabble-rousing son who ran a paper without "even the veneer of decency." He claimed that Hearst had spent millions in weak imitation of Pulitzer's "new journalism," and he dismissed both the *Journal* and the *World* as "fake mongers, chambers of horrors, cesspools, sloughs, purveyors of mendacity."[69] The *Press* had lost its business manager to the *Journal* in 1896 and was struggling to hold its circulation in an increasingly competitive market.[70]

Wardman is believed to be the first editor to publish the term "yellow journalism" in relation to Hearst and Pulitzer. Because it was never intended as a classification so much as as an epithet, Wardman never got around to defining the phrase. It appears to have been inspired by his loathing of the Yellow Kid cartoons—Wardman took their irreverent gutter humor as symbolic of everything foul in the *World* and the *Journal*. Whatever its derivation, it seems clear that Wardman intended "yellow journalism" to cover a gamut of journalistic sins, from unreliable information to dangerous politics, moral turpitude, sensationalism, and bad taste. It was soon ubiquitous as a term of abuse for both the Hearst and the Pulitzer papers, and it remains today as Wardman's principal contribution to the history of journalism.

In addition to sniping at Hearst and Pulitzer, Wardman joined Dana's *Sun* and the *New York Times*, recently purchased by Adolph Ochs, in fomenting a public uprising against the yellow menace through the winter of 1896 and well into '97. The *Times* acted as megaphone for a committee of the New York Ministers' Association that was complaining about the pernicious influence of the *World* and the *Journal,* papers "so low in moral tone as to make their toleration and success a reproach upon the community." The ministers encouraged the public to patronize "clean and wholesome" newspapers—papers like the *Times,* it went without saying.[71]

When trustees of the Newark Free Public Library voted on February 4, 1897, to remove copies of the *Journal* and the *World* from its files on the grounds that their "chronicles of crime, of lust, and of general nastiness" were offensive to decent people and corruptive of youth, Wardman and Dana could not contain themselves. "In decent public esteem yellow journalism occupies the same place as brothels," crowed the *Press.*[72] The *Sun* warmly congratulated the Newark trustees and encouraged other libraries, clubs, and reading rooms to institute similar bans. It claimed to see in the *World* and the *Journal* a licentious, vulgar, and criminal spirit and "an effrontery almost without example in the history of journalism."[73] Dana, a past master at counseling decency and restraint while displaying neither, echoed Wardman's whorish imagery: "The procuress corrupting her sex is not more an enemy to society than the 'new journalism,' with its prurient wares—the suggestiveness of the pencil and the salaciousness of the pen."[74] The *Times* lamented that so much of the public was "debased in soul and deed" and "vulgar in taste and thought," and sought to shame respectable men and women into dropping the yellow papers: "The moral disease germs of the new journals are as big and hideous as rattlesnakes."[75]

By spring, close to a hundred institutions had jumped on the banishment bandwagon, including the Yale University Library, the Harlem Branch of the YMCA, the Century Club in Manhattan, and the Flatbush Young Republican Club in Brooklyn. Hearst kept up his standing routine of printing religious features and sermons in order to "ingratiate ourselves with the Godly," but otherwise he ignored the hullabaloo.[76] Pulitzer lashed back, calling his critics malicious troublemakers jealous of his phenomenal success. But while giving no quarter publicly, Pulitzer was privately rattled by the banishment campaign. He lectured his executives on the importance of journalistic respectability and found occasion for yet another reorganization of his management suite. He needn't have worried. The protests petered out by summer, leaving the circulations of the *Journal* and the *World* undiminished. In all probability, the attentions of its rivals convinced more people to try the *Journal* than to shun it.

The morals campaign fizzled because readers liked the yellow papers and did not see anything terribly wrong with them. The watchdogs had failed to make a credible case that Hearst and Pulitzer were propagating evil or causing harm. As the newspaper historian Joseph Campbell notes, the attacks tended to be "invective-filled generalizations," short on specific grievance.[77] Indeed it was difficult to be precise because there was nothing the yellows could publish that their gray rivals wouldn't touch. All of the big papers on Park Row competed for sensational stories. The *Herald* ran the most explicit testimony from the Seeley trial, and even the sanctimonious *Times* found it necessary to mention, in a 4,500-word story on Mrs. Nack's confession, her strong and sensual features and "the high swell of her bust."[78] The yellow tricks of presentation were prevalent in the three-cent papers, too. The moralizers never really had a chance, and they should have known better—Dana in particular, who had trained readers to expect what he was now asking them to reject.

While the gray papers tried in vain to foment a popular revolt against Hearst, a more interesting and substantive discussion of yellow journalism was playing out in the trade press, as it made honest efforts to understand the sudden tumult in their industry. The trades picked up arguments on both sides of the question and distilled, elaborated, and tested them through the spring and summer of 1897.

While some trade commentators echoed Ervin Wardman and company, others were excited by the work of the yellow papers. The *Journal*'s proponents recognized the paper as a serious daily, and wondered why the "sober, clean, self-respecting" papers weren't providing their readers with work by top-drawer talent or matching the enterprise of Hearst and Pulitzer in their newsgathering.[79] They celebrated the efforts of the "sensational press" to fight corruption and expose fraud and help the needy. It wasn't drivel that drew readers to the *World* and the *Journal* but "the freshest news brightly presented, the sham sharply punctured and, above all, the feeling, justified or not, that behind and through the paper there beats a warm, generous, human heart alive to the troubles and miseries of humanity and anxious to alleviate them." The better papers, by contrast, seemed to have had all the humanity refined out of them.[80]

The trades were careful to separate real from imagined problems in the yellow press. For instance, they were not overly distracted by politics. Whereas the "wholesome" papers sought to stigmatize Hearst for his support of Bryan and progressive causes generally, industry professionals were generally tolerant of political differences, recognizing that no particular brand of politics made a paper good or legitimate. One man's vicious muckraking was another's "sham sharply punctured."

A trade critic who signed his pieces XYZ took up another supposed problem with yellow journals: charges of falsehood and fakery leveled at Hearst and Pulitzer. These did not come only from the gray papers; the *World* and the *Journal* frequently accused each other of getting things wrong and making things up. There was the usual amount of hyperbole in all these indictments; a paper's honest mistake would be discovered by an enemy and lustily denounced as a deliberate fraud. There is no question, however, that the yellows were fingered more often than the grays, a fact that troubled XYZ:

> The charge of lying against newspapers and newspaper men is so old and threadbare that those of us who have been ten years in the work sometimes smile when we recall how indignantly we repelled the accusation during our first year or two in harness. But there seems to be an added bitterness, a more convinced tone in the mouths of men when they speak of the *Journal* or the *World*. . . . Now, as a matter of fact, either Mr. Empson, the city editor of the *Journal*, or Mr. Russell, who holds the same position on the *World*, is just as insistent on verification of stories turned in as Mr. Rieck, of the *Herald*, ever dreamed of being. . . .
>
> Nor is this all. I have amused myself when I have heard such remarks made about the *World* or the *Journal*, by asking the one talking which paper he believed told the truth. The answer might be the *Herald*, the *Times* or any other. Procuring the two papers, that believed in and that denounced, I have asked for a comparison of the reports. Provided it was not a case of a "beat," the statements made have been identical to all intents and purposes with that of the "new" journal as usually the more conservative. Yet I have never found proof of this kind to have any effect on the belief or prejudice, if you will, of the objector, simply because that belief or prejudice is honest.[81]

While it is not unreasonable to assume that its exuberance and inexperience led the *Journal* to commit more error than its rivals, the paper has never been demonstrated to be unusually inaccurate or unethical. Like every other daily on Park Row, it sometimes made mistakes, embroidered stories, manipulated facts, rushed to judgment, and plagiarized competitors. But it also made best efforts to get things right, and its shortcomings were within the realm of acceptable practice for the times. Gilded Age journalism ethics were ad hoc and learned on the job, and most yellow journalists, including Hearst's top editors, were trained at the best papers in New York. That the Park Row dailies were hyper-vigilant about spotting and bewailing one another's mistakes was a huge deterrent to any sort of journalistic crime. The yellows probably felt the scrutiny more keenly than many of their competitors because market leaders were always prime targets for criticism. As Bradford Merrill, a Pulitzer editor, wrote James Creelman during the election campaign: "The *World* has ten times as many reasons to be careful as any other newspaper in this land. I am determined so far as eternal vigilance and earnest sincerity can prevent, not to let one canard or single unauthentic sensation get into the [paper]. We are absolutely surrounded by enemies—our deflated competitors, many of whom do not hesitate to lie to make any body believe that we are lying."[82]

A lot of trade commentators believed that the *Journal* and the *World* were more sensationalistic than other New York papers, an assessment that stands today. It is seldom clear, however, what is meant by "sensationalism." Like "yellow journalism," the term tends to be thrown around indiscriminately. By a plain definition, sensationalism denotes journalism that wallows in the lurid, shocking, and emotive. But, again, content of that sort was wallowed in by a variety of papers, gray and yellow. The gray editors described Hearst's paper as a chamber of horrors, a procuress, a brothel, a criminal, a moral disease, a rattlesnake, and a licentious vulgarian without example in the history of journalism— words that were nothing if not sensationalistic.

Hearst himself seems to have been uncertain about the word sensationalism. He could at times embrace it, and in the next breath modify it ("intelligent sensationalism"), and on other occasions eschew it in favor of "striking journalism." But most of his efforts to distance himself from the word came later in his career. At this point he appears to have enjoyed his sensations both for their own sake and for the readers they attracted. He always believed that a successful newspaper entertained as well as informed its readers.[83]

Over the years, there have been efforts to measure sensationalism empirically or to define it objectively, but they all founder on the same rocks. Who is to say how many murders, cartoons, and bold headlines are too many? Shouldn't sensational news receive sensational treatment? Who is to say what is genuine journalism and what is trivial or prurient? How do we know when an editor is genuinely outraged or excited by a story and when is he just trying to sell newspapers? (And what's wrong with selling newspapers?) These are all questions on which reasonable people (and reasonable editors) disagree. Sensationalism, in the end, is a highly subjective concept.

Subjective or not, few would disagree that the *Journal* and the *World* were more sensational than other Park Row sheets. Of course, in any crowded newspaper market, one daily is bound to be relatively sensational and another relatively dreary. The test is whether or not the sensationalism undermines the paper's credibility with its audience; readers who do not share an editor's excitement or concern over a story will consider his paper unreliable.

There is no question that some readers and critics believed that the *Journal* failed the test of reliability, but the *Journal*'s many regular patrons felt otherwise. They either liked the paper's style or tolerated it or discounted it in the same way that they were accustomed to discounting extreme political rhetoric in all newspapers. This is not a sad commentary on Hearst's readers. Again, everything Hearst was doing was different only in degree, not in kind, from the work of his competitors, and none of it was inherently incompatible with quality journalism. One might argue that the high color of the yellow papers led to distortions of reality, that the world was never so exciting or lurid as it seemed in their pages. But it is not at all clear that Godkin's *Evening Post*, the dreariest of the grays, got closer to real life by filling long columns of unbroken type "without prejudice, without color, and without style," as its alumnus Lincoln Steffens described it.[84]

The trades, on the whole, recognized that there was more than one correct way to make a newspaper and that differences in style had little to do with good and evil, right or wrong. Different dailies appealed to different tastes. "Approaching the subject from an unprejudiced standpoint," wrote one commentator in the *Journalist*, "I should say Mr. Hearst's gravest offense has been against good taste rather than morals." Like many traditionalists, this critic wished for more serious news of the commercial, scientific, and artistic worlds. He frankly admitted to preferring the rambling wit of the *Sun* to the shout and hurry of the *Journal*.[85] He nonetheless acknowledged that his own tastes were not representative of the greater reading public. There will never be a model journalism, he wrote, "until there shall be a model public to read and support it."

The paternalism of that last comment—assuming a low estimate of the public mind—runs through all discussion of sensationalism. As early as the 1840s, press critics had complained of penny papers' feeding "the depraved appetites" of their readers with exciting news.[86] The word "sensationalism" was first applied to journalism in an 1869 essay by E.L. Godkin that protested newspapers' squandering attention on the lives and opinions of people inherently unworthy of notice. Godkin was referring specifically to the vulgar human-interest journalism of the *Sun* and the *Herald*.[87] By showing high regard for popular sensibilities, he maintained, these papers were destroying the reverence of the people for their betters.

The same paternalism runs through the 1896–97 morals campaign against Hearst and Pulitzer. Wardman hated the Yellow Kid cartoon with its mockery of dress balls, horse shows, and much else that the privileged classes held dear. The Kid was wicked and subversive, the dirty emblem of the very same dirty sheet that had embraced Bryan's anarchic mob and ridiculed the Seeley clubmen. The gray editors believed themselves to embody the highest purposes and best practices of newspapering, and they considered the *Journal* an affront to their principles and tastes, as well as a menace to their ideas about society and culture. They understood themselves to be wrestling with the yellows for cultural authority, which, of course, they were. Wardman, Dana, and Godkin were in the newspaper business to wield influence and shape opinion, as well as to make a good living, and their pleas for moral and intellectual enlightenment were being overpowered by Hearst's ribald conversations with the common man.

Which brings us back to competitive realities on Park Row. Hearst's rise was fast and destabilizing. He was pulling readers and advertisers from other titles and no one knew for certain in 1897 if he was already peaking or just ramping up. The market shares of smaller dailies like the *Press*, the *Times*, and the *Sun* were shrinking, they were desperate for a competitive response, and it cost them nothing to fling mud at Hearst while promoting themselves as "decent" and "wholesome" newspapers.

They wrapped their elitism and conservative politics in a cloak of good-
ness, and sold their comparatively dreary presentation of news as a measure of their reliability and sobriety.

In this limited respect, the decency campaign was effective. It did not
ruin or even hurt the *Journal*, and it probably did not expand the audiences
of the gray papers, either—Wardman and his ilk were preaching to the
choir. But the choir was flattered. The gray editors made their journalists,
their readers, and their advertisers feel better about themselves and their
choice of newspaper. No one understood the commercial advantages of
journalistic "sanitation" better than Ochs at the *Times*.[88] He liked to publish letters from readers who got the spirit of it. The *Times*, wrote one fan,
was a "clean, wholesome family paper, bound to be appreciated by the
many thousands who have become ashamed to place some of our great
newspapers in the hands of their children."[89] Ochs used his cleansing campaign in a naked bid to win advertisers by claiming that "respectable men
and women" were abandoning the yellows.[90] He liked it so much that he
adopted it as a marketing slogan: "All The News That's Fit To Print."

The decency crusade was also effective in other ways. It prompted
many trade commentators to take sides on the merits of the yellow press;
the near universal applause that greeted Hearst in his first year would
henceforth be balanced by serious criticism of his politics, taste, and practices. What's more, while Hearst did not join a morals debate with the
gray editors, he did eventually react, and in a predictable manner. James
Gordon Bennett, target of the first great morals campaign, had emerged
from it a relentless self-promoter. He used his own pages to trumpet the
virtues and the success of his *Herald* in response to his critics. Hearst,
having promoted the *Journal* enthusiastically in his first year, would do so
maniacally in the months ahead. Sensationalism, the *Journal* would maintain, "is always the cry of the newspaper to the rival which passes it."[91]

CHAPTER NINE

Two Warm Babes and a Hot Hansom

I t is easy to forget that in 1897 the editor whose name was on every-one's lips, whose next moves were the subject of speculation and dread all along Park Row, was only thirty-three years old. Hearst was by no means the only young man in the newspaper business. There were plenty of boyish scribblers around when he hit town—the likes of Richard Harding Davis, Stephen Crane, and David Graham Phillips. There were also men of his vintage clawing their way into the management suite, including Ervin Wardman, Arthur Brisbane, Morrill Goddard, and Charles Edward Russell. But it was one thing to find gainful employment at a big city paper at an early age and quite another to be operating your own scorching entry in the high-stakes race for daily newspaper supremacy. Hearst's main competitors—Joseph Pulitzer, James Gordon Bennett Jr., Charles A. Dana, E.L. Godkin, and Whitelaw Reid—were all giants of the industry a generation or two older than he was. The next youngest of this bunch was Pulitzer, seventeen years Hearst's senior; Dana, the eldest, was twenty-eight years beyond Pulitzer. Even Adolph Ochs, recently arrived from Tennessee to purchase the struggling *New York Times,* was five years older than Hearst. The trades considered Ochs a whelp, and in journalistic terms they were correct: it would take him more than a decade to give the *Times* a commanding voice.

One has to reach as far back as the 1840s, when Horace Greeley took over the *Tribune,* to find another editor playing so significant a role as Hearst at so early an age. And it is unlikely that the priggish Greeley ever enjoyed the experience as much as the upstart Californian. However much turmoil Hearst was creating around him, however much effort and concentration he gave the *Journal,* he still managed to tend to his

pleasure. He was a dashing newspaper publisher with an ample
allowance, no attachments, and half a lifetime's experience of living on
his own, and the high life was in his blood. Both of his parents were
vigorously self-indulgent: his mother lived like a queen and his father
had lived as he pleased. Their son did a little of both. The bounteous
delights of Gilded Age New York were now laid out before him, and he
knew exactly what he wanted.

After his brief residence at the Hoffman House, Hearst moved to the
third floor of Worth House, across 25th Street, where he was refused a
long-term lease as the building was on the market. He nevertheless renovated, gutting the interior of his apartment and rebuilding it to his
own taste with beamed ceilings and antique mantelpieces. He furnished
the rooms with tapestries, paintings, and other pieces from his swelling
collection of European treasure. The Worth House was reportedly sold
shortly after he was settled in. Hearst salvaged some of his fittings and
furnishing and reinstalled them in his new home, an unpretentious
four-story residence previously owned by President Chester Arthur
and sitting at the unfashionable address of 123 Lexington and 28th
Street. Hearst dubbed it "the shanty." In addition to his own quarters,
he set aside rooms for his college friend Jack Follansbee, who spent his
winters running the Hearst ranch in Mexico, and his summers in New
York, following the ponies and entertaining his friends. The shanty's
other inhabitant was George Thompson, Hearst's fat, pop-eyed Irish
valet, hired away from service at the Hoffman House. Thompson
would maintain a precise and tactful domestic order in Hearst's life for
thirty years.

All three of the aforementioned Hearst residences were within a few
blocks of Madison Square Garden, in the center of town. This was the
rebuilt Madison Square Garden, Stanford White's Moorish pavilion
with its soaring mock minaret topped by an eighteen-foot nude statue of
the goddess Diana. As the Astors, Vanderbilts, and Whitneys migrated
north of 50th Street, the neighborhood was taking on a commercial cast,
but it suited a busy young press lord perfectly. On a typical day, Hearst
would start with meetings at the bar of the Hoffman House, followed by
a short walk to Delmonico's for a hearty lunch. Early in the afternoon,
he would hop into a carriage or hansom cab, and head south to the
Journal offices on Park Row, where he would catch up on the day's

news and prepare his next edition. By early evening he was bouncing back up Broadway to the theater. Sometime around midnight, after a late supper at Bustanoby's or Sherry's or Jim's Chop House, he would rush back to Park Row and see his paper to bed, returning to the shanty just before dawn.

Notably absent from Hearst's daily rounds were social obligations. Phoebe still longed for her only child to blossom into an impeccable gentleman, taking his rightful place among the New York elite, hiring a box at the opera, attending masked balls and cotillions and society weddings, perhaps summering in Newport. Hearst had been inundated with social invitations on his arrival in town. He accepted some, probably out of deference to his mother, who had many connections in New York. He may also have wanted to extend his commercial contacts and to bone up on local affairs prior to his newspaper launch. Once the *Journal* was up and running, however, he declined most invitations. He joined the exclusive Metropolitan and Union Clubs but seldom visited either, and, given his anti-establishment politics, he was probably not missed (any mention of Hearst's name in the haunts of capital and conservatism, remembered the critic James L. Ford, would cause the tables to be pounded with impotent fists).[1] Nor did Hearst believe he was missing anything. His attitude toward America's social elite was hardening— "he despised them," according to Flint.

The one club that did hold Hearst's interest was the American Yacht Club at Milton Point, a relatively new establishment founded by Jay Gould and friends, not for sailors but for steam craft owners. While it counted many wealthy and respectable gentlemen among its members, the AYC was regarded as a "rather 'fast' place where the more conservative members hesitated to bring their families." Hearst served as vice-commodore and berthed his new yacht at the club. His old boat, the *Vamoose*, might have been the fleetest thing on water but its builders had sacrificed everything in the way of comfort and stability to velocity, and Hearst had put it up for sale almost the moment it set its speed records. In 1896 he purchased the 138-foot *Unquowa*, "a large, powerful, and well-equipped yacht, and a very convenient passenger craft." It afforded him the odd day of recreation when news was slow.[2]

Another favorite pastime, and one that fit more easily into Hearst's busy schedule, was shopping. A quick stroll west from his Lexington home brought him to Manhattan's most opulent commercial strip. While still a rough stone road plied by horse-drawn omnibuses, Fifth above 23rd was lined at all hours of the day with the footmen, the toy dogs, and the gleaming lacquered carriages of New York's grand dames. Hearst was always in and out of the stores, dropping impressive sums at galleries, book dealers, and the haberdashers who supplied his favorite striped shirts and circus ties. (He once carried home a wild collection of new cravats and asked his butler for an opinion. "I doubt these are any worse than your others," Thompson replied.)[3]

Much as he enjoyed Fifth, greater thrills awaited Hearst a few steps farther west. New York's robust theater district was centered on a two-mile stretch of Broadway between 23rd and 42nd streets, spilling over onto Sixth and Seventh Avenues and assorted side streets. There were forty-one stages in total, more than in London's West End. Establishments at the southern extreme of the strip competed with the Tenderloin's cheap taverns and streetwalkers. Those in the middle and at the northern tip—Garrick's Majestic, Daly's, the Empire, the Casino, Weber and Fields' Music Hall—were surrounded by lobster palaces and sumptuous hotels. Broadway was lit like no other street in the world. It had glittering marquees, billboards for Coney Island and Heinz pickles, and New York's first electric street lamps. The boulevardier Diamond Jim Brady called it "the Street of the Midnight Sun."[4] The name that stuck was the Great White Way.

The Broadway stage offered everything from crude burlesque to song-and-dance variety to Shakespeare and Ibsen. Men arrived for opening nights in horse-drawn carriages, wearing white tie and tails or dinner coats with white silk scarves and black silk hats. Women wore high collars under ermine and sable, piled their hair under big feathered hats, and trailed clouds of perfume. A hit show at the popular Casino might attract the socialites Mrs. Stuyvesant Fish and Mrs. Herman Oelrichs, the millionaires Jesse Lewisohn and James Keene, the impresario Oscar Hammerstein, the voluptuaries Stanford White and Jim Brady, Tammany's Boss Croker, the author Richard Harding Davis, and the newspaper phenom William Randolph Hearst.[5]

Hearst had been drawn to the stage as a boy in San Francisco, haunting the new California Theatre on Bush Street where Edwin Booth performed his famous Hamlet and the gorgeous Adelaide Neilson her equally renowned Juliet. He was also fond of the great black entertainer Billy Emerson, king of the city's lively minstrel community. Hearst memorized Emerson's comic songs and practiced his dance steps until he had them cold. He would perform for his friends on makeshift stages and became good enough that his mother worried he might want a stage career. At Harvard, Hearst impressed his friends with his vaudeville shuffles and banjo playing. He took the comic role of Pretzel, a German valet with "a penchant for legerdemain," in the Hasty Pudding's historical burlesque *Joan of Arc, The Old Maid of Orleans.* He considered himself a highlight of the show. Apart from family entertainments and the odd newsroom jig, his performing days ended in college, but his love of theater endured.

Hearst's preferred Broadway fare was the musical comedy of Joe Weber and Lew Fields, a pair of East Side New Yorkers and one of the all-time top comedy teams. Weber and Fields had started on the vaudeville circuit and laughed their way up to an eponymous palace on the strip. Along the way, they gave the world the custard pie in the face and one of its most durable jokes: "Who was that lady I saw you with last night?"asked Weber. "She was no lady," snorted Fields. "She was my wife."[6] A typical Weber and Fields program opened with a flurry of song-and-dance numbers and comedy skits, and closed with a send-up of either a current Broadway hit or a dramatic masterwork—Molière, for instance, parodied as Cyrano de Bric-a-Brac.

Weber and Fields were no threat to Molière or any other serious playwright, but they were impressive in their own right—successful popular artists in the nascent world of American show business, forerunners of any number of Broadway, Vegas, and Hollywood acts. They forged a specialty in smart, funny, iconoclastic commentaries on New York life, drawing on class and ethnic conflict in the new urban jungle, exploring such topical phenomena as newspapers, bicycles, telephones, elevators, and Teddy Roosevelt. Their audiences were not as tony as those at established theatrical houses, but critics found them sharp: a wry social observation, a nimble physical comedian, or a catchy new tune would not pass unappreciated. Their patrons were also numerous and loyal enough that Weber and Fields were able to hire first-tier musical and dramatic talent. They signed Lillian Russell, the reigning queen of operetta and the highest-paid actress in America, at $40,000 a year.[7] They auctioned season seats to cover the cost, with Hearst among the buyers. (He would later confess that the teenage crush he had on Russell in San Francisco was so "tense, dramatic, and ecstatic" that he considered proposing.[8]) Weber and Fields presented their star in a spoof of Feydeau's *The Girl from Maxim's*. "You might bring me a demitasse," she tells a waiter. "Bring me the same," says her millionaire boyfriend, "and a cup of coffee."[9]

Hearst wasn't especially interested in high culture, with the exception of the visual arts. Years of ambling through European museums and galleries with his mother, combined with an art history course at Harvard and further study on his own time, had trained his eye and made him an astute collector. He was reasonably well read. His letters to his mother show a familiarity with Dickens and Thackeray and a keenness for Greek and Roman history. But he dodged the symphony and the grand opera, and he did not belong to a salon or write essays in the quarterlies. There were more sensitive aesthetes and deeper intellects all over New York. Aside from his areas of specialized interest, Hearst's tastes ran to popular American commercial entertainment, most of it clever and unapologetically middlebrow and entirely consistent with his "democratic tendencies" in social and political affairs. Hearst probably felt a kinship with Weber and Fields, who were in a sense the Hearsts of Broadway. By bringing new levels of talent and ambition to light musical entertainment, they expanded its appeal while raising its quality, much as Hearst was doing with one-cent papers.

Weber and Fields were experienced enough to know better than to trust their fortunes entirely to comedic timing and catchy tunes. They also had girls—nightly parades of comely singers, dancers, and bit players, collectively known as chorus girls. They were young, often teenagers, and the desired look was tall and athletic, with extra points for swan necks and pert noses. Physically, there was little to distinguish them from the new ideal of womanhood popularized by the magazine illustrator Charles Dana Gibson. But Gibson's girls existed in parlors and opera boxes, bearing the unmistakable stamp of social privilege, and however spirited, they also respected prevailing notions of virtue and female subordination. The chorus girl, gainfully employed and relatively independent thanks to her talent and looks, represented a different sort of glamour—less for marrying, more for sport. "She was gay," wrote Theodore Dreiser, "showy, sexy, youthful, of course—the type that had led the world to dancing and madness since the beginning of time." She ran with a set of millionaires and celebrities in a shimmering world of "yacht parties, midnight suppers, dances and backstage scenes." For many young men, Hearst included, her lack of social pedigree was either irrelevant or a bonus.[10]

The quintessential Gilded Age chorines were the Florodora girls. *Florodora*, imported from London, book and lyrics by Owen Hall, was a forgettable musical comedy but for a single song and dance piece known as "Tell Me, Pretty Maiden." This number, as staged at the Casino, featured six Gibsonesque darlings of impressive and equal height and fine identical figures. They were clad in matching black ostrich-plumed hats with long pink dresses and parasols. The girls strolled across the stage on the arms of handsome young men in evening attire. In response to a query from their escorts—"Tell me, Pretty Maiden, are there any more at home like you?"—they sang an unremarkable ditty answering in the affirmative. This pedestrian scene relied for its impact on the perfect similitude of the sextet and on a surprise ending: instead of smiling sweetly over the heads of their audience on the closing note, as was Broadway custom, the girls looked directly into the seats and winked. That cheeky twist brought the house down on opening night. The girls were called back for ten encores, and never for fewer than six through more than five hundred performances. The Florodora chorus was touted as the most attractive in the world and the girls were soon drawing salaries on par with newspaper editors. Every night they would exit the stage door to run a gauntlet of bachelors and sporting men offering flowers, pearls, furs, horses, stock tips, and real estate. All six would eventually marry millionaires, several of them titled.[11]

Hearst, who usually attended the theater in the company of his close friends Jack Follansbee, George Pancoast, and Cosy Noble, regularly made his way backstage to meet the cast and the starlets. He had a thing for performing women, the more beautiful and talented the better. His boyhood infatuations with Adelaide Neilson and Lillian Russell hadn't been passing fancies so much as the start of a pattern.

Sybil Sanderson, who had bewitched the teenaged Hearst in Monterey, was a gifted soprano. She had a pretty, round face, large dark eyes, porcelain skin, and an impressive figure. Like Hearst, she was the child of a successful California miner. They spent the summer in California swimming, riding horses, and walking on the beach, and might have married, had Phoebe not stepped in.[12] Hearst followed the same script a few years later in his affair with the dramatic actress Eleanor Calhoun, otherwise remembered as Phoebe's "Devil fish." Tall, slender, with brilliant blue eyes and a "thrilling" voice, she accepted his proposal only to have the engagement crushed under the heel of his mother.[13]

Both of Hearst's betrotheds would find success overseas. Sanderson, with her soaring vocal range, flourished in the Paris opera scene, becoming a favorite of the composer Jules Massenet and the most famous interpreter of his masterpiece, *Manon*. Calhoun distinguished herself as a fashion icon and actress in London. She received good notices as Dora in the play *Diplomacy* and enjoyed the company of Robert Browning, George Bernard Shaw, James McNeill Whistler, and Oscar Wilde. She would eventually marry Prince Stephen Lazar Eugene Lazarovich-Hrebelianovich of the royal house of Serbia.

The version of Will Hearst now presenting himself backstage on Broadway was more than a decade older than the youth known to Sanderson and Calhoun. Tall and slim, he had gained control of his gangly limbs, large hands, and feet, although he still tended to fidget. His face had settled into its mature form, with a little more flesh on his pale cheeks. His hair, parted in the middle, had begun its journey from blond to light brown and he remained clean-shaven. His tall forehead was unlined, and his close-set blue eyes were as striking as ever. His voice was unfortunate. It was said to bleat "thinly and flatly" like a toy flute, an odd sound from so large a man.[14] That was not the only incongruity. His rather loud wardrobe—checked suits, flashy neckwear, brightly colored bands on hard-brimmed straw hats, a long gold watch chain, and sporty high-laced shoes, light brown with fawn tops and mother-of-pearl buttons—was at odds with an otherwise reserved personality and his quiet good manners. The overall effect was not unpleasant, however, and his mother would not have been alone in thinking him a catch.

The showgirl who would win Hearst's heart in New York was younger than any of her predecessors but perhaps the most fetching of the bunch. Millicent Willson was appearing with her sister Anita in the musical comedy *The Girl from Paris* at the Herald Square Theatre. Hearst biographers have represented the production as a "risqué" show, undisturbed by plot, featuring girls who showed "as much leg as possible without getting arrested."[15] In fact, it was a rather decorous musical comedy by George Dance and Ivan Caryll, both of whom enjoyed enormous success on Broadway as well as in the West End. (Dance was knighted for his prodigious contributions to London theatre; Caryll collaborated with the D'Oyly Carte Opera Company when it wanted a break from Gilbert and Sullivan.) *The Girl from Paris* opened on December 6, 1896, and ran for the better part of a year. It was praised in the prudish *Times* for its "snap and vim." The show's "few suggestive hints" failed to shock the audience, according to the reviewer.[16] The Willson sisters performed in a dance number as "bicycle girls." The audience would have been lucky to see their ankles.

The review appears to have been the Willsons' first professional work. They subsequently appeared in *The Telephone Girl* at the Casino, a successful musical comedy adapted by Hugh Morton from a French play by Maurice Desvallières, who wrote *Hotel Peccadillo* with Georges Feydeau. The score was by Gustave Kerker, who also did the music for *Yankee Doodle Dandy* and *The Belle of New York*.

Theater was a Willson family business. The girls' father was George Leslie Willson, the scion of a prominent Maine family who had run off to make his name as a clog dancer in vaudeville. Performing under the name George Leslie, "he would top his old white hat, swing his cane merrily and go into his famous medley of coon dances, the 'Pasa-ma-la,' 'Mobile Buck' and 'Mule in the Sand.'"[17] He also gained modest fame singing the tune "I Met Her by the Fountain in the Park."

Willson married an ambitious Irish-American girl who made her own contributions to the family coffers through real estate investments. Hannah Willson owned properties on some of the livelier streets in Harlem and the Tenderloin, including at least one building that might have been home to a brothel. There have been whispers by gossips and Hearst's political enemies that Mrs. Willson was a madame or a prostitute, but there is no evidence to support the claims.[18] The Willson family lived on Gramercy Park, only a few blocks from the shanty. Millicent was sixteen at the time Hearst laid eyes on her; her sister, Anita, was eighteen.

At first it was not clear which of the Willson girls interested Hearst. He and George Pancoast caught the *The Girl from Paris* many nights from aisle seats at the Herald Square, after which they and the sisters would dine as a foursome somewhere along Broadway. Hearst was often spotted around town with a sister on each arm, ostentatious behavior even for a Manhattan newspaperman. Millicent would later tell a friendly reporter that Anita was along as her chaperone at their mother's insistence: "When he asked me to go out with him . . . my mother was against it," remembered Millicent. "I recall she said, 'Who is he? Some young fellow from out West somewhere, isn't he?' She insisted Anita had to come or I couldn't go. Well, he took us down to the *Journal*—the *New York Journal*—we'd hardly heard of it, and he shows us over it, *all over it*. I hadn't the foggiest notion what we were doing, walking miles on rough boards in thin, high-heeled evening slippers, and I thought my feet would kill me. Of course this wasn't our idea of a good time. We wanted to go to Sherry's or Bustanoby's. More than that, Anita kept whispering to me, 'We're going to get thrown out of here, Milly, the way he behaves you'd think he owned it.'"[19]

Even Hearst's cousin, Anne Apperson Flint, who took an instant dislike to Millicent, admitted she was enchanting—"one of the prettiest creatures that you could imagine."[20] Millicent had a small oval face with soft features and flawless skin. Her round brown eyes were frank and friendly, her lips a perfect bow. She wore her thick brown hair heaped high but still reached only to the chin of Hearst, who stood well over six feet. By all accounts, she was a vivacious girl, cheerful and gracious if not especially polished. Hearst was completely smitten. He would drop by the Willson home on his way to the office and stroll arm in arm with Millicent through Gramercy Park. He showered her with attention, notes, flowers, and gifts. According to his cousin, he presented her with a hansom cab drawn by a white horse; it became her calling card around town.

Hearst kept his mother informed of his relationship with Millicent. That was his way. She detested his choice, as was her way. Indeed, Will's new Broadway baby probably rivaled "that prostitute" Tessie for least welcome of his girlfriends. Anne Apperson Flint claimed that Mrs. Hearst was in a near constant "state of fury" about the Willson sisters and could not bring herself to mention their names. Never mind the Missouri dirt yet clinging to their own finery, Phoebe and her niece refused to meet Millie and went out of their way to avoid her on the

street. Flint was still wagging her finger at the match when she was interviewed by Swanberg more than sixty years later, although her only specific complaints were that Millicent was "common as anything," and that
the thirty-three-year-old Will showed poor judgment in not dating a girl
his mother could love—"He didn't care!"[21]

The trade papers, which covered Hearst intently, would occasionally
flick at his personal life. "Billy Hearst," one noted in the summer of 1897,
"is down the coast with a cottage, young friends and a yacht, sighing for
the unattainable. . . . Fully occupied with what he believes to be
Pleasure—with a capital P."[22] Another trade gossip columnist, claiming
to have worked for a spell at the *Journal,* described Hearst as "a very easy
mark for girls who like yachting, good feeding and jolly times in general;
for men with schemes and odd suggestions; for men about town, who can
post him in the ways of the world; for sharks and sharps, especially those
who were educated in what the *Sun* is pleased to call, 'The Academy of
Crime.' He is good-natured, kindly disposed, slow to suspicion, and very
proud of his father's money."[23]

The only print outlets to aim directly at Hearst's relationship with
Millicent were a clutch of cheerfully vicious gossip sheets, ancestors of
today's celebrity tabloids. *The New-Yorker* referred to the Willson girls as
the Sassafras Sisters, actresses who had "achieved immortal glory and
annexed themselves to the Hearst leg—no, to the Hearst millions."[24]

Town Topics was more aggressive in its taunts. Edited by the acid-
tongued Colonel William D'Alton Mann, *Town Topics* was a weekly com-
pendium of the social, financial, and sexual indiscretions of New York's
better families. It was unsourced, unreliable, and highly entertaining.
Mann ran a sort of reputational protection racket on the side, raking in
hundred of thousands of dollars in "loans" from the likes of J.P. Morgan
and William C. Whitney on the understanding that their names would
escape his magazine's notice. (Mann was belittled in *Collier's* for "printing scandal about people who are not cowardly enough to pay for
silence.")[25] Hearst appeared with some regularity in *Town Topics,* usually
identified as "Willieboy" or "Willie the Worst." It was noted that he had
been "burning up Broadway with two warm babes and a hot hansom."
He was also accused of penning editorials while "resting in the laps of the
lovely."[26] The arch-conservative Mann also used imaginative descriptions
of Hearst's lifestyle to attack his anti-establishment politics:

My vague allusions to his ways of sultanic languor and sybaritish luxury,
to his frantic imitations of Oriental schemes of festival, to his general
and presumably enjoyable disregard of the tiresome conventions of
sedate society, had no other object than the illumination of my comments
on the inconsistency of his course in damning and slandering and curs-
ing men and women for possibly wanting to do as he actually does. . . .
I hold that if sloth, idleness, loose gayety, riotous extravagance and general demoralization of manners and morals are to be publicly pilloried,
the editor and proprietor of the *Journal* is not the person appointed and
anointed for the mission.[27]

It is not difficult to imagine a jab like that driving Phoebe to her bed
with acute embarrassment. Her friends would have read it—*Town Topics*
was well thumbed in her set—and a lifetime of mortification over her
husband's personal habits had left her especially sensitive to loose talk
around Will, even the teasing of professional mischief-makers. She desperately wanted him to enhance the respectability of the House of
Hearst; instead, from her perspective, he was following in his father's
stubbornly shabby footsteps.

She was undoubtedly privy to other gossip about Will. He was a
much-discussed young man and he never cared to disguise his behavior.
He had trampled proprieties by living openly with Tessie Powers, and
there are hints of other indiscretions. "I was told," wrote Upton Sinclair
years later, "that when he first came to New York, [Hearst] made himself
a scandal in the 'Tenderloin.' I was perplexed about that, for the members
of our [generation] are generally well known in the Tenderloin, and
nobody calls it a scandal. But one young society man who had known
Hearst well gave me the reason—and he spoke with real gravity: 'It wasn't
what he did—we all do it: but it was the way he did it. He didn't take the
trouble to hide what he did.'"[28]

Further allegations of indecency were made against Hearst in 1897
on the floor of Congress by a disgruntled California representative.
Grove L. Johnson was one of the few remaining friends of the Southern
Pacific Railroad in Washington at a time when the railway was begging
for a long-term amortization of its debt to the federal government.
Hearst's *Examiner* was leading a campaign to hold the railroad to its

obligations. Congressman Johnson made the matter personal in a speech so exquisitely vicious that it is worth quoting at length:

He is a young man, rich not by his own exertions, but by inheritance from his honored father and gifts from his honored mother. He became possessed of the idea that he wanted to run a newspaper. Like the child in the song, he wanted a bow-wow, and his indulgent parents gave him the *Examiner*. By the reckless expenditure of large sums of money he has built up a great paper.

The *Examiner* has a very large circulation. It did have a great influence in California.

It has done great good in California. It has exposed corruption, denounced villainy, unearthed wickedness, pursued criminals, and rewarded virtue.

At first, we Californians were suspicious of "Our Willie," as Hearst is called on the Pacific Coast. We did not know what he meant. But we came to believe in him and his oft-repeated boasts of independence and honesty. Daily editorials, written by "Our Willie," hired men praising his motives and proclaiming his honesty, had their effect. Besides, "Our Willie" through his paper was doing some good.

We knew him to be a debauchee, a dude in dress, an Anglomaniac in language and manners, but we thought he was honest.

We knew him to be licentious in his tastes, regal in his dissipations, unfit to associate with pure women or decent men, but we thought "Our Willie" was honest.

We knew he was erotic in his tastes, erratic in his moods, of small understanding and smaller views of men and measures, but we thought "Our Willie," with his English plaids, his cockney accent, and his middle-parted hair, was honest.

We knew he had sought on the banks of the Nile relief from loathsome disease contracted only by contagion in the haunts of vice, and had rivaled the Khedive in the gorgeousness of his harem and in the joy of restored health, but we still believed him honest, though low and depraved.

We knew he was debarred from society in San Francisco because of his delight in flaunting his wickedness, but we believed him honest, though tattooed with sin.

We knew he was ungrateful to his friends, unkind to his employees, unfaithful to his business associates, but we believed he was trying to publish an honest paper. . . .

We thought he was running an independent newspaper on a plane far above the ordinary altitude of newspapers, with a sincere desire to do good to the world, with an honest wish to expose shams, to speak the truth, and to establish a paper that, while it might be a personal organ, would still be an honest one. We came finally to admire "Our Willie" and to speak well of him and his paper.

When William R. Hearst commenced his abusive tirades against C.P. Huntington and the Southern Pacific Company and the Central Pacific Railroad Company and all who were friendly to them, and to denounce the funding bill and all who favored it as thieves and robbers, we thought his course was wrong, his methods bad, and his attacks brutal, but we believed "Our Willie" to be honest.

When C.P. Huntington told the truth about "Our Willie" and showed that he was simply fighting the railroad funding bill because he could get no more blackmail from the Southern Pacific Company, we were dazed with the charges, and as Californians we were humiliated.

We looked eagerly for "Our Willie's" denial, but it came not. On the contrary he admitted that he had blackmailed the Southern Pacific Company into a contract whereby they were to pay him $30,000 to let them alone, and that he had received $22,000 of his blackmail, and that C.P. Huntington had cut it off as soon as he knew of it, and that he was getting even now on Huntington and the railroad company because he had not received the other $8,000 of his bribe. He admitted by silence that the Southern Pacific Company was financially responsible, but that he dared not sue it for the $8,000 he claimed to be due because of fear that his blackmail would be exposed in court.[29]

The allegations of bribery were unfounded. Hearst had indeed accepted an advertising contract from the Southern Pacific, one the company expected would buy it preferential treatment in the *Examiner*. Hearst printed the ads, cashed the checks, and stepped up his attacks on Huntington. He had no qualms about taking money offered in ambiguous circumstances so long as his own actions were correct. The SP refused to pay the final $8,000 owed. The suggestion of venereal disease is without evidence but impossible to disprove. It would be repeated years later by other political enemies, along with the suggestion that Hannah Willson ran a brothel catering to John D. Rockefeller and his associates, and that Hannah and Millicent had worked as prostitutes.[30]

All of the scandalous tales around Hearst make for juicy reading but they are invariably from second-hand or anonymous sources. There is nothing close to solid evidence to support any of them, despite years of digging by Hearst's political and publishing enemies. He took up with Millicent in the midst of the morals campaign launched against him by the gray papers. Given the enmity toward him at that moment, any demonstrable connection between Hearst—the journalistic "procuress"—and real live prostitution would have been investigated, exposed, and exploited to the fullest. The New York dailies were not at all shy about covering transgressions, real or perceived, of prominent citizens. In fact, they were packed with tales of physical attacks, financial embezzlements, divorces, elopements, and exposed love nests among Manhattan's elite. Hearst's courtship of Millicent did not trouble the respectable press. Johnson's accusations registered in Park Row only as a comment on the congressman's scurrility.[31]

That Phoebe Hearst and her niece, Anne Apperson Flint, considered Will's behavior outrageous is, to a certain extent, understandable. Appearances mattered in their social circles, and Will did not play by their rules. Yet however much her friends clucked their tongues at her son's antics, nothing he did impeded Phoebe's movements through the highest reaches of Anglo-American society.

As a counterbalance to Phoebe's perspective, Will's "scandalous" personal conduct can be measured against that of his peers, particularly James Gordon Bennett Jr., Park Row's virtuoso of debauchery. He is described in one reliable chronicle as a "swaggering, precociously dissolute lout who rarely stifled an impulse. He drank, wenched, yachted, and played polo with spectacular gusto, and when, late at night, he took it into his pickled brain to bound into the nearest Bennett coach and drive the team through the dark at a frothing pace, careening wildly around corners, thundering over bridges, bowling aside anything in his way, stripping off his clothing as the wayward vehicle flew along and caterwauling at the moon, no one afterward told him to behave."[32]

James Gordon Bennett Jr. was everything Hearst's worst critics have supposed Hearst to be: a reckless, dissipated, cruel, selfish, erratic, temperamental, and ruinously insecure product of inherited wealth. Handed the *Herald* and its income of a million a year in his early twenties, Bennett displayed the contempt for working men often identified in heirs to fortune. He ruled his newspaper by "caprice and fear," firing perfectly good employees if he didn't like their haircuts or if his dogs didn't take to them. He flew into furious rages when his reporters received more attention than he did. He used his letters columns to campaign against restaurants whose service had disappointed him. He would walk down the aisle of a world-class eatery, pulling the linen from each table just to hear the crockery smash on the floor. He rode his polo pony into the Newport Reading Room on a lark, and once threw a roll of banknotes into a fire because he did not like the way it was sitting in his pocket. Most famously, he celebrated New Year's 1878 at the elegant home of his intended, Caroline May, by telling crude jokes in front of the ladies and relieving himself into either the fireplace or the grand piano (accounts vary). The next day, May's brother, Fred, horsewhipped Bennett on the steps of the Union Club. The indignant publisher responded by challenging his assailant to a duel. Both men survived: May had aimed his pistol at the sky; Bennett shot to kill but missed. Suddenly unwelcome among New York's elite, he headed for Europe and spent most of the rest of his life in exile. He remained, throughout all this, an excellent newspaperman.

Compared with Bennett, Hearst seems a bit of a square. Even in the more general context of Gay Nineties, Seeley-era New York, he comes up short. It is possible that he whiled away some hours in the Tenderloin but, as Sinclair acknowledges, there was nothing remarkable in that; it is difficult to build a case for Hearst as a womanizer when his principal lovemaking strategy had always been to hand his whole heart to a winsome young woman and cling desperately to her until his mother broke things up. His approach to Millicent was true to form. He fell deeply in love with the beautiful, talented, fun-loving teenager. He took her everywhere. "[It] was such a love affair," said one acquaintance. "He was so terribly in love with her, you know. I mean, he wouldn't let her leave his side. . . . [Millicent] couldn't even go and buy a dress, he wanted to [go]. Sometimes it's sort of fun: 'Where are you going, Milly?' 'I want to go shopping.' 'You can't go without me.' And he went with her everywhere. Well, she was terribly in love with him so it was all right."[33] Mrs. Flint, for all her criticism of her cousin, admitted that he was "a very straight-laced, clean-living man" and "not as promiscuous as the world said he was."

Some aspects of Hearst's behavior might have been racy or brazen, but he did not drink or smoke or gamble or run afoul of the law. He stayed out of the spotlight and clear of the law. As a willful, high-spirited son of privilege in a wide-open city, with a standing invitation to every conceivable personal indulgence, he was a poor excuse for a devil.

The public scrutiny and gossip never seemed to bother Hearst. He understood that personal and political attacks accompanied success in newspapers as in politics (which was one of the reasons Phoebe detested both professions). It would also have helped that he felt at least as much contempt for the social universe of *Town Topics* as it harbored for him. Mann's mockery was a small price to pay for the freedom to disregard "the tiresome conventions of sedate society." But, contrary to Anne Flint's opinion, Hearst did worry about his mother's feelings. In letters home, he routinely reassured her about his activities and urged her to ignore the rumor-mongers. He kept his picture and his social affairs out of his own and other dailies and he gave interviews only on business matters and politics. (Phoebe by contrast, earned press by showing up at parties "blazing with diamonds," and by keeping company with elderly bachelors.)[34] Hearst did not end his romance with Millicent to please his mother, as he had ended previous relationships, but he was now in his thirties and Phoebe had not given the girl a chance.

One further blow to Hearst's image as a sultanic sybarite is the fact that most of his nights on the town ended at the office. Millicent and Anita probably never guessed the first time they traipsed across the *Journal's* wooden floors in evening slippers that they would be back again and again. Henry Klein, then a rewrite man at the paper, says the girls routinely arrived with his boss around midnight and stood around as Hearst spread the proposed layouts on the floor and got down on his knees to study them. Others nights Hearst would return to the paper alone. He would bust in, recalled Willis Abbot, "full of scintillating ideas and therewith rip my editorial page to pieces. Other pages were apt to suffer equally, and it was always an interesting spectacle to me to watch this young millionaire, usually in irreproachable evening dress, working over the forms."[35]

The fact is that while Hearst made time for recreation and romance, his overwhelming preoccupation was his newspapers. With his morning, evening, and Sunday editions, he had effectively launched three titles in close succession, without entirely removing himself from the newspaper war in San Francisco. He was up to his elbows in dozens of political controversies, some as local as a proposed new charter for New York City, some as large as Cuba. He did not write his own editorials, but he was the undisputed architect of his papers' policies. He was guardian of the front page, living and dying by its relative strength against the competition each morning. He was the repository of what we would now call the "brand"—his newspapers' vision, tone, and image—which made him crucial not only to editorial operations but also to marketing efforts, from posters to special events to promotional stunts. He was continually buying, installing, and upgrading his mechanical plant to accommodate a larger press run and enhanced color reproduction. Hearst delegated a lot of the *Journal*'s day-to-day business affairs, but he could not avoid monitoring its financial performance and cash flow, advertising bookings, ink and paper costs, and the distribution stream that daily delivered his wares to not only New York and its suburbs but as far away as Buffalo. He had a large staff to motivate, manage, and replenish. There were all manner of unscheduled problems that might interrupt his day: breaking news, attacks from rivals and wounded politicians, press failures. And then there were the unceasing, sleep-destroying pressures to always be fresh and lively, first and most compelling, to surprise and innovate and squeeze every ounce of competitive advantage out of available resources. It was a phenomenal workload and Hearst loved it. "To work hard, to study out intricate problems of newspaper detail . . . and to be anxious about many matters seems to be his ideal existence," wrote Charles Edward Russell.[36]

By the middle of 1897, with the election and the moral war behind him and with Millicent at his side, Hearst seems to have begun to relax and enjoy himself in New York. Charles Palmer was no longer writing Phoebe with concerns over Will's health. His own letters to his mother were brief and upbeat, and relatively free of the panic he had often displayed in San Francisco. Morale in his newsroom was high and the *Journal* shone with exuberance and confidence. Hearst was clearly having fun making everyone else on Park Row miserable. "We did have fun really and that is the right word for it," Hearst would say years later. "It was really fun, enjoyment. I don't think [we] looked upon it as work at all. We couldn't have been offered anything else that would have been as interesting as what we were doing, and as enjoyable as what we were doing."[37]

JOSEPH PULITZER, BY CONTRAST, was still not having fun. His problems started with his health. He spent the first few months of 1897 much as he had spent every other winter since his 1890 "retirement" announcement—in a futile search for relaxation and relief. Among his stops in the intervening years had been a sanitarium in Lucerne, a spa at Wiesbaden, and the mineral waters of Pfäfers-Bad. He'd consulted a long parade of medical specialists for his asthma, insomnia, nervous prostration, encroaching blindness, and general physical deterioration. The winter of 1897 took him to the German specialist Ernst Schweininger, who had made his reputation treating Bismarck. He examined Pulitzer at the Hotel Cap Martin, near Monaco, and for a gargantuan fee prescribed a new regimen of massage, baths, diet, and exercise. It did not help. If anything, his entourage believed, Pulitzer looked worse as a result. "I have never seen him so steadily and persistently gloomy," wrote his secretary, Alfred Butes, to Kate Pulitzer, "or in so deep a gloom." In his own letter to his wife, Pulitzer didn't disagree: "I stopped smoking with the new year, have stopped drinking claret; have never been more careful in eating, have never taken so much exercise . . . as during the last six weeks . . . yet in spite of, or perhaps on account of this I am more miserable in some respects (physical)—than I have been in years."[38]

While Pulitzer still unburdened himself to Kate and complained incessantly that his seven young children did not write him regularly, as per his demands, he made little effort to be with them. He had decided that family was disruptive of his work routine and emotional equilibrium. He lived and traveled instead with a household of aides and secretaries, six or more at a time, all of them male, most of them single. (It is curious that Pulitzer's sexuality has received far less attention than Hearst's.) The young men were recruited through newspaper advertisements seeking intelligent, erudite, widely traveled individuals who were good sailors and prepared to live abroad. Candidates were subjected to extensive interviews on such matters as their ancestry, education, livelihood, political prejudices, musical preferences, magazine subscriptions, facility with languages, memory, health, temper, sense of humor, tact, and discretion. They were requested to submit a life history of around two thousand words. The most promising applicants finally met the great man himself. "I sat next to him," wrote one in his diary, "and he pelted me with questions. Talk ranged from metaphysics to spiritualism, murder trials, and police reporting. A man with a most astonishing range of conversation. Tall, cadaverous, reddish beard . . . piercing but dead eyes, long bony hands; a fascinating yet terrifying figure. He is not quite blind, but cannot see to read even with the most powerful glasses."[39]

It was the combined job of successful applicants to minister to all of Pulitzer's personal and professional needs, keeping him active, informed, and entertained, and to suffer without complaint his unpredictable rages and depressions. The pay was good. The accommodations were always first rate. The other men in Pulitzer's service were capable and bright. It was nonetheless difficult work.

Restless and impulsive, Pulitzer was never in one place more than a few months at a time. He shuffled between his various North American homes with side trips to Washington or St. Louis, and crossed to Europe at least once a year. He expected everything to be just so wherever he landed, hence the advance guard of aides who preceded him, inspecting and photographing lodgings, listening for noisy plumbing or barking dogs or anything else that might interrupt his fragile sleep and force him on a moment's notice to pack up and leave. There was only so much the advance men could do: a stay at Moray Lodge, the estate of British publisher Alfred Harmsworth, was ruined by the squawking of the royal peacocks in nearby Kensington Garden. In Maine, Pulitzer's aides had gone so far as to ask the harbor authorities to silence a foghorn in murky weather (a request wisely refused).

Whether in transit or at home, Pulitzer worked constantly and, as a result, so did his secretaries, arranging meetings, managing his correspondence and appointments, reading him the newspapers, and running his errands. When he wanted to relax, they took turns reading to him from Thackeray, Trollope, and George Eliot, as well as from histories and biographies. It was not enough for the men to read well; they were also required to condense, on the fly, any discursive or descriptive passages that got between their impatient employer and the next plot development. They accompanied him to concerts and plays, often walking out if the pace was slow or there was a cougher in the audience. They put him on horseback and took him for boat rides. They ate their meals with him and scrambled to keep up with his singular notion of table talk.

Pulitzer did not converse with his secretaries and assistants so much as spar with them. A typical tactic of his was to force an opinion on a particular subject from one of his men and then humiliate the poor fellow with his own superior knowledge and judgment. Alleyne Ireland, one of Pulitzer's later secretaries, was once asked at lunch what he was reading. He rattled off a few titles. Pulitzer seized on one and asked for a report. Ireland obliged. He had barely got started when his host exploded: "My God! You don't mean to tell me that anyone is interested in that sort of rubbish. . . . Try something else. Do you remember any plays?"[40]

Pulitzer's moodiness kept his entourage in constant suspense. He could be chatting merrily in his high-pitched, clear voice on American politics or Shakespeare and then suddenly turn in fury on a guest who was being noisy with his cutlery; he could sit through an entire meal in wordless anxiety, refusing to be cheered or distracted, nervously stroking his bushy beard. His men watched his face for clues. Normally his skin was a youthful, healthy pink. When he was exercised about something, it flushed a deep red; when he was sleepless or depressed, it would turn gray. His range of expression was enormous. "No face was capable of showing greater tenderness," wrote Ireland, yet "none could assume a more forbidding expressing of anger and contempt."[41] And he could flash to both extremes in half a sentence. It took a nimble secretary to know how best to approach him at a given moment.

Telling Pulitzer a joke was an even riskier business. He was lustily appreciative if he got it, petulant if he did not, and furious if it was aimed at him. A safer way to lift his spirits was to let him exercise what Ireland called his zest for contradiction: "Indeed, nothing put him in such good humor as to discover a cleft in your intellectual armor, provided that you really possessed some talent, faculty, or resource which was useful to him."[42] That last point was important. Pulitzer held his intellectual punching bags in high regard; it gave him no pleasure to beat up on stiffs. They, in turn, were so impressed with his gifts and occasional displays of generosity that they tended to excuse his excesses. "When I recall," wrote Ireland, "the capaciousness of his understanding, the breadth of his experience, the range of his information, and set them side by side with the cruel limitations imposed upon him by his blindness and by his shattered constitution, I forget the severity of his discipline."[43]

On returning from Europe in 1897, Pulitzer set up at Bar Harbor for the summer. His estate, Chatwold, with its four-story soundproofed Tower of Silence, fronted on Frenchman's Bay. The cool sea air took the edge off his asthma. He saw something of his family, lodged in the main quarters. He also mixed selectively with local society, which included the university presidents Charles William Eliot (Harvard) and Seth Low (Columbia), a variety of diplomats, and Baron Hengelmüller, minister from Austria-Hungary. Society was important to Pulitzer. He had joined the better clubs in New York and it pleased him that his winter resort at Jekyll Island put him in the company of Morgans, Astors, Rockefellers, and Harrimans. But the idea of society was always better than the reality. His long career of anti-establishment crusades made him suspect in the eyes of the great families and, much as he wanted to be welcomed at their hearths, his convictions wouldn't permit him to forswear further attacks. As he complained to Alfred Harmsworth, "I am the loneliest man in the world. People who dine at my table one night might find themselves arraigned in my newspaper the next morning."[44]

One of Pulitzer's preoccupations that summer, as for the previous eighteen months, was the financial shape of his newspapers. At the start of the war with Hearst he'd been selling 185,000 copies of the morning World at two cents, another 340,000 of the Evening World, and about 450,000 of the Sunday World. The morning edition had hit a peak of 312,000 in the wake of his 1896 price cut but was now hovering around 300,000. The evening paper was down about 5 percent and the Sunday edition 10 percent. The World and the Journal each claimed a combined circulation in all weekday editions of 750,000. Pulitzer got to that figure by counting a triweekly summary of his paper published mostly for out-of-towners; Hearst inflated his numbers by throwing in the circulation of his German-language edition.

Whichever way circulation was tallied, Pulitzer's revenues were suffering because he had dropped his cover price. He had also had to ramp up editorial and promotional spending to keep pace with Hearst, and the Journal was likely cutting into his advertising business. Like every other proprietor on Park Row, Pulitzer was watching his margins shrink.

He was still a long way from poor. One estimate had his annual newspaper income falling from just under a million to just over half a million. On top of that he had solid profits from his St. Louis paper, and his earnings from his myriad non-publishing investments, but the decline unnerved him.

Pulitzer was already cutting costs, particularly by reducing the number of pages he published each day. He now went further, hauling his managers out to Chatwold for yet another lecture on economizing, and berating them in memos. "Ding Dong Ding Dong Ding Dong Ding Dong the word economy into [editor E.O.] Chamberlin until he has nervous prostration," read one missive.[45] He also tightened up his personal expenses, which were then running at about $350,000 a year. Rather than deal with the large burdens—his yacht, his entourage, his several homes—he challenged the coal bill at Bar Harbor, browbeat his doctors about their fees, and put the screws to Kate, who was spending $6,000 a month in support of the entire Pulitzer household. Incensed, she informed her husband's secretary, Alfred Butes, that without immediate relief she was headed for debtor's prison:

> Seriously, do get Mr. Pulitzer to attend to this at once, & send me a check at once. Don't let the paper, in this instance, come before his family. I hate to owe money. When I had probably nothing, I owed nothing. Now that I am supposed to have much, I owe much. This seems unfair & I will not consent to it. J.P. told me to pay all bills whether rightfully included in my allowance or not & let him have the totals. I hope there will be no brouhaha about this, but in any event I will not suffer any further worry. Money is such a contemptible thing to so constantly fight about. I wish there was no such thing as money in the world. Do make him careful in avoiding high winds, bright lights, glare, and sudden violent movements. As long as his eyes trouble him he should not go into the pool, nor ride horseback. These things, at least, he can do, even though it is impossible for him to stop worrying.[46]

While financial difficulties clearly contributed to Pulitzer's unease in '97, his confidence in his means seemed to blow hot and cold. When he was not trying to squeeze a few nickels out of the mechanic who repaired his steam launch in Maine, he was considering the purchase of William

Rockefeller's estate at Tarrytown, priced at $350,000. In the spring of '97, the trade press reported a rumor that he was purchasing the Calumet Place residence of Mrs. John A. Logan in Washington, DC. "It evidently pays to own a great paper like the New York *World*," wrote *The Fourth Estate*, noting that in addition to his 55th Street mansion and extensively renovated properties in Bar Harbor and Jekyll Island, Pulitzer also rented cottages from time to time at Newport, Lenox, and Lakewood.[47] One suspects the loss of income bothered him less than the threat to his stature on Park Row.

Pulitzer was immensely proud of what he had accomplished in New York. He considered himself a publishing genius, a journalistic and commercial innovator, a popular educator, a righteous crusader for justice and liberty, a friend to the poor and oppressed, a scourge of predatory wealth, as well as a presidential kingmaker and an international peace broker. Above all else, he cherished the role of trusted tribune of the great American people, whose faith in his powers was demonstrated every day by the unexampled sale of his newspapers. It was an impossibly grand self-image but one Pulitzer could sustain so long as the *World* continued to outsell all rivals. Hearst was ruining that. He had arrived from nowhere to challenge all of Pulitzer's roles. His was the paper with the strongest voice and the sparkling new features, the biggest names and brightest talent. His soup kitchens had the longest lines and his fireworks the loudest bang. He had all the energy and momentum, and his sales were going nowhere but up. For thirteen years Pulitzer had reigned supreme and unrivaled at the summit of Park Row. Suddenly it was all in jeopardy. Even worse, the conservative papers were lumping him in with Hearst in their condemnations of the yellow papers.

In his blacker moments, Pulitzer was withering in his assessment of Hearst and the *Journal*: "[He] is welcome to spend another million or two if he wants to advertise himself still more as the man who could not, like Bennett and Greeley, create a paper with brains and ideas of his own, but who did have the distinction of sinking millions."[48] When provoked, Hearst could be just as nasty about Pulitzer, calling him "a journalist who made his money by pandering to the worst tastes of the prurient and horror-loving, by dealing in bogus news, such as forged cablegrams from eminent personages, and by affecting a devotion to the interests of the people while never really hurting those of their enemies, and sedulously looking out for his own."[49]

But just as Hearst had admitted privately in letters to his father and through his own actions that he held the *World* in considerable esteem, Pulitzer, in the right mood, would confess an admiration for his young rival and his paper. Hearst, he wrote *World* executive Don Seitz, possessed both "brains and genius, not only brains for news and features but genius for the self-advertising acts which have no parallel."[50] Pulitzer refused to let his employees disparage the *Journal* and gave them his personal view that it was "a wonderfully able & attractive and popular paper."[51] On one occasion, he pointed out an ingenious item in the *Journal* and complained to his men, "That is the sort of brains the *World* needs. Pardon me for saying also, that with all [the *Journal*'s] faults, which I should not like to copy—though they have been exaggerated— it is a newspaper."[52] Interestingly, Pulitzer counted among the *Journal*'s strengths not only such obvious items as the quality of its pictures or the talent of its writers but also the fact that it stole the *World*'s best stories and ideas without reservation. He urged his managers to follow suit.

The big question for Pulitzer was how long Hearst could keep it up. He studied his opponent for signs of weakness. He knew as well as anyone the physical and mental strain of managing a fledgling property in the heat of a Manhattan newspaper war. Pulitzer had been almost as young as Hearst when he had bought the *World* and challenged Dana's supremacy. He had triumphed, but at the cost of his health. Pulitzer knew in his bones that no man could sustain Hearst's pace indefinitely. The competitive demands would wear on him, as would the attacks of his competitors. It would be difficult for the challenger to maintain his superhuman levels of concentration and fighting spirit when his flaws were exposed, his best ideas were copied or stolen, and his novelty and exuberance waned. There were no signs as yet, however, that the young man was anything but energized by the strife. Imagining his imminent physical collapse wasn't a sound business strategy.

Hearst's finances seemed to Pulitzer more vulnerable than his constitution. It was an open secret on Park Row that Hearst had drawn on his family's wealth to finance his ventures, but no one knew the size of his stake, or the extent of his mother's patience. Nor was there agreement on the magnitude of the *Journal*'s losses. Everyone, however, had a firm opinion. As the *Journalist* snickered, "The subject which is most vigorously discussed and upon which it is easiest to obtain exact and well vouched for information is the precise financial condition and money making or losing capabilities of the morning *Journal*."[53] Hearst's boosters swore the paper was already in the black: "I tell you, sir! The *Journal* is making money, making money hand over fist. A good deal of the dead wood has been lopped off. The salary list has been reduced to reasonable limits and the enormous circulation gives them absolute command over advertisers, and they are stiff in their rates, stiff as nails! They can afford to be, and they are simply coining money." His detractors saw red ink and conspiracy: "You can calculate it up for yourself easily enough. The *Journal* does not get any prices for its advertising; they have to take what they can get, and they carry very little in comparison to the circulation that they claim. Every paper that they sell is a dead loss; the white paper costs more than they get for the paper at wholesale. Mrs. Hearst is disgusted with the whole thing . . . and if it was not for a big syndicate of silver men, who are back of the paper, it would have to stop publication."[54]

Pulitzer did his best to persuade himself that Hearst was losing big and courting disaster. He ordered Don Seitz, Bradford Merrill, and other *World* managers to lunch with past and present *Journal* employees to glean what they could of the paper's performance. They learned that Phoebe's cousin and financial adviser, Edward Hardy Clark, had been assigned to monitor Will's expenses. Bradford Merrill told Pulitzer that Phoebe had sent "expert accountants" over the head of Will and his managers to examine the *Journal*'s books.[55] Another internal *World* memo estimated that Phoebe would not allow her son to spend a penny more than $5 million in New York and that most of that was already gone. Pulitzer's bean counters pored over Hearst's newspapers, counting inches of advertising and estimating expenses on wages, printing, paper, marketing, and other aspects of the business in the hope of arriving at a sound approximation of the *Journal*'s bottom line. Nothing they learned dissuaded Pulitzer from his strategy of protecting the *World*'s position as best he could until Hearst was financially gassed. Pulitzer did not think it would take long.

Protecting the *World*'s position was not a passive exercise. Pulitzer had not reached the top through a lack of challenge. He remained up to his elbows in the newspaper's operations, monitoring everything from the prices demanded by individual news dealers to the quality of the *World*'s weather reports.[56] He developed an elaborate secret code by which to communicate with his managers about competitive issues, and he tried to hire a spy in the *Journal*'s offices (he was convinced Hearst had one at the *World*). The volume of communications with his executives ran as thick as ever. Some of it was constructive; some of it was distracting, like his instruction to Don Seitz to have someone go "gently, softly, and early in the morning" to Bradford Merrill's office and erase the stenciled title "Editorial Manager" from his door.[57] Pulitzer was not keen on grandiose titles. He did appreciate the need to rebuild morale at the *World* and asked for recommendations of young men for special recognition and Christmas bonuses.

Some of Pulitzer's smartest moves were financial. He began to invest again in printing equipment and he made generous offers to good men at the *Journal,* putting more pressure on Hearst by driving up wages. When the United Press collapsed in the spring of 1897, Hearst and other Park Row proprietors who were left without a premium wire service—an essential for any competitive newspaper—applied to join the Associated Press. Pulitzer, a charter member of the AP, approved the other papers but vetoed the *Journal*. Hearst quickly managed to purchase the New York *Morning Advertiser,* a paper with an AP franchise, and merged it with his flagship, creating the *New York Journal and Morning Advertiser*. It was a nimble move and a necessary one if Hearst was to stick to his plan, but hideously expensive at an estimated $300,000. As Pulitzer hoped, Phoebe's patience was about to crack.[58]

Pulitzer's flurries of instructions to his executives stopped abruptly in the last week of 1897. His seventeen-year-old daughter, Lucille Irma Pulitzer, was stricken with typhoid. He hired the best care available but Lucille did not survive. She was buried at Woodlawn Cemetery in New York. Pulitzer was devastated. However unusual his family circumstances, he did love his children, and he had fancied Lucille the brightest of his brood, brimming with potential, closer to him in personality than any of her siblings. It wasn't until early February that Pulitzer returned to his desk to jolt his executives with fresh rounds of correspondence: "The new color [press] is all important and should receive the utmost attention and brains and advertising, to make a hit."[59]

The trade press had meanwhile grown concerned that the animosity between the *World* and the *Journal* was making both papers look ridiculous. *The Fourth Estate* admired the yellows for their "marvelous" zeal in newsgathering, "but when two newspapers find their time chiefly occupied in exaggeration of one another's faults it is then time to consider whether journalism is doing due justice to its high estate."[60] As if determined to prove *The Fourth Estate*'s point, the papers promptly opened an entirely new front in their war.

The *World* was drawing crowds to the steps of the Pulitzer Building with an electric bulletin board that displayed the latest baseball scores. The *Journal* erected a better scoreboard, "with figures illustrating the progress of the games between the New York club and its competitors," and the crowd moved to the *Journal*'s offices. A man who sold billboards offered the *World* an upgrade on the *Journal*'s contraption at a price of $700. The *World* instead asked the police to dismantle the *Journal*'s board on the grounds that it was a public nuisance. Chief of Police Conlin told the *Journal* to halt its bulletins. The *Journal* said it would comply with the chief's order only if the *World* shut down its board too. Back and forth it went until attorneys for the *Journal* won an injunction from the state supreme court preventing police from interfering with its baseball bulletins. In the meantime, the *Journal* bought the $700 scoreboard from the novelty salesman and set it up outside its offices. "The fight grows livelier with every issue," reported *The Fourth Estate*, "and is creating the deepest interest with both the public and the profession."[61]

CHAPTER TEN

Taking Chances No Correspondent Ever Took

T he largest and most important story Hearst would cover in New York surfaced eight months before he purchased the *Journal*. On February 24, 1895, a small band of rebels under the banner of the Cuban Revolutionary Party declared an insurrection against Spanish rule at Baire, near Santiago on the eastern tip of Cuba. News of the uprising bounced quickly from Havana to Madrid to New York, where all of the major dailies gave it coverage, although none took it too seriously at first. Cuba had rebelled on several previous occasions, most notably the Ten Years' War (1868–78). Some 200,000 combatants died in that conflict before an increase in Spanish troops forced a peace negotiation. In its aftermath, rebel leaders scattered to the Americas and it had become a standing joke on Park Row that the Cuban revolution was now being fought with excited speeches in the cafés of Key West and the cigar factories of Manhattan. So when Spanish officials dismissed the Baire proclamation as a nuisance created by a handful of bandits and horse thieves, New York editorialists were not inclined to argue. That would change, however, inside of a week.[1]

Gathering up reports of battles between revolutionaries and Spanish soldiers in such diverse locales as Baire, Cienfuegos, and Jaguey Grande, Pulitzer's *World* was among the first to guess that the uprising was more serious than Spain was admitting. The *Times* was soon wondering why Madrid needed to open new credit facilities to round up a handful of bandits and horse thieves. The *Tribune* doubted that eight thousand Spanish soldiers had been hurriedly dispatched to Cuba "for the benefit they may derive from the sea voyage."[2]

Spain more or less confirmed the magnitude of the revolt in early March 1895 when it extended martial law to a third of Cuba. Then came news from Madrid that the Liberal government of Premier Práxedes Mateo Sagasta had collapsed over its failure to contain the Cuban problem. The new Conservative premier, Antonio Cánovas del Castillo, sent Spain's most famous soldier, General Arsenio Martínez Campos, a veteran of the Ten Years' War, to crush the revolt. "We should never have thought of sending Grant to put down a railroad strike," quipped the *World*.[3]

Now confident they were on to a big story, the New York editors began dedicating generous space to the Cuban crisis. From the outset, two important trends emerged in the coverage—one entirely defensible, the other less so.

The defensible part was principled support for the Cuban people in their revolt against Spanish colonial rule. An editorial in the New York *Sun* spoke for the majority when it asked by what right the Spanish monarchy exercised "despotic authority over the people of the radiant island which is so near our own seaboard and is thousands of miles distant from the kingdom of Spain? Why should these people numbering over a million and a half be taxed to the amount of millions each year for the enrichment of Spain. . . . Should their aspirations for liberty under a Republic be crushed generation after generation?"[4]

It was no surprise that the progressive Pulitzer shared the *Sun*'s views, but even the conservative press was offended at Spain's pillaging of its possession. The *Times* accused Spain of treating Cuba as "a lemon to be squeezed" while the *Tribune* compared the island to America under British administration, a popular analogy on Park Row.[5] Of all the major New York dailies, only the *Herald* and the *Evening Post* showed much consideration for Madrid. Both argued that Spain's internal affairs were of no concern to the United States. None of the papers made much of the fact that a recent hike in the U.S. tariff on sugar imports had hurt Cuba's economy, unsettled the Cuban people, and advanced the rebellion.

Hearst may not have owned a New York paper during the initial months of the Cuban conflict, but his *San Francisco Examiner* took a lively interest in the story. It, too, expressed sympathy for the Cubans. When, in the summer of 1895, Spain declared its intention to fight the insurgents to the last peseta and the last drop of blood, the *Examiner* was outraged: "This document announces that the whole eastern end of Cuba will be freed from all rebels and their adherents, that it will be war to extermination, that no foes will be allowed to remain to create further disturbances, that Spain will enter the fall campaign with only one object in view—the immediate and absolute subjugation of the island—and that the portion of the rebels will be death."[6] The paper compared Spain's intentions to Turkey's contemporaneous slaughter of Armenian nationalists. The United States, it averred, "cannot permit the creation of another Armenia in this hemisphere." When Hearst arrived in New York, these same arguments were taken up by the *Journal*.[7]

The pro-Cuban newspapers all looked to Washington to assist Cuba, but they were cautious in their appeals, acknowledging the time-honored U.S. doctrine of nonintervention in foreign disputes. They dismissed any notion of intervening militarily on behalf of the rebels, or annexing the island, or otherwise expanding America's sphere of influence in the Caribbean. As Hearst's *Examiner* wrote, "we are not looking for new territory, especially when it is inhabited by over 1,600,000 Spaniards, Creoles and negroes. We should be glad to see Cuba independent or annexed to Mexico, or even in the enjoyment of an autonomous local government under the sovereignty of Spain. But the present condition of the island is an international scandal, and a reproach to the [United States]."[8] Even the *Tribune*, convinced that the island would some day fall under American protection, agreed that the United States had neither the duty nor the right to force the issue. Washington was instead encouraged to recognize the rebels as belligerents under the law of nations. Belligerent status would grant the insurgents certain rights of land and naval warfare affecting their ability to import arms and men, but the primary attraction was diplomatic. The *Journal* believed that recognition would legitimize the Cuban nation, its provisional government, and its bid for self-determination. It would also move President Cleveland off of his strict respect for Spanish sovereignty in Cuba, which was seen in some quarters as tacit approval of its oppressive rule.[9]

In touting the Cuban insurgency as "a humanitarian mission worthy of the generous sentiments of the American people," editors were taking not only a principled but a popular stand.[10] Their audience was by its own history and traditions sympathetic to the story of an oppressed nation struggling for independence from a severe colonial master. Americans also felt close to the Cuban people by virtue of geography, economic integration, and immigration. And they were in an unusually compassionate mood. Walter McDougall defines the spirit of the late Victorian age as progressive idealism, or what one journalist at the time called "a tremendous impulse to the work of reform."[11] This mindset was most obvious on the home front, where anti-poverty crusades, trust-busting initiatives, educational philanthropies, and suffrage movements were launched with impressive regularity, but progressive idealism also traveled. The same enthusiasms for social justice and public service in domestic matters were effortlessly transposed to campaigns to protect oppressed peoples from brutal occupiers. In fact, it was in some ways easier to be a reformer abroad. At home, the progressive agenda had come to include the eight-hour day and the income tax, innovations deemed radical by conservatives such as Charles Dana and Whitelaw Reid. Abroad, progressivism entailed the less controversial promotion of basic human and democratic rights. The Cuban rebellion thus became a lightning rod for the reform spirit: what better way to do good than to encourage and aid a subjugated people in its revolt against imperial despots?

Important as these high principles and humanitarian concerns were to the New York dailies in their treatment of the Cuban story, one does not read much about them in journalism histories. That is due to the less defensible parts of Park Row's work.

While several books have been written on the failure of the American press in Cuba, one example catches the gist of it. On March 8, 1895, two weeks after the insurrection began, the U.S. merchant vessel *Allianca* was returning to New York from Colón with a cargo of wine, bananas, cocoa, mustard seeds, and rubber. It crossed paths with the Spanish gunboat *Conde de Venadito* off Cape Maisi in the Windward Passage. According to the *Allianca*'s captain, the Spaniards demanded he halt and submit to a search. The captain refused, being well outside Cuba's three-mile limit. The *Conde de Venadito* opened fire and gave chase for twenty miles. New York editorialists were furious. This affront, thundered the *Tribune*, "would not have been more flagrant if the Spanish gunboat had entered the harbor of New York and bombarded the City Hall." The *Sun* demanded that Washington "vindicate the honor of our flag and the rights of our fellow citizens." The *Times* saw a "prima facie case for sober but decided action by the government of the United States." Several papers insisted that a U.S. fleet be deployed in Cuban waters.[12]

That the *Allianca*'s captain, a known gunrunner, was accused by impartial observers of drawing within 1.5 miles of the Cuban coast in an effort to land arms and men for the insurgents was barely mentioned in the U.S. papers. Spain acknowledged an error in order to smooth over relations with Washington, but its response did not soothe the American press. One of the few contrarians was Godkin, of the *Evening Post*. He blasted the *Tribune* for dramatizing the story with "fourteen headlines and a picture" and Pulitzer for an illustration that showed a shell exploding within ten feet of the American ship, "a fact that was not mentioned by the Captain." Godkin mocked all of his fellow editors for their excitability: "A look askance at the flag cuts them like a knife, a gun pointed our way makes their hearts quiver and their eyes fill with burning tears, and a shot, an actual shot, constitutes a deadly insult which cannot be wiped out, except in double-lettered editorials and a sale of at least eleven extra copies."[13]

New York papers produced so many inaccurate, exaggerated, and hysterical reports in the initial stages of the war in Cuba that just a year and a half into the conflict, *Herald* correspondent George Bronson Rea began compiling a thick catalog of purported journalistic crimes, published under the title *Facts and Fakes about Cuba*. He complained of erroneous accounts of battles between Spanish and Cuban forces and about fabrications of bloodcurdling Spanish atrocities—prisoners shot without trial or drowned in the night, women and children slaughtered and fed to dogs. Rea noted that rebel leader Máximo Gómez and Spanish general Arsenio Martínez Campos were repeatedly and wrongly reported to have been captured, wounded, killed, or recalled. He also found fictitious accounts of Amazon-like beauties overwhelming columns of Spanish soldiers, and silly reports of insurgent cannons fashioned from tree trunks. He accused many of his competitors of operating as propaganda arms for the rebels' Junta, the U.S.–based government-in-waiting. Rea, biased in favor of Madrid, was himself histrionic, taking Spanish claims at face value while overstating the sins of the pro-Cuban papers and branding their differences of opinion as mistakes, but he nonetheless identified reams of error.[14]

Coverage of the Cuban crisis and the ensuing Spanish-American War are often cited as low points in the history of the American press. The yellow papers are singled out for particular abuse. Hearst is said to have been the ringleader, encouraging hostilities and inciting direct U.S. involvement in Cuba with mindless daily orgies of jingoism, sensationalism, and outright fakery—"the most disgraceful example of journalistic falsehood

ever seen," according to Swanberg.[15] Hearst's motives are said to have
extended no higher than increased sales and a megalomaniacal desire to
influence events. Through most of the twentieth century, he stood accused
of dragging America against its better judgment into an unwanted war
with Spain. It is clear from the *Allianca* incident alone, however, that the
New York newspapers had found their pitch on the Cuba story eight
months before Hearst even arrived on the scene. Hearst would in time
contribute to all that is deplored in the newspaper treatment of the rebellion, but he was certainly not the instigator. He gets more of the abuse
because he came to dominate coverage of Cuba (among other reasons
apparent in later chapters). Their errors and excitability notwithstanding,
the yellow papers did far better work on the rebellion than the record
shows. Just as the democratic ideals and humanitarianism that inspired
their coverage are largely lost to history, so too are the journalistic accomplishments of the Hearst and Pulitzer papers in Cuba. Park Row made
some heroic efforts to find truth on the island under unusually difficult
circumstances, with the yellows leading the way.

HEARST'S FIRST SIGNIFICANT MOVE on the story, two months into his
tenure at the *Journal* and toward the end of the first year of the uprising,
was a reaction against all of the misinformation and conjecture appearing
in the pages of his rivals. He dispatched to Havana as his "special commissioner" the celebrated Murat Halstead who the previous summer had
defended Hanna in the *Journal*. Halstead's assignment was to gauge the
real state of play in Cuba and he was an inspired choice. In the course of
his long and prolific career, much of it spent at the *Cincinnati Commercial*,
he had witnessed the hanging of John Brown at Harpers Ferry and the
rise of Abraham Lincoln in the conventions of 1860, and he had reported
from the front lines of the Civil War and of the Franco-Prussian War of
1870–71. He enjoyed such high repute that a town in Kansas had already
been named in his honor. That he was a Republican reinforced Hearst's
commitment to an impartial report.[16]

A walrus-faced man with a mussy white Vandyke, Halstead arrived in
Havana by steamer from Florida and checked in at the Inglaterra, a luxuri-
ous hotel that served as an unofficial headquarters for the American press in
Cuba. An experienced traveler, he was pleased with the accommodations.

His sumptuously furnished room featured twenty-foot ceilings and a large four-poster bed with a mother-of-pearl inlaid headboard and red velvet canopy. Glass doors opened onto a wide white marble balcony. Halstead would press a button at the head of his bed at 7 a.m. and in precisely 150 seconds a bearded porter would arrive to take his order. In exactly five minutes more, coffee, hot milk, rolls, butter and perfectly peeled oranges would be delivered on a solid silver tray with a full breakfast to follow at 11 a.m. The quality of the food in Havana put Halstead in mind of Paris. He was also impressed with his local barber—"deliberate, artistic and couteous . . . almost the barber of my soul." But it was his barkeep who won Halstead's deepest admiration. The man managed to keep a steady supply of crushed ice no matter what the temperature out of doors. He mixed drinks with two crystal glasses, one large, one small. He filled the large glass with ice and the other with liquors, bitters, and sweets and splashed the ingredients back and forth between the glasses, "clinking the crystal in a way that would delight a German's sense of sound." He then flung the concoction through a strainer, filling the smaller glass to the rim, and then returned the large glass to the counter with a triumphant "thwack."[17]

Halstead soon learned that the Inglaterra stood in stark relief to much of its surroundings. Havana was a squalid city with crumbling infrastructure and a dispirited, frightened population. At all hours, the streets and cafés were awash in rumor, and there was no such thing as a dependable source of information. The local population, accustomed to an atmosphere of rebellion, was better trained in conspiracy than objectivity. "Nothing can be stated too wild to find believers," wrote Halstead, "and exaggerations are heaped upon each other until the truth is lost even in outline. . . . 'Perfectly trustworthy' correspondence by secret lines of communication arrives stating highly important matters altogether imaginary." The rebels, dependent on the United States for fundraising and moral support, regaled American reporters in Havana with claims of glorious victories while insisting on the iniquities of the Spanish leadership "to the last detail of infamy."[18] The Spanish government was less fanciful than the rebels but it had blown its credibility at the outset by misleading the press about the extent of the rebellion: it would admit only to success in its efforts to defeat the insurrection, and it further contributed to the general confusion by restricting the movements of reporters and vigorously censoring dispatches from Havana.

Though no stranger to war zones, Halstead found the overall volume of distortion on the Cuba story bewildering. That falsehood was finding its way into print, in his view, was due more to unreliable sources than to dishonest or incompetent reporters.[19]

However difficult the circumstances, Halstead managed to grasp the balance of forces on the island. Spain controlled the western and central parts of Cuba, including Havana, with a conventional army of 100,000 men; the insurgents dominated the mountainous east with less than 40,000 soldiers.[20] While they had proclaimed a provisional government, or Junta, the insurgents had no representative or parliamentary institutions, and their leaders were constantly on the move. Small bands of rebels had crossed into Spanish territory and were causing havoc in the countryside around Havana. Limited in strength and short of ammunition, they tended to avoid direct engagement with the Spanish army, choosing instead to burn cane fields and plantations. Their strategy was to cripple the imperial economy, defeating Spain financially rather than militarily. Spain had plenty of artillery and command of the railroads, but its large columns of infantry were too clumsy to catch the fleet insurgents and its generals were frustrated that their enemy would not march onto a battlefield and fight by conventional rules. The rebel's tactics of sabotage, sniping, ambush and strategic retreats violated the Spanish sense of honor in war. Halstead sympathized with Spain's generals but also recognized their impotence. He predicted that the rebellion was headed for a nasty stalemate, disastrous for noncombatants, particularly for the Cuban peasants whose livelihoods had been destroyed in the rebel raids. He was right on the money.

While Halstead grasped the insurgent strategy within weeks of arriving in Cuba and accepted it as practical, other observers, American and European, would never entirely come to terms with it. They were unaccustomed to a war without clashing armies, sackings, and sieges, and dumbfounded that the rebels were content to harass the Spanish forces and disappear into the weeds. During his tour with the Spaniards, young Winston Churchill wondered what kind of army would rather burn cane and shake down plantation owners than directly engage the enemy. It seemed an inglorious way to found a nation. Even before Halstead's visit, a *Journal* editorial had proclaimed the insurgent strategy the only possible path to success given Spanish superiority in numbers, arms, resources, and discipline. The paper recognized that torching plantations jeopardized the livelihoods of ordinary Cubans but it held Spain responsible for having mismanaged its possession in the first place, and argued that nothing was more likely to bring Madrid to negotiate with the rebels than a sharp decline in the revenue it received from the island. Other newspapers, including some that supported the rebellion, thought the rebel strategy shameful and cowardly. It was controversial even within the ranks of the insurgency.

Halstead's tour of Havana coincided with a changing of the Spanish guard: Captain-General Martínez Campos, hero of the Ten Years' War in Cuba, was recalled to Madrid for failing to quash the rebellion. He did not leave reluctantly. Campos had seen enough to know that the only way succeed in Cuba would be to make war on its rural population, which gave the rebels succor and shelter. He felt he had already violated his own notions of the limits of civilized warfare. "I lack the qualities," he told his superiors. "Among our present generals only Weyler has the necessary capacity for such a policy."[21]

Lieutenant-General Valeriano Weyler y Nicolau, Marquis of Teneriffe, Captain General of Catalonia, a veteran of the Ten Year's War, the Carlist Wars, the Moorish War, and the Philippine uprising, took command of the Spanish forces in Cuba on February 10. He was depicted as a savage barbarian all along Park Row, and even in leading Spanish papers, at least one of which was suppressed for detailing his record of ruthlessness. The *Journal* described him as "a fiendish despot" and an "exterminator of men," the "prince of all the cruel generals this century has seen." The *Tribune* recalled his "revolting acts" of "cruel persecution of the defenseless, wounded invalids and women." This was more abuse than Weyler deserved but only slightly, as events would prove. He immediately extended martial law on the island and attached the death penalty to crimes of disloyalty and treason. He also tightened up censorship of the press, expelling from Cuba reporters whose work he deemed offensive to the regime.[22]

Halstead gained one of the first interviews with Weyler, a fierce little man under five feet tall, whose thick dark sideburns met his long mustache to monogram his face with a perfect W. The captain-general was courteous and businesslike. He denied that the Spaniards were using Cuban prisoners for target practice, as rebel spokesmen had charged. He dismissed the insurgents as so many "fire-bugs," "murderers," "destroyers," and "ravishers." Halstead attempted to persuade the new commander that allowing correspondents to travel about the island would improve the quality of reporting on the conflict. Weyler wasn't buying. He saw the reporters as the problem: "One would think, from the writings of correspondents here, that they were . . . themselves sufferers from the severities they related when what they give out as news comes from agitators and conspirators."[23] He continued to expel reporters by the cartload, adding immeasurably to the problems Park Row and Hearst, in particular, met in covering the war.

The best news correspondent Hearst had stationed in Havana at the time of Halstead's visit was Charles Michelson. Typical of reporters attracted to the Cuba story, Michelson was an athletic young man with a taste for literature and adventure. He was the son of shopkeepers in Virginia City, Nevada, and the brother of Albert Michelson, who would win a Nobel Prize in physics for his exact calculation of the speed of light. Charles had clerked in company stores in the mining belt before finding his way into journalism. He was part of the *Examiner* team that hunted down a California grizzly to prove the species was not extinct in the state. When he was passed over for the position of editor of the Sunday edition he fled to the *San Francisco Call*, but Hearst soon tempted him back with an assignment to Cuba. "This," Michelson would later write, "was bait I could not resist."[24]

Michelson was a responsible reporter by the standards of the day. He filed to New York whatever seemed to be news as quickly as possible, seeking independent corroboration if time allowed, but more often using his best judgment to separate truth from rumor and doing further investigation afterward. He frequently used information from biased parties—rebel or government spokesmen—but he identified his sources, allowing readers to judge the content accordingly. He seldom admitted mistakes, preferring to write follow-up stories with corrective information. In early 1896, for instance, the insurgents surprised the Spanish by sweeping deep into western Cuba, almost to the suburbs of Havana, and Michelson (like all the reporters in the city) reported rumors that the city was in peril of falling. When it became clear that the rebels did not have the numbers, the arms, the expertise, or the intention to take a fortified city brimming with Spanish soldiers, Michelson wrote that "there is nothing to indicate that Havana is in immediate danger of an attack . . . notwithstanding the alarming rumors cabled to New York from here."

He added that Spanish officials, cognizant of the strength of their position, laughed at the rumors of their impending doom.[25] The better Havana correspondents all worked in this amend-as-you-go manner.

Reliable as he was, Michelson's career in Havana was short. Forbidden by the Spanish regime to contact insurrectionists or to travel about the island, and with his stories subject to censorship, he worked underground, as did most American reporters. He would arrange secret meetings with the rebels and smuggle his copy to Key West on passenger steamers with instructions that it to be forwarded to New York. He also tried to sneak out of Havana to get a better sense of what was happening in the field. In February 1896, he was arrested trying to slip past a military checkpoint on his way to investigate rumors of a massacre of twenty noncombatants by Spanish soldiers in a village west of the city. Michelson was interrogated and locked in a tiny cell in Morro Castle, the grand fortress guarding the entrance to Havana Bay. Murat Halstead, learning of his fate, quietly tried to negotiate his release. When the *World* reported the arrest, Halstead wrote it up as well, guessing that it was Michelson's Kodak camera that worried Spain most. Press reports of Michelson's incarceration eventually reached Madrid, where cooler heads prevailed. He was released and instructed to leave the country.[26]

Another *Journal* man, Charles Salomon, reached Havana in January 1896 with plans to steal into the countryside and travel with the rebels. Spanish customs agents found a letter of introduction from the U.S.–based leadership of the Junta in his bags and locked him up. When his *Journal* credentials were authenticated, he was marched aboard the next ship home.[27] No paper had more reporters expelled from Havana than the *Journal,* largely because no paper was sending as many and reporting as aggressively. On one of his trips through Florida, Rea counted eight *Journal* men attempting to arrange the difficult passage to rebel territory.

The expulsions caused Hearst fits. He was scrambling to build a foreign operation for his paper, which had no tradition of international reporting, and the turnover in his Havana staff produced some unfortunate results. Hearst was reliant for a time on the dubious talents of Frederick Lawrence, a former police reporter from San Francisco who Rea considered one of the worst correspondents to write from Havana during the conflict. Lawrence camped out at the Inglaterra and reported whatever was handed to him from rebel sources. According to Rea, he vastly exaggerated the size

of the insurgent army, gave detailed accounts of battles that never happened, and had the same band of Cubans attacking, in the same night, cities
hundreds of miles apart. About all that can be said for Lawrence (and what
Rea failed to mention) is that he clearly sourced his rebel propaganda to the
rebels and dutifully reported disavowals from Spanish officials.[28]

It is tempting to criticize Hearst and the rest of Park Row for the inexperience of some of their Cuban correspondents but, again, many seasoned
men were expelled and, as it happened, much of the best work as the war
progressed came from raw recruits. While most of their colleagues were
reporting on Cuba from Havana, Key West, or Fort Lauderdale, the
World's Sylvester Scovel, the *Journal*'s Grover Flint, and the *Herald*'s
George Bronson Rea took enormous risks to break through Spanish
lines and report the story from insurgent camps and the Cuban countryside. They did some of the most daring and important reporting of their
times, and none had any previous experience in journalism.

AT THE SAME TIME Murat Halstead was snuggling into the Inglaterra,
Sylvester Henry "Harry" Scovel was locked up in Morro Castle. He had
been arrested on January 12 while attempting to sneak into Havana
from the countryside with faked credentials. He had been mistaken for
El Inglesito, the legendary English-speaking rebel colonel, and threatened with a firing squad. Springing him from jail should have been easy,
but the newspaper to which Scovel had been filing, the *New York Herald*,
refused to recognize his credentials.

Morro Castle was an odd landing place for a young man descended
from three generations of American college presidents, but Scovel had a
flair for the unexpected. Just a year before his detention, he had been
working as the popular general manager of the Cleveland Athletic Club.
He directed several amateur sports teams, a poetry circle, and a dramatics
society, and lived in a suite of rooms off the lobby of the downtown
mansion that served as the clubhouse. In his spare time, he promoted boxing matches and billiard tournaments and performed in a well-reviewed
amateur operetta of his own composition. These pursuits brought the
boisterous and likable Scovel a buttery salary of $1,000 a month. He
committed all of it and more to what he termed "a good deal of riotous
living." By the autumn of 1895, his debts had caught up with him and he

had no choice but to turn to his father, who was the president of the University of Wooster and a stiff-necked Presbyterian minister given to railing against "popular corruption." The elder Scovel settled his son's debts on harsh terms. Harry was compelled to return to Pittsburgh and work in the insurance business, which he toiled at for three miserable months before scraping together $200 and setting off for Cuba. He told friends he wanted to see the fighting. He told his parents nothing.[29]

Scovel's writing credits at the moment of his departure were limited to his amateur operetta and a handful of dramatic notices. There was nothing in his background to suggest that he might become a great war correspondent except, perhaps, an affinity for danger. He had been so enamored of hazardous stunts as a boy that his father had encouraged him to attend funerals in order to contemplate his mortality. He survived to attend the University of Michigan, establishing himself as a leading student politician and one of the best athletes on campus before quitting from boredom midway through his sophomore year. His alumni maga-zine, remembering his "vivacity" and "impulsiveness," claimed that he had passed through so many perils before his majority that "he seemed to bear a charmed life."[30]

Scovel's personal qualities—his intelligence, resourcefulness, determi-nation, bravery, and affability—would more than compensate for his lack of education and experience as a reporter. On his way to Cuba, he stopped by the Manhattan offices of the *New York Herald*. The *Herald* may have had an insipid editorial page, but it was an aggressive news-gatherer, producing the best foreign file of any paper on Park Row. Its attention to international affairs was a reflection of the cosmopolitan interests and lifestyle of its owner, Bennett Jr., who still resided most of the year in Europe. Scovel told a *Herald* editor named Taylor of his intention to travel with the insurgent army; the editor promised him $24 a column for whatever copy he could smuggle out of Cuba.

That same day, Scovel visited Horatio Rubens, legal counsel and offi-cial spokesman for the Junta in New York. Rubens had gained prominence as host of the so-called Peanut Club, a daily news briefing where Park Row reporters were fed peanuts and the party line. Scovel told Rubens he intended to travel to Cuba to report the war. Rubens decided the young man was crazy but likable and he took him to dinner to talk some sense into him. He advised Scovel that Cubans spoke a language other than

English, and warned him that even if he managed to elude Spanish border guards, there was no guarantee that an American correspondent would be welcomed by the insurgent army. Undaunted, dreading only a return to the insurance industry, Scovel persisted and won a letter of introduction from Rubens on Junta stationary.[31]

The letter did Scovel no good. Detained by customs agents in Havana on his first attempt to get in, he tore it up and ate it before police arrived to interrogate him. He was sent back to the United States and made a second entry attempt in mid-October, this one by steamer to Cienfuegos on the southern coast of the island, where security was relatively lax. He arrived safely and began searching for a contact suggested by Rubens. Unable to find the man, Scovel determined to simply walk out into the countryside in search of insurgents. Spanish police picked him up as he tried to bluff his way past a military sentry on the road out of town. He was escorted back to his hotel and relieved of his cash and watch. Two days later, he slipped past the sentry and began wandering from village to village, asking if anyone spoke English and knew where he might find some insurgents. Despite the language barrier and his unfamiliarity with the island, Scovel fetched up in the camp of the rebel commander Máximo Gómez less than two weeks later, on November 1, 1895.

Scovel had caught up to Gomez just as the general was gearing up for his foray to the western provinces, which involved crossing the troches, a system of fortified blockades running the width of the island and designed to contain the insurgents in the east. Gomez was the architect of the theory that the rebels needed to take their campaign to the prosperous western region, the center of the sugar trade and the foundation of the island's economy. He sought not only to destroy the wealth that was keeping Spain in Cuba and funding the oppression of his people, but to make ordinary Cubans desperate enough to join the rebellion.

A few weeks into the westward campaign, Scovel witnessed the same skirmish between Gómez's men and Spanish regulars that was observed by Winston Churchill from the other side of the lines. While Churchill dismissed the insurgents as an undisciplined rabble, Scovel admired their unconventional methods and considered Gómez a minor military genius. He stuck with him as the rebels swept westward, evading Spanish columns and razing plantations. He witnessed Gómez's romp through the suburbs of Havana in December—the gambit that launched rumors that the capital would fall.

As he traveled, Scovel had been composing dispatches and sending them via rebel smugglers to the *Herald* in New York. But he had no idea whether his copy was actually getting into print. Desperate to know, he broke from Gómez in January 1896, and headed for the Inglaterra to learn from the American press corps if he was a famous correspondent. It was that mission that landed him in a cell in Morro Castle.

The *Herald*'s man in Havana should have vouched for Scovel and won his release, but instead George Bronson Rea made a special trip to the governor's palace to deny that the prisoner represented his paper. Rea's editors at the *Herald* said they had never heard of Scovel. The U.S. consul also contacted the paper on Scovel's behalf but no one would claim responsibility for him. He might have languished in Morro Castle for months had it not been for the *World*'s Havana correspondent, William Shaw Bowen. A diligent reporter, Bowen was in the habit of checking out the Americans who turned up in Cuban jails in hopes that one might amount to a story. He visited Scovel four days after his arrest. He was surprised to meet a likable young man from a prominent Cleveland family. Convinced that Scovel was sincere in his ambition to be a famous war correspondent, Bowen arranged for the *World* to vouch for his credentials. Thus Harry Scovel left the *Herald* and became an unshakably loyal *World* man, giving Joseph Pulitzer an enormous advantage over all other editors covering Cuba.

As Scovel waited for his papers to be processed by Spanish authorities, he was visited by a tall, red-headed, deeply apologetic George Bronson Rea, who explained that Taylor, Scovel's contact at the paper, had been dismissed and that no one else on staff knew of his assignment. It was nonetheless thoughtless of Rea to have disowned a fellow correspondent, particularly since he too had been mistaken for El Inglesito only days earlier. Scovel was disappointed to learn that most of his smuggled copy had been lost or destroyed en route to New York. Only one early piece had made it into print, and, as per the *Herald*'s policy, it appeared without a byline, so Scovel was not yet famous. The paper offered to pay him a modest fee for the single published article. Scovel magnanimously forgave Rea his behavior and the two became friends and collaborators, but he held a grudge against the *Herald* for the rest of his life.

REA, LIKE SCOVEL, was in his mid-twenties and of good family; his father was a successful Brooklyn banker. For the previous five years, Rea had been working as an engineer in Cuba. When the fighting spread to the western provinces, industrial activity stopped cold and he began looking for something else to do. He joined the *Herald* just two weeks before he met Scovel.[32]

Thanks to his engineering experience, Rea knew the country better than his fellow correspondents, and his view of the Cuban people was typical of American businessmen on the island: "I lived in Cuba for five years previous to the insurrection . . . and I must say that if the Cubans were oppressed, I failed to discover in what manner." He saw little support for the revolution in the western provinces: "The majority were not in favor of it, and desired to be quiet, so as to grind their cane, and only joined the movement when forced to do so by lack of employment, hunger, or the burning of their homes."[33] These attitudes made Rea a perfect correspondent for the *Herald,* which habitually defended Spanish war methods as severe but necessary. (A cut in tobacco exports to America was one of the few Spanish moves to draw heat from the paper: "To be compelled to smoke tobacco of the temperate zone while Spaniards monopolize the tobacco of Cuba . . . seems almost too much to bear," complained one editorial.)[34]

At the time he met Scovel, Rea had it in mind to gain an exclusive interview with Máximo Gómez. President Cleveland had just dismissed all talk of belligerent status for the Cubans and pledged the U.S. to respect Spanish sovereignty on the island and to maintain a pose of strict neutrality with regard to the rebellion. The rebel general's response was eagerly anticipated in the United States. Scovel, too, intended to return to the countryside and interview Gómez. Although the journalist had been released from Morro Castle under a deportation order, he had no intention of retreating stateside. He told Rea that while competitive considerations prevented him from leading a rival newspaperman to Gómez, he would be happy to make introductions if Rea were to find the general's camp on his own. Finding the rebels was not difficult, Scovel added, as most Cubans knew where they were at any given time and were happy to provide directions if approached the right way. As the historian Joyce Milton has pointed out, "Rea must have listened to all this with a good deal of skepticism. He had been in Cuba for five years, and here was

Scovel after three months, a buddy of the famously enigmatic Gómez . . .
and now an expert on how to talk to peasants."[35]

Rea was first to depart Havana. He left Scovel drinking whiskey in a
Havana café on January 18 and trudged a week through the countryside
of Havana province before stumbling across a band of rebels who led
him to Gómez's camp. The general was out when the reporter arrived.
When Gómez finally came riding back, Harry Scovel was on a horse
directly behind him having already filed his exclusive interview.[36]

Rea took an immediate dislike to Gómez. "All my preconceived ideas
of him," he wrote, "were shattered by a glance, for instead of the
martial-looking old gentleman, whose bearing conveyed the idea of a
thorough soldier, I found a chocolate-colored, withered old man, who
gave one the idea of a resurrected Egyptian mummy, with the face
lighted by a pair of blurry, cold, expressionless gray eyes, that at times
glowed like two red coals of fire, especially when in rage or passion."[37]
However jaundiced Rea's view of the general, it counterbalanced the
more familiar portrait of him as a Cuban George Washington.

In the seven or eight months he traveled with Gómez, Rea was witness to insurgent looting and burning of villages and plantations, as well
as some fifty "skirmishes and guerrilla fights that have been misnamed
battles."[38] His descriptions of these clashes, while colored by his contempt for Gómez, are some of the best on record. On a typical occasion,
Gómez's scouts had located a column of Spanish soldiers an hour away
from camp. Instead of hustling his men into position for battle, the general sent out a few marksmen to harass the enemy. He himself remained
in camp, reading, while his bodyguards lounged nearby singing. When it
was learned that the sharpshooters had failed to halt the progress of the
troops, Gómez ordered a colonel to occupy a stone house along the road
and hold it against the Spanish advance. The general continued to relax
in camp, rifle fire in the distance. It was not until a shell whistled over his
head that Gómez, by Rea's account, finally roused the five hundred or so
soldiers and "general scum" of the insurgent army. They picked up their
revolvers, shotguns and machetes and vanished like the mist.[39]

Such maneuvers delighted Scovel as much as they enraged Rea, but
their differences did not affect their working relationship. Together they
perfected techniques of smuggling their dispatches to the mainland—
dangerous work given the watchfulness of Spanish sentries. The pair

would sneak into railway towns guarded by troops. and freight their articles to agents in Havana, who in turn would send the stories to Key West by ship. From there the copy was telegraphed to New York. Some of their pieces got to their papers in a week; most took a month; some took three months. They had a number of close calls, including one at Quivicán. "Unfortunately for our plans," wrote Rea, "a Spanish column arrived there before us and saw us coming. Like the good soldiers that they were, they formed an ambuscade to capture us 'vivita' on entering the town. A fight was the result. On second thought, I think the letter 'l' inserted in the world 'fight' would probably express our conduct more clearly. Scovel was unhorsed, and narrowly escaped capture, and my own 'genuine Cuban plug' was killed. By a miracle we gained the shelter of the canefields and escaped."[40]

However much Rea hated Gómez, the feeling appears to have been mutual. Not only was the correspondent haughty and opinionated, his paper, to the extent that it had a discernable position, supported Spain. At one point Gómez asked Rea by what right he was traveling with the rebels and eating at the general's table. When he mused aloud about having the reporter shot, Rea reminded the general that harming an American newspaperman would hurt the rebel cause in the U.S. He understood, nevertheless, that he had worn out his welcome and made his way to the camp of another insurgent leader, Antonio Maceo. A brave and self-educated mulatto cavalryman with a fondness for French literature and no qualms about confronting Spanish troops, Maceo emerged in Rea's reports as the anti-Gómez: "As day after day I witnessed him at the head of his men, directing the fray from the front ranks of the firing line, I could not but feel a certain admiration for the man who, despite his color, was so far the superior of the many 'opera bouffe' generals in the Cuban Army of Liberation."[41]

SCOVEL, MEANWHILE, had been shot in the leg while traveling with the rebels and the wound became infected. His hosts smuggled him to Havana, where U.S. consular officials shipped him back to the United States disguised as a businessman requiring medical treatment for tropical fever. Scovel used his time stateside to meet, for the first time, his employer, Joseph Pulitzer, and his managing editor, Bradford Merrill. He was presented with a new contract at a respectable $60 per week and with a generous allowance for expenses that permitted him to pick up a fine saddle, a camera, and a typewriting machine (possibly the first to be taken to a war zone). Scovel was anxious to return to Cuba, but Pulitzer apparently had qualms about sending him back into harm's way and Merrill was uncomfortable with his close ties to the insurgents. Scovel promised not to put his life at risk and to conduct himself as a noncombatant and solely as a news correspondent. He was back in Havana by the spring of 1896.

Scovel did not stick to the letter of his promises to Pulitzer and Merrill. While he never carried a gun or engaged in combat, he did courier documents for the insurgents, and they valued his work highly enough to provide him with an armed escort of up to eleven men when he traveled in Cuba. The Spanish were not wrong to regard him as an enemy. Weyler, meanwhile, had read Scovel's interview with Gómez, conducted in defiance of Spain's ban on press contact with the rebels, and posted a $5,000 reward for the correspondent's capture, dead or alive. By simply being in Cuba with a price on his head, Scovel was putting himself at risk. When James Creelman arrived in Havana in April, he was astonished to find Scovel hiding in plain view amid Spanish officers at the Cafe Inglaterra. He was wearing a shabby business suit and pretending to be Mr. Brown, a salesman from New York.

Creelman, taking a break from his political assignments, was also in Cuba for Pulitzer, who was preoccupied with documenting Spanish atrocities against civilians. Probably with Scovel's assistance, Creelman slipped out of Havana to nearby Campo Florida to investigate another rumored massacre of noncombatants by Spanish soldiers. In a field not far from town, he and his Cuban guides found the fresh shallow graves of the slain, their hands tied behind their backs. Creelman gave Pulitzer the atrocity story he sought, with the names of thirty-three victims and the dates of their executions. It appeared May 1 on the front page of the *World* and continued over almost a full page inside. Creelman personally delivered a copy of his report to Weyler, who promptly ordered him deported. Creelman's response, on returning stateside, was one of the more notorious screeds of the war: "The horrors of the barbarous struggle for the extermination of the native population are witnessed in all parts of the country. Blood on the roadsides, blood in the fields, blood on the doorsteps, blood, blood, blood! The old, the young, the weak, the crippled, all are butchered without mercy. There is scarcely a hamlet that has not witnessed this dreadful work."[42]

The *World*'s editorial page responded to Creelman's report by calling for diplomatic pressure on Spain to end the conflict: "It is time that the government at Washington awoke to the fact that we have an Armenia at our very doors, and that the fair and fertile island of Cuba is not only being desolated by the torch of the insurgents but depopulated by the remorseless savagery of the Spanish soldiers. Intervention has become a duty."[43]

Notwithstanding his paper's position, Harry Scovel, still in Cuba, was skeptical of Creelman's story and began his own investigations into atrocity reports. In May, he visited a site near San Pedro where eleven unarmed civilians were said to have been slaughtered by Spanish troops. He then proceeded to several other sites of reported carnage. "I came here with the conviction that the reports of these slayings of unarmed men were much exaggerated," he wrote, but over two months of field work he collected 196 signed affidavits attesting to Spanish brutality resulting in 212 deaths. He had the names, addresses, and ages of his victims, and in some cases the identities of the soldiers who had ordered or committed the killings: "That extermination of the Cuban people under the cloak of civilized warfare is Spain's settled purpose is shown by facts already made public through the *World*." Scovel's conversion from skepticism would be repeated by many observers in the months ahead. Rea challenged his friend's reporting, pointing out that many of his examples came from rebel sources and that some of the names were repeated. Nonetheless, Scovel's reporting was unusually thorough for the time, and a British journalist who traveled in his footsteps through Havana province believed his work to be solid.[44]

Although one could read even in the *Herald* reports of Spanish forces raiding rebel hospitals, assassinating the wounded in their cots and burning the buildings over their heads to cover up the crime, the yellow papers clearly had the most enthusiasm for atrocity stories, a fact that has brought Pulitzer and Hearst heavy criticism over the years, a great deal of it unjust. The *Journal*'s headline "Feeding prisoners to sharks" is a frequently cited example of supposed excess, yet it ran over a well-reported story of how Havana policemen were executing prisoners outside the harbor and dumping the corpses in shark-infested waters. The *New York*

Times ran an almost identical piece on the same day: "The reason why [the prisoners] are taken out of the harbor is on account of the immense number of sharks which get hold of the bodies and leave no trace." The *Times* headline—"Cuban prisoners drowned"—was less emotive than the *Journal*'s, and in a sense less accurate for failing to convey that the victims were deliberately and not accidentally killed.[45]

THE ONLY OTHER AMERICAN NEWSPAPERMAN to spend significant time with the rebels in the early years of the conflict was Grover Flint of the *New York Journal*. Slightly older than Scovel and Rea, Flint came from a more illustrious background, being the son of the Civil War hero Major General Cuvier Grover and the grandson of the noted New York physician Austin Flint, president of the American Medical Association. Born Flint Grover, he reversed his name at the request of the Flint side of his family and received a substantial inheritance for his trouble. He graduated from Harvard and remained close to his alma mater, courting the daughter of Cambridge historian and philosopher John Fiske. It was in all probability a Harvard connection that brought him to Hearst's employ—both were associated with the *Lampoon*. Flint was unique among the early reporters in Cuba for having actual combat experience with the First Cavalry in the Indian Wars. He was also fluent in Spanish thanks to a year in Madrid with a friend, the American diplomat Edward Strobel.[46]

After connecting with Havana-based Junta agents, Flint hopped off a train at the port of Cárdenas on March 27, 1896, and began roaming the countryside in search of Gómez. He found a small crew of insurgents who led him to a larger group busily torching plantations. They were courteous to Flint, supplying him with a pair of porters and leading him eventually to Gómez, whom he described as a "gray little man" in ill-fitting clothes but impressive in his own way: "[T]he moment he turns his keen eyes on you, they strike like a blow from the shoulder. You feel the will, the fearlessness, and the experience of men that is in those eyes."[47] Flint disagreed with Rea's criticism of Gómez's leadership qualities, noting that the general managed to hold sway over a ragtag group of undernourished and poorly supported volunteers who were kept moving constantly through inhospitable terrain, even in the rainy seasons. Discipline was firm and morale was strong.

A stolen saddlebag reduced Flint to scribbling notes with pencil stubs, and he appears to have had trouble finding reliable couriers. He filed only four reports to the *Journal* in his four months in the field, but among these was a thorough sketch of one of the few direct engagements of the early part of the war. The forty-eight-hour battle began on the afternoon of June 9 in the thick hilly country near Puerto Principe. Gómez's ragged troops, including four hundred cavalry and a hundred infantry, confronted two Spanish columns comprising two thousand infantry and five hundred cavalry. Most of the time was spent in a tense standoff with the combatants firing at each other from safe distances, but when the action got hot, Flint recorded it minute by minute.

At 4:55 p.m. on the first afternoon, he described the Spanish forming "dark gray lines, splashed with the red of sashes." Their bullets were "coming thickly, but too high. You can feel them in the air. They make you wink. The smoke is getting thick. I can scarcely see the lines. Our men loom up in silhouette."

At 5:05 p.m.: "Our infantry are shooting into the enemy's right wing from the woods. The enemy are getting excited. They shoot higher and faster. General Gómez, followed by his staff, [is] riding placidly up and down, peering at the lines through the smoke. He has stationed his escort on the plain back of us as a reserve. . . . The Spaniards open on us with artillery, two guns well to the rear of the hill. It is inspiring to watch Gómez under fire. He looks twenty years younger."

At 5:20 p.m.: "They are beginning to bring the wounded from the front. Some are in the arms of comrades, riding double, to be left with the impedimenta. In the firing line some have had their horses shot, and are fighting on foot."[48]

By noon of June 11 the battle had ended, with a Spanish retreat to Puerto Principe. Flint rode through their abandoned positions, noting the bits of bloody clothing, empty cigar packages, and ammunition boxes that marked their presence. "I learned how the Spanish bury their dead," he wrote. "The graves were so hastily dug and covered that in many cases hands protruded and faces could be seen between clods of earth." His report was accompanied by six illustrations, including one of a cavalry charge and another of the graves of dead Spaniards. He estimated that Spain had lost fifty men. Soon after this incident he sailed from Cuba to Nassau in an open twenty-seven-foot boat, and from there returned to the United States.[49]

IT IS SIGNIFICANT that of the three American newspaper reporters to penetrate Spanish lines and travel for significant times with the insurgents, one worked for the *Herald*, with its great tradition of foreign reportage, and the other two worked for the *Journal* and the *World*. The same three dailies would continue to dominate coverage of events in Cuba. All three pursued the story in the spirit of journalistic enterprise and competitiveness, confident of their readers' interest. The yellows had none of the *Herald*'s international experience but they made up for the lack with fierce commitment, rooted in outrage at the plight of the Cuban people. Hearst and Pulitzer dedicated more resources to the story than other papers and saw more of their men arrested, expelled, and injured on the job. (Weyler treated *Herald* men lightly because of the paper's relatively sympathetic treatment of Spain.) The yellows routinely carried three or four pieces a day during the conflict, and at peak moments they published three, four, five, or more pages of coverage. More copy made more error inevitable, and Cuba was an especially tricky war, as Halstead and others noted.[50] With much of the action occurring in a hit-and-run manner in remote areas, journalists could see little for themselves and were dependent on unreliable sources on both sides. By taking a leading position in covering the conflict, the yellow press was more vulnerable to the difficulties such coverage presented.

Forgotten though they may be, the laudable aspects of the Cuban coverage were at least appreciated at the time. Richard Harding Davis had Grover Flint in mind when he wrote the following tribute to reporters in Cuba:

> They are taking chances that no war correspondents ever took in any war in any part of the world. For this is not a war—it is a state of lawless butchery, and the rights of correspondents, of soldiers, and of noncombatants are not recognized. Archibald Forbes and "Bull Run" Russell and Frederick Villiers had great continental armies to protect them; these men work alone with a continental army against them . . . and they are in the field now, lying in swamps by day and creeping between the forts by night, standing under fire by the side of Gómez . . . [and] going without food, without shelter, without the right to answer the attacks of the Spanish troops, climbing the mountains and crawling across the trochas,

creeping to some friendly hut for a cup of coffee and to place their despatches in safe hands, and then going back again.[51]

Davis's admiration was not misplaced. A case in point is the story of Charles Govin, as reported by the *Journal*'s Grover Flint. Yet another young man of good family determined to make a name for himself as a war correspondent in Cuba, Govin was twenty-three and a reporter for the Key West *Equator-Democrat*. On July 6, 1896, he crossed to Cuba on one of the many filibustering expeditions smuggling men and arms out of Florida. Three days after landing, he was marching in Havana province in the company of a rebel major named Valencia. The Cubans skirmished with a Spanish column under Colonel Ochoa. When Spanish reinforcements arrived on the scene, the Cubans disappeared into the bush. Govin, finding himself alone and lost, rode to a nearby hilltop to get the lay of the land. He saw Spanish troops advancing from three directions. He presented himself to the Spaniards waving a white handkerchief, confident of his rights as a U.S. citizen and neutral observer. He was detained by an advance guard until Colonel Ochoa arrived, dismounted, and addressed him with vehemence. According to Flint's account, "his papers were torn from his pockets, and his clothing hurriedly searched. No weapons were found." His papers were handed to Ochoa, who "glanced them over and scornfully threw them on the ground." Govin was then bound to a tree and hacked to death with machetes by two noncommissioned officers. A handful of Cuban soldiers witnessed the execution from nearby hiding places. They recovered and buried Govin's body and reported the incident to their superiors. Major Julio Rodríguez Baz of the Cuban army told the story to Flint.[52]

George Bronson Rea, skeptical as always of reports of Spanish atrocities, did his own investigation into Govin's death. He told a U.S. Senate committee in June 1897 that he could not find Flint's source, a Major Baz, but that his own sources corroborated the facts of the story.

CHAPTER ELEVEN

Only a Hero Can Sit for a Month
on a Hotel Porch

Richard Harding Davis's account of the Yale-Princeton football match during Hearst's first month in New York sold out the edition, earning the paper much praise and guaranteeing that Davis would be invited back to the pages of the *Journal*. After the game, he signed on to cover anticipated hostilities between the United States and Great Britain over the Venezuelan boundary dispute, but before he could sail, a diplomatic solution averted war and kept him at home. Five months later, in the spring of 1896, he had better luck, disembarking for Moscow to report on the coronation of Nicholas II as Czar of All the Russias for both the *Journal* and *Harper's* magazine.

Hearst may have considered royalty a tiresome anachronism, but many Americans felt otherwise, and Davis could be counted on to compensate for the publisher's relative lack of enthusiasm. According to his superb biographer, Arthur Lubow, Davis looked upon kings and queens with inexhaustible wonder, as though they belonged to a gorgeous "imperilled species."[1] He was a connoisseur of their pageants and spectacles, covering the coronation of Spain's King Alfonso XIII, and the millennial celebration of the Kingdom of Hungary. His passion for regal splendor was consistent with the Victorian era's nostalgia for a chivalric past. The Arthurian legends were much in vogue, as were heroic tales from classical and medieval mythology. Davis drew heavily on these traditions in his bestselling fiction: his virile Manhattan knights in dinner jackets and polished shoes traveled the Americas to rescue chaste maidens and slay metaphorical dragons. He crafted his own public image from romantic ideals of courtliness and valor, as the gallant, square-jawed, squeaky-clean gentleman adventurer, equally at home in the opera box and on the field of battle. So who better to travel four thousand miles to report on one of the most splendid imperial ceremonies of the age?

The trick to the story was gaining access to the Cathedral of the Assumption, where Nicholas would take his oath and begin his reign. The guest list was limited to eight hundred and the Russian court, European royalty and nobility, and international heads of state took most of the seats, leaving few for journalists. Twelve, to be precise. Davis began his campaign for admission at the top, asking President Cleveland to declare him part of the official U.S. delegation—after all, Richard Harding Davis was no ordinary hack—but his request was denied. Baffled but undeterred, Davis hustled to Moscow to try his luck with the Russian court, playing up his status as a "literary light of the finest color," one whose work would live forever, yet again he was refused. Much to his credit, Davis grew more determined in the face of rejection. "There is not a wire we have not pulled, or a leg, either," he wrote his family, "and we go dashing about all day . . . leaving cards and writing notes and giving drinks and having secretaries to lunch and buying flowers for wives and segar [sic] boxes for husbands, and threatening the Minister with Cleveland's name." His fierce lobby paid off. Davis finally gained one of only two blue badges of admission handed to U.S. correspondents.[2]

On the morning of May 26, Davis passed through some 300,000 people gathered outside the cathedral to take his place amid the crush of tiaras and uniforms inside. He watched the three-hour ceremony with awe. The grand dukes, carrying the royal robes of ermine to the front of the church, literally staggered under their weight. The dowager empress was all gems and tears. The czar placed his crown upon his own brow and took up his scepter, ornamented with the Orloff diamond. Davis was especially enchanted by the young czarina, Princess Alix of Hesse-Darmstadt, whom he had first glimpsed on an earlier trip to Athens. He had found her, on that occasion, so strikingly beautiful that he had followed her from the Acropolis to her hotel to learn her identity. His infatuation had blossomed into his bestselling 1895 romance, *The Princess Aline,* in which a young man (not unlike Davis) falls into a passionate but chaste affair with a princess (not unlike Alix). For the coronation, the czarina was "so simply dressed that, in comparison with the ladies of the Court and the Princesses and wives of Ambassadors rising in tiers around her, she was the most feminine looking woman in the Cathedral. Her shoulders were bare, even of straps; her hair was without ornament, and hung in two plaits, one over each shoulder. Around her neck was a single string of pearls. . . . [T]he contrast was striking."[3]

Davis had bribed the director of the telegraph bureau to ensure that his story would be transmitted first. It filled the first three pages of the *Journal* the next day, with his own portrait as the main art (pictures of the ceremony awaited shipment by sea). Unfortunately, Davis missed the biggest news of the coronation. A massive feast for a half million Russian commoners was held after the ceremony in a field outside of Moscow. The promise of free food and drink caused a stampede in which hundreds were trampled to death and thousands injured. Davis had already split for Budapest. He was spared great embarrassment, however, by a devastating cyclone that swept St. Louis the very same day; it claimed hundreds of lives and pushed the Russian disaster to inside pages.

Newspaper Maker called Davis's dispatch on the coronation a "fine specimen of special correspondence."[4] It marveled at the "modern methods" of progressive newspapers, sending famous writers to file long and instantaneous reports on great events when previously a short cable dispatch of half a column would have sufficed. Davis would later complain that the paper was late with funds to cover his telegraph fees and that Hearst's editors were impudent, but few publications ever treated him to his satisfaction. His association with the *Journal* would continue, and Hearst was about to entrust Davis with the biggest story of them all.

AS SOON AS THE 1896 ELECTION WAS DECIDED, Park Row scampered to catch up with events in Cuba. Fighting on the island had not merely resumed after the summer rains but intensified. Captain-General Weyler was spending more time in the field in pursuit of insurgents, apparently under compulsion from a home government anxious for results. He was unsuccessful, but his determination worried pro-Cuban editors. His treatment of the Cuban people was also living up to Park Row's dire expectations: stories of atrocities committed against noncombatants were increasingly frequent and credible. Weyler had taken the drastic step of ordering the rural populations of three western provinces moved to "reconcentration camps" on the outskirts of urban centers. His intent was to deprive the insurgents of protection and support in the countryside; the effect was to finish off the island's reeling economy and to inflict unimaginable suffering on innocent people. The rebels, for their part, vowed to fight to the finish even if Cuba was "drowned in blood and devoured by flames," and ordered that all emissaries of peace be killed on introduction.[5] A Russian diplomat in Havana sighed that both sides "have sworn to lay waste to this unfortunate country."[6]

The popularity of the Cuban cause was meanwhile mushrooming in the United States. Parades and rallies in support of *Cuba Libre* were popping up everywhere: the newspapers reported mass meetings across the country and petitions in support of the rebels with as many as 300,000 signatures.[7] Benefit societies were founded for relief of the wounded and sick. Gun clubs were organized to supply the insurgents with arms (the initiation fee at one such organization was a rifle or one hundred rounds of ammunition).[8] Although humanitarian concerns remained foremost in the popular mind, U.S. economic interests were a significant part of the story. Trade with Cuba had fallen to a quarter of previous levels. Plantations and commercial properties representing millions of dollars in direct American investment lay in ashes. The rebels had done most of the torching, but Spain was supposed to be keeping order on the island. The losses were drawing the United States more directly into the conflict.[9] So, too, were filibusters.

Filibusters were private oceangoing expeditions carrying arms and recruits to the insurgents, most often from ports in Florida. They sailed in violation of the U.S. Neutrality Act, which allowed only medical supplies and nonmilitary aid to leave the country for the island. Some of the boats arrived safely in Cuba and disgorged their cargo. More sank or turned back in rough seas, or were intercepted by the U.S. Coast Guard or, worse, by Spanish gunboats. Spain's efforts to prosecute captured gunrunners generated angry headlines in the United States, while Madrid accused Washington of doing too little to prevent the expeditions. President Cleveland, anxious to calm relations, issued a special proclamation against filibustering, much to the chagrin of pro-Cuban editors like Hearst, Pulitzer, and Dana, who continued to complain that the president's cold-blooded insistence on strict neutrality was sustaining Spanish despotism and starving the rebels of arms and recruits. Cleveland's special proclamation had little effect, however. As the

Commercial Advertiser noted, filibusters were impossible to stop when all of Florida was a Cuban refuge.[10] The expeditions continued, and international disputes kept bobbing up in their wake.

Impatience with Cleveland's strict neutrality was hardly limited to Park Row. All manner of community organizations petitioned Washington to protect Cuba (the Youngstown Chamber of Commerce distinguished itself by boycotting the Spanish onion). Governments of every level in every part of the country made declarations in support of the insurgents. In the first few months of 1896, senators and congressmen lined up to denounce Spain's cruel and inept management of the island and a deluge of resolutions and amendments hit both chambers. Sympathy for the insurgents was near unanimous, but there was little agreement on anything else. Was Spain fighting a war or putting down an insurrection? Should the United States express concern for the Cuban people or intervene to end the conflict? What form of intervention would be appropriate? Should the United States recognize Cuba as a belligerent, or as an independent nation, or should it encourage Spain to submit to arbitration, or present her with an ultimatum to end the fighting?[11]

Importantly, Republicans and not yellow newspapers were the jingoes at this point in the crisis, the most eager to send warships to Cuba and the first to talk of annexing the island. Republicans were the aggressors, writes the historian Walter Millis, in part because of their political opposition to the ruling Cleveland Democrats, but also because of their philosophical embrace of an expansionist foreign policy—territorial aggrandizement was seen as good for American business. The *Literary Digest* listed all the new bills drawn up in the name of preparedness, including one calling for $100 million in new armaments, another for six battleships at $4 million a piece and twenty-five torpedo boats at $175,000 each, another for $87 million in coastal defenses, another for reorganizing the army, another for refurbishing the naval reserve, another for issuing Springfield rifles to the National guard, and another proposing $100 million in new fortifications—all but one brought by Republicans. Teddy Roosevelt might have believed "this country needs a war" to bolster its character but no similar sentiment was ever uttered by Hearst. Rather, writes Millis, the yellow press and the progressive wing of the Democratic Party were "more deeply impressed with our Christian duty to right the wrongs of suffering in

Cuba." But whatever their motives, both sides often came across as bellicose and anxious for Washington to take action.[12]

After several months of closely reported debate, Congress determined
that a state of war existed in Cuba, that the insurgents should be accorded
the rights of belligerents, and that the United States should use its
friendly offices to encourage Spain to recognize the independence of the
Cuban people. Cleveland, however, remained firm in his neutrality with
the result that Congress, the press, and the American public now began to
look beyond him. The Democratic and Republican parties both emerged
from their summer conventions waving staunchly pro-Cuban policies.
The Republicans went furthest, vowing immediate recognition of Cuban
independence.[13]

In the wake of the congressional debates, Park Row papers sharpened
their positions. It was not until the summer of 1896 that Hearst moved
beyond his initial demand to extend belligerent status to the Cubans and
began calling for Washington to ensure the restoration of peace and order
in Cuba. Particularly, he wanted protection for American citizens and
investment in Cuba, aid to alleviate the suffering of the Cuban people, and
a halt to Spain's brutal suppression of the rebellion. Ultimately, he wanted
a free Cuba. "We have given Spain every opportunity and she has shown
that she can do nothing," the *Journal* declared. " . . . The truest kindness
we can do to Spain would be to cut once and for all the bond that fastens
her to the putrefying corpse of her American colonial empire, and give
her a chance to develop her domestic resources in health and peace."[14]

Hearst believed these goals were best accomplished through an ultima-
tum. The United States would choose the appropriate moment to tell
Spain the war must end, and it should be prepared to force its will if necessary (how exactly Washington might do this was left unsaid). This
position put Hearst at the leading edge of pro-Cuban commentary, but
Pulitzer's *World* and Dana's *Sun* adopted similar lines. None of the New
York papers was yet advocating direct military intervention, although the
Republican *Tribune* had come out in favor of spending tens of millions,
even billions, to make the United States the strongest military power on
the planet. If Spain insists on fighting the United States, it said, "the feeling here is that it can be accommodated."[15]

As 1896 wound down and McKinley won the presidency on a platform
that included an aggressively pro-Cuban plank, America succumbed to a

case of war jitters. Credible voices in both the United States and Spain suggested conflict was imminent. The stock market plunged. Volunteer militia groups sprang up from New York to Nebraska to California, attracting thousands of recruits in preparation for service in Cuba. Stories appeared in all of the dailies on the relative military preparedness of the United States and Spain, along with analyses of how the war might be fought and who would win. The *Journal* picked up an extensive comparison of the Spanish and American fleets undertaken by French experts (who predicted a U.S. defeat). The war panic lasted several weeks, and it spurred the New York press to make even greater investments in the Cuban story. Reporters and commentators who had recently been following Bryan and silver were redeployed in Havana and Florida. Acres of space recently committed to election news were now dedicated to stories and opinion on Cuban affairs.[16]

No paper pulled out more stops than the *Journal*. Hearst launched a series of editorials on Cuba, expressing hope that McKinley would wipe out "the standing disgrace" of U.S. inaction.[17] He dispatched senator-elect Hernando De Soto Money of Mississippi to Havana as another "special commissioner." He assigned the Yale rowing hero and upstart Philadelphia journalist Ralph Paine to join a filibuster and make his way to the insurgents. He scored a major competitive coup by poaching James Creelman, Pulitzer's celebrated but estranged reporter. Hearst paid Creelman $8,000 a year (a figure soon to escalate) and installed him in Madrid to report on the Spanish government and its diplomacy and to keep an eye on public sentiment—there had been a series of anti-American riots in Spain in 1896 and a student-led attack on the U.S. consulate in Cadiz.[18] George Eugene Bryson and Charles Michelson remained in Havana and Florida, respectively, for the *Journal*.

Hearst also moved to address a great logistical obstacle to his Cuban coverage: how to evade Spanish censors and ferry copy from Cuba to Key West in a timely fashion. On November 24, the *Journal* announced the acquisition of a new dispatch boat, none other than the 109-foot custom-built wonder of the yachting world, the "fastest craft that ever left a trail of foam up on the waters of New York," the *Vamoose*. Hearst had arranged to lease the vessel from its new owner and it now headed south to Florida, attracting admiring crowds at every stop along the route.[19]

Pulitzer reacted to Hearst's onslaught as he had during the election campaign, with boasting of his own and by building his coverage around one inimitable reporter—in this instance, Sylvester Scovel. Thanks to his exclusive interviews with insurgent generals and his catalog of atrocities against noncombatants, Scovel was becoming one of the most famous journalists in America. The paper promoted him as a man possessing "all the great and high qualities of the war correspondent—devotion to duty, accuracy, graphic descriptive power, absolute courage and skill."[20]

Pulitzer also kept pace with Hearst in the unofficial contest for the title of Cuba's best friend. Both editors cultivated close ties to the insurgents, and both ran letters from the Junta congratulating them on their enterprise and conveying the gratitude of the Cuban people (they both ran correspondence and official documents from the other side, as well). When a Spanish newspaper in Havana denounced Scovel's work as an attempt to deceive the American public, the *World* exulted in having been singled out for criticism. When Weyler blamed U.S. newspapers for fueling a rebellion that otherwise would have been easily suppressed, the *Journal* was quick to accept his "tribute" and "grateful compliment."[21]

The journalistic animosities that had boiled up during the election campaign were spilling over into the Cuban file. Pulitzer attacked senator-elect Money's reports as warmed-over Scovel. Hearst attacked the *Herald* as a pro-Spanish newspaper and suggested that Spain was "making better headway in this country against the Cuban insurgents than she is in Cuba."[22] The *Evening Post* called the *World* and the *Journal* "Cuban Junta newspapers" and blasted the *World* for continuing to insist that insurgent leader Antonio Maceo had been assassinated even after one of the *World*'s own correspondents had disproved the theory. The *Sun* cited its conservative peers as apologists for Spain and denounced their habit of first denying the truth of the reports of Spanish cruelty and then "insisting that it is a stern necessity."[23]

However loudly Hearst proclaimed that he was routinely beating "eminent exponents of the old journalism" to news, he obviously felt he had yet to put enough distance between himself and his competition.[24] His paper's stance on Cuba was not especially distinct from that of the *World*, the *Sun*, or even the *Tribune*, and rival correspondents were often matching and sometimes beating the *Journal*'s reporting. Thus, in December 1896, Hearst quietly hired Richard Harding Davis and the artist Frederic

Remington at fees of $3,000 apiece, plus expenses. The plan was to spirit the duo aboard the *Vamoose* to rebel-held territory, where they would spend a month traveling with the insurgents.[25]

Davis's fame made his assignment an event in itself, and he had the talent and authority to augment the *Journal*'s voice and extend its audience rather than duplicate the efforts of beat reporters. Hearst was taking a risk, however. Assigning Davis to football matches and coronations was easy. While the *Journal* took a professional interest in covering such events well, they were one-day wonders. Hearst considered Cuba the greatest moral and political issue facing America, yet he was handing it over to a high-profile writer who by temperament and politics was incompatible with his paper.

Hearst and Davis did have a few things in common. They were tall, attractive men of roughly the same age. Both were raised by ambitious and overweening mothers. Both had been noted in university more for their wardrobes than for their grades. Both loved spectacle and the theater (indeed, both would marry showgirls). Beyond that, they couldn't have been more different. Hearst, though the son of a senator, championed America's hustling spirit and egalitarian ethics. Davis, the son of a Philadelphia editor and the writer Rebecca Harding Davis, would have killed for what Hearst was throwing away. He was anxious to meet the best people and to join the best clubs. He affected English manners and customs: tweeds and khakis, clarets and cigars, and a vaguely aristocratic drawl. He firmly believed the bathtub to be the dividing line between civilization and barbarism. Some thought him "a prig, a snob, an affected little ass." (Asked his first name by a new acquaintance, Davis replied, "Mister.")[26] It is clear, however, that most people in the circles to which Davis aspired were impressed by him. In many ways, he was the son Phoebe Hearst had always wanted.

Davis was an unabashed elitist. He pronounced democracy a failure and derided popular causes. He disparaged the world of commerce and its new creature, the businessman. He joined the entire New York establishment in supporting the McKinley Republicans. Davis's elitism was also evident in his professional life. He aligned himself with the most reputable publishing houses and magazines. He was especially proud of his association with *Harper's Weekly* and its top-drawer audience. He saw it as his job to defend the established social order and to inform and comfort its leadership—one paper called him "the prose laureate of the snoboc-racy." After his initial enthusiasm for Hearst's paper, Davis had gained a clearer sense of its thoroughly democratic outlook and turned against it. Upscale and conservative sheets such as the *Tribune* and *Herald* were more his style, but they were not hiring big-name writers at fat fees. And there was Davis's problem: he needed his fat fees.[27]

As the *Book Buyer* noted, Richard Harding Davis was a man "addicted to double-breasted waistcoats, patent leather boots, twice-around ties, trousers turned up at the bottom, and all other things which make any-thing but great affluence quite intolerable."[28] His mother, during one of his recent European excursions, had been shocked on opening his mail to discover his enormous debts for dinners, gifts, and furnishings. He was constantly outrunning his means. He could not support his ostentatious lifestyle without stooping to write for the likes of Hearst. He blamed the popular publishers rather than himself for his degradation. He howled at their crass promotion of him, whined that he was being used for his name, but took their cash all the same.

The *Journal*'s Cuba assignment was doubly welcome to Davis as an opportunity to redeem a personal humiliation. Like many young men of his or any other generation, he had been ambitious since youth to see a war. When several reporters of his acquaintance dashed off to cover the Sino-Japanese conflict in 1894, Davis was determined to follow. It was a big war, and it involved Japan—a country that had fascinated him since Gilbert and Sullivan's *The Mikado* had toured the United States in 1885. Davis signed with *Scribner's* to write a series of articles on the conflict, with an eye to producing a book. He commanded a handsome fee, bought a complete war correspondent's kit, and booked passage across the Pacific via Vancouver.

On the eve of his departure for Japan, a group of friends staged a sur-prise farewell for Davis, decorating a room with Japanese lanterns and flower arrangements and dressing themselves in pigtails and silk robes. They hired six glamorous showgirls to dance in costumes from *The Mikado* and had them mince and bow when the guest of honor entered the room. Davis was touched, and he left New York by train the next day in a good frame of mind. By the time he hit Montreal, however, he was stricken with doubts. A few hours later, in Ottawa, he packed it in and returned home to redecorate his apartment. "I waited too long to be a war correspondent," he wrote his brother, adding that he couldn't face the three-week voyage to Tokyo and that he hoped some day to get a shot at another war, only closer to home. Cuba presented a perfect opportunity for Davis to erase painful memories of what he called his "retreat from Ottawa."[29]

Davis's traveling companion, Frederic Sackrider Remington, was also anxious to test his abilities in a war zone. He dreamed of a grand European battle between massive armies, with enough pageantry and bloodshed to fill an acre of canvas. So far he had settled for a few scrappy Indian fights and the Pullman strike of 1894. His hopes for real action were now pinned on Cuba.

Notwithstanding Davis's enormous fame, the *Journal* granted Remington equal billing in all its promotions, with good reason. He was an established author and sculptor, the nation's leading illustrator of military and frontier life, and an outstanding visual journalist besides. A native of Canton, New York, Remington had studied at the new Yale School of Art before heading west. He spent five years beyond the Mississippi, traveling the Santa Fe and Oregon trails, working as a rancher, military scout, hunter, and trapper. He kept his eyes open as he moved, meticulously recording a disappearing way of life. "I knew the wild riders and the vacant land were about to vanish forever," he later wrote, " . . . and the more I considered the subject, the bigger the forever loomed."[30]

On his return east, Remington made his living in magazines, churning out thousands of pictures to supply the bottomless demand for views and information about life on the frontier. He was a fixture at *Harper's* after 1886. Scrupulous about details, he transformed his studio into a museum of western artifacts—tools, costumes, weapons, animal skins. He drew hunters, trappers, Indians, lawmen, gunfighters, broncobusters, settlers, and horses. He specialized in thrilling scenes of action, with heroic individuals struggling against overwhelming forces. Some of the most enduring images of the Old West—the lone figure on horseback on a stark plain under a punishing sun—originate with Remington. The Victorian art establishment envied his commercial success and dismissed him as an illustrator rather than an artist, a verdict that stands today, although Remington did possess more talent and originality than many favorites of the academy.

Davis and Remington made an odd couple. They were both paid-up members of the nineteenth-century cult of manliness but belonged to different branches entirely. In place of Davis's cleanliness and parlor manners, Remington substituted an earthy machismo. In his younger days, he had been known to dip his football uniform in a pool of slaughterhouse blood before a big game. He enjoyed shooting and fishing and all things military (Nelson A. Miles, commanding general of the U.S. Army, was a hunting buddy). He liked to eat—"Fatty," Mrs. Remington called him, and "my massive husband." Even more, he liked to drink. On one visit to New York, he headed for the Players' Club while his wife retired early to their hotel room. She was awakened at 2 a.m. by the repeated slamming of doors, beginning at the far end of the corridor and moving toward her. When her own door opened, there stood her sodden husband with an embarrassed porter in tow. "It's all right," said Remington. "This one's my wife."[31] When his indulgences caught up with him, he would head north to Canada or west to Montana to "sweat & stink and thirst & starve & paint."[32]

Notwithstanding his occasional vulgarity and a long streak of racial chauvinism, Remington was one of very few journalists in 1896 sensitive to the price America would pay for any involvement in Cuba. As he wrote to his friend, the novelist Owen Wister, "I expect you will see a big war with Spain over here and will want to come back—and see some more friends die. *Cuba Libre.* It does seem tough that so many Americans have had to be and have still got to be killed to free a lot of d———niggers who are better off under the yoke. There is something fatefull [sic] in our destiny that way. This time however we will kill a few Spaniards instead of Anglo Saxons which will be proper and nice."[33]

Wary of Spanish spies in Manhattan, Davis and Remington met at the *Journal*'s offices after dark on December 19, 1896. They were dressed for the occasion, Remington straining the seams on his canvas Duke of Marlborough field jacket, Davis wearing "a pseudo-military uniform with white hunter trimmings" (he'd had his picture taken in the outfit and released it for publication). He carried in his luggage "a new saddle, bridle, horse blanket, pad and two leather trunks designed to be made into a field bed." Davis had also purchased, at the *Journal*'s expense, a fifty-dollar field glass, "which is a new invention," he wrote home, "and the best made."[34] He promised his mother that as soon as the shooting started, "I mean to begin to ride or run the other way—no one loves himself more than I do so you leave me to take care of myself."[35] The furtive adventurers left the *Journal*'s offices in a closed hack and boarded a Florida-bound train.

Davis and Remington were scheduled to meet the *Vamoose* in Key West. The yacht would drop the pair, along with medical supplies and nonmilitary aid (cargo permitted under the Neutrality Act), in the Santa Clara province of Cuba. They would be accompanied by two Cubans from the local Junta who would guide them to Gómez (a violation of Spanish law and dicey under the Neutrality Act). They planned to spend a month with the rebels, sending weekly files home via Michelson on the *Vamoose*. As Davis explained, "All we want to do is to get in and size Gómez up and see what sort of troops they have and listen to their stories and then get back here again quick take a special car home and draw out our 3,000 dollars and publish a book. If war comes between U.S. and Spain we will be able to speak with the authority at least of those who have been there."[36]

Davis was as impressed with his transportation—"the most marvelous thing on the water"—as he was impatient to get moving. The ship's engineer wasted a day by insisting on spending Christmas onshore, and then on Boxing Day, the *Vamoose*'s Newport-based crew, having heard one too many rumors of Spanish atrocities against captured filibusters, lost its nerve and had to be replaced. As the new crew made its training runs, the wind began to pick up, which delayed the crossing at least two more days. "I am ashamed to look people in the face," Davis wrote home. "I have said 'goodbye' so often."[37]

Still, Davis and Remington managed a tolerable existence in the interim. They would rise in the morning, take a swim in the bay, return to dress and eat breakfast, and sit on the hotel porch smoking huge Key West cigars while their boots were being polished. Evenings found them dining with the officers of a pair of U.S. Navy cruisers anchored at Key West.

> The officers of the *Raleigh* and *Newark* are agreeably engaged in rivaling each other by giving us meals, and it is great fun seeing uniforms again and playing with the guns and talking war. . . . Today Fred and I lunched on the *Raleigh* and during target practice Remington asked if he could shoot off the big ten inch gun with a sub caliber cartridge—his first shot

hit the buoy target on which the red flag waved and the second broke the flag shaft. You should have heard the sailors cheer.[38]

Finally, on December 30, the *Vamoose,* its new crew, the correspondents, and their guides were all ready to push off. Remington wrote his wife: "Dear Kid—It is now 4 o'c—we leave at six—the boat lies at the dock steaming up. The towne is wild with excitement—We have only the Custom House to fear. Two Cuban officers go with us—I am well—and feel that I am to undertake quite the most eventful enterprise of my life—I think there will be a war with Spain—I leave my effects at the Duval House *here*—Good bye little one—from Your loving old boy Frederic."[39]

Remington's letter was longer than his trip. The wind had calmed but the winter seas remained rough. The *Vamoose* was twenty miles out before the new crew declared it unseaworthy and the captain turned back for Key West. Remington and Davis commiserated on deck, clinging to the rails to avoid being swept over. A Chinese cook fashioned a crude life raft from rope, wooden boxes, and a door. Davis wanted to imitate him but Remington said, "Let him make his raft. If we capsize, I'll throttle him and take it from him." (Asked later about the morality of his plan, Remington replied, "Why Davis alone was worth a dozen sea-cooks— I don't have to talk of myself.")[40]

A despondent Davis wired home from Key West shortly after their return: "Unless we get steamer the game is off will either come home with Remington or return Via Havana as tourist guess I am done with Journal for ever Merry Christmas. . . ."[41]

Both Davis and Remington thought about packing it in at this point. They had signed on for a first-class ride to rebel headquarters, and the *Journal* had not delivered. Hearst was not quitting, however. He authorized Davis and Midelson to buy or lease any boat in Florida that would take them to Cuba, and when Davis petulantly demanded a $1,000 advance on his fee, the *Journal* wired the funds. With Hearst pressing and Michelson cabling nearby marinas in search of an alternate craft, Davis, with the retreat from Ottawa still on his mind, decided he was stuck with his assignment. He returned, sulkily, to his regimen of swimming, bicycling, smoking, dining, and boot blacking. Remington began to wear on his nerves. "He always wanted to talk it over," Davis wrote home, "and that had to be done in the nearest or the most distant café, and it always took him fifteen minutes before he got his cocktails to suit him."[42]

Davis was also beset with competitive jealousies. Cuba was the hot story in America, and Florida had become a magnet for ambitious reporters. Platoons of them were crowding hotels from Jacksonville to Key West, all looking for a ride to rebel territory. With a high proportion of filibusters failing to make the crossing, they were almost all as frustrated as Davis. But some correspondents at least had great stories to tell of their attempts to reach the island. One of these was his fellow *Journal* correspondent, the Yale rowing hero Ralph Paine.

ANOTHER MINISTER'S SON, and a native of Jacksonville, Paine had been working as a professional journalist since grade school, earning enough to pay his own way to university. At Yale, in addition to rowing, playing football, and winning the school's highest social honors, he wrote athletic news for more than twenty papers. He was two years into a thriving career as a Philadelphia news reporter when the insurrection in Cuba captured his imagination. He traveled to New York to coax the Junta into letting him join a filibuster and, with the Junta's approval, he visited Hearst at the *Journal* in hopes of a paying assignment. The two men chatted amiably, the editor sitting on the edge of his desk, his hands restless and his long legs swinging. Hearst told Paine of a recent benefit for Cuba held in Madison Square Garden where he had contribution $2,000 to a fund to purchase a ceremonial sword for General Gómez. He asked Paine if he would like to see the sword.[43]

> With dazzled eyes I beheld the costly weapon as it rested in a mahogany case. The scabbard was ornately adorned, the hilt plated with gold and sparking with small diamonds. It had been made by a famous firm of Fifth Avenue jewelers. Here was a sword which looked like two thousand dollars. Displaying the blade, Mr. Hearst called attention to the engraved inscriptions, such as "To Maximo Gómez, Commander-in-Chief of the Army of the Cuban Republic," and "Viva Cuba Libre."
>
> "Very handsome," said I. "Old Gómez will be tickled to death, when he gets it."

"That is the idea, *when he gets it*," observed the bland, debonair Mr. Hearst. "I have been trying to find somebody foolish enough to carry this elegant sword to Gómez. I am perfectly frank with you. These inscriptions would be devilish hard to explain to the Spanish army, if you happened to be caught, wouldn't they?"

"And you want me to try to present this eighteen-karat sword to Gómez, with your compliments?" I suggested.

"If you don't mind," was the hopeful reply. "I swear I don't know what else to do with the confounded thing. Of course if you are nabbed at sea, you can probably chuck it overboard in time—"

"And if I get surrounded on land, perhaps I can swallow it, Mr. Hearst. Never mind that. I am the damn fool you have been looking for. . . ."[44]

A few weeks before Christmas, Paine packed the sword with his two revolvers and headed for Jacksonville to meet his ship. He lounged around town a few days, renewing old acquaintances, before an anonymous Cuban sauntered up to him in a piazza and told him to report to a freight yard at midnight. Paine appeared at the appointed hour with his bags and his sword and found some forty Cuban and American volunteers ready to board a commandeered freight train loaded with machetes, Mauser rifles, field artillery, and millions of rounds of ammunition. As they all climbed aboard, Paine literally tripped over the very nervous man who would become his traveling companion: Ernest McCready of the *New York Herald*. The rebels fired up the engine and rolled for a few hours through the pines and palmetto to an isolated port where the filibuster the *Three Friends* was at dock.

The *Three Friends* was a seagoing towboat captained by the legendary "Dynamite Johnny" O'Brien. A graying terrier of a man, O'Brien had run guns all over Latin America. He served as the Junta's unofficial fleet commander, and he had never failed to make a landing in Cuba. Once the insurgents stowed their contraband belowdecks (in barrels and crates labeled "salted codfish" and "prime lard"), the captain pointed the *Three Friends* up the coast. The passage to Key West took four days. With dirty weather and rough seas, the Cubans spent much of the trip leaning over the rails. Paine and McCready slept fitfully on deck between sacks of coal. O'Brien dodged a U.S. Revenue cutter not far out of Jacksonville and later slipped quietly at night between Davis's favorite dining spots, the *Newark* and the *Raleigh,* anchored a mile apart off Key West for the purpose of discouraging filibusters. As the *Three Friends* steered into the Yucatán Channel, Paine was struck by the romance of the voyage: "It had the flavor of bygone centuries, of an era when the little ships of England had sailed to the West Indies and the South Sea to singe the beards of the viceroys of Spain and to laugh at all the tall galleons with their tiers of cannonades and culverins."[45]

The only unpleasantness on the trip, so far as Paine and McCready were concerned, was that Sylvester Scovel had boarded the *Three Friends* somewhere along its coastal route. The *World* had chartered him a dispatch boat in imitation of Hearst's *Vamoose* but, like the *Vamoose,* it had foundered in rough conditions. So Scovel used his impeccable connections among the insurgents to catch up with Dynamite Johnny. Paine and McCready would henceforth share their adventure with the famous correspondent.

On the evening of December 19, with the rebels singing on deck and Paine rehearsing a speech with which to present General Gómez his sword, the *Three Friends* approached the mouth of the Rio San Juan in Puerto Principe province. The ship's surfboats were just about to hit the water when someone spotted a shadow moving against the wall of the jungle inside the bay. It was a Spanish gunboat, and it almost immediately fired its engines to give chase. Dynamite Johnny lunged back to sea as the Spaniards lobbed shell after shell at his wooden hull, but despite smooth seas and a brilliant moon, none came close to landing. The insurgents fired back with their new Mausers. One of the Americans pulled a bugle out of his gear and let loose with a series of cavalry calls, a move that seemed to puzzle the Spaniards—the gunboat swerved and slowed. The insurgents next pulled out a Hotchkiss field gun and mounted it on the bow of the *Three Friends.* A first round spat a red streak but missed the mark. A second round swept the gunboat's decks. The Spaniards made a sudden halt and launched a series of distress rockets. The *Three Friends* had won the first naval battle of the insurgency.

Running low on coal and in need of a new plan, Captain O'Brien dumped his cargo and passengers on No Name Key for safekeeping while he headed back to the mainland. Paine and McCready were annoyed to be left behind, especially as the latecomer, Scovel, remained on board. The *World,* it appeared, had made the larger contribution to the expenses of the *Three Friends.* Captain O'Brien at least agreed to arrange for the stranded reporters' copy to be forwarded to New York. Out of tobacco and low on rations, Paine and McCready spent an unpleasant week marooned with the Cubans on the swampy islet with its "evil smell of rotten vegetation and tidal mud."[46] A Junta schooner finally arrived and sailed the ragged correspondents back to Key West.

The day after their return, Paine ran into Davis at a Key West barbershop and heard the good news that his bylined story had made the front page of the *Journal*. The bad news was that Scovel had beaten him into print by a week. Davis remarked that Paine's adventures had the delightful flavor of piracy, which turned out to be prescient. A few days later, returning from another ill-fated attempt to reach Cuba, Paine read that the *Three Friends* had been impounded and that he had been indicted by a federal grand jury, along with Dynamite Johnny and several others. The charge was indeed piracy, an offense carrying the death penalty. Paine went underground with the help of his father, who hid him in the home of a church elder. The charges were eventually dropped for lack of prosecution witnesses, but Paine's career as a filibuster was over. He reluctantly gave up his ambitions to reach Gómez, returned the jeweled sword to Michelson, and resumed his old newspaper job in Philadelphia.

Davis was cranky. "This new journalism is beyond my finding out," he wrote home. "It is not news they want. They send Gómez a two-thousand-dollar sword and two medicine chests and a keg of rum . . . and then the Journal publishes pictures of the sword and the *Vamoose* and the other fake freaks, and lets the news be written in the office or Key West." And yet he had done less: "Anybody can run a boat into a dark bayou and dump rifles on the beach and scurry away to sea again but only heroes can sit for a month on a hotel porch or at the end of a wharf, and wait."[47]

The most painful part for Davis was that he really had no appetite to do much beyond sit on that hotel porch. He was headed to Cuba out of fear of losing his self-respect and "getting laughed at and paragraphed as the war correspondent that always Turned Back."[48] One brief face-saving, image-burnishing tour of Cuba would allow him to pass on any future assignments in war zones, since he would have already had his moment. Paine, however ridiculous his luggage, could already say as much. So, too, could Stephen Crane.

CRANE HAD WAVED GOODBYE to New York and his Tenderloin troubles on November 27. He had boarded a train for Jacksonville carrying in his chamois belt seven hundred dollars in gold, courtesy of the Bacheller Syndicate. America's most notorious war novelist had accepted an assignment to sneak into Cuba and report on the fighting from the insurgent ranks. "The same lad who longs to fight Indians and to be a pirate longs to embark secretly on one of these dangerous trips to the Cuban coast," he wrote. Like Paine, he viewed filibustering as a "delicious bit of outlawry in the evening of the nineteenth century."[49]

Arriving in Jacksonville, Crane registered under an assumed name at the elegant St. James Hotel. He wrote his brother with instructions for his will and began looking for a ship. It would take him all of December to find one. Meanwhile, he expertly made his way to the backrooms of the dingiest waterfront taverns and a strip of brothels known collectively as The Line. Within two or three days of hitting town, he had won the heart of Cora Taylor, keeper of the Hotel de Dreme, the finest whorehouse in Jacksonville.

Miss Cora was a vivacious redhead from a Boston family of artists and art dealers. She had been married at least twice, once to a baronet. She shopped for clothes in Paris and had taken the Orient Express to Constantinople, and she was rumored to have landed in Jacksonville on a millionaire's yacht. In addition to a passion for literature—Shakespeare, Goethe, Ibsen—she possessed a complete indifference to conventional morality. "Sometimes I like to sit at home and read good books," she wrote, "at others I must drink absinthe and hang the night hours with scarlet embroideries. I must have music and the sins that march to music. These are moments when I desire squalor."[50]

Miss Cora happened to be reading one of Crane's novels when he walked into her sporting house for dinner. Straightaway, they recognized each other as soul mates. He wrote fond inscriptions in her book while still penning love letters to the sweetheart he had left up north (a woman to whom he owed a great deal of money). Within days, Crane was living at the Hotel de Dreme. Scovel joined him there regularly, and took him riding to improve his health. He believed Miss Cora was "just the woman" for his friend Stevie. Ernest McCready was impressed with her as well: "Fact is, she was a cut above us in several ways, notably poise and surety of command of herself and others."[51]

Crane finally tore himself away from his new love on December 31, feeling a little melancholy but, as he would later write, "When a man gets the ant of desire-to-see-what-it's-like stirring in his heart, he will wallow out to sea in a pail."[52]

His pail was the *Commodore*, a 123-foot tug commanded by a Captain Murphy. It left dock at 8 p.m., bound for Cienfuegos with a $10,000 payload including "203,000 cartridges, 1,000 pounds of giant powder, 40 bundles of rifles, 2 electric batteries," and 300 machetes. The voyage was trouble from the start. The *Commodore* ran aground on a mud bar before exiting the St. Johns River. When it finally hit open water, it ran directly into a thumping southeasterly squall. Even experienced hands were queasy. Crane stayed on deck with Captain Murphy, impressing the ship's cook by never quailing as the *Commodore* was tossed about.[53]

The tug was only a few hours out to sea when it sprang a leak in the boiler room and then with water accumulating, its bilge pumps failed. Crane joined a human chain passing bailing buckets back and forth, but the water only deepened. On deck, amid the wind and spray, the captain ordered the *Commodore*'s three large wooden lifeboats cut free and lowered into the now-monstrous waves. The crew and passengers piled in and began rowing to shore. Captain Murphy, with his arm in a sling, Crane, and two others remained on deck. They would take their chances in a ten-foot dinghy.

The captain insisted the dinghy stay close to the ship until it went down. Despite its heavy cargo and waves as high as the captain had ever seen in those parts, the pail was still afloat at dawn. As the four men sat bobbing in the dinghy, bailing to keep active and warm, one of the lifeboats returned. It carried seven men, including the first mate, who apparently wanted to retrieve something from the sinking tug. As the lifeboat approached, it was staved, either by contact with the tug or by a wave. While it disintegrated, the seven men clambered onto the stern of the *Commodore*. They fashioned a raft from planks and barrels and lowered it into the waves. The first mate fell in and was drowned. Three sailors made it onto the raft but it quickly broke to pieces and they too were lost. The other three went down with the *Commodore* a few minutes later. Cold, drenched, and exhausted, Crane and one of his dinghy mates now began to row—or, rather, steer—toward a tiny point of light some fifteen nautical miles in the distance.

The little dinghy bounced among the foaming waves all that day and through the night. The men alternately rowed and bailed, moving as gingerly as possible under constant threat of capsize. They had no food and they could not sleep. They shivered with cold and ached from the strain of the oars. Although haunted by the faces of the seven lost men, Crane felt a warmth of camaraderie in the little vessel. "The correspondent, who had been taught to be cynical of men, knew even at the time [that] this was the best experience of his life."[54]

The pinpoint of light for which they were aiming—the lighthouse at Mosquito Inlet—had grown to a milky smudge by dawn on January 2. They could make out land by late afternoon but saw no signs of life. Meanwhile, a fresh squall was whipping up and the seas were growing more treacherous, especially as they approached shore. Captain Murphy ordered the dinghy back out into deeper water, where they had more control. They spent another night riding tall, black waves, this time while being circled by a shark. At dawn they could see land again but still no human activity. They decided to crash into shore, come what may.

Three of the four survived, including Captain Murphy with his injured wing. Crane was dragged from the surf by one of the locals who had run down to meet the dinghy, bringing blankets, flasks, and coffee. The last thing he saw before collapsing on shore was the lifeless form of the ship's oiler, Billy Higgins.

Crane spent the night in a Daytona Beach cottage. Cora Taylor arrived the next morning, fearing the worst. The *Commodore*'s two other lifeboats had landed the previous day, and word had spread that the tug was lost, and her lover with it. A telegraph operator saw the two of them at the station in Daytona Beach, wrapped in each other's arms, awaiting a northbound train.

All of the major newspapers carried accounts of the *Commodore*'s wreck and Crane's ordeal. (At least one publication jumped the gun and published his obituary.) His companions in the dinghy praised his courage. "Crane is a man every inch of him," declared Captain Murphy.[55] The writer recovered quickly enough to deliver Bacheller a thousand-word account of his adventure, syndicated January 7. The new story did not bury memories of the Tenderloin scandal, but it did help to restore Crane's reputation. He would later rework "the best experience of his life" into what is arguably his finest short story, "The Open Boat."

ON JANUARY 9, Richard Harding Davis and Frederic Remington joined a passel of tourists and businessmen aboard the *Olivette*, a regularly scheduled passenger ship running from Key West to Havana. Davis was still in a foul mood: he was traveling neither on a luxury yacht nor on a swashbuckling filibuster but aboard a tourist tub, and he was about to become one of many reporters in Havana rather than one of a few with the insurgents. He was completely fed up with Remington: "I would rather manage an Italian opera company than him." He was cross with the *Journal*, too. "Had we not wanted to go so much," he wrote his family, "neither of us would have put up with the way we have been treated."[56]

Davis was somewhat mollified on landing when U.S. consul general Fitzhugh Lee turned out to meet him and promptly arranged an introduction to General Weyler. The Spaniard struck Davis as "a dignified and impressive soldier."[57] He extended his visitors all the usual courtesies and granted them permission to travel throughout the island, so long as they stuck to Spanish-run railroads and steamships—restrictions imposed on all foreigners. Weyler also promised Davis and Remington they could join him on his next campaign but said that he did not expect to be leaving any time soon.

Still hoping to meet up with some insurgents, and certain that he was not going to find any in Havana, Davis accepted an invitation from the proprietor of a sugar plantation in Santa Clara province. He and Remington, with an interpreter, boarded a train and passed through the Cuban countryside, noting its beauty and the distant smoke from burning cane fields. They spent a night in Jaruco amid cows and chickens in a flea-ridden barn. On January 15, they reached Matanzas, which Davis thought looked like Paris, at least compared to Jaruco. Remington was less impressed. He declared that he had seen enough of Cuba for his purposes. He had signed on with Hearst for a month, and his month was almost up. The United States was not going to invade Cuba in the three or four days left under his agreement, and the insurgents were nowhere to be found. He turned back to Havana and booked passage to New York.

It is to this moment that we owe one of the most remarkable anecdotes in the history of American journalism. James Creelman, in his 1901 memoir, *On the Great Highway*, reports the following exchange of telegrams between Remington and Hearst:

W.R. Hearst, *New York Journal*, N.Y.:
Everything is quiet. There is no trouble here. There will be no war. I wish
to return.
Remington

Remington, Havana:
Please remain. You furnish the pictures, and I'll furnish the war.
W.R. Hearst.[58]

Neither Remington's telegram nor Hearst's reply have ever been produced. Creelman is the sole source for the anecdote and he does not claim
to have laid eyes on the original documents. The story attracted little attention when it was published in Creelman's memoir amid a fanatical defense
of yellow journalism as a supreme force for justice and progress in the
world. But in 1907 a correspondent for *The Times* of London gave it new
life in an article, asking, "Is the Press of the United States going insane?"[59]

Hearst, in response to the *Times* piece, dismissed the alleged telegrams
along with the suggestion that he was chiefly responsible for a war as
"clotted nonsense." Nonetheless, "I'll furnish the war" has become his
most famous utterance. During the 1930s and '40s, when Hearst was
indisputably the most significant publisher in America as well as a frightening (to some) political force, it seemed entirely plausible to many commentators that he would attempt to start a war in order to sell newspapers,
and the anecdote enjoyed its heyday. It was Exhibit One in any discussion
of journalistic menace and the megalomania of press lords. In the 1960s,
biographer W.A. Swanberg took Creelman's story at face value and used
it to argue that Hearst suffered from a Napoleonic complex, among other
forms of psychological damage. By the end of the twentieth century,
Hearst had been dead for several decades and the fear and awe he had once
generated was giving way to dismissal and ridicule. Biographer David
Nasaw argues that the only reason anyone believed that Hearst played a
pivotal role in Cuba was because of Hearst's zealous self-promotion.[60]

It is probable that something like the exchange reported by Creelman
occurred: he was a generally reliable reporter and unlikely to fabricate
from whole cloth an anecdote about two men still active in journalism.
Remington's half of the conversation is believable. An alarmist about
Cuba, he was disappointed that the U.S. didn't invade while he was

there—"I think there will be a war with Spain," he had written to his wife from Key West.[61] The words attributed to Hearst cannot be dismissed out of hand given that he is on record as savoring an opportunity to push Spain out of the Caribbean, and only a year away from taking partial credit for furnishing a war (not withstanding his letter to the *Times*). But, that said, there are serious problems with Creelman's story.

In the paragraph introducing the telegrams in his memoir, Creelman writes that Hearst, with his alert "eye for the future," sent Remington and Davis to Cuba with instructions "to remain there until the war began." There is no doubt that by "war" Creelman means not the ongoing Cuban insurrection but military conflict between the United States and Spain. Creelman then presents the telegrams and claims that Hearst was "as good as his word" in furnishing the war and liberating Cuba.[62] But we have known since the publication of Richard Harding Davis's letters in 1918 that he and Remington were hired for exactly one month, not for however long it took for the United States to declare war on Spain, and that their mission was to meet and travel briefly with the insurgents.

Creelman is wrong in his facts and he fundamentally mistakes the nature of the Davis-Remington assignment. Given that the credibility of his report rests not on documentary evidence but on his own authority, Creelman's anecdote is highly suspect. In the absence of the original documents or further evidence, it is impossible to know exactly what was communicated between Hearst and Remington, and any speculation as to what might have been said or meant is futile.

If Hearst did send any kind of a message to Remington asking him to remain in Cuba, he was not heeded. Remington had contracted for a month and when his time was up, he flew the island, appalled at its condition: "more hell there than I ever read about. . . . small pox—typhoid—yellow jack—dishonesty—suffering beyond measure," he wrote the journalist Poultney Bigelow. He left a less encumbered and, hence, more cheerful Richard Harding Davis to continued his tour of the western provinces.[63]

DAVIS TRAVELED IN AN ARMORED TRAIN with a Swiss-born interpreter who insisted on calling him "my lord" and who doubled as his valet. The

U.S. consuls around the island knew Davis by reputation and offered their services in making his travel arrangements. He boasted in his letters of spending more of Hearst's money in one night at a Cárdenas hotel than Spanish officers would spend in a week. However much he was enjoying himself, Davis was aware that he was seeing only what Weyler was permitting him to see. He could not forget that the point of his journey was to join the rebels. He thought of Scovel, traveling under an assumed identity, with his eyebrows shaved and a bounty on his head, and he knew he could not match the *World* reporter for "deeds of daring." Davis reassured himself that he was at least getting closer to the truth than his colleagues back in Key West and Havana. He flattered himself that he brought unsurpassed perspective to the story, having read more about Cuba than the likes of Scovel, but he still could not shake his doubts.[64]

Davis never would meet a rebel on this trip, nor would he abandon his comfortable itinerary, but he did file three remarkable pieces. The first was on the effects of Weyler's reconcentration order, which now applied to Havana, Matanzas, and Santa Clara provinces. Spanish troops were burning fields, huts, and villages in order to drive hundreds of thousands of *pacíficos*, or noncombatants, from the countryside to fortified suburban encampments. In a story datelined Cienfuegos, January 22, 1897, Davis wrote that the order was proving "exceedingly short-sighted." Far from hurting the insurgency, it had the opposite effect: "The able-bodied men of each family who had remained loyal [to Spain], or at least neutral, so long as they were permitted to live undisturbed on their few acres, were not content to exist on the charity of a city, and they at once swarmed over to the insurgent ranks by the hundreds."

Not only was reconcentration counterproductive to the Spanish war effort, it was ruinous to the local populations. The camps, Davis observed, were filled with the old and infirm, with women and with children, living unsupervised in revolting conditions. At one facility in Jaruco, he reported, "the filth covered the streets and the plaza ankle deep and even filled the corners of the church, which has been turned into a fort and has hammocks swung from the altars. The huts of the *pacíficos*, with from four to six people in each, were jammed together in rows a quarter of a mile long, and within ten feet and parallel with the cavalry barracks, where sixty men and horses had lived for a month. . . .

No one was vaccinated, no one was clean, and all of them were living on half rations."[65]

As many as 400,000 Cubans would be relocated under Weyler's order. Tens of thousands, perhaps hundreds of thousands, would die of fever and disease. The reconcentration policy would do much to persuade the United States and Europe that the burden of the war was falling unduly on the helpless. Davis was one of the first newspapermen to the scene, and the first to write a substantial account of the effects of reconcentration. What he witnessed had a profound effect on him. He had gone to Cuba determined to be "fair to both sides," and with heavy skepticism of the pro-Cuban sympathies of the yellow newspapers. He had dismissed Remington as excitable and determined to see the worst in everything. But his views were shifting. He began to assign blame for the "wholesale devastation" on the island primarily to the Spanish, who were embarked on a policy of "extermination and ruin." Davis believed things could only get worse: "As soon as the rains begin the yellow fever and small-pox will set in and all vessels leaving Cuban ports will be quarantined and the island will be one great plague spot. The insurgents who are in the open fields will live and the soldiers will die for their officers know nothing of sanitation."[66]

His second piece, as good as any Davis would ever write, and the only story from the conflict still reprinted in our time, was an account of the last hour in the life of Adolfo Rodriguez, a twenty-year-old farm boy from Santa Clara province. He had been captured with a band of rebels two months earlier and charged with bearing arms against the government. A Spanish military court had sentenced him the previous day to die by fusillade before sunrise, one of thirty so condemned; they were being shot on consecutive mornings for maximum effect. Spanish officials frequently invited American journalists to witness these deaths. In fact, the execution story was already a staple of coverage from Cuba, which perhaps explains why Davis felt it necessary to rationalize his presence:

> I hope it is not impertinent for the writer to introduce himself, so far as to say that he did not go to see this man die through any idle or morbid curiosity. The young man's friends could not be present. It was impossible for them to show themselves in that crowd and that place with wisdom or

without distress, and I like to think that although Rodriguez could not know it, there was one person present when he died who felt keenly for him, and who was a sympathetic though unwilling onlooker.[67]

The procedings, as described by Davis, began at 5 a.m. under a full moon. Some three hundred Spanish soldiers marched in formation to an empty plain a half mile from town, led by a military band playing a jaunty quickstep. They found a spot on the grassy plain and waited patiently, the band still playing, as a second procession made its way from town, this one including Rodriguez. "I expected to find the man, no matter what his strength at other times might be, stumbling and faltering on this cruel journey, but as he came near I saw he led all the others, that the two priests on either side of him were taking two steps to his one, and that they were tripping on their gowns and stumbling over the hollows in their efforts to keep pace with him as he walked erect and soldierly at a quick step in advance of them."

Davis was impressed at the young man's appearance, his handsome, gentle face, "great wistful eyes," and curly black hair. He looked more Neapolitan than Cuban: "You could imagine him sitting on the quay at Naples or Genoa, lolling in the sun and showing his white teeth when he laughed." Davis thought him shockingly young for the sacrifice he was about to make, but was exhilarated by his bravery. "I confess," he wrote, "to have felt a thrill of delighted satisfaction when I saw, as the Cuban passed me, that he held a cigarette between his lips, not arrogantly or with bravado, but with the nonchalance of a man who meets his punishment fearlessly and who will let his enemy see that they can kill but not frighten him."

It was all over quickly. Rodriguez, his arms bound at the elbows, was positioned with his back to the firing squad; he looked out over the plain to the hills where he had lived most of his twenty years. One of the priests held a cross before him. Rodriguez dropped the cigarette from his lips and bent to kiss the cross. An officer drew his sword and gave the "make ready" signal. Only at the last second did he realize that some of his men, forming a U around the condemned man, were actually in the line of fire. Rodriguez, braced for the worst, was instead tapped on the shoulder and politely ordered to move a few steps. Davis wondered at his coolness—"snatched back to life" at the supreme moment, Rodriguez neither trembled nor broke down, but on steady legs advanced to his new position. He stood, alone among enemies, facing certain death with his back straight and chin high.

> The officer of the firing squad, mortified by his blunder, hastily whipped up his sword, the men once more leveled their rifles, the sword rose, dropped, the men fired. At the report the Cuban's head snapped back almost between his shoulders, but his body fell slowly, as though some one had pushed him gently forward from behind and he had stumbled. He sank on his side in the wet grass without a struggle or sound and did not move again. It was difficult to believe that he meant to lie there, that it could be ended so without a word, that the man in the linen suit would not go up and continue to walk on over the hills, as he apparently started to do, to his home, that there was not a mistake somewhere or that at least some one would be sorry or say something or run to pick him up.
>
> But fortunately he did not need help, and the priests returned—the younger one with the tears running down his face—and donned their vestments and read a brief requiem for his soul, while the squad stood uncovered, and the men in hollow square shook their accoutrements into place and shifted their pieces and got ready for the order to march, and the band began again with the same quickstep which the arrival of the prisoner had interrupted. The figure still lay on the grass untouched, and no one seemed to remember that it had walked there itself, or notice that the cigarette still burned, a tiny ring of living fire, at the place where the figure had first stood.

The front page of the *New York Journal* on February 2, 1897, was taken up almost entirely by an illustration of the brave Rodriguez, face to the reader, in his last moment standing. The moon in the sky is so bright that you can see the shadows of the soldiers aiming at his back, and behind them the outline of the town of Santa Clara. Remington's signature is low on the left-hand side. He drew the scene from Davis's report, as was customary for newspaper illustrators. The story opens on the front page and continues inside. It is not a long piece and it is sentimental in moments, but it is nonetheless transfixing. A Davis biographer says it anticipates Hemingway in its spare language and its theme of a death well met. But the mix of farce, pathos, and tragedy may be more suggestive of Orwell and his indictment of imperial cruelty in "Shooting an Elephant." Davis lacks Orwell's subtlety and self-awareness, but he makes the most of his material.

The Rodriguez piece notwithstanding, Davis still feared that his trip was a failure. He had not seen any fighting and he had yet to meet an insurgent. He twice tried to slip out of government-controlled territory to join the rebels, but both times his Cuban escorts backed out, wary of Spanish spies. In his last attempt, he arranged a rendezvous with George Bronson Rea and Sylvester Scovel in the seaside village where they were meeting their own Cuban guide.

The two reporters arrived in disguise, with their hair dyed. According to Davis, they were waving the January 17 edition of the *New York Journal* in which Davis's likeness was prominently featured along with a claim that he and Remington had "reached the insurgent army on the island of Cuba." Scovel told Davis the article had blown his cover. "Your paper has queered you, Davis," he said. "I never knew a case of a paper's treating a correspondent worse." Rea and Scovel said they could not assume the risk of added scrutiny on their hazardous mission and promptly disappeared, taking with them Davis's last hope of reaching the rebels.[68]

The January 17 story may have been a pretext for Scovel and Rea to dump Davis, given that he represented a competitive threat, and a large one, by virtue of his profile. He was also a security risk. Scovel and Rea were taking great pains to move by stealth through the countryside, and even if Davis agreed to abandon his folding bathtub and valet, he was ridiculously conspicuous. But Davis had every reason to be upset with the *Journal*. Running his picture at that moment only made his job more difficult, and besides, the claim was patently false— he was not riding with the insurgents. It is not clear whether the paper simply assumed Davis and Remington had achieved their goal of reaching rebel territory or if, as Davis suspected, it ran the promotion to provoke him into joining the rebels.[69]

Davis now surrendered his dream of finding Gómez and the rebels, and made preparations to return home. But he would stumble across one more story before leaving Cuba. Appropriately, given his red-carpet tour of the island, he found it at dinner.

LEAVING HAVANA AS HE CAME, aboard the passenger liner *Olivette*, Davis met at his table Señorita Clemencia Arango, a cultivated young Cuban woman who "spoke three languages and dressed as you see girls dress on Fifth Avenue after church on Sunday."[70] She told her new acquaintance she had been expelled from the island along with her sister, her younger brother, and two other women on suspicion of aiding the insurgents (she freely admitted her guilt). Davis wrote up the three women's experiences, including the following incidents:

> After ordering them to leave the island on a certain day, [Spanish officials] sent detectives to their houses on the morning of that day and had them undressed and searched to discover if they were carrying letters to the Junta at Key West and Tampa. They then, an hour later, searched them at the Custom House as they were leaving for the steamer. They searched them thoroughly, even to the length of taking off their shoes and stockings, and fifteen minutes later when the young ladies stood at last on the deck of an American vessel, with the American flag hanging from the stern, the Spanish officers followed them there and demanded that a cabin should be furnished them to which the girls might be taken, and they were then again undressed and searched for the third time.

The image of Spanish officers, "with red crosses for bravery on their chests and gold lace on their cuffs," plucking pretty maidens from the deck of an American ship and subjecting them to strip searches was too much for the chivalrous Davis. The executions, the atrocities, the suffering he had witnessed in Jaruco—all of it paled next to this base and insulting treatment of womanhood. He was furious. Under the headline "Does Our Flag Shield Women?" he announced a complete personal capitulation to a pro-Cuban position on the war. He was dropping his opposition to U.S. interference in the conflict, a stance he now blamed on his ignorance of reality on the island. He felt ashamed that America had stood by idly for so long. The young nation had been too considerate of European power, unintentionally giving free rein to a cruel and dishonest imperial regime.

> The British have just sent an expedition of 800 men to the west coast of Africa to punish a savage king who butchers people because it does not rain. Why should we tolerate Spanish savages merely because they call

themselves "the most Catholic," if they are in reality no better than this naked negro? What difference is there between the King of Benin crucifying a woman because he wants rain and General Weyler outraging a woman for his own pleasure and throwing her to his body guard of blacks, even if the woman has the misfortune to live after it, and still lives in Sagua la Grande to-day?

This unsourced attack on Weyler (the previously "dignified and impressive soldier") was followed by a more restrained enumeration of the reasons for U.S. intervention. The Spaniards had destroyed millions of dollars' worth of American property and ignored State Department demands for an explanation. They had imprisoned and shot U.S. citizens, sometimes after a trial, sometimes not. And now they were running amók on American vessels. If that were not reason enough to step in, Davis locked arms with Hearst, Pulitzer, and Dana and made the compassionate case for action against the "revivers of the Inquisition":

[Why not] interfere in the name of humanity, not because we are Americans, but because we are human beings and because within eighty miles of our coast Spanish officials are killing people as wantonly as though they were field mice, not in battle, but in cold blood: cutting them down in the open roads, at the wells where they have gone for water, on their farms where they have stolen away to dig up a few potatoes . . . ? This is not an imaginary state of affairs. . . . I am writing only of the things I have heard from eye witnesses and of some of the things I have seen.

Davis quoted President Cleveland's warning to Spain that if its efforts to defeat the insurgency degenerated into a "useless sacrifice of human life," America's obligations to respect Spanish sovereignty would be superseded by higher obligations. "These conditions," concluded Davis, "are now manifest."

The story ran in the February 12 edition of the *Journal*, halfway down the front page, which was prominent but not aggressive placement. The headlines scrupulously reflected Davis's reporting. The text continued to the second page, where it was accompanied by a Remington illustration that showed a cluster of Spanish officials in suits and straw hats pawing over the clothes of a young Cuban beauty, who stands before them shapely and naked, her backside to the reader.

The story raised an uproar unlike anything yet published about the war. Determined to horn in, the *World* sent staff to greet Señorita Arango as she disembarked in Tampa. When these reporters asked her to speak of being strip searched by Spanish soldiers, she was shocked. The searches, she protested, had been performed by matrons. The *Evening World* was jubilant: "Association for a few short weeks with the *Journal* has led Mr. Davis to write over his signature an atrociously exaggerated story of an alleged Spanish outrage upon a woman."[71] The *Commercial Advertiser* labeled the Arango incident the "most monstrous falsehood that has yet appeared even in the new journalism." It was suggested that Davis and Remington should be quarantined before being allowed to mingle again with reputable newspapermen.[72]

Davis, horrified at the error, wrote a letter to Pulitzer's paper disavowing Remington's illustration and Hearst's presentation of his story. He claimed to have been clear in his text that male Spanish officers directed rather than conducted the search. The outrage he expressed in his story, he continued, had nothing to do with gender: it had been prompted by the fact that the *Olivette,* an American ship, was searched in Havana harbor in violation of international law. He begged the *World* to print his statement as prominently as possible. He needn't have asked.

The Arango debacle has lived ever since as another example of how yellow journals trampled truth and accuracy in pursuit of tawdry sensations. Hearst, as editor of the paper, bears ultimate responsibility, but Davis deserves a share of the blame. His story describes three searches of the Arango girl: one at her home, one at the Customs House, one aboard ship. With regard to the first, Davis does say, as per his defense, that Spanish detectives "had" the women undressed, but he does not say by whom. Recounting the second search, Davis writes that "they" searched the women thoroughly, right down to their stockings. "They" refers either to the Spanish officials who ordered the women deported or to the Spanish detectives who ordered the first search. Spanish policemen and justice officials, as Remington knew, were uniformly male, and all the Spaniards identified by gender in Davis's piece are male. Davis is silent about who performed the third search but his phrasings, together with his numerous descriptions of Spanish officers strutting about, and his extreme indignation at the treatment of the señoritas, would lead a reasonable person to infer that the young women were searched by men.

Davis was perhaps too decorous to have quizzed Señorita Arango on the sordid details of the incident, but if he knew the searchers to have been matrons, he should have been precise about it. He was also wrong about the number of searches endured by Señorita Arango (there were two, not three). And he was wrong on the point of law: Spain was perfectly entitled to search foreign ships in its harbor. Regardless, Davis emerged from the incident unscathed. He had moved quickly to pin blame on the *Journal*, vowing never to write for the paper again. Rival editors were quite pleased to accept his version of events and blame Hearst, who took the criticism without comment, as did Remington.

In the end, the results of the great Richard Harding Davis experiment were mixed. Hearst got "The Death of Rodriguez," an unusually powerful piece for any daily to carry on its front page. He printed the first major report from the reconcentration camps, a story of enormous consequence. The Arango tale received its share of attention (a debate on Spain's right to search American vessels erupted in Congress), but the incident itself was insignificant. Remington provided dozens of sketches, primarily of Spanish troops training, standing for inspection, loading their dead—enough to last the paper for several months. His work had a detail and subtlety that stood apart from the usual clear, bold lines of newspaper illustration but it did not reproduce as well on newsprint as it would have in magazines. Remington's one illustration of the brave Rodriguez meeting his death easily matched Davis's story for emotional power.

It is ironic that an effort to bring first-rate journalistic talent to a mass-circulation paper should still be cited more than a century later as an example of cheap sensationalism, but one significant mistake will have that effect. We do not know whether or not Hearst thought the Davis-Remington experiment worth the criticism it engendered, or the expense, but something that would have interested him keenly was the frame of mind in which Richard Harding Davis left Cuba. The *Journal* had taken a gamble sending Davis to report on the conflict. The hope was that the ruthlessness of the Spanish war effort and the suffering of the Cuban people would be sufficient to stir in any reporter, whatever his ideological or partisan leanings, a modicum of sympathy for the insurgency. By his return, Davis was as fierce an enemy as Spain had in America.

CHAPTER TWELVE

To Slay a Dragon and Free a Damsel in Distress

Of all the advice Joseph Pulitzer hurled at Morrill Goddard before he departed to edit Hearst's Sunday paper, the one piece of lasting significance was contained in a simple observation. "Most men know very little about their own business," said Pulitzer, "and newspapermen least of all." This hit Goddard between the eyes. He determined to study his trade as a doctor studied medicine or a divinity student the Bible. As obvious as this notion may seem now, there were no schools of journalism at the time, and the literature on the subject was thin so Goddard had to devise his own course of study. What he came up with bears little resemblance to what we might today consider a proper education in print journalism, with emphasis on writing and editing skills, legal and ethical issues, the history of the press, and so on. It is not that those things were unimportant; they just were not what Pulitzer meant by the business of newspapermen. Goddard took another approach entirely.[1]

The business of an editor, as Goddard understood it, came down to two fundamentals: "to seize attention and deliver a compelling message." The first took priority because it allowed for the second. Goddard believed that the way to seize attention was to print stories of interest to readers. Too many editors, he felt, filled their papers with items they themselves found interesting, or that interested their peers or people in positions of authority. Others sought to impress their audiences with their own superior taste, judgment, or intellect—they were especially fond of stories they believed readers *ought* to appreciate. Goddard dismissed these approaches as impractical, self-indulgent, and condescending to readers. He wanted the newspaper to be a friend as well as a mentor to its audience. People expect their friends to respect their taste, judgment, and intellect. Why shouldn't an editor do his readers the courtesy of identifying and respecting their genuine interests and make his editorial choices accordingly? It followed that if an editor was to be successful, he needed to know what interested people, and why. That was the proper business of a newspaperman.[2]

Goddard studied this subject throughout a long career during which he remained the most successful features editor at any American newspaper. His Sunday magazine-style sections for Hearst's *Journal* evolved into the *American Weekly* supplement, which eventually achieved a circulation of 5.5 million in a nation of 75 million. At the end of his half century of practice, Goddard published a treatise entitled *What Interests People—and Why*. It is not a rigorous work, but it is probably the most serious attempt undertaken by an American practitioner of the craft to explore and codify human-interest journalism. Goddard adopts a very broad definition of his subject: human-interest journalism is journalism of interest to humans or, as he liked to say, journalism that sets the mind aglow. The mind, he wrote, is the seat of one's senses, emotions, and intellect, and it is in these fields, to use another of his metaphors, that the journalist plants his seeds. If an editor does not understand the human mind—the way people think, feel, and behave—he cannot expect a bumper crop of readers.[3]

None of that is terribly contentious. Goddard's more daring assertions begin from the premise that it is hard to make people think. He agrees that the power of abstract thought is the highest human faculty, but he nonetheless sees a lot of flattery in the notion that man is a rational animal. In Goddard's observation, people are far more interested in their sense perceptions and emotions than in their thoughts. He sees nothing particularly wrong or shameful in this, but puts it down to the fact that we have been sensing, feeling, and emoting since we lived in caves, while we have only lately begun to cultivate our rational faculties, public education and mass literacy being last-minute innovations in the life of man. Thus, while all mankind is capable of rational thought, most of us only use it with deliberate effort, after a good night's sleep, and for remuneration. Even then, our efforts are often halfhearted and the results mixed. Our senses and emotions, by contrast, are always engaged and rather quickly and effortlessly excited and acted upon. At any given moment, our feelings are far more likely to be governing our intellects than vice versa. If an editor, then, wants to set our minds aglow, he had better respect our natural human inheritance and approach us through the grand portal of feelings rather than through the sticky wicket of rational thought.

The appeal to feelings is not an end in itself. Goddard argues that our emotions tend to ignite our intellects: a story catering to a reader's feelings is more likely than a dry treatise to stimulate thought and persuade a reader to begin weighing facts and arguments. Goddard also considers it humane to approach the reader as a living, breathing whole rather than as a mere intellect. Great storytellers, he observes, have relied upon this approach from the Bible through Shakespeare to Dickens—aren't those works celebrated for stimulating and cultivating human feelings as well as intellects? Why should journalism aim for less?

Surveying the full range of stories he had edited over the years, Goddard identified sixteen universal elements of human interest: love, hate, fear, vanity, evildoing, morality, selfishness, immortality, superstition, curiosity, veneration, ambition, culture, heroism, science, and amusement. Some overlap, while others were subject to Goddard's own personal interpretations. For instance, he lumped stories about health fads under the label "fear," and fashion under "ambition." He also saw significance in the number sixteen: it allowed an editorial maestro two full octaves of emotions on which to play. Not surprisingly, Goddard's standard repertoire included pieces on money and status, sacrifice and devotion, beautiful women, passions and crimes, mysteries and discoveries, and the spiritual life (or, as he called it, the haunted universe), all of which appealed to natural and deeply rooted instincts.

Goddard made no apologies for the fact that he worked in a popular medium and that he edited for the popular mind. He was content to produce newspaper features that reached as close to universal appeal as any have ever managed. His work was plainspoken and unpretentious. He had no academic ambitions, nor any patience for the avant-garde. He was careful to note that recognizing the importance of the emotions was not an argument for vulgarity, lewdness, or appeals to base passions. He further insisted that the point of seizing a reader's attention was to deliver a message, preferably something bold and compelling. He did not waste much space on the nature of the message to be delivered; an editor without something to say, in Goddard's estimation, was beyond help.

There are obvious difficulties with Goddard's methodology. It can be read as a manual on how to manipulate reader emotions, an invitation to journalistic demagoguery. Constant appeals to feelings might actually discourage the hard and patient work of thought, and there is such a thing as prurient interest. Certainly not every lurid crime story that has lit up a newspaper audience reads like *Macbeth*. But just as Goddard's arts can be used irresponsibly, so too can they be neglected, which perhaps helps to explain the decline of human-interest journalism since his heyday, and why newspapers continue to lose their grip on the hearts and minds of mass audiences.

Goddard's book is mostly confined to feature journalism, but his insights into what works on the page, and why, apply to the newspaper as a whole. Indeed, those insights were applied to whole newspapers. Decades before Hearst arrived on the scene, Dana declared that newspapers "must be founded upon human nature" or they would never succeed.[4] All good yellow journalists, many of them trained in Dana's newsroom, sought the human in every story and edited without fear of emotion or drama. They wore their feelings on their pages, believing it was an honest and wholesome way to communicate with readers. It made their careers. It made for compelling and hugely popular newspapers. And it made for the Evangelina Cisneros story.

IN THE SUMMER OF 1897, *Journal* reporters in Havana picked up a rumor that an American female had been brought in chains from the countryside and dumped in the Real Casa de Recojidas, a notoriously foul prison for abandoned women. George Eugene Bryson and George Clarke Musgrave strolled over to investigate. They do not appear to have found an American, but then again, powerfully distracted, they might not have looked very hard. Out in the prison yard, among the prostitutes, murderesses, and lunatics who constituted the Recojidas population, the reporters noticed a startlingly beautiful young woman. She was seventeen years old, with pale skin, fine features, dark eyes, and masses of black hair, and she carried herself with unusual grace. She could not have been more conspicuous in her vile surroundings. Bryson learned from her jailers that she had been arrested for taking part in the attempted assassination of a Spanish military official. Her name was Señorita Evangelina Cossio y Cisneros.

Bryson could not get the girl out of his mind, nor could his colleague, George Clarke Musgrave, who wrote for both the *Journal* and the London

Chronicle. He thought that she "resembled the Madonna of an old master, inspired with life but plunged into Hades."[5] The journalists began frequenting the prison, as did staffers from the U.S. consulate. There is general agreement that Bryson, a former *Herald* correspondent who had also run a paper in Key West, was most assiduous in his attentions to the girl and was the one to piece together her story.

Evangelina was said to be a niece of Salvador Cisneros Betancourt, president of the Cuban revolutionary government. She had been raised "as carefully as the daintiest maid on Fifth Avenue," with servants to braid her dark hair and a coachman to drive her carriage. She was educated, refined, and "harmless as a babe in its mother's arms."[6] Her troubles had begun in June 1895, when her father, a veteran of the Ten Years' War, was arrested and sentenced to die for raising a rebel cavalry unit. Evangelina had managed, through personal appeals to Weyler and his predecessor, General Arsinio Martínez Campos, to have her father's sentence commuted from death to life imprisonment in a penal settlement on the nearby Isle of Pines. She and her sister had voluntarily joined him in his exile, cooking and caring for him (their mother had died when they were young). The alleged assassination attempt for which she had been arrested was said to have been part of an uprising at the settlement, which had happened nine months before Bryson found her.

Bryson did not immediately file anything to the *Journal*. He and his colleagues feared that publicity might increase Spanish resentment toward Evangelina and damage the odds on her release. They pinned their hopes to U.S. consul general Fitzhugh Lee, who had also been alerted to her plight. Lee convinced Weyler to move the girl and several other political prisoners to separate sleeping quarters in Recojidas. Bryson, according to Musgrave, also tried to spring her the old-fashioned way by offering a bribe to a military officer connected with her case. The man wanted $2,000 in gold, with $500 up front. When Bryson balked at the huge sum, the officer told him to pay up or Evangelina would get twenty years in Ceuta. Bryson responded with his first story, filed for publication on August 17 under the byline of Marion Kendrick, perhaps to keep Bryson from getting expelled.[7]

As James Creelman tells it, Hearst was lolling around the *Journal*'s editorial offices on a sultry afternoon when an attendant walked in with a telegram summarizing Bryson's story:

Evangelina Cisneros, pretty girl of seventeen years, related to president of Cuban Republic, is to be imprisoned for twenty years on African coast, for having taken part in uprising Cuban political prisoners on Isle of Pines.[8]

Hearst, by Creelman's account, read the cable once, read it twice, and whistled softly. He slapped his knee and called for his editor, Chamberlain.

"We've got Spain, now!" exclaimed Mr. Hearst. "Telegraph to our correspondent in Havana to wire every detail of this case. Get up a petition to the Queen Regent of Spain for this girl's pardon. Enlist the women of America. Have them sign the petition. Wake up our correspondents all over the country. Have distinguished women sign first. Cable the petitions and the names to the Queen Regent. Notify our minister in Madrid. We can make a national issue of this case. It will do more to open the eyes of the country than a thousand editorials or political speeches. The Spanish minister can attack our correspondents, but we'll see if he can face the women of America when they take up the fight. That girl must be saved if we have to take her out of prison by force or send a steamer to meet the vessel that carried her away—but that would be piracy, wouldn't it?[9]

Creelman's vignette, offered in the same chapter of the same book that contains the Remington-Hearst telegrams, rings with his usual mad insistence on the surpassing brilliance and omnipotence of the yellow press. The words assigned to Hearst are probably a conflation of hours (if not days) of musings and directives on the Evangelina file. Nonetheless, if Creelman says the story lit a fire under Hearst, it probably did. His account of Hearst's instructions is a reasonably accurate summary of the *Journal*'s actions in the coming weeks.

Hearst charged Bryson and his Havana contingent with filling gaps in Evangelina's story—"every detail of this case." The initial piece had said little about the circumstances of her arrest. The *Journal* now reported that the girl and her father had managed a tolerable existence at the Isle of Pines penal settlement until the arrival of its new military governor, Colonel José Berriz, a nephew of General Azcárraga, the Spanish minister of war. Berriz took an immediate shine to Evangelina or, as the paper put it, "his foul passions were aroused by the sight of this slender, helpless child." She repulsed his advances, her "only crime." Berriz locked her father away and tried again but she resisted still. And then, late one night, Berriz arrived unannounced in Evangelina's room, a struggle ensued, and several exiles ran to the girl's rescue or, as the *Journal* reported "the settlement rose in revolt." The Cubans knocked Colonel Berriz to the ground, restrained him with rope, and determined to deliver him to a judge. His shouts and threats, however, attracted a clutch of Spanish guards. They came running and the Cubans scattered. Some were captured and at least one was shot. Evangelina and others were imprisoned and charged with sedition and attempted assassination.[10]

The *Journal*'s correspondents waxed to exhaustion about Evangelina's sweet face and lustrous eyes. When they ran out of adjectives they simply declared her "the most beautiful girl in the island of Cuba." Their admiration for her physical charms was proportionate to their disgust at her treatment by the Spaniards. Her accuser, Berriz, was depicted as "a lecherous and foiled scoundrel." The prison to which she was consigned was a rat-infested pit overseen by a cruel and corrupt warden. She was forced to scrub floors and sleep on boards. Her health was suffering. Her cellmates, judging by the *Journal*'s illustrations, were swarthy, ugly, and obviously demented—poor company for a girl "as ignorant of the world as a cloistered nun." The paper doubted that any well-bred young woman in modern times had been subjected to such unwholesome scenes. And Recojidas was nothing compared to what awaited her in Ceuta. The latter was described as a Moroccan prison with nothing but the Atlantic before it and "wild Moors behind it." Vicious criminals and political exiles were shipped there in equal numbers, packed into unsanitary cells and fed like animals in a zoo, and forced to labor in chain gangs. Bryson allowed that Evangelina's sentence of twenty years in Ceuta had yet to be confirmed, but he believed her chances of survival if she were sent there were nil.[11]

In answer to Hearst's demand for an appeal for the girl's pardon, Creelman wired orders to some two hundred stringers to gain the signatures of prominent American women for a petition to Queen Regent Maria Christina of Spain. The response was overwhelming. Within a week, the *Journal* had more than ten thousand names. Among them were the wife of Secretary of State Sherman, the grandniece of George Washington, the mother of President McKinley, Mrs. Mark Hanna, and Clara Barton, founder of the American Red Cross. The paper was particularly pleased with the participation of the widow of Confederate leader Jefferson Davis, a Pulitzer relative. She confessed to being ignorant of all the facts but wrote that she knew the girl to be young and defenseless and "in sore straits."[12]

The campaign for Evangelina quickly took on a life of its own. Julia Ward Howe, author of the "Battle Hymn of the Republic," wrote His Holiness Pope Leo XIII, imploring him to emulate "the action of that Providence which interests itself in the fall of a sparrow" and intervene with Spain on the girl's behalf.[13] The Vatican was sufficiently moved to invite the Spanish ambassador for a long chat about the case. Before August was out, the queen regent, at her summer palace in San Sebastian, was digging out from under hundreds if not thousands of telegraphed pleas.

PULITZER COULD NOT SIT placidly through all this. He knew the popular appeal of Cuban martyrs. He had suffered through a similar episode earlier in the year when Hearst had championed the cause of Dr. Richard Ruiz. A Philadelphia-trained dentist and naturalized American, Dr. Ruiz had maintained a practice in Cuba until arrested and accused of robbing a train. He was placed in solitary confinement and denied communication with the U.S. consulate. Thirteen days later he was found dead in his cell and his Spanish keepers claimed he had committed suicide. Bryson, who was first to the story, argued that Dr. Ruiz's severe head wounds indicated he had been beaten to death. Consul General Lee accused Spain of either killing the dentist or driving him to suicide. He demanded the discharge of all American citizens in Cuban jails and requested that a U.S. warship be dispatched to Havana harbor.[14]

Hearst kept the Ruiz story on his front page for weeks, and among other scoops printed the man's naturalization papers to disprove a claim by Madrid that he was not an American citizen. The *Journal* argued that Washington should declare war against Spain if it was proven that his jailers had murdered Ruiz in his cell; it was the first truly bellicose statement by the paper, and its sentiments were echoed in Congress. The Senate passed a resolution requesting more information on the case, and the Foreign Affairs Committee voted to demand the release of other American prisoners in Cuba. For his finale, Hearst brought Mrs. Ruiz and her five children to Washington, where they met both President McKinley and Secretary of State Sherman. McKinley would later ask Spain for a

$75,000 settlement for Mrs. Ruiz. "The cruel murder of one Ruiz," wrote the *Mail and Express*, "does more to create sympathy for the revolutionists than a score of oily diplomats . . . can overcome in a year."[15]

But at least through the Ruiz chronicles, Pulitzer had been able to boast a martyr of his own, none other than his star reporter Sylvester Scovel. Traveling under the guise of Harry Williams, scrap-metal dealer, Scovel had visited the tiny port of Las Tunas on the southern coast of Cuba in February 1897 to send his copy out by boat. He was picked up by Spanish guards and charged with communicating with the insurgents and bearing false documents, among other crimes.

Scovel's incarceration was hardly agonizing. He was transported from Las Tunas to Sancti Spiritus and installed in a comfortable cell with food and fresh flowers. He continued writing for his paper, smuggling out his copy via friendly guards and proudly datelining his stories "Calaboose No. 1, Prison of Sancti-Spiritus, Santa Clara Province, Cuba." Pulitzer mounted a righteous campaign to have his man released, soliciting and winning support from the journalistic and political communities. The U.S. Senate and four-teen state legislatures passed motions requesting that the State Department intervene on Scovel's behalf.[16] The *Journal* neglected to report on his plight.

The *World* and its allies stressed that Scovel had never carried arms or acted in any capacity other than as a journalist in Cuba. This was not strictly true. Scovel's most recent visit to Gómez had come at the urging of Consul General Lee, who wanted the insurgent general's reaction to Washington's proposal that the rebels accept an armistice in return for home rule. He had also been running letters back and forth from the insurgent army to the Junta in New York and assisting the Cubans in the training of their recruits. Fortunately for him, proof of his undercover work was in short supply, and Pulitzer had raised enough of a stink that Enrique Dupuy de Lôme, the Spanish minister to Washington, wrote Madrid recommending the reporter's release. Weyler reluctantly com-plied and by early March the *World* had lost a martyr but regained its most valuable and celebrated correspondent.[17]

Pulitzer had nothing similar to throw up against Hearst's Evangelina story, but what he could not match he could always undermine. He now cabled Weyler for his thoughts on the Cuban girl's case and received a prompt and gratifying reply. "For judicial reasons," wrote the captain general, "there is on trial in the preliminary stages a person named

Evangelina Cossio Cisneros, who, deceitfully luring to her house the military commander of the Isle of Pines, had men posted secretly, who tied him and attempted to assassinate him. This case is in the preliminary stages, and has not yet been tried by a competent tribunal, and consequently no sentence has been passed nor approved by me. I answer the *World* with the frankness and truth that characterize all my acts. Weyler."[18]

Pulitzer was delighted to report that Hearst's "blameless flower of Cuba" was actually a ringleader in an assassination plot and that the *Journal* had greatly exaggerated her legal predicament. His *World* had also learned that Evangelina was not in fact a niece of President Betancourt, and that her life in Recojidas was nowhere near as onerous as advertised. Pulitzer editorialized that nothing could be gained for the Cuban cause by "inventions and exaggerations that are past belief."[19]

Dupuy de Lôme joined the assault on the Evangelina story with a letter to Mrs. Jefferson Davis, informing the grand lady that "a shameless conspiration to promote the interest of one or more sensational papers is at the bottom of the romance that has touched your good heart."[20] He reiterated Weyler's line that Señorita Cisneros had lured to her house the military commander of the Isle of Pines and that her case was still under consideration.

A third line of attack on the *Journal*'s scoop was opened by U.S. consul general Lee, who, on his arrival in New York for thirty days' leave on September 8, told a delighted New York *World* that he wished to correct "false and stupid" impressions of the imprisonment of Evangelina Cisneros. She had two clean rooms in the Casa de Recojidas, said Lee, and was well clothed and fed. He did not believe that the Spaniards had any intention of sending the girl to Africa and surmised that she would have been pardoned long before "if it had not been for the hubbub created by American newspapers." Lee also doubted Evangelina's innocence: "[T]hat she was implicated in the insurrection on the Isle of Pines there could be no question. She, herself, in a note to me, acknowledged that fact, and stated she was betrayed by an accomplice."[21]

As a sort of punctuation point to all this, Weyler notified the U.S. consulate that he was expelling *Journal* correspondent George Eugene Bryson from Cuba, along with Edouardo Garcia of the New York *Sun*.[22]

Far from being embarrassed by the attacks, Hearst reprinted both the Weyler and the Dupuy de Lôme letters in full and thanked the men for admitting the essential and indefensible fact that Berriz had ventured alone at night to the room of an attractive young woman who was entirely at his mercy. "This defense," the *Journal* argued, "by being made official, deepens Spain's disgrace." The paper also corrected de Lome's assertion that "one or more sensational papers" were responsible for the Cisneros romance—"only the Journal is entitled to the Spanish Minister's censure."[23]

Bryson, before being shipped out of Havana, managed to wire New York addressing Weyler's dismissal of the girl's jeopardy: he quoted legal sources confirming that prosecutors had demanded a sentence of twenty years in Ceuta and that the matter was now in the hands of the Judge Advocate General. The New York *Sun* quoted a Cuban lawyer who substantiated Bryson's account of her legal situation, no doubt contributing to Edouardo Garcia's simultaneous expulsion.[24]

As for Weyler's charge that Evangelina had been involved in an assassination plot against her guards, the *Journal* considered it ridiculous. The prisoners had not harmed Berriz despite plenty of opportunity. More interestingly, the *Journal* argued that even if she had been involved in an uprising, she was simply supporting the cause for which every man in her life was prepared to die. That demonstrated good breeding, not rebelliousness or criminality, and did not detract at all from her status as a "blameless flower of Cuba." The paper evoked the heroine of a much-recited John Greenleaf Whittier ballad to make the case that in a civilized country, women were not prosecuted for supporting their men: "When Barbara Frietchie was allowed to wave the Stars and Stripes in the face of a victorious rebel army the incident was characteristic of American methods of warfare. No American soldiers, of North or South, made war on women. . . . The idea of punishing a woman for her devotion to the cause of her family would have been revolting to the roughest band of bushwhackers on either side."[25] That explains the importance of Mrs. Jefferson Davis to the *Journal*'s coverage (beyond her connections to Pulitzer). Her request that Evangelina be granted clemency, "even though the provocation may have been great," was a common sentiment. None of the intervening parties—not the Vatican, nor American politicians—stipulated that the teenaged girl must be innocent of any wrongdoing to qualify for mercy.

The *Journal* quoted the prison physician at Casa de Recojidas as saying that Miss Cisneros was threatened with consumption and needed to be moved to better accommodations to protect her health. Former prison mates were found to attest to her mistreatment in jail. Colonel Berriz was said to be under pressure to withdraw his charge against Evangelina and let the matter pass. (The *Sun* wrote that Berriz was eager to reclaim letters in which he had allegedly made immoral propositions to the girl as the price of her father's liberty. These letters have never surfaced.)[26]

As for Pulitzer, Hearst lambasted him and Weyler both for libeling a young woman of irreproachable character. The *Journal* took every opportunity to link the pen pals in print, vowing to fight for Evangelina "in spite of Weyler and the *World*." Davenport contributed a cartoon of a fierce-looking Weyler leading columns of tall, skinny, bug-eyed Pulitzer clones. The caption read, "Calling Out the Reserves."[27] Hearst also mocked Pulitzer as snobbish for quibbling over Evangelina's family connections. In practice, however, the *Journal* quietly downgraded the girl from a niece to a "relative" of the Cuban president.

Consul General Lee's criticisms of the *Journal*'s work were in some ways the most serious since he was neither a Spaniard nor a publishing rival but a well-placed agent of the United States government. He was also a nephew of Robert E. Lee, a graduate of West Point, a Confederate cavalry officer, a veteran of the Indian Wars, and a former governor of Virginia. His words carried weight. Yet the *Journal* did not answer his charges, even though it knew them to be disingenuous. Bryson was well acquainted with Lee and his staff. The newspaper and the consulate shared an office building, the Casa Nueva in central Havana. Bryson knew that Lee had seen Evangelina in prison, that Lee broadly shared the *Journal*'s concerns for her treatment, that he had fought to improve her living quarters, and that Lee's wife and daughter had visited Evangelina in prison to offer her comfort and support. Other consular officials also called on her regularly and agitated for her release. The day after his first story appeared, Lee had echoed Bryson's descriptions of conditions at the prison in a letter to Weyler begging for the girl's release. Yet now Lee described the *Journal*'s reporting as "false and stupid," and the paper let it pass. The only explanation is that the consulate and the newspaper were in cahoots, as subsequent events make clear.[28]

In early September, the queen regent requested that Weyler treat Evangelina as a distinguished prisoner of the state and move her to a convent to await the completion of legal proceedings. Although Weyler did not regard the girl as particularly villainous—he had suggested to Lee that she would be released as soon as the newspapers lost interest—he refused to comply with the queen regent's request. He instead held Evangelina incommunicado at Recojidas so that no one knew her precise circumstances.[29]

Weyler's stubbornness was probably connected to momentous events in his home country. On August 8, days before the Evangelina story broke, an anarchist shot and killed Spanish premier Cánovas at Miramar. Cánovas's government had been in trouble before his assassination. The costly and difficult war in Cuba was increasingly unpopular, and rebellion had spread to Spanish-held Puerto Rico and the Philippines. With Cánovas gone, an interim Conservative government was appointed, but it was not expected to last. There was immediate speculation that the Liberals would regain power. Their leader, Práxedes Sagasta, had proposed political reforms aimed at bringing peace to Cuba and had denounced Weyler's methods as both severe and ineffectual, giving rise to rumors that the captain general would be recalled. Weyler was unrepentant about his ways: "How do they want me to wage war? With bishops' pastorals and presents of sweets and money?"[30] But the last thing he needed was what Hearst had brought him: an international scandal over his treatment of female prisoners. Hence his peevish response to the queen regent's order.

Hearst took the queen regent's promise of all possible consideration for Evangelina as a guarantee that she would not be harmed and as an opportunity to declare victory. He celebrated the paper's triumph for a few days in early September before allowing the story to go dormant. It remained dormant for a month. The only hint, a very slight hint, of its imminent return was an October 5 *Journal* editorial on the proceedings of a municipal affairs symposium in Columbus, Ohio. At the paper's invitation, the mayors of several large American cities had spoken approvingly of the daily newspaper as "agent and attorney" for the people, and the editorial now wondered how far a newspaper might go in this new role: "It is universally admitted that a newspaper may deplore the existence of destitution and distress, and may even urge its charitable readers to relieve sufferers, but can it save lives itself without convicting itself of sensationalism? It may criticize corruption and maladministration in office, but has it a right to protect the public interests by deeds as well as words?"[31]

Three days later, the *Journal* reported that Evangelina Cisneros had escaped from the Casa de Recojidas. The story announcing her flight was short. Datelined Havana, it said that the girl had failed to appear for roll call in the morning and that a search was undertaken. The guards found one of the bars of her room filed and bent outward. Evidence pointed to the cooperation of outsiders in her escape. Several prison employees had been placed under arrest. The authorities had no idea as to Evangelina's whereabouts.[34]

The following morning, October 9, the *Journal* announced that Weyler had resigned, having failed to gain the support of the new Spanish government. Adjacent on the page was a large picture of Evangelina with news that she was on her way to the United States, having been sprung from prison by concerned "friends."[33]

It was not until the next morning, October 10, that the whole stupefying story spilled out in a six-column headline:

EVANGELINA CISNEROS RESCUED BY THE *JOURNAL*

Beneath the headline was a story by Charles Duval, datelined October 7 Havana and October 9 Key West:

> I have broken the bars of Recojidas and have set free the beautiful captive of monster Weyler, restoring her to her friends and relatives, and doing by strength, skill and strategy what could not be accomplished by petition and urgent request of the Pope.
>
> Weyler could blind the Queen to the real character of Evangelina, but he could not build a jail that would hold against *Journal* enterprise when properly set to work.

"Charles Duval" was the pen name of Karl Decker, a *Journal* reporter who had arrived in Havana on August 28, shortly after Bryson's expulsion. A native of Harper's Ferry, Virginia, and the well-educated son of a Confederacy colonel, Decker had been a rising star in the paper's Washington bureau before his assignment to Cuba. The paper described him as a handsome young man, six feet tall, two hundred pounds, "straight and lithe as an Indian." It is not altogether clear why he was chosen for the assignment, beyond that he was strong, daring, and willing. Decker comported himself in Havana as a genial and carefree young man bent on having a grand time at his employer's expense, a role that fit him comfortably and that did nothing to incur the suspicions of Spanish spies. He gave expensive dinners to friends at the Inglaterra and drove about in an open carriage smoking cigars. Occasionally he filed a story to New York, but he avoided the *Journal*'s bureau so as not to implicate other reporters in what he was about to do.[33]

Knowing nothing of Spanish or Havana, Decker needed accomplices to complete his mission, and he found them at the U.S. consulate. The historian W. Joseph Campbell has uncovered startling evidence in the papers of Fitzhugh Lee that U.S. diplomatic staff were up to their necks in Decker's adventure. One of the reporter's key contacts on the island was Donnell Rockwell, a junior staffer at the consulate who nurtured a Bryson-like obsession with Evangelina. Lee's papers suggest it was Rockwell who first hatched the notion of springing the girl. He had already passed her an instrument with which to file through her prison bars, although she had not been able to use it effectively. It was by exploiting Rockwell's diplomatic privileges that Decker was able to visit Evangelina in jail before Weyler held her incommunicado. It was probably Rockwell, as well, who introduced Decker to the three men who would directly assist in the jailbreak: Carlos F. Carbonell, William B. MacDonald, and Francisco (Paco) De Besche. Carbonell, a Cuban banker, was an intimate of Consul General Lee who would later join Lee's staff.[35]

While there is no evidence that Fitzhugh Lee was directly involved in Decker's plot, it is difficult to imagine him an innocent bystander. Lee was something of a cowboy. Bluff and outspoken, he chafed at State Department procedure, sympathized with the Cuban insurgents, and reveled in covert operations. On arriving in Havana, he had developed a network of spies (or, as he called them, scouts) to keep him abreast of local developments. It is clear from his letters and an unpublished memoir that Rockwell was operating with at least his tacit blessing. Whatever his precise role, Lee would have been anxious that neither he nor the State Department be implicated in a jailbreak, so he left Cuba a week after Decker's arrival and on landing in New York made his public show of dismissing the *Journal*'s Cisneros campaign.[36]

Even with accomplices and local knowledge, Decker was still short a plan for rescuing the girl. The prison was located in one of the meaner sectors of Havana, surrounded, as Decker wrote, "by a huddle of squalid huts occupied by negroes and Chinamen and reeking to heaven by day and night."[37] He walked the crooked alleys on every side of the building, scanning its thick walls, barred windows, and parapets for an opportunity. He brainstormed with his associates, principally Carbonell and MacDonald. They considered a violent daylight raid, but with the well-guarded Havana arsenal in the next block and a military barracks directly behind the prison, they did not like their odds. They tried to bribe the Recojidas guards, apparently without success. They were down to dynamiting their way into the prison before someone thought to ask Evangelina if she had any suggestions. They smuggled her a note. The "innocent child" immediately replied with a comprehensive plan to drug her cellmates with opium-laced sweetmeats, dissolve the bars on her windows with acid, and scale the prison walls with a long rope. She offered diagrams and suggested a series of stop-and-go signals involving lit cigars and white handkerchiefs.

Decker and company discarded the acid idea as impractical but otherwise adopted Evangelina's plan. Scaling the prison walls with a rope was too daunting, so they rented, across a narrow alley from the prison, a house whose roof was level with a ledge on the prison wall. A long plank laid between would bring them within reach of Evangelina's cell block. They made their first attempt in the middle of a Tuesday night under a moon that seemed to Decker as bright as the midday sun. Instead of a plank, they stretched a twelve-foot ladder across the alley and clambered to the prison ledge. "No man engaged in that enterprise," wrote Decker, "will ever forget that twelve foot walk across the sagging, decrepit ladder." The rescuers advanced to the window identified by Evangelina in her diagram and found her behind it, dressed inconspicuously in a dark dress. She clasped the hands of her rescuers through the bars before they took out their saw and got to work. The iron seemed to ring like an alarm with each pass of the teeth. After an hour they were only partway through the bar and they decided to return the next night with better tools. Evangelina went back to bed.

On the second attempt, everything went like clockwork. The ladder was raised without a sound. The men slid across in their stocking feet, carrying a pair of Stillson wrenches, with which they snapped the half-cut bar. Decker used brute strength to bend it upward far enough for

Evanglina to slip through and taste freedom for the first time in thirteen months. He noticed "one fleeting smile of ineffable happiness" on her face before she scampered fearlessly across the ladder to the rented house. Minutes later she was rushing over the cobblestones in a closed carriage.[38]

The original Tuesday-night plan had called for Evangelina to be spirited aboard a regularly scheduled U.S.-bound steamship on Wednesday morning. The one-day delay meant the girl had to hole up in Carbonell's Havana home for forty-eight hours awaiting the next boat. Carbonell kept cash on hand to bribe any policemen who came looking for her, and a revolver in case money was insufficient. Lee's memoir says that as Evangelina read newspaper reports of her escape and the search for her, she became increasingly frightened and vowed to kill herself rather than surrender to the Spanish.

On the evening she was to leave, Carbonell dressed her as a boy, stuck an unlit cigar in her mouth, and walked with her the two blocks from his home to the wharf, where she safely boarded a launch to the passenger ship *Seneca*. As they approached the ship, Decker and the purser induced the Spanish policeman on board to take a drink with them in the dining room, and Evangelina was smuggled into a stateroom by the quartermaster. The steamer departed for New York without incident.

Evangelina spent much of her journey in the company of Walter B. Barker, a U.S. diplomatic staffer. Barker was another of Lee's confidants, a fellow veteran of the Confederate army, and a man of similar style. He had recently been reprimanded by the State Department for trying to smuggle correspondence from rebel soldiers to the Junta through consular channels. A week before Evangelina's escape, he had trampled protocol by cabling an urgent last-minute request for leave, pleading unspecified health concerns. He had all of his approvals in place by October 4. On October 8, the day after Evangelina's rescue, he hustled from his post to Havana, boarding the *Seneca* with her on the ninth. On disembarking in New York, he told the *Journal* that he had not seen Evangelina until the second day out and that he had no idea how she got on board. The *World*, however, quoted the ship's captain as saying that on her first evening at sea she took a promenade on deck and met some of the passengers. "Among them," the captain reported, "was Walter B. Barker, United States Consul at Sagua. She addressed him in Spanish with an air which seemed to me as if she had met him before."[39]

While Barker was acting as Evangelina's chaperone aboard the *Seneca*, his consular colleague, Donnell Rockwell, was being interrogated by Spanish officials who suspected him of connivance in the jailbreak. He refuted their accusations, but within hours of the grilling, he too had applied for unscheduled leave from Cuba, citing an unspecified illness. His request was quickly approved.[40]

In the days after the escape, the *Journal* reported that its offices in Havana were under close surveillance. The houses of several prominent Cubans were said to have been ransacked as part of a search ranging from "the brothels on Azuacata Street to a convent on the outskirts of the city." A Spanish cruiser launched a search in response to reports that Evangelina was headed to Key West in a small boat.[41]

Back in New York, Hearst hashed and rehashed the rescue story from every conceivable angle while awaiting Evangelina's arrival. The jailbreak was described as "the most daring coup in the history of the war." *Journal* writers strained to express the enormity of the achievement. General Bradley Johnson compared it favorably to Bollman's unsuccessful attempt to free Lafayette from an Austrian jail at Olmütz. Murat Halstead claimed that one had to go all the way back to the hairsbreadth escape of Mary Queen of Scots from her imprisonment in Loch Leven Castle for an appropriate parallel.[42]

Not content with tooting its own horn, the *Journal* filled its entire front page on October 11 with letters and accolades, some spontaneous, others no doubt solicited. Mrs. Ulysses S. Grant, Clara Barton, Lady Rothschild, and other signatories of the Evangelina petitions wrote to express their joy and gratitude. *The Times* of London and the Baltimore *Sun*, among other papers, doffed their caps to Hearst, as did rafts of governors, senators, and congressmen. "Surely no feat of American journalism can compare with the enterprise and chivalry displayed by the *Journal* in this, its latest triumph," declared Senator Stephen Elkins.[43]

One of the most thoughtful contributions was wired from Washington by the head of the papal delegation, Monsignor Sebastian Martinelli. It managed to be gracious and yet skeptical of yellow journalism:

> I was never so impressed with the wonderful resources of American journalism. It seems almost incredible that such an escape could have been accomplished so openly and with such apparent ease. Since my arrival in this

country the gigantic activity of the press, the tremendous influence which it exercises on public life and the individual industry and personal study which are given in every line of its daily work, have filled me with amazement. I have sometimes been forced to regret that so much space was devoted to unworthy or futile efforts, but never could I refrain from admiring the skill with which all subjects are handled and the untiring efforts on the part of the journalists who accomplish the mission to which they are assigned.[44]

The orgy of self-congratulation continued through the week as more telegrams and quotations were received from ever-higher offices. Secretary of State John Sherman commented that "every one will sympathize with the *Journal*'s enterprise in releasing Miss Cisneros. She is a woman." President McKinley, in the presence of his cabinet and a *Journal* reporter, allowed that the Secretary had "correctly voiced the unofficial sentiment of the Administration." The notes of chivalry struck by Secretary Sherman and Senator Elkins were often heard in discussions of the rescue. The *Pittsburgh Commercial Gazette* described Evangelina's liberation as "a dashing chapter to modern knight errantry, and the suggestion of chivalry is not less so because the men who risked their lives to execute the daring exploit were employed by a newspaper for the purpose."[45]

The jailbreak raised some vexing diplomatic questions. The British papers addressed them first, wondering if Evangelina was extraditable and, if so, if Spain would bother with a request. A lawyer for the Spanish legation in Washington argued that the United States would be honor bound to comply with a Spanish demand for the girl's return. New York legal eminence Elihu Root ventured that because Evangelina had been seized by individuals acting in their individual capacity on Spanish soil, the United States bore no responsibility for the escape and was unaffected in its friendly relations with Madrid. The *Journal*, for its part, was spoiling for a custody battle. It declared itself pleased with the "rank illegality" of its actions: "When right and wrong are turned upside down, when devilish ferocity and bestial lust are intrenched in power and innocence is under the ban of outlawry, there is a savage satisfaction in striking a smashing blow at a legal system that has become an organized crime." The paper acknowledged that its sentiments might be out of tune with a prosaic and commercial century, and it expected lectures on how "the age of knight errantry" was past. To that it answered, "if innocent maidens are still imprisoned by tyrants, the knight errant is yet needed. The *Journal* is boundlessly glad that it has rescued Evangelina Cisneros. . . . The *Journal* is ready to stand all the consequences of what it has done. The main thing is that the wronged and suffering girl is out of the Casa Recojidas, out of Cuba, out of Weyler's grasp, and safe under the Stars and Stripes."[46]

EVANGELINA COSSIO Y CISNEROS arrived in New York Harbor on October 13. She was met by a delegation of well-wishers and *Journal* staffers, who whisked her away in a *Journal* launch to meet the proper authorities. They then bundled her into a *Journal* carriage bound for the Waldorf Hotel. The reporters noted her every utterance and blink along the way: "It is a dream, a happy, happy dream," she said, and the quotes did not get much better in three days of heavy coverage.[47]

The thirteen-story Waldorf, built in 1893 at Fifth Avenue and 33rd Street, the current site of the Empire State Building, was the first Manhattan hotel to boast electricity throughout and private bathrooms in many of its one thousand suites. With its great courtyard and Peacock Alley, it was the grandest and most public of the city's hostelries, and thus a perfect stage for Evangelina. She found it a considerable improvement over Casa de Recojidas, even with the *Journal* at her door at 6:30 a.m. to awaken her for her first full day in New York. The paper had filled her room with boxes of dresses, lingerie, hats, and accessories from which to select a wardrobe. She went down to breakfast at 7:30 dressed head to toe in black. "I like myself best in the somber colors and often I think I may go into the convent, where I shall wear nothing else," she told a reporter. She added that the convent was on her mind because in prison she had promised God that if he she were ever released, she would forsake the love of mortals and dedicate herself to the Church.[48] (She would marry a Cuban-American businessman in a matter of months.)

The *Journal* stuck with Evangelina as she met Cuban and American dignitaries and other notables and took a tour of the city. She marveled at the streets, the carriages, the tall buildings, and the brass buttons on the policemen's uniforms. She took her first elevator ride and talked of her ambition to ride a bicycle. The newspaper was impressed by her good manners and her erudition (she was familiar with Victor Hugo). It was announced that at her own request she had visited the Naturalization

Bureau in the Supreme Court to swear her intention to become a U.S. citizen, a revelation that must have puzzled her fellow Cubans.

The crowning events of her New York tour were held on Saturday, October 16. Evangelina was met at the Waldorf by a guard of soldiers and naval cadets in gleaming uniforms and paraded through the streets of the city. She attended a reception in her honor at Delmonico's, with Cuban patriots, local dignitaries, and *Journal* staffers. Hearst himself made an appearance. "In the midst of the bizarre and pompeian reception which was given to the young woman at Delmonico's," wrote Frederick Palmer in *Collier's,* "the man who footed the bills came into the room where she stood among the palms, shyly shook hands with the heroine whom his wonder machine had created, and then excused himself and hastened away in his automobile."[49]

From Delmonico's, Evangelina was whisked to Madison Square, where music, searchlights, and a cheering throng of 50,000 awaited her. She stood on the platform hand in hand with Karl Decker, who had become a celebrity himself, greeted on his arrival in New York by a coterie of newsmen eager for a few more quotes. "The Prince of the Fairytale," as his own newspaper described him, had since been holding court at the Hoffman House, accepting congratulations and passing out souvenirs of Havana—long black cigars with Captain General Weyler's mug on the band. Now he pushed Evangelina forward "in silent deprecation of his own claim to the uproarious greeting." Fireworks burst and hissed in the air, the band played the Cuban anthem, and the girl, according to the *Journal,* stood like a beautifully chiselled statue, motionless, awed. Her eyes were dancing with excitement; her color was constantly changing; her bosom was heaving with indescribable emotion.[50]

While the *Journal* was busy with its Evangelina extravaganza, several of its rivals began to wonder if the whole thing was a hoax. Consul General Lee contributed to the skepticism by publicly commenting that the girl could not possibly have exited Cuba without the permission of the Spanish government. Officials in Havana, he surmised, must have "winked at" the jailbreak. Taking Lee's cue, the *New York Times* scoffed at "a remarkable case of unobstructed rescue."[51]

The "fake" theory gained general acceptance with the publication of Willis Abbot's memoir in 1933. Still editorials editor of the *Journal* at the time of Evangelina's rescue, he wrote that money had bought the girl's way out of prison and claimed it was only to exonerate the prison guards and to furnish newspaper material that an elaborate plan of rescue was developed. Abbot's take became the conventional view.[52]

His estimation of Hearst's state of mind during the Cisneros affair has also won broad acceptance: "If ever for a moment he doubted that he was battling a powerful state to save the life and liberty of a sorely persecuted girl martyr, he gave no sign of it. It was the one dominating, all-compelling issue of the moment for him. . . . . Hearst felt himself in the role of Sir Galahad rescuing a helpless maiden." Abbot's comments have been taken as evidence of Hearst's mental instability. Biographer W.A. Swanberg, for example, relies on Abbot for his diagnosis that Hearst suffered a "psychological aberration." He could at times become "a creature of pure fantasy. He *believed* that he had performed a gallant rescue. He *believed* what his newspapers said about it. He could enter into a dream world and, like a child, live out a heroic role in it, brushing aside humdrum reality. Those who thought him a mere cynical opportunist missed half the point. The Hearst reverie could become actuality."[53]

David Nasaw, too, sees a mix of cynicism and psychological damage in Hearst's handling of the Evangelina episode. His interest in the girl, argues Nasaw, was a desperate bid to juice the *Journal*'s front page in a slow news month. It was not important journalism: it was a "melodrama," a "sideshow," irrelevant to the "real story" of the war between Cuba and Spain, but at least it sold papers. The jailbreak, in Nasaw's estimation, stoked Hearst's megalomania and feelings of invulnerability.[54]

In fact, the rescue of Evangelina Cisneros from Casa de Recojidas was not a hoax. It was an audacious and purposeful exploit, and it happened pretty much as reported. Fitzhugh Lee's papers and other diplomatic archives corroborate the essentials of the *Journal*'s account, but there was plenty of evidence that the jailbreak was not a fake even before this material was released. The *New York Herald* had printed an account of Evangelina's escape, gathered from Spanish sources, in the hours before Decker's role in the affair was revealed. Her disappearance had "caused a sensation in Havana." The paper reported that police had found a filed and bent iron bar in a window in her wing of the prison, as well as a ladder, a guide rope, and a loaded revolver. Investigators suspected outside involvement and guessed that the escape had been "long and carefully planned." They confirmed that the house across the street had been rented by two young, well-dressed men who didn't bother to furnish it. The girl's cellmates claimed to have been drugged. "The police are hard at work," said the *Herald*, "and all the Spanish authorities along the coast have been communicated with in the belief that an attempt may be made to embark . . . for the United States or elsewhere." The jailer and four employees who were on duty the night of the escape were arrested.[55] The *Herald*'s story, coming as it did before the *Journal* announced its part in the escape, substantiates Decker's account—unless one wants to believe that a pro-Spanish competitor of Hearst's was in on the hoax, along with the Spanish officials who searched for Evangelina, grilled U.S. consular staff, and argued in Washington for her return to Cuba.

Decker may have induced a guard or two to look the other way. The *Journal* reported on its front page that its correspondent was carrying explicit instructions to do "all that man and money might" to bring about the escape of Miss Cisneros, and Decker appears to have bought off a policeman aboard the *Seneca*.[56] But he did not bribe the whole of the Spanish army, the imperial diplomatic corps, the Cuban police force, the prison guards, and the *New York Herald*. The contention that Hearst cynically manipulated Evangelina's plight merely to sell newspapers is itself cynical. The *Journal* was not in desperate need of front-page material when she came along. The Klondike gold rush was the paper's preoccupation through the summer of 1897, even after the Evangelina story broke; nor was Hearst short on Cuban-related news given the Cánovas assassination.

Hearst did enjoy the fact that the Cisneros saga was selling newspapers—he mentioned it to his mother when he thanked her for signing his petition. But he did not champion Evangelina's cause simply to build circulation. Nor is it necessary to put him on the couch to discern his primary interests: they were shouted in his editorials, incessantly. Hearst honestly believed the girl had suffered injustice at the hands of the Spanish and he wanted to expose her mistreatment, free her from "Weyler's ruthless grasp," and arraign her jailers "at the bar of civilization." He regarded Spain's treatment of the girl as the exemplification of its barbarous stewardship of Cuba and he was frustrated that successive administrations in Washington had refused to rally to the Cuban people. He believed that Cleveland and McKinley had been able to maintain attitudes of neutrality on the Cuban question because too many Americans were as yet unaware of the magnitude of Spanish savagery on the island. He hoped that the Cisneros story would rid America of its apathy. "The sufferings of a whole people," argued one editorial, "make no such appeal to the average imagination as does the atrocity of the sentence imposed on one young woman."[57]

GENERATIONS OF HISTORIANS and biographers have mistrusted Hearst's outrage at the rape of Cuba. Many, in fact, have mocked it. Nasaw and Swanberg devote more than a hundred pages to this period in Hearst's life but only a few sentences to reconcentration. Hearst's anger was well founded. It was not just scribblers for the yellow sheets—Creelman, Scovel, Davis, Bryson—who had chronicled and decried the brutality of Spanish dominion in Cuba. The *Herald*'s Stephen Bonsal was probably the most experienced foreign correspondent in America, and the most respected due in part to his occasional assignments as a State Department diplomat. He traveled to Cuba in the early months of 1897 and moved about the island in the company of the Spanish army. Bonsal was a skeptical reporter who made his reputation in part on an exposé of exaggerated Turkish atrocities in Macedonia, yet he was shocked by what he saw in Cuba. Weyler's method of war was "so barbarous, so blood-thirsty, and yet so exquisite, that the human mind refuses to believe it, and revolts at the suggestion that it was conceived, planned, and plotted by a man."[58] After watching several hundred executions of Spanish prisoners in just four days, and seeing first hand the horrors of disease and starvation visited upon the *reconcentrados*, Bonsal accused Spain of following a policy of "depopulation by proclamation" and predicted that Cuba was headed for something "that would not find a parallel in the history of human suffering."[59] That the U.S. was permitting these outrages to occur on its very doorstep, he believed, called into question its character as a nation. Bonsal testified to this effect before the Senate Foreign Relations Committee.

Information pouring into the White House and the State Department throughout 1897 confirmed the very worst of what Bonsal and the yellow press had predicted for and reported from Cuba. Donnell Rockwell had been sent by Fitzhugh Lee in July to investigate the effects of Weyler's reconcentration policy. He visited one "doomed settlement" at Artemisa, where disease and starvation claimed twenty-five to thirty-five victims a day. "The death cart makes its rounds several times daily, and into it the corpses are thrown without ceremony," he wrote with a further description of the mass graves in which victims were interred. "This state of affairs . . . is but a repetition of what is taking place in all the towns of reconcentration on the Island."[60]

Rockwell's colleague Walter B. Barker had written the State Department in July that what was happening in Cuba should no longer be considered war "but extermination of the inhabitants, with destruction of all property." In November, the U.S. Consul in Matanzas reported the following: "As I write . . . a dead negro woman lies in the street, within 200 yards of the consulate, starved to death; died sometime this morning, and will lie there, maybe, for days. The misery and destitution in this city and other towns in the interior are beyond description." Consular staff declared that during the first fifteen days of November, 275 deaths had been registered in Santa Clara, compared to a historic average of seventeen a month.[61] While the State Department kept most of this information to itself, Hearst and Pulitzer reporters were in constant contact with the U.S. legation in Cuba, and well aware of consular appraisals of the situation. These close relations and shared concerns go some way to explaining the willingness of consular officers to assist Hearst's men in a diplomatically indefensible rescue of a non-American citizen from a Cuban jail.

Not trusting the press or his diplomats, William McKinley, in one of his first acts as president, arranged to collect his own information in Cuba. He sent a friend, the former congressman William J. Calhoun, as his personal envoy to the island in the spring of 1897. Calhoun found that all classes of Cubans backed the insurrection, that the armies had fought to a standstill, and that the *reconcentrados* were dying in droves. Touring the depopulated countryside, he noted that "every house had been burned, banana trees cut down, cane fields swept with fire, and everything in the shape of food destroyed. . . . I did not see a house, a man, a woman or child; a horse, mule or cow, not even a dog; I did not see a sign of life, except an occasional vulture." In the reconcentration camps, he observed children with swollen limbs and "extended abdomens that had a dropsical appearance; this I was told, was caused by a want of sufficient food."[62]

Calhoun put the death count at 300,000 and believed that if the Spanish were allowed to fight the war to its conclusion, the island's entire population might be eliminated. His observations were seconded by C.F.

Koop, a Boston tobacco merchant who several months later testified to the Senate Foreign Relations Committee. By the end of 1897, Koop said, 80 percent of the *reconcentrados* in some camps had died. The Spanish policy, to his mind, amounted to genocide. He calculated that 500,000 to 600,000 people had perished in Cuba since the start of the conflict.[63]

Hearst's paper estimated 500,000 casualties in Cuba, and reported that Senator Gallinger, who had visited Cuba at the paper's behest, used the figure of 600,000 in a speech to his colleagues.[64] The *Sun* and the *World* printed comparable numbers while the *Tribune* preferred a toll of 400,000. Other observers who were not in competition with Hearst had arrived at similar counts. In March 1898, writes John Offner, the American minister told the Spanish prime minister that 400,000 had died in Cuba; the Spanish leader did not dispute the figure, since his sources reported a similar loss of life.[65] José Canalejas, a Madrid publisher and respected politician who toured Cuba late in 1897, wrote two extensive reports on the situation for Premier Sagasta. Everyone he encountered on the Spanish side, of whatever political persuasion, agreed "that the war and reconcentration policy [had] led to the death of a third part, at the very least, of the rural population, that is to say, more than 400,000 human beings." Canalejas put the total losses between reconcentration and fighting at 600,000, which represented close to 40 percent of the island's population, with no end in sight.[66]

At the start of 1898, there was a rough consensus in the United States that war, starvation, and disease had claimed at least 400,000 people in Cuba in very short order. More recent studies, working with data extrapolated from the last Spanish census and an American-led survey in 1899, have put the death toll in Cuba at less than 200,000.[67] The new numbers may be unduly conservative (there are serious problems with the data underlying these estimates).* In any event, the precise body

---

*Historians arguing for lower death tolls tend to trust projections based on a combination of Spanish and U.S.-led censuses. The Spanish numbers are unreliable. Fitzhugh Lee noted in *Cuba's Struggle Against Spain* (published in 1899) that "no trustworthy census has been taken" in Cuba for fifty years, a view echoed by the Harvard historian John Fiske in his introduction to Grover Flint's book, and the *Cambridge History of Latin America* (vol. iv). Of equal importance, the U.S.-led censuses of 1899 and 1907 admit to large and inexplicable anomalies. The only other empirical argument for the lower projections is based on reports of Spanish officials in Cuba, which are acknowledged as incomplete. Spanish officers couldn't even be counted on to report their own casualties reliably.

count does not much bear on the legitimacy of Spanish war measures: it is indisputable that Spain forced at least several hundred thousand noncombatants away from their land and their livelihoods into reconcentration camps, where they dropped like flies from disease and lack of food and clean water. The humanitarian case for U.S. action does not vary if 50,000 lives are lost or half a million. No one in American public life was telling McKinley to wait until the death toll reached a big round number before intervention in Cuba was worth the bother.

By the end of 1897, the McKinley administration had clearly signaled that it was coming around to Hearst's point of view. Coincidental to the Cisneros drama, the president had dispatched Stewart Woodford, his newly appointed envoy extraordinary and minister plenipotentiary, across the Atlantic to Spain, to inform Madrid that America was impatient with the "chronic condition of trouble and violent derangement" in Cuba. Woodford was to mention that the fighting had persisted through a period of twenty-nine years, dating from the start of the Ten Years' War, and that the last two years in particular had threatened "mutual destruction" for the warring parties while bringing unexampled devastation to the island. Significant U.S. investment in Cuba had been destroyed, the peace of the American people disturbed, and their sympathies aroused. Woodford was further instructed to admit that McKinley was under pressure from Congress and the American public to recognize the Cuban rebels as belligerents.[68]

The language of Woodford's brief is important. The yellow newspapers are often criticized for demonizing Spain and exaggerating both its sins and the suffering of Cuba, yet the minister was told to speak not only of chronic trouble and violent derangement but "grave disorder and sanguinary conflict," and he was told to chastise Spain for the "unparalleled severity" of its war measures. The administration described these measures as "horrible and unchristian and uncivilized," and "cruel, useless and horrid." Spain was begged to reconsider its methods "for the sake of humanity and civilization." In personal correspondence, Woodford worried that the Spanish were intent on bringing "the peace of a graveyard" to Cuba.[69]

McKinley himself used similar language in his first annual message to Congress on December 6, 1897. Nearly half of the speech was devoted to the Cuban insurrection. The president regretted the "devastation and ruin" of the island and the "horrors of starvation" that had visited the Cuban people and the "horrors and danger to our own peace." Weyler was singled out as the commander "whose brutal orders inflamed the American mind and shocked the civilized world." Reconcentration was described as a policy of "cruel rapine and extermination" that had "shocked the universal sentiment of humanity." The words "shocked," "cruel," "extermination," "ruin," "devastation," and "horrible" were all repeated. At more than a half-dozen points, McKinley charged Spain with violating international standards of civilized conduct. There was no mention of feeding prisoners to the sharks but the administration and the yellow press were now finding harmony.[70]

For all its flaws and melodrama, the Evangelina Cisneros story was an effective allegory of Spanish depredation, Cuban suffering, and American responsibility. The story did not drive the United States to confront Spain as its author, Hearst, had hoped. That decision was several months and three calamities away. It did, however, solidify popular sentiment against Spain and in favor of U.S. involvement. And when Washington finally chose to act, it followed to a remarkable extent Hearst's script, right down to the chivalrous ire. The American people and their government, writes the Pulitzer Prize–winning historian of U.S. foreign policy Walter A. McDougall, would be "swept by a hurricane of militant righteousness into a revolutionary foreign war, determined to slay a dragon and free a damsel in distress."[71]

CHAPTER THIRTEEN

Uncrowned King of an Educated Democracy

The very same Saturday that Evangelina Cisneros and her guard of naval cadets rode into Madison Square to the accompaniment of the Seventh Regiment Band, Charles Anderson Dana, editor of the New York *Sun,* lay dying of cirrhosis of the liver at his home in Glen Cove, Long Island. He was seventy-eight years old and it was the first major illness of his life. At one point in the evening, he slipped into unconsciousness and his doctors gave him up for dead. Some time after midnight, the embers of a brushfire lit earlier in the day by workers on his property were whipped into flames by a north wind. The fire consumed several outbuildings and threatened the main house and Dana's deathbed before it was brought under control around 4 a.m. The great editor did not stir throughout the emergency. He rallied in the morning long enough to murmur farewell to his assembled family and died in the early afternoon, knocking all other news, including Evangelina Cisneros, from the *Journal*'s front page.

Hearst's coverage of Dana's death was full and fair. It included an account of his final days, a review of his long and stormy career (highlighting his transition from youthful radical to archconservative), generous tributes from former colleagues and leading newspapermen, four front-page pictures, and the following editorial:

> A good fighter, he was hard fought; a consistent hater, he did not escape hatred. But those who fought and who criticized and who hated never for a minute questioned his brilliancy of intellect, his mastery of style or his effectiveness in combat.
>
> Charles A. Dana was a brilliant journalist. He was one of the last of the old-time "great editors"—a type which seems passing in journalism.

Perhaps he would be the last man to wish to be spared just, if hostile, criticism after his death, and yet, hard as has been the fight he has waged, it is doubtful whether even his enemies will remember their grievances against him when they reflect how great and vigorous was the intellect which was thus obliterated.[1]

Those were generous words considering what had transpired between the *Journal* and the *Sun* in the previous eight months. Not only had Dana tried to lead a moral revolt against the yellow papers, but in the midst of that campaign he had opened up a second front against Hearst with the aid of a cranky and little-known New York State Republican senator, Timothy E. Ellsworth. A practiced prude, Ellsworth had earlier contributed to the decency crusade by drafting a bill calling for fines and prison terms for anyone involved in the production and distribution of any licentious, indecent, corrupt, or depraved paper.[2] This ridiculous legislative gambit was laughed out of Albany, but Ellsworth returned with a better-focused effort to outlaw the publication of illustrated portraits, caricatures, and cartoons of identifiable persons without their prior consent. His so-called Anti-Cartoon Bill did not explicitly target Hearst, but no other paper used caricature as frequently and as effectively as the *Journal*. New York's most powerful Republican, Thomas Platt, whose own mug was routinely abused in the *Journal*, lent Ellsworth his support, and the Anti-Cartoon Bill passed the state Senate. Dana, who had been depicted by Davenport as a pint-sized prizefighter pummeling straw anarchists in the *Journal*'s election coverage, took up the cause from Park Row:

> No one can now be summoned into public view without the certainty of having not merely his portrait flaunted to the rabble, but of having the same subjected to every conceivable distortion and deformity. . . . If there ever was an evil that called for whole restraint by law, it is surely this.[3]

There was a touch of hypocrisy in Dana's position. He attacked public figures with relentless brutality, and while he seldom used cartoons, his prose was so evocative he hardly needed them: his jeremiad against Hearst's paper—"the procuress corrupting her sex is not more an enemy to society than the 'new journalism'"—was as vivid as anything Homer

Davenport might produce. Despite Dana's support, most editorialists and legislators dismissed Ellsworth's initiative as a gross attack on press freedoms, and it died in the lower house without coming to a vote.

However bitter these final quarrels, Hearst was right to give Dana a generous send-off. He owed more to the *Sun*'s editor than either party would have admitted. Dana's hatred of the yellow press, his high literary style, and his conservative visual tastes obscure the degree to which Hearst and Pulitzer benefited from his example. Dana taught them how to mix human-interest journalism, sharp rhetoric, and Democratic politics for a mass audience, and he trained many of the men crowding their executive suites. In fact, the biggest talent to leave the Dome for Hearst's employ in 1897 owed his start not to Pulitzer but to Dana. Arthur Brisbane was the third of three great editorial talents to abandon Pulitzer in a span of eighteen months, following Morrill Goddard and S.S. Carvalho out the door.

BRISBANE WAS A YEAR YOUNGER than Hearst, yet he had several more years' experience in journalism. He had been a teenager when his father, Albert, had arranged for him to meet Charles Dana, then at the peak of his success with the New York *Sun*. It was not just anyone who could walk in off the street and get his son an appointment with Dana: Albert Brisbane was a wealthy American socialist who had helped finance several Utopian communities in the United States, including Brook Farm, Dana's alma mater. Not content with proselytizing his radical social ideals, the elder Brisbane had also practiced them at home. Young Arthur and his brother were raised as close as possible to the state of nature on a farm in New Jersey. They spent their days running wild, forbidden all contact with clergy, teachers, doctors, barbers, or books. Eventually Mrs. Brisbane intervened and Arthur was sent to boarding schools in Paris and Stuttgart, where he received a solid education at safe distance from the corrupting influences of American materialism. He returned to the United States intending to study at Harvard, but his visit to the *Sun* changed his plans.[4]

Dana had a sixth sense for newspaper talent and he favored erudition: "I had rather take a young fellow who knows the 'Ajax' of Sophocles, and has read Tacitus, and can scan every ode of Horace—I would rather take him to report a prize fight or a spelling match, for instance, than to take one who has never had those advantages."[5] The nineteen-year-old Brisbane knew not only his classics but French and German literature besides. That he was a stranger to New York and had only a loose grasp of written English did not bother Dana—the young man was dazzling in every other regard. He stood just under six feet tall, with the broad shoulders and slim hips of a boxer. His tall forehead, keen blue eyes, aquiline nose, and strong chin made for a handsome, intelligent face under soft curls of fair hair. His manners were a tad artificial but nonetheless exquisite. He was bright, witty, brimming with confidence, and instantly likable. Dana hired him as a reporter on the *Evening Sun* at $15 a week.

Brisbane's early copy was awkward, largely because he wrote in French and used a pocket dictionary to translate into English. But as he grew comfortable with his mother tongue, he displayed an ear for idiom and the ability to write with both speed and clarity. He also became a hit with his fellow *Sun* reporters, who considered themselves the elite of Park Row. They had initially dismissed him on account of his manners and foppish wardrobe, but when they raced from the office to Mouquin's bistro on Fulton, Brisbane never lost and he was the only one among them who had sparred with Gentleman Jim Corbett. After eighteen months on the job, Brisbane was as diligent, popular, and valuable as any reporter on staff. When he announced he was quitting the *Sun* to join his father in England, Dana appointed him the *Sun*'s London correspondent rather than lose him.

Brisbane rented an excellent suite at the Victoria Hotel, freshened his wardrobe—hats from Lock's, shoes from Lobb's, socks specially designed with a stall for each toe—and announced the formation of the Albert and Arthur Brisbane News Service. He presented himself as a grand journalistic ambassador rather than a simple hack, and people took him at his own estimation. He was invited to the better parties and introduced to leading political figures, becoming intimate with the Gladstone family. He followed Jack the Ripper's trail through the slums of Whitechapel and traveled to the mainland to interview Pope Leo XIII. His most famous piece from this period was a ringside account of the John L. Sullivan–Charlie Mitchell fight at Chantilly in 1888. Brisbane quoted Mitchell's corner man pleading with him between rounds: "Think of the kids, Charlie. The dear little kids a callin' for you at home and a countin' on you for bread. Think of what their feelings will be if you don't knock the ear off him. . . ."[6]

When Brisbane returned to New York to serve as managing editor of the *Evening Sun*, an enormous responsibility for a man of twenty-four years, one of his first acts was to hire a young Richard Harding Davis. They became pals, a pair of dashing, athletic dandies who never missed a first night, spent afternoons at the track and weekends in the country, and still found time to exercise their prodigious journalistic talents. Although a half year older, Davis was Brisbane's protégé. As Arthur Lubow notes, Brisbane was a flesh-and-blood exemplar of the European manners and pretensions Davis knew only from literature and the stage. He would show up for dinner wearing "a pink evening coat, white waistcoat and . . . a white tie, somewhat sketchily arranged."[7] He was fond of grand gestures, never sending a bouquet when a crate of roses would do. "It is no wonder he is popular," Davis wrote of Brisbane. "He is a most remarkable young man."[8]

Joseph Pulitzer thought so too. He purchased the *World* around the time Brisbane started at the *Evening Sun*. In 1890, he outbid Dana for the young editor's services. Brisbane began at the *World* as a feature correspondent, covering among other events the first electrocution at Sing Sing prison, an event that turned his face a greenish white and left him shaking and sick. A more momentous assignment was the 1892 strike at Homestead, Pennsylvania, in which thousands of men, women, and children supporting the Amalgamated Association of Iron and Steel Workers engaged in low-grade combat with several hundred well-armed Pinkerton agents hired by the Carnegie Steel Company. It was one of the bloodiest episodes in American labor history and while the majority of Park Row dailies sided with Carnegie, the *World* backed the strikers, with Brisbane doing much of the reporting. His support was sincere. As Charles Edward Russell remembered, "We were a couple of radicals in those days and after the paper had gone to press, we would sit and talk for hours and hours on sociological matters. Brisbane at that time was at least as radical as I was. I heard him say on many occasions that he was more than willing to sacrifice himself for the cause of the common people. In fact, he declared himself willing to go to jail for them."[9]

Pulitzer, for his part, was not about to let Brisbane sacrifice himself to any cause but his employer. Growing fond of the young man, he adopted him as a traveling companion, taking him to Europe in the winter of 1893–94. Pulitzer wasn't the best company. His jangled nerves were once

again ruining his temper; he slept fitfully and ate heavily. Brisbane, something of a fitness nut, encouraged him to cut his food intake by half and
to take regular exercise. He got him on horseback, much to Mrs.
Pulitzer's amazement, and in time Pulitzer's health showed modest
improvement. Alone among *World* employees, Brisbane did not fear his
boss. He addressed him with mild impudence as "Uncle Joe," bore his ill
humors with equanimity, and took advantage of his blindness to rob him
at poker (a mischief Brisbane cheerfully confessed). Pulitzer offered him
the position of personal secretary but Brisbane turned it down, eager to
return to full-time journalism.

Brisbane had served Pulitzer for five years when Goddard and the
entire staff quit to join Hearst. Summoning what one colleague called his
"absolutely unassailable courage," Brisbane volunteered to assemble a
team and rebuild the Sunday edition.[10] To everyone's astonishment, circulation neither collapsed nor lagged but actually climbed. Brisbane's Easter
edition sold a whopping 600,000 copies. His Christmas special hit 623,000,
matching Goddard's Sunday *Journal* for wonder and excitement.[11]

Pulitzer was grateful for Brisbane's Sunday miracle for a few short
months until the conservative papers took up their decency crusade at the
end of 1896 and Pulitzer began looking for someone to blame. It was difficult to locate the sinners. To read the *Sun* and the *Press*, recalled Don
Seitz, one would think the *World* was staffed "by a combination of ghouls
and perverts," when in fact "at no time in its history had the paper been
so respectably manned."[12] Almost everyone on staff had been hired from
the *Sun* or the *Herald*, and quite a number were college-educated, or the
sons of clergymen or upstanding families. Eventually, Pulitzer put the
finger on Brisbane, not without some help.

One of Brisbane's internal rivals in Pulitzer's employ was E.O.
Chamberlin, another former *Sun* employee, whose news sense, according
to Russell, was that of a "dull, sane, Christian gentleman, solely desiring
to impart information."[13] He implicated Brisbane to Pulitzer and recommended his stodgy self as the solution to the paper's injured reputation.
Pulitzer made Chamberlin editorial manager in charge of everything.
No shrinking violet, Brisbane demanded to see the boss, but could not get
a meeting. On learning that Pulitzer was headed to Jekyll Island in his
private rail car, he bought a ticket on the same train and tried to barge
into Pulitzer's compartment, but his boss caught wind of his presence and

installed a guard outside the door. Brisbane remained on the train and finally gained a hearing at Jekyll Island. He could do nothing, however, to assuage Pulitzer's panic or to reverse his decision. Chamberlin remained in charge for three months until wobbly circulation numbers forced Pulitzer to reconsider his priorities and Brisbane was restored.

Indeed, by late May of 1897, Pulitzer, in yet another shuffle, appointed Brisbane to work his circulation magic at the *Evening World*.[14] Brisbane toiled around the clock and literally lived under the Dome—he converted a small square office space on the seventh floor into an apartment. Overlooking Park Row, the room contained a bed, a screen, a washstand, a chiffonier, and a small table and chairs; it was decorated with copper kettles and an array of French paintings. He was a committed *World* man. When Russell was offered a position at the *Journal*, Brisbane did his best to change his mind, keeping him up all night with his arguments. "Brisbane was eloquent and logical," recalled Russell, "and had me almost convinced that I had made a mistake."[15] With the sky turning red in the east, Brisbane made a final appeal to phrenology, insisting that Hearst could not win the newspaper war because Pulitzer had the better-shaped head, indicating superior intellectual endowments. Russell resigned from the *World* regardless. He was shocked, two months later, when Brisbane followed him to the *Journal*.

The conventional story is that Brisbane left Pulitzer over a byline dispute. It had long been Brisbane's ambition to write a column on the front page of either the morning or the evening edition of the *World* under his own name, independent of the newspaper's standing editorial policy. Pulitzer would not have it. There was only one editorial voice at the morning and evening *World*s, he insisted: "[These] newspapers belong to me and so long as I live, no one will express an independent editorial opinion in my newspapers."[16] Unhappy with that answer, Brisbane waited until Pulitzer was out of town and produced a first-person column that ran on the front page of the evening paper for several weeks. He thought it was working well and expected Pulitzer to wire him congratulations. Instead, he received an angry rebuke. Shortly thereafter, the story goes, Brisbane accepted Hearst's offer of a fat paycheck to edit the *Evening Journal*. That is hardly the only account of his defection, however.

Russell maintains that Brisbane left the *World* to pursue his dream of a more radical paper than could be realized in Pulitzer's shadow, and yet another story has Brisbane leaving after a quarrel over money. Pulitzer sometimes worried about the high salaries he paid. "It oughtn't to cost very much to get socialist editorials written," he would complain. And Brisbane would fire back: "It would cost a good deal to get them well written by a man who believes in them."[17] In a bout of cost consciousness in the summer of 1897, Pulitzer reportedly slashed Brisbane's bonus, precipitating his departure. Hearst himself, in an unpublished interview about Brisbane, endorsed this version of events:

> [Mr. Pulitzer] deducted the bonus . . . and that irritated Mr. Brisbane very much, and he left the *World* and he . . . came in to see me and I said I would like to have him with us, and told him to talk terms with Mr. Palmer our business manager, and Mr. Palmer engaged him for $10,000 a year. Now he had been getting $15,000 on the *World*, with the bonus in addition, and Mr. Palmer told me that he had made a very good business deal with Mr. Brisbane.
>
> I said, I didn't think it was a good business deal—it was a good deal—but not a good business deal [and] that Mr. Brisbane ought to have more money, and ought to have something to look forward to in the way of appreciation. So I made an arrangement, a circulation arrangement with him, lasting over a definite period.[18]

A schoolteacher named Anne Brown whom Brisbane was dating at the time also saw pecuniary interests behind his move. She disliked Hearst and his newspapers. She wanted Brisbane to strike out on his own and was crushed when he signed at the *Journal*. "I wouldn't dine with him or go out with him—didn't see him," she says. "I said he could have his choice, the Hearst paper or me, and he chose Hearst. . . . I didn't see him anymore."[19]

Brisbane may also have moved out of concern for his professional status. He had begun his journalism career at the top Democratic newspaper in New York; he moved from the *Sun* to the *World* when Pulitzer surpassed Dana; he now jumped again as the trades proclaimed Hearst to be trouncing Pulitzer. The *Journalist* had begun a running tally of the *Journal* news beats at the *World*'s expense: "That great paper which the genius of Pulitzer built up from the condition of a corpse on the dissecting table to the liveliest sheet in New York, if not in the United States, is scooped every day of its existence."[20]

Days before Brisbane announced his move, the *Journalist* marked the first anniversary of Hearst's evening paper by complimenting Richard Farrelly and S.S. Carvalho on its remarkable progress: "Its circulation is soaring upwards, like a crazy kite."[21] *The Fourth Estate* applauded its "vast popularity," "distinct individuality," daily scoops, and abundant advertising.[22] With Hearst making his charge in the afternoon market, Brisbane had to be worried about his own reputation and the standing of the *Evening World*. He had unshakable confidence in his own abilities, but Pulitzer's bouts of economizing, attacks of respectability, and erratic management style put Brisbane at a competitive disadvantage against the *Evening Journal*. If he stayed, he was facing an imminent eclipse.

The zaniest story of Brisbane's defection comes from the journalist Boyden Sparkes. In the course of researching an unpublished biography of Brisbane, Sparkes interviewed three sources, each of whom claimed to be the only person who knew the real reason Brisbane left the *World*. All of them maintained that he departed after fathering one of Mrs. Pulitzer's sons, presumably Herbert, born shortly before these events. Sparkes tried this theory on Russell, who was dubious and told him, "You'd better erase all of that."[23]

In the end, there were likely several motives for Brisbane's decision: he wanted a greater role in the direction of whatever paper he was working on; he was frustrated by his low profile at the *World;* he was losing competitive ground to the *Evening Journal;* his relationship with his proprietor was shaky; and, the last straw, an ungrateful Pulitzer was stingy about remuneration. But Brisbane was not "bought" by Hearst. In fact, he took a pay cut to leave and he had to talk his way into the *Journal,* presenting himself as a bargain. As one colleague noted, there was "some extraordinary hurt in Brisbane's mind" when he finally jumped ship.[24] Like Carvalho and Goddard before him, Brisbane was driven into the arms of Hearst. It was a colossal blunder by Pulitzer. He cared less for his raffish evening product than he did for his more prestigious morning edition, but the evening market was increasingly popular with advertisers, and the *World* was the strongest entry in the field. It was a bad time to be shaking up a moneymaker and making Hearst stronger. The *Evening Journal* had been competently staffed with Farrelly and Carvalho but now, thanks to Pulitzer's mishandling of a key employee, it was in the hands of the brilliant Brisbane.

Perhaps thinking the loss of Brisbane, Russell and others would rattle Pulitzer, Hearst chose that moment to propose a settlement: the *Journal* would raise its cover price to two cents if the *World* would follow suit and also endorse the *Evening Journal*'s application for an Associated Press franchise. Preliminary discussions were held not involving either principal, but Pulitzer, taking Hearst's move as a sign of weakness, insisted that the *Journal* rise to two cents on its own. The talks went nowhere.

THE *Evening Journal* WAS A BUSTLING SHOESTRING OPERATION published from ramshackle quarters on the second floor of the Tribune Building. The room had bare floors, unpainted board walls, and mountains of paper on every flat surface. Brisbane worked at a desk on an elevated platform protected by wire netting. "It made an incongruous background," said the journalist Dorothy Dix, "for the man who sat in the midst of the confusion—handsome and young and with still something of his gardenia and silk-hat days when he was the pet of London society and the boy wonder of the newspaper world about him."[25]

One of the first things his new colleagues learned about Brisbane was that he spoke at the same pace he worked. "He'd talk so fast," said the artist T.E. Powers, "get about four, five ideas mixed up in one, and he'd confuse you if you didn't get to know him."[26] Already renowned as a tireless worker, Brisbane found another gear at the *Evening Journal*. He started work at 4:30 a.m., roughly four hours earlier than was customary for afternoon editions, in order to get his paper on the street well before lunchtime, and far ahead of the competition. When the news was hot, he would publish in the immediate wake of the last editions of the morning dailies—as early as 8 a.m.

Brisbane favored large illustrations and streamers—oversized headlines across several columns, if not the whole of the front page. He'd watched how newsboys flashed papers in the street, and he wanted pedestrians to be able to take in his top news at a glance. Hearst recalled him once writing a headline that pretty near filled the front page: "I said, 'Now I think that is going a little strong. We had better modify these headlines, we will precipitate some criticism.' And then the *World* came out with headlines just about as big, and Artie and I arranged to put those big headlines back into the paper again."[27]

Brisbane's paper kept its stories short and its vocabulary simple.

"There's no need ever to use a word of more than three syllables in a newspaper," he would lecture reporters. "Remember that a newspaper is mostly read by very busy people, or by very tired people, or by very uneducated people none of whom are going to hunt up a dictionary to find out what you mean. And never forget that if you don't hit a newspaper reader between the eyes with your first sentence, there is no need of writing a second one."[28] Brisbane believed it was important for young men to cultivate their minds by reading widely and deeply, yet at the same time he encouraged them to protect their superficiality. He had seen too many journalists reach their thirties and become "too seriously interested in something" and thereby grow "heavy and monotonous."[29]

Surprisingly, the *Evening Journal* became known for its editorials during Brisbane's tenure. Brisbane avoided public policy and insider politics, the staples of most editorial pages, his notion being to chase readership and let the nation take care of its own business. This approach suited Hearst, who always suspected that readers avoided editorials because of editorial writers' stilted prose. Even a good journalist, he complained,

> if you tell him to write an editorial, will immediately stiffen up and become self-conscious and write something that nobody will read. Well, Brisbane had the faculty of writing editorials that people would read. In the first place, he wrote on subjects that people were interested in, not eternally on politics. The average editorial writer almost confines himself to politics and economics; very seldom does he discuss any of the human problems that people have to meet continually in their journey through life. But Brisbane wrote about those human problems, and some of them seem almost trivial, like what kind of hats a girl should wear . . . but he made it interesting to them, and after all, the girls are thinking about what kind of hats they shall wear. And I speedily found that his editorial columns weren't like other people's editorial columns. His were read.[30]

Like Morrill Goddard, Brisbane wrote a treatise on the interests of newspaper readers, and attempted to codify the primary elements of human-interest journalism, but it is not as illuminating or comprehensive as Goddard's effort. Perhaps the best summary of Brisbane's approach to journalism comes from his colleague, Russell:

His theory of it was this. You can't get people's attention without shouting at them. We shout at them in order to make them think. The most valuable function that any man can perform in this world is to cause people to think . . . . We use the big headline and the editorial and the picture to attract people's attention, get hold of their minds, then when we have gotten hold of their minds we stimulate them to think . . ."[31]

Years later, Russell would wonder how much thinking ever got done amid all the shouting, but he believed Brisbane to have been sincere in his intentions and infallible in his "extraordinary intuition" about the sympathies of the common man. "I never knew him to make a mistake in that respect," said Russell. "I have seen him handle hundreds, literally hundreds of stories that came up and give out instructions as to how they should be handled, treated and so forth. I never knew him to make a slip on any of them. . . . He would have what would be the popular response of everything that came up. . . . [H]e was able to put himself right in the position of the average man, how the average man would feel about the whole thing, how it would seem to them."[32]

Brisbane's *Evening Journal* certainly had appeal. He claims to have told his secretary, a gentleman named Flynn, that his ambition was to catch the circulation of the *Evening World* within seven years. He swore off all drink but milk and tea until he reached his target. It took him seven weeks. His exact sales can't be determined, but Hearst confirmed that circulation skyrocketed under Brisbane's leadership. He would collect about $50,000 in bonus payments before he and Hearst agreed to replace the commission schedule with a larger flat salary. By that time he was the highest-paid editor in the history of journalism, and it would be decades before anyone caught up to him.

To make his change of newspaper allegiance complete, Brisbane took up residence in the shanty. Hearst would drag himself home at 4 a.m. after seeing the morning edition to press and find Brisbane rising to start his day. "We lived together pretty much without seeing much of each other," said Hearst. "Because we divided the work and I worked on the morning paper most of the time and he worked on the evening paper. . . . [Brisbane] got up that early and I worked late and I frequently got home about five o'clock and I had my supper with him when he was having his breakfast."[33]

The roommates developed some peculiar ways of enjoying one another's company. In the morning, they would take off their shoes and socks, drop all of their pocket change on the floor, and race to pick up the coins using only their feet. Each man kept what he retrieved. Hearst was nimble but Brisbane had unusually prehensile toes and claimed the lion's share of the cash.

That was about as exciting as it got at the shanty unless Jack Follansbee happened to be in town. A female acquaintance once asked Brisbane about reports of raucous gatherings at his home address. Brisbane insisted that neither he nor Hearst entertained or drank—they were too busy at their respective papers. The woman was skeptical so Brisbane offered to march her over to Lexington for an immediate tour of his tranquil home. She accepted. They climbed the shanty's stairs to find the tall, handsome Follansbee in mid-bash with a crowd of well-refreshed friends. It was to such moments that Follansbee owed a controversial position in Hearst's circle. A friend of the family, Clara Anthony, wrote Phoebe to say she would like to see Follansbee, for one, "break his ugly neck, and every other fawning sycophant that exploits Will follow suit."[34]

Hearst and Brisbane were on their way to becoming lasting friends as well as colleagues, a relationship based on mutual respect for each other as newspapermen. "At the time I took the job," Brisbane remarked, "I thought Hearst didn't know much about the newspaper business. I was wrong."[35] Hearst valued Brisbane's companionship as well as his abilities: "He had a great charm. He was very interesting, not only to men, but to women . . . they loved to hear him talk—like Bernard Shaw in that respect."[36]

Hearst himself liked to hear Brisbane talk. Lincoln Steffens dined with the pair and Brisbane, as per usual, carried the conversation. Hearst spoke well when he felt the need, but he did not feel it often. "He does not want to win you," said Steffens. Brisbane was so much more voluble and assertive than Hearst that many guessed he was actually the brains behind the *Journal*. He sometimes received stock tips on the assumption that he was in charge.[37]

Hearst's relationship with Brisbane was typical of his male friendships. He was not close to any other publishers, nor to other men in public life, nor to any of his old college chums who did not work in journalism, except for Follansbee, who was away most of the year at the Babicora. Almost all of Hearst's friends were on his payroll—Brisbane would stay there for life—and their relationships were more collegial than intimate. Whether out of insecurity, or a simple preference born of his upbringing in a largely female world, Hearst preferred to confide in women, particularly his mother and his girlfriends. He rarely revealed his inner life to men and, in truth, he was a bit lost in any male society outside of his newsrooms. It took gregarious and self-assured individuals like Brisbane, Follansbee, and George Pancoast to conquer his reticence and become his friends, and Hearst was happy to let them serve as his front-men outside the office. At the same time, there was never any doubt among them as to who was in charge: they all lived in Hearst's house, attended shows he wanted to see, ate in his favorite restaurants, and vacationed where he wanted to travel, on his schedule. Someone had to lead and, however quiet his demeanor, Hearst understood himself as a great man on a great mission, somewhat beyond his peers and worthy of having friends and followers in subordinate positions. This made for sadly limited friendships but Hearst showed Brisbane and other select staffers unusual degrees of support, trust, loyalty, and freedom in their work, and they were all in it for the work.

Happy as he was with Hearst, Brisbane remained on good terms with his former employers. He dined occasionally on Pulitzer's yacht; they would tease one another over the circumstances of their parting, Brisbane insisting that he had jumped for less money, Uncle Joe answering with a snort. Brisbane would also speak warmly of Dana. Even after the *Sun*'s ferocious attacks on the yellow press, Brisbane described Dana in a trade journal as an avuncular codger with unsurpassed accomplishments and a taste for lemon meringue pie and watered whiskey. If journalism were a religion, Brisbane declared, "Dana would be the pope."[38]

It is one of the perversities of the "pope's" career that he wound up in opposition to so much of his own legacy, his politics hardening and his style dating as protégés like Brisbane filled the despised yellow journals with flash and progressivism. Nowhere was the debt of succeeding generations more evident that in the realm of newspaper crusades. The first purpose of a journalist, Dana liked to advise young newspapermen, was to "tell the truth and shame the devil."[39] The yellow editors had taken that mission to heart and developed it well beyond his original intentions. Whereas a young Dana had sympathized with the working classes and demanded that political and business elites play fair with the common man, his successors held out for a fundamental rebalancing of American politics in favor of the many at the expense of the privileged few. They expanded the investigative function of newspapers, sending out waves of reporters to expose social injustice and corruption in high places. It was no longer sufficient to deplore social and political problems from the sidelines; the new editors actively investigated injustices and promoted solutions, sometimes even taking matters into their own hands. When trouble hit town—a snowstorm, for instance, or a large fire—editors not only sent teams of reporters into the streets but gathered food and blankets for the relief of victims. Pulitzer was the first master of these techniques in New York. He raised funds to build a base for the Statue of Liberty and sponsored Nellie Bly's undercover exposés of official corruption and abuse, and helped to convince the Treasury to sell a billion-dollar bond issue directly to the people rather than through the sticky hands of J.P. Morgan & Co. (the *World* canvassed bankers across the country to prove there was popular demand for the notes at prices far better than what Morgan would pay).

Hardly a month went by without the *World*'s seizing the popular mind with one community-minded initiative or another. Pulitzer grasped more keenly than any editor before him how crusades, campaigns, investigations, and purposeful stunts could serve his business plan. They generated goodwill among the readers and enhanced a paper's prestige and authority, leading to improved circulation and advertising revenue. This commercial motive does not mean Pulitzer was insincere in combating social ills (although his enthusiasm did wane as his wealth and respectability climbed). He believed in what he was doing and saw his commercial success as confirmation of his paper's good character.

Hearst's ambitions as a crusader rose in stages. In San Francisco, he practiced a noisy, combative style of community leadership modeled primarily on Pulitzer's. In New York, he picked up his pace. Elizabeth Schauer, the young woman arrested for soliciting in a citywide crackdown on prostitution, was the first cause he championed in New York, with the *Journal* not only investigating and pleading her case but helping to pay her legal bills. Hearst collected blankets for the poor during a winter storm, raised money for the family of a slain New York policeman, and organized a strike fund for 24,000 New York tailors who walked off the job in protest of low wages in the garment industry. By the end of his first year, the *Journal* had supplanted the *World* as the most flamboyant activist on Park Row.

At the start of his second year, Hearst launched what came to be known as the "gas gift" campaign. On December 11, 1896, the *Journal* hired a lawyer and sought an injunction against New York Mayor William L. Strong and the Board of Aldermen, who were preparing to hand a new gas franchise to cronies. The deal would have paid the franchisees as much as $10 million to build miles of gas mains, needed or not. Hearst went to court as a citizen and taxpayer claiming the award was illegal and fraudulent—"a $10,000,000 steal."[40] Within three days of his intervention, the franchise was quietly withdrawn. The *Journal* celebrated with a page-one banner : "While Others Talk the *Journal* Acts." That headline was immediately adopted as a slogan for the paper and the basis for Hearst's own declaration of a "new journalism," a journalism that "does things" while old journalism "stands around and objects." As an editorial explained, "The *Journal* has adopted the policy of action deliberately and it means to stick to it. It thinks that it has discovered exactly the engine of which the dwellers in American cities stand in need. . . . It showed how the multitudes that are individually helpless against the rapacity of the few could be armed against their despoilers. With an advocate of the People to keep a vigilant eye on the proceedings of public servants and bring them into court when they prove unfaithful, our judges will have a chance to show that they are ready to render justice to all comers . . ."[41]

By the end of Hearst's second year, the *Journal*'s "policy of action" had become an integral part of its identity, and reporting on its own initiatives and successes was one of the paper's most regular activities. The *Journal* made its own front page virtually every day through the fall of 1897: in the week before announcing that it had sprung Evangelina Cisneros from prison, the paper railed against corruption in New York's Commissioner of Public Works, reported on a grand jury investigation into unfair taxation that the *Journal* had urged on behalf of organized labor, and took credit (on weak grounds) for a New York State investigation into irregularities in the insurance industry.

Not everyone endorsed the *Journal*'s new trajectory. There were critics inside and outside of publishing who believed that editors belonged on the sidelines, observing and commenting; they wondered what all this activism had to do with journalism. Boss Croker was among those who thought the *Journal* was overstepping its bounds. He had come under attack by Hearst for stacking a local Democratic slate with Tammany

lackeys. Through an intermediary, Croker objected to the *Journal*'s interference and sneered at what he viewed as an attempt at "government by
newspaper." The paper responded with a front-page Homer Davenport
cartoon, probably suggested by Hearst himself. It was a precise rendering
of Emmanuel Frémiet's famous sculpture *Gorilla Carrying Off a Woman*,
the inspiration for King Kong, among other twentieth-century bestial
fantasies. Davenport simply added labels to Frémiet's original: the gorilla
was "Bossism," the woman was "Democracy," and the chivalric arrow in
the gorilla's back was the "Journal." A caption read "The Press to the
Rescue! 'Government by Newspapers vs. Boss Rule.'"[42]

The cartoon was a cartoon and not a statement of editorial policy but
Hearst's paper had emerged as a remarkable political and social force, and
this was even before the revelation of the *Journal*'s most audacious
exploit—the rescue of a pretty Cuban girl from a foreign jail. When the
full Cisneros story came to light, the paper presented it as the culmination
of its policy of action and used the occasion for its most fulsome and triumphant declaration of a new journalism. The "journalism of action,"
operating in the service of humanity, represented "the final stage in the
evolution of the modern newspaper." The new daily did not wait for
things to turn up: "It turns them up." The *Journal* ran through a long list of
notable deeds—from its exposure of safety issues at railway crossings to its
cracking of the Guldensuppe case—before reaching a ringing conclusion:
"These are a few of the public services by which the *Journal* has illustrated
its theory that a newspaper's duty is not confined to exhortation, but that
when things are going wrong it should itself set them right if possible. The
brilliant exemplification of this theory in the rescue of Miss Cisneros has
finally commended it to the approval of almost the entire reading world."[43]

The notes Hearst was hitting in his campaigns had all been played
before by other newspapers. Advocacy and activism are as old as journalism itself, and the *Journal*'s crusades were not intrinsically different from
what had passed before or from what was being published simultaneously
in competing papers. The *Journal* was not the first newspaper to solve a
big crime: the *World* had proved the identity of the madman who blew
himself up in an attempt to bomb New York businessman Russell Sage. It
was not the first daily to undertake an audacious international adventure:
the *Herald*'s mission to Africa in search of Livingstone remained an
exploit with out equal. Even the *Journal*'s promotion of its enterprise was

unoriginal; all of the New York papers (including the stodgy *Evening Post*) were in the habit of publishing scads of congratulatory letters and telegraphs to celebrate their journalistic feats. Still, the music Hearst shook from these old notes sounded fresh to many ears.

The difference was primarily rhythmic. Hearst hammered away frenetically, day after day, week after week, at privately held trusts in ice, water, gas, sugar, rubber, coal, and railways, among other commodities and services. He accused the corporate combines and monopolies of foisting high prices on consumers, rallied opposition to them, attacked their supporters on the New York Board of Alderman and in the Republican administration at Albany, suggested legislative remedies, and occasionally resorted to the courts to press his point. Clarence Shearn, the lawyer who drew up Hearst's application for an injunction on the gas-grab story, was put on retainer by the *Journal* to find new ways to challenge corporate trusts and municipal boodlers through the courts. Hearst hired Edward W. Bemis, an economist and a leading progressive reformer who had been expelled from the University of Chicago for his radical views, to write and advise the *Journal* on the municipal ownership of public utilities.[44]

All of Hearst's activism operated at a similar pace. He not only ran an unofficial Democratic campaign on behalf of Bryan in 1896 but got up to his teeth in every local and state campaign as well. When a trade publication undertook a survey of acts of charity by Park Row papers, it was able to find two or three examples for all the dailies except Dana's; it didn't attempt to list the *Journal*'s activities, citing them as too numerous to mention and too familiar to require it. As an activist and community servant, Hearst was operating with a vigor, scope, and conviction unprecedented in American newspapers.[45]

AMID THE FLOOD OF CONGRATULATORY MESSAGES published in the *Journal* in the wake of the Cisneros rescue was one from distant lands: "As a journalist of the Old World I hail with pride and joy this splendid deed of knight-errantry. . . . No more worthy use can be made of the sceptre of modern journalism than this, to revive the traditions of the age of chivalry by delivery of the captive and bidding the oppressed to go free."[46]

That message was from William Thomas Stead, now best remembered for having gone down with the *Titanic*. After the ship hit its iceberg, he reportedly helped women and children into lifeboats before returning to the first-class smoking room, where he was last seen in a comfortable leather chair with a book in hand. Born in Northumberland in 1849, the son of a Congregational minister, Stead ran the *Pall Mall Gazette* through the 1880s and made himself the most famous editor in England. He specialized in anti-establishment politics and energetic crusades for social justice. He riveted London in 1885 with a series of articles on child prostitution, in the course of which, to demonstrate the extent of the problem, he arranged the "purchase" of the thirteen-year-old daughter of a London chimney sweep. The stunt landed Stead in jail, but it also speeded changes to the criminal law.

In 1890, Stead founded the *Review of Reviews,* a popular monthly based in London but with editions on both sides of the Atlantic. He also began churning out provocative books on peace movements and social reform, causing a sensation in the United States in 1894 with an early entry in the muckraking genre, an exposé of municipal corruption entitled *If Christ Came to Chicago.* It is said to have sold 70,000 copies on its first day of publication. Three years later, Stead probed the filthy underbelly of New York in *Satan's Invisible World Displayed.* A chapter of the latter was devoted to "the natural and inevitable emergence of the journalist as the ultimate depository of power in modern democracy."[47]

Stead ranked with Dana as the world's leading evangelist of newspapers, agreeing with the pope on their miraculous capacities and high public purpose. Stead went a step further, however, and wondered why newspapers should not begin to assume some of the functions of government. He dismissed contemporary politics as a hackneyed circus of partisan exhibitionism that contributed little to human progress. Politicians had left a vacuum in public governance, he argued, that editors were best suited to fill. Stead claimed that newspapers had already adopted many of the deliberative functions formerly monopolized by legislatures:

> The very conception of journalism as an instrument of government is foreign to the mind of most journalists. . . . [Yet in] a democratic age, in the midst of a population which is able to read, no position is comparable for permanent influence and far-reaching power to that of an editor who understands his vocation. In him are vested almost all the attributes of real sovereignty. He has almost exclusive rights of initiative; he retains a permanent

Homer Davenport drew "Dollar" Mark Hanna in a suit of plutocratic plaid.

William McKinley campaigning from his porch in Canton, Ohio.

William Jennings Bryan, the most dashing candidate anyone had ever seen.

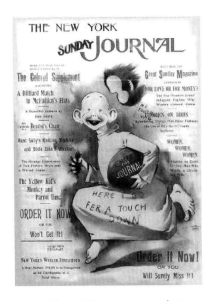

The Yellow Kid, an uppity ethnic urchin.

Election returns light up the Pulitzer building.

Little Egypt danced in "ze altogether."

Stephen Crane looking a little too distinguished.

NEW YORK JOURNAL
AND ADVERTISER.

Copyright 1897, by W. R. Hearst—NEW YORK, SATURDAY, OCTOBER 9, 1897.—16 PAGES.

EVANGELINA CISNEROS ON HER WAY TO THE UNITED STATES.

Señorita Evangelina Cosio y Cisneros.

Despite Weyler's Spies, the Guards in the Streets and the Cordon About the City, Her Friends Brought Her Safely Out of Havana.

"The Butcher," Valeriano Weyler y Nicolau, and the woman (left) rescued by the *Journal* from her prision.

Hearst's outrage at Spanish misrule in Cuba was not unfounded.

The wreck of the *Maine*.

The *Journal*
offers a reward.

NEW YORK JOURNAL

DAVIS AND REMINGTON TELL OF SPANISH CRUELTY.

The Pen of the Gifted
Writer and the Pencil
of the Brilliant Art-
ist Describe How
a Brave Cuban
Met Death.

Moonlight Execution of Young Rodriguez.

Frederic Remington
provided one of the
Journal's most dramatic
front pages (left), and its
single most controversial
story illustration
(below left).

SPANIARDS SEARCH WOMEN ON AMERICAN STEAMERS.

Frederic Remington.

Cuban and American flags, and headline bulletins outside the *Journal* and *Tribune* offices.

W.R. on deck, off the coast of Cuba, covering the Spanish-American War.

The only published wedding photo of Mr. and Mrs. W.R. Hearst.

William Randolph Hearst as he is most often remembered.

right of direction; and, above all, he better than any man is able to generate that steam, known as public opinion, which is the greatest force in politics.[48]

It seems a ridiculous idea, government by newspaper, but it's important to be precise about what Stead had in mind. He was not proposing a coup d'état. He was not suggesting editors assume direct authority for the public business. Rather, he wanted them to use their resources and their command of public opinion to raise and debate issues, and to rally both the people and their governments toward solutions. Stead had only contempt for journalists who treated newspapers as mere money machines or who argued that leadership, guidance, and governance were beyond the ambit of their craft. He called them eunuchs. The future, Stead declared, would belong to the journalist who possessed the instinct and capacity for government and who was bold enough to accept the challenge. He would be limited only by the scope of his knowledge and faculties and by the extent of his circulation.

Of all the editors then working in Europe and North America, Stead held that none was more likely to rise to the position of "uncrowned king of an educated democracy" than William Randolph Hearst. Much of Stead's chapter on government by journalism is devoted to Hearst, "the most promising journalist whom I have yet come across. He has education, youth, energy, aptitude, wealth, and that instinctive journalistic sense which is akin to genius." Stead applauded Hearst for choosing his staff "wisely and well," and for not being afraid to pay top dollar for top talent. But he fixes praise for the *Journal*'s success firmly on Hearst himself: "No one did more to give the newspaper character and success than the young millionaire, who was to be seen in his shirt-sleeves through the hottest nights in the sultry summer toiling away at proofs and forms until the early hours when he saw his paper to press. Members of his staff who worked like niggers could not complain when they saw their chief working harder than any of his salaried employees."[49]

Stead was struck, as were others, with the discrepancy between Hearst's personal modesty and his newspaper's style. He describes the *Journal* as "Broadway in print—Broadway at high noon, with cars swinging backward and forward along the tracks, and the myriad multitudes streaming this way and that, life everywhere." He claims that the direction or governing purpose of the paper was not always discernable amid

the fever and sensation but that it finally found expression in the slogan
"While Others Talk the *Journal* Acts." He ends the chapter by begging
Hearst to realize the possibilities of his position and embrace a supreme
ambition, such as making New York the most humane and habitable city
in the world. "Certainly no man in all New York," Stead concludes, "has
such a chance of combining all the elements that make for righteousness
and progress in the city as the young Californian."[50]

If there was ever a moment when editors could plausibly aspire to fill
the role Stead imagined for them, it was here in the waning days of the
nineteenth century. The contemporary view that the yellow press existed
on "the level of the *National Enquirer* and other supermarket tabloids" is
wildly off target.[51] Far from being shady, squalid, or trivial, the yellows
were big, rich businesses run out of towering buildings with elevators,
telephones, and electric lights. There seemed no limit to their potential size
and reach. Their dazzling color presses could spit out a million copies a day
for delivery over thousands of square miles. They could generate a fresh
edition with the latest news from a conflict halfway around the globe in a
matter of minutes. They were staffed with college graduates and first-rank
journalistic talent—men of high purpose and powerful expression who
daily held the attention of larger audiences than most candidates for the
presidency would address in an entire national campaign. They spoke to
the nation with a frankness and familiarity that politicians could only envy.

The very size of their circulations lent Hearst and Pulitzer authority.
Huge sales were a sign of broad public favor, which in itself was political
currency. The primacy of public opinion was still a "vital unifying tenet"
in the operations of U.S. governments at all levels in the nineteenth century, writes historian Gerald F. Linderman. "Americans assumed a priori
both the existence of public opinion and its accurate and automatic translation into political decisions."[52] Newspapers, in such a world, were crucial intermediaries. Politicians used the press to monitor the attitudes and
temper of electors; in the absence of broadcast, broadband, and organized polling, there were few other ways to keep up. They also responded
to issues and campaigns in the dailies, and deferred to them to an extent
today's politician would consider humiliating. They did so out of regard
for the public voice: "conciliating the priest in worshipping the deity," as
one historian puts it.[53] Hearst and Pulitzer, to extend the analogy, had by
far the largest parishes, and these were growing at intimidating rates.

Politicians could not afford to ignore the yellow press. Pulitzer had helped to bully Grover Cleveland into dropping his bond sale. Hearst had played as important a role in a national election as any newspaper in U.S. history. Congressmen, senators, and governors responded in impressive numbers to opinion surveys undertaken by the *Journal* and the *World*. When Sylvester Scovel was arrested, the Senate requested that the secretary of state intervene with Spain for his protection. The request was granted. A sizable party of congressmen and senators, including a member of the House Committee on Naval Affairs and a member of the Foreign Affairs Committee, accepted Hearst's invitation to join his newspaper's fact-finding tour of Cuba; when they returned, they vouched for the accuracy of their host's journalism. McKinley not only felt it advisable to meet Evangelina Cisneros in Washington after she had been illegally liberated from a Spanish jail, but also complimented the *Journal* on its enterprise.

Better evidence of how politicians were affected by what they read in the yellow press comes from Marcus Wilkerson's 1932 study of public opinion during the Cuban crisis. "Senators and representatives, seemingly moved by the atrocity stories found in the press, made stirring speeches in favor of Cuban belligerency, using portions of the news reports from Cuba. . . . The number of resolutions introduced in Congress dealing with Cuba and the speeches resulting from the introduction of such measures increased with the number of atrocity stories carried by the press." From late 1896 through the first half of 1897, the period in which atrocity stories were most plentiful, with Hearst and Pulitzer leading the way, twenty-five separate resolutions dealing with Cuba were introduced in Congress.[54]

The notion of the press filling a perceived political vacuum was far less ludicrous than we might assume today, writes Linderman.[55] So too was the prospect of Hearst as the uncrowned king of an educated democracy, operating in a whole new realm outside of governmental authority, beholden to none but his readers, with his newspapers and his influence still expanding. Early in 1898, the start of his third year in New York, Hearst bought the cream of Dana's collection of pottery and paintings at an estate auction, and his publishing rivals continued to worry.[56]

CHAPTER FOURTEEN

Suddenly the Dinnerware Began to Vibrate

A t the beginning of 1898, Hearst was more impatient than ever for a resolution of the Cuban crisis, and he was not alone. Spain and the rebels were locked in a stalemate. Credible accounts of Spanish atrocities against noncombatants continued to surface in the press, as did horrific reports of human suffering in reconcentration camps. The *Journal*, the *World*, the *Sun*, and other pro-Cuban papers kept urging the McKinley administration to fulfill its duties as steward of the Western Hemisphere and compel Spain to bring peace to its possession. Most members of Congress and, in all probability, a majority of the American people concurred, but the president, while not insensitive to the clamor for action, was determined to avoid any measures that might lead to a military confrontation. He had seen enough bloodshed in the Civil War, and was determined to use patient diplomacy and "every agency of peace" to negotiate a settlement mutually satisfactory to Spain, Cuba, and the United States.[1] He offered Madrid his friendly offices in coming to terms with the rebels and he suggested that Washington might be forced to act in the name of humanity and U.S. interests if Spain could not arrange a settlement, but he mentioned intervention as a remote and unpleasant specter, not as an imminent threat.

McKinley believed his strategy was working. Weyler, the reviled Cuban governor, had been recalled by Spain and replaced with General Ramón Blanco, a moderate who promised to temper the reconcentration program. Better still, Spain had granted a limited form of autonomy or self-government to Cuba. A hastily constituted Havana-based assembly took office January 1, 1898. It comprised hand-picked Cuban and Spanish representatives and was charged with a range of domestic administrative functions. Washington hailed these developments as major concessions from Madrid, and weeks earlier McKinley had proclaimed his faith in Spain's reforms in his annual address to Congress. He praised Sagasta as a conciliator and declared that Spain was sincere and "irrevocably committed" to its new path. In a crucial passage of his speech, McKinley admitted to having given his "most anxious and earnest consideration" to intervening in Cuba on humanitarian grounds but said his confidence in Sagasta's reforms restrained him. In the event that the new policies failed to bring a righteous peace to Cuba, the United States would answer its obligation to "intervene with force," in full knowledge that it would command the support and approval of the civilized world.

Deliberation is not a bad thing in a chief executive, and McKinley was right to give diplomacy every chance of success, but by this point, the odds on a negotiated settlement to the Cuban crisis were negligible. The rebels for three years had been firmly rejecting any solution short of outright independence, while Spain, even with Sagasta in office, was steadfastly refusing to put Cuban independence on the table, and both sides continued to fight in the countryside with what the historian John Lawrence Tone calls "apocalyptic determination."[2]

Hearst and the other pro-Cuban editors dismissed Sagasta's concessions as insufficient and insincere. The rebels and Cuba's hard-core Spanish loyalists were unrepresented in the new Havana assembly and both groups stood in the way of lasting peace. Madrid retained control of the judiciary, law enforcement, spending, and taxation policy in Cuba, and it could end the reform experiment at its discretion. The *Journal*, noting that Spain had not abandoned its larger strategy of killing insurgents accused Sagasta of pretending to grant reforms in order to buy time for a military victory. This sham of autonomy, it maintained, led nowhere: "After our forefathers had declared their independence, George III was willing to make almost any concessions for the sake of a restored empire. The Americans repulsed his advances, although their grievances were as light as snowflakes compared with the crushing wrongs that Cuba has suffered at the hands of Spain. The Cubans would be fools if they trusted Spanish promises, and we should be infamous if we tried to induce them to do it."[3]

Most of the conservative papers, eager for action under Cleveland's Democrats, now applauded McKinley's caution and his pursuit of a negotiated settlement with Spain. They accused Hearst and the pro-Cuban editors of warmongering for their insistence that Washington deliver an ultimatum to Spain, backed, if necessary, by force. Historians have tended to agree with the conservative papers, drawing a line in American opinion at this stage in the crisis between those striving for a negotiated peace and those eager for war, with Hearst usually presiding as jingo-in-chief. But Hearst's impatience with diplomacy was not motivated by martial ardor. He believed nothing short of a U.S. ultimatum would bring peace to Cuba, either by forcing Madrid to back down (which the *Journal* considered a real possibility) or by precipitating an armed intervention—the choice was Spain's. His view was shared not only by a large contingent of editors, activists, and congressional leaders but also by the American diplomat who knew Spain best.

Hannis Taylor, lawyer, constitutional historian, biographer of Cicero, and the Cleveland administration's last minister in Spain, had published in the November 1897 edition of the *North American Review* a comprehensive and insightful discussion of the Cuban crisis. Read closely in Washington and Madrid, his essay was far removed in tone from the yellow newspapers but consistent with them in its analysis and conclusions.

After four years in Madrid, Taylor believed the Spanish were impotent to resolve their Cuban problem. Unable to defeat the rebels militarily, they had lost control of the island yet they couldn't conceive of giving it up. One of the few things Spain's civil, clerical, military, and political elites could agree upon was that their sovereignty in Cuba was inviolable. As inheritors of an old-world monarchical society and owners of a paternalistic colonial system, the Spanish had no real conception of what words like "autonomy" and "independence" meant to Cubans or Americans. Madrid had steadfastly resisted substantive reforms during three decades of unrest in Cuba. Concessions were occasionally announced to divert public opinion in the United States and Europe, but they were never substantially implemented—the fighting had resumed in 1895 in large part because Madrid had failed to deliver on promised reforms. There was an economic dimension to Spain's recalcitrance: financially dependent on its colonies, it could not afford but to bleed them. Washington's offers of friendly and respectful mediation were fine, but they had been extended before; they were always politely received and quickly forgotten. Relations between Spain and the

United States were now so strained, and opinion in both countries was so inflamed, as to amount to a state of "semi-war."[4]

The United States, wrote Taylor, was down to two options. It could recognize the horrifying human cost of the Cuban rebellion and discharge its duty to humanity by confronting Spain, citing the Monroe Doctrine as well as "ancient rights of intervention" recognized by international law. Alternatively, it could dispense with moral dignity, frankly declare itself "incapable of protecting its own interests and of guarding the peace of the new world," and take a seat on the sidelines. Taylor favored confrontation. He believed that an ultimatum, sanctioned by the executive and legislative branches in Washington and backed by threat of force, might bring Spain to its senses.

Taylor was no jingo: he was a seasoned diplomat who had played a leading role in a Cleveland administration notable for its stubborn neutrality. That he drew a harder line on Cuba than anyone in McKinley's immediate circle is largely a result of his long experience of Spain and the Cuban crisis. McKinley had come to office in early 1897 with limited experience of international relations, no first-hand knowledge of Spain, and without having said a word about Cuba during his campaign or in his inaugural address. He had chosen as his secretary of state the septuagenarian John Sherman—who was almost completely deaf and racing toward senility—in part to make Sherman's Senate seat available to Mark Hanna. Sherman's assistant secretary, William R. Day, had all his marbles but he too was a novice on the international stage, as was Minister Woodford.[5] Notwithstanding their admirable patience and caution in dealing with Spain, it is hard to escape the conclusion that McKinley and his team placed a naïve faith in the possibilities of continued dialogue with Madrid. Three stunning events in the first seven weeks of 1898 would vindicate the judgment of Taylor and the yellow newspapers, and plunge America into war.

ON JANUARY 12, *El Reconcentrado*, a moderate Spanish newspaper in Havana, published an article critical of the recently departed Weyler and one of his key subordinates. Spanish loyalists, including many army officers, supported Weyler's harsh policies as the only means of holding the island. They took to the streets, razing *El Reconcentrado*'s offices and those

of several other pro-autonomy journals as well. While the primary target
of the rioters was the newspapers, Consul General Lee heard amid the
cries of "Viva Weyler" and "Death to Autonomy" a scattering of anti-
American slogans and rumors of a march on the consulate, where many
American citizens had taken refuge.[6] He worried that the new Spanish governor, Blanco, had lost control of his army, and warned Washington that he
might require naval support. Havana was calm again within forty-eight
hours, but Lee nonetheless signaled his intention to request a battleship for
Cuba just as soon as one might arrive without adding to local tensions.

Hearst is said to have exploited the riots to force the United States into
a war with Spain. One influential account claims that the January 13 edition of his paper exaggerated the threat to Americans in Havana with
careless reporting and the "screaming" full-page headline "Next to War
with Spain."[7] In fact, surviving editions of that day's *Journal* make no
mention of the riots—the news does not appear to have made deadline.
The offending headline appeared in the *Evening Journal,* which appealed
to a different audience than its morning sibling and was more excitable as
a matter of policy. The January 14 edition of the morning paper features
a matter-of-fact three-column headline, "Battle Ship Maine Awaiting
Gen. Lee's Direct Orders." The news story describes the riots and the
interruption of communications between Havana and Washington but
clearly states that few shots were fired and that Blanco had regained control of Havana. A front-page cartoon depicts Uncle Sam sharpening his
sword as a Spanish gunboat cruises between Cuba and Florida. The caption reads: "Uncle Sam Doesn't Seek Trouble, But—."An editorial
advised that naval vessels be dispatched to Havana without delay to protect the lives and property of Americans in the event of further riots.

Hearst's coverage was sufficiently aggressive to raise the ire of the
Tribune and other pro-McKinley papers, all of which sought to minimize
the clashes. The *Journal* answered that it was difficult to dismiss the riots
as insignificant when the Havana cable office had been shut down, the
guard doubled around the U.S. consulate, and Spanish artillery posted on
the city's principal streets. No American blood was spilled, it allowed,
but "the patriot armies are still in the field, the material ruin of the
island is progressing, the wretched comedy of autonomy has been
hissed off the boards, and the grim tragedy of a nation's starvation . . .
holds all eyes."[8]

The riots in fact did undermine the credibility of the Sagasta government and confirm in the minds of many observers the hopelessness of Spain's position. The Spanish minister in Washington, Don Enrique Dupuy de Lôme, noted an "abrupt" shift in American opinion at Madrid's expense. Second Assistant Secretary of State Alvee A. Adee wrote to Assistant Secretary Day (who had assumed most of the duties of the dotty John Sherman) that the riots had killed the autonomy initiative—a sentiment Fitzhugh Lee voiced publicly. Congress erupted in another round of fierce debates on recognition of Cuban belligerence and independence, and it was widely believed in Washington that the president was preparing for a decisive intervention. The navy, having already cancelled scheduled leaves for enlisted men and moved the North Atlantic squadron to the Gulf of Mexico for battle exercises, warned its major commands of possible trouble in Cuba and began gathering intelligence on possible landing sites on the island.[9] The administration asked Lee for a fresh report on the fighting strength of the Spanish army. McKinley continued to counsel patience, but he knew full well he would be blamed for any American losses in Cuba. He sent a ship to Havana without waiting for Lee's final okay, and regardless of the effect it might have on local tensions.[10]

The second-class battleship *Maine*, commanded by Captain Charles Dwight Sigsbee, had been stationed for several weeks at Key West. The 319-foot, 6,682-ton armored steel vessel was one of the most imposing things afloat, with towering masts fore and aft, two big smokestacks between, and four 10-inch guns in twin turrets. It carried 343 enlisted men in forward berths and 31 officers behind.[11] With its hull painted peacetime white, it steamed into Havana harbor thirteen days after the riots. Sigsbee moored within sight of the Spanish flagship *Alfonso XII* and assorted commercial and fishing craft. The *Maine* had a view "clear up the cobbled, portico-shaded streets, right into the white and pastel heart of the metropolis."[12]

Spain was not a happy host of the *Maine*. It had warned that it would consider the arrival of a U.S. warship in Cuba a hostile act. McKinley and his secretary of the navy, John D. Long, skirted this concern by announcing the *Maine*'s maneuver as the resumption of "friendly visits" to Cuban ports, as had been customary before the insurgency. Madrid gritted its teeth and joined the charade, dispatching the cruiser *Vizcaya* to New York in a "friendly" gesture of its own. But it also ramped up its munitions production, increased its naval capacities, and reproached Washington for answering Spain's grant of autonomy with a baldly aggressive move. Newspapers in New York and Madrid reported a hardening of popular and political sentiment. Tensions were highest in Havana, where the *Maine*'s captain was handed circulars on the street calling for death to autonomy and "Death to the Americans."[13] He cancelled shore leave for his sailors to avoid trouble. The *Evening Journal*'s headline, "Next to War with Spain," hadn't been far from the mark, after all.

THE SECOND SHOCK TO SPANISH-AMERICAN RELATIONS came within a month of the Havana riots. Don Enrique Dupuy de Lôme was a small, balding, dapper man with long waxed mustaches and five years' experience as Spain's minister to Washington. In late January he arrived at the annual White House dinner for foreign diplomats wearing a brace of medals on his gilded jacket and a handsome ceremonial sword. President McKinley sought him out, sat him down, and proudly noted that Republican forces in the Senate were holding the Capitol's pro-Cuban elements at bay.[14] The minister was pleased at McKinley's mood but under no illusions as to the real state of Spanish-American relations. He warned his colleagues to avoid any gestures or statements that might inflame Congress or public opinion in the United States, and then he himself sparked a conflagration.

Like everyone else concerned with Cuba, Dupuy de Lôme had paid close attention to President McKinley's recent address to Congress. He briefed his home office on the speech and also relayed his private thoughts in correspondence to José Canalejas, the Spanish editor and Sagasta confidant who had recently passed through Washington en route to Cuba. Dupuy de Lôme's letter was chatty, intelligent, cynical, amusing, and dangerously indiscreet. It was also intercepted.

Horatio Rubens, the New York–based Junta spokesman, claimed that a Cuban patriot with a friend in Canalejas's Havana office had acquired the letter on behalf of their cause. It may, in fact, have been lifted in Washington, but in any event, the document found its way to the Junta. Rubens took it first to the *Herald*, probably on the assumption that publication in a pro-Spanish paper would do maximum damage to Dupuy de Lôme and Spain. He had made a translation of the letter and gathered other samples of the minister's handwriting to demonstrate its authenticity. The

Herald, however, said it would not accept the document unless Dupuy de Lôme admitted authorship. Rubens walked down the street to Hearst, who, on the morning of February 9, ran a transcript of the letter in Spanish on the front page along with an English translation.

To a popular audience, the most obviously offensive part of Dupuy de Lôme's letter was his description of McKinley as a political pretender: "Besides the ingrained and inevitable bluntness with which is repeated all that the press and public opinion in Spain have said about Weyler, it once more shows what McKinley is, weak and a bidder for the admiration of the crowd, besides being a would-be politican who tries to leave a door open behind himself while keeping on good terms with the jingoes of his party."[15]

More consequential in the prevailing diplomatic environment was Dupuy de Lôme's admission that the autonomy initiative was a ruse designed to relieve Spain of "a part of the responsibility for what is happening" on the island. The minister hoped the Cubans, whom the Americans "think so immaculate," would by virtue of their participation in the governance of the island share blame for its sorry state. Spain would in the meantime continue to press for the military success without which, Dupuy de Lôme believed, nothing would be accomplished in Cuba. The minister allowed that Spain had been entertaining the idea of further reforms, particularly trade negotiations with the United States, primarily for purposes of "propaganda" and to buy time for further military actions. As an aside, Dupuy de Lôme rued the influence of the "newspaper rabble that swarms in [Havana] hotels," and singled out the *New York Journal*'s correspondents for special abuse.[16]

Hearst is accused by biographers and historians of making too much of a "comic diplomatic blunder" and of stoking tensions by publishing an inflammatory English translation of the letter, a charge that originated with the *Evening Post.*[17] In fact, the same translation was also used by the *Tribune* and other conservative papers, and several days after its initial complaint, the *Evening Post* reversed itself and admitted that the *Journal*'s published version was "sufficiently correct."[18] Hearst is also faulted for accepting a "stolen" document that had been rejected by the more scrupulous *Herald.* In fact, the *Herald*'s failure to take advantage of a hand-delivered scoop was probably due more to its pro-Spanish leanings than to its journalistic standards (the *Tribune* had no trouble printing the document). The *Journal* took some risk, but not a reckless amount, in running the letter without absolute proof of its authenticity. It was, in fact, the genuine article, and its significance is difficult to overstate.

More than the riots, more than any other event in this period, Dupuy de Lôme's letter exposed the folly of McKinley's peace strategy. The minister had involuntarily confirmed congressional and newspaper suspicions that Madrid was negotiating in bad faith. He had revealed that the good offices of the presidency were being manipulated in Spain's desperate bid to maintain its possession—a far greater insult to the United States than the personal slighting of McKinley. In sum, Dupuy de Lôme had destroyed the president's lone argument against the use of force in the name of humanity to bring peace to Cuba.

In the wake of the letter's publication, Dupuy de Lôme resigned his office and, after a week of diplomatic wrangling, Spain agreed to apologize to Washington and to reassert its commitment to its promised reforms. The damage, however, was done. The U.S. Senate heard three proposals for recognition of Cuba as an independent republic.[19] The Senate Foreign Affairs Committee entertained a resolution demanding from the administration all consular reports on the consequences of reconcentration and the progress of autonomy. The resolution passed unanimously, indicating the president's assent. It was understood, writes the diplomatic historian John L. Offner, "that the consular reports would provide Congress with the basis for intervention in Cuba."[20]

The notion that Hearst hyped the letter as a pretext for war persists to this day, but the *Journal* never advanced Dupuy de Lôme's indiscretion as a casus belli. It did pronounce the McKinley peace strategy dead, and it did, consistent with its standing policy, insist on immediate U.S. intervention in Cuba (a measure that might or might not lead to war, depending on Spain's response). What else, asked the paper, was Washington going to do—"wait for the autonomy burlesque to somehow bear fruit? Wait for Spain to arm itself and prepare for war?"[21] The most succinct expression of the *Journal*'s position was as follows: "Diplomacy can deal with de Lôme's folly at its leisure, but humanity calls for instant action in behalf of bleeding Cuba."[22]

There is some substance to the accusation by the *Tribune* that the *Journal* handled the letter with "baseness and malignity."[23] The *Journal* had history with the minister. They had sniped at one another over filibusters and atrocity reports, the expulsion of correspondents from Cuba, and the Cisneros affair, among other stories. Hearst did not simply publish the offending letter: he beat it to death for the better part of a week. He ran a banner headline characterizing it as the worst insult to the United States in its history, a blatant exaggeration, even considering Spain's trifling with the office of the president. He treated readers to comprehensive annotations of the letter to ensure that no deprecatory nuance was overlooked. He announced, precipitously, that Dupuy de Lôme had been handed his walking papers. He dredged up the minister's previous indiscretions, from blithe dismissals of the humanitarian disaster in Cuba to slighting remarks on American women (retrieved from a travelogue published in the 1870s). Even in an age of indecorous journalism, this was laying it on thick.

None of these antics endeared the *Journal* to Spain. When the paper's 138-foot yacht *Buccaneer,* a replacement for the *Vamoose,* arrived at Havana on February 11 carrying the writer Julian Hawthorne and his party, it was boarded by harbor police looking for Karl Decker. Unable to find him, they instead pointed to several small artillery pieces mounted on the *Buccaneer*'s decks and impounded the vessel. The *Journal* feigned outrage, declaring a "Spanish-*Journal* War" and asking why the seizure had been allowed to occur almost under the guns of the *Maine.*[24] Also around this time, dynamite was discovered at the *Journal*'s offices in Casa Nueva. Whether the bomb was intended for the paper or for the building's other prominent tenant, the U.S. consulate, is unclear, but the legation made its opinion clear by asking the newspaper to find new digs.

Hearst's papers had never been afraid to call attention to themselves, but somewhere between the Havana riots and the Dupuy de Lôme letter, the *Journal* began pushing the practice to extremes. Every insult from a Spanish source, every word of commendation from a congressional figure, however minor, was given excited display. In late January, two weeks after the Havana riots, Hearst ran a feature in a Sunday edition by one Rafael Guerra claiming that mobs had been determined not only to destroy *El Reconcentrado*'s offices but to attack the *Journal* as well. A headline suggested it was "only by a miracle that wholesale slaughter of Americans was averted."[25] The body of the story more soberly admits that no damage was done to the *Journal* or its staff.

Hearst was obviously feeling more than the usual competitive pressures. His editorial line had lost some of its distinctiveness as pro-Cuban and pro-intervention views gained currency. One way to compensate was to talk up the *Journal*'s exploits and grab recognition for the shift in public mood. Another was to use even flashier layouts. The front-page template was now routinely blown apart to make way for larger cartoons and illustrations and for multiplying layers of display copy. The strategies worked for Hearst in that his paper's circulation seemed to grow in proportion to the size of its headlines and the volume of its self-promotion. On many days, however, the self-promotion amounted to self-absorption, which would only get worse in the wake of the third great shock to Spanish-American relations.

ON THE EVENING OF FEBRUARY 15, 1898, the battleship *Maine* swung on its mooring so that its bow pointed out of Havana harbor, as if it were trying to escape its fate. The night was warm and still; the sky was overcast, and the air heavy. Captain Sigsbee, a straight and trim officer with thirty-five years of exemplary service and a long mustache overhanging his lips, was at the polished desk in his cabin, writing a letter home. When the marine bugler sounded taps at ten past nine, Sigsbee paused to listen. The enlisted men were already in their berths. They were also grumpy. It was the second day of Carnival in Havana, and the city's cantinas and palm-lined streets were bursting with revelers, the women wearing their longest earrings, the men their loudest trousers. The bells and drums could be heard across the water, but Sigsbee had still not allowed the sailors off the ship. The *Maine*'s officers had at least seen the city, its dances and promenades, and a handful of them remained on the decks this evening, smoking cigars and watching the lights twinkle ashore.

Sigsbee finished his letter and was reaching to put it in an envelope when he heard what sounded like a gunshot. It was followed a second later by a heart-stopping, bone-shaking explosion. The ocean floor seemed to heave up beneath him. Sigsbee heard "ominous, metallic sounds" as the ship lurched violently and listed, trembling, to port.[26] He fought his way from his quarters in the aft section of the ship through the blackness and smoke to the deck, knowing for certain that the *Maine* was destroyed and sinking beneath him.

Passengers on the deck of the commercial steamer *City of Washington* didn't so much hear as feel the blast from across the harbor. They saw a column of flame and white smoke shoot 150 feet over the *Maine*. It mushroomed, sending fire and metal debris hundreds of yards in every direction. They watched the bow of the battleship rear up before plunging beneath the water. They saw the foremast and smokestacks topple, and a fiery gash open in the starboard deck.

George Bronson Rea was dining that evening with Scovel and his wife in the glittering café of the Inglaterra, looking out on Parque Central. He noticed his dinnerware vibrating a split second before the shock of the explosion blew out the hotel's windows and sent diners scurrying for cover in doorways and under tables. The sky over the harbor flashed bright as day. The men deposited Mrs. Scovel in the safety of her rooms and sprinted for the wharves to find the *Maine* on its side, half sunk and burning, its artillery shells bursting at random. Rea and Scovel jumped into a rowboat with the chief of the Havana police and bent oars for the burning ship. Searchlights combed the water, turning up floating white shapes the men quickly realized were the bodies of crew. "Great God," Scovel said. "They are all gone. This is the work of a torpedo."[27]

It is not clear when the *Journal*'s Bryson arrived on the scene, but he reported that "after the big flash there was darkness. The night resounded with cries for help and inarticulate shrieks. The surface of the bay was alive with men swimming for their lives, and from the sky rained bits of pipe, small iron and other wreck dust."[28] Whatever triggered the initial explosion, it had ignited more than five tons of powder charges in the *Maine*'s magazines. The worst damage was to the forward third of the vessel, where the crew was berthed. The officers of the *Maine* lowered their few remaining lifeboats and began scooping up survivors and bodies from the harbor. They were joined by rescue parties from the *City of Washington* and the *Alfonso XII* as well as by boats from shore. Two hundred and sixty died at the scene, most of them instantly (another six died in hospital of their injuries).[29] Most of the officers survived.

Sigsbee reluctantly gave up the *Maine* for the safety of the *City of Washington*, where he jotted a telegraph to the secretary of the navy reporting the loss of his ship and many of his men. Although he believed that he had been sunk by a mine or a torpedo, a view he would never revise, delegations of Spanish officials offering assistance and sincerest sympathies moved him to include a line of caution at the close of his account: "Public opinion should be suspended until further report."[30] He gave his transcript to the *Herald*'s Rea to wire on his behalf. Rea and Scovel hurried to the telegraph office and found it already crowded with reporters. They elbowed to the front of the line, pleading official business, and sent Sigsbee's message. Only two other telegrams got out that night. One was a hundred-line Associated Press bulletin that would comprise almost the whole of Park Row's first-morning coverage. The other belonged to the endlessly resourceful Scovel, who had earlier filched from the censor's office a blank cable form with a preapproved seal; he carried it with him for just such an occasion. His brief report to the *World* added little to the AP account, but it more directly addressed the question of blame: "The injured do not know what caused the explosion. There is some doubt as to whether the explosion took place ON the Maine."[31] His paper would be first to hint that the blast had not been an accident.

After 2 a.m., a telegram was delivered to the front door of the Washington home of John D. Long, secretary of the navy, informing him of the destruction of his ship. He immediately telephoned the White House and instructed the duty watchman to rouse the president. McKinley reportedly took the news hard. Years later, the watchman recalled him walking the floor in shock, muttering to no one in particular, "The *Maine* blown up! The *Maine* blown up!"[32] Meanwhile, the newspapers in New York, having received the first news flash from Havana, had roused their Washington correspondents, who reached the secretary's home and the White House almost as quickly as did the official notification. They wanted information and comment but received little beyond expressions of sorrow.

Hearst, decades later, claimed to have returned home late that night from the newspaper to find his butler, George Thompson, waiting up for him: "There's a telephone from the office. They say it's important news."

When Hearst called the *Journal*, an editor told him that the battleship *Maine* has been blown up in Havana harbor.

"Good heavens, what have you done with the story?"

"We have put it on the first page, of course."

"Have you put anything else on the front page?"

"Only the other big news," said the editor.

"There is not any other big news," replied Hearst. "Please spread the story all over the page. This means war."[33]

That anecdote is the starting point for most accounts of Heart's coverage of the sinking of the battleship *Maine*. It was the biggest story he addressed during his years as a hands-on editor, and it is also the moment that has defined him as a journalist. As quickly as it rolled off the press, Hearst's coverage of the *Maine* explosion was attacked by rival editors as the most disgraceful display in the history of American journalism, and a century's perspective has done nothing to soften the reviews. Indeed, condemnations of the coverage have been so passionate, thorough, and numerous as to almost defy summary. Biographers, journalists, military historians, political scientists, and novelists have cited Hearst's response to the destruction of the *Maine* as the epitome of yellow journalism—the single point in time when all crimes of the craft were committed at once. Nothing in his journalistic career, not even his work in the 1896 election, has brought Hearst anywhere near so much opprobrium.

The criticism began even while bodies were still being lifted from Havana harbor. E.L. Godkin fired the first broadside and kept firing in both the *Evening Post* and *The Nation* for the next five weeks, setting the tone and isolating the targets for all subsequent criticisms. The following are among his most frequently cited remarks. Some are directed entirely at Hearst, while others implicate Pulitzer as well:

- The admirable conduct of the government officials at Washington renders the course of the sensational press in this city the more shameful by contrast. Nothing so disgraceful as the behavior of two of these newspapers this week has been known in the history of American journalism. Gross misrepresentation of the facts, deliberate invention of tales calculated to excite the public, and wanton recklessness in the construction of headlines which even outdid these inventions.[34]

- The reason why such journals lie is that it pays to lie, or, in other words, this is the very reason for which they are silly and scandalous and indecent. They supply a want of a demoralized public. Moreover, such journals are almost always in favor of war, because war affords unusual opportunities for lying and sensation. That war involves much suffering and losses, does not matter. Their business is not to promote public happiness or morality, but to "sell the papers."[35]

- The resources of type have been about exhausted. Nothing in the way of larger letters can be used, unless only a single headline is to be given on the first page. Red ink has been resorted to as an additional element of attraction or terror, and if we had a war, the whole paper might be printed in red, white, and blue. In that case, real lunatics instead of imitation lunatics should be employed as editors and contributors.[36]

- No one—absolutely no one—supposes a yellow journal cares five cents about the Cubans, the *Maine* victims, or anyone else. A yellow journal office is probably the nearest approach, in atmosphere, to hell, existing in any Christian state. As we see to-day, in spite of all the ridicule that has been lavished on the "yellow journals," in spite of the general acknowledgement of the mischief they do, in spite of the general belief in the baseness and corruption and Satanism of their proprietors, their circulation is apparently as large as ever.[37]

- A better place in which to prepare a young man for eternal damnation than a yellow-journal office does not exist.[38]

- A blackguard boy [Hearst] with several millions of dollars at his disposal has more influence on the use a great nation may make of its credit, of its army and navy, of its name and traditions, than all the statesmen and philosophers and professors in the country.[39]

Godkin, age sixty-seven, was a thick balding Irishman with a full gray beard and short features. Educated in the British Isles, he had covered the war in the Crimea before moving to New York, where he was made editor of *The Nation*, a weekly journal of opinion. Under his leadership, it became one of the more influential small publications in the United States. In 1881, Godkin added the *Evening Post* to his responsibilities. But he is remembered today as much for his denunciations of yellow journalism as anything else. Several of the most prominent journalism histories of the twentieth century hail him as a lonely voice of reason and sobriety amid the *Maine* madness. In 1934 Joseph E. Wisan published a comprehensive day-to-day study of Park Row's coverage of the Cuba story. He celebrates Godkin for his "devotion to the best standards in journalism" and fleshes out the editor's criticisms of Hearst with specific examples of erroneous reporting, inflammatory headlines, and generally irresponsible journalism.[40] Wisan's work, in turn, has been influential among Hearst's primary biographers and other chroniclers of the American press.

W.A. Swanberg's 1961 biography of Hearst relies on the vehement denunciations of Godkin and the specific examples produced by Wisan to denounce Hearst's coverage of the *Maine* as "the orgasmic acme of ruthless, truthless newspaper jingoism."[41] Hearst, according to Swanberg, wanted war with Spain and "fought for these ends with such abandonment of honesty and incitement of hatred that the stigma of it never quite left him even though he still had fifty-three years to live. Intelligent Americans realized the preposterousness of the idea that Spain had blown up the *Maine*. Proud Spain had swallowed insult to avoid a war she knew she would lose. Her forbearance had borne fruit until the explosion in Havana caused journalistic insanity in New York." Swanberg maintains that the *Journal* ignored the White House's appeal for the press to suspend judgment on the cause of the explosion until a Navy Department court of inquiry had opportunity to investigate and file its report. Instead, Hearst convicted Spain in a blink. While Hearst's editorials admitted disbelief that Spain had officially ordered the explosion, "this was tucked away in small type and later disavowed. The big type, the headlines, the diagrams, the cartoons, the editorials, laid the blame inferentially or flatly on Spain."[42] Swanberg cites a handful of screaming headlines (most of them first noted by Wisan) as proof of Hearst's deliberate efforts to mislead and inflame the public: "Warship Maine was Split In Two by an Enemy's Secret Infernal Machine"; "The Whole Country Thrills With the War Fever"; "How The Maine Actually Looks As It Lies, Wrecked By Spanish Treachery, in Havana Bay."

Whereas Godkin had seen a lust for circulation and Satanism behind Hearst's antics, Swanberg adopted a pop-Freudian approach: "His sympathies were swift and unreasoning. He was emotionally unstable, plunged into horror and indignation by the disaster. Since he wanted to believe the Spaniards guilty, he did. His ability to abandon reality and accept his own fantasies as facts absolved him from any obligation toward truth and led him into wild bypaths of error. Also, the megalomaniac in him delighted in making himself the author of mighty events."[43]

Godkin, Wisan, and Swanberg all blamed Hearst for America's eventual entry into war with Spain, as did a great many other commentators in the last century. Estimations of Hearst's power and influence have since ebbed. Nasaw's 1998 biography of Hearst minimizes his role, yet Nasaw too joins in the mockery and condemnation of the *Journal*'s coverage.

So what, exactly, did roll off the *Journal*'s presses in the wake of the *Maine* calamity?

If Hearst did, in fact, return home late on the evening of February 15 to relay instructions to his news desk over the telephone, he appears to have been disregarded by whoever received them. Judging from surviving editions and historical accounts, the *Journal*'s first-day coverage was not significantly different from that of any other paper (not surprising given that the news did not reach New York until about 2:30 a.m.). The paper's front page on the morning of February 16 carried a three-column factual headline: "Cruiser Maine Blown Up In Havana Harbor." The subhead added, "Disaster a Mystery and Loss of Life Said to Be Appalling." Captain Sigsbee's telegraph to Washington was quoted in full. A secondary story, perhaps lifted from Scovel's report in the *World*, stated that all boats from the Spanish cruiser *Alfonso XII* were assisting in rescue efforts, as were Spanish officers and soldiers, local firemen, policemen, and sailors. The cause of the explosion was not obvious; the wounded sailors of the *Maine* were unable to explain it. It was believed that the cruiser was totally destroyed. The only rumor presented by the *Journal* was that "it is believed the explosion occurred in a small powder magazine." In other words, the paper opened its coverage not with an assault on Spain but by suggesting an onboard accident.

The *Journal*'s second day of coverage, taking the entire front page and continuing for seven pages more inside, is closer to what we've been led to expect. The banner headline read "Destruction of the War Ship Maine Was the Work of an Enemy." (Swanberg's more colorful treatment, blaming a "secret infernal machine," appears in a later edition. It was not the product of Hearst's overheated imagination; an early edition of the *Herald* picked up the same rumor)[44] The source for the paper's declarative "work of an enemy" headline was revealed in the subhead: "Assistant Secretary Roosevelt Convinced the Explosion of the War Ship Was Not an Accident." That crucial line of attribution is not mentioned in discussions of Hearst's coverage. The assistant secretary of the navy was a significant source on the destruction of a U.S. naval vessel, and the fact that Roosevelt had ignored his department's cautions and advanced his own theory as to the cause of the *Maine* disaster warranted strong play. Roosevelt later denied the quote, but his personal correspondence reveals that he did believe the *Maine* to have been "sunk by an act of dirty treachery on the part of the Spaniards."[45]

The *Journal*'s early belief that the *Maine* was sunk by an external force was further bolstered by two sources in Havana. The paper was in close contact with Fitzhugh Lee, who immediately took the view that the ship was destroyed by a mine, as did Captain Sigsbee. Both the *Journal* and the *World* published news that Sigsbee had sent to Secretary of the Navy Long a secret or "suppressed" cable message suggesting an external cause. The Sigsbee cable has been received with snorts in the Hearst literature but the captain did indeed send the following message to Long in cipher on February 18: "Probably the *Maine* destroyed by mine, perhaps by accident. I surmise that her berth was planted previous to her arrival, perhaps long ago. I can only surmise this."[46] The *Journal* would have done better with a less categorical banner headline on its second day, but its statement carried an attibution and was nowhere near the acme of ruthless, truthless journalism.

The *Journal* did publish diagrams and headlines suggesting that the *Maine* could have been destroyed by a mine, and it was unquestionably fond of the theory, but Hearst did not invent this, either. One of his paper's sources was Polish-born Civil War veteran E.L. Zalinski, a retired munitions and submarine specialist who had taught military science at the Massachusetts Institute of Technology. Zalinski sketched scenarios of how a mine might have been rigged, explained patterns of damage caused by internal and external explosions, and interpreted photographic evidence of the wreck. Among the many experts cited in support of the external explosion theory were Rear Admiral George E. Belknap (retired), president of the Board of Commissioners of the Massachusetts Nautical Training School; Naval Constructor Philip Hichborn (soon to be Admiral Hichborn, chief constructor of the U.S. Navy); and Naval Constructor Francis T. Bowles of the Brooklyn Navy Yard, who oversaw construction of the battleship *Texas* and who had worked as assistant to Theodore D. Wilson, the late builder of the *Maine*. Bowles stated positively that "no destructive explosion was possible on board the vessel."[47] But the *Journal* still did not accuse Spain of sinking the *Maine:* the day's lead story, by George Eugene Bryson, stated that "nobody thinks the authorities were party to the crime, if crime there was."[48]

The third day's headline, "The Whole Country Thrills With the War Fever," does appear blatantly jingoistic when torn from context. It was, in fact, attached to reports that governors from New York, Tennessee,

Minnesota, Utah, and many states in between intended to raise militias for service in Cuba. There was also news of mass assemblies, flag-waving demonstrations, and belligerent speeches from church and campus groups, community associations, and labor unions. Many of these meetings gave birth to regiments of volunteer soldiers. The first installment of a two-day *Journal* straw poll of congressional opinion indicated overwhelming support for immediate U.S. intervention in Cuba (subsequent votes in both houses were consistent with these findings). Senators on both the Naval Affairs Committee and the Foreign Relations Committee were demanding an immediate investigation into the sinking of the *Maine* and talked openly of sending ships to the island. A rumor out of Washington held that McKinley would go to Congress for a war loan (the rumor proved to be accurate). So while it is not literally true that "the whole country" thrilled with war fever, Hearst's headline reflected the prevailing public sentiment.[49]

The *Journal*'s editorials clearly favored the external explosion theory but did not rush to judgment. In its first comment, on February 17, the paper pleaded for time and better information about the cause of the blast; it saw no reason to panic, nor any reason to believe official Spain could be culpable. The next day an editorial suggested Spain could bear some responsibility for a ship sunk in its waters but the paper did not think this fact especially consequential: "The fate of the *Maine,* heartrending as it is, profoundly as it has moved the American people, is only an episode in a drama that would have moved swiftly to its destined end without it. Intervention in behalf of Cuban independence was our duty before the *Maine* was destroyed; it was our duty before de Lôme wrote his letter, and it is our duty now."[50] In the days ahead, the paper's editorials would be inconsistent in their details and sometimes disingenuous in their arguments—talking of Spanish treachery and the "murder" of the ship's crew, for instance, while still professing to withhold judgment on the cause. It continued to argue that the U.S. had a moral and humanitarian obligation to bring peace to Cuba regardless of the calamity in Havana harbor. The *Journal* never isolated the loss of the *Maine* as grounds for war, but in the wake of de Lôme it no longer saw hope for non-military solution. The paper now clearly wanted a war.

Every day for a week after the *Maine* explosion, Hearst ran eight or more pages of news, comment, and speculation—more content than any other paper on Park Row. He carried descriptions of the blast and of rescue efforts, with close attention to the movements and utterances of Consul General Lee, Captain Sigsbee, and Spain's General Blanco. There were group pictures of the crew of the *Maine*, biographies of both the dead and survivors, and interviews with families of the victims. The administration's efforts to manage the crisis and formulate a response received a page or more a day, not including news from Congress and Wall Street. The paper played up differences as to the cause of the blast between the secretary of the navy and his belligerent assistant, Roosevelt. There were dozens of stories on war preparations in the United States and Spain.

Hearst was directly orchestrating coverage as evidenced by this flurry of telegrams to his European editor, Creelman:

> February 19: "MADRID SEEMS DOING NOTHING HERALD HAS FINE CABLE ON ATTITUDE OF WEYLER MAINE IS GREAT THING AROUSE EVERYBODY HEARST"
> February 22: "CRISPI STATEMENT GREAT CAN YOU GET MORE LIKE IT WORLD HAS STATEMENT INTERNATIONAL EXPERTS LEGAL ASPECTS HEARST"
> February 23: "STIR UP MADRID WORLD HAS CABLED MAN THERE TO GET FROM SPANISH GOVERNMENT STATEMENT WHETHER MINES IN HAVANA HARBOR SHOULD HAVE SOMETHING TO OFFSET THIS HEARST."
> February 24: "TRY FOR BIG INTERVIEW STATEMENT HERR KRUPP ON GUNS POSSIBLY FURNISHING QUICKLY HAS HE ANY READY MADE FOR SALE PART OF HEAVY ARTILLERY IN MODERN WARFARE LAND BATTERIES AGAINST FLEET DEFENSE HEARST"
> February 27: "FOREIGN STUFF SIMPLY GREAT THANKS IMMENSELY WOULD LIKE TO REACH ACROSS AND SHAKE HANDS HEARST"[51]

By the end of the first week of coverage, Hearst had three ships in or bound for Havana, carrying a who's who of special correspondents, among them Karl Decker, James Creelman, Alfred Henry Lewis, Julian Hawthorne, and Frederic Remington. He kept his presses running around the clock and produced new editions almost hourly. His circulation had doubled. On March 1 he wrote Creelman, who had taken Hearst's gratitude as an opportunity to renegotiate a contract now paying him $18,000 a year:

"ARRANGEMENT SUGGESTED YOUR LETTER SATIS-
FACTORY YOURSELF AS EUROPEAN EDITOR CIRCU-
LATION OVER MILLION DAILY DURING WAR SCARE
HOW IS THAT HEARST"[52]

There was a lot of solid work in the *Journal*'s eight pages a day and there was some indisputably bad journalism, as well. Hearst overreached in defense of the external explosion theory. It was not true that naval officers were "unanimous" that the ship had been purposely destroyed. Zalinski did not offer "indisputable evidence" of a submarine mine, merely a hypothesis, and the *Journal*'s photo-illustrations of the wreck in Havana harbor were not "proof of a submarine mine," as Hearst's headlines shouted.[53] Alfred Henry Lewis argued on no real evidence that Weylerites had blown up the *Maine*.[54] The paper reported erroneously that President McKinley believed the ship had been destroyed by an external blast and that "Official Washington Now Regards War as Inevitable."[55] The *Journal* printed on its front page a transcript of an alleged interview with Theodore Roosevelt in which he lauds the paper as "commendable," "accurate," "patriotic," and "loyal."[56] Roosevelt emphatically disavowed the interview, this time in private as well as in public. Pulitzer made the most of the spat, describing Hearst's Cuba news as "Written by Fools for Fools."[57]

There was also the usual mess of self-promotion in the *Journal*'s eight pages a day. Hearst offered a $50,000 reward for information leading to "the detection of the perpetrator of the *Maine* outrage" (on another occasion, "the persons, if any, criminally responsible for the destruction of the *Maine*").[58] Consistent with its practice of giving readers of its Sunday edition puzzles and diversions revolving around news themes, the *Journal* invented a board game involving a shootout between the Spanish cruiser *Vizcaya* and the *Texas*. It launched a campaign for funds to build a monument to the *Maine* victims. (Grover Cleveland refused to join the fundraising committee, saying, "I decline to allow my sorrow for those who died on the *Maine* to be perverted to an advertising scheme of the

New York Journal.")[59] There were dozens of self-promotional stories about the *Journal*'s scoops, the *Journal*'s efforts to crack the mystery of the *Maine*, the *Journal*'s influence in Congress, and the *Journal*'s special trains carrying news of the explosion at lightning speed in all directions, among other examples of *Journal* enterprise.

The worst aspect of Hearst's coverage crept into the paper five days after the *Maine* went down. Stung by accusations of warmongering from his competitors, he took refuge in nativist demagoguery, running a boldfaced front-page editorial presented against a backdrop of the American flag:

> The *Journal* is neither surprised nor affected by the abuse heaped upon it by newspapers whose owners either live in Europe, or, being native there, came to this country too late in life to absorb the spirit of American institutions or the temper of the American people. Men of this type are unfitted, by their environment, to gauge the force and trend of public sentiment in the United States. Their habits of mind are European; their instincts anti-American. The *Journal* is an American paper for the American people. It is not what the alien press, borrowing a phrase from British politics, calls a "jingo" newspaper. It does not urge war. It hopes for peace—peace in the United States and in Cuba—and it sees clearly enough that to enforce peace in the ravaged island is the surest way to assure it at home. The policy of the *Journal* is aggressive Americanism. The people have approved a course by swelling its circulation to more than a million copies a day. Peace with honor, peace with the maintenance of national dignity, peace without sacrificing the cause of humanity is the American ideal.[60]

Error, poor judgment, and bigotry are never virtues in newspapering, and there is no excusing them in this instance. It is one thing, however, to regret these failings, and quite another to describe them as damnable or lunatic, especially when they weren't even unusual. Again, context matters. Even before the *Maine* blew, Congress, the American people, and Park Row were deeply disturbed by events in Cuba. The destruction of the ship put them all in a frenzy. Hearst's coverage was part of an uproarious national dialogue. His voice sounds freakish when plucked out and examined in isolation, but in the context of the journalistic conversation that erupted as the *Maine* sank, it sounds quite different.

As Godkin noted, Pulitzer kept pace with Hearst in the days after the blast, promoting the external explosion theory, quoting many of the same sources and experts, claiming scoops, offering rewards, and making its share of mistakes. While it might be expected that the yellows would bark up the same tree, the *Sun*, more conservative in thought and style, was if anything more eager to link Spain to the sinking of the *Maine*. It gave prominence to a general in the Cuban army who claimed to know for a fact that Spanish authorities had torpedoed the vessel—"[I] would stake my life upon it."[61] It ran on its front page several reports that Spanish soldiers in small craft had made suspicious maneuvers in Havana Bay hours before the explosion. It carried rumors that Spanish women in Havana had been warned to avoid the wharves the day of the blast, and that a caller to the U.S. consulate alerted the Americans to an impending attack on the *Maine*. It laughed at the *Tribune* and the *Herald*, among other papers, for maintaining that the *Maine* had blown itself to bits. Its editorials insisted that the Spaniards were responsible for the *Maine* whether or not they had conspired in its destruction, and they openly encouraged U.S. military intervention in Cuba, expressing strong views on the proper procedure for a declaration of war and the most advantageous deployment of American fighting resources.

The *Tribune* demonstrated that a paper need not be pro-Cuban to be rash, wrong, or wildly partisan. It had been on press with an editorial pronouncing Spanish-American relations healed at the very moment the *Maine* was burning in Havana harbor, and having invested heavily in McKinley's diplomatic mastery, it remained anxious that the Havana riots, Dupuy de Lôme's revelations, and a single sunken battleship not count as setbacks. On February 17, the second day of coverage, the *Tribune* championed the theory of a spontaneous explosion in one of the ship's magazines and claimed that informed opinion was unanimously and unequivocally on its side: "It appears to be practically the consensus of the highest naval expert opinion that . . . the deplorable occurrence will become historical as a mysterious accident in which blame can never be positively attached. . . ." The paper continued to insist that the explosion was "inexplicable" even as it absolved the navy and the ship's officers of negligence, assembled forensic experts to argue against an external blast, and pointed to earlier explosions and fires aboard American naval vessels as examples of what must have happened to the *Maine*.

The *Tribune* was so eager to protect the supposed peace between

Washington and Madrid that it argued Spain had no obligation to disavow or even regret the sinking of the *Maine*. If the ship had been deliberately blown up, the culprit would have to be a "Cuban madman, hoping thus to embroil the United States and Spain to the advantage of the insurgent cause."[62] Who could blame friendly Spain for a lone madman?

The most striking aspect of the *Tribune*'s coverage was its insistence that the American people accept the administration's views as gospel. President McKinley and his cabinet had repudiated all theories of foul play and it remained for the public to fall in line: "It is the manifest duty of every American to trust [McKinley] in the present tragic crisis, to sustain him in the onerous tasks by emulating his own fortitude and forbearance, and above all scrupulously to refrain from any deed or words that may add to his burdens."[63] It is unusual for a newspaper to call for strict allegiance to the chief executive, especially outside of wartime. It is remarkable in this instance because the *Tribune* was calling for obedience while still insisting that McKinley had everything under control and that there was no crisis. Both the *Tribune* and the *Times* advocated legislative action against newspapers inclined to disagree with them on the *Maine* disaster.[64]

The *Herald* followed a similar line, but the most radical expressions of the conservative position came from the *Commercial Advertiser:* "The less said about the *Maine* the better. Apparently we have blown up a fine ship, killed several hundred sailors and sent $3,000,000 worth of property to the bottom of the sea by sheer carelessness. We have come to grief like a boy trusted with a real pistol after drilling and parading and fighting imaginary Indians with wooden dummies. The incident will be worth the cost if it teaches us humility and abates our thirst for war."

The fact is that newspapers up and down Park Row—whatever their political inclination—were as riddled with rumor and falsehood in the aftermath of the *Maine* as they had been since the start of the Cuban story. There was so much disinformation flowing from so many sources within forty-eight hours of the explosion that the Associated Press called for a time-out: "The cruiser *New York* has not been ordered to Havana; Consul General Lee has not been assassinated; there is no conference of the Cabinet; Congress is not in session tonight, both Houses having adjourned at the usual hour until tomorrow; President McKinley did not go to the Capitol, and the situation is decidedly quiet."[65] Hearst probably did publish more sloppy and inaccurate news than other papers, not to foment war but because he published more news than his rivals, good and bad. He had made a conscious choice to run the most aggressive news operation in New York. That put speed and comprehensiveness in competition with the paper's commitment to absolute accuracy. The *Herald*, reputed to be the best news operation in the country, played by the same rules.

As for Hearst's quickness to pronounce on the cause of the blast, no one in America—not even William McKinley—was waiting for the naval court to submit its report before voicing an opinion. Every major daily on Park Row staked out a position on the cause and defended it aggressively. Whether an editor believed the *Maine* was sunk by accident or by treachery wasn't determined by circulation concerns, journalistic standards, or the emotions of proprietors: it was largely a political decision. "Those who favored a peaceful settlement of the Cuban problem," writes John Offner, "believed [the explosion] was an accident, whereas those who wanted direct and immediate intervention in Cuba suspected foul play."[66] It is probably more accurate to draw the line between those who believed diplomacy would work and those who did not but, otherwise, Offner's formulation holds.

Hearst did wrap himself in the flag. He did preach a form of chauvinistic Americanism, and he belittled those of his rivals not native-born. But given the public mood, he was at worst encouraging sentiments that were already blazing. Today's journalist is likely to be offended by the idea of an editor seeking to ride or incite public sentiment rather than standing aloof from it or challenging it, but this was accepted practice in the Gilded Age. All of Hearst's principal competitors flattered the prejudices of either a popular audience or the better classes. Within weeks of these events, most of them would join Hearst in red, white, and blue, for, as Dana said, "You must be for the Stars and Stripes every time . . . [or] you won't sell enough papers to pay your expenses."[67]

The majority of the error and recklessness assigned to Hearst's coverage of the *Maine* is either overstated or unremarkable in light of prevailing journalistic standards. It is perhaps hard to believe that so many biographers and historians could have so profoundly misread Hearst's coverage, but most begin from the same point of reference: E.L. Godkin, the first and most vociferous critic of Hearst and the yellow press. Godkin himself has been profoundly misread, and that in turn has led to a serious misapprehension of Hearst.

E.L. GODKIN WAS BRILLIANT, witty, and influential, one of the more battle-hardened controversialists of the Gilded Age. He was anything but a voice of steady reason and cool judgment amid the Cuban crisis, as one might gather from his various descriptions of Hearst and the yellow press as lunatic, diabolical, eternally damned, and Satanic.

Godkin was the great reactionary of late-nineteenth-century American journalism—elitist and gloomy. He was sickened by the social and political trajectory of his adopted country, and he frankly admitted that all his hopes and ideals for America had been dashed. He was emerging as the arch-critic of popular government, writing a series of screeds against democracy, referring to the American people as "howling savages" and "lunatics" and "maniacs," and reserving his utmost disgust for the varieties of populism favored by the *Journal*.[68] According to his biographer, Godkin also wasted "an unconscionable amount of precious time envying young people," and he reserved the hardest corner of his heart for the western United States, despising California in particular.[69] It is no wonder that he seized upon Hearst, the young Californian, as the focus of his enmities.

Godkin wasn't much for war, either. A follower of Richard Cobden, he opposed armed conflict as injurious to the nation's finances. He considered patriotism and pro-Americanism unfortunate distractions from the business of life and, as such, "species of madness."[70] He feared U.S. involvement in Cuba would lead to annexation of a land of mongrel peoples who might corrupt American industriousness (perhaps the closest he came to a popular opinion).

Godkin's journalistic standards, against which Hearst is routinely and unfavorably measured, wilt under scrutiny. The *Evening Post* did less original reporting on the Cuban crisis than any other major daily on Park Row. Almost all of its news on the subject was gathered from administration sources in Washington. As a result, it did not cover the crisis so much as it covered the McKinley team's response to the crisis. In his initial editorial on the *Maine,* Godkin was surer than either Hearst or Pulitzer as to the cause of the explosion: "Taking it for granted that the explosion on the *Maine* was an accident pure and simple, we have only to remember that such things are among the risks which those taking service in the navy have to face. . . ."[71] Subsequent editorials argued the accident theory dogmatically and vociferously while belittling the coverage of Hearst and Pulitzer and wondering how they might be suppressed by "the hand of the law."[72] Godkin not only

wanted yellow newspapers held criminally accountable for their libels of
noble Spain but thought their readers should be considered accessories to
their crimes: "In the well-governed and highly civilized communities
of the future, they will be arrested at the newsstands and locked up."[73]

In yet another editorial, Godkin himself hit what might have been the
single-most diabolical note in all of Park Row's *Maine* coverage. Seizing
on the rumor that a wounded sailor had seen a small boat carrying a lit
fuse toward the ship seconds before it blew, he ventured the following:

> It is well known that [the *New York Journal*] sent a yacht down to Havana
> not long since. . . . Now, our theory is that it was a small boat from this
> yacht that was seen by the wounded sailor approaching the *Maine* with a
> lighted fuse. Of course much greater excitement could be made by the
> blowing up of a ship, and much larger sales of newspapers would result
> there from, than from the mere seizure of a yacht. We think that the naval
> court of inquiry should interrogate this sailor at once and find out
> whether he is sure that the boat and the fuse in question were not a part of
> the outfit of this American yacht.[74]

Godkin was only half-serious about his allegation but it has been
accepted as credible by subsequent writers, including biographer
Ferdinand Lundberg whose *Imperial Hearst* was published with a ringing
endorsement from Charles A. Beard, a president of the American
Historical Association (it was also the primary text for Orson Welles'
Citizen Kane.[75]) A surprising amount of the discussion of Godkin's lofty
standards revolves around newspaper style. Critics have always been
impressed by the *Evening Post*'s high tone: its tight focus on politics,
finance, and literature; its factual and succinct reporting; the formality of
its language; the restraint of its layout. There is something impressive
about the *Evening Post*'s style, even though (or perhaps because) it was
as reactionary as Godkin's opinions, but it reflected less his standards,
than his tastes and those of his audience. His ethics were unremarkable;
he was as concerned as any other editor on Park Row that his views find
readers and support his sales. Much as he complained of the circulation
antics of the yellow papers, he boasted to a colleague that his antiwar
crusade during the 1895 Venezuelan boundary dispute brought him "oral
applause of every description, and our circulation rose 1,000 a day."[76]

WITHIN TWO WEEKS OF THE EXPLOSION, there was unanimity on Park Row that an external explosion had destroyed the *Maine*. Swanberg and others have suggested that Hearst browbeat his rivals into adopting his point of view, but it was leaks to the Havana press corps from the naval court of inquiry that prompted the shift in opinion. Among other clues, investigators had found that the ship's keel had been bent upward, which they interpreted as evidence of a blast from below. After this revelation, the papers turned their attentions to debating whether or not Spain could be held responsible for failing to protect a visiting ship in Havana's harbor.

McKinley was still unwilling to give up on diplomacy, but Congress and public opinion were now firmly for intervention. Fearing for his own relevance, the president asked the chair of the House Appropriations Committee for $50 million for national defense. On March 9, Congress approved the funds by votes of 311 to 0 in the House (after 73 individual speeches), and 76 to 0 in the Senate. "Before it was over," one Senate clerk noted in his diary, "it seemed as though a hundred Fourth of Julys had been let loose in the House."[77] The *Journal*'s headline the next morning was "$50 Million For War!" Those words are sometimes criticized as being technically inaccurate because the money was designated for defense spending but the chairman of the House Committee on Appropriations recalled McKinley asking for the funds "for war."[78]

Another signal that the administration was about to capitulate to the interventionists came a week later in Washington. There had been regular reports to Congress from a variety of sources on the still-deteriorating situation in Cuba, some landing with more force than others. Senator Redfield Proctor was a Civil War veteran, a secretary of war in the Harrison administration, and a personal friend of William McKinley. He had toured Cuba of his own accord to gauge the progress of the insurgency and the welfare of the civilian population. On March 17, he told Congress that he had gone to the island convinced that "a few cases of starvation and suffering" had been subjected to the highly-cultivated imaginations of press correspondents and blown out of all proportion. He found that their reports were not overdrawn, that Cuba was in the ruinous grip of "desolation and distress, misery and starvation." Spain controlled only four western provinces, and every man, woman, and child in those parts was under guard in reconcentration camps. "Their huts are about ten by fifteen feet in size; and for want of space are usually crowded together very closely. . . . Conditions are unmentionable in this respect. Torn from their homes, with foul earth, foul air, foul water, and foul food or none, what wonder that one-half have died and that one-quarter of the living are so diseased that they cannot be saved? . . . Little children are still walking about with arms and chest terribly emaciated, eyes swollen, and abdomen bloated to three times the natural size." Proctor compared the human tragedy to the French Wars of Religion and the Spanish Inquisition. Because Spain could not defeat the insurgency and the rebels would not accept autonomy, Proctor saw no alternative to U.S. intervention.[79]

Proctor said nothing that Hearst, Pulitzer, Dana, and many other pro-Cuban voices in the United States hadn't been saying for many months, but it meant something for the Republicans and their press to hear it from their own. One of Proctor's Senate colleagues confessed to a sense of shame that "we, a civilized people, an enlightened nation, a great republic, born in a revolt against tyranny, should permit such a state of things within less than a hundred miles of our shore."[80] The *Tribune* now found "convincing force" in the call for intervention, but not all of the conservative papers were impressed.[81] The *Herald* ignored the speech entirely. Godkin's *Evening Post,* which had initially called for the suppression of Proctor's report, dismissed it, in twelve lines flat, as old news. Hearst and Pulitzer both reported Proctor's speech in its entirety, hailing it as a vindication of their long campaigns on behalf of the insurgents. "Senator Proctor," crowed a *Journal* editorial, "yesterday administered the finishing stroke to the self-styled 'better element' that has allied itself with tyranny and inhumanity in Cuba."[82]

Vindicated or not, the *Journal* lost its bearings through the month of March. On March 9, it was encouraging Americans to rally around the president now that he had found his spine. On March 11, the paper announced incorrectly that the court of inquiry had found that Spanish government officials had blown up the *Maine.* On March 12, it gave over two pages to a review of the paper's coverage of the crisis under the premature heading "The Part the *Journal* has Played in Making Cuba Free." By March 19, the paper was back on McKinley's case, finding weakness and timidity in yet another bid for a diplomatic solution.

The naval court of inquiry delivered its report to the White House on March 24, attributing the destruction of the *Maine* to "the explosion of a submarine mine, which caused the partial explosion of two or more of the forward magazines."[83] It was beyond the court's mandate to affix responsibility, but no one else in the country felt constrained. All fingers pointed to Spain. An exhausted, distraught McKinley still could not bring himself to give up on diplomacy. He tried belatedly to coax Spain out of Cuba with an ultimatum. It was ineffective. He considered further maneuvers, despite overwhelming public support for military intervention, pressure from Congress, and a threatened revolt in his own party.

The president's stubbornness drove the *Journal* to distraction, and Hearst produced what can only be described as atrocious journalism in the first week of April. He accused McKinley of tricking Congress and the American people by delaying intervention and asking for more time, and called the state of affairs in Washington "the most scandalous in the history of the country."[84] But the *Journal* was finally about to find relief.

McKinley's war message to Congress on April 11 confessed that all diplomatic solutions had been exhausted and that the time had come for America to act. His rationale for intervention relied in part on the national interest: the conflict in Cuba had placed in jeopardy the lives and liberty of U.S. citizens, destroyed U.S. property in Cuba, and compelled Washington to remain on a "semi-war" footing. The president argued that concern for Cuba had distracted Congress from "that close devotion to domestic advancement that becomes a self-contained commonwealth whose primal maxim has been the avoidance of all foreign entanglements." McKinley included the destruction of the *Maine* in his tally of damages suffered by America. He did not suspect that Spain was directly responsible. Rather, the tragedy was "a patent and impressive proof of a state of things in Cuba that is intolerable. . . . [The] Spanish Government can not assure safety and security to a vessel of the American Navy in the harbor of Havana on a mission of peace, and rightfully there." These were not the president's strongest arguments. Damage to U.S. interests certainly warranted indemnities and apologies from Madrid, but what little Cuban-American trade remained certainly wasn't worth a fight. Nor were there many American lives left to protect in Cuba: the vast majority of U.S. nationals had evacuated. Nor was a distracted Congress a powerful reason for war. The call to avenge the *Maine* had popular appeal, but should a "self-contained commonwealth whose primal maxim has been the avoidance of all foreign entanglements" plunge into a foreign adventure over what the president was describing as an issue of harbor safety?

McKinley was on firmer ground in citing as his "first" reason for intervention the cause of humanity: "Our people have beheld a once prosperous community reduced to comparative want, its lucrative commerce virtually paralyzed, its exceptional productiveness diminished, its fields laid waste, its mills in ruins, and its people perishing by tens of thousands from hunger and destitution." Spain's exercise of "cruel, barbarous, and uncivilized practices of warfare," had "shocked the sensibilities and offended the humane sympathies" of the American people. McKinley described Spain's war method as a species of inhumanity unprecedented in the modern history of civilized Christian peoples. "In the name of humanity," he summed up, "in the name of civilization, in behalf of endangered American interests which give us the right and the duty to speak and to act, the war in Cuba must stop."[85]

With that, the president asked Congress to authorize him to go to war. Congress quickly approved resolutions demanding Spain withdraw from Cuba. Some fifty representatives gathered in the lobby to belt out the "Battle Hymn of the Republic" and "Dixie." To the delight of Hearst and Pulitzer, the Senate also passed the Teller amendment, forswearing any intention to annex or establish sovereignty over the island and asserting the objective of leaving Cuba in the hands of Cubans. It would be a war for liberty and humanity, they exulted, not one of opportunism and territorial aggrandizement.

News of the war resolution was breathlessly awaited across America and especially on Park Row. Ray Stannard Baker, already on his way to becoming one of the finest reporters of the early twentieth century, tells how the *Journal* got the news out first:

A correspondent was on watch in Congress; a score of feet away a telegraph operator sat ready with his finger on the key; the wire was wide open, and in the composing-rooms of at least two New York papers a linotype operator, who was also a telegraph operator, sat at his machine ready to tick the words into type the moment they sprung from the wire. Three minutes after the declaration of war was passed, the newsboys were struggling up out of the Journal delivery room crying and extra announcing the news. In three minutes the correspondent had gathered and written the news—just a line or two of it—the dispatch had been sent from Washington to New York, had been set up in type, printed, and delivered on the street, ready for sale at a penny. This remarkable time record was rendered possible by a process known as 'fudging.' The type lines set by the lineotype-telegraph operator . . . are firmly clamped in an ingenious little supplemental machine consisting of a cylinder and an inking roll for red ink. This is attached to a revolving shaft a the top of one of the huge printing presses, and so arrange that when the paper comes rushing through from the regular type cylinders below, the 'fudge' prints a big red 'war' and a few lines of extra news in spaces left for that purpose in the right hand columns of the edition. This is the genesis of the 'Red Extra' and it is a typical development of modern journalism.[86]

OVER THE YEARS, Hearst's biographers and critics have gleefully enumerated and inflated the failings of his Cuban coverage. Much less has been said about what his paper got right, although the list is rather impressive. It was right about the intractability of the Spanish-Cuban war. It was right to call attention to Spanish atrocities and to the suffering of the *reconcentrados*. It was right about the inadequacy and insincerity of Spain's reforms. It was right about the futility of further negotiations with Madrid. It was right about the consequences of the riots in Havana. It was right about the significance of the Dupuy de Lôme letter. It had a reasonably firm grasp of the sentiments of Congress and the American people. Most importantly, the arguments the *Journal* advanced for U.S. intervention in Cuba were consistent with the arguments advanced by McKinley in his war message. The gray papers, excepting the *Sun*, have a relatively weak record on these fundamental points.*

Through the first half of the twentieth century, scholars tended to see Hearst and yellow journalism as the cause behind America's war against

---

* Hearst was probably wrong about the cause of the destruction of the *Maine*, although there is still some uncertainty on that front. McKinley's naval court of inquiry determined that the ship was sunk by an external blast, as Hearst believed; a second inquiry in 1911, which raised the wreck from Havana harbor and studied it minutely, reached the same conclusion. A 1976 investigation overseen by Admiral Hyman G. Rickover, relying on forensic knowledge collected from ships damaged in the Second World War, decided that the explosion likely occurred within the *Maine*, probably as a result of a fire in a coal bunker. In 1999, the National Geographic Society sponsored a computer-aided analysis of the wreck that supported the conclusion of the two initial inquiries. The sinking of the *Maine* is still a mystery but Rickover's analysis is persuasive.

Spain. The oft-cited Joseph Wisan, among others, argued that "the Spanish-American War would not have occurred had not the appearance of Hearst in New York journalism precipitated a bitter battle for newspaper circulation."[87] W.A. Swanberg wrote: "It was an unnecessary war. It was the newspapers' war. Above all, it was Hearst's war." Through the second half of the twentieth century, scholars began to downplay the role of the newspapers. Some argued that technological, economic, and social developments made U.S. involvement in Cuba more or less inevitable. Others emphasized the domestic political situation in 1898 and congressional anxieties about the approaching mid-term elections. A shrewd McKinley took the lead of pro-Cuban forces in advance of the mid-term elections, securing a Republican triumph (alternately, he was stampeded into a declaration of war by a Congress nervous about its re-election prospects). The yellow press is little more than a nuisance in these accounts. The latest Hearst biography argues that the United States would have crossed the Straits of Florida on much the same timetable as it did had Hearst never set foot in New York. That Hearst was mistaken as a critical player in Cuba is attributed to his "genius for self-promotion."[88] It is a long fall from primary instigator of an international conflict and liberator of an oppressed people to bit-playing object of ridicule.

A certain amount of correction was overdue. Hearst was by no means solely responsible for the U.S. intervention. War between Spain and America may not have been inevitable but it was probable, for the simple reason that the interests of the rebels, Washington, and Madrid were fundamentally irreconcilable. At the moment of truth, President McKinley and Congress made up their own minds to intervene. Hearst was not in the cabinet room and he did not have a vote in Congress; he was on the sidelines with the rest of the press corps. That said, he was far more influential than is presently understood.

That the press made a difference in the Spanish-American War can be seen in several realms, starting with public opinion. While the was no unanimity on the subjects, the cause of *Cuba Libre* and, ultimately, the decision to intervene were wildly popular. "The American people took a deep interest in the Cuban revolution," writes Offner. "They sympathized with Cuban independence, favored the underdog, looked with horror on the numerous deaths in Cuban reconcentration camps, wanted to avenge the *Maine*, and by March 1898 were willing to use military force to remove Spain from Cuba."[89] Or, as President McKinley said, the "temper and forbearance of our people have been so sorely tried as to beget a perilous unrest among our own citizens."[90]

It was highly unusual for the American public to get wound up about an international conflict. Nineteenth-century politics were parochial. The conduct of foreign policy was an elite preoccupation more or less immune to popular sentiment.[91] It is true that the American people had rattled sabers over the Venezuelan crisis in 1895, but only after being invited to do so by Washington's aggressive posturing. The moment President Cleveland resolved matters to his satisfaction, he was able to throw a wet blanket over the affair. *Cuba Libre* had a birth and life independent of Washington. Both Cleveland and McKinley tried to smother it. Both failed. The Cuban cause captivated millions of people who had no material stake in the outcome of the rebellion. How do we account for their knowledge and passion? Junta propagandists? Community activists? Local homilists? Perhaps to some extent, but would the whole nation have been "swept by a hurricane of militant righteousness" into a campaign to "slay a dragon and free a damsel in distress" without the influence of the press?

Newspapers were by far the dominant communications medium of the day. All of the important New York papers contributed to coverage of the Cuban story, and several news outlets, including the *New York Herald* and the Associated Press, played major roles, but the yellow papers were predominant. They were among the leading sources—usually *the* leading sources—for information on just about every angle of the story from the progress of the insurgency to the *Maine* explosion. They had the most reporters in the field. They conducted special investigations, straw polls of state and national politicians, and their own commissions of inquiry into affairs in Cuba. They developed the narrative lines that kept Cuba alive and vivid in the public mind: the murder of Dr. Ruiz, the trials of Evangelina Cisneros, the imprisonment of Sylvester Scovel. They were leading promoters of the progressive ideology that inspired so many Americans to want to do good in Cuba. They articulated on an almost daily basis the moral and political arguments eventually adopted to justify U.S. intervention. The Cuban story as it played out in their pages was the same Cuban story that existed in the public imagination—the same plot, the same themes, the same villains. The influence of the yellows was extended through their own circulations, which were easily the largest in the country, and through their proprietary news syndicates and the Associated Press, as well as by example. There was often a correspondence between the progression of opinion in regional papers and those of Hearst and Pulitzer.[92] And all observers cite Hearst as leader of the yellow press.

In addition to affecting the political process indirectly through public opinion, the yellow papers directly influenced Congress. Representatives and senators relied heavily on the press for what they knew of Cuba and Spain and all related issues. They had few other sources. The administration wasn't forthcoming. Seeking to lower the temperature around the conflict and negotiate quietly with Spain, it offered only infrequent presidential addresses or public statements and the odd leaked diplomatic letter. With minimal expertise and research capacity, the administration had trouble assembling reliable data even for its own purposes. McKinley is said to have followed the movements of his fleet in these months on a page ripped from a school geography text.[93] Consular reports from Cuba were fitful, not always reliable, and limited in circulation. Newspapers with correspondents in Havana had better access to the views of consul staffers than all but the highest-ranking officials in Washington. Not always satiated by what it read, Congress routinely summoned journalists for briefings. A series of reporters with first-hand experience of Cuba, including at least two from the *Journal,* were interviewed by the Senate Foreign Relations Committee. Scovel briefed the secretary of war on the progress of the U.S. official inquiry into the *Maine* explosion. As previously noted, the number of congressional resolutions dealing with Cuba ebbed and flowed with atrocity stories in the yellow newspapers.[94]

It would be an overstatement to say newspapers drove congressional debate. The relationship between the politicians and the press was, as per usual, symbiotic. Each viewed the other as a barometer of public sentiment. Each took the other's leadership. Politicians were influenced by editorial commentary (far more so than today); editors adjusted their views in light of political opinion and of the passage or defeat of congressional resolutions. The endless debates, speeches, petitions, and resolutions out of Congress were welcome fodder for the dailies; representatives loved to be seen working for a cherished cause by a vast newspaper audience. It must also be said that a lot of bad information and rash opinion washed back and forth between Congress and the papers.

Expert testimony as to the influence of the press on the U.S. political process comes from none other than Enrique Dupuy de Lôme. He firmly believed that the yellow papers influenced the temperature in the Capitol, and that the best way to hold the House in check was to avoid making headlines. He considered the *Journal* his most dangerous enemy and cursed its influence in the letter that brought about his resignation.[95] While Dupuy de Lôme railed against Hearst in Washington, Weyler blamed American newspapers for all his problems—"the poison everything with false-hood"—and made *Journal* correspondents his favorite targets for expulsion from Havana.[96] Prime Minister Cánovas marveled to the *Journal*'s James Creelman that "the newspapers in your country seem to be more power-ful than the government."[97] About the only thing Spanish officials and the Junta could agree upon was that the insurgency had important allies in the yellow press. The rebel generals relied on steady coverage in the yellows to raise funds in America and to keep pressure on Congress. They gave interviews and stories to the papers and showed New York correspon-dents elaborate courtesy in their travels through Cuba, offering them security details to rival those of their own generals.[98] The Junta, knowing it had a bombshell in the Dupuy de Lôme letter, released it not to a politi-cian but to the press. General Garcia would soon present his battle flag to Hearst because he considered the publisher a critical ally and, even after the declaration of war, a more reliable one than McKinley.

Newspaper influence on the public and Congress mattered because the men in charge—the president and his cabinet—were sincere in their regard for the voice of the people. McKinley mentioned the agitations of the American people and their elected representatives in his instructions to his envoy, Woodford, as well as his first annual address to Congress and again in his war message. All of McKinley's biographers acknowl-edge his reverence for and keen sense of the public will.

The motives behind McKinley's ultimate decision to force Spain from Cuba are still hotly debated. Some historians argue that public and congressional opinion forced the president's hand: with midterm elections looming, he "made war on Spain in order to keep control of Washington."[99] Others see the president as master of the whole Spanish-American affair, dampening public enthusiasms and fending off congressional jin-goes until such time as he himself was convinced of the advisability of a fight.[100] The latter would be an easier argument to make if McKinley had not made such a large and public display of trust in Spain and of his hopes for a negotiated settlement. The more important point, however, is that even those historians who credit McKinley with making his own decision agree that he believed the sentiments of Congress and the American people to be highly relevant.

Hearst and the yellow newspapers can not be purged from the Cuban story. As advocates, narrators and weathervanes, they played a significant role in shaping public opinion, congressional sentiment, and the domestic political environment of 1898—all of which influenced McKinley's decision to make war.[101] The *New York Journal* was the leading pro-Cuban paper in America and its vigorous coverage of all aspects of the story encouraged its major competitors to devote more attention and resources to it. In the end, Hearst's voice was not decisive in America's decision to fight, but it was certainly instrumental. The *Journal* probably exerted as much influence in those decisive months as a newspaper can exert.

In dismissing Hearst and the yellow papers as jingoes or circulation-hungry cynics, and in underestimating the role of the American people in forcing action against Spain, historians have obscured an interesting angle to the story. In her 2002 book, *A Problem from Hell: America and the Age of Genocide,* Samantha Powers reviews the twentieth century's horrible record of mass killings—non-Serbs by Bosnian Serbs, the Ottoman attempts to eradicate Armenians, the Nazi Holocaust, Pol Pot's murderous regime in Cambodia, Saddam Hussein's attempted extermination of Iraq's Kurds, the Hutus' slaughter of Tutsis in Rwanda—and discerns a pattern of U.S. reaction to these monstrous events. Early warnings go unheeded, reports of violence are rejected as exaggerations by impartial sources, or rationalized as typical of warfare, or dismissed as none of America's business. The United States, writes Powers, has "never in its history intervened to stop genocide" and has "rarely even made a point of condemning it as it occurred."[102] American policy makers, journalists, and citizens have been "extremely slow to muster the imagination needed to reckon with evil. Ahead of the killings, they assume rational actors will not inflict seemingly gratuitous violence. They trust in good-faith negotiations and traditional diplomacy."[103] Politicians read the silence of their constituents as "public indifference" and the battle to stop genocide is repeatedly lost.[104]

The term "genocide" was not available in the nineteenth century and it is beyond the scope of this book to determine if what Spain inflicted on Cubans in the 1890s meets the United Nations criteria for genocide (it appears to, but the related terms "democide" or "policide" might fit better). Journalists who visited the island, and Spanish and American officials—not least of all McKinley—found the word "extermination" adequate to describe policies they believed would lead to the eradication of a subject people ("extermination" also sufficed, at the time, for the Turkish massacre of Armenians, the opening act of the Armenian genocide). Hundreds of thousands of Cubans died as a result of Spain's policies, and many more might have perished had the outside world not protested and, ultimately, interceded. As with most of the genocides cited by Powers, there were many ways for the United States to rationalize a hands-off approach to Cuba: the rebels were contributing to the humanitarian crisis; Spain had a sovereign right to pursue a counterinsurgent strategy; reports of atrocities were often exaggerated and inseparable from Junta propaganda. Yet the American people, with leadership from their newspapers, did in this instance "muster the imagination needed to reckon with evil," prompting the intervention.

Hearst celebrated the congressional declaration of hostilities with a volley of fireworks from the roof of the *Journal*'s offices on Park Row. Spain severed diplomatic relations with Washington on April 21. The next day, on McKinley's orders, the U.S. Navy began a blockade of Cuban ports. On April 24, 1898, Spain declared war on the United States, and on April 25 Congress passed a resolution declaring that a state of war had existed since April 21.[105] Hearst turned his mind to what role he would play in the Spanish-American War.

CHAPTER FIFTEEN

As I Write, Ambulance Trains
Are Bringing the Wounded

In April, everywhere over this good, fair land, flags were flying. Trains
carrying soldiers were hurrying from the North, from the East, from the
West, to the Southland; and as they sped over the green prairies and the
brown mountains, little children on fences greeted the soldiers with flapping
scarves and handkerchiefs and flags; and at the stations, crowds gathered to
hurrah for the soldiers, and to throw hats in to the air, and to unfurl flags.
Everywhere it was flags: tattered, smoke-grimed flags in engine cabs; flags
in button-holes; flags on proud poles; flags fluttering everywhere.
—WILLIAM ALLEN WHITE[1]

The Spanish-American War may well have been the most popular
in U.S. history. Over a million men, far in excess of requirements, offered their services. It was the best chance for adventure and honor at arms available to young American men since the Civil
War, and everyone wanted in on the action. William Jennings Bryan
signed up with a Nebraska militia. Five hundred Westchester businessmen volunteered en masse. William F. "Buffalo Bill" Cody proposed to
sweep the Spanish out of Cuba with a force of thirty thousand Indian
braves. A Colorado matron named Martha Shute bid to organize an all-
female cavalry unit. Frank James, brother of Jesse, mused about assembling a cowboy regiment (two such organizations actually materialized,
under the leadership of Melvin Grigsby and Jay Torrey). Hearst's
Journal suggested a fighting team of America's finest athletes, including
boxers Bob Fitzsimmons and Jim Corbett, football great Red Waters, and
baseball hero Cap Anson, men who would "overawe the Spanish by their

mere appearance."² It seems a silly notion, but the most famous regiment
of the war turned out to be Teddy Roosevelt's Rough Riders, a mélange
of frontiersmen, Indian fighters, and some of the best football, polo, golf,
and tennis players from Ivy League clubs in Manhattan.

McKinley and his Secretary of War, Russell Alger, more than doubled
the size of the regular army to 58,688 and backed it with 200,000 volunteers. Combined with the navy's 26,000 crew and officers, America's
fighting force weighed in at 290,000 men.³ It was more than enough to
handle a Spanish army estimated to have less than 100,000 healthy regulars and volunteers in Cuba, but hardly sufficient to satisfy the fighting
ardor of the American male: hundreds of thousands of volunteers were
turned away, and only a very small proportion of those accepted got anywhere near the action. There was even more disappointment among those
seeking high command: the White House appointed and commissioned
roughly 1,000 officers from a pool of 25,000 applications.⁴

Hearst was among the snubbed. At the declaration of war, he wrote the
White House offering to fully outfit a cavalry regiment, modestly requesting for himself a position "in the ranks." McKinley politely rebuffed him.
Hearst next offered the navy the use of his yacht, *Buccaneer*. He wanted a
command on the boat and promised to write all necessary qualifying
examinations. The yacht was accepted; Hearst's commission did not
arrive until several weeks after the fighting had ended, and even then the
navy appointed him an ensign, its humblest rank, which had to be a calculated insult.⁵ Spurned as a combatant, Hearst would take his place in
the conflict, more fittingly, as a journalist.

THE SPANISH-AMERICAN WAR was as big an opportunity for newspapermen as it was for soldiers. Willis Abbott reports that everyone
with any influence on Hearst's staff became a war correspondent—
"The office was depopulated."⁶ A *Journal* editorial boasted of the "journalistic army" the paper had assembled to cover the war: it featured
Langdon Smith, George Eugene Bryson, Alfred Henry Lewis, Frederic
Remington, James Creelman, and Walter Howard, among many others.
These correspondents, artists, and photographers would travel about on
the *Journal*'s own "navy of dispatch boats," including the *Anita*, the

Buccaneer, the *Ely,* the *Simpson,* the *Baracoa,* the *Diamante,* and two or three tugs.[7]

The queues of prospective war correspondents were equally long at other addresses on Park Row. Approximately three hundred American journalists would win assignment to the Spanish-American conflict, including such unlikely figures as Alexander Kenealy, humor writer for the *World,* and Acton Davies, drama editor of the *Evening Sun.*[8] Even before Congress had declared war, dozens of reporters gathered with the likes of Richard Harding Davis, Stephen Crane, and the novelist Frank Norris on the piazzas of Key West, where the North Atlantic Squadron was stationed. They paid exorbitant rates to sleep on iron cots in the hallways of crowded hotels, bobbed around the harbor in their dispatch boats, and fought among themselves for telegraph time and privileged access to admirals and battleships. They waited impatiently at the cable office for their turn on the single wire not reserved for government use, "their copy growing stale in their hands," according to one observer, "as the sweat beaded on their necks."[9] That the fighting was many weeks away and there was precious little news to report did nothing to dampen their excitement.

Not all of the New York papers initially shared the enthusiasm of their correspondents. The conservative dailies fought the call to arms until the last minute. The *Herald* dismissed the war as an impulsive, illogical, and "sentimental" adventure.[10] The pro-McKinley *Tribune* made the clearest antiwar statement of any New York daily in this period: "War is not purification. It is debauchery. War is not an uplifting. It is a degradation. War does not lend the national mind to higher thoughts, but to lower and less worthy ones."[11] But all of the conservative papers, with the notable exception of Godkin's *Evening Post,* reluctantly buried their misgivings once war became inevitable. As the *Tribune*'s Reid advised his managing editor, "it would be unwise for us to be the last persons to assent to it, or to seem to be dragged into the support of it."[12] With an enthusiasm bordering on funereal, they adopted the line that America was fighting for humanity and liberty in the face of Spain's obstinacy and the oppression of the Cuban people. Their spirits lifted, however, with the first whiff of gun smoke. Within a week of Congress's declaration, these papers would leap to the front ranks of what they had previously called the jingo brigades.

The most startling changes occurred at the venerable *Herald.* James Gordon Bennett, no longer boasting that he could acquire all the talent he needed at $25 a week, was now employing and granting bylines to Richard Harding Davis at $400 a week plus expenses. With his earlier failure to reach the Cuban insurgents for the *Journal* still on his conscience, Davis embraced this new assignment as completely as any he had undertaken in his life. He arranged contracts not only with the *Herald* but with *The Times* of London, *Scribner's* magazine, and a book publisher. "I expect to make myself rich on this campaign," he wrote his family.[13] As per his custom, he assembled a new quasi-military costume for the adventure—canvas shooting jacket, holster and cartridge belt, leather flask, gloves, and top boots—and distributed a new photo of himself to the press. ("There will be terrific ink shed when he reaches the front," winked the *Springfield Republican*).[14] He also equipped himself with a letter of introduction to Rear Admiral William T. Sampson of the North Atlantic Squadron from his acquaintance Teddy Roosevelt, assistant secretary of the navy. Roosevelt didn't much like Davis. He describes him in private correspondence as an "everlasting cad," but the publicity-happy Roosevelt knew how to work the papers.[15] His letter was a factor in Davis's gaining access to Sampson's flagship, the *New York*. "It is like a luxurious yacht, with none of the ennui of a yacht," Davis wrote home. "The other night, when we were heading off a steamer and firing six-pounders across her bows, the band was playing the 'star' song from *Meistersinger*. Wagner and War struck me as the most *fin de siècle* idea of war that I had ever heard of."[16]

It was aboard the *New York* on April 27 that Davis witnessed one of the first actions of the war, the U.S. naval bombardment of Matanzas on the northern coast of Cuba. A long-range artillery salvo does not make for scintillating copy, and this one was of little consequence (the Spanish reported the loss of a single mule) but thanks to the *Herald*'s system of dispatch boats, Davis was able to file his breathless account ahead of any competitors. "The guns seemed to be ripping out the steel sides of the ship," he wrote. "The thick deck of the superstructure jumped with the concussions and vibrated like a suspension bridge when an express train thunders over it." His scoop was splashed on the paper's first news page under what was by the *Herald*'s standards an enormous, double-decker, four-column, all-caps headline, illustrated with a sprawling artist's conception of the shelling prepared in New York. An account of how Davis reported the incident and then boarded a dispatch boat to file his story received almost as much space on the page as the bombardment itself. The *Herald* milked its exclusive for several editions under such headings as "Take That For the *Maine!*" It continued to celebrate in lead stories and editorials its "brilliant achievement" in newsgathering. It exulted at length over the paucity of coverage in rival papers: "The only news our morning contemporaries were able to give on going to press was a bare bulletin of the bombardment gathered from hearsay at Key West after the arrival of the *Herald*'s dispatch boat.[17]

The zeal of the *Herald*'s Matanzas coverage was nothing compared to what followed a few days later. The paper was fortunate enough to be one of few witnesses to the single-most critical battle of the Spanish-American War. At first light on May 1 on the other side of the globe, Commodore George Dewey's Asiatic squadron attacked Admiral Patricio Montojo's Spanish fleet in Manila Bay and in just over six hours had destroyed or captured every one of Spain's ships without the loss of a single American life.[18] It was a crushing blow to the enemy in almost the first week of war, and the *Herald* couldn't contain itself. This "Glorious American Victory," declared the paper, was the reward of Providence to Spain for having trifled with the American people and for "the unspeakable crime of the destruction of the *Maine.*"[19] Dewey was hailed as a modern-day Columbus whose historic victory had opened a whole new world to the Stars and Stripes: "An event like this of Manila, which passes into history as among the decisive battles of the world, cannot be dismissed as an accident. Ours was a just cause. . . . every gun spoke the voice of humanity."[20]

The *Herald*'s ardor spilled over into other aspects of its war coverage. It jolted its readers with a menacing illustration of the Spanish armada and the startling headline "Spain's Fleet Steaming Toward American Waters."[21] It launched a series of cartoons mocking the Spanish war effort and shouting "Remember the Maine!", and gave another set of bold headlines to wild (and false) rumors that both the Spanish colonial minister and former governor general of Cuba, Martínez Campos, had been assassinated.[22] It wrongly accused a clutch of U.S. congressmen and senators of being in the pay of a rival newspaper proprietor.[23] It boasted not only of its feats of journalism but of its "enormous increase in circulation" as well.[24] Giddy in the wake of Manila Bay, it published a recipe for a Dewey cocktail: "One of them will make you feel like a true American;

two will cause you to wonder why you are not fighting for your country; and five or six will make you believe yourself to be as big a man as Dewey."[25] At moments such as these the *Herald* reads like an E.L. Godkin caricature of yellow journalism, but on the whole the paper's reportage on the Spanish-American War was thorough and, by the standards of the day, accurate.

The *Tribune*, too, let all its misgivings sink with Montojo's fleet. The paper trumpeted Dewey's "crushing blow" to the enemy with waving flags and multi-column, all-caps headlines—one reading "Remember the *Maine!*"[26] It decorated its front page with patriotic poetry and images of the wrecked Spanish ships. The city of New York, it reported, was "Ablaze with Joy," and a spirit of "exaltation" filled "every American heart." The paper boasted of having been first with news of the victory and of having informed the president and the secretary of the navy of Dewey's battle. Even more boldly, with its protest against war as debauchery and degradation still hanging in the air, the *Tribune* now presented Dewey's success as proof of the superior character of the American people: "That in such circumstances the Americans won is to be attributed to the simple fact that they are Americans. That is, they are intelligent, well disciplined and drilled, clear-sighted and steady of nerve, fully understanding their ships and guns, and able to use them in the most effective manner. . . ."[27] The *Tribune* topped all this with an early grab for the spoils of battle, troubling itself over which Philippine islands to keep and which to discard: "The nation that, for self-protection or in the cause of humanity, is compelled to go to war and bear its dreadful burdens, is entitled to enjoy the fruits of the victory it wins."[28] (The *Herald*, similarly, could not send enough troops to the Philippines to hold the islands and demonstrate to the world the methods of responsible imperial power.)[29]

Decisive moments are uncommon in newspaper wars: there is no adjudication; no one keeps score; all parties claim victory at every turn; no one admits defeat. Such performance metrics as exist—circulation and advertising numbers—are easily inflated, manipulated, and challenged. The winners and losers are generally sorted out years later when one title or another falls into obvious decline, or is shut down or sold or merged with a rival. But if there was a definite point at which Hearst clearly emerged as the leading voice on Park Row, it is in these very first days of the war with Spain. The evidence of his editorial, operational, and stylistic influence on his peers, for good and bad, is overwhelming. For almost three years, Hearst's newspaper had been lambasted as a warmonger for urging U.S. intervention in Cuba. Its motives had been impugned, its techniques ridiculed. Now some of its fiercest critics were appropriating for themselves its adopted role as humanitarian avenger of oppressed peoples, and with it every big-spending, self-promoting, eye-catching, crowd-pleasing, circulation-building trick in the yellow arsenal. They had all dabbled in these methods before and at certain moments they had all blasted Spain for its sins, but this was different. This was a phenomenal reversal of judgment on the part of the gray papers, executed without hesitation or the slightest blush.

Hearst did not miss his opportunity to declare victory. A May 6 editorial proclaimed "a time of full justification" for the paper and its proprietor: "This war has been called a war brought on by the *New York Journal* and the press which it leads. This is merely another way of saying that the war is the war of the American people, for it is only as a newspaper gives voice to the American spirit that it can be influential with the American masses. The *Journal* is powerful with the masses because it believes in them—because it believes that on large questions of right and wrong, on issues of national policy, their judgment is always likely to be sounder than that of the objecting few."[30]

On May 8, Hearst printed the slogan "How do you like the *Journal*'s War?" on either side of his front-page nameplate, a move that has been criticized as both tasteless gloating and the delusional raving of a man overstating his own importance to events. Hearst did believe his paper had done much to furnish the war but the slogan was, in fact, a riposte to critics of the paper's editorial leadership. It first appeared in a headline on Hearst's editorial page of May 2, the first day of reporting on Dewey's heroics above a reprint of the *Evening Post*'s complaint that a "blackguard boy" with millions at his disposal was exercising too much influence over American foreign policy: "Some People Say the *Journal* Brought On the War. How Do You Like It So Far as It's Gone?"[31]

Intent on maintaining his leadership, Hearst spared no expense in coverage of the war, never mind that he was out of funds. He had run through his initial $1 million sometime in 1897 (probably early) and ever since he had been drawing on family money—drawing so deeply that Phoebe made him sign over to her the deed to the Babicora ranch. Her

intention was to put a brake on his spending but she also wanted to protect the ranch in the event of a *Journal* bankruptcy. Will, confident of his
ultimate success and anxious to keep spending, transferred the property, a
gift from his father, on February 19, 1898.[32]

Brisbane would estimate the cost of the *Journal*'s coverage at $3,000
a day in excess of normal requirements, a rate of an additional $1 mil-
lion a year. The bulk of the money went to personnel, dispatch boats,
and the telegraph companies. All of the soldiers in the *Journal*'s "journalistic army"—including some thirty-five correspondents bound for
Cuba, dispatch boats and navy ships, and others in Washington, foreign
capitals, and Caribbean ports—would have collected large salaries.
Each vessel in the paper's journalistic navy cost $5,000 to $9,000 a
month (not counting insurance, at as much as $2,000 a month, and
coal).[33] The cable tolls were breathtaking. A man in Key West filing
daily could ring up bills of $7,500 a month, an amount far in excess of
his annual wages. A single story filed from Jamaica or Haiti at the
"urgent" rate of $1.65 a word could top out at $5,000 (by comparison,
an entire roster of war correspondents at one large New York paper was
costing $1,464 a week).[34]

Strong as its "journalistic army" may have been, there was one warrior
still coveted by the *Journal:* Sylvester Scovel of the New York *World.* He
and Brisbane had become acquainted in Pulitzer's employ. Scovel valued
their relationship enough to recommend stringers to Brisbane and to
smuggle photographs out of Cuba for the *Evening Journal*—a generosity
Uncle Joe would not have appreciated. But there would be no reunion.
Scovel believed he owed his career to the *World* and he remained loyal,
despite Brisbane's flattery and a promise of more money.[35]

The *Journal* spent still more to improve its operations on the home
front. Hearst built a war desk where a dozen men worked day and night
at a long table, sifting through acres of copy flowing in from around
the globe, separating as best they could fact from rumor, rushing the
most important news into print within minutes of its receipt. The
evening paper alone could spit out as many as forty editions in a single
day, a pace that required new battalions of pressmen, stereotypers,
engravers, compositors, mechanics, and office boys. Special trains were
hired to satisfy the demand in markets outside of New York, including
20,000 copies a night for the after-theater crowds in Buffalo. At the

height of the conflict, Hearst's presses ran almost around the clock. The *Evening Journal* once printed just short of 1.1 million copies in a day and still fell short of advance demand by 200,000. The morning paper was now routinely selling more than a million copies a day; its single best day was 1.6 million.

For the benefit of readers who could not wait ten minutes for his next edition, Hearst, like other publishers, erected bulletin boards on Park Row and at strategic points throughout the city. Orchestras played to attract crowds as the latest headlines were displayed; sketch artists kept everyone entertained when, as Brisbane said, "the work of killing Spaniards progressed too slowly."[36] The *Journal* also hosted midday sing-along concerts beside the bulletin boards throughout the spring. A cornetist and a clutch of singers would lead crowds in the "Star-Spangled Banner" and other patriotic songs. One day in June, Hearst happened to stroll out of his offices to find the little band in full flight. He paused on the steps of the Tribune Building to enjoy the full effect of several thousand voices in unison. They finished one anthem or another before bursting into a lusty drinking song. Hearst ran upstairs and cancelled all future concerts.[37]

DESPITE ALL OF ITS PLANNING, expenditures, and enthusiasm, the *Journal* failed to distinguish itself in any positive manner in the first two months of the Spanish-American War. One reason was the competitive environment. Every other paper on Park Row had also devoted vast resources and endless pages to war news. The *World*, the *Herald*, and the Associated Press spent at close to the *Journal*'s pace.[38] Each hired several dispatch boats, and collectively, they would field some seventy war correspondents.[39] All the major dailies had roughly the same access to sources and scenes, and all were subject to U.S. government censorship. The *Journal*'s foreign reporting on events in Spain and the European reaction to the war was often strong and distinctive but otherwise it had trouble finding an edge. It pushed to extremes and often landed in embarrassment.

One of its worst moments came after Manila Bay. The paper had not been with Dewey. Only three reporters were: John T. McCutcheon, a cartoonist with the *Chicago Record;* Edward Harden, a financial writer stringing for Pulitzer's *World* and the *Chicago Tribune;* and Joseph L. Stickney of the *New York Herald*. They witnessed the Battle of Manila

Bay from the decks of the revenue cutter *McCulloch*. They could not immediately file, however, because Dewey had cut the telegraph cable at Manila. The first news of the defeat of the Spanish fleet thus reached the United States from European sources. It was enough to start the celebrations, but days passed without confirmation from Dewey or any American witness. In the interim, no one knew the details of the clash, including the extent of Dewey's losses, and every newspaper in the country wanted the scoop. The three men aboard the *McCulloch* were positioned to deliver. Dewey eventually gave their ship permission to steam for Hong Kong to dispatch its cargo of copy. He asked that his official report be filed ahead of the newspaper stories, but Harden preempted it with a thirty-word dispatch cabled at the "urgent" rate of $9.90 a word:

WORLD, NEW YORK
JUST ARRIVED FROM MANILA. MCCULLOCH.
ENTIRE SPANISH FLEET DESTROYED. ELEVEN SHIPS.
SPANISH LOSS THREE HUNDRED KILLED, FOUR HUNDRED
WOUNDED. OUR LOSS NONE KILLED, SIX SLIGHTLY WOUNDED.
SHIPS UNINJURED. BULLETIN. HARDEN.[40]

The scoop arrived on a Saturday morning at the news offices of the *World,* just after its morning edition had left the building. Unluckily for Pulitzer, a *Chicago Tribune* reporter playing cards in the *World*'s newsroom picked up the phone and received the dispatch from the telegraph office. Because of the time-zone difference, he was able to relay the news to Chicago in time for his morning edition, winning the beat for the *Tribune.*[41] The *World* was first with the news in New York.

Although it did not have its own man aboard the *McCulloch*, the *Journal* did have a copy-sharing arrangement with McCutcheon of the *Chicago Record*. McCutcheon filed a 600-word summary of the battle later the same Saturday. He reserved the bulk of his copy—a 2,500-word report—for transmission on Sunday because the *Record* didn't publish again until Monday. That left Hearst in a bind. The *Herald* and the *World* were certain to produce many thousands of words on Dewey's triumph in their Sunday editions and the *Journal* had only McCutcheon's brief file. Charles Michelson and others in the *Journal* newsroom were assigned to

make up the difference. They bolstered McCutcheon's copy with information gleaned from previously published reports, the AP wire, competing papers, and European sources. What was still missing they supplied
from their imaginations. They had soon puffed out McCutcheon's 600
words to 3,000. They ran it under his byline and shamelessly claimed for
it the "Greatest Beat of Modern Times."[42]

McCutcheon, neither recognizing nor approving of the words attributed to him by the *Journal,* was mortified, all the more so because the
Chicago Tribune, a subscriber to the Hearst news service, picked up the
Journal's piece and ran it in the Chicago market on the Sunday, ahead of
his own 2,500-word masterwork, which appeared in the *Record* on
Monday. He vented his frustration to his employer: "You may imagine
how I felt when I read the *Chicago Tribune* account over which my name
appeared and saw what ridiculous and preposterous things I was credited
with having sent. . . . It read as if the one who wrote it did it out of pure
malice and to make me appear a gigantic idiot. . . . The officers on the
McCulloch read the report amidst howls of laughter and naturally I felt
like a yellow dog."[43]

Michelson defended the *Journal*'s "bit of fakery" as common practice,
which it was, but the paper nonetheless embarrassed itself in a crucial
moment.[44] McCutcheon had every reason to feel humiliated. The con-
cocted report had some dreadful writing. "I confess that my teeth chattered
and I felt qualmish," McCutcheon was said to have muttered to himself as
the battle got underway. "Perhaps I had rather been at home. . . ."

THROUGH MAY AND INTO JUNE, the U.S. Fifth Army assembled and
trained on the mainland, awaiting deployment in Cuba. Just where it
would land—Mariel, Matanzas, a point east of Havana—was undecided
until events at sea settled the matter. The Spanish Caribbean Squadron,
the bulk of what was left of its navy, had been discovered in port at
Santiago de Cuba by elements of U.S. commodore Winfield Scott
Schley's "Flying Squadron." Schley set up a blockade with reinforcements from Rear Admiral William T. Sampson's Atlantic Squadron.
They considered entering the port to destroy the Spanish ships, but the
channel entrance was mined and protected by shore batteries. Spanish
admiral Pasqual Cervera appeared content to wait in port for support,

or for bad weather to interrupt the blockade. Sampson called for a land invasion and the administration obliged, but the army was still weeks from ready.

The lack of action frustrated the legions of correspondents in Florida and off Cuba, all of whom were under pressure from editors at home to fill acres of space devoted to the war. The reporters answered the demand with speculation and exaggeration. No incident or rumor was too minor to escape a headline. Stephen Crane mocked stories that arrived in Key West as mice only to be cabled north as elephants.[45] The *Journal* was as guilty of these excesses as any. It reported that U.S. ground forces had disembarked for Cuba or were hours from disembarking almost every day for a month before transports actually left Tampa. In early June, the paper offered readers running accounts of nonexistent skirmishes between Spanish and U.S. troops in Santiago. A report datelined Cape Haytien, June 5, announced that five thousand U.S. soldiers had landed at Punta Cabrera, six miles west of Santiago, and were preparing to meet the Spanish army; among the troops were Karl Decker, rescuer of Evangeline Cisneros, and Martin Seeley, of the infamous bachelor party. The report was entirely false.[46]

The day after the *Journal*'s Cape Haytien story, the *Herald* carried its own account of a nonexistent battle between U.S. and Spanish forces in Cuba; it also announced the sinking of several Spanish battleships that were still, in fact, afloat. The Associated Press and the *Journal* both ran rumors picked up from English sailors that Santiago had fallen, before U.S. troops had actually left Tampa. Even the Manhattan newsboys tired of the sham and hype, much of which was rushed to readers in extra editions. One took up the cry, "Here's yer latest extra. Fake extra! All the fakes. Exclusive fakes! Extra! Extra! Fake extra!!" According to the *Fourth Estate*, he sold out in an instant and all his colleagues copied his sales pitch.[47]

As stories were now routinely inflated, so too was typography. Even the conservative papers, said Brisbane, suddenly looked as though they were interested in news, while the penny papers grew to look like "aggravated circus posters." Soon, he added, half-jokingly, "a new genius was in demand, the man who could think of short words with energy . . . suitable for the construction of headings. The fact that there were only three letters in 'war' was the greatest blessing."[48] On its good days the *Journal* had a bright and startling appeal; on others it seemed to have declared war on the eyes of its readers.

Yet another lamentable element of the coverage was the tendency of journalists to fill the lull in action by turning guns on one another. It became a sport to impugn the loyalty of a rival newspaper; words like "unpatriotic" and "treasonable" flew like bullets. When the journalist Poultney Bigelow published an article in *Harper's Weekly* doubting America's preparedness, Richard Harding Davis leapt to the Fifth Army's defense and blasted Bigelow for his "un-American" sentiments and for giving succor to the enemy. Hearst seized on the fact that Bennett Jr. and Pulitzer were overseas in May and, noting that the former was a European resident and the latter European-born, challenged their commitment to the fight. Pulitzer's *World* reported that U.S. soldiers had boarded a *Journal* dispatch boat to prevent the paper from publishing war secrets: "It is said the correspondents on that vessel are suspected of having obtained government plans and documents and intended to sail for some port where they could send the matter by wire."[49] Hearst responded with a $500,000 libel writ charging Pulitzer with impugning his patriotism and used the occasion to make public his offers to equip a regiment of cavalry and to lend his yacht *Buccaneer* to the navy. The *Journal* capped its reply with the most amusing prank of the Spanish-American War.

The major Park Row dailies were all assiduous in stealing one another's news; it generally took less than half an hour for a scoop in one paper to appear in some form in the pages of its rivals. Most of the poaching appears to have occurred among the *World*, the *Sun*, and the *Herald*, but no paper was exempt. Brisbane had noted that the *World* was making a regular diet of news from the *Evening Journal*; after Pulitzer's smear of Hearst, Brisbane laid a trap. The following item appeared in his June 8 edition: "Colonel Reflipe W. Thenuz, an Austrian artillerist of European renown, who, with Colonel Ordonez, was defending the land batteries of Aguadores . . . was so badly wounded that he has since died."[50]

The *World* spotted the item and published a rewrite in its next edition, dressed up with a grandiose dateline:

On Board the World's Dispatch Boat Three Friends, Off Santiago de Cuba, via Port Antonio, Jamaica:
Colonel R. W. Thenuz, an Austrian artillerist well known throughout

Europe, who, with Colonel Ordonez, was defending the land batteries of Aguadores . . . was so badly wounded that he has since died.[51]

The following day, the *Journal* published an ecstatic page-three headline: "The World Brands Itself a Pilferer of the News by Published Confession!"[52] It explained to readers that Reflipe W. Thenuz was an anagram for "We Pilfer the News." Not content with proving Pulitzer's depredations, the *Journal* returned to Colonel Thenuz almost every day for the next several weeks. It published poetry in memoriam of the late fictional colonel. It ran a cartoon of his framed portrait with the caption, "Specially taken for the *World*, by the *World*'s special photographer."[53] It launched a fundraising campaign and a design competition for a monument to Thenuz. Readers played along, sending in Confederate currency and expired bonds as contributions. The *World* attempted to strike back by planting stories in its pages in hopes that the *Journal* would poach them. Brisbane not only eluded the snares but sent good-natured notes to the *World* teasing its editors for their clumsiness. "Great was Brisbane," writes his colleague, A.P. Terhune.[54]

Hearst now contemplated a stunt even more audacious than his Evangelina escapade. With a Spanish naval squadron rumored to be disembarking from Cadiz to attack Dewey in the Philippines, Hearst wrote Creelman as follows:

> I wish you would make necessary preparations, so that in case the Spanish fleet actually starts for Manila we will be prepared to buy or charter some English tramp steamer on the Eastern end of the Mediterranean and take her to some narrow and inaccessible portion of the Suez Canal and sink her where she will obstruct the passage of the Spanish fleet. I do not know that we will want to do this, but we may, in case the American boats from San Francisco have not reached Dewey and he should be placed in a critical position by the approach of the Spanish vessels. I understand if a British boat were taken and sunk under such circumstances as above outlined, the British government would not allow her to be blown up to clear the passage, and it might take enough time to raise her to put Dewey in a safe position.
>
> I merely want you to be in a position to do this in case it should be decided upon later."[55]

Hearst never ordered this act and, in any event, it proved unnecessary as the Spanish squadron returned to port soon after leaving in response to false rumors of an approaching U.S. fleet. Creelman, in his memoir, offers Hearst's letter, with all reservations carefully excised, as a piece of "heartfelt, practical patriotism" and a "Napoleonic stroke" of newspaper promotion—yet another proof of yellow journalism's alertness to its public duty. He also allowed that sinking a steamer in the canal would have been "a grave breach of international law," but that is probably not what held Hearst back, given his defense of the "rank illegality" of his Cuban jailbreak.[56] Any number of practical considerations, from the expense and difficulty of the operation to the disruption of international trade and travel it would have caused, could have brought him to his senses.

Strange as it may seem, Hearst's Suez whim was not unusual in one respect: all of the Park Row papers were putting resources at the disposal of the U.S. war effort. The *World*'s Scovel spent the spring of 1898 performing secret service work on behalf of a government woefully short of intelligence capacity. He gathered information on Spanish military preparedness and coastal defenses, recruited agents from among his acquaintances, provided them with press credentials, and helped them land in Cuba using *World* dispatch boats. He ran messages between the insurgents and the U.S. Navy and helped to negotiate the terms of cooperation between them. He reported some of the information gathered in these pursuits without revealing his official role, and when he eventually did he was widely applauded for his patriotism. The *Herald*'s George Bronson Rea ran errands for Captain Sigsbee and gathered intelligence for the U.S. in Puerto Rico while his editor floated trial balloons with Spanish officials on behalf of the State Department. It is a safe bet, however, that Hearst was alone in contemplating an independent contribution to the fight.

RUMORS THAT HEARST HIMSELF was headed to the battlefields of Cuba began to circulate on Park Row in early June. They were met with silence from the *Journal*, but on June 18, 1898, the *Times* reported the following:

> The British steamer *Sylvia*, Quebec Steamship Line, which arrived from Barbados a few days ago with a load of asphalt, will leave the docks of the Barber Asphalt Company, Sixth Street and East River, Long Island

City, to-day bound for Cuba. The steamer has been chartered by William R. Hearst, proprietor of the *New York Journal,* who proposes to publish the first paper printed in English in Cuba. He will personally superintend its production.

Besides editors and skilled workmen the vessel takes a complete printing outfit, including stereotyping apparatus and an army hand-press.

The party expects to reach Santiago by Wednesday, and will effect a landing at the safest point in the vicinity.

Hearst had received permission from Secretary of War Alger to take the *Sylvia* to Cuba as part of the press corps. "Goodbye Mother dear," he wired Phoebe. "Take good care of yourself. You are much more likely to get sick than I am to get injured and your life and health [are] just as dear to me as mine is to you. Your loving son, etc."[57]

In addition to his printing facilities and pressmen, Hearst loaded his boat with provisions, field equipment, medical supplies, and an entourage that included his printing expert and jack-of-all-trades George Pancoast, his star correspondent James Creelman, the photographer John C. Hemment, motion-picture cameraman Billy Bitzer, and old friend Jack Follansbee. He outfitted a complete darkroom in the bowels of the ship to allow Hemment to develop photographic plates at sea for immediate shipment on arrival in port. He also carried Bitzer's unwieldy Biograph motion-picture camera, an early prototype requiring two thousand pounds of storage batteries. Hearst was the only publisher to take a press or a darkroom, let alone a motion-picture camera, to war. According to Bitzer, he was also the only newspaperman with a set of sisters in his cabins: the Willson girls were along for the ride.

Hearst's journey to Cuba was smooth. The *Sylvia* docked first at Kingston, Jamaica, where Hemment took on a supply of ice for his darkroom and Hearst and Follansbee wandered a few miles out of town to purchase polo ponies from a racetrack. The entire *Sylvia* party then ate a sumptuous meal at the Crystal Springs Hotel, loaded the horses, and shoved off for Cuba. After ten hours on a rough sea they caught sight of the blockading U.S. squadron at the mouth of the harbor at Santiago de Cuba on the southeast coast.

The Fifth Army had also just arrived off Santiago. After two false starts, complete with bands playing and flags waving, its transports had finally steamed out of Tampa on June 14, a week after they had been boarded, this time without so much as a goodbye or a backward glance. Traveling much of the way at a 6-knot crawl, the convoy of 35 vessels carried 819 officers and over 16,058 soldiers, including 3 regiments of volunteers and 23 of regulars—the largest military force to depart from the United States before the Great War.[58] The men endured two weeks of jostling in the stinking bowels of the transports, with nothing to drink but fetid water, before they finally received instructions to land.

The *Sylvia* buzzed through the blockade and located Admiral Sampson's flagship, the *New York*, directly in front of Santiago's Morro Castle. As twilight fell, Hearst, Creelman, and Hemment ventured out in a launch and clambered up the flagship's rope ladder to present their credentials. They were warmly received by the admiral and allowed full run of the fleet. Hearst would describe Sampson as a quiet, conservative man with thin features, a snowy beard, and melancholy eyes,[59] which, judging by Hemment's photographs, is accurate:

> As he sat under a sailcloth awning on the quarterdeck and talked in a soft voice it was hard to imagine we were lying in front of a great stronghold of the enemy. Ships stretched out on both sides in perfect order. Everywhere were signs of intelligent method. "We have had men ashore," [Sampson] said, "and have located the position of Cervera's entire fleet. Every one of his vessels is lying safe from our guns behind that high hill there with such a narrow entrance and with thick fields of mines that the navy can do nothing but stay here and prevent any egress. [The Army] must first drive the enemy out of Santiago forts and capture Morro Castle before we can remove the mines and enter the harbor."[60]

Hearst and the *Journal* crew next sought to introduce themselves to Major General William Rufus Shafter, commander of the Fifth Army Corps. They learned that he was quartered on the transport *Seguranca* at Guantanamo Bay, forty-five miles east of Santiago, but finding him after sundown was no easy task. The waters between Santiago and Guantanamo were crowded with American vessels—warships, supply ships, transports, dispatch boats—and very few were using their lights. The *Sylvia* bumped around in the dark for several hours until at last they discovered the *Seguranca* and all three hundred pounds of General Shafter.

Cranky, wracked with gout, stripped of his jacket yet still sweating profusely, the 63-year-old Civil War veteran was in the process of disgorging his enormous cargo, which in addition to his officers and troops included 2,295 horses and mules, 10 million pounds of rations, field guns, howitzers, siege rifles, mortars, Hotchkiss mountain guns, four Gatlings, an experimental dynamite gun, and an ill-fated observation balloon.[61] Shafter was putting all this ashore at the tiny villages of Daiquiri and Siboney, the latter a dozen miles east of the strategic target of Santiago. It was not a graceful landing. Neither village had a port or a useful pier. The Fifth Army was simply dumped into the surf with bands playing and men singing—anything was preferable to another night on a miserable transport ship—yet Shafter drowned only two soldiers and a handful of animals in the operation. The Spanish had unaccountably decided against defending the beaches.

Shafter had already had his fill of journalists by the time Hearst arrived. His supercargo included eighty-nine reporters (as against just seventeen ambulances).[62] Richard Harding Davis was one of the eighty-nine. On the first day of the landing, Davis had objected to the general's order that everyone not on immediate duty stay afloat until the beaches were secure. Shafter dismissed his complaint but Davis persisted, using the line that he wasn't some hack newspaperman but a "descriptive writer." The general exploded: "I don't care a damn what you are. I'll treat you all alike."[63] Shafter suffered in Davis's copy for the duration of the conflict, but the general nonetheless received Hearst and company with civility and treated them to an extensive briefing.

Shafter's assignment was to fight his way west from Siboney and Daiquiri by an inland route to take Santiago and its shore defenses, leaving Cervera's warships in the harbor at Sampson's mercy. The destruction of Spain's Caribbean squadron, combined with Dewey's work, would give the United States effective control of the seas and a stranglehold on Spanish Cuba. Shafter, who struck Hearst as a "bold, lion-headed hero . . . a sort of human fortress," told the *Journal* that Spain had 12,000 troops deployed in strategic and well-protected positions in and around Santiago.[64] He doubted the fighting spirit of the Spaniards and predicted that he would require only a short campaign to reach Santiago. Hearst, Hemment, and Creelman presented their papers, which the general countersigned, allowing them the right of uninterrupted travel in and out of combat lines. "We then returned to our ship and retired for the night," writes Hemment. "Next morning we were awakened early, and we got all things in readiness and went ashore."[65]

Hearst and friends landed at the village of Siboney, where the Fifth Army continued to unload personnel and supplies. Hearst, carrying a camera and with a pistol strapped to his belt, was dressed in light flannels with a gaily-colored band on his panama hat. Creelman, a veteran of many war zones, wore a khaki uniform with bright buttons, polished leather boots, and puttees. It is probably true, as W.A. Swanberg has suggested, that the "slightly older and immensely more self-assured Creelman" would have struck the uninitiated as the employer of the quiet and slightly awkward Hearst.[66] They made their way to the outskirts of town, where scores of newspaper correspondents had constructed a village of white tents. The *Journal* had established headquarters in what Hemment described as a "cosy little Cuban dwelling" next to the Red Cross offices.[67]

Hearst's first objective ashore was a meeting with a third leader in the war against Spain, General Calixto García, commander of the Liberating Army, which was the eastern half of the rebel force under Commander-in-Chief Gómez. García had already agreed to support the U.S. landing and the advance on Santiago, although his ragged and emaciated army would fight as a separate force, the Americans not wanting direct responsibility for Cubans. The insurgent general would deploy several thousand men inland from Guantanamo to shelter the U.S. presence there, and thousands more at various inland approaches to Santiago to prevent the Spaniards from reinforcing their garrison in the city.

García and his staff had taken quarters outside Siboney near the rail tracks in a blue and white shanty with a broad veranda and a red-tiled roof. The general was a tall, graceful old warrior with flowing white mustaches, a frank and appealing nature, and a deep, hollow scar in the lower middle of his forehead, a souvenir of a suicide attempt during the Ten Years' War (captured by Spaniards, he had fired a bullet under his chin, only to have it emerge above the bridge of his nose). "When he stood up on his veranda and bade us welcome," writes Hemment, "we saw a man between sixty and seventy years of age, with a physique and frame which had doubtless once been ideal in its massiveness and strength. He was clad in a pair of light brown leather boots, the inevitable blue-striped trousers, a white duck coat, and a large wide-brimmed panama."[68]

The *Journal* men were served coffee and introduced to García's son and other members of his staff. The general regaled them in English with stories of the hardships and trials on the long road to Cuba's liberation, and apprised them of the insurgent army's movements. García's son brought forward a gift which his father offered with great ceremony to Hearst: "I present to the *New York Journal,* in commemoration of its services to liberty, the headquarter flag of the Eastern Department of the Republic. You see upon it the marks of Mauser bullets. This flag has been borne through many battles, and hundreds of brave men have died under it. Its colors are faded but it is the best thing the Cuban Republic can offer to its best friend. You were our friend in the dark days when we had few friends, and now that we have many friends, we do not forget what you did for us when we were weak and alone."[69] García then shouted "*Viva Cuba Libre.*" All returned his call.

There was more than gratitude in the Cuban general's embrace of Hearst and the *Journal.* García harbored doubts about the intentions of President McKinley and his armed forces. In a letter to Palma in New York, he confided his fear that the administration would think better of granting the Cubans self-government once the Spaniards were defeated. García was pinning his hopes on the good faith of the American people: "I do not doubt that before concluding the campaign all the people of the United States will be convinced to leave to us conditions for governing ourselves and for organizing all the necessary institutions for realizing the ends of an independent state." Hearst was thus welcomed as a key ally and installed in comfortable quarters while his competitors rested in tents.[70]

While Hearst was getting acquainted with García, one of his reporters, Edward Marshall, was traveling with the First United States Volunteer Cavalry, better known as Teddy Roosevelt's Rough Riders, who belonged to a dismounted cavalry division of 2,700 men under Major General Joseph Wheeler. They had been first off the transports at Daiquiri, and as quickly as Wheeler was able to gather his troops on the beach, he began a march in oppressive heat over steep coastal hills to Siboney, the army's second landing site. He arrived on the morning of June 23 after an uncomfortable night of camping amid rain and giant land crabs. The cavalry's instructions were to secure the area and wait for the rest of the Fifth Army to reach shore, but Wheeler was in a hurry to meet the enemy. Early on the morning of the twenty-fourth, after another near sleepless night, he dispatched two regular regiments and the Rough Rider volunteers up a narrow jungle trail on an armed reconnaissance.

Stealth was not a priority on the march. Stephen Crane, who had joined Marshall, Richard Harding Davis, and a handful of other reporters on the trail, was alarmed at the Rough Riders' cheerful lack of discipline: they "wound along this narrow winding path, babbling joyously, arguing, recounting, laughing; making more noise than a train going through a tunnel."[71] The happy troops more or less walked into an ambush.

Named for a stand of nut trees, Las Guasimas was the site of the first serious land battle of the Spanish-American War. It was a high ridge with stone breastworks and several blockhouses—nothing imposing, but it offered Spain a solid defensive position with good angles on the approaching troops. At 8 a.m., the 1,500 men under General Antero Rubín, Spanish military commander at Las Guasimas, began firing their German-designed rifles in disciplined volleys. A handful of Wheeler's soldiers fell dead in the first hail of bullets, among them the great collegiate athlete and society scion Hamilton Fish, a member of the Rough Riders. "The shots came thicker and faster every moment," the *Journal* reported, "and the air seemed filled with the singing and shrieking sound of the Mauser bullets. The short pop of the Spanish rifles could be distinguished easily from the heavier reports of the American weapons."[72]

Edward Marshall and Richard Harding Davis stuck close to the Rough Riders, and to Theodore Roosevelt in particular. When the advance guard of his regiment came under heavy attack, Roosevelt hustled his men across a barbed-wire fence and through a thick ravine to offer assistance. They emerged in deep grass under bright, clear skies and a hail of bullets. They were eager to return fire but could not locate the enemy (the Spaniards, unlike most of the Americans, used smokeless gunpowder). Davis, scanning the hillsides with his high-powered binoculars (probably the same glasses bought for his earlier expedition with *Journal* expense money), spotted Spanish sombreros on a ridge amid thick vegetation. He pointed them out to Roosevelt. The Rough Riders redirected their fire and succeeded in breaking Spain's front line and eventually claiming the ridge. Roosevelt put Davis forward for an official commendation and continued to enjoy stellar press in the *New York Herald* for the duration of the conflict.

That is not to say praise of Roosevelt was unwarranted. Marshall had watched the lieutenant colonel help a dozen men through the barbed wire and into the tangled ravine: "Then he stepped across the wire himself. . . . It was as if that barbed-wire strand had formed a dividing line in his life, and that when he stepped across it he left behind him in the past all those unadmirable and conspicuous traits which have so often caused him to be justly criticized in civic life, and found on the other side of it, in that Cuban thicket, the coolness, the calm judgment, the towering heroism, which made him, perhaps, the most admired and best beloved of all Americans in Cuba."[73]

Marshall was himself in the front lines of the fight. At one point he emptied his revolver in the direction of the Spanish positions. Davis picked up a carbine from a wounded soldier and drained it in similar fashion. They felt, Marshall explained, "that every man who was hit was my personal friend, and there was nothing professional in the interest which I took in each one of them."[74] Firing or not, Marshall continued to make professional observations as the action unfolded around him. He noted the sickening smells of the crushed jungle vegetation and the way men fell in silent heaps when shot. He was one of several Americans fascinated by the noise of the Mauser bullet. As one soldier wrote, it was "not impressive enough to be really terrifying until you have seen what it does when it strikes. It is a nasty, malicious little noise, like the soul of a very petty and mean person turned into sound."[75]

Marshall did not hear the shot that ripped through his own body. He didn't even feel it. He simply found himself collapsed on the ground, unable to use his legs, feeling "perfectly satisfied and entirely comfortable in the long grass." The regiment's surgeon found him where he fell and after a quick examination told Marshall that if he wanted to dictate any letters home, he had better hurry. Marshall was on his third letter before the burden of the surgeon's remarks hit him.[76]

Marshall has no profile in journalism lore except as the *Journal* correspondent shot in the spine at Las Guasimas. He was, in fact, a prolific (if not a celebrated) playwright and a well-regarded newspaperman. Four years before the war, as Sunday editor of the *New York Press,* he had been in the habit of publishing the street sketches of an as yet unknown literary talent, Stephen Crane. They had met as members of the Lantern Club, a loose society of young authors and newspapermen that dined, drank, and argued daily on William Street near Park Row.

Crane distinguished himself at Las Guasimas, as he would throughout the war, with a reckless disregard for his own safety. (The *Journal*'s reporter Langdon Smith at one point noticed him standing under a tree, calmly rolling a cigarette as Spanish bullets cut the leaves to either side of him and other men fell a few feet from him.) Crane heard a passing soldier speak of a correspondent "all shot to hell," went to investigate, and found Marshall where the surgeon had left him.[77]

"Hello, Crane!" said Marshall.

"Hello, Marshall! In hard luck, old man?"

"Yes, I'm done for."

"Nonsense. You're all right, old boy. What can I do for you?"

"Well, you might file my dispatches. I don't mean file them ahead of your own, old man—but just file 'em if you find it handy."[78]

Crane believed Marshall was doomed. "No man," he later wrote in the *World*, "could be so sublime in detail concerning the trade of journalism and not die."[79] He put aside his own duties and walked five miles to the cable station to wire Marshall's copy to the *Journal*. He then gathered a handful of correspondents, including George Coffin of the *Journal* and Acton Davies of the *Sun*, to carry Marshall back through the jungle to a field hospital, where the battlefield surgeon Dr. William Gorgas operated on him by candlelight under a mango tree. Gorgas amputated Marshall's left leg and saved his life. The patient was subsequently transported to the *Olivette*, now serving as a hospital ship. Giddy with shock, Marshall bellowed "On the Banks of the Wabash Far Away" from his stretcher.

After performing his heroic act of friendship, Crane spent the evening smoking and chattering, unable to eat. He startled Davies and Coffin with gruesome deliberations on what it must be like to be shot, describing in minute detail how soldiers had fallen through the day. Sixteen American soldiers died at Las Guasimas. While the *Journal* was filled with praise of the valiant performance of the Rough Riders and army regulars, it did note that during the fight in the thicket several of the troops "did some wild shooting into the troop ahead of them, and a part of the American loss is due to this fact."[80]

Amid its reports on the battle, the *Journal* profiled several of the prominent casualties, including Hamilton Fish. He was remembered as a rower, a footballer, a society favorite, and a practical joker who had once tied "a little darky" to a telegraph pole and hired a band to play "I

Wish I Was in Dixie" to the helpless fellow.[81] The sacrifice of Edward Marshall was prominently treated: he had proved his courage by pushing himself to the front lines of the fight, and he was yet another example of the dedication of yellow journalism to the cause of Cuban freedom. His injuries occasioned a tribute to the role of the battlefield reporter, who must face the hardships and dangers of battle, including being fired upon, without shooting back. The editorial desk of the *Journal* probably didn't know that its correspondent had done his best to thin the Spanish lines.

Hearst and his entourage did not venture inland until after the skirmish at Las Guasimas. Hard rains had by then swamped the road inland from Siboney. Hemment complained of "mud, fetid odours, miasmatic mists, and biting insects."[82] Hearst studied the battle-scarred ridge captured by Wheeler's troops while Hemment photographed the graves of the fallen American soldiers and captured the massive figure of General Shafter performing a reconnaissance on horseback. Returning to the *Sylvia* that night, the *Journal* men polished off a hearty meal served by Hearst's steward before setting off to Jamaica and the cable office (thus bypassing the censors at Key West). As they steamed south into the night, Hemment went below to his makeshift darkroom and developed the three dozen plates he'd exposed that day. The next morning he sent a set of prints to New York aboard a Boston Fruit Company steamer.

After cabling their copy to New York, the *Journal* men replenished the *Sylvia*'s stores of ice, fruit, and fresh meats and returned to Cuba. It was a delightful passage on a gentle sea. All of the journalists and the ship's crew, from cabin boy to captain, were invited to eat and drink, and an unexpected camaraderie infused the yacht. Billy Bitzer, the Biograph cameraman, said the "champagne and lively companionship" relieved tension and did wonders for the spirit. The Willson girls, "full of fun and laughter," raced about the boat. They were dressed in male attire so as not to attract the attention of the sailors on the blockade. "We were in the delirious state of being under fire in war time," wrote Bitzer, "and we got more friendly than we would have at home."[83]

When the *Sylvia* reached Santiago, the newsmen aboard wanted an update from the battleship *Texas*. Press boats, however, were prohibited from sailing amid the blockading vessels. A bribe of fresh bananas was offered and gratefully received and the *Journal* men were advised that a bombardment would begin at 8 a.m. The *Sylvia* scooted outside the lines as the *New York,* the *Indiana,* the *Texas,* the *Brooklyn,* the *New Orleans,* the *Massachusetts,* the *Iowa,* and the *Oregon* opened up on Morro Castle at the mouth of Santiago harbor from a range of 2,000 yards. Their fire was returned by Spanish shore batteries. Shells flew thick and fast. The noise was terrifying. The sky filled with sulfurous smoke. Hemment saw earth and stonework bursting skyward from the fortifications ashore. With shells whistling overhead, the *Sylvia* crept in closer to the action to give its various cameramen better angles. Hemment was in the bow of the vessel with his 11-by-14 camera, peering through the smoke in hopes of a clear shot:

> We were cautioned once or twice to keep out of the line of fire, but, as we were determined to stay as long as we could, we let this advice go by unheeded until ordered peremptorily by one of the American captains to get out of the way.
>
> At one time we were in danger of being hit ourselves, for several large shells landed quite close to our boat. One shell in particular, which seemed to be an eleven-inch shell, struck the water not more than one hundred yards from our starboard quarter, ricocheted, and passing over our ship, landed two hundred feet beyond us. It was then that we received the peremptory order to move away and get out of range at once. Mr. Hearst reluctantly ordered the captain of the *Sylvia* to pull out.[84]

After the bombardment, Hemment left the *Sylvia,* returning to Siboney with a load of fruit and iced delicacies and a note from Creelman for Edward Marshall on the *Olivette.* He found the correspondent convalescing in a cot: "I approached with a feeling of tenderness and sympathy, as I knew the terrible ordeal through which he had passed. As soon as he saw me his face lit up with joy, and he bade me welcome. I told him I had a few small things for him, together with the note. He thanked me, and begged me to read the note to him, as it would distress him too much to move." Creelman had written him as follows:

> My dear Marshall: Cheer up, old man! I hear you have been trying to stop Spanish bullets, and were successful. I trust you have passed the worst, and that you may never again experience what you did in the battle with the Rough Riders at Las Guasimas. I trust you may have a speedy recovery.

Keep up a good heart, and reserve the cot next to yours for me, as I may be with you before long. I am, etc.[85]

To this point on his journey, Hearst had been content to watch and direct his correspondents as they went about their work. That was consistent with his role as editor, one he'd filled for a decade without ever turning his hand to reportage or commentary. Whether Hearst arrived in Cuba with an intention to act as his own correspondent or was pressed into action by Marshall's incapacitation, the first story under his byline appeared in the June 29 edition:

> It is satisfactory to be an American and to be here on the soil of Cuba, at the very threshold of what may prove to be the decisive battle of the war. The fight for possession of the City of Santiago and the capture of Cervera's fleet seem to be only a few hours away, and from the top of the rough, green ridge where I write this, we can see dimly on the sea the monstrous forms of Sampson's fleet lying in a semi-circle in front of the entrance to Santiago harbor, while here at our feet masses of American soldiers are pouring from the beach into the scorching valley, where smells of stagnant and fermented vegetation ground under the feet of thousands of fighting men rise in the swooning hot mists through which vultures that have already fed on corpses of slain Spaniards wheel lazily above the thorny, poisonous jungle.
>
> Santiago and the Flower of the Spanish fleet are ours, although hundreds of men may have to die on the field before we take possession of them.
>
> Neither Cervera's crews nor General Linares's battalions or squadrons can escape, for the American fleet bars the way by sea and our infantry and dismounted cavalry are gradually encircling the city, driving the Spanish pickets backward toward the tiers of trenches in which the defenders of the Spanish aggression must make their last stand.
>
> . . . I have talked with [Sampson, Shafter, and Garcia], and each has assured me that victory is absolutely certain.

The piece ran close to 3,000 words, and aside from the personal note at the top, it was a fair-minded summary and analysis of the American position on the eve of what would indeed be the decisive battle of the war. Hearst is clearly impressed with the operation to date, calling it "almost a miracle" that Shafter landed 16,000 soldiers and all their supplies in "small boats through a rough surf on the steep dangerous beach, between ugly reefs in almost killing heat." He even went so far as to reverse his criticism of President McKinley's war strategy: "Now that I am here on the spot . . . I am satisfied that McKinley is right in deciding to attack Santiago rather than Havana."

The conclusion of the article looks forward to a quick U.S. victory and expresses the hope, soon realized, that Washington would strip Spain of its major possessions: "It may be that the taking of this seaport and capture of what must be considered all that there is of an effective Spanish navy will induce the great powers of Europe to compel Spain to sue for peace, but every officer and every private in the American forces on land and sea hopes that no peace will be granted till the American flag is nailed to the flag staffs of Porto Rico and the Philippines—not simply hoisted there, but nailed."

While Hearst largely kept himself out of his copy and was absent entirely from Hemment's published photos, his editors in New York did not share his reserve. His article was followed a day later by several columns of front-page congratulations wrung by *Journal* reporters from statesmen and soldiers, including the commanding general of the U.S. Army, Nelson Miles, and Vice President Hobart, who suggested that Hearst's presence in Cuba set a praiseworthy example for his fellow proprietors. Some of the applause for Hearst was even spontaneous: the *New York Times* allowed that "the editor and proprietor of the *Journal* of this city showed more than usually good judgment when he assigned Mr. W. R. Hearst to duty as a staff correspondent at the campaign of Gen. Shafter, with instructions to interview that grand old soldier and Admiral Sampson, and particularly Gen. Garcia. We do not know if the assignment was made in order to provide an object lesson to the other correspondents, but the copy turned out is notably superior to that which generally passes the censorship of the *Journal* telegraph desk. It is straightforward, clear, and readable, with the exception of a little nervousness at the start."[86]

After taking Las Guasimas, the Fifth Army had a clear run to within several miles of Santiago, setting up the major offensive of the Cuban campaign. On July 1, General Shafter intended to meet the Spaniards at their main line of resistance in the San Juan Heights, a set of low-lying hills commanding the eastern approach to Santiago. He hoped to claim the heights by midday and drive ahead to take Santiago before dinner. The sun would set with the United States in command of the harbor—the principal objective of Shafter's expedition.[87]

Before leaving the *Sylvia* for the grand battles he expected would decide the war, Hearst wrote a letter home, misleading his mother as to both his intentions and his safety:

> Dear Mother: I am at the front and absolutely safe, so don't worry. Since poor Marshall was shot the General has made strict rules limiting newspapermen to certain localities that are well within the lines so that there is no opportunity for any of us to get hurt even if we wanted to.
>
> The landing of troops, guns and horses is most interesting and [the] march to the front very impressive. I have interviewed Admiral Sampson, General Shafter and General Garcia. The last named gave me his headquarters flag which has seen much service and is riddled by bullets. He said the Journal had been the most potent influence in bringing the United States to the help of Cuba and that they would always remember the Journal as a friend when friends had been very few. Now he said that they had many friends but ranked the Journal above all others.
>
> I have been greatly interested in everything and of some service to the hospital ship providing them with ice and delicacies which they lacked. I think the standing of the paper will profit by me being here. Other proprietors are safely at home—and I will be soon. I hope you are well and not at all alarmed about me for honestly there is no occasion.[88]

Frederic Remington wrote a similar letter before the assault on Santiago. Attached to the Sixth Cavalry, his experience of the war bore little resemblance to that of Hearst. Ill equipped and grossly overweight, he spent the week slogging on foot in the heat and mud, struggling to keep up with his regiment, before finally buying a horse from an ailing American officer. He shared his discomfort with his wife, Eva:

> My dear Kid: . . . [We] are about 5 miles from Santiago and except the fight which the cavalry brigade had the other day the Spanish have not opposed us—I—Davis and [the novelist] John Fox went to within 2 miles or nearly 11/2 miles of Santiago yesterday on a reconnaissance—everything is quiet in and about the city—what one might call an ominous lull—

The first night ashore it rained and I slept all night wet. . . . I have an awful cold—and can't get over it. . . .

John Fox and I sleep on the same blanket. We burn at Genl Chaffee mess—crackers, coffee and bacon—by God I haven't had enough to eat since I left Tampa—I am dirty—oh so dirty. I have on a canvas suit and have 2 shirts—my other shirts as the boys call them—I have no baggage which I do not carry on my back—

I bought a horse and equipment from Col Benham 7ᵗʰ Inf for $150 gave my check last night—he goes home sick—so now I wont have to suffer—If I could get my hammock some cegar and a quart of whiskey I would be it. . . .

Hearst is at the port I understand I hope to get home soon—I hope I don't get ten days quarantine either—Yours lovingly. . . .[89]

Hearst, Hemment, Creelman, and Follansbee left the *Sylvia* by steam launch for Siboney well before dawn on the decisive day of July 1. The *Journal*'s headquarters had been appropriated for use as a hospital to accommodate the multitudes of feverish soldiers dropping back from the lines. After locating their horses, the *Journal* men found some empty space on the mosquito-ridden veranda and slept, or tried to sleep, until sunrise. After packing Hemment's camera equipment and saddling up, they headed up the muddy road toward the Fifth Army's forward position a few miles from Santiago.

Charles Johnson Post, a one-time *New York Journal* artist who had enlisted as a private with the 71st New York Infantry (and who, despite his new role, contributed a valuable series of sketches from the field), was surprised to run across his former employer that morning in a clearing. He left perhaps the best image of Hearst in Cuba:

The horse was not big but the man was, and tall: his legs and white socks hung well below the horse's belly. Dressed in black civilian clothes as if he had just stepped over from New York, he wore a jaunty felt-brimmed straw hat with a scarlet hatband and a scarlet tie to match. It was William Randolph Hearst. . . . We hailed him joyously—he was someone we knew! "Hey, Willie!" The hail went up and down the column, and it was all friendly. Someone from New York! He never moved a muscle. Always poker-faced, he never cracked a smile. If he thought we were jeering he was wrong. We were just glad to see someone from home. James

Creelman, the correspondent, came galloping back from ahead and con-
ferred with Hearst. . . . Creelman turned in his saddle and called out to us:
"Boys, you're going into battle. Good luck!" Then he spoke and turned to
Hearst. Hearst made a gesture in our direction with his scarlet-banded
hat. He almost smiled. "Good luck!" he called mildly. "Boys, good luck be
with you," and then he stiffened again.[90]

General Shafter started his attack with an artillery barrage. Four 3.2-
inch field cannon under Captain George Grimes were positioned atop a
hill known as El Pozo and trained on Spain's forward position, the San
Juan Heights, 2,600 yards away. Shafter intended to soften up the enemy
and provide cover for 8,000 U.S. soldiers advancing toward the heights.
The black-powder smoke from Grimes's cannon, however, revealed the
position of his battery. Spanish gunners easily found their range and
harassed Shafter's assembled divisions with heavy return fire.[91]

Hearst and Hemment were riding among the American troops when the
Spanish shells began to fly. Hemment heard "a screech through the air as I
had never heard before and another and more in quick succession." He
remembers next hearing an officer of the Rough Riders shrieking at him:

"What in hell are you fellows doing? Don't you see you are drawing the
fire from those batteries? For God's sake, men, get off your horses!"
Hearst turned his horse to Hemment, smiled, and said, "Well, I guess possibly we are drawing the fire, but we are not the only ones around here."[92]

After dismounting, they scrambled toward El Pozo for a closer look at
Grimes's artillery. Again, they were admonished by the soldiers—"Have
you fellows no sense?" They reluctantly moved back among the reserves,
avoiding censure but still finding danger. Shrapnel burst over their heads.
Mauser bullets whizzed past their ears and snapped through the tall grass
and cactus stalks. In every direction, soldiers were falling. "A man was
hit," observed Hemment, "and he simply sagged down in a heap, sinking
into the low bushes without a murmur, without a word."[93] The effective-
ness of the Spanish response quieted Grimes's guns and left 8,000 Fifth
Army soldiers to advance with almost no artillery support.

Creelman had meanwhile lit out in another direction. As part of the
drive to Santiago, Shafter had ordered a morning attack on the hamlet of

El Caney, six miles northeast of the city on the strategically important road from Guantanamo. He anticipated that one division under General Lawton could take El Caney in two hours—between 7 and 9 a.m.—and then advance to reinforce the Fifth Army's principal assault on the San Juan Heights late in the morning. A friendly general had told Creelman that Lawton would have the toughest fight of the day. The correspondent thus walked the five miles from El Pozo to El Caney under an already scorching sun. The narrow trail was littered with giant land crabs— "green and scarlet, with leprous blotches of white"—and interrupted by suffocating thickets and slimy shallow swamps. Vultures slouched in the tall palms. When he finally reached the battle site it looked idyllic by comparison: "a rumpled landscape of intense green," with "flowering hills, tall, tossing grasses, and groves of palm trees."[94] To one side was a misty range of mountains, stretching toward a sea ridge on which Creelman could make out the ancient form of Morro Castle. It yielded just the battle he expected.

El Caney's central feature was a stone fort surrounded by a well-sheltered system of trenches and blockhouses. This proved a strong defensive position for the Spanish. A small garrison of just over five hundred soldiers, armed only with light weapons, fought like lions against a much larger American force.

Guns were already blazing by the time Creelman arrived. He was determined to creep forward and observe the Spanish position from close range. The high calling of reportage, he would later write, allowed no consideration for one's mortal safety. The newspaperman "must be in the very foreground of battle, if he would see with his own eyes the dread scenes that make war worth describing." He got close enough to peer into the outlying Spanish trenches. He saw a row of straw hats under which young Spanish soldiers—"not a beard among them"—projected the shiny barrels of their Mausers over the earthworks.[95]

Creelman next made his way to the U.S. lines and stuck to the side of Brigadier General Adna R. Chaffee, whose brigade was firing upward from a position below the old stone fort. He watched Chaffee rage up and down his infantry lines, oblivious to the heat and smoke and noise, his eyes flashing fire, "the soul of war incarnate." Creelman thought nothing of interrupting him for comment. As they chatted, a bullet clipped a button from Chaffee's jacket and another ripped the cape from Creelman's raincoat ("Looks better without it," observed the general). They retreated under a tree to continue the conversation. In addition to gathering quotes, Creelman told the general what he'd seen of the Spanish positions and suggested a route for a bayonet charge. He was aware that it wasn't his place, as a correspondent, to make such a proposal. It had always struck him as strange yet necessary to sit quietly, pencil in hand, setting down the sounds and colors of a battle scene "as a matter of business—to be in the midst of the movement, but not a part of it."[96] Something was different about the El Caney battle, however. He was, for the first time, watching American soldiers in combat, and they fought in service to a cause dear to his own heart. He was passionately committed to this war, to the liberation of Cuba, and to the ouster of Spain from the Caribbean. And so he set aside his customary detachment and laid out his plan for Chaffee, who was not immediately persuaded.

By late morning, Hearst and Hemment had also abandoned El Pozo. Following the sound of bursting shells, they reached El Caney around noon. Shafter's expected two-hour fight was still running hot, with casualties mounting on both sides. Chaffee's men were advancing slowly; his artillery was blasting away at the old stone fort, weakening the structure but failing to destroy it. Hearst watched it all through field glasses:

> As the cannon at our side would bang and the shell would swish through the air with its querulous, vicious, whining note, we would watch its explosion and then turn our attention to the little black specks of infantry dodging in and out between the groups of trees. Now they would disappear wholly from sight in the brush, and again would be seen hurrying along the open spaces, over the grass-covered slopes or across plowed fields. The infantry firing was ceaseless, our men popping away continuously as a string of firecrackers pops. The Spaniards fired in volleys whenever our men came in sight in the open spaces.
>
> Many times we heard this volley fire and saw numbers of our brave fellows pitch forward and lie still on the turf while the others hurried on to the next protecting clump of trees.
>
> For hours the Spaniards had poured their fire from slits in the stone fort, from their deep trenches and from the windows of the town. For hours our men answered back from trees and brush and gullies. For hours

cannon at our side banged and shells screamed through the air and fell upon the fort and town. And always our infantry advanced, drawing nearer and closing up on the village, till at last they formed under the mangrove tree at the foot of the hill on which the stone fort stood.

With a rush they swept up the slope and the stone fort was ours.

Then you should have heard the yell that went up from the knoll on which our battery stood. Gunners, drivers, Cubans, correspondents, swung their hats and gave a mighty cheer.[97]

It is not clear if Hearst noticed the familiar goateed face of James Creelman at the head of the storming party in that final uphill dash. The correspondent had finally coaxed one of Chaffee's field commanders into taking up the bayonet charge. When it got underway, he took his revolver firmly in hand—the same revolver he had carefully holstered and slung behind his back so that he would not be tempted to draw—and broke into a run. "Foolishly or wisely, recklessly, meddlesomely, or patriotically," he became by his own admission a part of the army, "a soldier without warrant to kill." Creelman made the three-hundred-yard uphill charge to the old fort with his heart leaping wildly and his eyes on a Spanish flag as "a glorious prize for my newspaper."[98]

The few remaining soldiers in the stone fort now finally gave up the fight. Half of their garrison had been killed; many others had scattered. Creelman was shocked at the scene inside the battered structure, the "dead and wounded strewn across the floor in every conceivable position. Men writhing and wailing in their own blood."[99] He ran back outside to claim the red and yellow Spanish flag that had drawn him up the hill. It was now lying in the dust, a fragment of the staff still attached. He picked it up and began waving it in celebration, attracting to himself the fire of lingering Spanish snipers. He felt what seemed like a punch in the upper part of his left arm; it whirled him around. The next moment he felt numb, and the next brought a darting pain as his arm fell loose and he collapsed to the ground. He was pulled back into the fort and helped onto a hammock.

The bullet had entered Creelman's left shoulder, shattering the blade and exiting high on his back. He lay listening to his own blood drip on the floor until a half dozen soldiers carried him down the hill with the other wounded, the captured flag thrown over his body. The shock of his wound and the terrific heat blurred his vision, making everything around him swim. He later wrote,

> Someone knelt in the grass beside me and put his hand on my fevered head. Opening my eyes, I saw Mr. Hearst, the proprietor of the *New York Journal,* a straw hat with a bright ribbon on his head, a revolver on his belt, and a pencil and note-book in his hand. The man who had provoked the war had come to see the result with his own eyes and, finding one of his correspondents prostrate, was doing the work himself. Slowly he took down my story of the fight. Again and again the tinging of Mauser bullets interrupted. But he seemed unmoved. That battle had to be reported somehow.
>
> "I'm sorry you're hurt, but"—and his face was radiant with enthusiasm—"wasn't it a splendid fight? We must beat every paper in the world."
>
> After doing what he could to make me comfortable, Mr. Hearst mounted his horse and dashed away for the seacoast, where a fast steamer was waiting to carry him across the sea to a cable station.[100]

Hearst's account of this meeting, published in the *Journal,* was shorter but corresponds in its essentials: "When I left the fort to hunt for Creelman I found him bloody and bandaged, lying on his back on a blanket on the ground, but shown all care that a kindly skillful surgeon could give him. He was pretty well dazed and said, 'I'm afraid I can't write much of a story. If you will write it for me I will describe it the best I can.'"[101]

Hemment says Hearst left Creelman with the surgeons and proceeded to Siboney to file his report. It opened with a dramatic dateline and ran a full page on July 4:

> With the army in front of Santiago, July 1, midnight, via Kingston, Jamaica—To-night as I write, ambulance trains are bringing wounded soldiers from the fierce battle around the little village of El Caney.
>
> Siboney, the base of the army, is a hospital, and nothing more. There is no saying when the slaughter will cease. Tents are crowded with wounded, and hard worked surgeons are busy with medical work. There is an odor of antiseptics, and ambulances clatter through one narrow street.

Hearst went on discuss the early morning artillery barrages, and complimented the soldiers for doing their best with inadequate guns. He criticized Shafter's decision to locate a battery at El Pozo on the grounds
that the Spaniards, having formerly occupied it as a fort, knew the precise range and were able to make it unpleasant for U.S. troops. He noted
that when he stopped for lunch he discovered that a piece of shrapnel
had passed clean through a can of pressed beef carried by his pack mule.
He discussed with some precision the positioning of forces and angles
of attack at El Caney, and described General Chaffee flashing about
"with his hat on the back of his head like a magnificent cowboy." He
paid tribute to the discipline of the Spanish soldiers and closed with his
account of the final charge, quoted above.

As Creelman lay bleeding at El Caney, General Shafter was
failing in his objective of overrunning Santiago in a day, stallling a mile
away at the San Juan Heights. General Linares, commander of Spain's
Santiago Division, had kept his main body of 10,000 troops garrisoned
in Santiago. He was holding the heights, a series of sun-baked hills,
including San Juan Hill and Kettle Hill, with a deployment of 750 men.
Nestled into a line of well-constructed hilltop trenches, the Spaniards
took advantage of good sightlines to pick off American troops as they
made their approach below through thickets, clearings of long slippery
grass, and tangles of barbed wire. With Lawton still tied up at El Caney,
Shafter aimed two divisions at the heights and suffered three times the
losses of the enemy. If it had not been for the timely appearance of a
Gatling-gun detachment, the slaughter would have been worse. Firing
3,600 rounds per minute, the Gatlings forced the Spaniards from their
positions, allowing the U.S. infantry to climb San Juan Hill. Meanwhile,
Lieutenant Colonel Roosevelt, tired of catching bullets at the base of
Kettle Hill and emboldened by the arrival of the Gatlings, led his Rough
Riders on a charge for the summit. It was one of the most dramatic acts
in U.S. military history. As the *Journal* reported it,

Roosevelt [on horseback] was in the lead, waving his sword. Out into
the open and up the hill where death seemed certain in the face of the
continuous crackle of the Mausers came the Rough Riders with the

Tenth Cavalry alongside. Not a man flinched, all continuing to fire as they ran.

Roosevelt was a hundred feet ahead of his troops, yelling like a Sioux, while his own men and the colored cavalry cheered him as he charged up the hill. There was no stopping as men's neighbors fell, but on they went, faster and faster.

Suddenly Roosevelt's horse stopped, pawed the air for a moment and fell in a heap. Before the horse was down Roosevelt disengaged himself from the saddle and landing on his feet again yelled to his men and, sword in hand, charged on afoot. It was something terrible to watch these men race up that hill with death. Fast as they were going it seemed that they would never reach the crest.

They did not stop to fire, but poured in rifle shots as they marched in the ranks. We could clearly see the wonderful work the dusky veterans of the Tenth were doing. Such splendid shooting was probably never done under these conditions.

As fast as the Spanish fire thinned their ranks the gaps were closed up, and after an eternity they gained the top of the hill and rushed the few remaining yards to the Spanish trenches.

Had the enemy remained staunch the slaughter at close range would have been appalling, but the daring of the Americans dazed the [Spaniards]. Their fire driveled to nothing. They wavered and then ran. Our fellows dropped to one knee and picked them off like partridges in the brush. The position was won.[102]

That un-bylined report ran in the *Journal* on July 4, along with Hearst's account of the Battle of El Caney, giving the paper the best and earliest reports of the most consequential land battles of the war (the *Herald* would take more than a week to publish Richard Harding Davis's dispatch from San Juan Heights). Shafter decided against another attack on Santiago. Ill and weak and discouraged by the Spanish resistance of July 1, which cost him 1,200 casualties, he had to be talked out of a retreat. He lay siege to the city, a difficult operation that left his men exposed to extreme heat, torrential rains, and Spanish gunfire. The shortcomings of the army's planning revealed themselves as the troops ran short of food and supplies and succumbed to fever at a shocking rate. Shafter was not holding the heights so much as clinging to them by his fingernails and, but for a rash move by the Spanish navy, the results could have been disastrous.

Early on the beautiful morning of Sunday, July 3, Admiral Cervera made a break from Santiago harbor. His flagship, the *Maria Teresa,* steamed out to sea followed by the *Vizcaya* and five other vessels, with cover from the Spanish land batteries. The American squadron picked up the Spanish movements immediately and opened its big guns. The second great naval battle of the Spanish-American War lasted just over four hours. One by one, the Spanish ships were chased down, fired upon, and either run aground or sunk. The last ship, the *Colon,* was run onto the beach at Rio Tarquino, about fifty miles from Santiago.

Hearst returned from Jamaica on time to observe the last of the fighting from a distance of three or four miles. With the smoke of battle still heavy in the air, the *Sylvia* approached the wreck of the *Vizcaya.* Hemment was eager to take pictures:

> We passed close to her and took views from all possible positions, after which we put off in a whaleboat and boarded her. As we came alongside the Viscaya, in climbing up the sea ladder, we found it almost too hot to place our hands upon her. Our party consisted of Mr. Hearst, Mr. Follansbee, the ship's mate, and several others, and we boarded her and saw the terrible havoc that fire and shell had wrought. The girders which supported the main deck were twisted into every conceivable grotesque shape. The gun deck and the superstructure were totally demolished; all the woodwork, which had been so beautifully cleaned and polished, was destroyed. Nothing combustible could be found. The charred remains of many of the sailors were strewn around, some hanging from the iron girders and beams in all sorts of positions. Carcasses of animals were also to be found. We made a thorough investigation and secured a great many souvenirs, consisting of Mauser rifles, revolvers, and bunches of keys.[103]

Hearst's party left the *Vizcaya* for the *Oquenda,* which was still burning. Hearing an explosion from one of the ship's guns, evidently caused by the intense heat, they decided against boarding. They proceeded to the ruin of the *Maria Teresa* and, while taking pictures there, spied on shore a large party of men waving white flags. Hearst, Hemment, and an assistant put off in a steam launch to investigate. They found twenty-nine stranded

Spanish sailors, most from the *Vizcaya*, many of them naked but armed with machetes and rifles. Relieved to have been discovered by American journalists rather than by marauding Cuban troops, the Spaniards cheerfully surrendered their weapons and agreed to be taken as prisoners aboard the *Sylvia*. Hearst treated his captives graciously, giving them food and drink, dressing their wounds, and clothing them as best he could. The Spaniards reciprocated by giving three cheers for the Fourth of July as the *Texas* sailed by. They also described for the benefit of the *Journal* correspondents the havoc aboard their ships as they came under fire that morning: knowing the fight was lost, crews had abandoned their guns and fire rooms and had crowded the upper deck in hopes of abandoning ship. The *Sylvia* eventually steamed alongside the *St. Louis* and transferred the prisoners to the proper authorities. Hearst demanded a receipt for them; it was printed along with the story on the *Journal*'s front page. The *Times* opined that the prisoners represented "the most genuine as well as the most legitimate increase in circulation" Hearst had yet achieved: "We admit that we cannot imagine Mr. Pulitzer in the act of corralling shipwrecked Spaniards for the glory of his journal and the country . . . "[104]

The *Journal* crew now returned to Siboney to pick up the wounded Creelman. In the forty-eight hours since he had been shot, the $18,000-a-year correspondent had been more or less abandoned, spending the first two nights on a litter in a field by a stream outside of El Caney. Lawton's division had moved on to Santiago, leaving the wounded behind without adequate protection or provisions—victims of the army's growing logistical problems. Creelman and the other casualties were exposed to rain and sun and occasional sniper fire from Spanish sharpshooters. "Vultures gathered around the camp," he wrote, "and waited in the wet grass. Nearer they came, with hesitating, grotesque hopes, watching, watching, watching."[105] Finally, on July 3, an army surgeon returned to camp and told the men they were under orders to abandon the site and walk to Siboney unless absolutely incapacitated. Creelman had already penned a desperate letter to his employer:

Dear Mr. Hearst,

After being abandoned without shelter or medicine and practically without food for nearly two days—most of the time under constant fire—you can judge my condition. My shoulder was as you know. That I am here and alive is due simply to my own efforts. I had to rise from my litter and stagger seven miles through the hills and the mud without an attendant. . . . Mr. [Follansbee] stayed one night with me and got a fever. We are both here without clothes. I must get to the United States in order to get well. I expect no gratitude but I do expect a chance for my life.[106]

Hearst appears to have asked his friend Follansbee to look out for Creelman. Neither a writer nor a soldier, Follansbee had gone to Cuba simply for the adventure. Like Creelman, he had been unable to remain detached during the action at El Caney. Fluent in Spanish, he volunteered to lead a post-battle search party through the village of El Caney. He went house to house rounding up Spanish combatants, including several found hiding in a locked closet. If Follansbee did fall sick after attending to Creelman for a night, they appear to have been reunited at the Siboney field hospital, where Hearst finally collected his correspondent.

WITH THE SMOKING HULKS of Cervera's squadron littering the coast of Cuba, the Spanish-American War was for all intents and purposes over. Some 1,700 Spanish sailors and naval officers had been captured. The seige of Santiago would drag on a while longer. Shafter never did succeed in storming the city and his position was worsening, but fortunately for the U.S. Army, Spanish forces at Santiago felt at least as vulnerable and agreed to negotiate a settlement. Talks on the terms of capitulation began on July 14. The U.S. Army would take Puerto Rico against token resistance later that month, prompting Spain to sue for peace and bringing hostilities to an official close on August 12.

Even as the Spanish-American War wound down, the newspaper war raged on. The *Journal* seized on an unsigned *World* story dated July 15 that suggested the officers of the 71st New York regiment had demonstrated a want of mettle on coming under Spanish fire at the San Juan Heights. The *Journal* torqued it as a "slur on the bravery" of the boys of the Seventy-First, a regiment that had suffered a high casualty rate.[107] Hearst himself vouched for the character of these "brave" soldiers in a bylined report of his own interactions with them (although, as he admitted, he had not witnessed the battle in question). The *World* tried to fight back, arguing that it had not printed a single derogatory word about the regiment—a statement nearer the truth than the *Journal* allowed. Pulitzer began a face-saving campaign to raise funds for a memorial to American volunteers who fell at Santiago. The *Journal* mocked it all as a groveling admission of libel and coaxed veterans of the regiment into rejecting the *World*'s tribute, and the monument campaign was soon dropped.[108]

Simultaneous with this embarrassment, the *World*'s ace, Sylvester Scovel, brought his spectacular run as a war correspondent to an igno-minious climax. On Sunday, July 17, Spanish and American officials gathered in a plaza outside the governor's palace in Santiago for a formal ceremony of capitulation. General Shafter, sensitive about his press, had banned reporters from the city. A handful snuck into the plaza unnoticed. After a series of greetings, the Spaniards dropped their colors from a flagstaff atop the governor's palace. Three U.S. officers clambered onto the roof to hoist the Stars and Stripes. To Shafter's astonishment, they were joined by a fourth individual, none other than Scovel. He had no business in town, let alone on the palace roof, and Shafter ordered him down. The two squared off in the plaza, with Shafter apparently taking the first swing. Scovel made the mistake of striking back and wound up in prison facing a court-martial.[109] Already under attack for smearing the Seventy-First, the last thing the *World* needed was a fight with a brigadier general. It made a show of cutting Scovel loose, only to come under fire from the reporter's many friends and the *World*'s publishing rivals for abandoning a valiant employee who had risked his life in Pulitzer's service. Sheepishly, the *World* hired Scovel back.[110]

Hearst himself was caught in a blunder in the last days of the war. One of his reports mentioned that Honore Laine, a sugar planter turned rebel warrior and part-time *Journal* correspondent, had gone out on patrol after the fight at El Caney and captured forty Spaniards in a blockhouse. Hearst asked Laine what he had done with the prisoners and quoted him as answering, "We cut their heads off, of course."[111] This news alarmed officials in Washington who cabled Shafter seeking confirmation of Hearst's story. The general replied that it was completely false. A subse-quent *Journal* editorial claimed that Hearst's original copy had said "four" Spaniards were decapitated, not "forty," and that the error was made by the telegraph operator. Walter Howard, the *Journal* reporter who had cabled Hearst's story, corroborated his boss's claim, but the damage was done. "The *Journal* men are mightily cut up over the bad break made by Hearst and [Laine] in the matter of the 'forty beheaded Spaniards,'" wrote the *Journalist*. "It was bad enough as it stood, but when Hearst explained that he meant four instead of forty, he gave the *World* a chance to show him up, because, according to Shafter and all the rest, there wasn't a single instance of the kind, not one."[112]

The *Journal* also ran afoul of General Shafter for plastering Santiago with advertisements for a forthcoming Cuban edition of the paper. The large, illustrated posters were headlined "Remember The Maine." Shafter, responsible for a thousand Spanish prisoners of war and Cuban allies who were not ready to quit fighting, considered the advertisements an unnecessary provocation. He arrested several *Journal* men and charged them with attempting to create disorder. Secretary Alger, knowing Shafter to be in poor health and worse temper, wrote a polite letter from Washington asking him to reconsider. The *Journal*, he said, was "in terrible distress because of their exclusion from Santiago." The general insisted that the culprits "deserved death" but he did eventually release them.[113]

Hearst delivered on his promise of a battlefield newspaper. During the siege of Santiago, a mechanical department under the endlessly resourceful George Pancoast set up shop at Siboney in a wood-paneled cabin with open rafters. Hand presses were mounted on planks suspended over barrels. Pressmen and correspondents labored with cigars in their teeth at makeshift composing tables, the floor strewn with waste paper. On July 10 they produced a four-page newspaper, seven columns to the page, containing not only the latest from *Journal* war correspondents but reports from Washington and Europe and an assortment of sports and entertainment news as well. The English-language edition was called the *Examiner-Journal;* the Spanish, *El Journal de Nueva York.* Copies were circulated among American and Cuban soldiers at Santiago and among Sampson's sailors. The front page featured pictures of William McKinley and Vice President Hobart with a message from J. Addison Porter, the president's private secretary:

The President takes great pleasure in commending the enterprise of Mr. Hearst in publishing an American newspaper under the stars and stripes on Cuban soil. He regards it as a unique exemplification of modern journalism, and has no doubt that the Army and Navy at Santiago will receive the publication with the utmost cordiality. The President extends the thanks of the country to the soldiers and sailors for their gallant conduct. The eyes of the world are upon them, and they are furnishing an inspiration that will last forever.[114]

Hearst himself did not linger in Cuba. The day after his Cuban edition rolled off the press, Sam Chamberlain in New York relayed a message to Phoebe on her son's behalf: "Don't worry. Everything is over here now, and we are coming home."[115] The *Sylvia* sailed for Baltimore with the convalescing correspondents, Marshall and Creelman, and the cameraman Billy Bitzer, who had developed a fever, probably typhoid, after drinking murky water. Bitzer lay in his bunk listening to the onboard revelry of the Willson sisters, getting up only to collect the food left at his door. Anxious to avoid quarantine, the party sailed into Baltimore late at night. Bitzer disembarked and took a train to New York, where he would require sixteen weeks to recuperate, his weight having fallen from 165 to 96 pounds.

Marshall would also recover and return to a vigorous career in journalism despite his amputation. He is said to have later survived three train collisions, the wreck of a lake steamer, and two hotel fires. He was aboard the British channel steamer *Sussex* in 1916 when it was destroyed by a torpedo. Unable to swim, Marshall clung to wreckage for several hours before being rescued. He died in 1933. Creelman drifted in and out of journalism over the next decade and a half—writing editorials for the *World*, also working for the state of New York. He returned to Hearst to cover the Great War, and died suddenly of nephritis in Berlin.

Richard Harding Davis had avoided Spanish bullets but suffered from sciatica throughout the fighting; the best reporting appeared not in newspapers but months later in magazines. However, Davis had impressed his colleagues with his "white-faced persistence" despite racking pain, and had proved his manhood after his previous failures to reach war zones.[116]

CHAPTER SIXTEEN

Standing in the First Rank of American Journalism, Feeling Blue

Perhaps the last moment of full-throated martial celebration in 1898 occurred on Saturday, August 20, with the return to New York of Sampson, Schley, and the fleet that had destroyed Cervera. Several days in advance of the homecoming, the *Journal* had begun talking up what it hoped would be "the grandest naval and military demonstrations ever known in the history of the United States" (a boast later amended to recognize the Civil War). Sampson's fleet was expected to reach Sandy Hook by Friday night and the North River by Saturday morning. It would fire a salute opposite Grant's Tomb at Riverside Park and then return to anchor. The *Journal* decided Saturday should be a holiday to "give everybody, rich and poor, high and low, laborer and idler, a chance to properly greet the great fighting machines of our navy as they steam up North River, showing their scars of battle to a proud people."[1] The paper persuaded leading businesses, including Macy's and Lord & Taylor, to close for the day so their employees could greet the ships. Thomas Edison agreed to shut his laboratory in Orange, New Jersey. A long roster of state and civic politicians hopped on the bandwagon. At the *Journal*'s request, Mayor Robert Van Wyck called upon the citizens of New York to give up business as fully as possible during the review and to decorate their streets and residences with flags and bunting.

The weather on the appointed day was perfect. Enormous crowds gathered to wave and cheer on the slopes of Staten Island, on roofs and balconies in Battery Park, and at Grant's Tomb. Hundreds of pleasure crafts and ferryboats sailed out to meet the fleet and the *Journal* counted as many as a million people along the route (more conservative sources estimated

750,000.) The mayor himself was on hand. A *Journal* balloon floating a thousand feet over Grant's Tomb alerted the throngs to the progress of the warships by spraying clouds of color-coded confetti: purple meant the ships had reached the Statue of Liberty, and so on. At the height of the festivities, Hearst literally upstaged the fleet. He had sent a team of men on the *Anita* to intercept Sampson as he steamed up the Jersey coast, and when they crossed paths at 3 a.m. Saturday morning, the *Journal*'s emissary advised the admiral's officers of the reception awaiting them and the hour at which they were expected or, rather, the hour at which the *Journal* had told its readers to expect them. The *Anita* then chugged ahead and, assuming for itself the role of parade master, led Sampson's flagship up the river with *Journal* banners waving.

With that, the celebratory mood quickly passed. Days after the fleet review, the *Journal*, like every other paper on Park Row, was filled with horror stories on the condition of returning American troops. Tropical disease and the combined effects of inadequate food, clothing, and shelter wound up doing far more damage to the Fifth Army Corps than the Spanish had managed. The newspapers and their readers were outraged at the desperate state of the hale young men who had landed in Cuba less than two months earlier. By the time the Fifth Army Corps formally disbanded, it had lost 771 men to fever, more than three times the number who died in combat.[2] In addition to this toll came daily accounts of bungling and scandal at the War Department, including accusations that troops had been served "embalmed beef." A commission of inquiry struck by President McKinley would later report that the War Department had indeed been guilty of administrative incompetence. A separate court of inquiry found the embalmed beef story to have been overblown, although other criticisms of the army's provisioning were upheld. Coverage of these controversies brought the summer's giddiness to a sharp halt and marked the beginning of a Spanish-American hangover.

Hearst was among those who returned from Cuba in rough shape. He had many reasons to celebrate—the Cuban people were rid of their oppressor, he had made a successful debut as a correspondent, he had dodged his share of Spanish bullets—but he was nonetheless a troubled man. He moved into a suite at the Waldorf, presumably to be alone. He uttered in two letters some of the gloomiest sentiments found in his lifetime of correspondence. One letter was to his reporter James Creelman, now nursing his wounded shoulder in Ohio: "I hope you are getting along well. I feel like hell myself. I sit all day in one place in a half trance and stare at a spot. I'm afraid my mighty intellect is giving way. Anybody can have Cuba that wants it."[3]

The second letter was to his mother:

> I guess I'm a failure. I made the mistake of my life in not raising the cowboy regiment I had in mind before Roosevelt raised his. I really believe I brought on the war but I failed to score in the war. I had my chance and failed to grab it, and I suppose I must sit on the fence now and watch the procession go by. It's my own fault. I was thirty-five years of age, and of sound mind—comparatively—and could do as I liked. I failed and I'm a failure and I deserve to be for being as slow and stupid as I was. Outside of the grief it would give you I had better be in a Santiago trench than where I am. . . . Goodnight, Mama dear. Take care of yourself. Don't let me lose you. I wish you were here tonight. I feel about eight years old—and very blue.[4]

Hearst was normally a resilient individual, loaded with energy, self-confidence, and optimism. He had suffered bouts of homesickness as a young man at school, he had fallen into funks at the end of romances, his letters to his parents occasionally betray moodiness and anxiety, but he had always managed to rebound quickly. Whatever was bothering him when he moved into the Waldorf that summer, however, was still dogging him in November after the midterm elections. Still more unusual was his choice of confidants. Hearst generally kept his private affairs private. His emotional life was open to Phoebe and, one presumes, his girlfriends, but it was entirely out of character for him to unburden himself to a colleague. There is no evidence that he was particularly close to Creelman, a relatively new employee and one of the few individuals ever to get under Hearst's skin. "[I] am very sorry to have 'shown temper,'" Hearst wrote him at one point, "but I felt deeply humilated at your rising contemptuously and leaving when we were in the middle of the discussion we had assembled to hear."[5] Their shared Cuban adventure may have brought them closer but it was nonetheless rare for Hearst to share confidences in this manner. He was obviously deeply upset, quite possibly depressed.

Part of the problem might have been physical. Hearst appears to have been slightly ill with a tropical fever. One of the trade papers reported that he was suffering from fatigue "as a result of exposure to inclement weather and the hardships peculiar to the campaign. Shortly after his return the fever developed but was proved to be slight."[6] He would later mention a relapse of his Cuban illness in a letter to his mother.

It may also be that his mental health was affected by Cuba. While the Hearst record does not need another bout of amateur psychologizing, it is not far-fetched to suggest that he was troubled by his exposure to the traumas of war. His enthusiasm for the invasion may have been high, and his coverage may have lacked complete solemnity, but he did witness serious battles at El Caney and the San Juan Heights. He had seen young men wounded, maimed, killed, and destroyed by disease. It is not at all uncommon for witnesses to war to experience depression, cognitive problems, and feelings of estrangement. It may go against the grain of Hearst's biographical literature to suggest that he was capable of normal human emotions; on the other hand, it is harsh to deny the possibility.

Still, whatever part ill health played in Hearst's condition, it was probably an aggravating factor rather than the primary issue. His letters suggest he was preoccupied with the state of his career: he uses the word "fail" five times in one paragraph to his mother. He had not got what he wanted from the war, but it is not immediately clear why he saw himself as a failure.

Hearst's claim to Phoebe that he had blown his opportunity to score in the war by not raising a cowboy regiment cannot be taken too seriously. He is often facetious with his mother and he appears to have been so here, notwithstanding the depth of his feelings. Even if he was only of sound mind "comparatively," he could not have forgotten that his offer to equip a cavalry regiment and to enlist in its ranks had been rejected in Washington and that the navy had belatedly offered him only a useless minor commission. He had not failed to grab an opportunity for Rooseveltian military distinction; no such opportunity had ever existed.

It is sometimes suggested that Hearst hated Roosevelt and was unhinged at his sudden emergence as a war hero and as the Republican nominee for governor of New York.[7] The two men had crossed paths at

Harvard, and they would later be political rivals. Roosevelt, however, was treated by the *Journal* better than most Republicans in the months leading up to the Spanish-American War, and during the fighting Hearst's paper did as much as any other to raise Terrible Teddy to mythic stature, lauding him for his valor and leadership: "No finer picture of young American manhood in war has ever been presented than that of Teddy Roosevelt at the head of his Rough Riders."[8] If Roosevelt was on Hearst's mind, it was not because of schoolboy rivalries or cowboy regiments but simply as an example of a man who had made the most of the war. He was not the cause of Hearst's distress but a measure of his disappointment. Like the vast majority of soldiers and correspondents who had crowded into Cuba, Hearst had smelled a chance for glory. Roosevelt had got his. Hearst felt empty.

Given that Hearst had gone to Cuba as a newspaperman and that his entire involvement in the conflict had been through the *Journal,* it makes sense that his self-assessed failure was rooted in journalism.

By the late summer of 1898, when the carpenters arrived to dismantle the special war bulletin boards on Park Row, there were good reasons for all New York newspaper executives to be upset. The dailies themselves were among the casualties of war. Not only had the conflict been expensive to cover but advertisers, worried about the stability of the economy in wartime, reined in their spending, some by as much as 60 percent, doing further damage to the bottom lines of the big papers. Godkin might have thought his rivals were profiting from war, but all those dispatch boats were floating on seas of red ink. Worse, publishers had not much in the way of great journalism to show for their pains.[9]

The war had been a disappointment as stories go, a lopsided contest with a minimum of real action. The decisive battle—Dewey's victory—was played out on the other side of the globe. The Santiago actions were brief and witnessed by hordes of journalists, allowing for little in the way of sustained reportage or scoops. *The Fourth Estate* found it difficult to determine which of the papers published the best correspondence: "A singular thing about the war news service . . . was that none of the men engaged in news gathering at the front specially distinguished himself for brilliant newspaper writing."[10]

Of the two- and three-cent papers, the *Herald* alone had a decent war. It endured its share of mistakes and criticisms and it executed a stunning reversal of judgment on the advisability of the conflict, but its traditions of comprehensive and straightforward coverage of international affairs served it well in Cuba. "We may criticize the *Herald* on minor points," wrote the *Journalist*, "but when a great crisis comes; when we want the news promptly and accurately reported, [it] is always in the front."[11]

The *World* landed the biggest scoop of the war with its full account of Dewey's triumph in Manila Bay, and Scovel did some good reporting from the ground in the vicinity of Santiago in advance of the Fifth Army's arrival, but pretty much everything else went miserably for Pulitzer.[12] His overzealous effort to find the *Journal* guilty of un-American activities in the *Buccaneer* incident backfired, bringing Hearst sympathy and providing him an opportunity to make public his munificent offer to grant the war effort a yacht and a fully funded regiment.[13] It also triggered Brisbane's great prank, the unmasking of Reflipe Thenuz, one of the great embarrassments of Pulitzer's career. The so-called slur on the Boys of the Seventy-First, Scovel's crashing of the Santiago ceremony, and the paper's dismissal of its star correspondent did nothing to assuage the harsh impressions of the trades that the *World* was "hopeless, vile beyond redemption."[14] At one point during the fighing, Pulitzer lost complete faith in himself and his staff and offered the Chicago newspaperman Melville Stone free run of the *World* at $50,000 a year. Stone, knowing Pulitzer's capriciousness, declined.[15]

The excitement of war did bring out the garish hues of the yellow papers, hardening opposition to both Pulitzer and Hearst in some quarters. One outraged critic wrote in the *Journalist*, "For 'offensive partisanship' and 'pernicious activity,' there has been nothing in human experience so far as I can call to mind to exceed the course of a certain portion of the New York press in the last six months."[16] Yet all of the trade papers noticed that the flaws of the yellow press were also abundantly evident in the "respectable" dailies. One theory was that the better sheets had been dragged down market by "the morbid, craving, sensation loving public," while another held that they had been infected by a one-cent journalism toxin: "The taint of the yellow sheet has seemed to reach all."[17] These reviews notwithstanding, many critics continued to rate the *Journal* an excellent all-around newspaper and credited it with forcing its Park Row rivals to raise their games.[18]

If one individual gained a lion's share of acclaim from his journalistic peers in the wake of the war, it was Hearst. His decision to go to Cuba captivated Park Row. His movements were closely followed in the trades and the applause began the moment he embarked. "It must be evident to even Mr. Hearst's most bitter enemies that he is not lacking in personal courage," wrote *The Fourth Estate,* "for if there is any one man the Spaniards would like to have in any of their several Morro castles it is the proprietor of the *New York Journal.* He is blamed by them with causing the war which has proven so disastrous. Then, too, they object to the habit of the *Journal* of printing the news just as fast as it happens, telling of the defeats of the Spanish arms as they come in rapid succession."[19] As to Hearst's copy, *The Fourth Estate* judged that he summoned the atmosphere of the battlefield and told truth in a straightforward fashion without the "pat picturing" of competing reports. The whole effect was "enormously attractive."[20]

The *Journalist* was amazed that a proprietor would stoop to reportage. It seemed to upset the natural order of things on Park Row. Generally speaking, men who achieve high executive office or an ownership stake in a newspaper not only quit writing for its pages but put as much social distance as possible between themselves and front-line hacks. Hearst had led his journalists by example: "That the editor and proprietor of the *Journal* is willing to share with his subordinates the heats of the day and its toils has been amply demonstrated within the last few weeks, and only a churl would deny him his just mead of praise."[21] It was not public knowledge that Hearst was only sharing the toils of his men by day, retiring at night to the comforts of the *Sylvia* and his beloved Millicent.

Hearst made an even stronger impression with his successful printing of a Cuban edition. The trades recognized that the endeavor had no commercial value and that it was at least as much a promotional vehicle as a public service, but they were nonetheless wowed. Publishing an edition in Cuba was an idea that could only have sprung from the mind of a newspaperman who "loved his profession, as an artist does his art; for its own sake and not for what he can make out of it," according to the *Journalist.*[22] In its view, Hearst's success in New York and the unquestionable appeal of the *Journal* were due to the fact that Hearst was a newspaperman first and "only incidentally a proprietor." He now stood "in the first rank of American journalism."

Newspaper Maker celebrated Hearst as the embodiment of an emerging national spirit.[23] With his singularly American "nerve and pluck," the relative newcomer had shown the old-timers how to be progressive. "This hustling young millionaire," the *Newspaper Maker* wrote, "has astonished the newspaper world during the past three years by the magnitude of his enterprises, and although some of his methods are open to question, the dry bones that were rattled among his contemporaries made them put a little more vim in their efforts."[24] It was Hearst's accomplishments that *Newspaper Maker* had in mind when at the close of the war it celebrated the "newspaper age" with a rhetoric of transformative change later echoed by enthusiasts of the space age and the digital age:

> Here is the raw event on one side of the earth; and before you can turn around the account and explanation has not only been thought out and written out and filed at the telegraphic office and ticked off to the home office; but it has been assigned its proper page and place and type, it has been set up, cast and printed, it has been delivered to the newsboys and agents and carried by trains to all points of the compass. And this is not done during certain special office hours, but it is done every hour of the four-and-twenty; you have no sooner read the first edition than the second is ready, with the third in sight, and so on all day long. Energy! Where in all fairy-tale is there an enchanter who could achieve anything half so marvelous? Every man who can read, and is not himself at the front in the present crisis, will practically be present at operation and turn of fortune and will be able to tell the veterans when they return home more about what they have been doing than they know themselves. Space and time, as hindrances to knowledge, have ceased to be. . . . It is revolutionary. . . . [I]t is magnificent. The modern newspaper introduces a new age, unlike anything imagined heretofore.[25]

Although mixed with fierce criticism, the shower of approbation Hearst received on his return from Cuba shows that the consensus within his profession was that he had, in fact, made a success in Cuba. He had scored in most of the ways it was possible for a newspaperman to score at war: his dispatches brought him critical applause, the *Journal* was hugely influential and more popular than ever with its readers, and the Cuban edition of his paper was a smash. Yet somehow it was not enough.

THIS WAS HEARST'S REAL PROBLEM. Newspapers had consumed him
since he had taken the reins of the *San Francisco Examiner* in 1887. He
had studied and mastered the trade and he had dedicated every ounce of
his intelligence, imagination, talent, and ambition to his publications.
He had arrived in New York in 1895, unbidden and unheralded in the
greatest newspaper city in the world, and set for himself the ridiculously high goal of supplanting Pulitzer as king of Park Row, champion
of the Democratic Party, and popular voice of the great American people. He had met that challenge. He had followed Dana's instruction to
use his high position for good, pushing the boundaries of editorial influence and activism far beyond what some thought advisable and most
thought possible—to the point where some serious observers began to
think newspapers really did command the public agenda, that they were
indeed the greatest force in civilization. Hearst had done all this happily,
at the expense of his youth and a good part of his fortune, at risk to his
health and reputation. Yet at the very pinnacle of his achievement in
New York he had slammed face-first into the hard limits of his profession. The role of the press, however grand his aspirations for it, was
essentially one of observation and criticism.

At some level, Hearst had believed all that was said about the high
purpose and unprecedented capacities of newspapers, that they did
"control the nation because they REPRESENT THE PEOPLE," and that,
as the biggest editor on Park Row, he just might deserve the title of
"uncrowned king of an educated democracy." But nothing was calibrated
to crush these conceits so decisively as a shooting war. When the boots hit
the ground and the big guns boomed, all eyes shifted to the commander-
in-chief, his admirals and generals, their decisions and their arms. The
publisher and his newspaper, notwithstanding their unprecedented
resources, their unmatched audacity and ambition, their evangelical
promotion of "The Journalism That Acts," were left shouting from ringside. Wielding influence, in the end, was something quite different
from wielding power. Roosevelt would articulate the difference between
the roles a dozen years later in a famous speech at the Sorbonne: "It is
not the critic who counts. . . . The credit belongs to the man who is actually in the arena, whose face is marred by dust and sweat and blood."

In fairness, Hearst got his hands dirty. He sweated and struggled as
much as anyone in his chosen line. He had not been found wanting in

courage or ability, but at the critical moment, he was not in command of anything he did not own or lease, he was merely witness to those who did control the nation, and that was not enough for Hearst. He never expressed disappointment with his profession or disavowed his faith in the power of the press. He would continue in the months and years ahead to exhort his editors to practise the journalism of action in pursuit of social improvements, but without comment or explanation, he now pointed his life in a different direction.[26] He began to remove himself from the *Journal*'s daily operations and to concentrate his efforts on expanding his publishing empire and finding a place in the political arena. His mood brightened considerably.

As part of his transition, Hearst made his first serious effort to stem his losses at the *Journal*. Whatever progress he had made toward profitability through 1897 had been wiped out by the war. The estimate of $3,000 a day in additional editorial expenditures comes from Brisbane, who was in a position to know. That would have brought the total cost of the *Journal*'s war coverage in the direction of $500,000, a hefty sum even if it was amortized over morning, evening, and Sunday editions, the *Morgen Journal*, the *San Francisco Examiner*, and the Hearst syndicate (some years later the *Journal* would claim to have spent $750,000 on the war).[27] The gossip sheets suggested that Phoebe Hearst was so disturbed by her son's finances that she had decided to replace him with professional managers; there is no evidence to support the claim, but Phoebe was certainly troubled by the *Journal*'s expenses. Her accountant, Clark, was sweating over the paper's books and writing reports to Phoebe throughout the summer and had the war dragged on she might indeed have interfered.[28]

Hearst dialed back his spending in every direction, reducing the color pages in his Sunday edition, discharging as many as a hundred employees and cutting his circulation to a level slightly above the *World*'s.[29] Given that he had always resisted economizing lest it affect his sales, this suggests not only that he was out of money but that he now considered the *Journal* established and that a new phase of his career was underway. He sued for peace with rival publishers by printing a statement in the *Journal* lamenting the infighting on Park Row and the lack of collaboration among newspapers on items of shared editorial concern—public safety, for instance, and better schools. He pledged the *Journal* to the support of all good measures proposed by other dailies and to working constructively with them in the public interest.[30] Hearst's efforts to increase market share at their expense were over, and a period of consolidation had begun.

In this same spirit, Hearst sent an emissary directly to the Pulitzer camp. S.S. Carvalho met with *World* lieutenant Don Seitz in the late summer of 1898 to begin negotiations toward a Hearst-Pulitzer peace protocol. They settled on mutual cuts to expenditures and the curtailing of certain circulation and advertising practices (including, one presumes, rate reductions) and they also agreed to stop "the unfriendly utterances" between their papers.[31] Seitz took the proposed terms to Pulitzer.

It was not a hard sell. Pulitzer had to be regretting his decision to snub Hearst's prewar overtures. He had watched in horror through the summer as his advertising lineage shriveled, and his margins with it. When he tallied up the costs of the *World*'s extra correspondents and dispatch boats and the returns from his unsold papers, he found that his mighty money machine was operating at a loss for the first time since he had purchased it. Even as Cervera's fleet lay burning off Santiago, Pulitzer was desperate for a truce with Hearst. He accepted the negotiated terms, instructing Seitz to "tell every night editor, city editor, managing editor & editorial writer, to let the *Journal* alone as long as they let us alone—and possibly even longer."[32] Pulitzer would backslide from that position. He accused Hearst of violating Associated Press guidelines by running its copy in the *Evening Journal* (which was not party to the morning *Journal*'s AP franchise). He pressed the matter in the courts. When Hearst found himself being tailed through the streets of New York by process servers, he had Carvalho write his counterpart at the *World* that if Pulitzer didn't back down, the *Journal* would terminate its good relations with his newspaper and "begin a personal assault on Mr. Pulitzer," making it "as personal and as powerful" as possible. The sniping would continue for another year but, commercially, "good relations" were maintained.[33]

Pulitzer did some serious cost-cutting of his own after the war and suffered another bout of respectability, leading to sweeping changes to *World* operations. Murder and crime stories were banished to inside pages. Limits were placed on the size and number of illustrations; those deemed unnewsworthy were banished entirely. The flagrant use of "extras" to plump sales was curbed. Front-page fonts came under review, especially in the evening edition. "Mr. Pulitzer endured the screaming typography until the end of the fighting," recalled Seitz, "then he ordered the foreman to collect all large letters and melt them up. This he did, but they refused to stay dead."[34] In keeping with the new emphasis on restraint, Pulitzer instructed his executives to re-educate newsroom employees on proper editorial practice. A notice was posted around the Pulitzer Building calling staff to a meeting at 11 a.m. on November 28. A series of managers stood to confess their journalistic sins and confess that the *World* had lost its way over the previous two years. As Bradford Merrill said, "In strenuous competition a man may do a thing for a newspaper which he would not do as an individual. It is Mr. Pulitzer's desire that no man should ever do anything as a member of the staff of the *World* which he would not do or believe in doing as a man. The great mistakes which have been made [and] I have made a number of them myself—have been caused by an excess of zeal. Be just as clever as you can. Be more energetic and more entertaining than any other man if you can, but above all, be right."[35]

This forced ritual of penitence was typical of Pulitzer, but hair shirts were not the style at the *Journal*. For the most part, Hearst would defend his paper against charges of sensationalism in its Cuban coverage: "There is a good deal that is sensational about a war," he told one interviewer, and the *Journal* wrote "to the temper of the people."[36] He had nothing but praise for his newspaper staff, writing Brisbane: "All must be congratulated on this tremendous job . . . It must be remembered as we embark on a movement to upgrade social conditions that through efforts of exposure and exploitation public opinion will compel anything to be done that is right. The war with Spain was our war but the credit goes to the nation. Let us always remember the power of an informed public mind . . ."[37]

All the same, Hearst joined the rest of Park Row in moderating his style and tone through the autumn of '98. He brought the pitch of the *Journal* down at least an octave, using far fewer streamer headlines, and making massive front-page illustrations relatively rare. That was as close as Hearst came to acknowledging that his paper had lost its composure at the height of the conflict.

IN THE SPRING OF 1899, Hearst began showing up at Democratic fundraisers in New York. In an undated letter to Phoebe, he talked of running for governor of the state (likely in 1900). She agreed to bankroll him. "I went home full of gratitude for your great generosity and kindness in letting me go into this political contest," he wrote Phoebe. "I got hold of Brisbane and talked to him for hours about politics and the paper. Brisbane is sure the nomination will do the paper an <u>immense</u> amount of good. He says just think how it would help the *World* if Pulitzer were nominated and elected Governor of the state of New York. Would there be any doubt in our minds as to how that would dignify the *World* and raise it in public esteem, especially if he gave a good administration. The *World* would be the mouthpiece of the Democracy and we would feel that the *Journal* was unutterably insignificant and would doubtless see another political field. That is a fair way to look at it."[38]

While that letter suggests Hearst's political activities were supporting his journalism, it was soon apparent that his papers were directly serving his ambitions for office. Hearst was pestered by the Democratic National Committee to launch a daily in Chicago. Weak in the Midwest, Bryan's people desperately wanted Hearst on their side against Chicago's largely Republican press corps. They baited him with the presidency of the National Association of Democratic Clubs, an organization dedicated to publishing and distributing campaign literature. Hearst was intrigued, but Phoebe was appalled at the prospect of another newspaper in the family. She wrote Orrin Peck from Paris in May 1899:

I have been feeling greatly depressed and did not feel like writing. Will is <u>insisting</u> upon buying a paper in <u>Chicago</u>. Says he will come over to see me if I do not go home <u>very</u> soon. It is <u>impossible</u> for me to throw away more money in <u>any</u> way, for the simple reason that he has already absorbed almost <u>all</u>. In a few months there will <u>actually</u> be <u>no</u> money, and we must then sell anything that can be sold to keep on. It is <u>madness</u>. I never know when or how Wm will break out into some <u>additional</u> expensive scheme. I cannot tell you how distressed I feel about the heavy monthly loss on the *Journal*. And then to contemplate starting another nightmare is a hopeless situation. I have written and telegraphed that <u>no</u> argument can induce me to commit such a folly as that of starting another newspaper.[39]

Never mind the underline on the word "no," Phoebe did contribute to the Chicago venture. Her affairs were nowhere near as desperate as she claimed. Rather, her gold and copper mines were throwing off stupendous returns. She did insist that the *Journal* reduce its losses before Chicago got underway, and further letters from Will indicate that she was keeping close tabs on his operations. Will told her that Brisbane would be installed as publisher of the morning and evening editions, with Sam Chamberlain editing the former and Richard Farrelly the latter. He had given Brisbane "full authority to make changes we discussed which would result in saving five thousand a month more than Clark's figures. We believe we can bring the loss down to twenty five thousand a month including the Evening, which will be $300,000 for the next year at the present rate of advertising. I believe the advertising can be increased $300,000 so that for the year of 1899 I will show you a profit on the *Journal*." He advised Phoebe to keep his letter: "I think this will be one time that my financial predictions will come true."[40] Whether or not he met his target is unclear, but the *Journal* was soon operating in the black.

Late in 1899, Hearst made a long trip to Europe and Egypt with Millicent, her sister, and her parents. The journey restored his spirits and improved his health. He visited some archeological digs Phoebe was funding in the Nile region. "I am going to write a book about the conquest of Egypt by Mrs. P.A. Hearst," he wrote her. "In Cairo, the dragomen sailors and waiters besieged me with recommendations from Mrs. P.A. Hearst, on the boat I am entertained with tales of the generosity of Mrs. P.A. Hearst, and here at Luxor I am overwhelmed with antiquity dealers (guaranteed) who were the particular favorites of Mrs. P.A. Hearst. The wide swath you cut through Egypt is still distinctly visible. Seriously you must have had a great time and everybody speaks of you with so much admiration and affection that I am very proud to be my Mother's son."[41]

On his return to the United States, Hearst told the Democrats he would indeed launch a Chicago daily, but only after he had laid down a marker with Bryan himself. "The undertaking is big and the prospect of another period of work and strain is not pleasant to contemplate," he wired the candidate. "I would like to know how important you consider such a paper, what real benefit to the party it would be. . . . These things being determined I suppose the satisfaction of being of some value would lead me to disregard all other considerations."[42]

Bryan's response must have been satisfactory. S.S. Carvalho launched the *Chicago American* in a miraculous six weeks. Its first edition was on the press July 2, timed for the national holiday and the height of the electoral season. Bryan would lose, again, in 1900. Hearst would not run for governor of New York that year, but he did win election to Congress in 1902. He soon after established two new papers in Los Angeles and Boston, fulfilling the prophecy he had made to George Pancoast as they ferried across San Francisco Bay in 1889, circling cities on a railway map—"a paper there, and there, and there."

AS HEARST WAS RAMPING UP his political career, the U.S. military was bogging down on the other side of the Pacific. After Dewey's triumph in Manila Bay and the Spanish capitulation at Santiago, McKinley had decided that America had a duty to uplift and Christianize the Filipinos and nurse them to independence. The Paris peace conference held to settle the Spanish-American War became what historian David Trask describes as a "territorial grab of significant proportions, something neither planned nor even anticipated before the brief conflict with Spain over Cuba."[43] The Filipino freedom fighters who had been struggling for their independence from Madrid long before Dewey sailed onto the scene saw little difference between American and Spanish occupation and soon resumed their war of independence against their supposed deliverers. In no time, a large U.S. expeditionary force was hunting rebels in the hills and jungles of the Philippines and, inevitably, the American army adopted many of the counter-insurgent tactics that Spain had applied in Cuba, including reconcentration of the civilian population and savage treatment of captured rebels. All of this would have a grave effect on history's judgment of Hearst's work at the *Journal*.

The Philippine war triggered a reconsideration of 1898's harsh judgments against Spain and its colonial methods—Congress went so far as to recognize Weyler as a misunderstood soldier who had bravely met the requirements of a nasty situation in the Caribbean. As more time passed, McKinley's Far Eastern adventure came to be understood, not incorrectly, as an act of "brutal aggression" and "adolescent irresponsibility" on behalf of a young country; the president had succumbed to a "national egoism" entirely divorced from the national interest.[44] Less reasonably, historians cast the whole Spanish-American experience, start to finish, as a grievous error. Cuba lost standing as a discreet event and was viewed as a symptom of the same malignancies that produced the Philippine fiasco. The suffering of the Cuban people was downplayed, and America's humanitarian concerns were dismissed as a cover for less worthy imperialist motives. The original advocates of Cuban intervention, like Hearst, were scorned as the jingoes or cynical profiteers who had dragged an innocent America into a wholly unnecessary imperial disaster.

It is true that Hearst, McKinley, and almost everyone else who supported the Cuban intervention of 1898 gave insufficient attention to the practical outcomes of war with Spain, including the possibility that America might wind up holding far-flung territories. Unforeseen consequences are the constant plague of humanitarian initiatives in foreign policy, and the best argument against them. All the same, Cuba did not make the Philippines inevitable: McKinley, on settling with Spain, could have chosen not to acquire and fight for the archipelago.[45] As Mark Twain wrote in 1901, Cuba and the Philippines were separate wars undertaken with different motives. McKinley had seen in Cuba an "oppressed and friendless little nation" that was willing to fight to be free, and he put the strength of seventy million sympathizers and the resources of the United States behind it, making America proud. In the Philippines, America played a European-style imperial game with utterly different consequences: "We have stabbed an ally in the back . . . we have robbed a trusting friend of his land and his liberty . . . we have debauched America's honor and blackened her face before the world."[46] Hearst supported the Phillipines acquisition as yet another humanitarian mission, and wound up apologizing for U.S. agression.[47]

In 1903, Hearst married the twenty-one-year-old Millicent Willson in a small ceremony at Grace Church in New York City. Phoebe, strenuously opposed to the match, refused to attend the wedding of her only child, pleading an illness. Will wrote her a play-by-play:

> The day of the wedding was very fine. . . . I got out with Orrin and went to the Holland House and we sat around in our frock coats and white ties waiting for the time. We went to the church a little before eleven. Millie was there. She had been crying a little with excitement, and happiness, too,

I think. Orrin and I went back to the chantry and waited for the sound of a little bell which gave us our cue.

The chantry was very beautifully decorated with colored roses and apple blossoms. Our wedding was cheerful and not to be mistaken for a funeral. Some thirty of our friends were present. Orrin and I stepped out to the altar. The bishop looked very grand and solemn. Anita came up with Millie and her pa. They didn't have any bouquet. I had forgotten to bring it. Millie didn't mind. She stepped up alongside me trembling and frightened. The bishop married us. Then he kissed Millie quite a smack and patted her on the head and told her he wanted her to come and see him when she returned and that she and he would "keep tabs" on me. Then I kissed Millie and the audience *applauded*. The bishop hushed them and appeared to be rather shocked but wasn't. He went away after shaking hands with everybody. All seemed pleased. . . . The bishop said "Hearst you are the right sort" so I guess he was pleased too.[48]

Phoebe's contribution to her son's nuptials was limited to a wedding telegram and an emerald brooch for the bride. Millicent wrote a gracious reply and invited her new mother-in-law to join them on their extended honeymoon overseas. On arriving in London, Millicent tried again, promising "we will try hard to make you as happy as you have made us."[49] Phoebe kept her distance for several months but eventually relented, throwing Millicent a grand birthday party, and by the time the first of five grandchildren arrived, relations were much improved, although never warm.

Finally surrendering to her son's ways, Phoebe concentrated on her own responsibilities as the first female regent of the University of California and one of the nation's most pre-eminent philanthropists. Energetic and curious as ever, she maintained an active social life on both sides of the Atlantic, read incessantly, traveled to Japan and India, and dabbled in the Baha'i faith. She gave up her home in Washington and took a twenty-room apartment in Paris with a prized view of the Eiffel Tower. When home in California, she divided her time between San Francisco, the Hacienda del Pozo de Verona—a fifty-three-room faux-Spanish estate amid the orchards of Pleasanton—and Wyntoon, her five-story Germanic castle in the forests near Mount Shasta.

No sooner was Will Hearst married than he traded in his circus ties and bright hatbands for sober black suits and made an unsuccessful bid for the 1904 Democratic presidential nomination. He would continue to expand his publishing concerns and to fail to win high office deep into the twentieth century. The quality of his newspapers diluted as their number increased and their profits soared, and they were further undermined by their owner's electioneering. Interestingly, Phoebe Hearst saw this clearly, writing shortly before her death of her hope that her son would abandon his political ambitions because "the moment his name is mentioned as a candidate for office, his papers lose their influence for good and are accused of being used solely to further his own personal desires."[50]

With all his wealth, influence, and ambition, and with his remote, somewhat impenetrable personality, Hearst cut an ever more disquieting figure in American life. He lived by his own lights, in his own world, without apology or explanation. He created a distance around himself that his enemies filled with suspicion and loathing, and even those who should have been his allies were often against him. In the early innings of his political career, Hearst sat for an interview with Lincoln Steffens, one of the finest reporters of his own or any other generation. Steffens was writing a profile for the new *American Magazine*, which he had founded along with several other refugees from the magnificent muckraking monthly, *McClure's*. Steffens put a great deal of work into the piece, and Hearst, probably at the urging of Brisbane, and out of regard for Steffens' reputation, gave him closer access than he would allow any other journalist at any point in his long life. During their interactions, Steffens found his subject not simply at ease but "utterly indifferent" to his purpose. Hearst answered questions in a matter-of-fact way but volunteered nothing, not information or elaborations or ideas. He was all business. Steffens was impressed by his "absolute self-sufficiency," a level of independence that was easily misread as indifference. "Mr. Hearst doesn't count on anything that may be said about him, one way or the other," he wrote, "he counts on himself and his own. . . . That's the way to get done the thing you want to have done. Do it yourself."[51]

It was a mistake for Hearst to sit for the profile, entitled "Hearst, the Man of Mystery." Steffens gave him marks for intelligence and fortitude and the odd good intention, however, he depicted Hearst, at core, as a ruthless and dangerous bully, a man with power and money but without friends or a home or scruples, a man manipulated by his employees, living in shadows, psychologically damaged, obsessed with stories of murder and vice. Swanberg called the Steffens piece a "miracle" of reportage and "by far the most searching effort" by a Hearst contemporary to understand the man.[52] "Hearst, the Man of Mystery" became a foundation stone of a Hearst legend that would continue to grow in scale and perversity and culminate in the fine but scurrilous motion picture, *Citizen Kane*.

It is never noted in Hearst lore that years after "Hearst, the Man of Mystery" was published Steffens returned to his subject. In his autobiography, a classic of American literature and the book for which he is best remembered, Steffens recounted the pressure he came under from his editors at the *American Magazine* to take a hatchet to a man they hated. They broadly shared Hearst's politics but his style offended their taste. He was "an innovator who was crashing into the business," Steffens wrote, "upsetting the settled order of things, and he was not doing it as we would have had it done. He was doing it his way." Steffens' editors thought Hearst's way was simple, crude, and demagogic, and they wanted to believe that he was stupid and that his hirelings were responsible for what passed for his successes. "I compromised . . . with my colleagues," Steffens wrote, "to keep my job."[53]

What Steffens really thought of Hearst at the time, and still believed many years later, was that Hearst "was a great man, able, self-dependent, self-educated (though he had been to Harvard) and clear-headed; he had no moral illusions; he saw straight as far as he saw, and he saw pretty far, further than I did then; and studious of the methods which he adopted after experimentation, he was driving towards his unannounced purpose: to establish some measure of democracy. . . . [He] proposed to give the people democracy, as others of this sort give charity or an art museum. . . ." At the end of the day, the only criticism Steffens thought worth writing of Hearst was that his patience, "his superb tolerance," prevented him from imposing himself sufficiently on his publishing managers and as a result his many newspapers—he had dozens by then—did not meet the measure of the man.

THE LAST GASP of the Hearst-Pulitzer newspaper war occurred in 1906 in the offices of the *St. Louis Post-Dispatch* where Joseph Pulitzer Jr. was beginning his career as a newspaperman in his father's service.

Hearst, passing through town in his private railway car, stopped by the *Post-Dispatch* offices to visit a representative of the Associated Press who shared the premises. He found the AP man at the back of the building and on his way out again he encountered young Pulitzer, who nodded amiably and started a conversation, the results of which were reported by the St. Louis *Republic*:

> For a moment the two seemed to be conversing in a friendly way . . . when suddenly Mr. Hearst seemed to become somewhat excited. His head bobbed up and down emphatically as he spoke to Mr. Pulitzer, and all who were watching were wondering what was going on.
>
> Then Mr. Hearst walked away a few feet, took off his overcoat, laid it on the railing, and returned to where Mr. Pulitzer was standing. Mr. Hearst folded his arms and again began speaking to Mr. Pulitzer in emphatic fashion.
>
> Suddenly, without either man having raised his voice loud enough to be overheard, Mr. Pulitzer struck at Mr. Hearst two blows, which the latter warded off with his two hands, which had been crossed over his chest as if he had been expecting an attack.[54]

The combatants were separated by *Post-Dispatch* staffers before any damage was done. Hearst retrieved his overcoat, smiled at the men who had come between him and Pulitzer Jr., and walked out of the building. A newsroom full of reporters had witnessed the scuffle but none could shed any light on its cause. Joseph Pulitzer Sr. died on his yacht in 1911 and was eulogized by Hearst as "the founder and foremost exemplar of modern journalism—the great originator and exponent of the journalism of action and achievement." He wrote that Pulitzer was an able businessman who had accumulated a vast fortune but it was as an editor and a democrat that he was to be remembered, a man who "understood the aims and aspirations of the people, sympathized with the sentiments of the people and labored to express in his newspapers the popular need and the popular will." The nation, wrote Hearst, had lost a great leader: "May his sons continue his far reaching work . . . for the public good."[55]

HEARST'S GROWING NEWSPAPER chain produced enormous returns but bank borrowing and prodigious spending would keep his finances in a perpetually precarious condition throughout his career. When the Great War brought sharp decreases in newspaper advertising, Hearst was in worse straits than usual. Phoebe, who had always kept careful track of her son's withdrawals from the family accounts (often putting them on the books as loans requiring payments of interest and principal), recognized his distress and in February 1919 released him from all obligations to her in order to improve his standing with his bankers. In so doing, she considered herself to have fulfilled George's instruction to make "suitable provisions" for their son. In typical Phoebe fashion, she demanded in return for her magnanimity a commitment from Will in writing that he would build a $300,000 building for one of her pet projects at the University of California.[56] She died of pneumonia two months later at age seventy-six, with her son at her bedside. She was given the high honor of a state funeral and laid to rest in the Hearst Mausoleum at Cypress Lawn Cemetery just outside San Francisco.

Phoebe's estate, worth approximately $7.5 million and consisting largely of mining stock and real estate (including the Babicora ranch), fell primarily to her son, with certain properties and legacies assigned to his children and other relatives. Will was dismayed to learn he owed $949,101 in inheritance taxes, particularly when his mother had left only $90,000 in cash.[57] It is interesting to note that while Hearst's biographies, relying on Phoebe's correspondence, present him as a reckless marauder of the family purse, he appears to have taken only $10 million from his mother over the three decades in which she controlled the senator's estate. During that time she consumed not only many of the millions in income produced by George's fortune but much of the capital besides, with $20 million going to her charities and uncounted sums to her building projects and extravagant lifestyle.[58] If, as she appeared to acknowledge in private correspondence, her son was morally due half of the estate, he was shortchanged.

Fortunately for Hearst, the end of the Great War brought financial relief for newspapers and within a couple of years his chain was producing annual revenues of $100 million and profits of $12 million a year.[59] He was still often pressed for cash, though, for the simple reason that he never stopped spending on his businesses, his collections, and his estates. He was the only man alive, said Brisbane, who simply couldn't get by on less than $10 million a year. His unconventional attitudes toward money and his several brushes with insolvency (including one major bust) tend to obscure Hearst's most impressive accomplishment as a publisher and a businessman. The vision he had first articulated as a twenty-six-year-old ferrying across San Francisco Bay was perfectly realized: with $10 million in family funds, he had built a newspaper empire that now returned more than the initial investment on an annual basis. The relatively paltry sums he threw at the likes of Richard Harding Davis and Morrill Goddard on his arrival in New York, the outlays for extra editions and special promotions, seem less outrageous in light of his long-term ambitions and accomplishments. No doubt he could have spent less but Hearst always knew that his dream of a nation-spanning, multi-paper news operation was impossible without a triumph in New York, without a firm foothold in what was, and would remain the news hub and the commercial capital of the world. Had he been beaten down by Pulitzer and the rest of Park Row, his career would have been markedly different and almost certainly smaller.

By the late 1920s, Hearst owned twenty-six papers in eighteen cities, a large and profitable stable of magazines (including *Cosmopolitan, Good Housekeeping,* and *Harper's Bazaar*), a burgeoning radio network, a motion-picture studio, vast property holdings (including many blocks of prime Manhattan real estate), and one of the world's great art collections. He was also in the early stages of building what would become the country's most spectacular private residence: a 71,000-square-foot hilltop castle packed with his personal collection of European antiques and art and surrounded by 127,000 acres of gardens, pools, and ranchland above the old Pacific whaling station of San Simeon. It would serve as Hearst's home for the remainder of his active years. He would continue to spend time in New York, but reluctantly. Manhattan felt to him "like one big office building. . . . [Y]ou do not really get out to breathe good air and get good sunshine until you get at least west of the Mississippi."[60]

Another reason for Hearst's bicoastal existence was his complicated personal life. Still a Broadway habitué and a Backstage Johnny at fifty-two, Hearst, in late 1915 or early 1916, met and fell in love with Marion Davies, the Brooklyn-born daughter of a minor politician who had kicked her way into the chorus of the latest Irving Berlin musical. She was eighteen years old, roughly a third of Hearst's age, willowy, with blonde curls and a delightful stutter. She was soon starring in his motion pictures and taking up what would become permanent residence with him on the West Coast.

Millicent, meanwhile, had matured into a significant personage in her own right, with five sons and a palatial apartment comprising the top five floors of the Clarendon on Riverside Drive. Intelligent, charming, and ambitious, she had followed Phoebe into respectable society and committed herself to an impressive array of philanthropic activities. She knew of her husband's affair and there were scenes over it, but divorce was out of the question. She began to live an increasingly independent life in New York and would always be known publicly as Mrs. William Randolph Hearst.

By the late 1920s, Hearst was at the zenith of his career in terms of influence and financial might. Certainly no media figure had ever loomed as large—one in four Americans, it was said, got their news from Hearst. Silas Bent, a noted practitioner, professor, and historian of journalism, wrote in *Outlook* magazine of the "imperial glamour" surrounding the man: "No President has ever been more gossiped about: Hearst's dalliances, his extravagances, his whims, his bursts of generosity and moods of icy wrath, the magnificence of his Riverside Drive apartment and his neckties, the sudden transfer of his subordinates and his incalculable changes of editorial front, afford endless food for small talk."[61]

Hearst was arguably the most important private citizen in America and he gave no signs of slowing down, yet Bent believed that his best years were already behind him. Never mind the publishing concerns, the movies, the residences, and the spectacle of his life, Hearst was at core a newspaperman, and it was as a newspaperman that Bent judged him. Hearst, he said, was still capable of "virtuosity of showmanship" and some "genuinely praiseworthy" crusades, but his dailies weren't the same without his constant presence, and his reputation in the business had suffered as a result.[62]

Bent might have added that the business of newspapering itself was drastically changed. Hearst had reached the top of the heap when the heap was highest: newspapers would never again be so expansive, competitive, and influential as they were in the last decades of the nineteenth century. The twentieth century brought an extended (and ongoing) era of profit-taking and consolidation. Advertising came to dwarf circulation as a source of newspaper revenue, and advertisers found it more cost-effective to reach a whole reading public with one or two ad placements than with many. The big papers got richer, the smaller ones disappeared, to the point where many metropolitan dailies enjoyed local monopolies. With reduced competition, newspapers lowered their voices and brought in their elbows. The aggressive, crusading, politically charged, self-promoting, polarizing, audience-building antics of the old warrior owner-editors gave way to the relatively bland consensual habits of the business manager who wanted only as many readers as would keep his advertisers happy. Papers relied less on their ability to move the hearts and minds of the public and more on the utilitarian attractions of basic news coverage, sports scores, show times, grocery prices, and classifieds. The belief that a newspaper ought to cater to the tastes and sentiments of the people lost ground to the new imperatives of objectivity and detachment. Whereas the Victorian era had brought a flurry of innovations aimed at pleasing readers (women's sections, sports sections, op-ed sections, signature columnists, illustrated supplements, color comics, flexible typography, photo-illustration, photojournalism, humor sections, games, and bigger and better stunts and crusades) the twentieth century's principal contribution to newspapering was the advertising environment (real estate, food, travel, and auto sections). As a newspaper-chain owner, Hearst had helped to drive the changes and he had reaped enormous profits from them, but as an editor he was a victim of the shifting priorities and values. Adherents of the new journalism looked with contempt upon Hearst and his anachronistic ways. As Bent wrote: "[His] life is now an anticlimax. Its apex was reached in his middle thirties, and has been a steady decline since then. Only an incorrigible appetite for power in its spectacular manifestations drives him on. The spectacle never quite comes off. He has never since approached that peak, when he stood on a battlefield in Cuba and received as his personal souvenir a shell-torn Spanish standard. . . . [It] is safe to say that this was the proudest moment of his life, his dramatic apex of power."[63]

Hearst, who always considered newspapering his principal occupation, would probably have accepted Bent's conclusion. Several years before his death in 1951, while writing a regular column for his own dailies, he looked back at his early years as a practicing journalist with a wistful pride:

Those were the wonderful days, and happy achievements of youth. No grandiose performance of later years ever equaled them in satisfaction.

Life was not "one damn thing after another" then. It was one wonderful adventure after another.

The competition of journalism was a glad sport; and yet back of it all was a due sense of responsibility—a genuine desire to use the powers and opportunities of the press to serve and to save.

There was delight in work, happiness in service, joy in life—for we were young.[64]

NOTES

PROLOGUE: NOTHING BY HALVES

1. Don C. Seitz, *Joseph Pulitzer: His Life & Letters* (New York: Simon & Schuster, 1924), 187–188, 289; Richard O'Connor, *The Scandalous Mr. Bennett* (Garden City: Doubleday & Co., Inc., 1962), 241.

2. Mrs. Fremont Older, *William Randolph Hearst: American* (New York: D. Appleton-Century Co., 1936), 165–166.

3. Eric Hofman, *The Steam Yachts* (Tuckahoe: John De Graff Inc., 1970), 4–19; Richard M. Mitchell, *The Steam Launch* (Portland: Elliot Bay Press, 1994), 26–36; Ross MacTaggart, *The Golden Century: Classic Motor Yachts, 1830–1930* (New York: W.W. Norton & Co., 2001).

4. Judith Robinson, *The Hearsts: An American Dynasty* (Newark: University of Delaware Press, 1991), 248.

CHAPTER 1: WHEN HE WANTS CAKE, HE WANTS CAKE

1. Theodore Dreiser, *Newspaper Days: An Autobiography*, ed. T.D. Nostwich (Santa Rosa: Black Sparrow Press, 2000), 436.

2. *The Journalist*, February 19, 1887

3. Older, *William Randolph Hearst*, op. cit., 96–97; John K. Winkler, *William Randolph Hearst: A New Appraisal* (New York: Hastings House, 1955), 59.

4. Robinson, op. cit., 224.

5. William Randolph Hearst (WRH) to his father, George Hearst (GH), undated, Hearst family papers, Bancroft Library, University of California, Berkeley; hereafter cited as Bancroft Papers.

6. Robinson, op. cit., 221.

7. Ibid., 235.

8. Ibid., 248–249.

9. *New York Times*, March 1, 1891.

10. Ibid.; Robinson, op. cit., 235.

11. David Nasaw, *The Chief: The Life of William Randolph Hearst* (Boston: Houghton Mifflin, 2000), 7, 22, 24, 41, 61.

12. *New York Times*, June 25, 1886.

13. *Washington Post*, February 20, 1889; Robinson, op. cit., 230–231.

14. *San Francisco Examiner,* March 16, 1891.

15. Ibid.

16. *New York Times,* March 27, 1891.

17. Robinson, op. cit., 238.

18. Ibid., 242.

19. WRH to GH, undated, Bancroft Papers.

20. *New York Times,* June 25, 1886.

21. Discussion of the timing and records of Hearst's birth in Robinson, op. cit., 60.

22. Phoebe Apperson Hearst (PAH) to GH, June 29, 1873, PAH papers, Bancroft Papers.

23. PAH to GH, August 6, 1889, Bancroft Papers.

24. PAH to Orrin Peck, April 8, 1896, Orrin Peck Papers, Huntington Library; hereafter cited as Peck Papers; Robinson, op. cit., 257.

25. PAH to GH, January 4, 1885, Bancroft Papers.

26. Robinson, op. cit., 229.

27. Robinson, op. cit., 228–230.

28. Robinson, op. cit., 216–217.

29. Ibid., 89.

30. Ibid., 97–98.

31. PAH to GH, June 5, 1873, Bancroft Papers; PAH to Orrin Peck, April 8, 1896, Peck Papers.

32. Robinson, op. cit., 162.

33. Edward D. Coblentz, *William Randolph Hearst: A Portrait in His Own Words* (New York: Simon & Schuster, 1952), 9–10; Robinson, op. cit., 84.

34. Coblentz, ibid., 9–19; Robinson, ibid., 159.

35. Robinson, op. cit., 163.

36. Nasaw, op. cit., 320.

37. Nasaw, op. cit., 33.

38. *New York Press,* undated, WRH papers, Bancroft Papers.

39. WRH to PAH, April 27, 1884, Bancroft Papers.

40. WRH to PAH, undated, Bancroft Papers.

41. PAH to GH, November 12, 1885, Bancroft Papers.

42. PAH to WRH, November 10, 1884, PAH papers, Bancroft Papers.

43. A.A. Wheeler to WRH, March 15, 1885, WRH papers, Bancroft Papers.

44. WRH to PAH, undated, Bancroft Papers.

45. Ibid.

46. Nasaw, op. cit., 42.

47. WRH to GH, November 23, 1885, WRH papers, Bancroft Papers.

48. WRH to GH, December 30, 1882, Bancroft Papers.

49. WRH to GH, undated, Bancroft Papers.

50. GH to PAH, December 16, 1882, Bancroft Papers.

51. WRH to PAH, undated, Bancroft Papers.

52. Lincoln Steffens, "Hearst, the Man of Mystery," *The American Magazine* 63 (November 1906): 10–11.

53. Ibid.

54. WRH to GH, January 26, 1886, Bancroft Papers; WRH to GH, January 4, 1885, Bancroft Papers.

55. PAH to GH, June 4, 1885, Bancroft Papers.

56. WRH to GH, undated, Bancroft Papers.

57. WRH to PAH, undated, Bancroft Papers.

58. Ibid.

59. WRH to GH, undated, Bancroft Papers.

60. WRH to GH, undated, Bancroft Papers.

61. John Tebbel, *The Life and Good Times of William Randolph Hearst* (New York: EP. Dutton & Co., Inc., 1952), 95.

62. Nasaw, op. cit., 54; Coblentz, op. cit., 30–31; "Walks and Talks," by Carlos, undated clipping, Bancroft Papers.

63. W.A. Swanberg, *Citizen Hearst* (New York: Charles Scribner's Sons, 1961), 37.

64. Tebbel, op. cit., 95.

65. Swanberg, op. cit., 43.

66. George P. West, "Hearst: A Psychological Note," *American Mercury*, November 1930.

67. Robinson, op. cit., 225.

68. Ben Procter, *William Randolph Hearst: The Early Years, 1862–1910* (New York: Oxford University Press, 1998), 62–63.

69. WRH to PAH, undated, Bancroft Papers.

70. WRH to GH, undated, Bancroft Papers.

71. WRH to GH, 1887, Bancroft Papers.

72. WRH to GH, undated, Bancroft Papers.

73. Robinson, op. cit., 216.

74. Ibid.

75. WRH to PAH, August 17, 1891, Bancroft Papers.

76. Robinson, op. cit., 244.

77. WRH to PAH, 1892, Bancroft Papers.

78. Ibid.

79. WRH to PAH, undated, Bancroft Papers.

80. Robinson, op. cit., 244–245.

81. Ibid., 243–244.

82. Ibid., 256.

83. Ibid., 203–210.

84. "Interview with Mrs. Joseph Marshall Flint," January 18, 1960, W. A. Swanberg Papers, Columbia University; hereafter cited as Swanberg Papers; see also "Interview with Mrs. Fremont Older," October 18, 1959, Swanberg Papers.

85. WRH to GH, undated, Bancroft Papers.

86. WRH to PAH, 1889, WRH collection, Bancroft Papers.

87. PAH to GH, September 28, 1889, PAH papers, Bancroft Papers.

88. "Interview with Mrs. Fremont Older," October 18, 1959, Swanberg Papers.

89. "Interview with Mrs. Joseph Marshall Flint," January 18, 1960, Swanberg Papers.

90. Robinson, op. cit., 245.

91. WRH to PAH, undated, Bancroft Papers.

92. Nasaw, op. cit., 92.

93. Swanberg, *Hearst,* op. cit., 68.

94. WRH to GH, 1889, Bancroft Papers.

95. WRH to PAH, undated, Bancroft Papers.

96. Ibid.

97. WRH to PAH, November 1894, Bancroft Papers.

98. Louis Pizzitola, *Hearst over Hollywood: Power, Passion, and Propaganda in the Movies* (New York: Columbia University Press, 2002), 26–27.

99. Robinson, op. cit., 255.

100. WRH to PAH, January 16, 1895, Bancroft Papers.

101. Edward Clark to PAH, August 1, 1895, Bancroft Papers.

102. PAH to Irwin Stump, undated, Bancroft Papers.

103. Irwin Stump to PAH, September 18, 22, 29, 1895, Bancroft Papers; Irwin Stump Correspondence, undated, PAH papers, Bancroft Papers.

104. Irwin Stump to PAH, September 18, 1895, Bancroft Papers; Robinson, op. cit., 254; H.B. Parsons to PAH, July 3, 1896, Bancroft Papers.

105. Irwin Stump to PAH, September 29, 1895, Bancroft Papers.

CHAPTER 2: IS GOD IN?

1. Henry Kellett Chambers, "A Park Row Interlude: Memoir of Albert Pulitzer," *Journalism Quarterly,* 539–547.

2. *New York Times,* May 8, 1895, October 5, 1909.

3. *Washington Post,* May 8, 1895, May 12, 1895.

4. Mark Lipper, "John R. McLean," *Dictionary of Literary Biography: American Newspaper*

Journalists, 1873–1900, vol. 23 (Detroit: Gale Research Co., 1983), 216.

5. *The Fourth Estate,* September 5, 1895; see also *The Newspaper Maker,* September 5, 1895.

6. *Printers' Ink,* June 27, 1894, 793.

7. All circulation claims were unaudited and unreliable. In 1895, no less than five papers advertised themselves as the best-selling daily in New York. *Printers' Ink* did its best to analyze circulation data and rank the contenders but it acknowledged a large margin of error. Even those papers that got notarized statements of their circulation—for instance, Pulitzer's *World*—could still misreport their sales by 19%. Ted Curtis Smythe, *The Gilded Age Press, 1865–1900* (Westport: Praeger Publishers, 2003), 87.

8. Irwin Stump to PAH, September 18, 1895, Bancroft Papers.

9. Irwin Stump to PAH, October 3, 1895, Bancroft Papers.

10. Sidney Kobre, *The Yellow Press and Gilded Age Journalism* (Tallahassee: Florida State University, 1964), 102.

11. Ibid., 109.

12. Sidney Kobre, *Development of American Journalism* (Dubuque: Wm. C. Brown Co. Publishers, 1969), 401.

13. Ibid., 376.

14. Susan E. Tifft and Alex S. Jones, *The Trust* (Boston: Back Bay Books, 2000), 34–40; Kobre, *Development,* op. cit., 404.

15. *Printers' Ink,* December 4, 1895, 17.

16. Terry Hynes, "Charles A. Dana," *Dictionary of Literary Biography: American Newspaper Journalists, 1873–1900,* vol. 23 (Detroit: Gale Research Co., 1983), 72.

17. Janet E. Steele, *"The Sun Shines for All: Journalism and Ideology in the Life of Charles A. Dana* (Syracuse: Syracuse University Press, 1993), 78.

18. Allen Churchill, *Park Row* (New York: Rinehart & Co. Inc., 1958), 14.

19. Smythe, op. cit., 107.

20. Charles A. Dana, *The Art of Newspaper Making* (New York: Arno Press, 1970), 12.

21. James Melvin Lee, *History of American Journalism* (Boston: Houghton Mifflin Co., 1917), 328.

22. Kobre, *Yellow,* op. cit., 34.

23. Louis J. Budd, "Color Him Curious about Yellow Journalism," *Journal of Popular Culture,* 15 (Fall 1981): 25–33.

24. W. A. Swanberg, *Pulitzer* (New York: Charles Scribner's Sons, 1967), 20.

25. Ibid., 10–11.

26. Denis Brian, *Pulitzer: A Life* (New York: John Wiley & Sons, Inc., 2001), 12.

27. Swanberg, *Pulitzer,* op. cit., 12.

28. Brian, op. cit., 17.

29. Swanberg, *Pulitzer,* op. cit., 27.

30. Brian, op. cit., 64.

31. "Jay Gould, Railroad Tycoon, Visits the City of Ottawa," October 15, 1886, in the Franklin County Kansas Genealogical Society Quarterly Online.

32. Seitz, *Pulitzer*, op. cit., 136.

33. Swanberg, *Pulitzer*, op. cit., 70.

34. Alleyne Ireland, *Joseph Pulitzer: Reminiscences of a Secretary* (New York: Mitchell Kennerley, 1914), 115.

35. Smythe, op. cit., 123, 209.

36. Swanberg, *Pulitzer*, op. cit., 70.

37. Ibid., 74.

38. Brian, op. cit., 66.

39. Swanberg, *Pulitzer*, op. cit., 49.

40. Ibid., 80.

41. *New York Times*, November 5, 1884.

42. Swanberg, *Pulitzer*, op. cit., 111; Thomas J. Schlereth, *Victorian America: Transformations in Everyday Life, 1876–1915* (New York: HarperCollins, 1992), 78.

43. Brian, op. cit., 104.

44. Seitz, *Pulitzer*, op. cit., 21.

45. Brian, op. cit., 119.

46. Jean Strouse, *Morgan: American Financier* (New York: Harper Perennial, 2000), 194.

47. Steele, op. cit., 144.

48. Brian, op. cit., 129.

49. George Juergens, *Joseph Pulitzer and the New York World* (Princeton: Princeton University Press, 1966), 357.

50. Brian, op. cit., 130–132.

51. Steele, op. cit., 149.

52. Brian, op. cit., 152.

53. Seitz, *Pulitzer*, op. cit., 180.

54. Brian, op. cit., 153.

55. Dana, op. cit., 22.

56. Ibid., 62.

57. Dreiser, op. cit., 608.

58. Ibid., 545, 608, 609, 619.

CHAPTER 3: A GREAT DEAL MORE THAN MONEY

1. Swanberg, *Hearst*, op. cit., 80–81.

2. Nasaw, op. cit., 102.

3. *Printers' Ink,* June 27, 1894.

4. W.T. Stead, *Satan's Invisible World Displayed* (New York: R.F. Fenno & Co., 1897), 22.

5. Smythe, op. cit.,130.

6. O'Connor, *The Scandalous Mr. Bennett,* op. cit., chapter 9.

7. *New York Times,* September 30, 2004; Willis J. Abbot, *Watching the World Go By* (Boston: Little, Brown and Co., 1934), chapters 3–5.

8. Willis Abbot, *Watching the World Go By* (Boston: Little, Brown and Co., 1934).

9. Irwin Stump to PAH, October 8, 1895, Bancroft Papers.

10. *The Fourth Estate,* October 17, 1895.

11. Nasaw, op. cit., 311.

12. *Printers' Ink,* December 4, 1895, 18.

13. *The Fourth Estate,* March 19 1896; see also *The Fourth Estate,* October 10, 1895.

14. Irwin Stump to PAH, September 22, 1895, Bancroft Papers.

15. Stephen Crane, *Active Service* (Boston: Little, Brown and Co., 1934), 20.

16. *New York Morning Journal,* October 7, 1895.

17. *New York Journal,* November 7, 1895.

18. Irwin Stump to PAH, October 8, 1895, Bancroft Papers.

19. Nasaw, op. cit., 101.

20. *New York Journal,* November 9, 1895, November 10, 1895.

21. *New York Journal,* November 25, 1895.

22. *New York Herald,* November 8, 1895.

23. *New York Journal,* November 12, 1895.

24. *Printers' Ink,* November 20, 1895.

25. *New York Journal,* November 4, 1895.

26. *New York Journal,* December 8, 1895.

27. Christopher P. Wilson, "Stephen Crane and the Police," *American Quarterly,* June 1996, 273–315.

28. *New York Journal,* December 9, 1895, December 10, 1895.

29. *New York Journal,* December 22, 1895.

30. *The Fourth Estate,* November 7, 1895; *The Newspaper Maker,* November 14, 1895.

31. *Printers' Ink,* August 15, 1894; *The Fourth Estate,* December 26, 1895.

32. *The Fourth Estate,* January 2, 1896, February 13, 1896; *The Newspaper Maker,* January 30, 1896, February 13, 1896, February 20, 1896, March 5, 1896, March 19, 1896.

33. *Printers' Ink,* December 4, 1895, 18.

34. Nasaw, op. cit., 111, 131.

35. A.J. Liebling, "The Man Who Changed the Rules," in *Just Enough Liebling* (New York: North Point Press, 2004), 243.

36. Brian, op. cit., 185.

37. Richard Kluger, *The Paper* (New York: Vintage Books, 1989); "Whitelaw Reid," *Dictionary of Literary Biography: American Newspaper Journalists, 1873–1900*, vol. 23 (Detroit: Gale Research Co., 1983).

38. O'Connor, *The Scandalous Mr. Bennett*, op. cit.; Kluger, ibid.; Richard O'Connor, "The Wayward Commodore," *American Heritage Magazine* (June 1974).

39. Don S. Seitz, *The James Gordon Bennetts: Father and Son* (Indianapolis: Bobbs-Merrill Co., 1928), 218; Kluger, op. cit., 141–145, 162; Brian, op. cit., 254, 283–284; O'Connor, *The Scandalous Mr. Bennett*, op. cit., 222; Swanberg, *Pulitzer*, op. cit., 279.

40. Irwin Stump to PAH, October 8, 1895, Bancroft Papers.

41. Steffens, "Hearst, Man of Mystery," op. cit., 11.

42. Tebbel, op. cit., 308.

43. Hosmer Parsons to PAH, 1896, PAH Papers, Bancroft Papers.

CHAPTER 4: A KIND OF RUMBA ACCOMPANIED BY SNAPPING FINGERS

1. Swanberg, *Pulitzer*, op. cit., 170–173.

2. *The Journalist*, October 2, 1897.

3. Swanberg, *Pulitzer*, op. cit., 177.

4. *The Fourth Estate*, September 30, 1897.

5. Swanberg, *Pulitzer*, op. cit., 177.

6. Brian, op. cit., chapters 15–16.

7. Swanberg, *Pulitzer*, op. cit., chapter 4.

8. Ibid., 169.

9. Churchill, *Park Row*, op. cit., 64.

10. Ibid., 72.

11. James Wyman Barrett, *Joseph Pulitzer and His World* (New York: Vanguard Press, 1941), 154.

12. Swanberg, *Pulitzer*, op. cit., 206.

13. Frank Luther Mott, *American Journalism, A History of Newspapers in the United States Through 260 Years: 1690 to 1950*, revised edition (New York: Macmillan Co., 1950), 482.

14. *The Fourth Estate*, April 16, 1896.

15. Nasaw, op, cit., 107.

16. Swanberg, *Pulitzer*, op. cit., 206.

17. Winkler, op. cit., 65–66.

18. Winkler, ibid., 68–69; Barrett, *Pulitzer*, op. cit., 172.

19. Swanberg, *Pulitzer*, op. cit., 206; Seitz, *Pulitzer*, op. cit., 212; *The Fourth Estate*, February 6, 1896.

20. WRH to Boyden Sparkes, Arthur Brisbane Papers, Special Collections Research Center, Syracuse University; hereafter cited as Brisbane Papers.

21. Seitz, *Pulitzer*, op. cit., 213.

22. *The Newspaper Maker*, February 13, 1886.

23. *The Fourth Estate*, February 13, 1896.

24. *Printers' Ink*, February 26, 1896.

25. Seitz, *Pulitzer*, op. cit., 213; Brian, op. cit., 99.

26. *The Newspaper Maker*, February 20, 1896.

27. *The Newspaper Maker*, March 19, 1896.

28. Seitz, *Pulitzer*, op. cit., 164.

29. Brian, op. cit., 168.

30. *The Fourth Estate*, March 19, 1896.

31. Seitz, *Pulitzer*, op. cit., 216–217; *The Fourth Estate*, March 26, 1896.

32. *The Fourth Estate*, January 7, 1897.

33. *The Fourth Estate*, June 4, 1896.

34. Ibid.

35. *The Newspaper Maker*, March 26, 1896.

36. Abbot, op. cit., 140.

37. Ibid., 137.

38. Charles Edward Russell, "William Randolph Hearst," *Harper's Weekly*, May 21, 1904.

39. Driscoll to Boyden Sparkes, Brisbane Papers.

40. Crane, *Active Service*, op. cit., 50.

41. Churchill, *Park Row*, op. cit., 70.

42. Driscoll to Boyden Sparkes, Brisbane Papers.

43. Churchill, *Park Row*, op. cit., 80.

44. Charles Edward Russell, "William Randolph Hearst," op. cit.

45. James L. Ford, *Forty-Odd Years in the Literary Shop* (New York: E.P. Dutton & Co., 1921) 259–260.

46. Swanberg, *Hearst*, op. cit., 51.

47. Ibid.

48. Irvin S. Cobb, *Exit Laughing* (New York: Bobbs-Merrill Co., 1941), 123.

49. Abbot, op. cit., 142.

50. Swanberg, *Hearst*, op. cit., 61.

51. Ibid., 70.

52. Swinnerton to Boyden Sparkes, Brisbane Papers.

53. Swanberg, *Hearst*, op. cit., 60.

54. Ibid., 73.

55. Ben Procter, op. cit., 62.

56. Steffens, "Hearst, Man of Mystery," op. cit., 6.

57. Winkler, op. cit., 43.

58. Cobb, op. cit., 123.

59. Churchill, *Park Row,* op. cit., 79.

60. *Printers' Ink,* April 22, 1896.

CHAPTER 5: LIKE A BLAST FURNACE, A HUNDRED TIMES MULTIPLIED

1.   Mr. and Mrs. Fremont Older, *George Hearst: California Pioneer* (Los Angeles: Westernlore, 1966), 187–196, 221, 226; Robinson, op. cit., 188.

2.   Robinson, ibid., 234.

3.   Steffens, "Hearst, Man of Mystery," op. cit., 8.

4.   Robinson, op. cit., 331.

5.   WRH to PAH, undated, Bancroft Papers.

6.   Abbot, op. cit., 147, 151.

7.   Stanley L. Jones, *The Presidential Election of 1896* (Madison: University of Wisconsin Press, 1964), 99 ff.

8.   John Whiteclay Chambers, *The Tyranny of Change* (New Brunswick: Rutgers University Press, 2000), 40–41; Thomas J. Misa, *A Nation of Steel* (Baltimore: Johns Hopkins University Press, 1999), 138–140; Jones, op. cit., 36–49; Harold U. Faulkner, *Politics, Reform and Expansion, 1890–1900* (Harper & Row, 1959), 141–142; H. Wayne Morgan, *From Hayes to McKinley* (Syracuse: Syracuse University Press, 1969), 447–448.

9.   Margaret Leech, *In the Day of McKinley* (New York: Harper & Brothers, 1959), 34–49.

10. *New York Journal,* May 11, 1896, April 23, 1896.

11. *New York Journal,* April 2, 1896, April 3, 1896, April 15, 1896.

12. Jones, op. cit., 8–12.

13. *New York Journal,* April 15, 1896, April 18 1896.

14. *New York Journal,* April 16, 1896, April 18, 1896.

15. New York *World,* April 17, 1896.

16. New York *World,* June 15, 1896, June 18, 1896, June 27, 1896.

17. *New York Journal,* May 20, 1896, June 17, 1896, June 18, 1896.

18. *New York Journal,* July 5, 1896.

19. *New York Journal,* July 6, 1896; James T. Havel, *U.S. Presidential Candidates and the Elections* (New York: Macmillan Library Reference/Simon & Schuster, Macmillan, 1996), Vol. II, 70.

20. *New York Journal,* July 4, 1896, July 8, 1896.

21. *New York Journal,* July 8, 1896.

22. *New York Journal*, July 9, 1896; George F. Whicher, *William Jennings Bryan and the Campaign of 1896* (Boston: D.C. Heath and Co., 1968), 33, 37.

23. *New York Times*, September 5, 1896.

24. Jones, op. cit., 173.

25. *New York Times*, September 5, 1896.

26. *New York Journal*, July 9, 1896.

27. H. Wayne Morgan, *William McKinley and His America* (Syracuse: Syracuse University Press, 1963), 240.

28. *New York Journal*, July 10, 1896.

29. Ibid.

30. Ibid.

31. Ibid.

32. Ibid.

33. Ibid; William Jennings Bryan, "The Cross of Gold," ed. Robert W. Cherny, (Lincoln: University of Nebraska Press, 1996).

34. *New York Journal*, July 10, 1896.

35. *New York Journal*, July 11, 1896.

36. Ibid.

37. Ibid.

38. *New York Times*, July 10, 1896.

39. New York *World*, July 10, 1896, July 12, 1896.

40. New York *World*, July 12, 1896.

41. New York *World*, July 10, 1896, July 11, 1896.

42. New York *World*, July 21, 1896.

43. Seitz, *Pulitzer*, op. cit., 226.

44. Swanberg, *Pulitzer*, op. cit., 212.

45. Winkler, op. cit., 82.

46. Ibid.

47. *World's Work*, October 1922.

48. *New York Journal*, July 3, 1896.

49. *New York Journal*, July 10, 1896.

50. *New York Journal*, July 11, 1896.

51. Rodney P. Carlisle, *Hearst and the New Deal: The Progressive as Reactionary* (New York: Garland Publishing, Inc., 1979), ix.

52. Michael Kazin, *A Godly Hero: The Life of William Jennings Bryan* (New York: Anchor Books, 2007), xix, xv; Jones, op. cit., 68.

53. Charles Palmer to PAH, April 16, 1896, Bancroft Papers.

54. Ibid.

55. *The Fourth Estate*, July 23, 1896, April 16, 1896, October 15, 1896; Bradford Merrill to James Creelman, James Creelman Papers, Rare Books and Manuscript Library, University of Ohio; hereafter cited as Creelman Papers.

Chapter 6: A Large Brute of Some Utterly New Species

1. *New York Journal*, May 19, 1896.

2. *New York Journal*, September 2, 1896.

3. *New York Journal*, August 30, 1896.

4. *New York Journal*, September 13, 1896.

5. *New York Journal*, June 19, 1896.

6. Abbot, op. cit., 124.

7. Abbot, ibid., 125; Robert L. Gates, "Alfred Henry Lewis," *American National Biography* (New York: Oxford University Press), 557–558.

8. Abbot, ibid., 124.

9. Albert Payson Terhune, *To The Best of My Memory* (New York: Harpers, 1930), 122.

10. Edith Garrigues Hawthorne, ed., *The Memoirs of Julian Hawthorne* (New York: MacMillan Co., 1938), 286–287.

11. *New York Journal*, April 13, 1896.

12. Ibid.

13. Leech, op. cit., 58–59.

14. Ibid., 62–65; Jones, op. cit., 103–105, 128.

15. *New York Journal*, April 14, 1896.

16. Ibid.

17. *New York Journal*, May 4, 1896.

18. Ibid.

19. Ibid.; *New York Times*, October 24, 1884.

20. Leland Huot and Alfred Powers, *Homer Davenport of Silverton* (Bingen: West Shore Press, 1973), 19–22.

21. Ibid., 3.

22. Ibid., 4.

23. Ibid., 39–41.

24. Ibid., 61–62.

25. Ibid., 65–73, 94.

26. Ibid., 77–79.

27. Ibid.; *New York Times*, January 2, 1910.

28. Huot and Powers, op. cit., 81–82.

29. Ibid., 115–124.

30. *New York Journal,* May 7, 1896.

31. *New York Journal,* November 8, 1896.

32. Lewis L. Gould, "William McKinley," *American National Biography* (New York: Oxford University Press, 1999), 122–125.

33. Huot and Powers, op. cit., 98–99; *New York Journal,* May 20, 1896.

34. *New York Journal,* September 8, 1896, August 4, 1896.

35. New York *World,* August 9, 1896.

36. New York *World,* June 20, 1896.

37. James E. Pollard, *The Presidents and the Press* (New York: Macmillan Co., 1947), 559; Kevin Phillips, *William McKinley* (New York: Henry Holt and Co., 2003), 72; David Herbert Croly, *Marcus Alonzo Hanna: His Life and Work* (New York: MacMillan Co., 1912), 224.

38. Charles William Calhoun, *The Gilded Age: Perspectives on the Origins of Modern America* (Plymouth: Rowman and Littlefield, 2007), 241.

39. *New York Journal,* May 23, 1896.

40. *New York Journal,* August 7, 1896, June 19, 1896.

41. *New York Journal,* May 6, 1896.

42. *New York Journal* June 19, 1896; see also April 13, 1896, May 27, 1896, June 21, 1896.

43. *New York Journal,* May 18, 1896.

44. *New York Journal,* April 22, 1896, June 13, 1896.

45. *New York Journal,* August 2, 1896.

46. *New York Journal,* June 11, 1896.

47. Morgan, *William McKinley and his America,* op. cit., 184.

48. Leech, op. cit., 38.

49. Francis Russell, *President Makers,* op. cit., 19.

50. Clarence A. Stern, *Resurgent Republicanism: The Handiwork of Hanna* (Ann Arbor: Edwards Brothers, 1968), 19.

51. Leech, op. cit., 83; Thomas Beer, *Hanna* (New York: Alfred A. Knopf, 1929), 142; Stern, op. cit., 39.

52. *New York Journal,* August 21, 1896.

53. Leech, op. cit., 99.

54. Croly, op. cit., 170; Quentin R. Skrabec Jr., *William McKinley: Apostle of Protectionism* (New York: Algora Publishing, 2008), 253.

55. Stern, op. cit., 11.

56. Morgan, *William McKinley and His America,* op. cit., 199.

57. H. H. Kohlsaat, *From McKinley To Harding* (New York: Charles Scribner's Sons, 1923), 77; Beer, op. cit., 165.

CHAPTER 7: SKIN THE EAST AND SKIN THE RICH

1. Charles Edward Russell, "William Randolph Hearst," op. cit.

2. *New York Journal*, September 4, 1896.

3. Frank Luther Mott, "Newspapers in Presidential Campaigns," *Public Opinion Quarterly* 8
    (1944): 348.

4. New York *World*, September 29, 1896.

5. David Traxel, *1898: The Birth of the American Century* (New York: Alfred A. Knopf,
    1998), 19.

6. Phillips, op. cit., 74.

7. *New York Journal*, August 11, 1896.

8. Henry Russell, "Julian Hawthorne," *American National Biography*, vol. 10 (New York:
    Oxford University Press, 1999), 356; Harold P. Miller, "Julian Hawthorne," *Dictionary of
    American Biography*, vol. 21 (New York: Charles Scribner's Sons, 1944), 386.

9. Ronald S. Marmarelli, "James Creelman," *Dictionary of Literary Biography: American
    Newspaper Journalists, 1873–1900*, vol. 23 (Detroit: Gale Research Co., 1983), 56.

10. James Creelman, *On the Great Highway* (Boston: Lothrop Publishing Co., 1901), 62.

11. Joseph Pulitzer to James Creelman, February 18, 1896, Creelman Papers.

12. New York *World*, October 24, 1896.

13. New York *World*, November 1, 1896.

14. Morgan, *William McKinley and His America*, op. cit., 230–233.

15. Leech, op. cit., 94.

16. *New York Journal*, August 5, 1896; Morgan, *William McKinley and his America*, op. cit., 228.

17. Jones, op. cit., 282; Patrick J. Kelly, "The Election of 1896 and the Restructuring of Civil
    War Memory," *Civil War History* 49 (September 2003): 261.

18. Kazin, op. cit., 66.

19. Jones, op. cit., 279.

20. Roy Everett Littlefield III, *William Randolph Hearst: His Role in American Progressivism*
    (Lanham: University Press of America, 1980), 34.

21. Jones, op. cit., 297, 302.

22. *New York Journal*, September 17, 1896.

23. Jones, op. cit., 311.

24. Patrick J. Kelly, op. cit., 261.

25. Kazin, op. cit., 66.

26. *New York Journal*, September 5, 1896.

27. Kazin, op. cit., 66.

28. Abbot, op. cit., 181–182.

29. *New York Journal*, August 1, 1896, August 8, 1896, September 5, 1896, September 22, 1896.

30. Patrick J. Kelly, op. cit., 272.

31. *New York Tribune,* October 30, 1896.

32. Patrick J. Kelly, op. cit., 276–278.

33. *New York Journal,* August 11, 1896, September 20, 1896.

34. *New York Journal,* October 12, 1896.

35. *New York Journal,* October 14, 1896.

36. New York *Sun,* July 10, 1896.

37. *New York Times,* July 26, 1896.

38. *New York Herald,* July 11, 1896.

39. *New York Tribune,* July 9, 1896, July 10, 1896, July 13, 1896; Richard K. Scher, *The Modern Political Campaign* (Armonk: M.E. Sharpe, Inc. 1997), 46.

40. *New York Journal,* September 26, 1896.

41. New York *Sun,* July 11, 1896.

42. *New York Journal,* August 1, 1896.

43. *New York Times,* September 27, 1896, September 29, 1896, October 1, 1896, October 8, 1896.

44. *New York Times,* September 30, 1896.

45. *World's Work,* October 1922.

46. Hosmer Parsons to PAH, July 14, 1896, Bancroft Papers.

47. Seitz, *Pulitzer,* op. cit., 227.

48. *New York Journal,* September 28, 1896.

49. New York *World,* October 21, 1896.

50. New York *World,* October 17, 1896.

51. New York *World,* September 22, 1896.

52. New York *World,* September 22, 1896, October 1, 1896, October 3, 1896.

53. New York *World,* October 27, 1896.

54. New York *World,* September 21, 1896, September 24, 1896, September 28, 1896, October 1, 1896.

55. *New York Journal,* September 29, 1896, October 4, 1896.

56. *New York Journal,* October 2, 1896, October 24, 1896.

57. Cartoon Research Library Collection, Ohio State University; Robert C. Harvey, *Children of the Yellow Kid: The Evolution of the American Comic Strip* (Seattle: Frye Art Museum, University of Washington Press, 1998).

58. Oliver Carlson and Ernest Sutherland Bates, *Hearst: Lord of San Simeon* (New York: Viking Press, 1936), 92.

59. *New York Journal,* November 1, 1896.

60. *New York Journal,* October 29, 1896.

61. *New York Journal*, November 3, 1896.

62. *New York Journal*, November 1, 1896.

63. *New York Journal*, November 2, 1896.

64. New York *World*, October 20, 1896.

65. New York *World*, November 1, 1896.

66. *New York Journal*, November 3, 1896.

67. Richard Harding Davis to his brother, November 12, 1896, Richard Harding Davis Papers, Clifton Waller Barrett Library, University of Virginia; hereafter cited as Davis Papers.

68. *New York Journal*, November 4, 1896.

69. New York *World*, November 4, 1896.

70. *New York Tribune*, November 4, 1896.

71. *New York Journal*, November 4, 1896.

72. WRH to PAH, November 4, 1896, Bancroft Papers.

73. *New York Journal*, November 6, 1896.

74. *New York Journal*, November 8, 1896.

75. Croly, op. cit., 228.

76. Francis Russell, *The President Makers*, op. cit., 35; Beer, op. cit., 175, 178.

77. Jeffry A. Frieden, "Monetary Populism in Nineteenth-Century America: An Open Economy Interpretation," *The Journal of Economic History* 57 (June, 1997), 374.

78. Sean Dennis Cashman, *America in the Gilded Age: From the Death of Lincoln to the Rise of Theodore Roosevelt*, 3ᵈ ed. (New York: New York University Press, 1993), 337.

79. Whicher, op. cit., 88.

CHAPTER 8: FOUR SENSATIONS AND THE MORALS POLICE

1. *The Fourth Estate*, November 12, 1896.

2. *The Fourth Estate*, December 3, 1896.

3. *The Fourth Estate*, March 25, 1897.

4. *The Journalist*, June 5, 1897.

5. Smythe, op. cit., 175.

6. *The Fourth Estate*, July 2, 1896.

7. *The Fourth Estate*, August 27, 1896, January 7, 1897.

8. *The Fourth Estate*, July 9, 1896, October 15, 1896; *The Newspaper Maker*, March 5, 1896.

9. Smythe, op. cit., 9.

10. Dana, op. cit., 11.

11. O'Connor, *The Scandalous Mr. Bennett*, op. cit., 24.

12. Marion Elizabeth Rodgers, *Mencken: The American Iconoclast* (New York: Oxford University Press, 2005), 38.

13. Joseph Conrad in *Stephen Crane: A Collection of Critical Essays,* ed. Maurice Bassan (Englewood Cliffs: Prentice-Hall, 1967), 123.

14. John Berryman, *Stephen Crane: A Critical Biography* (New York: Cooper Square Press, 2001), 54.

15. Rodgers, op. cit., 38.

16. Berryman, op. cit., 298.

17. Keith Gandal, *The Virtues of the Vicious: Jacob Riis, Stephen Crane, and the Spectacle of the Slum* (New York: Oxford University Press, 1997), 15.

18. Stephen Crane, *The Correspondence of Stephen Crane,* vol. 1, ed. Stanley Wertheim and Paul Sorrentino (New York: Columbia University Press, 1988), s255.

19. Luc Sante, *Low Life: Lures and Snares of Old New York* (New York: Farrar, Straus and Giroux, 2003), 19.

20. *New York Times,* June 29, 1897.

21. *New York Journal,* September 20, 1896.

22. Ibid.

23. *New York Journal,* September 17, 1896.

24. Ibid.

25. Ibid.

26. Ibid.

27. Ibid.

28. Ibid.

29. Linda H. Davis, *Badge of Courage: The Life of Stephen Crane* (Boston: Houghton Mifflin Co., 1998), 32.

30. Ibid., 81.

31. Ibid., 164.

32. Ibid., 163; *Harper's Weekly,* October 10, 1896.

33. *New York Journal,* October 17, 1896.

34. Ibid.

35. Ibid.; New York *World,* October 17, 1896; *New York Press,* October 17, 1896.

36. *New York Journal,* October 18, 1896.

37. *New York Times,* July 31, 1915.

38. M. H. Dunlop, *Gilded City: Scandal and Sensation in Turn-of-the-Century New York* (New York: HarperCollins Publishers Inc., 2000), 171–192.

39. Ibid., 173.

40. *New York Journal,* December 24, 1896.

41. Ibid.

42. *New York Journal,* January 8, 1897.

43. *New York Journal*, January 10, 1897.

44. *New York Journal*, January 18, 1897.

45. Ibid.

46. Dunlop, op. cit., 189.

47. *New York Journal*, January 18, 1897.

48. *New York Journal*, January 17, 1897.

49. *New York Journal*, January 11, 1897.

50. *New York Journal*, December 4, 1896.

51. Ibid.

52. Dan Streible, *Fight Pictures: A History of Boxing and Early Cinema* (Berkeley: University of California Press, 2008), 93.

53. *New York Journal*, February 16, 1897.

54. Streible, op. cit., 97–100.

55. *New York Journal*, February 21, 1897, March 8, 1897.

56. *New York Journal*, March 18, 1897.

57. Ibid.

58. Ibid.

59. Ibid.

60. *New York Journal*, June 27, 1897.

61. *New York Journal*, June 28, 1897.

62. *New York Journal*, June 29, 1897.

63. *The Journalist*, July 3, 1897.

64. *New York Times*, July 10, 1897.

65. *New York Journal*, June 30, 1897.

66. Ibid.

67. *New York Times*, November 11, 1897.

68. *New York Times*, August 2, 1898; Richard Halworth Rovere, *The Magnificent Shysters: The True and Scandalous History of Howe and Hummel* (New York: Grosset & Dunlap, 1947), 148.

69. W. Joseph Campbell, *Yellow Journalism: Puncturing the Myths, Defining the Legacies* (Westport: Praeger Publishers, 2003), 30–32.

70. *The Fourth Estate*, January 7, 1897.

71. *New York Times*, January 26, 1897.

72. Campbell, *Yellow*, op. cit., 34–35.

73. Ibid.

74. W. Joseph Campbell, *The Year That Defined American Journalism: 1897 and the Clash of Paradigms* (New York: Routledge, 2006), 26.

75. *New York Times*, March 4, 1897.

76. WRH to James Creelman, undated, Creelman Papers.

77. Campbell, *Year*, op. cit., 26.

78. *New York Times*, November 11, 1897.

79. *The Journalist*, May 1, 1897.

80. Ibid.

81. *The Journalist*, June 1, 1897.

82. Bradford Merrill to James Creelman, June 5, 1896, Creelman Papers.

83. W. R. Hearst, "Pacific Coast Journalism," *Overland Monthly*, April, 1888; Steffans, "Hearst, Man of Mystery," op. cit., 11–12.

84. Harry H. Stein, "Apprenticing Reporters: Lincoln Steffens on 'The Evening Post,'" *The Historian* 58 (1996).

85. *The Journalist*, July 17, 1897.

86. Hazel Dicken-Garcia, *Journalistic Standards in Nineteenth-Century America*, (Madison: University of Wisconsin Press, 1989), 138.

87. Ibid., 189.

88. *New York Times*, March 4, 1897.

89. Dunlop, op. cit., 176.

90. *New York Times*, March 12, 1897.

91. *New York Journal*, October 12, 1897.

CHAPTER 9: TWO WARM BABES AND A HOT HANSOM

1. Ford, op. cit., 263.

2. *New York Times*, March 28, 1895, July 16, 1896; Ruth Woodman, "A Brief History of the New York Yacht Club," 1952, Ruth Cornwall Woodman Papers, University of Oregon Libraries, Eugene, Oregon.

3. Winkler, op. cit., 180.

4. Allen Churchill, *The Great White Way* (New York: E. P. Dutton, 1962), 13.

5. Churchill, *The Great White Way*, op. cit., 6.

6. Ibid., 30.

7. Felix Isman, *Weber and Fields* (New York: Boni & Liveright, 1924), 253.

8. Nasaw, op, cit., 27.

9. Churchill, *The Great White Way*, op. cit., 34–35.

10. Dreiser, op. cit., 542.

11. Churchill, *The Great White Way*, op. cit., 3–10.

12. Nasaw, op, cit., 28.

13. Older, *William Randolph Hearst*, op. cit., 58.

14. Cobb, op. cit., 123.

15. Nasaw, op, cit., 114.

16. *New York Times,* December 9, 1896.

17. Winkler, op. cit., 131.

18. Pizzitola, op. cit., 14.

19. Adela Rogers St. Johns, *The Honeycomb* (New York: Doubleday, 1969), 132.

20. Anne Apperson Flint to W. A. Swanberg, Swanberg Papers.

21. Ibid.

22. *The Journalist,* August 14, 1897.

23. *The Journalist,* October 9, 1897.

24. Nasaw, op, cit., 161.

25. *New York Times,* March 9, 1906.

26. Nasaw, op, cit., 134–135.

27. Ibid., 135.

28. Upton Sinclair, *The Industrial Republic,* (New York: Doubleday, Page & Company, 1907), 203.

29. Grove L. Johnson, Congressional Record, 54th Congress, January 8, 1897.

30. Pizzitola, op. cit., 14.

31. *New York Times,* January 13, 1897.

32. Kluger, op. cit., 141–145.

33. Mrs. Brisbane to Boyden Sparkes, Brisbane Papers.

34. *New York Times,* January 5, 1896; Robinson, op. cit., 255–256.

35. Henry Klein, *My Last Fifty Years* (New York: Isaac Goldmann Company, 1935), 14; Abbot, op. cit., 145.

36. Charles Edward Russell, "William Randolph Hearst," op. cit. .

37. WRH to Boyden Sparkes, Brisbane Papers.

38. Swanberg, *Pulitzer,* op. cit., 215.

39. Brian, op. cit., 206.

40. Ireland, op. cit., 48.

41. Ibid., 41.

42. Ibid., 81.

43. Ibid., 141.

44. Swanberg, *Pulitzer,* op. cit., 192.

45. Ibid., 220.

46. Brian, op. cit., 218.

47. *The Fourth Estate,* April 9, 1897.

48. Swanberg, *Pulitzer,* op. cit., 231.

49. Ibid., 230.

50. Nasaw, op, cit., 111.

51. Swanberg, *Pulitzer*, op. cit., 231.

52. Ibid., 240.

53. *The Journalist*, May 15, 1897.

54. Ibid.

55. Swanberg, *Pulitzer*, op. cit., 223.

56. Ibid., 219–220.

57. Ibid., 219.

58. *New York Times*, April 2, 1897.

59. Swanberg, *Pulitzer*, op. cit., 221.

60. *The Fourth Estate*, March 25, 1897.

61. *The Fourth Estate*, July 22, 1897.

CHAPTER 10: TAKING CHANCES NO CORRESPONDENT EVER TOOK

1. *New York Times*, February 27, 1895, February 28, 1895; Charles H. Brown, *The Correspondents' War: Journalism in the Spanish-American War* (New York: Charles Scribner's Sons, 1967), 2.

2. *New York Times*, March 10, 1895; *New York Tribune*, March 10, 1895; Brown, ibid., 3; Joseph E. Wisan, *The Cuban Crisis As Reflected in the New York Press, 1895–1898* (New York: Octagon Books, 1965), 40.

3. Wisan, op. cit., 50; Ivan Musicant, *Empire By Default: The Spanish-American War and the Dawn of the American Century* (New York: Henry Holt and Co., 1998), 51–53.

4. Wisan, ibid., 42.

5. *New York Times*, March 5, 1895; Wisan, ibid., 43.

6. Ian Mugridge, *The View from Xanadu: William Randolph Hearst and United States Foreign Policy* (Montreal & Kingston: McGill–Queen's University Press, 1995), 9; John Lawrence Tone, *War and Genocide in Cuba, 1895–1898* (Chapel Hill: University of North Carolina Press, 2006), 49.

7. Mugridge, op. cit., 9; New York *Journal*, October 11, 1895.

8. Mugridge, op. cit., 8.

9. *New York Journal*, January 19, 1896, October 11, 1895, November 11, 1895, May 11, 1896.

10. New York *World*, April 7, 1895.

11. Walter A. McDougall, *Promised Land, Crusader State: The American Encounter With the World Since 1776* (Boston: Houghton Mifflin Co., 1997), 120.

12. *New York Times*, March 15, 1895; *New York Tribune*, March 14, 1895; New York *Sun*,

March 14, 1895; March 22, 1895; *New York Tribune*, March 30, 1895; Marcus M. Wilkerson, *Public Opinion and the Spanish-American War: A Study in War Propaganda* (Baton Rouge: Louisiana State University Press, 1932), 19; Wisan, op. cit., 70, 85; Musicant, op. cit., 81–82; Walter Millis, *The Martial Spirit* (Chicago: Ivan R. Dee, 1989), 28.

13. Wisan, ibid., 72–73; Tone, op. cit., 51; *New York Evening Post*, March 14, 1895; *New York Times*, March 20, 1895, September 7, 1895.

14. George Bronson Rea, *Facts and Fakes about Cuba* (New York: George Monro's Sons, 1897); Brown, op. cit., 88.

15. Swanberg, *Hearst*, op. cit., 108.

16. Joseph P. McKerns, "Murat Halstead," *Dictionary of Literary Biography: American Newspaper Journalists, 1873–1900*, vol. 23 (Detroit: Gale Research Co., 1983), 155.

17. Murat Halstead, *The Story of Cuba: Her Struggles for Liberty; the Causes, Crisis and Destiny of the Pearl of the Antilles* (Chicago: Cuba Libre, 1896), 206.

18. Ibid., 112.

19. Ibid., 111–115.

20. Musicant, op. cit., 52.

21. Musicant, ibid., 53, 66; Tone, op. cit., 121.

22. Musicant, ibid., 67, 75; David F. Trask, *The War With Spain in 1898* (Lincoln: University of Nebraska Press, 1996), 8; Wisan, op. cit., 88–89, 203; Tone, op. cit., 154; Hannis Taylor, "A Review of the Cuban Question in Its Economic, Political, and Diplomatic Aspects," *The North American Review* 165, no. 492 (November 1897): 610–636.

23. *New York Journal*, February 24, 1896.

24. Charles Michelson, *The Ghost Talks* (New York: G.P. Putnam's Sons, 1944), 85; James Boylan, "Charles Michelson," *American National Biography* (New York: Oxford University Press).

25. *New York Journal*, January 7, 1896, January 10, 1896.

26. *New York Journal*, February 26, 1896; Brown, op. cit., 30–32.

27. Brown, ibid., 29.

28. *New York Journal*, April 2, 1896, April 4 1896; Rea, op. cit., 162–163.

29. Joyce Milton, *The Yellow Kids: Foreign Correspondents in the Heyday of Yellow Journalism* (New York: Harper & Row, 1989), 60, 65; Brown, op. cit., 45; Sylvester Scovel Papers, Missouri Historical Society; hereafter cited as Scovel Papers.

30. Milton, ibid., 61–62.

31. Ibid., 59.

32. Rea, op. cit., xiii; Milton, op. cit., 74–75.

33. Rea, ibid., 37.

34. Wisan, op. cit., 157.

35. Milton, op. cit., 72.

36. Ibid., 73; New York *World*, February 10, 1896.

37. Rea, op. cit., 236.

38. Rea, ibid., xiii.

39. Brown, op. cit., 48; Rea, ibid., 252.

40. Rea, ibid, 276.

41. Ibid., xvi.

42. New York *World*, May 17, 1896.

43. Brown, op. cit., 37.

44. Ibid., 49–50; George Clarke Musgrave, *Under Three Flags in Cuba* (Boston: Little Brown and Co., 1899), 10–11.

45. *New York Herald*, July 23, 1896; Wisan, op. cit., 201; Campbell, *Yellow*, op. cit., 11; *New York Times*, October 7, 1896.

46. *New York Times*, June 29, 1894, October 1, 1915; Ethel F. Fisk, ed., *The Letters of John Fiske. Edited By His Daughter* (New York: Macmillan Co., 1940), 612, 672; Grover Flint, *Marching with Gomez: A War Correspondent's Field Note-Book Kept During Four Months with the Cuban Army* (Boston: Lamson, Wolffe and Co., 1898).

47. Flint, op. cit., 119.

48. *New York Journal*, July 5, 1896.

49. Ibid.; Fisk, op. cit., 652.

50. Millis, op. cit., 31.

51. Richard Harding Davis, *Cuba in War Time* (New York: R.H. Russell, 1897), 61.

52. Flint, op. cit., 277–278; Brown, op. cit., 65; Rea, op. cit., 178–179.

CHAPTER 11: ONLY A HERO CAN SIT FOR A MONTH ON A HOTEL PORCH

1. Arthur Lubow, *The Reporter Who Would Be King: A Biography of Richard Harding Davis* (New York: Charles Scribner's Sons, 1992), 4, 131.

2. Charles Belmont Davis, ed., *Adventures and Letters of Richard Harding Davis* (New York: Charles Scribner's Sons, 1917), 178–179.

3. *New York Journal*, May 23, 1896, May 27, 1896.

4. *The Newspaper Maker*, May 28, 1896.

5. Tone, op. cit., 57, 61.

6. Musicant, op. cit., 71.

7. Wilkerson, op. cit., 58.

8. Wisan, op. cit., 229.

9. Trask, op. cit., 12.

10. *New York Journal*, January 1, 1896; Wisan, op. cit., 142–154.

11. Wisan, ibid., 132, 102–114; Trask, op. cit., 11–16.

12. Millis, op. cit., 29, 45, 38, 62–63.

13. Trask, op. cit., 11–12; Millis, op. cit., 44–50.

14. *New York Journal,* June 29, 1896.

15. Wilkerson, op. cit., 27; Wisan, op. cit., 162–163; Musicant, op. cit., 86.

16. Wisan, ibid., 167–169; Millis, op. cit., 64–65; Musicant, ibid., 93–95.

17. *New York Journal,* November 4, 1896.

18. WRH letter to James Creelman, November 19, 1896, Creelman Papers.

19. *New York Journal,* November 24, 1896.

20. New York *World,* January 12, 1897.

21. *New York Journal,* December 6, 1896.

22. *New York Journal,* December 16, 1896.

23. Wisan, op. cit., 191–192.

24. *New York Journal,* January 19, 1897.

25. Charles Belmont Davis, op. cit., 187; Richard Harding Davis (RHD) to his mother, December, 1896, Davis Papers.

26. Lubow, op. cit., 21, 30.

27. Lubow, op. cit., 5, 25.

28. Gerald Langford, *The Richard Harding Davis Years: A Biography of a Mother and Son* (New York: Holt, Rinehart and Winston, 1961), 112.

29. Lubow, op. cit., 116.

30. Peggy Samuels and Harold Samuels, *Frederic Remington: A Biography* (Garden City: Doubleday & Co. Inc., 1982), 34; *Collier's,* February 1905.

31. Samuels, ibid., 128, 238–239, 249.

32. Allen P. Splete and Marilyn D. Splete, eds., *Frederic Remington-Selected Letters* (New York: Abbeville Press, 1988), 217.

33. Splete, ibid., 216–217.

34. Samuels, op. cit., 245–46; Lubow, op. cit., 137.

35. Charles Belmont Davis, op. cit., 188.

36. RHD to his mother, December 1896, Davis Papers.

37. RHD to his family, December 25, 1896, Davis Papers; RHD to his family, December 27, 1896, Davis Papers.

38. RHD to his mother, December 1896, Davis Papers.

39. Splete, op. cit., 218.

40. Lubow, op. cit., 138.

41. RHD to his family, December 30, 1896, Davis Papers.

42. Lubow, op. cit., 140.

43. Milton, op. cit., 115–116; Ralph D. Paine, *Roads of Adventure* (Boston: Houghton Mifflin Co., 1922), 62–63.

44. Paine, ibid.

45. Ibid., 82.

46. Ibid., 118.

47. Lubow, op. cit., 138–139; Charles Belmont Davis, op. cit., 191.

48. Davis, ibid., 190.

49. Linda H. Davis, op. cit., 172–173.

50. Milton, op. cit., 128.

51. Ibid., 129; Linda H, Davis, op. cit., 177.

52. Davis, ibid., 178.

53. Ibid.

54. Ibid., 183.

55. Ibid., 187.

56. Lubow, op. cit., 139, 140.

57. Ibid., 139.

58. Creelman, *On the Great Highway,* op. cit., 178–179.

59. Campbell, *Yellow,* op. cit., 85.

60. Ibid.; Nasaw, op. cit., 127–128; Swanberg, *Hearst,* op. cit., 107–108.

61. Splete, op. cit., 218.

62. Creelman, *On the Great Highway,* op. cit., 177–178.

63. Splete, op. cit., 218–219.

64. Lubow, op. cit., 140; Charles Belmont Davis, op. cit., 196–198.

65. *New York Journal,* January 31, 1896.

66. Lubow, op. cit., 140–141; Charles Belmont Davis, op. cit., 194, 197, 199.

67. *New York Journal,* February 2, 1897.

68. *New York Journal,* January 17, 1897; Lubow, op. cit., 142.

69. *New York Journal,* February 12, 1897.

70. *New York Journal,* February 12, 1897.

71. Lubow, op. cit. 143; Brown, op. cit., 82.

72. Wisan, op. cit., 191; Lubow, ibid.

CHAPTER 12: TO SLAY A DRAGON AND FREE A DAMSEL IN DISTRESS

1. Morrill Goddard, *What Interests People and Why* (New York: Published Privately, 1935), 8.

2. Ibid., 55.

3. Ibid., 10.

4. Dana, op. cit., 11.

5. Musgrave, op. cit., 93.

6. *New York Journal,* August 17, 1897.

7. Musgrave, op. cit., 100.

8. Creelman, *On the Great Highway,* op. cit., 179.

9. Ibid., 180.

10. *New York Journal,* August 22, 1897, August 18, 1897, August 19, 1897.

11. *New York Journal,* August 22, 1897, August 26, 1897, August 17, 1897.

12. *New York Journal,* August 19, 1897.

13. Ibid.

14. *New York Journal,* February 20, 1897, February 21, 1897, February 22, 1897.

15. John L. Offner, *An Unwanted War: The Diplomacy of the United States and Spain over Cuba, 1895–1898* (Chapel Hill: University of North Carolina Press, 1992), 34–35, 56; *Mail and Express,* February 24, 1897; Wisan, op. cit., 222–224, 226.

16. Brown, op. cit., 85–87; Wisan, ibid.; Milton, op. cit., 145–149.

17. Milton, ibid., 143.

18. New York *World,* August 21, 1897; Brown, op. cit., 98.

19. New York *World,* August 21, 1897; Swanberg, *Hearst,* op. cit., 121.

20. *New York Journal,* August 26, 1897.

21. New York *World,* September 8, 1897; Swanberg, *Hearst,* op. cit., 124.

22. *New York Journal,* August 21, 1897.

23. *New York Journal,* August 26, 1897.

24. *New York Journal,* August 28, 1897, New York *Sun,* August 27, 1897.

25. *New York Journal,* August 18, 1897.

26. *New York Journal,* August 28, 1897; New York *Sun,* August 27, 1897.

27. *New York Journal,* August 22, 1897.

28. Campbell, *Year,* op. cit., 166–167, 178; *New York Journal,* September 9, 1897.

29. *New York Journal,* September 9, 1897; New York *World,* September 8, 1897.

30. Musicant, op. cit., 69.

31. *New York Journal,* October 5, 1897.

32. *New York Journal,* October 8, 1897.

33. *New York Journal,* October 9, 1897.

34. *New York Journal,* October 15, 1897.

35. Campbell, *Year,* op. cit., 161–200.

36. Musicant, op. cit., 90–91; Musgrave, op. cit., 103; Campbell, ibid., 167.

37. *New York Journal,* October 11, 1897.

38. Ibid.

39. New York *World*, October 14, 1897; Campbell, *Year*, op. cit., 182–183.

40. *New York Journal*, October 12, 1897; Campbell, ibid., 181.

41. *New York Journal*, October 12, 1897.

42. *New York Journal*, October 10, 1897, October 11, 1897.

43. *New York Journal*, October 13, 1897.

44. *New York Journal*, October 11, 1897.

45. *New York Journal*, October 13, 1897, October 15, 1897.

46. *New York Journal*, October 11, 1897, October 12, 1897.

47. *New York Journal*, October 14, 1897.

48. *New York Journal*, October 15, 1897.

49. Frederick Palmer, "Hearst and Hearstism," *Collier's Magazine*, September 22 and September 29, 1906.

50. *New York Journal*, October 15, 1897, October 17, 1897.

51. Campbell, *Year*, op. cit., 169–170.

52. Abbot, op. cit., 215–216

53. Ibid., 216; Swanberg, *Hearst*, op. cit., 126.

54. Nasaw, op. cit., 129.

55. *New York Herald*, October 9, 1897.

56. *New York Journal*, October 15, 1897.

57. *New York Journal*, August 28, 1897, August 23, 1897; see also *New York Journal*, August 24, 1897, August 25, 1897, August 26, 1897, August 27, 1897, August 29, 1897.

58. Stephen Bonsal, *The Real Condition of Cuba To-Day* (New York: Harper & Brothers, 1897), 147.

59. Ibid., 111, 141.

60. Campbell, *Year*, op. cit., 180.

61. Ibid., 184; Offner, op. cit., 80–81.

62. Robert Dallek, *1898: McKinley's Decision, The United States Declares War on Spain* (New York: Chelsea House Publishers, 1969), 32–43; Offner, ibid., 46–47.

63. Offner, ibid., 112–113.

64. *New York Journal*, February 17, 1898, March 24, 1898; Wisan, op. cit., 402–403.

65. Offner, op. cit., 241.

66. Offner, op. cit., 78–80.

67. Millis, op. cit., 76; Musicant, op. cit., 63.

68. Offner, op. cit., 57.

69. Ibid., 61 and 63; Dallek, op. cit., 47–52.

70. William McKinley, "State of the Union Message, December 6, 1897," from John T. Woolley and Gerhard Peters, The American Presidency Project (online).

71. Walter A. McDougall, *Promised Land, Crusader State: The American Encounter With the World Since 1776* (New York: Mariner Books, 1997), 118.

CHAPTER 13: UNCROWNED KING OF AN EDUCATED DEMOCRACY

1. *New York Journal,* October 18, 1897.

2. *New York Times,* January 24, 1898.

3. Campbell, *Year,* op. cit., 28.

4. Oliver Carlson, *Brisbane: A Candid Biography* (New York: Stackpole Sons, 1937); Lubow, op cit., 43–45.

5. Frank M. O'Brien, *The Story of the Sun, New York: 1833–1928* (New York: D. Appleton & Co., 1928), 157.

6. Carlson, *Brisbane,* op. cit., 92.

7. Milton, op. cit., 37.

8. Lubow, op. cit., 49.

9. Carlson, *Brisbane,* op. cit., 97.

10. Charles Edward Russell interviewed by Boyden Sparkes, Brisbane Papers.

11. Brian, op. cit., 212.

12. Seitz, *Pulitzer,* op. cit., 230.

13. Charles Edward Russell to Boyden Sparkes, Brisbane Papers.

14. *The Fourth Estate,* May 27, 1897.

15. Carlson, *Brisbane,* op. cit., 107–108.

16. Ibid., 101.

17. Ibid., 109–110.

18. WRH to Boyden Sparkes, 1937, Brisbane Papers.

19. Anne Brown to Boyden Sparkes, Brisbane Papers.

20. *The Journalist,* September 18, 1897.

21. *The Journalist,* September 11, 1897.

22. *The Fourth Estate,* September 30, 1897.

23. Charles Edward Russell to Boyden Sparkes, Brisbane Papers.

24. Unidentified source to Boyden Sparkes, Brisbane Papers.

25. Carlson, *Brisbane,* op. cit., 113–114.

26. T. E. Powers to Boyden Sparkes, Brisbane Papers.

27. WRH to Boyden Sparkes, Brisbane Papers.

28. Carlson, *Brisbane,* op. cit., 115.

29. Lubow, op. cit., 145.

30. WRH to Boyden Sparkes, Brisbane Papers.

31. Charles Edward Russell to Boyden Sparkes, Brisbane Papers.

32. Ibid.

33. WRH to Boyden Sparkes, Brisbane Papers.

34. Nasaw, op. cit., 161.

35. Carlson, *Brisbane*, op. cit., 111.

36. WRH to Boyden Sparkes, Brisbane Papers.

37. Steffens, "Hearst, Man of Mystery," op. cit., 4.

38. *The Journalist*, May 15, 1897.

39. *The Fourth Estate*, September 9, 1897.

40. Winkler, op. cit., 80.

41. *New York Journal*, December 27, 1896.

42. *New York Journal*, December 8, 1897.

43. *New York Journal*, October 13, 1897.

44. Kobre, *Yellow*, op. cit., 77.

45. *The Journalist*, October 3, 1899.

46. *New York Journal*, October 13, 1897.

47. Stead, op. cit., 227.

48. Ibid., 227.

49. Ibid., 231.

50. Ibid., 236–237.

51. Smythe, op. cit, 191.

52. Gerald F. Linderman, *The Mirror of War: American Society and the Spanish-American War* (Ann Arbor: University of Michigan Press, 1974), 149.

53. Ibid., 15

54. Wilkerson, op. cit., 64.

55. Linderman, op. cit., 152.

56. *New York Times*, February 25, 1898; February 26, 1898.

CHAPTER 14: SUDDENLY THE DINNERWARE BEGAN TO VIBRATE

1. Lewis L. Gould, *The Spanish-American War and President McKinley* (Lawrence: University Press of Kansas, 1982), 18.

2. Tone, op. cit., 49.

3. *New York Journal*, November 27, 1897.

4. Taylor, op. cit., 610–636.

5. Offner, op. cit., 37; Gould, *Spanish-American War*, op. cit., 28.

6. Gould, *Spanish-American War*, op. cit., 32; Musicant, op. cit., 119.

7. Wisan, op. cit., 374; see also Brown, op. cit., 110; Wilkerson, op. cit., 100; Brian, op. cit., 228.

8. *New York Journal*, January 14, 1898.

9.   Gould, *Spanish-American* War, op. cit., 32–33.

10. Offner, op. cit., 95–98.

11. Musicant, op. cit., 116–117; H. G. Rickover, *How the Battleship* Maine *Was Destroyed* (Annapolis: Naval Institute Press, 1976), 1.

12. Musicant, ibid., 126.

13. Ibid., 129.

14. Gould, *Spanish-American War,* op. cit., 33.

15. Dallek, op. cit., 110.

16. Ibid., 110–111.

17. Swanberg, *Hearst,* op. cit., 136; Nasaw, op. cit., 131; Smythe, op. cit., 188; *New York Evening Post,* February 10, 1898.

18. *New York Evening Post,* February 10, 1898.

19. Traxel, op. cit., 99.

20. Offner, op. cit., 121–122.

21. *New York Journal,* February 13, 1898.

22. *New York Journal,* February 15, 1898.

23. *New York Journal* February 13, 1898.

24. *New York Journal,* February 10, 1898, February 12, 1898.

25. *New York Journal,* January 23, 1898.

26. Musicant, op. cit., 137.

27. Milton, op. cit., 219.

28. *New York Journal,* February 17, 1898.

29. Rickover, op. cit., 1; "The Destruction of USS Maine," Department of the Navy, Navy Historical Center website.

30. Musicant, op. cit., 141.

31. Brown, op. cit., 121.

32. Traxel, op. cit., 108.

33. Coblentz, op. cit., 58–59.

34. *New York Evening Post,* February 19, 1898.

35. *New York Evening Post,* February 21, 1898.

36. Carlson and Bates, *Hearst: Lord of San Simeon,* op. cit., 105.

37. *New York Evening Post,* March 17, 1898.

38. *New York Evening Post,* March 21, 1898.

39. *New York Evening Post,* April 30, 1898.

40. Wisan, op. cit., 30.

41. Swanberg, *Hearst,* op. cit., 137.

42. Ibid., 137.

43. Ibid., 145.

44. *New York Herald,* February 16, 1898.

45. H.W. Brands, *T.R. The Last Romantic* (New York: Basic Books, 1997), 325.

46. Rickover, op. cit., 45; Kobre, *Development,* op. cit., 500; Wilkerson, op. cit., 101.

47. *New York Journal,* February 17, 1898.

48. *New York Journal,* February 17, 1898.

49. *New York Journal,* February 18, 1898.

50. Ibid.

51. WRH to James Creelman, Creelman Papers.

52. Ibid.

53. *New York Journal,* February 20, 1898, February 21, 1898.

54. *New York Journal,* February 26, 1898.

55. *New York Journal,* February 23, 1898

56. *New York Journal,* March 19, 1898.

57. Brian, op. cit., 231.

58. *New York Journal,* February 17, 1898.

59. Swanberg, *Hearst,* op. cit., 138.

60. *New York Journal,* February 20, 1898.

61. New York *Sun,* February 19, 1896.

62. *New York Tribune,* February 17, 1898.

63. *New York Tribune,* February 17, 1898.

64. *New York Times,* February 18, 1898; *New York Tribune,* February 19, 1898.

65. Millis, op. cit., 108.

66. Offner, op. cit., 123.

67. Dana, op. cit., 43.

68. The *Nation,* March 3, 1898, cited in Campbell, *Yellow,* op. cit., 103; William M. Armstrong, *The Gilded Age Letters of E.L. Godkin* (Albany: State University of New York Press, 1974), 177.

69. Armstrong, ibid., 170.

70. Ibid., 177.

71. *New York Evening Post,* February 16, 1898.

72. *New York Evening Post,* February 19, 1898.

73. *New York Evening Post,* February 21, 1898.

74. *New York Evening Post,* February 18, 1898.

75. Ferdinand Lundberg, *Imperial Hearst: A Social Biography* (New York: Equinox Cooperative Press, 1936).

76. Armstrong, op. cit., 177.

77. Offner, op. cit., 129.

78. Walter LaFeber, *The New Empire* (Ithaca: Cornell University Press, 1963), 349.

79. Redfield Proctor, "Cuban Reconcentration Policy and its Effects—A Speech," The Spanish American War Centennial Website.

80. Gould, *Spanish-American War,* op. cit., 40.

81. Wisan, op. cit., 416.

82. *New York Journal,* March 18, 1898.

83. French Ensor Chadwick, *The Relations of the United States and Spain: Diplomacy* (New York: Charles Scribner's Sons, 1909), 561.

84. *New York Journal,* April 7, 1898.

85. Dallek, op. cit., 203–212.

86. Ray Stannard Baker, "How the News of the War is Reported," *McClure's,* XI (September, 1898): 491–495.

87. Wisan, op. cit., 458; Swanberg, *Hearst,* op. cit., 144; Brown, op. cit., 440, 445; Marcus M. Wilkerson, *Public Opinion and the Spanish-American War: A Study in War Propaganda* (Baton Rouge: Louisiana State University Press, 1932), 131; Carlson and Bates, *Hearst: Lord of San Simeon,* op. cit., 92.

88. Nasaw, op. cit., 125.

89. Offner, op. cit., ix.

90. Dallek, op. cit., 203–212.

91. Linderman, op. cit., 148–151.

92. Several studies [all cited in Richard F. Hamilton, *President McKinley, War and Empire* (New Brunswick: Transaction Publishers, 2006)] purport to show that regional newspapers were more cautious and deliberate than the Hearst and Pulitzer dailies in response to the Cuban story. But the flows of opinion they find in the regional press are often consistent with the actual contents of the yellow press.

93. Linderman, op. cit., 152.

94. Brown, op. cit., 57; Linderman, ibid., 163; Brown, op. cit., 107–108.

95. Wisan, op. cit., 379; Millis, op. cit., 98.

96. Swanberg, *Hearst,* op. cit., 119; Swanberg, *Pulitzer,* op. cit., 230.

97. Linderman, op. cit., 168.

98. Brown, op. cit., 52.

99. Offner, op. cit., ix, 192; Hamilton, op. cit., 234; Leech, op. cit., 180–182.

100. Phillips, op. cit., 94–96; Gould, *Spanish-American War,* op. cit., 52.

101. James Bryce, *The American Commonwealth,* vol. II (New York: Macmillan, 1920), 275.

102. Samantha Power, *A Problem from Hell: America and the Age of Genocide* (New York: Harper Perennial, 2003), xv.

103. Ibid., xvii.

104. Ibid., xviii.

105. Offner, op. cit., 190–191.

CHAPTER 15: AS I WRITE, AMBULANCE TRAINS ARE BRINGING THE WOUNDED

1. William Allen White, *Forty Years on Main Street* (New York: Farrar & Rinehart, 1937), 348–349.

2. Swanberg, *Hearst,* op. cit., 143.

3. Trask, op. cit., 155–56.

4. Brown, op. cit., 156; Trask, ibid., 156–157.

5. *New York Times,* August 7, 1898.

6. Abbot, op. cit., 223.

7. *New York Journal,* May 5, 1898.

8. Brown, op. cit., 446.

9. Baker, op. cit., 491–495.

10. *New York Herald,* April 2, 1898, April 6, 1898.

11. *New York Tribune,* April 1, 1898.

12. Dallek, op. cit., 216.

13. Lubow, op. cit., 155–156.

14. Ibid., 158.

15. Ibid., 166.

16. Charles Belmont Davis, op. cit., 174.

17. *New York Herald,* April, 28, 1898, April 29, 1898, April 30, 1898; Lubow, op. cit., 158; Brown, op. cit., 163.

18. Trask, op. cit., 95–105.

19. *New York Herald,* May 2, 1898, May 3, 1898.

20. *New York Herald,* May 8, 1898.

21. *New York Herald,* May 1, 1898.

22. *New York Herald,* April 22, 1898, May 7, 1898, May 4, 1898.

23. *New York Journal,* May 8, 1898.

24. *New York Herald,* May 6, 1898.

25. Brown, op. cit., 183.

26. *New York Tribune,* May 2, 1898.

27. Ibid.

28. *New York Tribune,* May 12, 1898.

29. *New York Herald,* May 6, 1898, May 8, 1898

30. *New York Journal,* May 2, 1898.

31. *New York Journal,* May 2, 1898, May 6, 1898

32. Charles S. Wheeler, "Brief on behalf of the executors of the estate of Mrs. Phoebe A. Hearst. . . ." Charles S. Wheeler Papers, Bancroft Library, University of California, Berkeley, 7, 8.

33. Baker, op. cit., 491–495.

34. Brown, op. cit., 445; *The Fourth Estate,* July 21, 1898; Baker, ibid.

35. Arthur Brisbane to Sylvester Scovel, March 3, 1898, Scovel Papers.

36. Arthur Brisbane, "The Modern Newspaper in War Time," *Cosmopolitan,* September, 1898.

37. *The Newspaper Maker,* June (date unknown), 1898.

38. Smythe, op. cit., 190.

39. *The Newspaper Maker,* July 15, 1898; Brown, op. cit., 446.

40. New York *World,* May 8, 1898.

41. Barrett, *Pulitzer,* op. cit., 178.

42. *New York Journal,* May 8, 1898.

43. Brown, op. cit., 201.

44. Michelson, op. cit., 90.

45. Milton, op. cit., 285.

46. Brown, op. cit., 266; New York *Journal,* June 6, 1898.

47. *The Fourth Estate,* April 14, 1898.

48. Brisbane, "The Modern Newspaper in War Time," op. cit.

49. New York *World,* June 8, 1898.

50. Swanberg, *Hearst,* op. cit., 148.

51. New York *World,* June 9, 1898.

52. *New York Journal,* June 10, 1898.

53. Swanberg, *Hearst,* op. cit., 149.

54. Terhune, op. cit., 133.

55. WRH to James Creelman, May 26, 1898, Creelman Papers.

56. Creelman, *On the Great Highway,* op. cit., 189–191.

57. WRH to PAH, undated, Bancroft Papers.

58. Trask, op. cit., 190; Musicant, op. cit., 354.

59. John C. Hemment, *Cannon and Camera: Sea and Land Battles of the Spanish-American War in Cuba, Camp Life, and the Return of the Soldiers* (New York: D. Appleton & Co., 1898), 72–73.

60. *New York Journal,* June 29, 1898.

61. Trask, op. cit., 190; Musicant, op. cit., 354.

62. Milton, op. cit., 309; Musicant, ibid.

63. Lubow, op. cit., 172.

64. *New York Journal*, June 29, 1898.

65. Hemment, op. cit., 76.

66. Swanberg, *Hearst*, op. cit., 153.

67. Hemment, op. cit., 79.

68. Hemment, op. cit., 81.

69. *New York Journal*, June 29, 1898.

70. Trask, op. cit., 209; Older, *William Randolph Hearst*, American, op. cit., 191.

71. Brown, op. cit., 315.

72. *New York Journal*, June 26, 1898.

73. Edmund Morris, *The Rise of Theodore Roosevelt*, (New York: Ballantine Books, 1979), 643–644.

74. Lubow., op. cit., 177.

75. Dale L. Walker, *Death Was the Black Horse: The Story of Rough Rider Buckey O'Neill* (Lincoln: University of Nebraska Press, 1997), 171.

76. Edward Marshall, "How It Feels To Be Shot," *Cosmopolitan*, September, 1898; Edward Marshall, "The Santiago Campaign, Some Episodes: A Wounded Correspondent's Recollections of Gausimas," *Scribner's Magazine*, September, 1898; Lubow, op. cit., 177.

77. Linda H. Davis, op. cit., 259.

78. Lubow, op. cit., 177

79. Ibid.

80. Trask, op. cit., 222.

81. *New York Journal*, June 27, 1898.

82. Hemment, op. cit., 96.

83. G.W. Bitzer, *Billy Bitzer, His Story* (New York, Farrar Straus & Giroux, 1973), 36.

84. Hemment, op. cit., 110–111.

85. Ibid., 112–113.

86. *New York Journal*, June 29, 1898; *New York Times*, July 1, 1898.

87. Trask, op. cit., 232–234.

88. WRH to PAH, undated, WRH Papers, Bancroft Papers.

89. Frederic Remington to Eva Remington, June 29, 1898 in Splete, op. cit., 224.

90. Charles Johnson Post, *The Little War of Private Post* (New York: New American, 1961), 114–115.

91. Trask, op. cit., 238–242.

92. Hemment, op. cit., 148–149.

93. Ibid., 150, 153.

94. Creelman, *On the Great Highway*, op. cit., 190.

95. Ibid., 196.

96. Ibid., 199.

97. *New York Journal*, July 4, 1898.

98. Creelman, *On the Great Highway*, op. cit., 205.

99. Ibid., 207–208.

100. Ibid., 211–212.

101. *New York Journal*, July 4, 1898.

102. *New York Journal*, July 4, 1898.

103. Hemment, op. cit., 215–216.

104. *New York Times*, July 7, 1898.

105. Creelman, *On the Great Highway*, op. cit., 214.

106. James Creelman to WRH, July 5, 1898, Creelman Papers.

107. Brown, op. cit, 430–432.

108. *The Newspaper Maker*, July 28, 1898.

109. Brown, op. cit., 402; Milton, op. cit., 349–351.

110. *The Newspaper Maker*, August 4, 1898.

111. *New York Journal*, July 6, 1898.

112. *The Journalist*, July 16, 1898.

113. Brown, op. cit., 429–430.

114. *New York Journal*, July 11, 1898.

115. Sam Chamberlain to PAH, July 10, 1898, Bancroft Papers.

116. Lubow, op. cit., 188.

CHAPTER 16: STANDING IN THE FIRST RANK OF AMERICAN JOURNALISM, FEELING BLUE

1.   *New York Journal*, August 16, 1898; August 17, 1898.

2.   Trask, op. cit., 335.

3.   WRH to James Creelman, July 25, 1898, Creelman Papers.

4.   WRH to PAH, undated, Bancroft Papers.

5.   WRH to James Creelman, undated, Creelman Papers; WRH to James Creelman, September 27, 1897, Creelman Papers.

6.   *The Fourth Estate*, July 28, 1898.

7.   Nasaw, op. cit., 147.

8.   *New York Journal*, July 5, 1898, November 14, 1897, November 17, 1897.

9.   *The Fourth Estate*, May 5, 1898.

10. *The Fourth Estate*, January 12, 1899.

11. *The Journalist*, July 23, 1898.

12. *The Fourth Estate*, June 12, 1898.

13. *The Fourth Estate*, June 16, 1898; *New York Times*, June 10, 1898.

14. *The Journalist*, February 12, 1898.

15. Swanberg, *Pulitzer*, op. cit., 241.

16. *The Journalist*, August 13, 1898; *The Newspaper Maker*, September 22, 1898.

17. *The Newspaper Maker*, August 11, 1898; *The Newspaper Maker*, July 20, 1899.

18. *The Fourth Estate*, June 9, 1898, July 28, 1898, November 24, 1898; *The Journalist*, July 16, 1898, August 20, 1898; *The Newspaper Maker*, May 5, 1898, June 30, 1898.

19. *The Fourth Estate*, June 23, 1898.

20. *The Fourth Estate*, July 7, 1898.

21. *The Journalist*, July 16, 1898.

22. Ibid.

23. *The Newspaper Maker*, June 23, 1898.

24. *The Newspaper Maker*, June 30, 1898, July 14, 1898.

25. *The Newspaper Maker*, August 4, 1898.

26. Littlefield, op. cit., 52.

27. *New York Journal*, January 12, 1902.

28. Edward Clark to PAH, June 9, 1898, Bancroft Papers; Nasaw, op. cit., 146.

29. Swanberg, *Pulitzer*, op. cit., 259.

30. *New York Journal*, September 25, 1898.

31. Seitz, *Pulitzer*, op. cit., 240–242.

32. Ibid., 240–2.

33. Nasaw, op. cit., 148–149.

34. Seitz, *Pulitzer*, op. cit, 242.

35. Brian, op. cit., 241.

36. WRH interview with Boyden Sparkes, Brisbane Papers.

37. Littlefield, op. cit., 52.

38. WRH to PAH, undated, Bancroft Papers.

39. PAH to Orrin Peck, May 3, 1899, Peck Papers.

40. WRH to PAH, undated, Bancroft Papers.

41. Robinson, op. cit., 329.

42. Nasaw, op. cit., 153.

43. Trask, op. cit., 483.

44. Jerald A. Combs, *American Diplomatic History* (Berkeley: University of California Press, 1983) 77 ff; Ephraim K. Smith, "William McKinley's Enduring Legacy: The Historiographical Debate on the Taking of the Philippine Islands," in *Crucible of Empire: The Spanish-American War and Its Aftermath*, ed. James C. Bradford (Annapolis: Naval Institute Press, 1993), 205 ff.

45. McDougall, op. cit., 111.

46. Mark Twain, "To The Person Sitting in Darkness," *Mark Twain: Collected Tales, Sketches, Speeches, & Essays 1891–1910* (New York: Library of America, 1992), 465, 471.

47. *New York Journal,* February 7, 1899, February 8, 1899, February 9, 1899.

48. Robinson, op. cit., 335.

49. Ibid., 336.

50. Ibid., 21.

51. *The American Magazine,* November 1906.

52. Swanberg, *Hearst,* op. cit., 246.

53. Lincoln Steffens, *The Autobiography of Lincoln Steffens* (New York: Grosset & Dunlap, 1931), 539–543.

54. James W. Barrett, *The World, The Flesh and Messrs. Pulitzer* (New York: Vanguard Press, 1931), 52–54.

55. Hearst, William Randolph, *Selections from the Writings and Speeches of William Randolph Hearst,* ed. E.F. Tompkins (San Francisco: Published Privately, 1948), 49–50.

56. "Brief on Behalf of the Executors of the Estate of Mrs. Phoebe A Hearst," 2.

57. Robinson, op. cit., 385–387; Nasaw, op. cit., 279.

58. Swanberg, *Hearst,* op. cit., 321.

59. Ibid., 363.

60. Nasaw, op. cit., 251.

61. Silas Bent, *Strange Bedfellows: A Review of Politics, Personalities and the Press* (New York: Horace Liveright, 1928), 229.

62. Ibid., 229–230.

63. Ibid., 227

64. Coblentz, op. cit., 48.

SELECTED SOURCES AND BIBLIOGRAPHY

The many newspapers and trade publications used in the preparation of this manuscript are sourced either in the text or in endnotes. Michigan State University and The Library of Congress have, between them, a complete set of the *New York Journal* for the relevant years. Citations for documents in the William Randolph Hearst, Phoebe Apperson Hearst, and George Hearst collections at Bancroft Library are not sourced to particular boxes and folders in the collections; the library changed its classification system in the midst of my research, and there is no concordance between the old system and the new. Nevertheless, the Bancroft Papers are well organized and researchers should not have trouble finding the materials cited.

The principal archives relied on:

Brisbane Family Papers, Special Collections Research Center, Syracuse University.

Cartoon Research Library collection, Ohio State University.

James Creelman Papers, Rare Books and Manuscript Library, University of Ohio; hereafter cited as Creelman Papers.

Richard Harding Davis Papers, Clifton Waller Barrett Library, University of Virginia.

William Randolph Hearst Collection, Bancroft Library, University of California, Berkeley.

George and Phoebe Apperson Hearst Collection, Bancroft Library, University of California, Berkeley.

Orrin M. Peck Papers, H. E. Huntington Library.

Sylvester Scovel Papers, Missouri Historical Society.

W.A. Swanberg Papers, Rare Book and Manuscript Library, Columbia University.

Charles S. Wheeler Papers, Bancroft Library, University of California, Berkeley.

The principal texts relied on:

Abbot, Willis J. *Watching the World Go By*. Boston: Little, Brown and Co., 1934.

Allen, Robert Clyde. *Horrible Prettiness: Burlesque and American Culture*. Chapel Hill: University of North Carolina Press, 1991.

Armstrong, William M. *E.L. Godkin: A Biography*. Albany: State University of New York Press, 1978.

Baldasty, Gerald J. *The Commercialization of News in the Nineteenth Century*. Madison: University of Wisconsin Press, 1992.

Berryman, John. *Stephen Crane: A Critical Biography* rev. ed. New York: Cooper Square Press, 2001.

Brands, H.W. *Bound to Empire: The United States and the Philippines*. New York: Oxford University Press, 1992.

————. *The Reckless Decade: America in the 1890s*. Chicago: University of Chicago Press, 2002.

————. *T.R. The Last Romantic*. New York: Basic Books, 1997.

Brian, Denis. *Pulitzer: A Life*. New York: John Wiley & Sons, Inc., 2001.

Brown, Charles H. *The Correspondents' War: Journalists in the Spanish-American War*. New York: Charles Scribner's Sons, 1967.

Burrows, Edwin G. and Mike Wallace. *Gotham: A History of New York City to 1898*. New York: Oxford University Press, 1999.

Calhoun, Charles William. *The Gilded Age: Perspectives on the Origins of Modern America*. Plymouth: Rowman & Littlefield, 2007.

Campbell, W. Joseph. *Yellow Journalism: Puncturing the Myths, Defining the Legacies*. Westport: Praeger Publishers, 2003.

————. *The Year That Defined American Journalism: 1897 and the Clash of Paradigms*. New York: Routledge, 2006.

Carlson, Oliver. *Brisbane: A Candid Biography*. New York: Stackpole Sons, 1937.

————and Ernest Sutherland Bates. *Hearst: Lord of San Simeon*. New York: Viking Press, 1936.

Cashman, Sean Dennis. *American in the Gilded Age: From the Death of Lincoln to the Rise of Theodore Roosevelt* 3d ed. New York: New York University Press, 1993.

Chadwick, French Ensor. *The Relations of the United States and Spain: Diplomacy*. New York: Charles Scribner's Sons, 1909.

Churchill, Allen. *Park Row*. New York: Rinehart & Co. Inc., 1958.

————. *The Great White Way*. New York: E. P. Dutton Cp. Inc., 1962.

Coblentz, Edward. D. *William Randolph Hearst: A Portrait in His Own Words*. New York: Simon & Schuster, 1952.

Crane, Stephen. *Active Service*. London: Heinemann, 1899.

Creelman, James. *On the Great Highway*. Boston: Lothrop Publishing Co., 1901.

Crockett, Albert Stevens. *When James Gordon Bennett was Caliph of Baghdad*. New York: Funk and Wagnalls Co., 1926.

Croly, Herbert. *Marcus Alonzo Hanna: His Life and Work*. New York: MacMillan Co., 1912.

Dallek, Robert. *1898: McKinley's Decision, The United States Declares War on Spain*. New York: Chelsea House Publishers, 1969.

Dana, Charles A. *The Art of Newspaper Making*. New York: Arno Press, 1970.

Davis, Charles Belmont, ed. *Adventures and Letters of Richard Harding Davis*. New York: Charles Scribner's Sons, 1917.

Davis, Linda H. *Badge of Courage: The Life of Stephen Crane*. Boston: Houghton Mifflin Co., 1998.

Davis, Richard Harding. *Cuba in War Time*. New York: R.H. Russell, 1897.

Dicken-Garcia, Hazel. *Journalistic Standards in Nineteenth-Century America*. Madison: University of Wisconsin Press, 1989.

Dreiser, Theodore. *Newspaper Days: An Autobiography*. Edited by T.D. Nostwich. Santa Rosa: Black Sparrow Press, 2000.

Dunlop, M. H. *Gilded City: Scandal and Sensation in Turn-of-the-Century New York*. New York: HarperCollins Publishers Inc., 2000.

Ellis, Edward Robb. *The Epic of New York City: A Narrative History*. New York: Kondansha International, 1966.

Flint, Grover. *Marching with Gomez: A War Correspondent's Field Note-Book Kept During Four Months with the Cuban Army*. Boston: Lamson, Wolffe and Co., 1898.

Gandal, Keith. *The Virtues of the Vicious: Jacob Riis, Stephen Crane, and the Spectacle of the Slum*. New York: Oxford University Press, 1997.

Glad, Paul W. *McKinley, Bryan, and the People*. New York: J. B. Lippincott Company, 1964.

Goddard, Morrill. *What Interests People and Why*. New York: Published Privately, 1935.

Gould, Lewis L. *The Spanish-American War and President McKinley*. Lawrence: University Press of Kansas, 1982.

Harvey, Robert C. *Children of the Yellow Kid: The Evolution of the American Comic Strip*. Seattle: Frye Art Museum, University of Washington Press, 1998.

Hawthorne, Edith Garrigues, ed. *The Memoirs of Julian Hawthorne*. New York: MacMillan Co., 1938.

Hearst, William Randolph. *Selections from the Writings and Speeches of William Randolph Hearst*. Edited by E.F. Tompkins. San Francisco: published privately, 1948.

Hemment, John C. *Cannon and Camera: Sea and Land Battles of the Spanish-American War in Cuba, Camp Life, and the Return of the Soldiers*. New York: D. Appleton and Co., 1898.

Huot, Leland and Alfred Powers. *Homer Davenport of Silverton*. Bingen: West Shore Press, 1973.

Ireland, Alleyne. *Joseph Pulitzer: Reminiscences of a Secretary*. New York: Mitchell Kennerley, 1914

Jones, Stanley L. The *Presidential Election of 1896*. Madison: University of Wisconsin Press, 1964.

Juergens, George. *Joseph Pulitzer and the New York World*. Princeton: Princeton University Press, 1966.

Kaplan, Richard L. *Politics and the American Press: The Rise of Objectivity, 1865–1920*. Cambridge: Cambridge University Press, 2002.

Kazin, Michael. *A Godly Hero: The Life of William Jennings Bryan*. New York: Anchor Books, 2007.

Kluger, Richard. *The Paper*. New York: Vintage Books, 1989.

Kobre, Sidney. *Development of American Journalism*. Dubuque: Wm. C. Brown Co. Publishers, 1969.

———. *The Yellow Press and Gilded Age Journalism*. Tallahassee: Florida State University, 1964.

Lee, James Melvin. *History of American Journalism*. Boston: Houghton Mifflin Co., 1917.

Leech, Margaret. *In the Day of McKinley*. New York: Harper & Brothers, 1959.

Linderman, Gerald F. *The Mirror of War: American Society and the Spanish-American War*. Ann Arbor: University of Michigan Press, 1974.

Littlefield III, Roy Everett. *William Randolph Hearst: His Role in American Progressivism*. Lanham: University Press of America, 1980.

Lubow, Arthur. *The Reporter Who Would be King: A Biography of Richard Harding Davis*. New York: Charles Scribner's Sons, 1992.

Lundberg, Ferdinand. *Imperial Hearst: A Social Biography*. New York: Equinox Cooperative Press, 1936.

McDougall, Walter A. *Promised Land, Crusader State: The American Encounter With the World Since 1776*. Boston: Houghton Mifflin Co., 1997.

McGerr, Michael E. *The Decline of Popular Politics: the American North, 1865–1928.* New York: Oxford University Press, 1986.

Millis, Walter. *The Martial Spirit.* Chicago: Ivan R. Dee Inc., 1989.

Miraldi, Robert. *The Pen is Mightier: The Muckraking Life of Charles Edward Russell.* New York: Palgrave Macmillan, 2003.

Milton, Joyce. *The Yellow Kids: Foreign Correspondents in the Heyday of Yellow Journalism.* New York: Harper & Row, 1989.

Morgan, H. Wayne. *America's Road to Empire: The War with Spain and Overseas Expansion.* New York: Alfred A. Knopf, 1965.

———. *William McKinley and His America.* Syracuse: Syracuse University Press, 1963.

Morris, Edmund. *The Rise of Theodore Roosevelt.* New York: Ballantine Books, 1979.

Morris, Lloyd. *Postscripts to Yesterday.* New York: Random House, 1947.

Mott, Frank Luther. *American Journalism, A History of Newspapers in the United States Through 260 Years: 1690 to 1950.* Rev. ed. New York: Macmillan Co., 1950.

Mugridge, Ian. *The View from Xanadu: William Randolph Hearst and United States Foreign Policy.* Montreal & Kingston: McGill–Queen's University Press, 1995.

Murat, Halstead. *The Story of Cuba: Her Struggles for Liberty; the Causes, Crisis and Destiny of the Pearl of the Antilles.* Chicago: Cuba Libre, 1896.

Musicant, Ivan. *Empire By Default: The Spanish-American War and the Dawn of the American Century.* New York: Henry Holt and Co., 1998.

Nasaw, David. *The Chief: The Life of William Randolph Hearst.* Boston: Houghton Mifflin Co., 2000.

Nevins, Allan and Frank Weitenkampf. *A Century of Political Cartoons: Caricature in the United States from 1800 to 1900.* New York: Charles Scribner's Sons, 1944.

O'Connor, Richard. *The Scandalous Mr. Bennett.* Garden City: Doubleday & Co. Inc., 1962.

Offner, John L. *An Unwanted War: The Diplomacy of the United States and Spain over Cuba, 1895–1898.* Chapel Hill: University of North Carolina Press, 1992.

Older, Mr. and Mrs. Freemont. *George Hearst: California Pioneer.* Los Angeles: Westernlore, 1966

Paine, Ralph D. *Roads of Adventure.* Boston: Houghton Mifflin Co., 1922.

Phillips, Kevin. *William McKinley.* New York: Henry Holt and Co., 2003.

Power, Samantha. *A Problem from Hell: America and the Age of Genocide.* New York: Harper Perennial, 2003.

Procter, Ben. *William Randolph Hearst: The Early Years, 1863–1910.* New York: Oxford University Press, 1998.

Rea, George Bronson. *Facts and Fakes about Cuba*. New York: George Monro's
    Sons, 1897.

Reid, Whitelaw. *Making Peace With Spain: The Diary of Whitelaw Reid September-
    December, 1898*. Edited by H. Wayne Morgan. Austin: University of Texas
    Press, 1965.

Rickover, H. G. *How the Battleship Maine Was Destroyed*. Annapolis: Naval Institute
    Press, 1976.

Robinson, Judith. *The Hearsts: An American Dynasty*. Newark: University of
    Delaware Press, 1991.

Revere, Richard H. *Howe & Hummel: Their True and Scandalous History*. Syracuse:
    Syracuse University Press, 1996.

Russell, Charles Edward. *Bare Hands and Stone Walls: Some Recollections of a Side-
    Line Reformer*. New York: Charles Scribner's Sons, 1933.

Russell, Francis. *The President Makers: From Mark Hanna to Joseph P. Kennedy*.
    Boston: Little, Brown and Co., 1976.

Samuels, Peggy and Harold Samuels. *Frederic Remington: A Biography*. Garden City:
    Doubleday & Co., Inc., 1982.

Sante, Luc. *Low Life: Lures and Snares of Old New York*. New York: Farrar, Straus &
    Giroux, 2003.

Schlereth, Thomas J. *Victorian America: Transformations in Everyday Life,
    1876–1915*. New York: HarperCollins, 1992.

Schudson, Michael. *The Power of News*. Cambridge: Harvard University Press, 1995.

Seitz, Don C. *Joseph Pulitzer: His Life & Letters*. New York: Simon & Schuster, 1924.

————. *The James Gordon Bennetts: Father and Son*. Indianapolis: Bobbs-Merrill
    Co., 1928.

Shikes, Ralph E. *The Indignant Eye: The Artist as Social Critic in Prints and Drawings
    from the Fifteenth Century to Picasso*. Boston: Beacon Press, 1976.

Smythe, Ted Curtis. *The Gilded Age Press, 1865–1900*. Westport: Praeger Publishers,
    2003.

Splete, Allen P. and Marilyn D. Splete, eds. *Frederic Remington: Selected Letters*. New
    York: Abbeville Press, 1988.

Starr, Paul. *The Creation of the Media: Political Origins of Modern Communications*.
    New York: Basic Books, 2004.

Stead, W. T. *Satan's Invisible World Displayed*. New York: R.F. Fenno & Co., 1897.

Steele, Janet E. *The Sun Shines for All: Journalism and Ideology in the Life of Charles
    A. Dana*. Syracuse: Syracuse University Press, 1993.

Stern, Clarence A. *Resurgent Republicanism: The Handiwork of Hanna*. Ann Arbor:

Edwards Brothers, 1968.

Steffens, Lincoln. *The Autobiography of Lincoln Steffens.* New York: Grosset & Dunlap, 1931.

———. "Hearst, the Man of Mystery." *The American Magazine* 63 (Nov. 1906): 3–22.

Stevens, John D. *Sensationalism and the New York Press.* New York: Columbia University Press, 1991.

Swanberg, W. A. *Citizen Hearst.* New York: Charles Scribner's Sons, 1961.

———. *Pulitzer.* New York: Charles Scribner's Sons, 1967.

Tebbel, John. *The Life and Good Times of William Randolph Hearst.* New York: E. P. Dutton & Co., Inc., 1952.

Tifft, Susan E. and Alex S. Jones. *The Trust.* Boston: Back Bay Books, 2000.

Tone, John Lawrence. *War and Genocide in Cuba, 1895–1898.* Chapel Hill: University of North Carolina Press, 2006.

Trask, David F. *The War with Spain in 1898.* Lincoln: University of Nebraska Press, 1996.

Traxel, David. *Crusader Nation: The United States in Peace and the Great War, 1898–1920.* New York: Vintage Books, 2007.

———. *1898: The Birth of the American Century.* New York: Alfred A. Knopf, 1998.

Whicher, George F., *William Jennings Bryan and the Campaign of 1896.* Boston: D.C. Heath and Co., 1968.

Whyte, Frederic. *The Life of W.T. Stead.* Vol. 2. London: Jonathan Cape Ltd., 1925.

Wilkerson, Marcus M. *Public Opinion and the Spanish-American War: A Study in War Propaganda.* Baton Rouge: Louisiana State University Press, 1932.

Winkler, John K. *William Randolph Hearst: A New Appraisal.* New York: Hastings House, 1955.

Wisan, Joseph E. *The Cuban Crisis as Reflected in the New York Press, 1895–1898.* New York: Octagon Books, 1965.

IMAGE PERMISSIONS

"The young San Francisco publisher . . ."
Courtesy of Hearst Castle, San Simeon, California.

"W.R. considered himself . . ."
From the author's private collection.

"Phoebe Apperson Hearst . . ."
Copyright Bettmann/CORBIS.

"Senator George Hearst . . ."
Courtesy of the Bancroft Library. University of California Berkley.

"Hearst's *Vamoose* . . ."
Published with permission from www.jsjohnston.org.

"The newspaper buildings . . ."
Picture Collection, The Branch Libraries, The New York Public Library, Astor, Lenox and Tilden Foundations.

"A confident W.R. . . ."
Courtesy of Hearst Castle, San Simeon, California.

"W.R. sent up . . ."
Library of Congress, Prints and Photographs Division.

"Homer Davenport . . ."
Library of Congress, Prints and Photographs Division

"Joseph Pulitzer . . ."
Copyright CORBIS.

"Millicent Willson . . ."
Courtesy of the Bancroft Library. University of California Berkley.
From *Hearst over Hollywood*, by Louis Pizzitola. Copyright (c) 2002. Columbia University Press. Reprinted with permission of the publisher.

"Homer Davenport drew "Dollar" Mark Hanna . . ."
Courtesy of the Serial and Government Publications Division, Library of Congress.

"William McKinley . . ."
Spencer Arnold/Hulton Archives/Getty Images.

"William Jennings Bryan . . ."
Copyright Bettman/CORBIS.

"The Yellow Kid . . ."
Courtesy of the Richard D. Olsen Collection.

"Election returns light up . . ."
Courtesy of the Serial and Government Publications Division, Library of Congress.

"Little Egypt . . ."
Courtesy of the Serial and Government Publications Division, Library of Congress.

"Stephen Crane . . ."
Courtesy of Christopher P. Wilson.

Evangelina Cisneros
Newspaper clipping courtesy of the Serial and Government Publications Division, Library of Congress.

"'The Butcher' Valeriano Weyler y Nicolau . . ."
Copyright CORBIS.

"Hearst's outrage . . ."
Archivo Nacional de la República de Cuba. Fototeca. C8 S77 R79

A C K O W L E D G E M E N T S

I should start with Michael Levine, without whose coaxing I might still be thinking about writing this book. A month or two after I began, Heather Munro-Blum, principal of McGill University, invited me to her campus as a visiting scholar. I spent two stimulating years at the McGill Institute for the Study of Canada, in the company of its director Antonia Maioni, and her wonderful colleagues and staff. I am most grateful to Heather, Antonia, and the McGill community for that opportunity and for many additional kindnesses.

I could not have hoped for a more talented and dedicated editor than Anne Collins at Random House Canada. We worked together years ago in the magazine business and I always held her in high regard but I am newly astonished at her capacities, and this manuscript has been immeasurably improved by her attentions. I also want to thank Jennifer Shepherd, Craig Pyette, and Sharon Klein at Random House for their hard work and professionalism.

I have benefited from the work of Judith Robinson, who has done a superb job of sorting out the Hearst family papers, and steered me to some materials I had overlooked, and who gave me her thoughts on several chapters of this manuscript. David Nasaw's thorough biography, *The Chief*, was useful and thought provoking, and an inspiration for my different take on Hearst. W. Joseph Campbell has done some truly original research in the field of newspaper history and I learned a great deal from his publications. The reference staffs at the Bancroft Library, the New York Public Library, and The Library of Congress went out of their way to be helpful. A kind assistant at the Michigan State Library taught me how to scan newspapers from microfilm.

Nancy Macdonald (McGill) was of enormous assistance as a researcher on this project. Patricia Treble (*Maclean's*) was indispensable as a fact-checker and bibliographer. Thanks as well to Julien-Russell Brunet (University of Toronto), Matthew Hogan, George Serhijczuk (*Maclean's*). The redoubtable Chris Johnston kept me as functional and organized as it is in me to be. John Fraser, Master of Massey College at the University of Toronto, was generous with his hospitality. Brian Segal, Leanne Shapton, Andrew Tolson, Lenny Blum, Florence Richler, Sasha Josipovicz, and Dianne de Fenoyl all contributed in different ways. Robert Fulford read the entire manuscript and gave me his thoughts.

This is a book about journalism and journalists, and much of what I know on these subjects has been gleaned from the many hundreds of writers, editors, and publishers I've been privileged to know over the years. I am beholden to them all, and this story is intended in part to give something back to a trade we love. Finally, and most importantly, my deepest gratitude to Tina Leino-Whyte and Thea Whyte for their love and support.

One of Canada's preeminent journalists, KENNETH WHYTE is the publisher and editor-in-chief of *Maclean's*, Canada's weekly current affairs magazine. He served as editor of the monthly *Saturday Night* magazine at the peak of its popularity and as founding editor-in-chief of the *National Post*.